THE MYRIAD CHRIST

BIBLIOTHECA EPHEMERIDUM THEOLOGICARUM LOVANIENSIUM

CLII

THE MYRIAD CHRIST

PLURALITY AND THE QUEST FOR UNITY IN CONTEMPORARY CHRISTOLOGY

EDITED BY

T. MERRIGAN AND J. HAERS

LEUVEN
UNIVERSITY PRESS

UITGEVERIJ PEETERS
LEUVEN – PARIS – STERLING, VIRGINIA

2000

ISBN 90 5867 009 0 (Leuven University Press)
D/2000/1869/9
ISBN 90-429-0900-5 (Peeters Leuven)
D/2000/0602/105

Library of Congress Cataloging-in-Publication Data

The myriad Christ: plurality and the quest for unity in contemporary christology / edited by T. Merrigan and J. Haers.
  p. cm. -- (Bibliotheca Ephemeridum theologicarum Lovaniensium; 152)
  Includes bibliographical references and index.
  ISBN 9058670090 (University Press: alk. paper) -- ISBN 9042909005 (Uitgeverij Peeters: alk. paper)
  1. Jesus Christ--Person and offices--Congresses. I. Merrigan, Terrence. II. Haers, Jacques. III. Series.

BT202 .M94 2000
232--dc21   00-058022

Leuven University Press / Presses Universitaires de Louvain
Universitaire Pers Leuven
Blijde-Inkomststraat 5, B-3000 Leuven (Belgium)

© 2000 – Peeters, Bondgenotenlaan 153, B-3000 Leuven (Belgium)

PREFACE

The papers gathered here are the fruit of an international congress held at the Faculty of Theology of the Katholieke Universiteit Leuven, 18-21 November, 1997. The theme of the congress serves as the title of the present work, *The Myriad Christ: Plurality and the Quest for Unity in Contemporary Theology*. The title of the congress and the book is largely self-explanatory. What is at issue is the multiplicity of portraits of Jesus which characterizes the contemporary theological landscape, and the challenges thrown up by this multiplicity. To survey the state of contemporary christology is to be reminded of those celebrated lines from William Butler Yeats' poem, *The Second Coming*:

> Turning and turning in the widening gyre
> The falcon cannot hear the falconer;
> Things fall apart; the centre cannot hold;
> Mere anarchy is loosed upon the world,
> The blood-dimmed tide is loosed, and everywhere
> The ceremony of innocence is drowned;
> The best lack all conviction, while the worst
> Are full of passionate intensity.

Can properly Christian discourse survive if its traditional center, the God-man, Jesus Christ, is dissolved into a myriad of disparate and even conflicting images and notions? Is the quest for unity in christology illusory and even counterproductive? And what are the preconditions for authentic christological discourse? In an age such as ours when the discipline has been opened up to all comers, Yeats' vision of a situation in which "the best lack all conviction, while the worst are full of passionate intensity" does not seem so farfetched. But how are we to acquire the insight which will allow us to know when that state of affairs has been reached? Where are we begin our quest? These are the sorts of questions which this collection considers.

The first group of papers assembled here: "The Quest for a Theological Norm", addresses the question of the starting point of christology, especially in the light of the contemporary experience of pluralism. The second group, "Biblical and Patristic Perspectives", examines some of the 'classical' sources of, and approaches to, christological discourse. The third group, "The Plurality of Religions and Cultures", reflects on the development of christology as the discipline spread beyond the 'classical' world into cultures with a very different world view. The fourth group, "The Myriad Christ in Theological Reflection", examines a variety of attempts to translate 'Christ-faith' into a concrete agenda for life in particular contexts.

To read the entire collection of papers is to recognize that the myriad Christ has always eluded theology's grasp. But it is also to realize that he continues to challenge every presupposition we bring to our quest for him. As Tennyson observed, "our little systems have their day... and cease to be", while the myriad Christ continually shows himself to be "more than they".

The congress out of which this collection grew was a cooperative endeavor involving many generous men and women. We would especially like to thank the contributors to the Congress, both for their participation in the event and for their patience in awaiting this publication. We would also like to thank the following people, in particular, for their assistance: the Chancellor of the University, Cardinal Godfried Danneels, and the Rector, Professor André Oosterlinck, for accepting to act as patrons of the gathering; Professor Herman De Dijn, Vice-Rector of the University and Chair of the Dondeyne Foundation for his active interest and encouragement; Professor Marc Vervenne, Dean of the Faculty of Theology and all our colleagues, for their unstinting support; the members of the Department of Dogmatic Theology, Professors Robrecht Michiels (Chair), Georges De Schrijver, and Lieven Boeve, and the assistants Dr. Peter De Mey and Drs. Johan Leemans for their hard work and unfailing good will; Professors Lambert Leijssen and Kristiaan Depoortere and their staffs at the Pope's College and the Holy Spirit College for their hospitality; the staff of the Faculty library for organizing an excellent exhibition of christological art by Luc Hoenraet; the secretarial and logistic staff of the Faculty of Theology for their patient and generous assistance; the students of the Faculty who took upon themselves all sorts of vital tasks, from acting as chauffeurs to preparing coffee; special mention must be made here of Dieter van Belle, Christopher Robinson, Gino Mattheeuws, Kristof Struys, Andy Raes, Arul Pragasam, Jeffrey Goh, Myriam de Klerck, and Sydney Palmer.

We would like to express our profound thanks to the Fund for Scientific Research (F.W.O.-Vlaanderen) for its generous support. Similar thanks are due to the Research Council (Onderzoeksraad) of the Katholieke Universiteit Leuven and the Dondeyne Foundation. It was above all due to the latter's generosity that we were able to organize a very successful 'Flemish Day' on the Congress themes which resulted in a separate Dutch-language publication[1].

We are grateful to Professor Frans Neirynck, general editor of BETL, and Peeters Publishers for the opportunity to publish this collection in the series. That the book has seen the light of day is due, in no small part, to the expertise of Mrs. Rita Corstjens whose help has been invaluable.

We are aware of our debt to all those named here and to many others, and we are grateful to them for sharing with us something of the riches of the myriad Christ.

Terrence MERRIGAN
Jacques HAERS

---

1. J. HAERS & T. MERRIGAN, *Christus in veelvoud. Pluraliteit en de vraag naar eenheid in de hedendaagse christologie*, Leuven, Acco, 1999.

CONTENTS

PREFACE VII

I

THE MYRIAD CHRIST
THE QUEST FOR A THEOLOGICAL NORM

Stephen J. DUFFY (New Orleans)
The Stranger Within our Gates: Interreligious Dialogue and the
Normativeness of Jesus   3

Roger HAIGHT (Boston)
The Impact of Pluralism on Christology 31

Sean KEALY (Pittsburgh)
Reflections on the Third Quest for the Historical Jesus 45

Terrence MERRIGAN (Leuven)
The Historical Jesus and the Pluralist Theology of Religions . 61

Jacques DUPUIS (Rome)
Trinitarian Christology as a Model for a Theology of Religious
Pluralism 83

Bruno FORTE (Naples)
Jesus of Nazareth, History of God, God of History: Trinitarian
Christology in a Pluralistic Age 99

W.G.B.M. VALKENBERG (Nijmegen)
Christ and the Spirit: Towards a Bifocal Christian Theology of
Religions 121

II

THE MYRIAD CHRIST
BIBLICAL AND PATRISTIC PERSPECTIVES

Adelbert DENAUX (Leuven)
The Monotheistic Background of New Testament Christology:
Critical Reflections on Pluralist Theologies of Religions . . . 133

Reimund BIERINGER (Leuven)
'My Kingship is not of this World' (Jn 18,36): The Kingship of
Jesus and Politics 159

Bianca LATAIRE (Leuven)
Jesus' Equality with God: A Critical Reflection on John 5,18 . 177
Frances YOUNG (Birmingham)
Christology and Creation: Towards an Hermeneutic of Patristic
Christology 191
Johan LEEMANS (Leuven)
'God Became Human in Order that Humans Might Become
God': A Reflection on the Soteriological Doctrine of Divinization 207

III

THE MYRIAD CHRIST

AND THE PLURALITY OF RELIGIONS AND CULTURES

Michael AMALADOSS (Delhi)
Jesus Christ in the Midst of Religions: An Indian Perspective . 219
Keith WARD (Oxford)
Christian Vedanta: An Absurdity or an Opportunity 235
Catherine CORNILLE (Leuven)
Buddhist Views of Christ and the Question of Uniqueness . . 249
Wiel LOGISTER (Tilburg)
The Challenge of Mohammed about the Place of Jesus Christ . 263
Harald SUERMANN (Bonn)
The Rational Defense of Christology within the Context of
Islamic Monotheism 273
Diane STINTON (Edinburgh)
Jesus of Africa: Voices of Contemporary African Christology 287
Achiel PEELMAN (Ottawa)
The Native American Christ 315

IV

THE MYRIAD CHRIST

IN THEOLOGICAL REFLECTION

Henk J.M. SCHOOT (Utrecht)
Friars in Negative Christology: Thomas Aquinas and Luis de
Léon 331

Peter DE MEY (Leuven)
Ernst Troeltsch: A Moderate Pluralist? An Evaluation of His
Reflections on the Place of Christianity among the Other
Religions   349

John PAWLIKOWSKI (Chicago)
Christology after the Holocaust   381

Marie BAIRD (Pittsburgh)
Jesus at Auschwitz? A Critique of Post-Holocaust Christologies   399

Bernhard KÖRNER (Graz)
'Jesus must be catholic': The Uniqueness and Universality of
Christ in the Work of Hans Urs von Balthasar   417

Jerry FARMER (New Orleans)
Four Christological Themes of the Theology of Karl Rahner .   433

Declan MARMION (Dublin)
The Christocentric Spirituality of Karl Rahner   463

Georges DE SCHRIJVER (Leuven)
Christology from the Underside of History: The Case of Jon
Sobrino   493

Chester GILLIS (Washington)
Radical Christologies? An Analysis of the Christologies of John
Hick and Paul Knitter   521

Arul PRAGASAM (India)
The God of Religious Pluralism and Christology   535

Nico SCHREURS (Tilburg)
A Non-Sacrificial Interpretation of Christian Redemption . . .   551

Martien E. BRINKMAN (Utrecht)
Christological Implications of the Ecumenical Agreement on
Justification   567

Lieven BOEVE (Leuven)
Christus Postmodernus: An Attempt at Apophatic Christology .   577

Index of names   594

I

THE MYRIAD CHRIST

THE QUEST FOR A THEOLOGICAL NORM

THE STRANGER WITHIN OUR GATES

INTERRELIGIOUS DIALOGUE AND THE NORMATIVENESS OF JESUS

Concern about the other is a subject for thought at least as old as humankind. Today the concern of Christians about the faiths of others has entered a new phase. Global economic and political interdependence, rapid transportation, and the expanding communications superhighway have given rise to a situation in which different cultures and their religious traditions are encountering each other as never before. In addition, an influx of immigrants from East to West, fueled by poverty and ethnic, political and religious turmoil is contributing to the growth of multicultural and multireligious societies that present possibilities for conflict or enrichment. While these technological and demographic changes and the challenges they place before Western societies are largely twentieth-century phenomena, the intellectual challenge to Western Christianity has an earlier provenance in the Enlightenment and in the fact that, from the seventeenth century on, the East has been seeping into Western consciousness[1].

Until relatively recently, diverse faiths existed almost in isolation from one another. When cultures did meet, the encounters were often marked by bloodshed and cultural vandalism because one would not acknowledge the moral standing of the other[2]. Only with expanding colonialism, interlacing international networks, innovations in communications, and snowballing economic and ecological interdependence did the fact of plurality erupt into serious questions. The stranger stood within the gates of Western consciousness; he was our neighbor. The Western ego was decentered; so, too, its Eurocentric history. As long as it was assumed that Western values and beliefs had scaled the apex of human evolution, other cultures and belief systems presented no challenge. But

---

1. See R. SCHWAB, *The Oriental Renaissance: Europe's Discovery of India and the East, 1680-1880*, New York, NY, Columbia University Press, 1984.
2. The language of the "other" invites misunderstanding, for it suggests ontological cleavage where there is only anthropological distinction. The language of "difference" is preferable. "Difference" is relational, relative, "otherness" absolute. "Otherness" obstructs understanding; "difference" solicits understanding, interaction. "Difference" (from *differre*) is an active term, suggesting a sifting out of what can be grasped as the "same". "Other" has no verbal form, except, possibly, "alienate", most frequently in the passive.

no more. The diverse family of faiths to which our planet is home raises questions about their coexistence that demand address.

All this has moved the West to recontextualize itself in a larger world. Although Christianity, even in its beginnings, was already seriously addressing non-Christian religions (e.g., Justin, Origen), in the closing third of the twentieth century it entered into dialogue with the religions in a way unknown before. Christianity can no longer read its tradition apart from the other great traditions. The encounter is somewhat similar to that of the fledgling Christian community facing the Greco-Roman world in its dawning centuries. Now, as then, Christianity confronts a new frontier. Encountering the stranger at close quarters necessitates a shift in horizon, no easy challenge when commensurate precedents are lacking[3]. Modern religious pluralism has plunged Christianity into a new conceptual crisis, one every bit as formidable as the crisis it faces in the large, public phenomenon of unbelief that was unleashed with modernity[4]. In this liminal state Christianity is forced to probe its identity, to take again its bearing. Christendom and Western empire-building are long dead. Christianity, no longer gripping Western imagination, no longer drives the intellectual, spiritual, and cultural climate. Until it entered the modern era, Christianity never had to deal systematically and from a position of equality with the other great traditions[5]. Christians seeking dialogue with the non-Christian faiths can ill afford postures of superiority or supersessionism, nor dreams of missionary conquest. There is no need to see in all this a turn for the worse. The liminal state that crisis throws us into can prove a fertile seed bed.

Christianity is not, however, pushed into encounter with the other religions merely by reason of its new situation in a global city that is secularized and culturally polycentric. It is impelled to dialogue by the logic of its own deepest conviction. Christianity's central affirmation, that divine Wisdom is incarnate in Jesus, ought not be construed to mean that Jesus is the sole medium in which God's creative and reconciling agency may be present in the world. No understanding of the religions is acceptable that

---

3. R. WILKEN, *Religious Pluralism and Early Christian Thought,* in *Pro Ecclesia* 1 (1992) 89-103 thinks there are precedents. I think the differences in the situations faced by early Christianity and by modern Christianity, while similar at points, are not commensurate.

4. See M. BUCKLEY, *At the Origins of Modern Atheism,* New Haven, CT, Yale University Press, 1987.

5. On the paradigms used through Western history – demonology, epistemology, developmental time, culture – to interpret non Europeans as inferior, see B. MC GRAVE *Beyond Anthropology: Society and the Other,* New York, NY, Columbia University Press, 1989.

denies the love of God for all of creation or holds hostage in one small
corner of the world the power of God to overcome the alienation of
humanity from its ground. The Word incarnate in Jesus is the discourse
that enlightens everyone; the Wisdom met in Jesus is the Wisdom already,
always, and everywhere at work. The Christocentrism of sectarian isola-
tionism is misguided because it misunderstands the incarnation and makes
its god a tribal deity. To place Jesus at the center of history, as Christians
do, is not to make him the whole human story. Too often the problem with
the way Christians tell their story is not that Jesus is at the center, but that
the circumference is far too constricted. As Rahner has pointed out, com-
fortably ensconced for too long, Constantinian Christianity came to view
itself as Western and European with annexes in North and South America.
Now comes the challenging opportunity to truly be, for the first time, a
world community, which will entail reassessing what Christians mean by
"we"[6]. This is not to remove Jesus from the center, but to transform all
that revolves around that center. Precisely because Wisdom incarnate is its
center, Christianity is thrust outward toward a more inclusive history.
While there must be boundaries, and doctrines do, among other things,
draw boundaries, we are often too quick to draw them, failing to see the
wisdom on both sides of the lines. Can we ignore what we take to be wisdom, divine wisdom, in the other? Can we afford the idolatry that makes
our small understanding the whole of the story?

I. SITUATING THE OTHER

In the waning decades of this century, theologians concerned with the
relationship of Christianity to the world religions adopted a paradigm
that maps out a typology of three possible ways of conceiving the relationship. The categories employed are exclusivism, inclusivism, and pluralism, and the compass points are soteriology and christology. Who gets
saved? How? And by whom? The paradigm runs, crudely, as follows.
Exclusivism affirms that truth is found in only one religion, Christianity,
for salvation and revelation are found only in Jesus; the Christ event is
constitutive of any authentic encounter with God, always and everywhere[7]. Thus other traditions are marginalized as flawed human attempts

---

6. K. RAHNER, *Basic Theological Interpretation of the Second Vatican Council*, in ID.,
Theological Investigations 20, New York, NY, Crossroad, 1981, pp. 72-89.

7. Exclusivists pin salvation to explicit confession of Christ, some prior to death,
while others entertain *post mortem* solutions to avoid mass non-culpable perdition. Salvation *solo Christo* does not necessitate juridical church membership.

at self-salvation, deformed by error and vice. Because exclusivism is preoccupied with guarding and maintaining its own house, the center of the universe, it shrinks the hermeneutical circle. Dialogue, therefore, if not ignored, is for proselytizing. Inclusivism, officially espoused by Roman Catholicism at Vatican II, expands the hermeneutical circle. Venturing beyond its borders, it maintains that the saving self-revealing God of Christians, "who desires everyone to be saved and come to knowledge of the truth" (1Tim 2,4), is present and at work in and through the world's religions[8]. However, whatever truth and saving power are found in other faiths is already included in Christianity and found there more fully, more certainly. The aims, doctrines, and forms of life of other religions may have significant material commonality with those of Christianity, but where so, they are superseded or fulfilled by Christianity, basically because the Christ encompasses the others by being present in them anonymously or by fulfilling them. In a sense, the others are implicit forms of Christianity. Jesus remains, if not constitutive of, at least normative for, all religious experience[9].

As for pluralism, it contends that many, or even in extreme versions, all religions are formally true and equivalent. Jesus is unique, but so are all great religious figures. Moreover, Jesus is neither constitutive of nor normative for authentic religious experience. Initially, pluralists opposed theocentrism to christocentrism. In other words, Jesus is but one manifestation, one incarnation of God's revelation and salvation in history[10].

---

8. See Vatican II's *Declaration on the Relationship of the Church to Non-Christian Religions; Dogmatic Constitution on the Church*, n. 16-17; *Dogmatic Constitution on Divine Revelation*, n. 3 and 14; *Declaration on Religious Freedom*, n. 4; *Decree on Ecumenism*. Also, J. DINOIA, *The Diversity of Religions: A Christian Perspective*, Washington, DC, Catholic University Press, 1992, pp. 26-29, 161-182.

9. Many Protestant thinkers have tended to recognize a general revelation in history but not to view the high religions as ways to salvation. Catholic theologians have, in this century tended to affirm these religions are possible ways of salvation. See P. KNITTER, *No Other Name? A Critical Survey of Christain Attitudes Toward the World Religions*, Maryknoll, NY, Orbis Books, 1985, pp. 97-184.

10. One criticism of theocentrism is that it is a Western category, an imperialist imposition. Some pluralists shifted to soteriocentrism or "kingdom-centrism" as hermeneutical keys. Again, Western categories, and the latter, some charge, monarchical. See M. SUCHOCKI, *In Search of Justice; Religious Pluralism from a Feminist Perspective*, in J. HICK & P. KNITTER (eds.), *The Myth of Christian Uniqueness: Toward a Pluralistic Theology of Religions*, Maryknoll, NY, Orbis Books, 1987, pp. 149-161. Moreover, the God of love championed in theocentric models is known through Jesus. Hence, they are redolent of the very Christocentric models pluralists eschew. For examples of soteriocentric approaches see P. KNITTER, *Toward a Liberation theology of Religion*, in this same work, pp. 178-200; ID., *One Earth Many Religions: Multifaith Dialogue and Global Responsibility*, Maryknoll, NY, Orbis Books, 1995; J. HICK, *An Interpretation of Religion: Human Responses to the Transcendent*, New Haven, CT, Yale University Press, 1989. Beneath

Jesus, therefore, may have universal relevance, but he is not the absolute savior, definitive and unsurpassable. A fourth possibility, though generally not included in the paradigm, is sheer conceptual relativism. It maintains that there are no universal norms. Lacking a normative critique of norms, which would make comparisons possible, each tradition is best by it own norms. The incommensurability of ultimate systems is unbridgeable. Each discursive universe, limited by its own horizon, is hermeneutically sealed, inaccessible to outsiders and relevant to itself alone. Radical relativism does not deny that beliefs and practices can be validated, but their validity and the process of validation itself are relative to the culture they inhabit. One cannot assess the truth of other religions from outside their circle. Things stand with the stranger as they did with Wittgenstein's lion: "If he could talk, we could not understand him"[11]. While appearing to do equal justice to all, relativism in fact cancels the claims of all, since all claim universality. Implied is refusal to acknowledge the other as one who can challenge one's own positions. The communicative purpose of language is thus privatized, immunized to critique, hence undermined.

Finally, it is worth noting three things about this paradigm. First, the three approaches boldly state their position in the indicative mood, as factual: Christianity is the only true religion; whatever truth is found in other faiths is already included, preeminently, in Christianity; all faiths are true and roughly equivalent. A more simplistic labeling of the three reduces them to ecclesiocentrism, christocentrism, and theocentrism, respectively. Second, as is the case with many Christians, exclusivist and inclusivist positions are often espoused by non-Christian believers as well, who place their own tradition at the center, outsiders on the periphery[12]. Third, all members of the paradigm draw cross-cultural judgments about other traditions. At issue is not the fact that such judgments are made, but whether compelling arguments can be marshaled for them, so that they are more than simply reflections of one's own cultural and religious commitments.

diversity inclusivists and pluralists detect a common soteriological structure. All seek salvation, blandly identified with overcoming egoism and fellowship with the transcendent or with the just society. Comparative study and self-description by believers fly in the face of these assumptions. Christian soteriology cannot be assumed analogous with any and every program for human amelioration. See D. DAVIES, *The Notion of Salvation in Comparative Study of Religions,* in *Religion* 8 (1978) 85-100; DINOIA, *Diversity of Religions* (n. 8), pp. 43-47, 53-55.

11. L. WITTGENSTEIN, *Philosophical Fragments*, New York, NY, Macmillan, 1985, p. 223.

12. See P. GRIFFITHS (ed.), *Christianity Through Non-Christian Eyes,* Maryknoll, NY, Orbis Books, 1990.

II. A CRITIQUE OF THE PARADIGM IN VOGUE

Such *a priori* paradigm building is, at least, premature, if, indeed, even possible. The relationship of Christianity to the other religions requires recasting in a way that, while exploiting resources available in the Christian tradition, also respects the complex particularities of other traditions and studies them for their own sake. In other words, one needs to attend to both the *a priori* and the *a posteriori* aspects of theology of the religions if it is to be a viable theology. The *a priori* aspect derives from what can be said about religious pluralism by appealing solely to the faith commitments and theological axioms of the Christian community. While diverse strands of the tradition may produce diverse *a priori* theologies of the religions, all *a priori* approaches are formally alike in that they derive from no knowledge of other religious communities aside from the bare fact of their existence. Obviously, *a priori* theory building, necessary as it is, cannot by itself constitute a full-blown theology of the religions. At best, it lays bare Christian presuppositions, maps out Christian doctrines concerning other religions, sketches a methodology, and thus delineates constraining parameter for dialogue and study[13]. Hermeneutical honesty demands as much. The exclusivist, inclusivist and pluralist positions are the result of such *a priori* theologizing.

The constructive *a posteriori* dimension of a theology of the religions, on the other hand, demands a knowledge of other traditions. It follows and derives from a critical understanding of other belief systems that has been integrated into the diverse areas of Christian theology. Because until recently few theologians have been concerned with comparative study, little *a posteriori* understanding born of comparative analysis has been incorporated into Christian theology. Theologies of the religions remain, for the most part, *a priori*. This essay is itself just such an *a priori* theologizing. And while *a priori* theologizing is necessary, the danger is that it begets a complacency that one's work is finished. This illusion blunts any sense of need for detailed study of the aims and forms of life pursued by non-Christians. Certainly, lack of concern for specifics is not ingredient to an *a priori* theology of religions, but it is fairly common. The thinking seems to be that obstacles impeding understanding of the relationships between traditions can be eliminated if only we get our doctrines about the others right.

---

13. Dinoia's *Diversity of Religions* (n. 8) attempts such an *a priori* theology of the religions.

Yet we have to distrust any theology of the religions that promises too much, too quickly, too cheaply. What is to be feared is neither the prospect of disagreement nor the weariness of a long impasse, but an undisciplined rush to simplistic positions whose easy certitudes allay our anxiety. Anxiety, however, is the specter that will continue to dog the faith of Christians in a post-Christian world. In encounter with the non-Christian world Christians will rediscover themselves as a community and where they stand in relation to the God of Jesus Christ. Christians can make clear the sincerity with which they enter conversation with other faiths only by placing beyond doubt their preparedness to face others' claims and to let the others test their very identity by putting at risk their present Christian self-understanding. This does not mean that Christians enter dialogue empty-headed, stripped of their commitments. Still, any half-serious Christian will find that serious engagement with non-Christian life worlds may entail significant soul-searching, an unnerving test of one's intellectual, moral, and religious mettle. Faced with a plurality of faiths, what am I to think about my tradition, about myself in relation to the others? In what follows, even if I fail to construe or analyze correctly the tangled web of issues that must concern any theology of religions, I hope at least to identify those issues and to make some generalizable points.

I turn first to a more specific critique of the paradigm in vogue. In a state of post-conciliar euphoria many theologians gladly embraced inclusivism, often as it was elaborated by Karl Rahner. Some went beyond Vatican II and Rahner to endorse the pluralism of a thinker like John Hick. There was comfort in both. These positions fostered openness, respect, the commonality of our humanity. They also provided an explanatory power as reassuring as it was beguiling. And they seemed blessed by a congruity with Christian teaching concerning God's universal salvific will that rendered them coherent with a magnanimity in the Catholic tradition tracing at least as far back as Justin the Apologist. Besides, who in those bracing post-conciliar days of theological renaissance would have wanted to be a benighted Feeneyite exclusivist dispatching "non-Catholics" to hell[14], or even a benign exclusivist, who by seeming theological sleights of hand made it possible for God to snatch unbelievers from the jaws of perdition[15]?

---

14. Leonard Feeney, expelled from the Jesuits and excommunicated in 1949, denied the possibility of salvation to non-Roman Catholics. See F. SULLIVAN, *Salvation Outside the Church? Tracing the History of the Catholic Response*, New York, NY, Paulist Press, 1992, pp. 3-5, 134-136.

15. *Ibid.*, provides a fine history of theological responses to the whether and how of salvation for those outside Catholicism.

Nonetheless, the lack of sympathy that the so-called exclusivist position meets with today appears unduly one-sided. What we label "exclusivism" and equate with imperialist adventures and colonialist abuse was, in its origins, not an expression of arrogance but of the absoluteness of religious commitment, of ultimate concern, an expression of heartfelt loyalty to meanings and values a community judged true and to the conviction that salvation is by the grace of God in Christ, not by any human achievement. Sensitivity to others' commitments was not always lacking in exclusivists, though there was deep conviction that one's own religious vision was definitive, warranted by experience and reason in a way that other visions of reality were not. We solidify our own group by distinguishing it from groups that are other, even alien. Identities, national or religious, cannot help but be shaped negatively as well as positively, for confessional claims grow into consciousness of their uniqueness by contrast with the claims of others. Thus all the great traditions make particularistic claims to universality; paradoxically, believers give themselves absolutely to an absolute they can grasp only relatively, for the absolute meets us and grasps us only in the relative, the particular. It seems there must be something like this absolutist sentiment in the heart of every serious believer, though to label it "exclusivism" in every case seems misleading. However, Kantian limitations on reason and modern relativism weakened confidence in reason where religion is concerned. This, along with the modern pluralistic and secular nation-state, which privatizes and trivializes religious commitment, has sapped the strength of religious commitment for many[16]. So much so, that serious religious conviction often meets a wall of incomprehension, even denunciation in secularized Western consciousness, especially when those convictions are voiced in "the naked public square" in an attempt to shape public policy.

As for inclusivism and pluralism, they rest upon the unwarranted *a priori* assumption that religions with aims, doctrines, and patterns of life that do not appear readily reconcilable are, nonetheless, in their deepest reality "about the same thing". Their diverse finalities and soteriologies, it is assumed, ultimately converge. More precisely, the same set of beliefs and norms, or an identical referent (reality with a capital R, or Ultimacy, or the Sacred, etc.) for beliefs and norms not shared, are assumed to be characteristic of all religions. This may be the case in some or in many instances. But we cannot assume it to be so. Are they

---

16. On the difficulties modernity creates for belief see P. BERGER, *The Heretical Imperative: Contemporary Possibilities of Religious Affirmation*, New York, NY, Doubleday, 1979.

all "about the same thing"? Can we even say that all religions have a soteriology? That diverse doctrines are identical, or similar, or complementary, or contrary, or dialectically related or have the same referent, these are judgments to be arrived at only after long, patient study and dialogue. Long and patient, because given the indeterminacy of meaning and the limits of understanding, dialogue is never easy. Profound commonalities are not presuppositions of dialogue; they are, perhaps, its conclusion. As it stands, inclusivists and pluralists presuppose commonality and elide the particularities of diverse traditions with an assertion proper to some pallid theory of religion, the vagueness and banality of which captures the commitments of no actual religious community. Meanings buried deep in culturally conditioned religious symbols, moreover, cannot effortlessly and objectively be sniffed out in their pure state much as muzzled truffle hunters might efficiently and harmlessly scent out the precious quarry of their search[17]. Difficult spade work is required, long and patient study.

Hans Küng has said (in a half-truth), "There can be no world peace without religious peace"[18]. We can add that religious peace comes largely with understanding. But to understand is to interpret and interpretation demands conversation and textual study. Yet it is the urgency of conversation and the rigors of interpretation that the logic of exclusivism, inclusivism, and especially pluralism undercut. More is needed than romantic celebration of multiculturalism. And that is painstaking comparative analysis of the aims and practices of particular traditions, dialogue that uncovers the life-possibilities the other may yield. Failing that, we are left with ungrounded assumptions about an identical abstract "Other" experienced by all in ineffable personal encounter. Here is an effective strategy to dampen the need for the textual analysis and critical comparative work that would in turn entail the rereading of one's own texts with new eyes. The major religious families tagged Hinduism, Buddhism, Judaism, Christianity, Islam are ahistorical reifications abstracted from the living flow of ordinary persons, prophets, mystics and their practices and symbols. Shorthand descriptions are blind to the many different ways of being Jew, Muslim, or Buddhist. Pluralists and inclusivists compound the reification by submitting the flow to a further level of abstraction, running it again through their homogenizing grids that filter out dense particularities and intractable specificities and categorize them as merely mythological or culture-specific. All phenomenal

17. DiNoia, *Diversity of Religions* (n. 8), pp. 133-138.
18. H. Küng, *Christianity and the World Religions: Paths to Dialogue with Islam, Hinduism, and Buddhism*, New York, NY, Doubleday, 1986, pp.440-443.

differences, even when acknowledged, are evaded by preoccupation
with a noumenal Real assumed common to all, the Mystery beyond all
grasping.

One need not be much concerned about detailed analyses of the doctrines and practices of others if they are discounted as merely culturally
generated expressions of a deeper, more important reality universally
shared by all religions that renders them alike, even equivalent. Interest
in the other may wane when one already knows what one will find in a
study of the other's beliefs and practices. There is something very wrong
about a theory that pronounces judgments on other faiths, yet whose
logic absolves us from serious study of the other. In this regard, theology, like politics, makes strange bedfellows. Even Karl Barth in his radical exclusivism, like inclusivists and pluralists, knew prior to detailed
study what he would find in the religions: *Unglaube,* human attempts at
self-justification, idols that cannot save.

Prolonging the Enlightenment dream, inclusivism and pluralism are
propelled by a foundationalist mode of thought so focused on elements
presumed universally shared by all that they are insufficiently attentive
to the stubborn, messy particulars of the goals, doctrines, and life patterns that color the religious landscape. The Enlightenment project
sought to eradicate the supposed prejudices of "local" reasonings and to
set reason on a secure, universal foundation. Yet it is precisely these
full-blooded realities of "local" reasonings, now leveled out by inclusivists and pluralists, that fire hearts and imaginations and energize the
wills of believers. The formalities shared by the great traditions that pluralists make so much of may be difficult to disagree with, but equally
difficult to get excited about or build one's life upon. No one dies for a
generic religion.

Inclusivists and pluralists envision a new kind of subject, one that is
placeless, universal, global. At work in their thinking is the assumption
that they have achieved an Archimedean point, a neutral, objective vantage point, a "view from nowhere", outside all religious, philosophical,
and cultural traditions. From this pure space far from the noise of culture, they survey the sweep of history and detect in all the great religions
a common denominator, a shared inmost core, a forever elusive
noumenon that is present but absent in some transcendental experience
or in some never finished struggle for liberation. Around this noumenal
center swirl a galaxy of less important phenomena (doctrines, rituals,
myths, forms of life), all born of the faith of believers fated to be forever
"almosting it". Pluralist maneuvers converge in considering all religions
partial instantiations of an elusive truth, a universal religiosity. Thus all

"positive religions" are relativized as sub-species. Given such a globe-straddling standpoint, one can, in one sense, better comprehend the great religions than their own faithful might.

There is in all this a large irony. In a repentant post-colonial era, pluralist theory is willy-nilly implicated in a subtle intellectual super-sessionism, a neo-colonialist form of discourse that constructs its other. Others are stripped of the radical historical particularity that constitutes them as other and domesticated, assimilated to one's own projects and assessed, even invented accordingly[19]. The other as genuinely other is disdained. There is even a kind of colonial justice at work here. Pluralists have peace of mind knowing they are open and accepting of all as equals, while at the same time they nudge into oblivion the justice they fail to do to the concrete beliefs and practices of Christians and non-Christians as all differences are counted as epiphenomenal. Inclusivists and pluralists may be open to Buddhists in a way that exclusivists were not. But they may hear them in the calm confidence that in the final analysis what these others have to say is not all that important, because it is not really different from what believers everywhere say. Pluralism especially is insistent on the rough parity of the diverse discursive spaces occupied by different traditions. All faiths voice the same enlightenment or pursue the same goal of liberation. Thus pluralism melts into a monism that brackets, reinterprets, or relativizes particular truth claims in deference to an alleged anthropological constant. The other is respected simply as image of oneself. Sympathy masks subtle betrayal. The others are reduced to being utterly transparent; we preempt their voice and presume to speak for them. Perhaps yesterday's missionaries were more accurate observers of the other religions than today's questers after Eastern wisdom. For even in their hostility or superiority they registered differences that go unseen by the glossing eye of the open-minded, tolerant pluralist.

If, however, doctrines as speech acts are, among other things, declarative and cognitive, if religious discourse must be given realist construal, and if humans are inescapably immersed in their communal history and stand always contextualized within a tradition and culture tied to particular systems of meaning, then wholesale degutting of diversities in the interest of some imposed idealization, a contentless universalism, will not

19. On invention of the "other" see C. LONG, *Significations: Signs, Symbols, and Images in the Interpretation of Religion*, Philadelphia, PA, Fortress Press, 1986; on the British "invention" of Buddhism see P. ALMOND, *The British Discovery of Buddhism*, Cambridge, Cambridge University Press, 1988.

do[20]. Is the Theravadin seeking Nirvana really seeking beatific vision of the triune God? Are Eckhart and Nagarjuna experiencing the same reality? Is the Zen master's *satori* what Christians mean by salvation? Is the Vaish-navite's devotion to Krishna really love of Jesus? Is Mahayana Buddhism's *sunyata* simply what Christians name God? Are the complex anthropologies of Buddhism and Christianity ultimately equivalent? The tendency of inclusivism and pluralism is to underplay *prima facie* differences as salvifically irrelevant, to mute the possibility that there are deeply ingrained, cognitively significant incompatibilities among the doctrines and practices that communities consider salvifically crucial. Profound similarities that are similarities-in-difference, analogies, there may be. But pluralism and inclusivism tend to paper over differences as due to a misapprehension of their own tradition by believers. This, of course, evidences pluralism's ambivalence about language and texts, both of which appear purely instrumental, secondary, and divisive in the world of experience as pluralism conceives it.

Finally, it would seem that mutual understanding is arrived at not by an immediate *a priori* adoption of a higher viewpoint, but by first adopting a lower viewpoint. What makes mutual interpretation possible is the natural hermeneutical competence that brings together strangers at sixes and seven about one another, the intuition and wager that they are in their differences, their otherness, mutually interpretable. All seek to understand; even more, to be understood. All are relatively intelligent and intelligible. A theology of the religions cannot start with a hermeneutics of suspicion. Rather, starting from below with distinctive differences, it proceeds in modesty and restraint. A theology of religions, confident of the ubiquity of grace, will affirm the possibility that God is at work in the lives of non-Christians. However, providing a detailed account of how this may be risks underestimating the distinctiveness of the religious aims they so fervently pursue. We can agree with pluralists that we need to probe beneath what is said to be something deeper. But the deeper something may not prove to be a common essence, but diversity. Nonetheless, the wager is that apparent contradictories can also often be resolved into non-contradictory differences, that what is intended by those who have lived, felt, and reflected deeply is apt to be true; their formulations, however, may exclude other truths that ought not be excluded[21].

---

20. On problems connected with pluralism's functionalist approach to doctrines see P. GRIFFITHS, *The Uniqueness of Christian Doctrine Defended,* in G. D'COSTA (ed.), *Christian Uniqueness Reconsidered: The Myth of a Pluralistic Theology of Religions,* Maryknoll, NY, Orbis Press, 1990, pp. 157-173.

21. See the insightful remarks on the hermeneutics of dialogue by F. J. VAN BEECK, *Faith and Theology in Encounters with Non-Christians,* in *Theological Studies* 55 (1994) 58-59.

All this leads us to again avert briefly to a matter crucial to the question at hand. In reflecting on these issues one keeps hearing other voices that in some subterranean passage are engaged in debate, a debate between foundationalists and nonfoundationalists[22]. Foundationalists stress universally shared foundational elements readily discernible to any reasonable person; nonfoundationalists, cultural diversity and unrepentant particularities that, despite family resemblances, resist philosophical or theological reduction to a common denominator or ready translation that warrants a facile explanation of the relationship among cultures and value systems. Foundationalists seek explanation of diversities by weaving them into a grand texture; nonfoundationalists, by positioning them within concrete cultural-linguistic frames of reference that build different worlds. The drift of the nonfoundationalist turn is to exchange a set of well-charted problems for a set of uncharted ones. These voices are a pertinent sub-text for a theology of the religions. Our theological problem is partially in function of this basic philosophical problem.

III. A PROPOSAL

Given this critique of the theology of religions as it stands, how are we to proceed? First, following the lead of Schubert Ogden and Paul Griffiths, but enlarging upon it, it seems preferable to modalize the three positions in the paradigm, to recast them in terms of possibility, to throw them into the subjunctive mood[23]. Transposed into a new key, the three play as follows. Exclusivism: it is possible that Christianity is the only true and salvific religion. Inclusivism: it is possible that whatever salvific truth might be found in other faiths is already included preeminently in Christianity. Pluralism: it is possible that many or all religions are true and salvific. Modalization makes for a more nuanced *a priori* theology of religions and opens the door more widely (and more logically) to an *a posteriori* theology of religion that feeds off comparative analysis.

Second, constructing a theology of the religions that does justice to both the *a priori* and *a posteriori* phases means that theologians have to

22. The philosophical literature of this debate abounds. J. Thiel sorts out the issues and provides essential bibliography in his *Nonfoundationalism,* Minneapolis, MN, Fortress Press, 1994.

23. S. OGDEN, *Is There Only One True Religion or Are There Many?* Dallas, TX, Southern Methodist University Press, 1992; P. GRIFFITHS, *Modalizing the Theology of Religion,* in *Journal of Religion* 73 (1993) 382-389.

work within a set of constraints levied by the faith commitments of their
community and the discipline of theology. But no less has to be said of
any believer encountering faiths other than his or her own. These constraints are parameters of the theological enterprise and meant to insure
fidelity to the tradition they express and derive from; they are directives
as to what positions are choice-worthy. They are not meant to impede
creativity, but are conditions of the possibility of dialogue.

The *a priori* stage of a theology of religions would lay down, for
example, the following constraining parameters (the listing is not taxa-
tive). First, and most basic, the incarnate presence of God in Jesus Christ
heightens the human solidarity rooted in the creation of all in the image
of God. All human conversation involves God's incarnate presence.
Traces of God incarnate mark the countenance of the stranger, the
uncomprehended other. And eucharistic living in the dialogue of life
provides hospitality to the other, especially the stranger and the outcast.
Genuine conversation, therefore, requires non-exclusive concern for the
flourishing of the other. A Christian is constrained, secondly, by the conviction that salvation is attainable through the grace of Christ. Many add
"always and only"; some do not. A third major constraint upon a theology of religions is that it must seriously address the commitments,
beliefs, and practices of the non-Christian religions in all their rich particularity. Christians cannot gratuitously assume that other communities
offer their members exactly what Christianity offers its members in a
different guise. Hasty assimilation of non-Christian doctrinal and practical commitments to those of Christians must be resisted. This third constraint rests upon a fourth, viz., that because God's love is unbounded,
we expect that love to be active in other communities. Thus, non-Christian traditions may be playing out a role in the divine plan, though the
role is not clearly discernible while details of the divine plot are veiled
to us. God's salvific will, Christians believe, ranges universally and the
Word incarnate in Jesus is the Wisdom, "the true light which enlightens
everyone" (John 1,9). A fifth constraint, as many construe Christian
self-understanding, would perhaps be this: even if the aims and forms of
life of any non-Christian communities share significant material commonality with those of Christianity, Christianity supersedes and fulfills
them. This constraint derives from the belief that salvation is always
solo Christo. Of course, it is possible there may be religious communities whose aims share no significant commonality with Christianity. In
that case Christians might attempt to discern what wisdom they might
offer and their role, if any, in the divine economy, recognizing that
eschatologically God may bring members of such communities and

Christians to a convergence. Possibly, such communities can bring their members to the goals they pursue, goals that may not be in contradiction to those pursued by Christians, but which ought not to be assumed to be latently or imperfectly Christian.

Given these constraints, a theology of religions cannot commit itself to an easy *a priori* inclusivism or pluralism that assimilates the others and makes them crypto-Christians or reduces all to a generic religion, in which no real, living community might recognize itself. Both moves turn a deaf ear to claims by the other and assume that other traditions are not really talking about what they take themselves to be talking about, nor valuing what they take it they are valuing. Such a posture is not conducive to substantive concern about the beliefs and practices of others. Transposing the members of the current paradigm into the mode of possibility is so conducive. Indeed, it demands critical study of non-Christian communities. There is no way to know in advance whether or not there is significant material commonality among the religions. Moreover, such study and dialogue open the way to diverse possibilities. First, it might be that the aims and practices of other traditions are diametrically opposed to Christian aims. The appropriate Christian response then might be civil criticism or an apologetic. Second, it might be that the aims and forms of life of other traditions are not opposed to those of Christianity but are simply different. Christians may in this case have something to learn and should be ready to recognize in the other a truth not taught in their own community. Disparate histories may play against each other to produce not harmony but polyphony. Vatican II allows acknowledgment of truths unearthed in non-Christian communities only when they are already taught by the church. Surely we need to go beyond that and gratefully acknowledge truth's manifestation wherever it occurs[24]. Perhaps the church will come to teach the truth contained in the others' doctrines because they are of value in grasping and living the gospel. True conversation lays open the possibility of deepening one's conviction but also of revising, qualifying, or abandoning strongly-held convictions. Only if we are disposed to change, do other religions cease being merely objects of proselytization and become partners in a common quest for truth. Thirdly, the doctrines and practices of other traditions might be neither opposed to nor different from those of Christianity, but substantively identical[25]. This possibility will be vehemently

---

24. *Declaration on the Relationship of the Church to Non-Christian Religions, n. 2-4.* See DINOIA, *Diversity of Religions* (n. 8), p. 29.

25. These possibilities open new worlds. Until now the remoteness of other traditions and the perception that they did not share our history led to indifference. Christians did

rejected by some because of their version of the second *a priori* constraint, the faith stance that salvation is always and only through the grace of Christ and that Christianity is the sole community which professes this. Hence the Christian community is the unsurpassable vehicle of salvation and no other shares precisely its aims. Of course, theologians who claim as much have proven endlessly generous and fertile in finding imaginative ways of rescuing those lost in a sea of confusion, sweeping them into Peter's bark and bringing them to safe harbor[26].

Nonetheless, to take the aims of others seriously and precisely as *religious* aims, whether consonant with Christian aims or not, is to recognize that all faiths entail commitments that claim universal relevance and esteem their aims as salvific and generally, unsurpassable. Religious commitment is driven to suffuse every dimension of life, to penetrate every corner and crevice; it is one's most intensive and comprehensive way of valuing, the all-encompassing horizon[27]. But more. Believers find it unthinkable that their aims might be embraced within, subsumed and superseded by any other community's aim, or shown to be penultimate, merely preparatory to higher aims and forms of life. An irenic and tolerant inclusivism can thus become intolerable, misguided in the eyes of serious believers of other communities. In one sense, inclusivistic supersession may even imply that other believers are mistaken, that their superseded aims are not strictly *religious* aims, lacking as they do comprehensiveness and unsurpassability. In this sense, amid the varieties of aims only one set of truly *religious* aims can emerge, for only one set can be unsurpassable and wholly comprehensive.

Inclusivism now appears to bleed into exclusivism. Both are instances of a salvational monism, the view that there is, in the end, only one, definitively salvific religion, indeed, strictly speaking, only one religion. For both exclusivism and inclusivism, the Christ event uniquely constitutes the possibility of salvation and is the formal norm judging the truth of any tradition claiming to be a religion. They differ only in how this formal norm, the Christ event, is accessible to people[28]. Perhaps, too,

---

not think much about the otherness of remote others. Any thought about otherness was directed against other Christians, Jews, near neighbors, and "descendants", especially Muslims.

26. See SULLIVAN, *Salvation Outside the Church?* (n. 14); DINOIA, *Diversity of Religions* (n. 8), pp. 98-103 shows the difficulties connected with appeals to implicit faith as a way of "saving" non-Christians.

27. S. CARTER, *The Culture of Disbelief,* New York, NY, Basic Books, 1993, shows how secularized American society attempts to confine religion to the private, inner life of individuals and silence its public voice.

28. OGDEN, *Is There Only One True Religion?* (n. 23), pp. 4-5, 31, 38-39.

both exclusivism and inclusivism risk offending against Christian self-understanding, which views Christians and all others as alike the object of God's all-embracing love, by allowing that some have privileged access to God's love solely for contingent reasons, such as the accidents of birth. Ironically, this makes darker still the mystery of evil[29]. At any rate, both claim that all meaning, that every assertion about the significance of life and reality, is to be judged by reference to a fleeting set of contingent happenings in the life of a "marginal Jew" in first-century Palestine. This is a faith claim.

Herein arises the problem of Jesus' uniqueness and universal, definitive normativeness as Christ[30]. Obviously, one must not identify Jesus, the Christ, and Christianity. The faith claim that Jesus is absolute, normative savior does not entail the empirical claim that Christianity as an ambivalent historical religion shares the same absoluteness, normativeness, and unsurpassability (pace Hegel)[31]. Head and body, vine and branches, shepherd and sheepfold know a unity, but remain distinct. This is why Christians must be critical of their community as *semper reformanda*[32]. It was precisely confusion of the two claims, not the logic of the first claim, that led to the religious imperialism and exploitation which pluralists rightly bewail but illogically point to as ground for total abandonment of the first claim. To draw this distinction is not to erase the ambiguity of Christianity's history or absolve Christians of the horrors of their misdeeds. It is naive to think, however, that if all religious claims to superiority and uniqueness were surrendered, evils too often associated with such claims would be drastically reduced[33]. We all need

---

29. *Ibid.*, p.45.

30. On this problem see HICK & KNITTER (eds.), *Myth of Christian Uniqueness* (n. 10) and the response of D'COSTA (ed.), *Christian Uniqueness Reconsidered* (n. 20); see also S. DUFFY, *The Galilean Christ: Particularity and Universality*, in *Journal of Ecumenical Studies* 26 (1989) 154-174; P. PHAN, *Are There Other Saviors for Other Peoples?* in ID. (ed.), *Christianity and the Wider Ecumenism*, New York, NY, Paragon Press, 1990, pp. 163-180.

31. It is impossible to determine historically whether a particular human is normative for all humans. Such significance eludes historical demonstration. The question concerning Jesus' universal normativeness can be answered only in belief. A positive reply is a matter of faith. Still, this faith response must have a basis in the history of Jesus, in reality; otherwise it is ideological. See E. SCHILLEBEECKX, *Jesus: An Experiment in Christology*, New York, NY, Seabury Press, 1979, p. 604.

32. For an appeal to empirical warrants to establish the superiority of Roman Catholic Christianity, see Vatican I's *Dei Filius*, c. 3.

33. Any salvo against the absoluteness of Jesus Christ must be fired on better grounds than an appeal to a contingent (often weak) link between its profession and the evil which pluralists rightly want to obliterate: anti-semitism, patriarchalism, colonialist domination, etc. Should one reject all of Indian metaphysics because many embracing key elements of it condone caste and a sexist social order?

to say of ourselves, as Prospero did of Caliban: "This thing of darkness I acknowledge mine".

But what are we to make of the claim that Jesus is the absolute savior? Perhaps there is a way to reconceive it. Perhaps the large raft of difficulties towed in the wake of exclusivism and inclusivism can be made less burdensome by a modalized pluralism. Then our more modest position, more in keeping with the finitude and relatedness of all knowledge[34], would be that possibly many faiths as quests for understanding about ourselves and our place in the universe attain truth, but all are surpassable; therefore, the faith that carries one's allegiance may be, at best relatively adequate, given one's time and place on history's stage. Perhaps differing faiths can reflect, correct, complement, and challenge one another. Many find it unacceptable that there could be many true religions. But mark well: the pluralism asserted here is stated as a possibility, not as established fact known *a priori*. Hence, the need to engage the others in serious dialogue without *a priori* assimilation of the commitments of the others to those of Christians or reduction of all to a vapid generic religious core, moves typical of inclusivism and pluralism. Note secondly, this position seems to imply a representative rather than a constitutive Christology and ecclesiology, though it leaves open the possibility of the truth of a constitutive Christology and ecclesiology[35]. Third, and most importantly, for a Christian, this "pluralistic inclusivism" or "relative absoluteness", which acknowledges real difference without necessarily implying exclusion, pivots on a decisive faith commitment not to be overlooked[36]. That is the faith claim that the Christ is decisive

---

34. "Aquinas knew that the experience of intelligence in us is an experience not so much of fullness as of hollowness, not so much of power as of desire, not so much of actual knowledge as of luminous affinity with all that is potentially intelligible". VAN BEECK, *Faith and Theology in Encounter with Non-Christians* (n. 21), 59; as K. Rahner notes, our everyday knowledge is a small island floating in a measureless, untraversed sea, though we are more familiar with it than with the sea that bears it. *Foundations of Christian Faith,* New York, NY, Seabury Press, 1978, p. 22.

35. A constitutive Christology considers Christ's mediation essential to salvation; he is the efficient cause of God's saving grace. Without the incarnation, none could be saved. Christ is the condition grounding any possibility of salvation. A constitutive reading of Christ's mediation leads to exclusivist or inclusivist Christologies. A representative Christology perceives the Christ as normative manifestation of the kingdom. While not constitutive medium of salvation, he is the criterion to assess, correct, fulfill whatever other mediations of grace may have occurred or will. While normative, Jesus is not the exclusive, constitutive way, but the regulative representation of the truths of existence. See P. SCHINELLER, *Christ and Church: A Spectrum of Views,* in *Theological Studies* 37 (1976) 545-567.

36. OGDEN, *Is There Only One True Religion?* (n. 23), pp. x-xi. On the paradox of a "relative absoluteness", see L. GILKEY, *Plurality and Its Theological Implications,* in HICK & KNITTER (eds.), *Myth of Christian Uniqueness* (n. 10), pp. 37-53.

in one's life but is also of universal significance, and that Christianity holds "for me" truth and life and the most adequate of self-understandings. A pluralistic inclusivist is not looking to adopt Hindu, Buddhist or Muslim commitments and is not going to envision the world as framed by those traditions. One will continue to read the world in Christ. Certainly, such faith is not without cultural conditioning. Can any faith be? There is wisdom in an observation central to Rahner's *a priori* theology of the religions: grace always incarnates itself; God's work is not carried out only in the secret recesses of individual hearts. Because we are social beings, faith commitments issue in communal expression; people are shaped by, and formative of, the religions accessible to them in their culture, religions that, for them, mediate "salvation" in their small acre of the universe, which is marked by its own epistemic contextuality[37].

Christians want to believe that God is present always and everywhere in history making authentic existence a universal possibility. The Christian claim that Jesus Christ is decisive is not a claim that God is found only in Jesus and nowhere else, but that the only God one might possibly discover elsewhere is the God made known in the life and death of Jesus. God's action in Jesus does not differ essentially from the divine action that may occur in other persons and events. Divine presence in Jesus is considered objective, attribution of Lordship and normativeness to him, subjective. The Lordship of Jesus is decisive for those who experience it to be so[38]. But if authentic existence is experienced as mediated through another, and Lordship as residing in that other, then exercise of that Lordship, a Christian believes, can assume no other structure than one homologous with the demand and promise re-presented for Christians in Jesus. What humans hunger for and find in Jesus' message and mode of being is the meaning of life, a reason for the hope they dare not surrender, liberation from sin, suffering, and death, a ground for the perduring value of their loves and their work. All this, re-presented for Christian definitively in Jesus, may be re-presented for non-Christians, wholly or partially, in other ways. To believe that the Christ as central symbol of Christian tradition is normative and decisively powerful is not to assert that the reality symbolized by him cannot be mediated efficaciously by another symbol for another tradition. Given the ambiguity

---

37. K. RAHNER, *Christianity and the Non-Christian Religions,* in *Theological Investigations* 5, Baltimore, MD, Helicon Press, 1966, pp. 115-134; ID., *On the Importance of the Non-Christian Religions for Salvation,* in *Theological Investigations* 18, New York, NY, Crossroad Press, 1983, pp. 288-295.

38. E. SCHILLEBEECKX, *Christ: The Experience of Jesus as Lord,* New York, NY, Seabury Press, 1980, pp. 27-64.

and diversity of our many human worlds, the universal significance of any particular historical person remains a faith hypothesis. We may test it in our own lives, but ultimate verification remains eschatological.

Two observations are now in order, one an attempt at a clarification of terms, the other the entertainment of a possibility. First, I want to suggest that the terms "uniqueness" and "finality" may lead to confusion. The logic of uniqueness does not carry on its coattails claims to exclusiveness or 'onlyness'. Uniqueness is rooted in particularity and distinctiveness. Mahler's 5th symphony is unique. This does not mean there is nothing else comparable, far less that it is the decisive, normative, unsurpassable, only symphony, but simply that it reveals in its own way what beauty is; in its glorious specificity it embodies preeminently what all art has to do with. Further, the particular and the universal, or the relative and the absolute relate dialectically. The former in each pair mediates and reveals the latter in a concrete entity; the latter in each pair gives birth to and renders itself present in the former. A poem may, in its unique disclosure of life and death, achieve, in its limited way, universal relevance, despite its cultural and historical relativity. In this sense a cumulative case can be made for the uniqueness of Jesus and Buddha in their distinctiveness. Such a claim to uniqueness is an inductive historical claim. But the claim to absoluteness, unsurpassability, normativeness and definitiveness (preferable to "finality" in this context) marches to a different logic, the logic of faith, though believers may attempt to ground its credibility in cumulative historical evidence. Such a claim leads us to ask how a particular historical person, admittedly unique, can be the absolute savior and definitive, normative revelation of the Absolute Mystery. Herein lies the idiosyncrasy of faith, and it is not susceptible to purely scientific or even historical kinds of argument. Historical knowledge of Jesus cannot establish that he is the absolute savior; such a claim is the confession of those who experience God's healing presence in Jesus as the key to a new humanity. So much so that Jesus becomes part of the referential meaning of God.When Christians claim that Jesus is the absolute savior, they do so because of who Jesus was and is and what he did and does for them and in them. As Newman had it, Jesus grasps the believer's intellect and imagination, creating a certitude born of varied and converging evidence too powerful for refutation. Involved is a participatory knowing leading to a complex faith act of inference and love, an act not irrational but transcending reason[39]. Something

39. As Newman had it, Jesus grasps the believer through intellect and imagination, creating a certitude "by arguments too various for direct enumeration, too personal and deep for words, too powerful and concurrent for refutation". Involved is Newman's "illative

similar occurs in serious life situations, in aesthetic and even scientific intuitions.

Such a claim need not entail a demeaning, arrogant exclusivism, nor the inaccessibility of the Absolute in other traditions, where religious ardor will surely, as always, stake claims to uniqueness and absoluteness. All such claims must be contextualized within an awareness that the Absolute mystery is our absolute future and not yet, if ever, fully revealed within the borders of our particularities. Possibly all traditions attain truth but all, as traditions borne by fallible humans, are surpassable. Meanwhile, as we await with hope eschatological verification, the truth of our faith claims may begin to appear solely in dialogue and in being tested in the human struggle for transformation.

It does not follow that commitment to Christianity is a bias that vitiates conversation and study. All thought, choice and action imply at least inchoate metaphysical and faith commitments as to how things actually are with us and our world and what courses of behavior are to be embraced or shunned. This is so of believers and unbelievers alike. Metaphysical neutrality is an impossibility. Any Christian theology is a critical, imaginative construction of a world whose compass points are God, the cosmos, humanity, and the Christ, a creative response to find an orientation for life in a particular situation. One should strive to be as self-conscious and intellectually honest about these bedrock commitments as possible; neutrality is feigned or fallacious. To come to dialogue empty-headed and empty-hearted is to have nothing to converse about. To think one can and should enter conversation with a mental *tabula rasa* is pure self-deception, in Gadamer's words, "the prejudice against prejudice". Indeed, commitment to Christianity's inherent impulse to catholicity compels Christians to dialogue and comparative analysis of the practices, texts, and practitioners of other traditions[40]. Conversely, Christians cannot expect their dialogue partners to step outside their own commitments.

Second, since two of the compass point of an *a priori* theology of the religions are Christology and soteriology, I want to rummage about in the realm of possibility by way of a question. Is it possible that there is a variety of salvations or fulfillments? Or could it simply be that one

sense". J.H. NEWMAN, *An Essay in Aid of a Grammar of Assent,* Westminster, MD, Christian Classics, 1973, pp. 492, 341-383.

40. A case can be made that the ascendancy of Christianity over neo-Platonism in the struggle for the commitment of the intelligentsia of late antiquity was partly due to Christianity's ability to assimilate neo-Platonic wisdom, while neo-Platonists were not equal to assimilation of Jewish and Christian wisdom.

and the same salvation is available inside and outside Christianity (as inclusivists maintain) though mediated in diverse ways (as pluralists maintain)? If the former, all these fulfillments would be, from a Christian perspective, at best penultimate or purely anticipatory and prospective to the extent they are not incompatible with the finality of humans as Christianity sees it. Or could they be enduring and definitive for those who attain them, though falling short of the saving fulfillment Christians strive toward? Against the case for one, same salvation inside and outside Christianity (or any "home" tradition), one might argue that there is no cogent reason to assume that those outside the "home tradition will experience, contrary to their prior conditioning and desire, the same fulfillment as those within the "home" tradition. These questions are raised not simply to pique idle curiosity, but rather because they have the heuristic value of pointing up the true otherness of the religions and of fostering dialogue[41].

IV. THE NEED FOR A DOCTA IGNORANTIA

Having wrestled with these issues, we would be well advised to recognize that the "followability" of the religions in their relationship to one another is rimmed by nescience. We always want to see farther than we can, to turn search into possession, to impose on history an intelligibility that eludes our grasp of the whence and whither of us and all else. And so a theology of the religions, like all good theologies, should be guardian of the *docta ignorantia futuri*[42]. In our study of the beliefs and practices of faithful non-Christians we should rein in curiosity about who gets "saved" and how. Confident of God's universal salvific will and of the ubiquity of grace, however, Christians will affirm the possibility and the hope that God's salvific work goes on in all, ourselves included. Judgments, nonetheless, about the sweep of history are God's (1 Cor 4:5); it is not for us to field detailed accounts of how God may be operative in our wounded selves and our flawed communities. We cannot lift the curtain hung over our history and the love that moves the moon, the sun and other stars. It is for us, rather to meet the more difficult but rewarding challenge of interreligious dialogue.

41. See S. M. HEIM, *Salvations: Truth and Difference in Religion*, Maryknoll, NY, Orbis Books, 1995.
42. K. RAHNER, *Possible Courses for the Theology of the Future*, in *Theological Investigations* 13, New York, NY, Seabury Press, 1975, pp. 32-60.

A *docta ignorantia* can help Christians put their faith in perspective. There is, for example, a pronounced eschatological emphasis in the Christocentrism of much contemporary theology that often spills over into the theology of religions. Though biblically warranted, the emphasis (often sheathed in mythological language) needs rethinking in a world newly educated by astrophysics and space exploration (50 billion galaxies we now estimate!). Can the whole of reality revolve around humanity's salvation history? The anthropocentrism that glorifies "man and his world" seems wrongheaded when we view minuscule planet earth moving within unimaginable vastness. The eschaton of our, perhaps, very brief history may be only remotely related to a boundless beyond that is independent of human history and impervious to its course. Such a perspective begets a humility that affords more realistic assessment of our place in the universe than do eschatological visions bloated with anthropocentrism. We are adrift on a small orb in an immense sea of interstellar space. Are we the center of it all? Are we alone graced with the incarnate revelatory Wisdom of a self-giving God? Or are there possibly many incarnations, many Christ's? Should we sing with the poet?

> ...In the eternities
> Doubtless we shall compare together, hear
> A million alien gospels, in what guise
> He trod the Pleiades, the Lyre, the Bear.
> O be prepared, my soul,
> To read the inconceivable, to scan
> The infinite forms of God those stars unroll
> When, in our turn, we show to them a man[43].

The stage is larger by far than we thought; the drama more complex. The human journey is but a moment in nature's untractable span. This is not to assert the meaninglessness of our history. Basic to Christian faith is the conviction that our history has been assumed as God's own. It is, however, to throw our story and all traditions into a larger perspective. No longer can the West read itself as the obvious center of the universe and its history; no longer can Christianity read itself as the obviously unsurpassable, solely valid religious self-understanding[44].

---

43. A. MEYNELL, *Christ in the Universe*, in *Selected Poems of Alice Meynell*, London, Burns, Oates, Washbourne, n.d., pp. 47-48.

44. RAHNER, *Christianity and the Non-Christian Religions* (n. 37), pp. 116-117.

V. THE CHALLENGE OF ONE WORLD

A sea change is occurring in the theology of religions. We are moving beyond the exclusivism-inclusivism-pluralism paradigm. This paradigm is a rush to judgment. Displacement of exclusivism by pluralism and inclusivism is understandable in terms of Enlightenment modernity's dream and transcendental theology's sensitivity to the universality of grace, hitherto often considered scarce[45]. Still, the paradigm reduces complexity to a programmatic proposal that on its own logic is restrictive of, rather than open to, the possibilities that comparative theology might unleash. Now, however, a new generation of scholars, many expert Buddhologists, Indologists, Islamicists, bring to the problematic new eyes. They confront divergences among traditions rather than vaporizing them away in a haze of presumptive generalities and assumed convergences. Their counterpoint awakens us to the possibility that there may be sand at the foundations of the unmodalized paradigm. These area specialists amplify non-Western voices. Through their work, detailed data is accumulating that is not as painlessly translatable without distortion or remainder into Christian categories, as we had thought. To translate is to interpret, alter, transform. *Traduttore-traditore*!

Numerous are the trials of translation; we note but four. First, while humans resort to plain language, they also resort to signals, allusions, indirect expression, which resist immediate deciphering. There is also the modesty of wordlessness, a sense of a realm language points to but cannot name, a realm that in Eckhart's words is *innominabile et omninominabile*, a realm that only those living in the interpretive community can inherit. We have our music, but also an imagined music in our music. Second, because languages are to some extent governed by existing politico-economic power relations, the languages of Third World traditions may be weaker in relation to Western languages and subjected to forcible transformation in translation. There are no innocent interpretations, nor innocent interpreters. Western epistemologies produce and deploy desired knowledge and languages more readily than do Third World mind sets. The discourse furnishing the favored categories for interreligious encounter are embedded in globally dominant Western discourse. The danger is intellectual re-colonialization, obliteration of the other as other by Western norms and notions[46]. Doctrines

---

45. On the history of this development, see S. DUFFY, *The Dynamics of Grace: Perspectives in Theological Anthropology,* Collegeville, MN, Liturgical-Glazier, 1993.

46. See TALAL ASAD, *The Concept of Cultural Translation in British Social Anthropology,* in J. CLIFFORD & G. MARCUS (eds.), *Writing Culture: The Poetics and Politics of Ethnography,* Berkeley, CA, University of California Press, 1986, pp. 157-158.

and practices of the other may be corralled within categories deriving from exported Western presuppositions of what constitutes religious thought and practice. These categorizations may even be accepted by Western educated elites representing the other religions. Empire lingers everywhere[47]. A neo-colonial metalingual approach supplants a needed bilingual competence. Third, the difficulties of translation are compounded by a growing diversity of theologies inside the Christian household (and by increasing numbers of historians of religion not well versed in the Christian traditions). No longer does one mode of theological discourse articulate what is Christian, and by implication, not Christian. Finally, and most difficult of all, learning the semantic registers of the other may require learning to live another form of life. There is no hermeneutical *intelligentia* or *explicatio* without *applicatio*, praxis[48]. We do not merely think words, we feel them. Because frequently, no amount of listening and watching brings us to see with our own eyes the dreams of another, the hermeneutical task is never purely cognitive, but existential and ethical as well. Sometimes symbols cannot be known from without but only by indwelling them, by participatory knowing. In the end, however, all translations are tentative, provisional, in process.

Many comparativists, therefore, have no desire to prematurely translate or to take the measure of Eastern traditions by simple appeal to what are considered Christian standards. In the complexity of dialogue, reading, and rereading the evaluation of truth claims must be deferred. Meanwhile, in a hermeneutics of wager, other religions may be presumed to be sources of a truth about the human and the transcendent that is not disclosed in Christianity. Probably many theologians of the future will sink intellectual roots in multiple traditions. In a new pluralistic inclusivism the non-Christian will come to live within the Christian as non-Christian traditions are transcribed within Christians who integrate them into a new articulation of Christian identity, one better suited to a post-Christian world[49]. Boundaries may at some points blur. For now, however, ours is a situation of pluralistic complexity that defies easy *a*

---

47. See J. MILBANK, *Beyond Secular Reason: Theology and Social Theory*, Oxford, Blackwell, 1990 and K. SURIN, *A Politics of Speech*, in D'COSTA (ed.), *Christian Uniqueness Reconsidered* (n. 20), pp. 192-212.

48. D. TRACY, *Plurality and Ambiguity: Hermeneutics, Religion and Hope*, San Francisco, CA, 1987, p. 101.

49. See, e.g., F. CLOONEY, *Theology After Vedanta: An Experiment in Comparative Theology*, Albany, NY, State University of New York Press, 1993; J. COBB, *Beyond Dialogue: Toward a Mutual Transformation of Christianity and Buddhism*, Philadelphia, PA, Fortress Press, 1982. For further examples see F. CLOONEY, *Comparative Theology: A Review of Recent Books*, in *Theological Studies* 56 (1995) 521-550.

priori theory construction. Nor are we in a position to mount an *a pos-*
teriori theology of the religions. Larger syntheses are at least a generation away; comparativists are still learning their trade. For now, we have
to be content to live in conversation with the luxuriant diversity pervading religious worlds that contextualize our own.

This challenge to interaction with the great ways of humankind is
daunting. Having barely begun, we cannot envision the transformations
to occur in Christianity. A fearful journey, but Christocentric faith grav-
itates toward catholicity. Christianity will be parochial as long as its history is parochial; the only history suited to a faith whose lodestar is
incarnate Wisdom is the history of planet earth. For a catholic Christian,
love of home gives way to love of every soil, a chance of "belonging"
to more than one history.

Christian theology of the religions, however, would lose its identity
were it to ground its interaction with the religions not primarily in the
universality of divine Wisdom disclosed in the Christ, but solely in some
putative religious *a priori* or anthropological constant. The particularities of one's religion are the door to the universal. To be centered in the
particularity of Jesus, is to enter into his openness to all and his hope for
the coming reign of God. It is to cultivate caring openness, not only to
one's own, but to the stranger as well. That surely draws into one's circle adherents of other faiths. A tricky coinage this. Needless to say, to be
open to the voice of the other is not to deny the need to resist it when
necessary. Genuine conversation recognizes and does not retreat from its
moments of conflict with the other, nor from the fruitful conflict of interpretations in conversations at home. Conversation may require argument
and refutation as well as explanation and understanding. Intellectual
honesty cannot politely sidestep argument when those who take seriously what they believe converse with others seriously committed to
their own beliefs. To shy away from the *agon* is a hollow irenicism, a
cruel kindness that trivializes deep-running convictions. Airing differences, real and radical or merely rhetorical, is profoundly important to
anyone committed to truth and its vital import to the well-being of the
other[50].

In sum, to be religious today is to be interreligious. Interreligious dialogue will have to become integral to all Christian theologizing. The
demands placed upon scholars will be great, but so too the new possibilities for the Christian community as it is challenged to become ever

50. P. GRIFFITHS, *Why We Need Interreligious Polemics,* in *First Things* (June/July
1994) 31-37; ID., *Apology for Apologetics: The Logic of Interreligious Dialogue,* Maryknoll, NY, Orbis Books, 1991.

more catholic. Christianity will be changed, as it was by Paul's march-
ing it into the Gentile world, by Augustine's neo-Platonic Christianity,
by Aquinas' integration of Aristotle and the wisdom of the Arabs, and
again by Rahner's incorporation of lessons culled from modern philosophy[51]. To do as well in the years ahead in relation to Hindu and Buddhist
wisdom, will demand equal daring and discipline. To contextualize
one's tradition along with other traditions is to tap into lodes of new
meanings. Neglected riches of the Christian tradition may be retrieved.
Established meanings may be extended and enhanced. Meanings perhaps
unintended by authors of our texts will occur to newly situated readers.
Norms by which we judge ourselves and others will be enlarged by new
appreciation of the importance of the linguistic, cultural, and theological
contexts that make each tradition what it is. Christian theology will
undergo rewriting as it inscribes transformative reading of non-Christian
traditions and accordingly reappropriates and reconstructs its identity as
catholic[52]. If Christian interpretation of the other is appropriation of a
larger framework of meaning and of new possibilities, the possibilities
do not remain exactly as they were in their original context. Western
Christians turn East only as Western Christians. Eastern traditions
change when they travel West. Consider Buddhism's metamorphosis as
it entered new contexts. Thus John Cobb can speak of a Christianized
Buddhism or a Buddhistic Christianity. Horizons are expanded within an
analogical imagination exploring a new "this" in terms of a newly perceived "that"[53].

Aside from the Christian imperative to catholicity, there are today
moral exigencies that cry out for an interreligious dialogue of liberative
praxis. Diverse cultural and religious communities are networked in
interdependence as never before. Human survival and flourishing on our
planet are threatened by ethnic, tribal, and religious conflicts, ecological
crises, nuclear proliferation, and poverty amidst affluence. Massive public suffering abounds as never before. One has to hope that interreligious

51. The best Catholic theology has always honored diversity while searching out
analogies in the diversity. Difference need not mean dialectical opposition. The classic
strategy of Catholic intellect has been cultivation of an analogical imagination that holds
to a unity-in-diversity. D. TRACY, *Dialogue With the Other: The Interreligious Dialogue*,
Grand Rapids, MI, Eerdmans, 1990, p. 30.

52. See F. CLOONEY, *Reading the World in Christ*, in D'COSTA (ed.), *Christian
Uniqueness Reconsidered* (n. 20), pp. 63-80; ID., *The Study of Non-Christian Religions in
the Post-Vatican II Roman Catholic Church*, in *Journal of Ecumenical Studies* 28 (1991)
482-494.

53. TRACY, *Plurality and Ambiguity* (n. 45), pp. 63-80; J. COBB, *Toward a Christocentric Catholic Theology*, in L. SWIDLER (ed.), *Toward a Universal Theology of Religion*,
Maryknoll, NY, Orbis Books, 1987, pp. 86-100.

understanding will make a modest contribution to human cooperation in enhancing the lives of all. The great faiths share, at least, important formal conmonalities: the convictions that human fulfillment is dependent on a transcendent source of meaning; that where humans are alienated from it, a self-destructive potential in unleashed; that this transcendent source grounds the possibility of forms of life that lead to justice and peace; that arrogant absolutizing of human autonomy, the root of so many threats to our humanity, is to be rejected. These common convictions always appear enfleshed in the irreducible particularities of each faith. This leads to diverse, even conflicting, doctrinal formulations and practices that generate antagonism[54]. Diversity, however, does not necessitate divergence; collaboration need not wait for justification derived from doctrinal consensus. Shared formal commonalities and ever-tightening global interdependence should spur us to unearth buried common ground for shared responsibility for prospering the planet. Interreligious dialogue focused on global responsibility and liberative praxis can serve to motivate and enhance the dialogue of shared religious experience and dialogue concerning doctrines[55].

To what extent Christianity will open itself to the stranger remains to be seen. Commitment to Jesus Christ has frequently been idolatrously ideological when the relative is absolutized and a partial wisdom triumphally equated with the whole truth. To the extent that Christianity opens itself to other traditions it will become different. Not that it will be less Christian or cease to be Christian altogether. It will simply be taking one more step toward catholicity, the fullness it claims to anticipate in the coming reign of God.

Dept. of Religious Studies   Stephen J. DUFFY
Loyola University
New Orleans, LA 701 18
USA

---

54. See W. SCHWEIKER, *One World, Many Moralities: A Diagnosis of Our Moral Situation,* in *Criterion* 32 (1993) 12-21; T. KOPFENSTEINER, *Globalization and the Autonomy of Moral Reasoning,* in *Theological Studies* 54 (1993) 485-511.

55. See P. KNITTER, *One Earth Many Religions* (n. 10) weds his theology of the religions to liberation theology, though he still labors under all the difficulties that beset his pluralistic position.

THE IMPACT OF PLURALISM ON CHRISTOLOGY

I suppose that everyone living in western developed societies is aware of pluralism. It is a feature of the culture of western industrial and democratic societies that young people today spontaneously internalize. The question that I shall entertain in this paper is the impact of this pluralism within the churches and specifically on christology. By christology I refer simultaneously to the understanding of Jesus Christ and the discipline by which that understanding is mediated. I will engage three aspects of that impact in a kind of ascending order: the first is the *fact* of pluralism in the churches; the second is the *necessity* of such a pluralism; and the third is the *possibility* of Christian theology being open to and accepting this pluralism.

I. THE FACT OF PLURALISM IN CHRISTOLOGY

I begin this discussion with what most can agree on, namely, the fact of pluralism. This point of departure will allow me to outline what I mean by pluralism, and to introduce more precisely the issues to be addressed and proposals to be put forward.

Pluralism means differences within a wider unity. In the case at hand, I refer to human beings and their cultures and ideologies. This pluralism obtains among people and their worldviews, understandings, ideas, values, and correlative behaviors. Pluralism, as I understand it, presupposes a larger unity. Some common denominator, some defining element, or context, or sphere of interaction, constitutes a unity that is differentiated. Pluralism, therefore, means that real, solid, and persistent differences prevail between people, between their views, between who they think they are as human beings, between the ways in which they act, and thus between the peoples themselves. But these differences are not all that characterize the relations between the people in question. The differences are not complete; they subsist within a larger framework of something shared, some sameness or unity: of the species, or of historical interaction, of a region, a society, a loyalty to a country, a common religion. This means that at some level one can find commonalities among the differing parties that bind them together, even though the term pluralism emphasizes differences[1].

---

1. Nicholas Rescher defends a doctrine of cognitive and social pluralism in these terms: "As pluralism sees it, a variety of distinct, mutually incompatible resolutions on

At its base, pluralism is an element of the human condition. It is not something that will disappear or gradually evanesce. Wherever there is more than one human being, there will be pluralism in some degree. What has emerged in the course of the 20th century is a reflective awareness of differences among human beings, indeed, a heightened consciousness of and sensitivity to differences.

Anyone who considers the whole Christian movement, either across history or in its actuality today, cannot fail to note that Christians understand Jesus Christ differently. A survey of the beliefs of any large Christian church, even the doctrinally controlled and conservative Roman Catholic Church, would show a wide variety of christological views among active and fervent believers. Pluralism in Christianity is a fact. But is such a pluralism something negative, or may it be construed positively? How are we to read it? In response to these questions, I am not addressing the place of Jesus Christ in a situation of religious pluralism, but the impact of the internalization of a consciousness of pluralism, generally, as an intrinsic dimension of our historical existence, on the church's understanding of Jesus Christ. How does this actual pluralism affect a Christian understanding of Jesus Christ? What bearing does this internalized consciousness of pluralism have on the suppositions and methods of the discipline of christology?

I offer two theses in response to this question. The first thesis is proposed against a view of christological uniformity, the conviction that there can only be one christology in the church at large or any given church. The first thesis is that a pluralism of christologies is theologically necessary. The second thesis addresses the menacing aspect of pluralism in christology; it is proposed against the conviction that pluralism in christology necessarily leads to relativism and undermines the foundation of the church's faith. The second thesis is that pluralism in christology is theologically possible, when it is contained within certain theological and christological boundaries[2]. Both theses presuppose that

any controvertible issue is in principle 'available'". N. RESCHER, *Pluralism: Against the Demand for Consensus*, Oxford, Clarendon Press, 1993, p. 96. Rescher's emphasis is on differences in understanding. As distinct from consensus, he insists that the common basis for human communication consists in a shared real world outside the self. "Our concept of a *real thing* as a commonly available focus is accordingly a fixed point, a shared and stable centre around which communication revolves, the invariant focus of potentially diverse conceptions". *Ibid.*, p. 140.

2. The argument here is developed on the supposition that Christian theology cannot be reduced to describing the beliefs and actions of the church, but that theology is a critical and normative discipline that seeks the most adequate expression of truth in theological beliefs according to certain criteria. See D. KELSEY, *The Uses of Scripture in Recent*

pluralism in christology already exists. The point of this discussion is to show how one might conceive of it being authorized theologically.

One final introductory comment regarding the implied audience of this essay may sharpen its point still further. The discussion aims at defining a position in the center between two extremes. Those extremes are represented among theologians by biblical or doctrinal fundamentalism on the right and, on the left, a sociological reductionism and latitudinarianism that judges every christology equally acceptable. But perhaps more importantly, these theological extremes loosely correspond to two broad constituencies or tendencies within the body of Christians who do not claim any theological expertise. They are people who, on the one hand, were formed in a narrow christological tradition which has become increasingly less credible in a postmodern situation, and who have welcomed the pluralism that now reigns. On the other hand, one finds in the churches today, especially among a younger generation, people who have been brought up in a pluralistic environment, but who are extremely uncomfortable with the lack of clarity and implied relativism that seem to accompany the pluralism of christological languages. I want to address both sides of this tensive christological situation. It should be clear, however, that the goal can be no more than to provide a formal structure that legitimates a pluralism of christologies. The discussion does not engage the concrete moves that are needed to determine the adequacy of any particular christology.

II. The Necessity of Pluralism in Christology

I propose that one must view the pluralism in christology as both necessary and positive. I argue this from the following criteria of a theological position: its fidelity to scripture and the doctrinal tradition, its intelligibility, and its ethical credibility or power to empower a moral life[3].

Theology, Philadelphia, PA, Fortress, 1975, pp. 159-160. I do not, however, use the terms "norm" and "criterion" in the hard sense that Kelsey assigns them.

3. For an account of the criteria of appropriateness to scripture and intelligibility, see S.M. OGDEN, On Theology, San Francisco, CA, Harper & Row, 1986, pp. 4-6. Ogden employs the criterion of ethical or moral credibility in his liberationist interpretation of Jesus Christ in S.M. OGDEN, The Point of Christology, Dallas, TX, Southern Methodist University Press, 1992, pp. 148-168. Ethical credibility also includes factoring Christian piety and spirituality into the balance. See F. SCHÜSSLER FIORENZA, The Jesus of Piety and the Historical Jesus, in Proceedings of the Catholic Theological Society of America 49 (1994) 90-99, and R. HAIGHT, Critical Witness: The Question of Method, in L. O'DONO-VAN & H. SANKS (eds.), Faithful Witness: Foundations of Theology for Today's Church, New York, Crossroad, 1989, pp. 202-205. Finally, these three criteria could be expanded;

The New Testament Prescribes Pluralism in Christology.

Relative to the first criterion for discussing the adequacy of a theological position, its fidelity to scripture, the following syllogism argues that Christian faith demands christological pluralism: The New Testament is normative for christology; but the New Testament contains a pluralism of christologies; therefore pluralism is normative for christology.

The New Testament is normative for christology. I will not dwell on this proposition which enjoys a common acceptance among Christian theologians. The New Testament is the source of almost all of our information about Jesus of Nazareth and the first layers of interpretation of his person and mission. But it may be useful simply to mention that the way one understands and applies this normativity is critical and carries consequences. Modern and Neo-orthodox theology have added considerable nuance to the understanding of the relation between scripture and revelation; propositional revelation, revelation as objective information about God, and proof-texting have been largely discredited. We must think historically in terms of a variety of different communities and authors bearing witness to their faith in Jesus Christ and expressing themselves in symbolic religious language. The New Testament gathers together in one book or bible the testimonies of different and separate, or loosely bound together, communities. Bringing this testimony to bear on present-day understanding requires hermeneutical expertise.

But the New Testament contains a pluralism of christologies. For some time now biblical scholars have underlined the fact of the pluralism of christologies in the New Testament. What is significant in this pluralism for theologians is not simply the fact that the New Testament portrays different understandings of Jesus Christ, but more importantly the irreducibility to each other of many of these different christologies. In some cases, if one accepts integrally and at face value one christology, one would not be able to accept another in the same way. For example, if one accepts literally the integral christological witness of Luke's writings, one cannot at the same time accept the christology of the Prologue of John's gospel. The differences between these two christologies are real and at certain points they exclude each other. In fact, there is no question of contradiction here because these christologies really represent holistic religious experience and interpretation of Jesus

they include other criteria which, in a fuller account, might be usefully distinguished and discretely employed. For example, I have expanded the criterion of scripture to include the classical doctrines of Nicaea and Chalcedon. The criterion of continuity with the past implicitly suggests a criterion of communion with the larger church at any given time.

Christ expressed in symbolic or analogous language. It would be practically impossible to line up the presuppositions, perspectives, and other variables of such witnesses in order to determine strict contradictions. To establish pluralism it is sufficient to note sharp differences in the common understanding that Jesus is the mediator of salvation from God[4].

Therefore pluralism is normative for christology today. Since the New Testament is normative and pluralistic, it seems to follow that the New Testament prescribes pluralism in christology. But this follows only if scripture is normative in that particular respect. Is it the case that the New Testament is normative precisely in the pluralism of its christologies? It is. The conclusion is sound not because of a necessary logic of the terms as given, but because the reasons for the pluralism in the New Testament are paradigmatic and are applicable universally. New Testament christologies differ because they are historical: the texts making up the New Testament were written by different authors, representing different communities, writing for different audiences, facing different problems. These different communities had different cultures, with different traditions, interests, and styles of speaking, understanding, and writing. Also, the subject matter, Jesus, displays any number of different facets for religious interpretation[5]. Each New Testament text is historically situated and contextualized; it is the product of the inculturated interpretation and appropriation of Jesus of Nazareth. The logic of the syllogism, then, is the following: christology should be a pluralistic discipline today because Jesus Christ must be interpreted and culturally appropriated by particular communities today even as he was in the formation of the New Testament[6]. To summarize this first point in a sharp phrase, the New Testament does not merely tolerate a situation of pluralism in christology, it prescribes it.

4. This pluralism is sometimes understood within a framework of a teleological development towards a single dominant christology in relation to which other christologies are subordinate. But an historical understanding of the development of New Testament christologies does not confirm an organic progression in the genesis and interrelationships between the various understandings of the person and work of Jesus Christ. One must accept a pluralism of christologies in the New Testament, without synthesis and harmonization into one, and, because of their differences, without holding all christologies in play at the same time on equal terms assigning equal validity to each. J.D.G. DUNN, *Christology in the Making: A New Testament Inquiry into the Origins of the Doctrine of the Incarnation*, Philadelphia, PA, Westminster Press, 1980, pp. 266-267.

5. See, for example, Edward Schillebeeckx's account of the development of christologies in the New Testament period in E. SCHILLEBEECKX, *Jesus: An Experiment in Christology*, New York, Seabury, 1979, pp. 401-515.

6. The New Testament canon itself illustrates the point. Although the New Testament is a bond of the unity of the early churches, it also symbolizes in its composition the diversity of churches within that unity.

This historically and pluralistically conscious reading of New Testament christology implicitly offers a critique of reading classical conciliar christological doctrine as a universally relevant christology. It suggests that a distinction be made between the christology of a classical doctrine and its doctrinal function. I will argue in the second thesis regarding the possibility of pluralism that as classical doctrines Nicaea and Chalcedon have a normative function in the Christian tradition. But as actual christologies these doctrines are historically conditioned and thus subsist along side others.

The Historicity of Human Existence Necessarily Entails Pluralism

The necessity of pluralism in christology can be argued on the basis of the criterion of intelligibility by a negative and a positive logic. On the one hand, a uniform mode of understanding Jesus Christ by all Christians in the world is historically impossible, so that, on the other hand, it is readily intelligible that the pluralism that characterizes all historical understanding also obtains in christology.

Pluralism is a consequence of the historicity of all human knowledge, including the interpretation of reality resulting from divine revelation. Because the human spirit is tied to matter, and a particular world of space and time, all appreciation of reality is historically mediated and thus shares a measure of particularity. It is this particularity, as determined by historical specificity, that accounts for pluralism. The sociology of knowledge, critical theory, and language philosophy have analyzed the social determinants that bestow particular accents and biases on all human appreciations of reality. Theology, in its methods and resultant interpretations of Jesus Christ, cannot be and demonstrably is not exempt from these social determinants.

But this very situation can also be represented in a positive and constructive rhetoric. Human beings understand reality within the framework of their language, their situation in their society, and the context of their culture. The principle that Thomas Aquinas laid down relative to personal appropriation of knowledge, can be rephrased in social terms: whatever is learned or known is appreciated according to the social historical form of the community who learns it[7].

The principles of the historicity of human existence and the pluralistic character of how reality is construed within different cultural and linguistic

---

7. "Cognita sunt in cognoscente secundum modum cognoscentis". Thomas Aquinas, S.T. II-II, q. 1, a. 2. See Hick's appropriation of this in J. HICK, *An Interpretation of Religion: Human Responses to the Transcendent*, New Haven, CT, Yale University Press, 1989, pp. 240-241.

frameworks have been driven home to the Christian churches during the second half of the 20th century. With the independence won by many nations after the Second World War, we have witnessed the development of national pride and indigenous cultural movements which have underlined distinctive social and ethnic identities around the world. Within the churches, these quests for cultural identity have taken the form of a demand for an indigenous or inculturated theology. What ordinarily goes on spontaneously over a long period of time has become an urgent conscious demand on the part of Christians all over the world. Christians outside as well as inside the West are no longer satisfied with a christology that has been formulated in terms that are foreign to their particular cultures; they are asking for an inculturated appreciation of Jesus Christ[8].

In sum, therefore, the historicity of human existence necessarily entails pluralism[9]. The growth towards a more explicit and extensive pluralism is not only intelligible, it is a positive value if people are to appropriate Jesus as being *"pro me"* in a large sense of the distinctive ways of knowing and acting of a culture.

Openness to Pluralism Models a Credible Morality of Belief

A third criterion for the authenticity of a theological position is its ability to empower a moral life in a particular situation. The situation that I envisage here is the situation of our world at the beginning of the third millennium. And the particular aspect of that situation is the frequently highlighted dialectical movements toward a so-called "smaller" globe in which people are more interdependent, and a simultaneous demand for more regional identity and autonomy. As the world becomes more interactive, threatening homogenization at various levels, distinctive cultural identity reasserts itself self-consciously. The tensive character of the very definition of pluralism, differences amid unity, plays itself out in sometimes dramatic fashion.

To understand the moral demand for pluralism one must begin one's reflection with a global understanding of the church as one. Christianity is a distinctive religion, not to be confused with religion itself or other religions. I suppose too that the Christian church is a world church, a

---

8. For examples, consult R.J. SCHREITER (ed.), *Faces of Jesus in Africa*, Maryknoll, NY, Orbis Books, 1991, and R.S. SUGIRTHARAJAH (ed.), Maryknoll, NY, Orbis Books, 1993.

9. "Different social, temporal, and historical contexts equip different inquirers with different experiential resources. And this will, in the end, equip them with very different cognitive products as well". RESCHER, *Pluralism* (n. 1), p. 67.

church that in principle includes people from all places and cultures, including subcultures that cut across ethnic cultures. At the present time the church is right on the threshold in which people in the West are becoming a minority of its membership.

From the perspective of the universality or catholicity of the church, two reflections support the moral credibility of pluralism in christology as the doctrine that lies at the defining center of Christianity itself. First, pluralism in the appreciation of Jesus Christ already exists. Moreover, I have argued, it necessarily exists, and it is positively salutary. It follows that the church, in its public and institutional face, should reflect within itself and promote this necessary dimension of its historical existence. Negatively, efforts by the centers of world churches to impede indige-nous appropriations of Jesus Christ at the periphery can only appear, in the light of the ideal of inculturation, as imperialistic and a morally questionable use, or abuse, of authority.

Second, recognition of the historical necessity of pluralism in all human understanding has been gradually undermining an extrinsicist understand-ing of authority and replacing it with a more intrinsic and dialogical con-ception. The unity of faith does not depend exclusively upon a this-worldly external and historical authority. Even the most common bond of all Chris-tians, its scripture, has been proven historically to be unable to serve as a bond uniting all Christians. Although external bonds are absolutely neces-sary, Christians are ultimately bound together by their common faith that in every case is appropriated by the human spirit freely as from the grace of God. God as Spirit unites Christians of every age and across the ages with those who first formed the scriptures. Within the context of this growing conviction of religious freedom, institutional churches cannot give the impression that the unity of Christians and Christianity as such can be reduced to the adherence to external ritual, discipline, or doctrinal formula. The moral credibility of the church as institution in contexts that are increasingly inculturated depends upon its ability to encourage the freedom to develop a distinctive appropriation of Jesus Christ. In sum, an explicit openness to pluralism on the part of the world church can serve as a model for a morality of belief in the postmodern world that is credible. Such is my argument for the necessity of pluralism.

III. The Possibility of Pluralism in Christology

I move now to the question of the possibility of pluralism in christol-ogy. The first thesis regarding the necessity of pluralism in christology begs the question of whether it is allowed by Christian faith itself. Surely such a pluralism cannot mean that all christologies are acceptable or adequate to Christian faith. What, then, are the norms for the relative adequacy, orthodoxy, and truth of christology in a pluralist situation? This is the question I wish to entertain in the second thesis.

The context of this discussion is different from the first, which viewed Christian faith as a whole and presupposed a certain unity of the church in the argument to justify pluralism. In this discussion I presuppose the pluralism within Christianity that we now see, and which threatens still more fragmentation among Christians, leading to a serious weakening of the church's moral and religious authority. This is perhaps the more pressing problematic for a younger generation, which presupposes pluralism, and wonders whether the historicity and relativism it reflects undermines the very truth of Christianity itself. Given pluralism, therefore, how are we to reclaim the moral and religious truth of Christology so that witness to it carries the moral and religious authority of a common faith?

Once again, I want to sketch an argument for the possibility of pluralism in christology by showing how the three norms for theology with which I have been working are able to perform their tasks within a pluralistic situation. In other words, these three criteria can be applied to insure that within our historicist and pluralistic situation the truth of Christian faith in Jesus Christ is preserved.

The New Testament and Tradition Function as Criteria for an Adequate Christology

Although the New Testament prescribes pluralism in christology, it also provides norms by which one can measure the adequacy of any given christology. Two elements of the New Testament's representation of Jesus function criteriologically: the portrait of Jesus that can be reconstructed from them, and the series of christologies that interpret him.

Faithful to Jesus. Jesus, as Jesus can be known by historical research, offers a first criterion for an adequate christology. This normativity functions in two ways. Negatively, a christology cannot contradict something that is established about Jesus on the basis of historical research. Docetism is a good example of a christology ruled out by the historical Jesus. More positively, because christology is precisely an interpretation of the historical person, Jesus of Nazareth, and because ordinarily interpretation must keep close to the object of interpretation, the historical person of Jesus as he is depicted by the consensus of historians must enter into the imagination in any portrayal of Jesus Christ.

Consistent with the point of New Testament christologies. The other way in which the New Testament provides a criterion for christology centers on the christologies that are found in the New Testament. But because there are many such christologies, this normative function cannot consist in making one of these christologies a norm for all others. Rather, the christologies of all ages must compare themselves with the "point" of all New Testament christologies, namely, that God was so encountered in Jesus that salvation from God is mediated through him. I will deal with this "point" further on under the criterion of intelligibility. What needs to be underlined relative to norms for christology is that an adequate christology must consider, interpret, and appropriate the classical christologies of the New Testament in order to be faithful to the foundational statement of Christian faith.

Congruent with classical christology. The classical and foundational expression of christological faith did not really end with the New Testament. Certain questions not answered by the New Testament were entertained in the patristic period. The formal doctrines of Nicaea and Chalcedon, for example, have been considered as classical expressions of Christian faith by the majority of the Christian churches. Because of this historical status, an adequate christology must enter into dialogue with this classical language, and allow itself to be shaped by these doctrines in the act of interpreting and appropriating them[10].

This dialogue with and interpretation of the tradition represent the way any given christology in any given community should enter into dialogue with other Christian communities and the church at large at any given time. The pluralism of christology should not be understood as a movement towards isolation of a particular community, or breaking communion with the wider church. Such communion and dialogue could readily be developed as a distinct criterion for christology.

In sum, the sources of christology contained in the New Testament and the classical christological doctrines of the foundational period of the church provide objective norms for the adequacy of christology. Because all religious language about transcendent reality is symbolic or analogous, it is possible for these classic expressions to be normative in communicating a formal content without being prescriptive in their particular

---

10. Ultimately, the reason why Chalcedon achieved the status of a classic doctrine is that its fundamental symbolic meaning represents the internal logic of christological faith itself. Chalcedon, therefore, must be interpreted in such a way that it is consistent with its own norm, that is, the intrinsic intelligibility of New Testament christology.

language and conceptualization, but by remaining open to reinterpretation and appropriation. I will explain how such normativity functions in the discussion of intelligibility as a criterion for christology.

The Function of the Criterion of Intelligibility as Intrinsic to Christology Itself

A second norm for the adequacy of a christology is its intelligibility. This intelligibility may be understood in relation to the intellectual context in which it is proffered. In dealing with the necessity of christological pluralism, I showed how intelligibility within a specific historical context urges such pluralism: if a christology is not credible against the background of the vision of reality that is commonly accepted as true, then it cannot be an object of belief[11]. But intelligibility may also be understood on the basis of the intrinsic structure of christological belief. This intrinsic structure or logic of Christian faith refers to the christomorphic character of Christian faith in God: specifically Christian faith is in God mediated by Jesus Christ. A consideration of this foundational aspect of the intelligibility of christology will account for the possibility of normativity in a pluralistic Christian church.

Because of pluralism, one christology of itself cannot be an excluding norm for another christology. This proposition, that argues against one particular christology of itself being a norm which can rule out another christology, has as its basic reason pluralism itself. In a pluralistic situation, one that not only allows but demands different christologies, one cannot simply appeal to one christology to negate another. For example, one cannot rule out of court the christologies of Mark or Luke on the basis of the christology of John. I add the qualification "of itself" because I do not wish to imply that all christologies are valid. Some christologies can be judged not to represent Christian faith adequately or satisfactorily. But this judgment of the adequacy of a christology cannot be made simply on the basis of a citation of another christology. Rather such a theological judgment can only be made on the basis of the internal criteria which govern the disciplines of theology and christology. And thus it follows that the external norms for christology considered in the last section are not sufficient in themselves but must be understood

---

11. Although this general statement could be parodied in a reductionist way, I do not propose such a reduction. This criterion simply says that faith in Jesus Christ cannot be described as *fides quia absurdum est*; faith is not belief in what everyone knows is untrue. Christology, as the formulation of Christian belief in Jesus Christ on the basis of faith, must be reasonable.

within the context of the logic, the method, the intelligibility of christology itself.

Working "from below", from a consideration of the epistemology of faith, the historical genesis of christology, and a conception of its structure or logic, one can discover the intrinsic norm for christology in the recognition of what a christology must express or explain. On this premise I propose that a christology must "explain" two things: how Jesus is a mediator of God's salvation, and why he is the object of Christian worship. This proposal introduces those elements in the experience of the Christian community which are distinctively christological. These two elements also isolate the primal christological experience, that which provides the basis for the full range of the conceptions of salvation and Jesus' divinity found in the New Testament.

The first element of the intrinsic intelligibility of christology lies in the common conviction, despite the pluralism of soteriologies and christologies in the New Testament, that Jesus is the mediator of a salvation that comes from God. The genesis of New Testament soteriologies and christologies all stem from the primal experience of an encounter with God in Jesus in such a manner that Jesus mediates God's salvation. The recognition of Jesus' divinity is a function of an experience that he is the bearer of a salvation which is from God and would not be salvation were it not. A second element lies in the cult of Jesus, which began quite soon after his death and the experience of his resurrection or exaltation. This worship of Jesus was the principal reason which lead to the clear and explicit affirmation of the divinity of Jesus in the patristic period. These two elements are common within the pluralism of New Testament christologies. Because they represent the experiential data upon which christology rests, they represent as well the groundwork for the intelligibility of any christology. And because they represent the genetic basis out of which all christology arises, they are precisely that which is being expressed and explained in all christology. This aspect of the norm of intelligibility in christology is experiential and as such intrinsic to the discipline itself.

In sum, the criterion of intelligibility includes an understanding of the very logic and coherence of Christological faith. Intrinsically the faith that generates christology is an encounter with God mediated by Jesus in such a way that Jesus is recognized as the bearer of God's salvation. *Therefore, any christology which explains within a given context how Jesus mediates salvation from God and is therefore the object of Christian worship is orthodox, and christologies that fail to do so are inadequate.* This structure also explains how the doctrine of Chalcedon, which insists on the humanity and divinity of Jesus, can be formally normative without implying an extrinsicist normativity for its specific language.

The Criterion of the Praxis of Faith

The third criterion of an adequate christology is its ethical credibility and its ability to empower a moral Christian life. A descriptive explanation of this criterion entails a formulation of the relationship between theory and practice. The scope of this discussion prevents me from dealing with this relationship in any detail, and I will have to be content with a definition of praxis as a form of life or pattern of behavior that is driven by a fundamental faith commitment to a certain vision of reality and shaped by theory. Praxis thus integrates understanding and knowledge on the one hand and action or practice on the other.

Because of the close interdependence of knowing and doing, and because of the structure of human existence itself in which they are bound together, action, in the sense of a free moral behavior that is consistent with christological faith, becomes another criterion for the adequacy of a given christology. This criterion allows one to suspect that a christology that allows or consistently generates behavior that is commonly judged to be unethical is less than adequate[12]. Conversely, one probably cannot say that a christology that generates certain religious and moral behavior is by that criterion alone orthodox. But a christology that is consistent with and encourages certain practical attitudes, convictions, and patterns of religious attachment to Jesus, as well as concern for justice on religious grounds, is at least morally credible.

This criterion has roots in the New Testament; the pragmatic principle is enshrined in the gospels. Axioms such as the love of neighbor being the measure of love of God (Lk 10,29-37), and principles such as "You will know them by their fruits" (Mk 7,16), are explicit and formal. Although this criterion is quite general, it is nonetheless practicable and effective in certain situations. For example, the rise of the social gospel movement at the turn of this century, and its reprise as liberation theology in the last third of this century, show that in situations of social suffering that mark our world an individualistic christology is simply inadequate. An adequate christology in an interdependent world cannot fail to represent Jesus Christ in a morally credible way that engages people's freedom at the point where they are inserted into the social, political world.

---

12. Many questions concerning the character and meaning of the "ethical" are being begged at this point. This fact is consistent with the largely formal character of these reflections.

CONCLUSION

I conclude with an observation concerning the possible usefulness of these reflections. It is difficult to approach the new century and millennium without a sense that a new world is being opened up before the Christian churches. Whether or not the term "postmodernity" helps to describe developments in western culture and its situation in an interdependent world, people throughout the world are daily being schooled in the degree to which ours is a pluralistic world. The church in its churches must reckon with this pluralism as it moves towards the future.

The church is fixed by many coordinates, two of which are its being bound to the past as an historical religion, and its being bound to the realities of the present and the future. If the church only looks back to the past, so that it walks backwards into the future, the pluralism that characterizes the present and the future can only appear as a negative threat. By contrast, if the churches look resolutely into the future through the lens of a critical analysis of their past experience, the pluralism of historical existence can be construed positively as an open field for a new self-understanding and mission.

I have outlined three levels of consciousness at which pluralism can have an impact and bearing on christology which lies at the heart of Christian faith and the church: the levels of fact, of necessity, and of positive potential. An appropriation of pluralism by the church at each of these levels represents a further step in being in contact with our human reality. Most of the churches are becoming aware of the fact of pluralism as it exists in varying degrees within the churches themselves. But the churches generally are not fully convinced that such a pluralism is a necessity. This pluralism is still appreciated negatively as a threat by large portions of Christians and church leaders. And the church still has some way to go before it understands how, while accepting the necessity of pluralism, it can still be confident that such a pluralism need not threaten the substance of Christian faith but may even enhance it.

Weston Jesuit School of Theology   Roger HAIGHT
3 Phillips Place
Cambridge, MA 02138-3495
U.S.A.

REFLECTIONS ON THE THIRD QUEST FOR THE HISTORICAL JESUS

"SIR, WE WOULD LIKE TO SEE JESUS" (JOHN 12,21)

The preacher who climbs the pulpit in one of the main churches in Pittsburgh is confronted with the Johannine reminder: "Sir, we would like to see Jesus". Yet not a few today would agree with the best selling spiritual writer M. Scott Peck (who became a Christian after writing *The Road Less Traveled*) that the Jesus of the Gospels – whom some suggest is the best kept-secret of Christianity – is not the "wimpy Jesus" of unflappable, unshakeable equanimity, who went about with a sweet unending smile, patting little children on the head, an image which three quarters of Christians still seem to be trying to create.

Peck insists that he himself was "absolutely thunderstruck by the extraordinary reality of the man I found in the Gospels. I discovered a man who was almost continually frustrated. His frustration leaps out of virtually every page: 'What do I have to say to you? How many times do I have to say it? What do I have to do to get through to you'? I also discovered a man who was frequently sad and sometimes depressed, frequently anxious and scared. A man who was prejudiced on one occasion, although he was able to overcome that prejudice and transcend it in healing love. A man who was terribly, terribly lonely, yet often desperately needed to be alone. I discovered a man so incredibly real that no one could have made him up"[1].

I. THE FIRST QUEST

It has become quite convenient to divide modern research on the historical Jesus into three historical periods[2]. The classic survey of the First Quest by Albert Schweitzer (1906), rejected the optimism of the late nineteenth century, and showed that the eschatological and apocalyptic areas of Jesus' life and teaching were widely neglected. Rather than lead

---

1. M. SCOTT BECK, *Further Along the Road Less Traveled*, New York, Simon and Schuster, 1993, p. 160.
2. Cf. my survey *The Third Quest for the Historical Jesus*, in *Proceedings of the Irish Biblical Association* (1996) 84-98.

to an authentic encounter with Jesus, the historical critical method tends
more to domesticate him. Further, the so-called objective historical critical method failed to produce an objective historical Jesus. In fact it produced a Jesus who was little more than a projection of contemporary
prejudice and culture. Schweitzer's own view was that the true historical
Jesus should overthrow the modern Jesus because he was not a mere
teacher but "an imperious ruler" ("Son of Man") who comes to us "as
one Unknown", summoning followers to learn "an ineffable mystery"
as he sets new tasks for each generation. The rather arrogant Schweitzer
did not see any use in studying English or American lives of Jesus. He
did, however, venture to France to accuse the French of perfuming the
life of Jesus with sentimentality. Significantly in 1878, P. Schaff
(*Through Bible Lands*) introduced the term "eisegesis" for exegetes
"who make the Scriptures responsible for their own pious thoughts and
fancies". In 1892 Johannes Weiss produced a book which introduced the
theme of apocalyptic into the debate. In 1898 the Lutheran scholar Martin Kähler, who saw the entire Life-of-Jesus movement as a blind alley
with something alluring about it, warned that, because the Evangelists
did not write historical studies but aimed at arousing and strengthening
faith, it was no longer possible to go back behind the Gospels to the real
Jesus, the unpretentious rabbi that he was. We should concentrate on the
biblical Christ and not produce propaganda-type social programs dis-
guised as lives of Jesus, as was so often done in the nineteenth-century
lives. Bultmann would reduce this view "ad absurdum". Fortunately, as
Robert L. Wilken pointed out[3], most Christians, who read the Bible for
edification and instruction, were calmly indifferent. More ominously, the
nineteenth century concluded with the very popular liberal, Adolph von
Harnack, the admirer of Marcion, who produced "a de-Judaized Jesus
with a social programme"[4]. This de-Judaized Jesus would have lead to
disastrous consequences. This was the liberal Christology so devastat-
ingly critiqued by Helmut Richard Niebuhr[5]: "A God, without wrath,
brought men, without sin, into a kingdom, without judgment, through
the ministrations of a Christ, without a cross". Further, as Leander Keck
put it, "the historical Jesus often has an anti-dogmatic, anti-theological,
even anti-Christian ring"[6].

---

3. R.L. WILKEN, *Harper's Bible Commentary*, San Francisco, CA, Harpers Row,
1985, p. 64.
4. N.T. WRIGHT, *Jesus and the Victory of God*, Minneapolis, MN, Fortress, 1996,
p. 58.
5. H.R. NIEBUHR, *The Kingdom of God in America*, New York, 1937, p. 193.
6. L. KECK, *A Future for the Historical Jesus*, Nashville, TN, Abingdon, 1971, p. 18.

II. The Second Quest

The 'Second Quest' was launched by Bultmann's independent disciple, E. Käseman of Tübingen, in a lecture in 1953. Calling for a new debate on the historical Jesus, he accused J. Jeremias of "historicism", but he also warned Bultmann and his disciples against docetism. He insisted that "there are still pieces of the Synoptic tradition which the historian has to acknowledge as authentic if he wants to remain a historian at all"[7]. However, Käsemann, like Kähler, von Harnack and many others was too concerned to distance Jesus from the Judaism of his time. Jesus was a dialectical theologian, a teacher of wisdom, who rejected the distinction of sacred and profane and the existence of demonic powers.

The most significant work in this school was Günther Bornkamm's *Jesus of Nazareth* (1956), which confidently asserted: "Quite clearly what the Gospels report concerning the message, the deeds and the history of Jesus is still distinguished by an authenticity, a freshness and a distinctiveness not in any way effaced by the Church's Easter faith. These features point us directly to the earthly figure of Jesus"[8]. Bornkamm's sketch of the life of Jesus, stressing his authority, his deeds, his difference from the contemporary experts in Scripture, his inclusivism which was so radically different from that of the people of the Dead Sea Scrolls, and his goad-like capacity to make people think, was still that of a cautious disciple of Bultmann.

However, John Reumann's survey, up to about 1980, of some twenty categories of lives, indicates the true range of lives which were, in fact, being written in this period[9]. In 1985 Jaroslav Pelikan provided an excellent survey of Jesus in the history of culture[10]. Unfortunately, culture meant "Western" culture, since Gandhi seems to have been the only non-Western interpreter of Jesus who is given adequate attention, apart from a footnote reference[11] to Gustavo Gutierrez, the founder of liberation theology. In 1986, the Dutch scholar, Anton Wessels, surveyed a number of non-European portraits of Jesus, thus reflecting a more inclusive approach to the wider world[12]. In 1992, Priscilla Pope-Levison and

7. *Essays on NT Themes,* London, 1964, p. 46.
8. G. BORNKAMM, *Jesus of Nazareth*, New York, Harper, 1960, p. 24.
9. J. REUMANN, *The New Testament and Its Modern Interpreters*, E.J. EPP and G. MACRAE (eds.), Missoula, MT, Scholars Press, 1989, 520ff.
10. J. PELIKAN, *Jesus Through the Centuries, His Place in the History of Culture*, New Haven, NJ, Yale University Press, 1985.
11. *Ibid.*, p. 257 n. 38.
12. A. WESSELS, *Images of Jesus: How Jesus is Perceived and Portrayed in Non-European Cultures*, Grand Rapids, MI, Eerdmans, 1990.

John R. Levison, in *Jesus in Global Contexts,* presented a fresh tour of the christologies emerging in Latin America, Asia and Africa, in addition to North American feminist and African American theologies, stressing such ways of viewing Jesus as liberator, ancestor, cosmic Christ and Black Messiah. They concluded that liberation theologians, who are often quite competent exegetes, are not concerned merely to establish objective data or to recover exactly what Jesus said and did but rather to understand the relevance of the historical Jesus for their own situations. Thus, R.S. Sugirtharajah, in the book which he edited[13], insists that the original sin of the historical-critical method is the hermeneutical gap between the biblical milieu and the present day. For him, the quest of the historical Jesus is not only to find the truth about the man from Nazareth but to fight for the truth which will liberate people. He strongly criticizes Western exegesis for subjecting the Bible to abstract, individualized, neutralized readings which rarely focus on people's experience of hunger, sickness and exploitation. Likewise, Elizabeth Schüssler-Fiorenza[14] rejects the prevailing division of labor in which exegesis expounds what a text *meant* while proclamation expounds what it *means* today. In another book[15], she incisively noted that historical scholarship interprets the past from its own values and concepts. Thus, it does not see the history of early Christianity as the history of a missionary endeavor but as an inner-Christian doctrinal struggle because mission, religious propaganda and apologetics are not fashionable themes in the current theological scene.

III. THE THIRD QUEST

The 1980s and 1990s have seen an extraordinary renewal of historical-Jesus studies. Especially in North America, scholars from E.P. Sanders (*Jesus and Judaism*) to John Dominic Crossan (*The Historical Jesus*) to John Meier (*A Marginal Jew*) and Luke Timothy Johnson (*The Real Jesus*) have made major contributions to the modern quest. The millennium celebration of Jesus' coming has added focus to this revival[16]. Clearly it is more an American quest and less dominated by narrow theological issues.

13. R.S. SUGIRTHARAJAH, *Voices from the Margin*, London, SPCK, 1991, p. 436.
14. E. SCHÜSSLER – FIORENZA, *Revelation: Vision of a Just World*, Edinburgh, T. & T. Clark, 1993.
15. E. SCHÜSSLER – FIORENZA, *Aspects of Religious Propaganda in Judaism and Early Christianity*, South Bend, IN, Notre Dame Press, 1976, p. 1.
16. W.E. ARNAL and M. DESJARDINS (eds.), *Whose Historical Jesus?*, Ontario, Wilfred Laurier University Press, 1997.

For Ben Witherington III[17], the Third Quest was fueled by "some new archaeological and manuscript data, some new methodological refinements and some new enthusiasm that historical research did not need to lead to a dead end." James H. Charlesworth[18] asks perceptively whether there is any consensus among scholars or is there "chaotic creativity?" Surprisingly, he lists twenty areas of consensus among experts involved in what he prefers to call Jesus research. Let me list them, with some comments, however brief, from his "terrifyingly rapid review":

1. In contrast to the position in Germany at the beginning of this century, it is widely accepted that Jesus was a Jew.
2. It is widely accepted today that it is not possible to write a biography of Jesus. Nevertheless, the appearance of the Gospels shows that the earliest followers had some interest in Jesus' life and teaching.
3. Many scholars today, in contrast to twenty years ago, admit that we posses considerable knowledge about the historical Jesus. Charlesworth gives a list of "far too many international authorities to mention" who accept that, "in its outline, the Gospels' account of Jesus is substantially reliable".
4. Scholars are now trying to understand Jesus in his own time and within the Judaism which produced him.
5. Many scholars have concluded that Jesus led a renewal movement.
6. Many critics agree that Jesus' attack against the money-changers was probably "the major stimulus to his condemnation and death".
7. Galilee has become such a major emphasis that one of the leading experts, Sean Freyne, remarks that, in recent times, the quest for the historical Jesus is rapidly in danger of becoming the quest for the historical Galilee.
8. Jesus is now recognized as having been a devout Jew who went to Jerusalem on the Passover pilgrimage and revered the Temple.
9. The past twenty years have "seen an incredible increase in primary sources from Jesus' time," most importantly the Old Testament Pseudepigrapha and the Dead Sea Scrolls. However, as Michael Cahill points out[19], it is well to keep in mind Dieter Georgi's surprise at the "explosive spread" of the "so-called New Quest" in the absence of new data: "The reversal of the burden of proof in favor of those who claimed authenticity of material that was obviously and thoroughly [sic] shaped by faith in the continued presence of Jesus

17. B. WITHERINGTON III, *The Jesus Quest*, Downers Grove, IL, Inter Varsity Press, 1997[2].

18. J.H. CHARLESWORTH and W.P. WEAVER (eds.), *Images of Jesus Today*, Valley Forge, PA, 1994, p.1. In *Jesus and the Dead Sea Scrolls*, New York, Crossroad, 1990, he lists 24 major points of similarity between Jesus and the scrolls and 27 major differences (pp. 9-35).

19. M. CAHILL, *An Uncertain Jesus: Theological and Scholarly Ambiguities*, in *Irish Theological Quarterly* 63 (1998) 26, note 23.

after his death did not happen by methodological argument but by way of decree"[20].

10. It is widely accepted that Jesus frequently quoted the accepted authority of the Old Testament collection of scrolls but not the other contemporary writings.

11. Most experts on Jesus and the Judaism of his time agree that he was significantly influenced by apocalyptic thought and that his message was eschatological as he proclaimed the dawning of God's rule, the Kingdom of God. There is wide agreement, based on Mark 9,1, that he expected the Kingdom to "erupt dynamically from above and during the lifetime of Jesus' contemporaries".

12. Jesus' parables are thoroughly Jewish and paralleled by other ancient Jewish parables, especially those in rabbinic tradition.

13. The archaeology of pre-70 Palestine is now providing a major challenge and stimulus, for example, with the "mikvaot" or Jewish purification baths, showing that Jesus' view of purity was markedly different from that of the rich Jerusalem aristocrats.

14. There is a growing importance in Jesus Research of sociology, anthropology and some branches of psychology.

15. It is quite clear that Jesus was seen as unusual because of his unparalleled authority (Martin Hengel) or because he was a "prophet or teacher extraordinary" (Hugh Anderson).

16. More and more scholars defend the possibility that Jesus thought of himself in messianic and eschatological ideas.

17. More and more acknowledge the importance of Jesus' miracles and the authenticity of many of the healing miracles.

18. It is widely accepted that Jesus began his ministry with John the Baptizer and that his message had similar eschatological tones.

19. Scholars have tended to conclude that Jesus did not belong to the Pharisees, Zealots or Essenes but that he had clashes with all known Jewish groups.

20. Jesus was sometimes disturbingly offensive, as F. F. Bruce showed in his careful study of the command "Let the dead bury the dead."

For Charlesworth there are four challenges to this consensus. There is, first, the claim to reunderstand Jesus in the light of what we knew of the Cynics. The Cynic view of Jesus is an addition to such modern portrayals as healer, charismatic, magician, prophet, revolutionary prophet. There is, secondly, Marcus J. Borg's rather inoffensive non-eschatological Jesus whose way to holiness was the path of dying to the self and the world. There is, thirdly, the extra-canonical literature and the view that the gospels are not the only repository of reliable traditions. There are, finally, the stimuli deriving from a sociologically sensitive examination of Jesus' life.

---

20. D. GEORGI, *Interest in Life of Jesus Theology as a Paradigm for the Social History of Biblical Criticism*, in *Harvard Theological Review* 85 (1992) 80-81.

According to Graham N. Stanton, most historians would accept a sketch along the following lines:

> ...Jesus was a prophet-teacher who had healing gifts and whose teaching methods were (in part) unconventional. Jesus certainly did not intend to found a new religion. He did not repudiate Scripture, though on occasion he emphasized some scriptural principles at the expense of others. With a few rare exceptions, he did not call in question the Law of Moses. Jesus believed that he had been sent by God as a prophet to declare authoritatively the will of God for his people. The key to the story of Jesus is its ending. Jesus went up to Jerusalem for the last time in order to confront the religio-political establishment with his claim that the kingdom of God was at hand. On the basis of his convictions about the presence, power and will of God, Jesus called for a re-ordering of Israel's priorities. In that sense, he sought the renewal of Judaism[21].

IV. RECENT STUDIES

A selection of seven authors[22] will give a good indication of the continuing flood of books and the variety involved.

Jesus at 2000[23] contains the proceedings of the national forum for the discussion of Jesus at Oregon State University, down-linked by satellite to 312 other sites. Witherington concludes that, of the key participants, Segal is far closer than either Borg or Crossan to what many mainline Christian scholars conclude about Jesus, insisting "that a non-Jewish, noneschatological, nonapocalyptic, nonprophetic and in some sense a nonmessianic Jesus makes no sense of the origins or character of either early Christianity or of the Jesus tradition after the criterion of dissimilarity has been applied to it"[24].

In *The Real Jesus*[25], Luke Timothy Johnson launches a badly needed broadside on the doubtful approaches of the Jesus Seminar. With some reminiscences of Martin Kähler's approach, he reminds us of the limitations of historical criticism and focuses the discussion on the relationship between history, tradition and liturgical faith, life and experience. However, it is important to remember that Christianity is an incarnational religion and that its New Testament does make historical claims about Jesus which can be examined.

---

21. G.N. STANTON, *Historical Jesus* in R.J. COGGINS and J.L. HOULDEN (eds.), *A Dictionary of Biblical Interpretation*, London, SCM, 1990, p.289.
22. This develops B. Witherington's postcript to his second edition of *The Jesus Quest*.
23. M. BORG (ed.), *Jesus at 2000*, Boulder, Col., Westview Press, 1996.
24. *Ibid.*, 259.
25. L.T. JOHNSON, *The Real Jesus*, San Francisco, CA, Harper, 1996.

In two detailed studies[26], Richard Horsley examines the social realities and situation of first-century Galilee, while, surprisingly, ignoring
both the key dimension of religious life and the Jesus movement in particular. His major assumptions, which include an enormous tax burden,
the absence of synagogues and Pharisees on a permanent basis, the
rejection of Theissen's hypothesis of a wandering charismatic Jesus, or
the Cynic Jesus, the dominance of Aramaic as a spoken language, and
the absence of any real Christian presence in Galilee during the last two
thirds of the first century C.E., have given much room for thought.

John Dominic Crossan, who has emphasized a Mediterranean instead
of a more precise Galilean background for Jesus, has continued his
rather quirky odyssey with his popular, historically minimalist study,
Who Killed Jesus? In direct contradiction to Raymond Brown's magis-
terial *The Death of the Messiah*[27], he holds that 80% of the passion narratives are prophecy while only 20% are history remembered, of which
a sizeable part is Christian propaganda. Crossan makes the following
claims[28]:

1.   The historical Jesus had both a personal or individual vision and a cor-
     porate or social program for the kingdom of God, there and then, in
     Lower Galilee, during the early first century C.E.
2.   Negatively, Jesus' program opposed the systemic injustice and struc-
     tural violence (as distinct from, but also including, personal or indi-
     vidual evil) of colonial oppression by Roman imperialism.
3.   That program's implementation involved a network of missionaries,
     of individuals willing to live like Jesus and empowered to announce
     the kingdom's presence in and by their lifestyle.
4.   That mission involved an absolute reciprocity of healing and eating,
     not just an imbalance of charismatic begging and sympathetic alms-
     giving.
5.   Theissen is quite correct in emphasizing the Cynic-like lifestyle of
     Jesus and those first missionaries – the knapsack's absence pro-
     claimed self-sufficiency for Jesus' missionaries as its presence did for
     the Cynics.
6.   Most of the first missionaries were probably from the rural poor and
     many may have been forced off the land so that Jesus' mission repre-
     sented an alternative to beggary or banditry.
7.   Theissen's "ethical radicalism" (to be distinguished from ascetic or
     apocalyptic, or esoteric or gnostic radicalism) is a very good descrip-
     tion of this program. It is above all a political statement of dissocia-
     tion from a systematically unjust situation.

    26. R. HORSLEY, *Galilee History, Politics, People*, Philadelphia, PA, Trinity Press
International, 1995; *Archaeology, History and Society in Galilee*, Philadelphia, PA, Trinity Press International, 1996.
    27. R. BROWN, *The Death of the Messiah*, New York, Doubleday, 1994.
    28. CROSSAN, *Whose Historical Jesus?*, pp. 9-11.

8. On the one hand, that mission, by its immediate lifestyle, obviated any need for a theoretical schooling process before those first followers could themselves perform the kingdom just as well as Jesus. On the other hand, there was necessarily a paradoxical relationship between itinerants and householders. Were all supposed to become itinerants?

Robert Funk, the controversial founder, in 1985, of the Jesus Seminar, published in 1996 *Honest to Jesus: Jesus for a New Millennium*[29], a study aimed at a wider audience and intended to set Jesus free from the dogmatic and ecclesiastical cages which Funk himself no longer found to be credible. He concluded that the earliest window on Jesus was to be seen in the earliest strata of the hypothetically reconstructed Q and in the earliest form of the Gospel of Thomas, both of which date to the 50s. Jesus steadily refused to be explicit in his teaching. He was not an eschatological prophet but quite simply an "irreligious, irreverent and impious" pungent pundit. Jesus was a secular sage, who may have more relevance to the spiritual dimensions of society at large than to institutionalized religion. Mark invented the mainly fictional passion narrative – Judas, for example, was not a historical person.

E.P. Sanders, in his *The Historical Figure of Jesus*[30], insists he is speaking as a historian and does not discuss either what God did or did not accomplish through Jesus' life and death. He believes that Jesus did not come into fundamental conflict with "Judaism", that is, with opinions and views which were shared by most of the people. Thus, he believes that the issues of food and Sabbath are so prominent in the Gospels because of the importance which they assumed in the early Church. While he accepts that Jesus proclaimed a future eschatology, he doubts that Jesus ever spoke of the kingdom as already present in his ministry. He summarizes:

> Much about the historical Jesus will remain a mystery. Nothing is more mysterious than the stories of his resurrection, which attempt to portray an experience that the authors could not themselves comprehend. But in the midst of mystery and uncertainty, we should remember that we know a lot about Jesus. We know that he started with John the Baptist, that he had disciples, that he expected the "kingdom," that he went from Galilee to Jerusalem, that he did something hostile against the Temple, that he was tried and crucified. Finally we know that after his death his followers experienced what they described as the "resurrection": the appearance of a living but transformed person who had actually died. They believed this, they lived for it, and they died for it. In the process they created a movement, a movement that in many ways went far beyond Jesus' message. Their movement grew and spread geographically.

29. R. FUNK, *Honest to Jesus: Jesus for a New Millennium*, San Francisco, CA, Harper, 1996.
30. E.P. SANDERS, *The Historical Figure of Jesus*, London, Penguin Books, 1993.

Twenty-five or more years later, Paul – a convert, not an original disciple –
still expected Jesus to return within his own lifetime. But Jesus tarried. The
delay led to creative and stimulating theological reflection, seen especially in
the Gospel of John; but the synoptic material was by no means immune from
theological development. Meanwhile, the man behind it all became remote.
The consequence is that it takes patient spadework to dig through the layers of
Christian devotion and to recover the historical core. Historical reconstruction
is never absolutely certain, and in the case of Jesus it is sometimes highly
uncertain. Despite this, we have a good idea of the main lines of his ministry
and his message. We know who he was, what he did, what he taught, and why
he died. Perhaps most important we know how much he inspired his followers, who sometimes themselves did not understand him, but who were so
loyal to him that they changed history[31].

John P. Meier has continued his "limited consensus statement", his
major contribution to Jesus research, with volume two of *A Marginal
Jew: Rethinking the Historical Jesus,* subtitled *Mentor, Message and
Miracles*[32], a work which has been praised as the most carefully presented historical-critical statement about Jesus in this century. Jesus
accepted the baptism of John, his mentor, and his message of the necessity of eschatological repentance if the imminent disaster which was
threatening Israel was to be avoided. But this ministry was a wider one
than John's, since Jesus went to different geographical regions, to Jews
of all socio-religious persuasions, and preached not only repentance and
judgment but also the good news of God's coming. The distinctive
phrase, "kingdom of God", which was not widely used, was central to
his proclamation. God's rule was present, somehow, for Jesus, but there
would also be a final coming with a reversal of injustices. It was not the
result of a political movement or a social improvement program. As for
his miracles, Meier rejects the view that they were merely ancient magical procedures. He also denies Sanders' "a priori" attitude which begins
from the conclusion that miracles cannot and therefore did not happen. It
is sufficient for a historian to know that Jesus performed deeds which
many people, both friends and enemies (and probably Jesus himself),
considered miracles. They were an integral part of Jesus' ministry, and
there is as much historical corroboration for them as there is for almost
any other statement which we can make about the Jesus of history.

N.T. Wright, in *Jesus and the Victory of God*[33], part of his multi-vol-
ume, as yet incomplete, study of *Christian Origins and the Question of*

---

31. *Ibid.,* pp. 280-281.
32. J.P. MEIER, *A Marginal Jew: Rethinking the Historical Jesus,* vol. 2, *Mentor,
Message, and Miracles,* New York, Doubleday, 1994.
33. N.T. WRIGHT, *Jesus and the Victory of God,* Philadelphia, PA, Fortress Press, 1996.

God, has produced the most positive, comprehensive and consistent study of Jesus in the "Third Quest". Wright had invented the phrase, "Third Quest", to describe one particular dimension, namely, "that which regards Jesus as an eschatological prophet announcing the long-awaited kingdom, and which undertakes serious historiography around that point"[34]. However, some use the phrase to indicate all current study of Jesus. For Wright, the search is of very specific relevance for those who profess some kind of Christian faith. If people such as Crossan (a "rather skeptical New Testament professor with the soul of a leprechaun", one of the most brilliant New Testament scholars alive today whose book is "almost entirely wrong")[35] and Mack are right, then the churches would need very radical changes today. He quotes the wry comment of a recent survey of the Church of England on the manifold reasons why people do not go to church:

> Part of the reason is simply a lack of belief that the death of Christ was the turning point of history....It all seems less likely to be true, the more you discover about those maniacs in the first century who were expecting a Messiah and getting ready for the end of the world[36].

The main task of Wright's book is to discuss the mindset of Jesus, within the total world view of first-century Judaism, as he goes to the cross. He follows a four-fold path of praxis, story, symbol and ideas. He uses a criterion of "double similarity" and "double dissimilarity" according to which the words and works of Jesus are "decisively similar to both the Jewish context and the early Christian world and at the same time importantly dissimilar"[37]. Jesus is a monotheistic Jew who focused on eschatology and election, on God and, in particular God's action in the present, bringing to a climax in Jesus' ministry both his redemption, critique and judgment on his people. Central to Wright's interpretation are his views on eschatology and, in particular, his conclusion that sayings, which are frequently seen as predicting a literal end to the world of space and time, are in fact to be seen as metaphorical. Further, he insists that the Jews of Jesus' time saw themselves as still "in exile" and expected that their God would restore them to their land and forgive their sins. Did Jesus fail also like so many others? The answer is given in the resurrection to which the early church witnessed. They insist, in the face of the Romans and failure, that the decisive victory has been achieved. Their answer was just as

34. *Ibid.*, p. 14.
35. *Ibid.*, p. 44.
36. *Ibid.*, p. xiv.
37. *Ibid.*, p. 132.

"maniac" and unbelievable to most people in the ancient world as it is today: "Would any serious-thinking first-century Jew claim that the promise of Isaiah 40-66 or of Jeremiah, Ezechiel or Zechariah, had been fulfilled? That the power and domination of paganism had been broken? That Yahweh had already returned to Zion? That the covenant had been renewed, and Israel's sins forgiven? That the long-awaited new exodus had happened?"[38].

For Wright the key questions are, firstly, how did Christianity begin and why did it take the shape it did? And, secondly, what does Christianity believe and does it make sense? To postpone the effectiveness of Jesus' victory to an after-life or to transform it into the victory of the true ideas of idealism over false ones, is to de-Judaize Jesus' program completely.

In Wright's popular *Who was Jesus?*[39] there are five key questions which are serious and legitimate if anyone wants to get to grips with modern Jesus-studies:

1. In Jesus' relationship with Judaism, did he share or challenge his contemporaries' aspirations and hopes for the immediate future?
2. What were Jesus' aims that led him on in his day to day ministry and what was he wanting people to do if they were to respond to him appropriately?
3. Why did Jesus die? The truth lies between the view, not found in our sources, that Jesus was a revolutionary killed by the Romans and the bland mild view of Jesus whom no one would have opposed. Did Jesus see himself called to meet a violent death?
4. Why did the early Church begin? Or what really happened at Easter? While the theories of Thiering ("Jesus in Code") and Wilson ("a moderately pale Galilean") are frankly laughable, the "Third Quest" has so far little to say, but serious historical scholarship cannot remain silent here.
5. Why are the Gospels, written by Christians (perhaps not exclusively) for Christians, the way they are? Are they substantially true but slanted like the better newspapers? Or like the worst newspapers substantially slanted and largely untrue?

Wright grants that it is "actually highly likely, that the Church has distorted the real Jesus, and needs to repent of this and rediscover who its Lord actually is". This does not mean the Church has been wrong in everything but that "real no-holds-barred history" is the approach to take in resisting the likes of Thiering, Wilson and Spong. Serious history is the answer to those who offer a Jesus of their own imagination.

38. *Ibid.*, pp. xvii-xviii.
39. N.T. WRIGHT, *Who was Jesus?*, London, SPCK, 1992, p.17.

V. Conclusions

There is widespread approval among scholars of E. P. Sanders' conclusion: "The dominant view today seems to be that we can know pretty well what Jesus was out to accomplish, that we can know a lot about what he said, and that those two things make sense within the world of first-century Judaism"[40]. This quotation comes from his study, *Jesus and Judaism,* which has been the most widely discussed scholarly study of Jesus in the "Third Quest". He sees three types of information as central, the fact about Jesus' career, the outcome of his life and teaching and knowledge of first-century Judaism. Jesus was a restorationist prophet who announced the doom of the Temple[41]. The work of B. J. Meyer, *The Aims of Jesus*[42], has been widely influential here. Methodologically rigorous, drawing on the philosophy of Bernard Lonergan, Meyer sees the restoration of Israel as the basic theme of Jesus' kingdom proclamation. He accepts the gospel distinction between the public and private teaching of Jesus who envisaged a new reborn covenant community in which sins would be forgiven.

The historical problems in reconstructing Jesus of Nazareth are well outlined by John Meier's *A Marginal Jew*. He carefully distinguishes the real Jesus from the historical Jesus, a fragile reconstruction based on available evidence and dealing with probabilities rather than certainties, providing fragments of the real person, but nothing more. His Jesus is a marginal Jew who lived on the edge of the empire ("a blip on the radar screen") in a smallish area where he identified with those in the margins of society.

For Luke Timothy Johnson one of the great deficiencies of the historical critical method is its disregard for the literary complexities of the texts, leading to the fragmentation of the texts into smaller pieces which are then used as historical sources. It is the final literary form of such texts which are canonized. Only when we attend to this literary dimension (he notes how most modern research begins by eliminating the literary structure of the Gospels) are we engaged in the interpretation of the New Testament. To read these texts as merely sources of historical information is "to miss the most important and explicit insight they offer the reader, namely, how the experience of the powerful Spirit of God that came through the crucified Messiah, Jesus, created not only a new understanding of who Jesus was but, simultaneously, a new understanding of

---

40. E.P. Sanders, *Jesus and Judaism*, Philadelphia, PA, Fortress Press, 1985.
41. *Ibid.*, p. 17.
42. B.J. Meyer, *The Aims of Jesus*, London, SCM, 1979.

God and God's way with the world"[43]. Johnson is in a long line of theologians such as Martin Kähler (the biblical Christ) and Rudolph Bultmann (the kerygmatic Christ) who insist that historical research cannot deny or confirm Christian faith. While a historian can produce a mini-biography of Jesus, a believer knows that they are addressed by the living, real yet mysterious Jesus and therefore can say much more about his deeper significance.

After more than a century of the almost total dominance of the historical-critical method among Western scholars, with an emphasis on origins and the development of texts, tentative approaches towards a new paradigm are emerging. There is an emphasis on the biblical texts as wholistic documents, as literary units, with a stress on the role of readers in the hermeneutical process. This approach is already producing a new type of Gospel criticism. According to John Barton's reflections on James Barr's 1977 inaugural lecture at Oxford, "Does Biblical Study still belong to Theology?", there is "a widespread perception of professional biblical scholarship as concerned only to talk to itself, taking the Bible away from the believing community and encapsulating it in a small world with its own rules"[44]. People, he suggests, feel that the Bible needs to be given back to the Church and the gap bridged between the professionals and ordinary Christians. The non-western approaches have much to teach the West here, a West which has been bedeviled by compartmentalization. As William M. Thompson put it, "the gospel-like critical spirit is far preferable to anythng to be had from hacksawers of the Gospels, whose critique is from without"[45].

A modern approach should of necessity be a much humbler approach. Martin Hengel pointed out in a lecture at the Roman Pontifical Institute[46] that "most of the great early Christian literature from the 1st and 2nd centuries has been lost, probably more than 90%". While these remains are far more than we have from contemporary religions and cults it is essential to remember that the historical reconstruction of earliest Christianity "will always be a search and that we do not arrive at a genuine continuous history or a full picture with always clearly-defined figures and traits". How abundantly rich must have been the oral teaching and how little do we really know about it. Radical critics with their enlightened feeling of superiority have concluded that everything is completely

43. L.T. JOHNSON, *Who is Jesus?* in *Commonweal*, December 1995, p.13.
44. *Expository Times* 100 (1989) 443.
45. W.M. THOMPSON, *The Struggle for Theology's Soul,* New York, Crossroad, 1996, p. 65.
46. M. HENGEL, *Problems of a History of Earliest Christianity,* in *Biblica* 78 (1997) 131.

uncertain. The most depressing problem in modern biblical scholarship since the Enlightenment is, according to Hengel, on the one hand, "the careless disregard of sources and, on the other hand, the fantastic over-interpretation" of a remote, strange and difficult world far removed from the world of a central European, "a mythic world full of angels, demons and apocalyptic hopes"[47]. I often recall the famous cartoon in a French journal during Vatican II. The picture was of pompous theologians proudly scanning the horizon for Jesus while behind them, hidden by a large rock, was Jesus talking to some children. The word *eisegesis* has recently entered our dictionaries. No method seems to have escaped its embrace. John Meier, rereading such classics as Bultmann's *History of the Synoptic Tradition* and Bornkamm's *Jesus of Nazareth*, notes the disconcerting way in which great authors like these "would decide the weighty question of the historicity of the material in a few sentences or at times with an airy wave of the hand"[48]. The fact is that all recon-structions of Jesus inevitably produce a Jesus of faith.

An honest view of the "strangeness" and "uncomfortableness" of Jesus should always be respectfully treated. Comments of writers stand-ing outside Christianity should be noted. Thus, in *Jesus, The Unan-swered Questions*[49], John Bowden summarizes Richard Robinson's *An Atheist's Values* where he notes the element of harshness in Jesus' teach-ing, its obscurity and paradoxical character, and the absence of the ideal of truth and knowledge.

> Jesus poured contempt on the professors of knowledge and declared that the kingdom of heaven is hidden from the wise and prudent. There is no place for beauty or justice. Above all, Robinson points out, Jesus says nothing on any social question except divorce, and all ascriptions of any political doctrine to him are false. He does not pronounce about war, capi-tal punishment, gambling, justice, the administration of law, the distribu-tion of goods, socialism, equality of income, equality of sex, equality of colour, equality of opportunity, tyranny, freedom, slavery, self determina-tion. There is nothing Christian about being for any of these things, nor about being against them, if we mean by Christian what Jesus taught according to the Synoptic Gospels.

According to the Gospels, the "quest" was already alive in Jesus' own time and the results were as varied. According to Mark 6,1-6, Jesus' fellow townspeople thought he was an ordinary person no more distin-guished than themselves. In Mark 3,19-21 his family is convinced he is mad. The scribes from Jerusalem believed he was in league with the

---

47. *Ibid.*, pp. 133-134.
48. MEIER, *A Marginal Jew*, vol 2, p. 2.
49. John BOWDEN, *Jesus: The Unanswered Questions*, London, SCM, 1988, p. 107.

devil. How otherwise could he cast out demons (Mark 3,22)? Some thought he was a prophet like the Baptist or Jeremiah or one of the prophets or even the Messiah! The evidence of the Gospels is that no one appreciated him adequately during his public ministry. His own answer is that he was the son of the owner of the vineyard, but that unless one (even a flesh and blood historian) was born from above, one could not see the kingdom which was Jesus.

Duquesne University   Seán P. KEALY
Dept. of Theology
Pittsburgh, PA 15282
U.S.A.

THE HISTORICAL JESUS
IN THE PLURALIST THEOLOGY OF RELIGIONS

I. INTRODUCTION: CLARIFYING OUR TERMS

The title of this article is unavoidably ambiguous. Both the notion of the "historical Jesus" and the notion of the "pluralist theology of religions" are controverted. Both expressions need to be clarified before the discussion can even begin.

John Meier can help us as far as the "historical Jesus" is concerned. Meier insists that the "historical Jesus" must not be confused with the "real Jesus". By the "real Jesus", Meier means either Jesus in his "total reality", or a "reasonably complete biographical portrait" of Jesus. Neither is accessible to us today. "The real Jesus... is unknown and unknowable"[1]. By the "historical Jesus" or the "Jesus of history", Meier means what he describes as "a modern abstraction and construct..., the Jesus whom we can 'recover' and examine by using the scientific tools of modern historical research"[2]. (One author has suggested that it might have been better if Meier had spoken of the "historians' Jesus" in this regard)[3]. According to Meier, "the historical Jesus is not the real Jesus, but only a fragmentary hypothetical reconstruction of him by modern means of research"[4]. I would like to adopt Meier's understanding of the "historical Jesus" for this discussion. By the "historical Jesus", I mean,

---

1. J.P. MEIER, *A Marginal Jew: Rethinking the Historical Jesus*, vol. 1, New York, 1991, pp. 24, 22.

2. *Ibid.*, p. 25.

3. C.S. EVANS, *The Historical Christ and the Jesus of Faith: The Incarnational Narrative as History*, Oxford, 1996, p. 10.

4. MEIER, *Marginal Jew*, vol. 1, p. 31. Meier also refers to the notion of the "historic Jesus", i.e., the Jesus who is the "highly significant source and center of Christian thought and life down through the ages". The notion of the "historic" Jesus was developed in contrast to the historical Jesus by German authors who distinguished the "historisch" from the "geschichtlich". While the former "refers to the dry bare bones of knowledge about the past", the latter "refers to the past as it is meaningful and challenging, engaging and thought-provoking for present-day men and women" (p. 26). Meier rejects this distinction on several grounds: i. the diversity of usages to which it is put by different authors; ii. the tendency to portray the two approaches as rivals; iii. the inapplicability of the distinction to the complexity of the case of Jesus; and iv. the untenable presupposition that a totally neutral study of Jesus is a genuine possibility for researchers (pp. 27-30). For Meier, it is not possible, "in practice", to "adequately disentangle" the historical and the historic Jesus.

therefore, the Jesus of modern historical research, the portrait of Jesus which is sketched on the basis of the historical-critical reading of the New Testament.

By the "pluralist theology of religions", I mean the current in the theology of religions which is characterized by the "move away from insistence on the superiority or finality of Christ and Christianity toward a recognition of the independent validity of other ways"[5]. Within the framework of pluralist discourse, the term, 'plurality', no longer denotes the mere fact of multiplicity or diversity. It now includes the concept of "parity", or at least of "rough parity", that is to say, "the quality or state of being equal or equivalent". By the pluralist theology of religions, then, I mean that theology which advocates the "recognition of the co-validity and the co-efficacy of other religions"[6].

---

5. P. KNITTER, *Preface*, in J. HICK – P. KNITTER (eds.), *The Myth of Christian Uniqueness*, Maryknoll, NY, 1988, p. VIII. Within the theology of religions, pluralism is usually distinguished from inclusivism and exclusivism. According to the exclusivist position, salvation cannot be conceived apart from an explicit faith in Christ. Inclusivism, the model associated especially with Karl Rahner and implicitly espoused by Vatican II, acknowledges the positive role played by other religious traditions, but regards Christ as the ultimate source and/or normative symbol of all salvation, and conceives of explicit Christian faith as the completion of every religious system. For a discussion of the three 'classical' tendencies, see A. KREINER, *Die Erfahrung religiöser Vielfalt*, in A. KREINER, P. SCHMIDT-LEUKEL (eds.), *Religiöse Erfahrung und theologische Reflexion. Festschrift für Heinrich Döring*, Paderborn, 1993, pp. 323-335. For Catholic inclusivism, Christ is always implicated in the salvific process, either as the *font* of saving grace (including that grace which is operative in the non-Christian religions), or as the *goal* of all of humanity's religious striving (in which case he is the norm against which all religious systems are to be measured) or as the *catalyst* for the operation of "the Spirit of truth" who fills all of creation and draws all women and men to the Father (via diverse religious traditions). As example of these three approaches, one thinks of Karl Rahner, Hans Küng and Gavin D'Costa respectively. See, for example, K. RAHNER, *Christianity and the Non-Christian Religions*, in *Theological Investigations*, vol. 5, Baltimore, pp. 115-134; H. KÜNG, *The World's Religions in God's Plan of Salvation*, in J. NEUNER (ed.), *Christian Revelation and World Religions*, London, pp. 25-66; G. D'COSTA, *Towards a Trinitarian Theology of Religions*, in C. CORNILLE – V. NECKEBROUCK (eds.), *A Universal Faith? Peoples, Cultures, Religions and the Christ* (Louvain Theological and Pastoral Monographs, 9), Leuven – Grand Rapids, 1992, pp. 139-154. For a discussion of the relationship between pluralist thought and traditional Catholic theology, see T. MERRIGAN, *The Anthropology of Conversion: Newman and the Contemporary Theology of Religions*, in I.T. KER (ed.), *Newman and Conversion*, Edinburgh,1997, pp. 117-144; *'For us and for our salvation': The Notion of Salvation History in the Contemporary Theology of Religions*, in *Irish Theological Quarterly* 64 (1999) 339-348.

6. L. GILKEY, *Plurality and its Theological Implications*, in J. HICK – P. KNITTER (eds.), *The Myth of Christian Uniqueness*, Maryknoll, NY, 1988, p. 37. See P.F. KNITTER, *The Pluralist Move and its Critics*, in *The Drew Gateway* 58 (1988) 4-10. K. YANDELL observes that the pluralist school itself is characterized by a plurality of approaches. See his *Some Varieties of Religious Pluralism*, in J. KELLENBERGER (ed.), *Inter-Religious Models and Criteria*, London, 1993, pp. 187-211. In *Five Misgivings*, in L. SWIDLER – P. MOJZES (eds.), *The Uniqueness of Jesus: A Dialogue with Paul F. Knitter*, Maryknoll,

My aim in this article is to reflect on the pluralist approach to the historical Jesus. More specifically, I would like to examine three issues: (1) the pluralist approach to the historical Jesus; (2) the pluralist portrayal of the historical Jesus; and (3) the pluralist understanding of the salvific significance of the historical Jesus. Of course, it is not possible to canvas the work of all those theologians who qualify for inclusion in the pluralist camp. I will therefore limit myself to two representative thinkers, namely, Paul Knitter and John Hick. A word of explanation about this choice is in order. Knitter is one of the most prolific pluralist theologians and the most prominent Catholic theologian in the pluralist camp. Hick is by far the most important theorist of pluralist theology and, to my mind, the most consistent in his development of pluralist thought. These two will therefore serve as paradigms of the pluralist approach, though we shall refer to other pluralist authors.

II. THE PLURALIST APPROACH TO THE HISTORICAL JESUS

Pluralist theology claims to do more justice to the world's distinctive religious traditions than either of the two major alternative approaches. Exclusivist theology, which makes salvation dependent on the explicit confession of Jesus Christ, assigns the world's religions an essentially negative role. They are, at best, expressions of humanity's flawed quest for the transcendent and, at worst, expressions of a sinful attempt to manipulate the deity. Inclusivist theology, which holds that Jesus Christ is at least implicated in the salvation of every man and woman, appears to accord other religions a more positive role in the salvific process, but cannot grant them equal status with Christianity.

According to pluralist theologians, exclusivism and inclusivism exhibit two major shortcomings. In the first place, they are unable to integrate in a convincing fashion the doctrine of God's universal salvific will. Secondly, they cannot provide an adequate theological account of the manifest achievements, whether ethical, doctrinal, or devotional, of the world's major religious traditions. Pluralist theology, on the other

NY, 1997, p. 80, John Hick chides Knitter for describing pluralism as recognizing only the "probability" of other true and valid religions. According to Hick, religious pluralism involves "the affirmation not merely of a possible or probable but of an actual plurality of authentically true-and-salvific religious traditions". In a response (*Can our 'One and Only' also be a 'One among Many'?: A Response to Responses*, p. 54 n. 2), Knitter acknowledges that "practically and experientially" he does in fact agree with Hick. The basis for this agreement is Knitter's observation of the "the ethical and spiritual fruits" manifest among the adherents of other traditions.

hand, regards the achievements of other religions as empirical evidence of the operation of God's universal salvific will in history[7]. In line with this conviction, it recognizes the other religions as equal players in the economy of salvation.

The combined appeal to the concrete religious history of humanity and the doctrine of God's universal salvific will is characteristic of pluralist theology. Indeed, one might say that pluralist theology in general is shaped by both an *empiricist* tendency and a *universalist* tendency (a combination reflected in the pluralist determination to give equal weight to both the comparative study of religion and a selection of classical theological doctrines such as the universal salvific will of God)[8]. According to pluralist theologians, the fact of religious diversity demonstrates that the ultimate reality, which Christians call God, has continually engaged men and women throughout history. The medium for this engagement is what is generally called "religious experience"[9]. There are wide 'varieties of religious experience' depending on, among other things, the culture of the experiencer. Given the ineffable character of all human experience and the partial and historically-conditioned character of all human knowledge, it is not possible to ascribe definitive status to any one of the religious systems which have emerged in the course of history. Given the manifest diversity of the world's religious traditions and their often incompatible claims, it seems advisable to regard the object of religion as essentially impervious to adequate description and as perhaps even multifarious by nature. The concern of religious men and women ought therefore not to be which description of the transcendent is superior, but what contribution each religion can make to humanity's historical project.

7. See, for example, P. KNITTER, *One Earth Many Religions: Multifaith Dialogue and Global Responsibility*, Maryknoll, NY, 1995, p. 33; *Jesus and the Other Names: Christian Mission and Global Responsibility*, Maryknoll, NY, 1996, pp. 29, 32-33, 41.

8. I have discussed the theological doctrines inspiring the pluralist system in *The Challenge of the Pluralist Theology of Religions and the Christian Rediscovery of Judaism*, in D. POLLEFEYT (ed.), *Jews and Christians: Rivals or Partners for the Kingdom of God?* (Louvain Theological and Pastoral Monographs, 21), Leuven – Grand Rapids, 1997, pp. 95-132. In addition to God's universal salvific will, pluralists appeal to the ineffability of the transcendent.

9. This notion is given clear expression by Wilfred Cantwell Smith when he describes humankind's religious history as a process of "continuous creation" in which "the transcendent, indeed infinite, truth ('God'), beyond history and continuingly contemporaneous" with it has been engaging religious men and women. According to Smith, "all human history is a divine-human complex in motion", the "process of humankind's double involvement in a mundane and simultaneously a transcendent environment". See W. Cantwell SMITH, *Theology and the World's Religious History*, in L. SWIDLER (ed.), *Toward a Universal Theology of Religion*, Maryknoll, NY, 1987, pp. 67, 59. See also KNITTER, *Can Our 'One and Only' also be a 'One Among Many'?*, p. 166 where Knitter invokes Raimundo Panikkar in this regard.

Accordingly, soteriology, understood as human well-being, replaces theology, understood as reflection on the nature of the transcendent, as the focus of pluralist theology. The fact that the world's major religious traditions are more or less equally well-matched as regards their practical effects confirms the decision to suspend judgement on their relative adequacy as theological systems. Within this framework, orthopraxis replaces orthodoxy as the criterion of religious truth.

The empiricist/universalist vision of pluralist theology might be summarized as follows: (1) Humanity's religious history is can only adequately be understood as a *single, universal process*[10]. (2) From a religious point of view, this process has its source/goal in an *ineffable mystery*. (3) Humanity's one religious history is played out in *diverse cultural forms* (the world's religious traditions). (4) The truest expression of this history is that practice (*praxis*) which promotes human well-being[11].

This is the framework within which Christian pluralists must develop their understanding of Christ and Christianity. In line with the *empirical* thrust of pluralist thought, it is not surprising that they appeal to the "history" of Jesus[12]; in line with the *universalist* thrust of that same thought, it is not surprising that they situate Jesus' history within the broader framework of universal religious history. The results of these two tendencies are clearly visible. Empiricism gives rise to a focus on the historical Jesus or, more accurately, the history of Jesus. Universalism gives rise to the development of what has traditionally been called Spirit-Christology. These two themes will form the subject of the next two sections.

---

10. See, for example, J. HICK, *God Has Many Names*, London, 1980, pp. 74-75. The reference is to a chapter entitled "Jesus and the World Religions". This chapter was originally published as Hick's contribution to *The Myth of God Incarnate*, 2nd ed., London, 1993, pp. 167-185. The original *Myth* was published in 1977.

11. For an analysis of the epistemological framework of pluralist thought, see T. MERRIGAN, *Religious Knowledge in the Pluralist Theology of Religions*, in *Theological Studies* 58 (1997) 686-707.

12. John Galvin has reflected on the turn to the "historical Jesus", especially as this evident in Catholic systematic theology. According to Galvin, "the change in reference from the humanity of Christ to the Jesus of history" represents "a paradigm shift necessitated by engagement with a new set of issues and distinctions". Galvin identifies two major factors in this regard: (1) the concern to provide historical and christological grounds for faith, and (2) the concern to clarify the content of traditional christological affirmations. Both concerns are certainly evident among pluralist theologians. However, it seems to me that their turn to the history of Jesus is inevitable given their basic epistemology. See J. GALVIN, *From the Humanity of Christ to the Jesus of History: A Paradigm Shift in Catholic Christology*, in *Theological Studies* 55 (1994) 252-273, esp. 256, 258.

III. The Pluralist Portrayal of the Historical Jesus

It is beyond the scope of this article to reflect on the nature of the links between the so-called 'Third Quest of the Historical Jesus'[13], and the pluralist theology of religions. What is clear is that pluralist theologians share with the major exponents of the 'Third Quest' a confidence in the ability of historical-critical scholarship to discern the main features of the self-understanding and ministry of Jesus of Nazareth.

Of course, like all practitioners of the 'Third Quest', the pluralists recognize that no single portrait of Jesus commands the support of everyone[14]. Their own portraits, too, differ in particular details. Knitter, for example, has followed the lead of Marcus Borg in downplaying "the image of Jesus as an eschatological prophet", a notion which is still very important to Hick[15]. Nevertheless, pluralist authors are confident that a sufficient consensus exists among exegetes to sketch at least a basic likeness of Jesus of Nazareth. And they invoke this consensus in their own attempts at portraiture[16]. Those attempts display a remarkable parallelism. Indeed, one might even speak of a "family resemblance" among the many portraits of the historical Jesus developed by pluralist theologians. This family resemblance is the product of two tendencies in pluralist christology. The first and most important is the tendency to portray Jesus as a person who enjoyed a remarkably intense consciousness

13. For a discussion of the character of the so-called New Quest, see B. Witherington, *The Jesus Quest: The Third Quest for the Jew of Nazareth*, Downers Grove, IL, 1995.

14. For a discussion of the portraits of the historical Jesus which are characteristic of the Third Quest, see Witherington, *The Jesus Quest*. Witherington identifies at least six: i. Jesus the itinerant cynic philosopher (John Dominic Crossan, Burton Mack, F. Gerald Downing); ii. Jesus, man of the Spirit (Marcus Borg, Geza Vermes, Graham H. Twelftree); iii. Jesus the eschatological prophet (E.P. Sanders, Maurice Casey); iv. Jesus the prophet of social change (Gerd Theissen, Richard H. Horsley, R. David Kaylor); v. Jesus the sage – the wisdom of God (Elisabeth Schüssler Fiorenza, Ben Witherington); vi. Jesus the marginal Jew or Jewish messiah (John P. Meier, Peter Stuhlmacher, J.D.G. Dunn, Marinus de Jonge, Marcus Bockmuehl, N.T. Wright).

15. See Knitter, *Jesus and the Other Names*, p. 173 n. 4; Hick, *The Metaphor of God Incarnate*, pp. 19-20. But compare P. Knitter, *No Other Name? A Critical Survey of Christian Attitudes Toward the World Religions*, Maryknoll, NY, 1985, p. 174 where he observes that "the total picture of what [Jesus] said and did indicates that he most likely experienced himself as the eschatological prophet – the final prophet". See also Knitter, Can our 'one and only' also be a 'one among many'?, p. 169 nn. 7, 8.

16. See, for example, Knitter, *Jesus and the Other Names*, p. 86; Hick, *The Metaphor of God Incarnate*, p. 18. Marcus Borg, one of Knitter's favored sources, has observed that "we can sketch a fairly full and historically defensible portrait of Jesus". See M.J. Borg, *Jesus: A New Vision*, San Francisco, 1987, p. 15, quoted in C.A. Evans, Life-of-Jesus Research and the Eclipse of Mythology", in *Theological Studies* 54 (1993) p. 14. See also pp. 15, 34.

of God. We might describe this as the focus on Jesus' *religious experience*. The second is the tendency to portray Jesus as a person who was radically committed to the well-being of his fellow men and women. We might describe this as the focus on Jesus' *liberating praxis*. The upshot of both these tendencies is a portrait of Jesus as a religiously-gifted genius and a doer of good deeds. It is not too much to say that the pluralist portrait of Jesus bears a striking resemblance to the stereotypical Jesus of Romantic and liberal Protestantism, that is to say, the remarkable religious personality who proclaimed the spiritual 'Fatherhood' of God and promoted the ethical brotherhood of 'man'[17].

Of course, individual pluralists tend to highlight one or other of these features. Knitter is most concerned with Jesus' praxis, though he also displays a real interest in Jesus' religious experience[18]. Hick is most

17. Note the emphasis on "ethical" brotherhood, a theme very prominent in the theology of Albrecht Ritschl, the 'father' of Liberal Protestantism. See A. McGRATH, *The Making of Modern German Christology*, Oxford, 1986, p. 56. McGrath notes that, according to Ritschl, "the calling (Beruf) of Christ was 'the establishment of the universal ethical fellowship of mankind' ('die Gründung der universellen sittlichen Gemeinschaft der Menschen')". See A. RITSCHL, *Die christliche Lehre von der Rechtfertigung und Versöhnung*, 3 vols., Bonn, 1870-1874, 3, 48, 423. (ET: *The Christian Doctrine of Justification and Reconciliation*, Edinburgh, 1900, 3, 449). I am using the notion of liberal Protestantism here in a very broad sense to denote that tradition in Protestant theology, represented by both Schleiermacher and Tillich, which is concerned with "the reconstruction of belief in response to contemporary culture". See A. McGRATH, *Christian Theology: An Introduction*, Oxford, ²1997, p. 103. The attention to religious experience is clearly most at home in the tradition of Schleiermacher, while the emphasis on the ethical implications of Christianity is more at home in the Protestant Liberalism of the nineteenth and early twentieth centuries. Frans Jozef Van Beeck brings these strands together while discussing "the original agenda" of the movement to reconstruct the historical Jesus which, he suggests, began with G.E. Lessing (1729-1781). According to Van Beeck, while Lessing "may not accept Christianity as a system of theological beliefs, he can understand it as true religion". The "central experience" of Christianity "is twofold: toward[s] God, it consists in an upright life, lived in abandon to divine providence; toward[s] humanity and the world it consists in loving all that is truly good". According to Van Beeck, "Lessing's program became the impetus of an impressive series of critical reconstructions of the life of Jesus sceptical of Christian doctrine and intended as imaginative, liberating, provocative clarion-calls for human and theological renewal. Names like Friedrich Schleiermacher, David Strauss, and Ernest Renan, Albrecht Ritschl and Johannes Weiss, and of course Albert Schweitzer, come to mind. They all attempt to render Jesus historically real by being meticulously biblical; but all of them also try to make him theologically appealing by cultivating universalism – that is, by casting him as the historic proponent of the most attractive humanism imaginable: authentic and thus universally appealing". See F.J. VAN BEECK, *The Quest of the Historical Jesus: Origins, Achievements, and the Specter of Diminishing Returns*, in J. CARLSON – R.A. LUDWIG (eds.), *Jesus and Faith: A Conversation on the Work of John Dominic Crossan*, Maryknoll, NY, 1994, pp. 83-99, esp. pp. 87-88.

18. In *No Other Name?*, p. 174, Knitter invokes Edward Schillebeeckx's claim that Jesus' "'original Abba-experience' provides the 'source and secret of his being, message and manner of life'". See E. SCHILLEBEECKX, *Jesus: An Experiment in Christology*, New York, 1979, pp. 256-271.

concerned with Jesus' consciousness of God, and less interested in Jesus' praxis. Nevertheless, both work with a portrait of Jesus which is most at home in the liberal Protestant tradition.

Hick is quite explicit about this connection. In *The Metaphor of God Incarnate* (1993), he declares forthrightly that his "mental picture" of Jesus "falls within the tradition of 'liberal' interpretation established by Schleiermacher, Strauss, Harnack and others"[19]. More specifically, Hick portrays Jesus as one possessed of "an extremely intense God-consciousness". This consciousness involved "a direct sense of a supernatural loving, judging, forgiving presence", which Jesus identified and interpreted using the categories provided by his Jewish tradition. In Hick's view, "religiously the most important fact about Jesus must have been his strong and continuous awareness of God as abba, 'father'"[20]. This awareness was the source of Jesus' prophetic vocation, of his call to repentance and radical love of neighbor, and of his charismatic power. "God was evidently so real to Jesus that in his presence the heavenly Father became a living reality to many of his hearers"[21].

Hick situates Jesus' contemporary appeal precisely in his "universally relevant religious experience" and his "ethical insights", provided that "these are freed from the mass of ecclesiastical dogmas and practices that have developed over the centuries reflecting cultures as widely different from ours as the Roman empire and medieval Christianity"[22].

What is true of Jesus is also true of other great religious figures in history. According to Hick, all the founders of the post-axial religious traditions[23] were inspired religious leaders, who enjoyed "powerful and persistent" religious experiences of unusual intensity[24], and all "have in

---

19. HICK, *The Metaphor of God Incarnate*, p. 18; *An Inspiration Christology for a Religiously Plural World*", in S.T. DAVIS (ed.), *Encountering Jesus: A Debate on Christology*, Atlanta, 1988, pp. 5-22. See p. 22. (The latter article was reprinted in J. HICK, *Disputed Questions in Theology and the Philosophy of Religion*, London, 1993, pp. 35-57; see p. 55). For evidence of Hick's concern with the historical Jesus, see *The Metaphor of God Incarnate*, pp. 26, 31, 77, 80, 82, 97, 98, 109, 110, 125, 127, 131. Leonard Swidler also acknowledges the parallelism between the Jesus of pluralism and the Jesus of Liberal Protestantism. See L. SWIDLER, *Interreligious and Interideological Dialogue: The Matrix for all Systematic Reflection Today*, in *Toward a Universal Theology of Religion*, p. 49 n. 38.

20. HICK, *The Metaphor of God Incarnate*, p. 18.

21. *Ibid.*, p. 18.

22. *Ibid.*, pp. 13, 98.

23. John Hick borrows the term, 'post-axial', from the work of Karl Jaspers, who spoke of the "Achsenzeit", to describe the period between 800 and 200 BC, when an evolution found place "from archaic religion to the religions of salvation or liberation". See J. HICK, *An Interpretation of Religion: Human Responses to the Transcendent*, London, 1989, pp. 29-33.

24. *Ibid.*, p. 154.

their different ways 'incarnated' the ideal of human life lived in response to the divine Reality"[25].

Unlike Hick, Knitter acknowledges no debt to the Liberal Protestant tradition. Indeed, the main sources for his portrait of Jesus would appear to be contemporary Catholic theologians (especially liberation theologians) and, more recently, certain practitioners of the Third Quest, especially Marcus Borg. In fact, Knitter devotes remarkably little space to the discussion of Jesus' life and ministry. To enter into the discussion of "what we can and cannot know about the historical Jesus", he observes, "is like stepping into a minefield where, with every assertion about what Jesus really said or did, one fears that the ground will blow up beneath one's feet"[26]. In the final analysis, though, Knitter does not step into the minefield at all. He circumvents it by focusing his attention on what he regards as the "the heartbeat of the being and practice of Jesus", namely, the Reign of God, the *Basileia tou Theou*[27]. Somewhat to his dismay, however, this notion, too, has proved to be something of a minefield.

Knitter has been inclined to interpret the notion of the Kingdom primarily as "an active commitment to this-worldly well-being", including the well-being of the planet. (His shorthand expression for this is "eco-human well-being")[28]. His most important source for this view is liberation theology[29]. According to Knitter, the cause of the Kingdom takes priority over every other dimension of Christian life, including Jesus himself. Jesus is to be understood in the light of the Kingdom, not the other way around. According to Knitter, "the promotion of human welfare and the transformation of this world – as either a commitment, concern, or question – is a condition for the possibility of knowing and responding to Jesus"[30].

The decision to accord "epistemological priority"[31] to praxis is a feature of all pluralist theology[32]. Knitter, however, has made more effort

25. HICK, *The Metaphor of God Incarnate*, pp. 13, 98.

26. KNITTER, *Can our 'One and Only' also be a 'One among Many'?*, p. 169.

27. KNITTER, *Jesus and the Other Names*, p. 89.

28. KNITTER, *One Earth Many Religions*, pp. 12, 17.

29. See especially P. KNITTER, *A Liberation-Centered Theology of Religions*, in *The Drew Gateway* 58 (1988) 17-53; *Toward a Liberation Theology of Religions*, in *The Myth of Christian Uniqueness*, pp. 178-200.

30. KNITTER, *A Liberation-Centered Theology of Religions*, pp. 38-39.

31. See D.J. KRIEGER, *The New Universalism: Foundations for a Global Theology*, Maryknoll, NY, 1991, p. 126; see KNITTER, *Jesus and the Other Names*, p. 94.

32. See MERRIGAN, *Religious Knowledge in the Pluralist Theology of Religions*, in *Theological Studies* 58 (1997) 698-702.

than most to justify this priority by an appeal to the historical Jesus. Indeed, in his most recent writings, he has identified the distinctive feature of Christianity among the world religions, as the radicality of its commitment to this-worldly liberation, in imitation of Jesus' commitment to the Kingdom[33]. As he expresses it: "Today, the unqiueness of Jesus can be found in his insistence that salvation or the Reign of God must be realized in this world through human actions of love and justice, with a special concern for the victims of oppression or exploitation"[34]. Accordingly, "the primary business of being a Christian is doing the will of the Father, imitating the commitment of Jesus, rather than having clear and correct ideas about the nature of God, or knowing and insisting that Jesus is the one and only or the best of the bunch"[35].

Knitter's decision to identify the distinctiveness of Christianity with Kingdom-centeredness, understood as a commitment to this-worldly liberation, has drawn criticism from a number of quarters, including his pluralist colleague, John Hick[36]. In response, Knitter has acknowledged that the "historical foundations" for his portrait of Jesus' understanding of the Kingdom are moot. All is not lost, however. Even if the critics are right, "another pivotal piece of Jesus' message would remain firmly in place: his call for radical love of neighbor". Knitter appears to equate this with commitment to the Reign of God[37], and he is prepared to use both notions interchangeably in his discussion of Christian uniqueness.

The upshot of all this is that Knitter's Jesus emerges as the "man for others", the preacher and practitioner of radical love of neighbor, who was possessed by a "vision of a humanity united in love and justice as children of a God of love and justice"[38].

As far as their portrayals of the historical Jesus are concerned, Hick and Knitter complement one another. While Hick focuses above all on Jesus' internal life, Knitter directs his attention mainly to Jesus' concrete practice.

Both authors acknowledge that their decision to focus on a particular aspect of Jesus' religious personality is somewhat personal (which is, of course, not to say that it is arbitrary). Hick invokes the example of the

33. KNITTER, Can our 'One and Only' also be a 'One among Many'?, pp. 161-174, esp. 164, 171-172.

34. Ibid., p. 171.

35. KNITTER, A Liberation-Centered Theology of Religions, p. 44.

36. The criticisms and Knitter's response are contained in The Uniqueness of Jesus. See especially 161-174, where Knitter responds to the various criticisms.

37. KNITTER, Five Theses on the Uniqueness of Jesus, p. 12; Can our 'One and Only' also be a 'One among Many'?, p. 172.

38. KNITTER, Can our 'One and Only' also be a 'One among Many'?, p. 15.

divergent portraits of Jesus in the New Testament and declares that he is "doing what... everyone else does who depicts the Jesus whom he calls Lord: one finds amidst the New Testament evidences indications of one who answers one's own spiritual needs"[39]. Knitter admits that his decision to focus on "liberation or emancipation as the heart of the Gospel" is inspired by "our contemporary need for liberation and global responsibility", as well as by the New Testament witness[40]. In any case, he argues, there is "no one way of stating, once and for all, what is for Christianity its 'canon within the canon' or its 'tradition within the tradition'"[41]. "The heart of the gospel or the core of Christian revelation is a pluriform, adaptive, changing reality. What Christians find to be most important or meaningful or saving in the good news of the living Christ has been experienced and formulated differently according to different stages of history and cultures"[42].

Knitter's remarks should not lead us to conclude that pluralist theology ultimately abandons the Jesus of history for the Christ of faith. Pluralist theology will continue to nail its flag to the mast of historical research. There are two reasons for this. First, it has no real alternative, since it regards the church's tradition of faith (and dogma) as at best excessive and at worst positively alienating[43]. Secondly, it hopes to find

---

39. HICK, *God has Many Names*, pp. 64-65. See also HICK, *An Inspiration Christology for a Religiously Plural World*, pp. 5-6 where Hick answers the question, "Where should we begin?", i.e., with "the man Jesus of Nazareth", or with the Second Person of the Trinity, by declaring that: "I propose to resolve the methodological dilemma by beginning with the historical Jesus". Hick explains that this involves an act of the "imagination", which will be influenced by "our knowledge of other religiously impressive people", our choice of historical data, and "our own varying spiritual needs".

40. KNITTER, *Jesus and the Other Names*, p. 88.

41. KNITTER, *Can our 'One and Only' also be a 'One among Many'?*, p. 165. See also *Jesus and the Other Names*, pp. 85-86; 88-89; 91; *One Earth Many Religions*, pp. 34-35; *No Other Name?*, 172-173. Regarding the significance of the pluralist appeal to the contemporary context, see MERRIGAN, *Religious Knowledge in the Pluralist Theology of Religions*, in *Theological Studies* 58 (1997), p. 693.

42. KNITTER, *Jesus and the Other Names*, pp. 85-86. Compare J.D. CROSSAN, *Responses and Reflections*, in *Jesus and Faith*, p. 143: "I would... define my own 'essence of Christianity'... not as some unchanging content but as an enduring formal dialectic between... an historically-read Jesus and a theologically-read Christ".

43. This is strikingly illustrated by L. SWIDLER, *Interreligious and Interideological Dialogue: The Matrix for All Systematic Reflection Today*, in *Towards a Universal Theology of Religion*, p. 33: "The historical person Jesus of Nazareth must be the primary standard for what is Christian. The historical Jesus naturally includes the Hebraic and Judaic traditions as they had developed up to his time, with the particular interpretation he gave them, but equally naturally does not include later 'Christian' reflections about him unless they agree with the *Urstandard*. I am aware of the grave difficulties of arriving at an authoritative, clear image of the historical Jesus. But to the extent that we can, there is the standard". See also p. 34: "... It seems to me that the best image of the historical Jesus that we are able to attain at a given moment has priority over all explanations

in the historical Jesus a convincing witness against that faith. Precisely twenty years ago, *The Myth of God Incarnate*, under the editorship of John Hick, made its appearance. Don Cupitt's contribution to that controversial volume was an essay entitled *The Christ of Christendom*. Cupitt contended that the Chalcedonian definition was damaging for both belief in God and for our conceptions of the relationship between God and humankind. However, Cupitt found solace in the fact that a critical reading of the Gospels was leading to a revision of our understanding of Christ. Cupitt wrote that "enough remains of Jesus to challenge us to rethink our ideas of Christ. In doing so", he continued, "we will be furthering the theological task of the modern period, that of shifting Christianity from the dogmatic faith of Christendom to the critical faith which is to succeed it". This shift will be difficult, Cupitt admitted, "but it will not take us further from Jesus: it will bring us closer to him. It will enable us to recover truths which have been largely lost"[44].

It seems to me that pluralist theology regards the reconstructed historical Jesus as a means to recover truths which traditional Christian faith has lost. Not surprisingly, those truths are the very ones which pluralist theology exists to promote. The most prominent among them are the universality of God's salvific will and the relativity of all historical expressions of that will, including the ones dearest to traditional Christian orthodoxy. The pluralist understanding of God's salvific economy, especially as this comes to expression in Jesus, is the subject of the next section.

---

as to his meaning. What Jesus thought, taught, and wrought is the 'Jesuanic', if not the 'Christian', gospel, even though we only learn it through what others have told us he thought, taught, wrought". Swidler then goes on to acknowledge that this task would have been made easier if the evangelists had been intent on doing this but, of course, they were not. However, despite their interference with Swidler's ideal, we might say, he is mild in his judgement of the evangelists. Their failure to provide Swidler with the standard he has set up "makes this task [of reconstructing the historical Jesus] more difficult, but not impossible". Swidler is obviously unhappy with the designation, Christian and would clearly prefer something like "Jesuitical", but this term, he says, "has come to mean quite the opposite of wht the historical Jesus supposedly stood for". This is a remarkable text, since the process of religious reflection on the historical Jesus is explicitly excluded from the definition of his significance although, paradoxically, the process of religious/theological reflection preceding Jesus is included. Regarding Swidler's predilection for Jesus instead of Christ, see his *The Meaning of Life at the Edge of the Third Millennium*, New York, 1992, pp. 71 ff.

44. D. Cupitt, *The Christ of Christendom*, in *The Myth of God Incarnate*, pp. 133-147, esp. p. 145.

IV. The Pluralist Understanding of the Salvific Significance of
the Historical Jesus

I have already suggested that the pluralist portrait of the historical
Jesus bears a striking resemblance to the gifted religious genius and
humanitarian, so dear to the liberal Protestant tradition. The affinity with
liberal Protestantism is not confined to the portrait of the historical
Jesus, however. It also extends to the nature of Jesus' salvific significance, that is to say, the question of how Jesus is significant for men and
women today[45]. Both Hick and Knitter, and other pluralists, equate
Jesus' saving significance with the history of his effects, so to speak. In
other words, Jesus can be described as "savior" because of the concrete,
salutary effects that his personality and his story have had on human history. He is savior to the degree that his history, which has been recycled
in myth and ecclesiastical tradition, makes a difference in the lives of
particular men and women. To put it another way, Jesus' relationship to
God's saving power is historical rather than theological, or representa-
tional rather than constitutive. Jesus does not belong to the definition of
God. Instead, he belongs to the history of God's encounter with particular men and women; he is an instance of God's saving presence, not its
source or its cause[46].

Pluralist theologians have sought to develop this understanding of
Jesus' salvific role – and remain within the framework of traditional
Christian discourse – by appealing to what can best be described as a
form of Spirit Christology (or, as it is sometimes called, inspiration
christology)[47]. For better or worse, this is a notoriously vague

45. Leonard Swidler is aware of the link between the pluralist approach to Christ's
salvific significance and Liberal Protestant theology. Swidler describes the task of christology as the "attempt to recapture the original 'historical' significance of what Jesus
thought, taught, and wrought, and express it in contemporary historical, deabsolutized,
critical-thought categories". He then goes on to say that "traditionalists" will undoubtedly object that "this description of the meaning of Jesus Christ – christology – is simply
that of nineteenth-century liberal Protestantism". Swidler insists that "despite surface
similarities, the diffferences between the two positions will also be significant". Beyond
suggesting that the latest position is based on better exegesis, he does not, however, specify what these differences consist in. See L. Swidler, *Interreligious and Interideological
Dialogue: The Matrix for All Systematic Reflection Today*, in *Toward a Universal Theology of Religion*, pp. 43, 49 n. 38.
46. For my understanding of the soteriology of Liberal Protestantism, I am indebted to
A. McGrath, *The Making of Modern German Christology*, pp. 53-68, especially his discussion of Adolf von Harnack (pp. 59-64).
47. Both words are used interchangeably by G.W.H. Lampe. See his *God as Spirit*,
Oxford, 1977, pp. 34, 96; *The Holy Spirit and the Person of Christ*, in S.W. Sykes – J.P.
Clayton (eds.), *Christ, Faith and History*, Cambridge, pp. 123, 125.

notion[48]. At its simplest, it consists in the affirmation that the human person, Jesus of Nazareth, was totally imbued by the divine Spirit[49]. As a theological device, however, it is often used to redress the perceived inadequacy of the classical doctrine of the hypostatic union. As is well known, that doctrine gave rise to the idea of the *anhypostasis*, namely, the view that the personal identity of Jesus is determined by the presence of the divine Logos[50]. Advocates of Spirit christology wish to undo this apparent denial of Jesus' full humanity by portraying his life and ministry as an instance of a cooperative endeavor between God, conceived as Spirit, and Jesus, understood as a fully human and historical person. G.W.H. Lampe, one of the greatest defenders of Spirit christology, expresses it as follows:

> A christology of inspiration and possession states no less clearly than a christology of substance that in the person of Jesus Christ God has taken human nature and from the moment of birth or before has made it his own; but it envisages this as a personal taking which involves a reciprocal relationship of inspiring and guiding influence and trusting and obedient response, and not as the hypostatic union was conceived of in ancient metaphysics[51].

In its fully-developed form, Spirit christology almost inevitably gives way to Unitarianism or modalism (though it can exist as a form of binitarianism)[52]. While Trinitarian language might be retained, Trinitarian

---

48. See H. HUNTER, *Spirit Christology: Dilemma and Promise (1)*, in *Heythrop Journal* 24 (1983) 127-140, esp. pp. 127-128. This article was continued as *Spirit Christology: Dilemma and Promise (2)*, in *Heythrop Journal* 24 (1983) 266-277.

49. See LAMPE, *The Holy Spirit and the Person of Christ*, pp. 111-130. "This union might be envisaged as 'indwelling', or as the descent of 'Spirit' from heaven and its incarnation as man" (p. 118); Lampe also speaks of Spirit-Christology as follows: "the 'possession' of a man by God" (120); "God-in-man and man-in-God" (p. 127); "Christ was a man indwelt by the Spirit" (p. 128); "Christ's possession by the Spirit" (129); "the perfection of his [Christ's] unity with God" (p. 129); "Jesus of Nazareth, the man fully possessed by the Spirit and thus united with God" (p. 130).

50. For a discussion of the evolution of this doctrine, see D. FERRARA, *'Hypostatized in the Logos': Leontius of Byzantium, Leontius of Jerusalem, and the Unfinished Business of the Council of Chalcedon*, in *Louvain Studies* 22 (1997) 311-327.

51. LAMPE, *The Holy Spirit and the Person of Christ*, pp. 125-126. See also p. 118-119: "This not an impersonal and quasi-mechanical process, but a relationship between persons. It consists, in its perfection, of the total response of the human spirit to the fully pervasive influence of the divine Spirit, so that the human attains its highest fulfilment in becoming the free and responsive agent of the divine".

52. See B. HEBBELTHWAITE, *The Incarnation: Collected Essays in Christology*, Cambridge, 1987, pp. 126-139 (*Contemporary Unitarianism*). In this essay, Hebbelthwaite discusses the work of Lampe. See also C. MOULE, *Three Points of Conflict in the Christological Debate"*, in M. GOULDER (ed.), *Incarnation and Myth: The Debate Continued*, London, 1979, pp. 134, 140.

doctrine must be rejected[53]. Lampe is well aware of this fact. In the final analysis, Spirit christology operates with a radically "monistic" concept of God[54]. The Spirit *is* "God the Father, God in Jesus Christ, God in every other mode of his self-revelation to [humankind] and his contact with the world of his creation". In short, the Spirit is "simply synony-mous" with God, understood as "the transcendent and immanent Cre-ator, the mover and inspirer and savior of all that is"[55]. Accordingly, as Lampe acknowledges, "Spirit christology cannot affirm that Jesus *is* 'substantivally' God [emphasis Lampe]"[56]. Instead, it prefers to regard him as God in an 'adverbial' sense. This means that the term, "divine", is used with reference to Jesus' actions. In Jesus a remarkable "unity of will and operation" has been established between God and a particular human person. Hence, we can say that "in all his actions the human Jesus acted divinely. In his teaching, healing, judging, forgiving, rebuk-ing, God teaches, heals, judges, forgives and rebukes, without infringing the freedom and responsibility of the human subject"[57].

Clearly, Spirit christology requires us to dispense with the time-honored notions of a pre-existent personal Son or pre-existent Christ. These will have

53. LAMPE, *God as Spirit*, pp. 33, 139-141; see also LAMPE, *The Holy Spirit and the Person of Christ*, p. 129.

54. The term, "monistic", is Lampe's. See his, *The Holy Spirit and the Person of Christ*, p. 123: "... Whereas the concept of incarnation seems to necessitate a pluralistic trinitarian doctrine, that of inspiration or possession is compatible with a monistic theol-ogy, a full recognition that Jesus was genuinely a man, and an equally full acknowldge-ment that his deeds and words were done and said divinely: that his Person mediates true God to man [sic]".

55. LAMPE, *God as Spirit*, pp. 222-223.

56. LAMPE, *The Holy Spirit and the Person of Christ*, p. 124. Lampe immediately goes on to note that the affirmation that Jesus is "substantivally" God "is in the last resort incompatible with the belief that Jesus truly and fully shares in our humanity". It is strik-ing that Knitter, in *Can our 'one and only' be a 'one among many'?*, p. 159 argues that while "the Council of Chalcedon spoke of one person in two natures, they did not iden-tify the trinitarian Second person with the person of Jesus. Such a replacement of the human person by the divine Person would have resulted in a dehumanized humanity of Jesus: a divine person walking around in a human costume. But if the Second Person is not identified with the person of Jesus, then that Person or Word of God is, as the early Fathers insisted, free to operate and take seminal form elsewhere". Clearly, this view of the incarnation is only possible if one restricts incarnation to the presence of the divine in a human form, that is to say, if one disregards the historical and cultural context which are an integral part of the definition of any person. As a corrective to this limited and limit-ing understanding of the incarnation, see K. WARD, *Religion and Revelation*, Oxford, 1994, p. 272, where Ward explains that incarnation "gives the whole cultural and histor-ical context that gives rise to this [incarnate] life an important part in the revelatory process, which is not repeatable in human history". See also FERRARA, *'Hypostatized in the Logos': Leontius of Byzantium, Leontius of Jerusalem, and the Unfinished Business of the Council of Chalcedon*, 324-325.

57. LAMPE, *The Holy Spirit and the Person of Christ*, p. 124.

to be "to be re-expressed in terms of the eternal Spirit who was manifested at a particular point in history operating humanly in the person of Jesus Christ". Lampe rightly recognizes that this raises "a major question" about "what Christians mean when they claim to 'encounter Jesus Christ', and to worship Jesus Christ here and now as contemporary". Strictly speaking, Spirit christology only allows Christians to say that the object of their encounter and their worship is "God, the Spirit who was in Jesus", and who meets them "with the identical judgment, mercy, forgiveness and love which were at work in Jesus". The specifically Christian vocation can only be to reproduce in one's own life the union of Spirit and person which reached its zenith in Jesus of Nazareth. Jesus serves here as the "source", "archetype", "model", "example", and "norm" for all subsequent instances of "indwelling"[58]. The upshot of this is a "degree christology", that is to say, an understanding of Jesus as unique or distinct because he possessed the Spirit to an unparalleled degree. "Degree" christologies are contrasted with traditional approaches (such as the 'substance' christology of Chalcedon), which regarded him as different in "kind" from other persons[59].

The appeal of Spirit christology for pluralist theologians is obvious. It allows the 'domestication' of Jesus as one inspired religious leader among others. As far as this use of Spirit christology is concerned, it is important to note a distinction between the earliest proponents of the theory and the pluralists. The former, including Lampe, were apparently convinced that while Jesus was 'only' different in degree, he had no equal. The latter appear to be convinced of the probability (and perhaps even the actuality) of an equal to Jesus[60]. This will become obvious as we reflect on the inspiration christologies of Hick and Knitter.

Hick is quite explicit about his theological debt to Lampe and other proponents of Spirit christology, and about the fact that "the basic ground plan" of this christology is evident in "older liberal theologians, such as Harnack"[61]. For Hick, Jesus is best understood as a "a man living in a startling degree of awareness of God and of response to God's presence"[62]. "He was a soul liberated from selfhood and fully open to the divine Spirit"[63]. From within Christianity, one can, of course, regard

58. *Ibid.*, p. 129.
59. See, for example, HICK, *God and the Universe of Faiths*, p. 157.
60. HICK, *An Inspiration Christology for a Religiously Plural World*, pp. 21-22.
61. Hick also mentions D. BAILLIE, *God was in Christ: An Essay on Incarnation and Atonement*, New York, 1948. See HICK, *An Inspiration Christology for a Religiously Plural World*, pp. 18-22.
62. HICK, *The Metaphor of God Incarnate*, p. 106.
63. HICK, *God and the Universe of Faiths*, p. 115. Roger Haight points out that in his earlier writings (Haight mentions *Jesus and the World Religions*, which dates from 1977),

Jesus as "God's agent on earth", as one who "incarnates" "the divine purpose for human life"[64]. Indeed, Hick is prepared to say that "God in Christ has acted *within* and *through* man's life by influencing the course of our history from the inside"[65]. In so far as Jesus was "responsive to God's loving presence" and thus reflected the divine love on earth in a "humanly limited way" – albeit "to an eminent degree" – Jesus can be described as incarnating God's love. However, it must be borne in mind that "the 'incarnation' of divine love occurs in all human lives" in so far as these constitute responses to and reflections of the divine love[66].

It is important to note here that human lives, including Jesus' life, only *reflect* the divine love to the degree that they are indeed '*responses*'. That is to say, Hick's conception of "incarnation" or "inhistorisation" is, to use a phrase borrowed from moral theology, decidely 'act-centered'[67]. It was in Jesus' *actions* that God's Agapé was enacting itself and God's Kingdom was being created"[68]. What is being described here is not the unity of "some kind of static substance but of volitional attitudes and operations"[69]. Hick describes the "continuity" between God's Agapéing and the agapéing of Jesus as "a continuity of event rather than of entity,…. a continuity of agapéing considered as an activity, rather than of agapé considered as some kind of substance or essence"[70].

Hick preferred "the symbol of Logos in a way analogous to [Raimundo] Panikkar". This is certainly the case. However, the passage quoted here dates from 1972. Moreover, in an article first published in 1966 and reprinted in *God and the Universe of Faiths*, Hick (p. 161) quoted Tertullian's remark (*Apology*, ch. 21) that "Christ is Spirit of Spirit, and God of God, as light is kindled of light". See R. HAIGHT, *Jesus and World Religions*, in *Modern Theology* 12 (1996) 344 n. 51.

64. HICK, *The Metaphor of God Incarnate*, p. 12.

65. J. HICK, *God and the Universe of Faiths*, London, 1973, pp. 152-153. The quotation is taken from the chapter entitled *Christ and Incarnation*, which was originally published in 1966.

66. HICK, *The Metaphor of God Incarnate*, 76-77. Of course, it is difficult to imagine what this divine love can be said to consist of, independently of the history of Jesus' life, death and resurrection. This is a constant problem for pluralist theology. The 'democratic' approach to all traditions makes it nearly impossible to deploy particular religious categories outside the confines of one's own tradition.

67. HICK, *God and the Universe of Faiths*, 153-154. See G. LOUGHLIN, *Preaching Pluralism: John Hick and the Mastery of Religion*, in *Modern Theology* 7 (1990) 43 where Loughlin points out that, for Hick, any particular manifestation of the Real is "never more than a moral example, as also the Real that is said to lie behind it". Loughlin continues: "For religious pluralism the Real is really only an heuristic or ethical goal that enables or motivates a concern for the other".

68. HICK, *God and the Universe of Faiths*, p. 163.

69. *Ibid.*, p. 158.

70. *Ibid.*, 160, 162-163. The "identity" between Jesus and God which Hick posits is "a continuous identity of *actions*", involving at least an identity of "moral pattern" ("a qualitative identity"), and at most "a direct causal connection between Jesus' attitudes to his fellow human beings and God's attitudes to them" ("a numerical identity"). In the latter

This limitation of Jesus' identity with God to the realm of action has as a consequence that Hick can find no real theological use for the traditions of Jesus' death or resurrection. In his most recent writings, these serve, respectively, as an expression of Jesus' earthly commitment, and of the "inner spiritual experience" which was enjoyed by the so-called 'witnesses' to the resurrection[71]. It also leads inevitably to the "degree" Christology which is very evident in *The Metaphor of God Incarnate*. According to this view, Jesus might well have undergone and exhibited "ethical flaws". Indeed, the biblical record suggests as much. The most that can be claimed is that he incarnated God's love to an "eminent degree"[72]. This leaves open the question of how the particular "exemplification" of God's love which found place in Jesus "stands in relation to other exemplifications, such as those in some of the other great religious traditions"[73] – and, presumably, in any and every human life[74].

In Hick's hands, the Trinitarian symbol becomes "three ways in which the one God is humanly thought and experienced", namely "as creator, as transformer, and as inner spirit"[75]. The doctrine of the Trinity is not to be understood "as a literal claim with universal implications, but as internal Christian metaphorical discourse"[76]. It is a form of God-talk shaped

case, what is at stake is a causal link between "a noumenal divine *activity* and its phenomenal correlate in the life of Jesus". See p. 160. The article from which this quotation is taken dates from 1966. The reference to the noumenal/phenomenal distinction is interesting because it dates from long before Hick actively began employing Kantian categories in his religious philosophy. According to Brian Hebbelthwaite, Hick only explicitly transferred the Kantian distinction to the epistemology of religion in 1986-1987, on the occasion of the Gifford Lectures at the University of Edinburgh. These lectures were the basis for Hick's *An Interpretation of Religion*. See B. HEBBELTHWAITE, *John Hick and the Question of Truth in Religion*, in A. SHARMA (ed.), *God, Truth and Reality: Essays in Honour of John Hick*, New York, 1993, p. 126. Regarding the influence of Kant on Hick, see also D. MCCREADY, *The Disintegration of John Hick's Christology*, in *Journal of the Evangelical Theological Society* 39 (1996) 258-259.

71. HICK, *Metaphor of God Incarnate*, pp. 15-26, esp. pp. 23, 25. See also HICK, *An Inspiration Christology for a Religiously Plural World*, pp. 10-13. Hick seems to hold that Jesus probably saw his death as vicarious suffering for the good of Israel. See *The Metaphor of God Incarnate*, p. 23.

72. *Ibid.*, p. 77; see also J. HICK, E.S. MELTZER, *Three Faiths – One God: A Jewish, Christian, Muslim Encounter*, London, 1989, p. 208.

73. HICK, *An Inspiration Christology for a Religiously Plural World*, p. 21.

74. See HICK, *The Metaphor of God Incarnate*, p. 154 where Hick observes that "the way to salvation/liberation [for the followers of religious giants, like Jesus] involves a gradual or sudden conversion to [the] new way of experiencing" the self and the world, disclosed by the founder though, in the case of "ordinary believers, the new mode of experiencing usually occurs only occasionally and is of only moderate intensity".

75. HICK, *The Metaphor of God Incarnate*, pp. 149, 152-153. See J. HICK, *The Rainbow of Faiths: Critical Dialogues on Religious Pluralism*, London, 1995, p. 136.

76. *Ibid.*, p. 88. It is interesting to note that Hick's language here comes very close to George Lindbeck's description of doctrinal formulations as "communally authoritative

by the theistic culture of the ancient Judaeo-Hellenistic world[77]. As such, it is an obstacle to the meaning it was originally intended to convey, namely, that in Jesus of Nazareth we are confronted with "the ideal of humanity living in openness and response to God"[78].

Knitter's christology, though less well developed than Hick's, also takes its lead from the omnipresence of the transcendent reality. Knitter apparently accepts the view that "all religions take their origins from some kind of a primordial liberative experience", such as, for example, the Jewish experience of the Exodus, "Jesus' proclamation of the Kingdom of God, the Meccan experience, [or] Buddha's leaving the palace for a life of homelessness". These experiences testify to a "common source" which manifests itself as an "energy of liberation". Knitter repeats Aloysius Pieris' claim that this source can be identified symbolically as a "liberating Spirit", which is described differently in the world's religious traditions[79].

In line with his praxis-oriented theology, Knitter proposes commitment to human (and ecological) well-being as the surest way to knowledge of this source. As we have seen, Knitter's Jesus exemplified this commitment to an impressive degree. In his most recent writings, Knitter has opted to describe Jesus as a *spirit person, one of those figures in human history with an experiential awareness of the reality of God*". But he insists that the portrait of Jesus as a mystic must be complemented and corrected by the portrait of him as "a social prophet", one committed to the transformation of the status quo[80]. And it is above all here that Knitter locates the lasting significance of Jesus.

He is relevant to the degree that he promotes the Christian acceptance of the challenge which he embodied, namely, the challenge to pursue eco-human liberation. Where this challenge is taken up, Jesus of Nazareth becomes the Christ of faith, the Christian savior. Christians who continue Jesus' commitment to the Kingdom can be said to be living in the Spirit

rules of discourse, attitude and action". For Lindbeck, doctrines function primarily as rules governing the way in which members of a given faith-community speak, feel and act. They are primarily "regulative devices", and not first-order truth claims. See G. LINDBECK, *The Nature of Doctrine: Religion and Theology in a Postliberal Age*, Philadelphia, 1984, p. 8. Of course, Lindbeck's confessionalism is far removed from Hick's pluralism.

77. *Ibid.*, p. 278.

78. HICK, *The Metaphor of God Incarnate*, pp. 12-13.

79. KNITTER, *One Earth Many Religions*, p. 100. See A. PIERIS, *Faith-Communities and Communalism*, in *East Asian Pastoral Review* 3 (1989) 294-309. See p. 297.

80. KNITTER, *Jesus and the Other Names*, pp. 92-93, 173 n. 4. Knitter's primary source for this view appears to be Marcus Borg. See also KNITTER, *Five Theses on the Uniqueness of Jesus*, p. 12 n. 16; *Can our 'One and Only' also be a 'One among Many'?*", p. 169 n. 8.

of Christ. Indeed, the entire Christian confession of faith can be said to
have its goal in the *reproduction*, among Christians, of Jesus' liberating
practice. Even the most exalted christological titles are to be understood
in the first place as "calls to action". They are intended "to empower
and guide Jesus' disciples in acting within our culture and social world".
Such action enables Christians to enjoy "the same Spirit-experience" as
Jesus himself[81].

However, we must be careful not to limit the work of the Spirit to
Christ's Spirit (which Knitter apparently equates with the Holy Spirit).
The Spirit is not exhausted in the Spirit of Christ[82]. In Knitter's view,
there may be "an economy of grace genuinely different from the one
made known through... Jesus"[83]. What unites these "different"
economies is, of course, the Reign of God which, as we have seen, is
convertible into the practice of radical love of neighbor.

As I have already indicated, it is striking that Knitter's christology,
which is so historically-oriented, should display such a lack of interest in
the reconstruction of Jesus' actual ministry. However, on closer examination this apparent paradox is easily dissolved. Knitter's Jesus, like

81. KNITTER, *Jesus and the Other Names*, pp. 92-93. See also "*Can our 'One and
Only' also be a 'One among Many'?*", p. 170: "... Every Christian prophet or activist
must, like Jesus, be Spirit-filled".

82. There is a tendency in Knitter's works to invoke the Spirit where the more or less
inexplicable or at least completely unpredictable is at stake. See, for example, *Jesus and
the Other Names*, p. 75; *Five Theses on the Uniqueness of Jesus*, p. 8; *Can our 'one and
only' be a 'one among many'*", pp. 148, 178.

83. KNITTER, *Jesus and the Other Names*, pp. 88, 112. Knitter almost seems to suggest
that Christians are 'saved' by Christ while non-Christians are saved by the Spirit. See
P. KNITTER, *A New Pentecost: A Pneumatological Theology of Religions*, in *Current Dialogue* 19 (1991), pp. 36, 38, and esp. p. 40. The source which Knitter invokes in this
regard does not justify the conclusions he draws. In the latter, and in *Jesus and the Other
Names*, Knitter refers to G. KHODR, *An Orthodox Perspective of Inter-Religious Dialogue*,
in *Current Dialogue* 19 (1991), pp. 25-27. However, Khodr's position, even as Knitter
presents it, is clearly inclusivist. It seems to me that the following remark, formulated by
Knitter in the context of his presentation of Khodr, cannot bear a pluralist interpretation:
"Thus the genuine difference of the Kingdom in other religions must be related, understood, and clarified within the Word incarnate in Christ and living in the church". See
Jesus and the Other Names, p. 114. See KHODR, *An Orthodox Perspective of Inter-Religious Dialogue*, p. 27. Moreover, Knitter (*Jesus and the Other Names*, p. 75) invokes
John 16,12-13 as proof-text to defend the view that the Spirit may well disclose more than
has been revealed in Jesus. This is exegetically dubious, however. The "Paraclete" fur-
thers knowledge of what has been revealed in Christ. 'He' cannot be seen as disclosing
something entirely novel. See, for example, P. PERKINS, *The Gospel According to John*, in
R. BROWN et al. (eds.), *The New Jerome Biblical Commentary*, Englewood Cliffs, NJ,
1990, p. 977: "The 'truth' in which the Paraclete guides the community must have the
same sense as 'truth' elsewhere in the Gospel: belief in Jesus as the sole revelation of
God and the one who speaks the words of God". See also KNITTER, *Can our 'One and
Only' also be a 'One among Many'?*", pp. 180-182.

Hick's, is no more (but also no less) than the representative of the universal love-ethic which is God's will for humankind. In other words, for Knitter as for Hick, the story of Jesus of Nazareth is the story of an ideal embodied in history. And it is the ideal that counts. The story is only relevant to the degree that it illuminates the ideal. Knitter says as much when he writes that: "... If we look at what we can know of Jesus based soley on historical or so-called scientific procedures, we have to recognize that we can't know enough to paint a crystal-clear, certain picture of who he was and what he said and did, but we can know enough to keep on the right track of following what he set in motion for ensuing history". "We can know enough about Jesus to feel his challenge and to know when we are turning our backs on it"[84]. It is neither realistic nor necessary to ask for more[85].

V. CONCLUDING REMARKS

At first glance, pluralist theology, with its celebration of religious 'otherness', looks strikingly postmodern. Appearances can deceive, however. In at least one important respect, pluralist theology is in fact remarkably 'modern'. I am thinking of its view of humanity's religious history. Pluralist theology purports to know the outcome of that history and the place to be assigned to each of its major players. One might object that inclusivism and exclusivism make the same claim. To some degree this is indeed true. What distinguishes pluralist theology, however, is the fact that it makes its claim without reference to any particular religious tradition. Or, to put it more accurately, particular religious traditions only serve to illustrate the claim. The tradition concerning Jesus of Nazareth is a case in point. In pluralist hands, Jesus of Nazareth becomes one more player on the world's religious stage, an exemplary actor who delivered an inspired performance. The record of his acheivements has been inevitably embellished, but enough reliable data remains to enable us to recapture the essential spirit of that performance. And that is all that really matters.

The basis of pluralist theology is the universal movement of the Spirit, or the movement of the universal Spirit. Within this movement, individual saviors are assigned relatively small parts. This is inevitable since

---

84. KNITTER, *Jesus and the Other Names*, pp. 86, 87.

85. For Knitter, it is not Jesus' person or even his history which is "universal, decisive, [and] indispensable". It is his message. See KNITTER, *Can our 'One and Only' also be a 'One among Many'?*", pp. 171-172.

the progress and outcome of the movement are guaranteed by the Spirit as such.

Pluralist theology is characterized, at its heart, by a profound paradox. The paradox consists in the fact that a system of thought which is ostensibly committed to the *particular*, gives birth to a universalistic vision which threatens to rob the particular of any real content. John Hick has written that the shift to the pluralist understanding of religion amounts to a Copernican revolution in theology[86]. This may be true, but it is good to bear in mind what the twentieth century has surely taught us, namely, that revolutions have a tendency to devour their children, even the 'sons of God'.

Faculty of Theology   Terrence MERRIGAN
Katholieke Universiteit Leuven
St. Michielsstraat 6
B-3000 Leuven

---

86. HICK, *God and the Universe of Faiths*, p. 131.

TRINITARIAN CHRISTOLOGY
AS A MODEL FOR A THEOLOGY OF RELIGIOUS PLURALISM

It has become commonplace, while reviewing the main positions in today's ongoing debate on the theology of religions, to distinguish three basic paradigms, namely, ecclesiocentrism, Christocentrism, and theo-centrism; or, equivalently, exclusivism, inclusivism, and pluralism. Account must, however, be taken of the different models which these general – and partly deceptive – labels do cover. In a volume published in English six years ago, I demonstrated that so-called "Christocentric inclusivism" somewhat ambiguously includes both the "fulfilment the-ory" of J. Daniélou and H. de Lubac, for example, and the "anonymous Christianity" of K. Rahner and others, the vast difference between these two positions notwithstanding[1].

Moreover, the threefold categorization just mentioned no longer suf-fices to account for the debate in its more recent developments. In my study, *Toward a Christian Theology of Religious Pluralism*[2], after reviewing the successive paradigm-shifts from ecclesiocentrism to Christocentrism, and, thereafter, from Christocentrism to theocentrism, I reflected on the other models have cropped up among the entire range of opinions[3]. The new version of John Hick's theocentrism has taken the form of "reality-centeredness", while Paul F. Knitter has substituted for his own form of theocentrism a certain "soteriocentrism"[4]. I further indicated two seemingly new models which, though not always explic-itly formulated, are not without significance, namely, logocentrism and pneumatocentrism[5].

It is well known that the debate between Christocentrism and theo-centrism arose because the protagonists of the latter position held that traditional Christian Christocentrism had become untenable in the pre-sent situation of religious pluralism. Among other things, it was argued that the traditional position made a positive appraisal of other religious traditions and an open attitude in interreligious dialogue impossible. I

---

1. See J. DUPUIS, *Jesus Christ at the Encounter of World Religions,* Maryknoll, NY, Orbis Books, 1991, pp. 126-130.
2. J. DUPUIS, *Toward a Christian Theology of Religious Pluralism*, Maryknoll, NY, Orbis Books, 1997.
3. *Ibid.*, pp. 180-201.
4. *Ibid.*, pp. 193-195.
5. *Ibid.*, pp. 195-198.

have attempted to show in the first volume referred to above that the different arguments advanced in favour of that thesis are not altogether convincing. Christian theocentrism cannot but be Christocentric. "Inclusive pluralism" then would seem to be the correct position[6]. This implies that Jesus Christ is and remains the universal Saviour and the Christ-event the climax of God's self-manifestation in history. However, the universal operative presence of the Christic mystery guarantees the positive significance of the other religious traditions as channels of the divine mystery of salvation within the one, complex and manifold, plan of God for humankind.

I. THE PRESENT STATE OF THE QUESTION

The positions which I described above as logocentrism and pneumatocentrism both tend to qualify the centrality of Jesus Christ in a way that raises new problems. This needs to be explained. Reference is made – rightly – to the universal active presence in the world and history of the Word of God, on the one hand, and of the Spirit of God, on the other. According to these models, the Logos and the Pneuma, "the Word and the Breath" of God[7], whom St. Irenaeus saw as the "two hands of God"[8] conjointly doing his work, tend to be severed from the Christ-event, to be viewed as autonomous and independent agents, transcending the historical and the particular, whose distinct action constitutes alternative economies of divine salvation.

Where the Word of God (*Logos*) is concerned, it is remarked – rightly – that the revealed message itself witnesses to his universal action throughout world history; the postbiblical tradition of the early apologists does likewise. But the conclusion is being drawn that in every event and in all circumstances it is the Word of God who saves, not precisely the Word-of-God-made-flesh, that is, Jesus Christ[9]. Aloysius

---

6. DUPUIS, *Jesus Christ* (n. 1), pp. 113-247.

7. See Y. CONGAR, *La parole et le souffle*, Paris, Desclée, 1984 (English translation: *The Word and the Spirit*, London, G. Chapman, 1986).

8. IRENAEUS LUGDUNENSIS, *Contre les hérésies* IV,7,4, ed. A. ROUSSEAU (SC, 100), Paris, Cerf, 1965, 462-465.

9. Such a tendency is found in A. PIERIS, *An Asian Paradigm: Interreligious Dialogue and Theology of Religions*, in *The Month* 26 (1993) 129-134. See also ID., *Universality of Christianity*, in *Vidyajyoti* 57 (1993) 591-595; *The Problem of Universality and Inculturation with Regard to Patterns of Theological Thinking*, in *Concilium* 1994/6, 70-79; *Inculturation in Asia: A Theological Reflection on an Experience*, in *Jahrbuch für kontextuelle Theologien*, Frankfurt am Main, IKO-Verlag für interkulturelle Kommunikation, 1994, 59-71.

Pieris writes: "He who reveals, who saves and transforms is the Word himself"[10]. "The Christ" is a title; a title does not save. As for Jesus, he is "he in whom Christians recognize the Word, as seen, heard and touched by human senses"[11]. The "singularity" of Jesus consists in the fact that he seals God's covenant with the poor. Such "singularity" is accessible to members of other religious traditions, while the "ontological oneness" of the Word incarnate is not. Jesus Christ is he in whom the saving Word is recognized by Christians.

In a somewhat similar fashion, Carlo Molari substitutes for the centrality of Jesus Christ that of the Word of God who reveals himself in Jesus. It is in Jesus, "the man who is the sacrament of God", that Christians have access to the revealing and saving Word. In fact, the person of Jesus is not the principle of universal salvation; he is the one who has lived the universal values which the eternal Word of God reflects, in the most radical manner[12].

Similar remarks are in order where the universal economy of the Spirit of God tends to be viewed as prescinding from the historical event of Jesus Christ. This time, the suggestion is made that, in order to avoid the blind alley which emerges out of a narrow Christological perspective, there is need for a new theology of religions built on a "pneumatical" model. Paul F. Knitter writes in this direction: "A pneumatical theology of religions could dislodge the Christian debate from its confining categories of 'inclusivism or exclusivism' or pluralism"[13]. And, more clearly: "The Reign of God, as it may be taking shape under the breath of the Spirit, can be seen as 'an all-comprehensive phenomenon of grace'; that is, an economy of grace genuinely different from the one made known through the Word incarnate in Jesus"[14].

Unlike the economy of the Christ-event, unavoidably limited by the particularity of history, the economy of the Spirit knows no bounds of

10. PIERIS, *Inculturation in Asia* (n. 9), p. 60.

11. *Ibid.*

12. C. MOLARI, *Assolutezza e universalità del Cristianesimo come problema teologico*, in *Credere oggi* (1986) 6, 17-35. See also ID., *Introduzione* to J. HICK & P.F. KNITTER (eds.), *L'unicità cristiana: un mito?*, Assisi, Cittadella, 1994, 11-48; *Introduzione* to G. D'COSTA (ed.), *La teologia pluralista delle religioni: un mito?*, Assisi, Cittadella, 1994, 11-37. See on this, C. CANOBBIO, *Gesù Cristo nella recente teologia delle religioni*, in *Cristianesimo e religioni in dialogo* (Quaderni teologici del Seminario di Brescia, 4), Brescia, Morcelliana, 1994, 86-88.

13. KNITTER, *A New Pentecost,* in *Current Dialogue* 19 (1991) 32-41; see p. 35. See also G. KHODR, *An Orthodox Perspective on Interreligious Dialogue*, in *Current Dialogue* 19 (1991) 27-31.

14. KNITTER, *Jesus and the Other Names. Christian Mission and Global Responsibility,* Maryknoll, NY, Orbis Books, 1996, p. 113.

space and time. Free of all constraints, the Spirit "blows where it wills" (see Jn 3,8). The Spirit of God has been universally present throughout human history and remains active today outside the boundaries of the Christian fold. He it is who "inspires" in people belonging to other religious traditions the obedience of saving faith, and in the traditions themselves a word spoken by God to their adherents. Could it not, in effect, be thought that, while Christians secure salvation through the economy of God's Son incarnate in Jesus Christ, others receive it through the immediate autonomous action of the Spirit of God? The "hypostatic independence", or personal distinction between God's "two hands", is warrant for the two distinct channels through which God's saving presence reaches out to people in distinct economies of salvation. In short, the Holy Spirit, as God's necessary "point of entry" into the life of human beings and of peoples, his immediate action – which bypasses the punctual event of Jesus Christ – opens up the way for a distinct model of a Christian theology of religions, one no longer Christocentric but pneumatocentric.

There is much truth in the Logos or Pneuma perspective for a theology of religions. The fact remains, however, that, while clearly professing the universal presence of the Logos, the "true Light that enlightens every human being by coming into the world" (Jn 1,9) even before his incarnation in Jesus Christ (Jn 1,1-4), the New Testament nonetheless clearly assigns to the Son of God, or the Word of God made human in Jesus Christ, the universal salvation of humankind (Jn 1,14). Logocentrism and Christocentrism are no more separable than Christocentrism and theocentrism. Rather than being mutually opposed, they call to each other in a unique dispensation. Again, that the Holy Spirit is God's "point of entry" wherever and whenever God reveals and communicates himself to people, is certain. However, it does not seem that a model for salvation centered on the Holy Spirit can be separated from the Christological model. One needs to affirm clearly the universal action of the Spirit throughout human history, before and after the historical event Jesus Christ. But Christian faith affirms that the action of the Spirit and that of Jesus Christ, though distinct, are nevertheless complementary and inseparable. Pneumatocentrism and Christocentrism cannot be construed as two distinct eonomies of salvation, one parallel to the other. They constitute two inseparable aspects, or complementary elements, within a unique economy of salvation.

My aim in this article is to show how these complementary elements combine in one and the same economy of salvation; how in God's design for humankind the universal significance of the punctual, historical – and thereby particular – event of Jesus Christ harmonizes with the universal active presence of the Word of God and his Spirit. In the process, it will likewise appear that the universal, constitutive, saving function of Jesus Christ can be held in creative tension with the saving value of other paths open to people in the various religious traditions and the significance, as channels of salvation for their members, of their respective saving figures.

II. A TRINITARIAN CHRISTOLOGY AS A HERMENEUTICAL KEY

To show that the Christ-event finds its place and its universal significance precisely within the full ambit of God's history with humankind through his Word and his Spirit, a Trinitarian and pneumatic Christology serves as a useful hermeneutical key. In *Toward a Christian Theology of Religious Pluralism*, I sought to propose such a hermeneutical key, one which allows for an integral model that can move us "toward a Christian theology of religious pluralism"[15]. Such a Christology will place in full relief the interpersonal relationships between Jesus and the God whom he calls Father, on the one hand, and the Spirit whom he will send, on the other. These relationships are intrinsic to the mystery of Jesus' person and of his work. Christology ought always to be imbued with these intra-Trinitarian relationships. But this requirement obtains all the more in the context of a theology of religious pluralism. Indeed, it may be thought that the mistaken development of Christocentrism into a closed and restrictive paradigm, one incompatible with theocentrism, was due to a past failure to pay adequate attention to the interpersonal dimension of Christology.

What then would be the implications of a Trinitarian Christology for a theology of religious pluralism? With respect to God, Jesus Christ must never be regarded as a substitute for the Father. The unique closeness which exists between God and Jesus by virtue of the mystery of the incarnation must never be forgotten. However, the same is true of the unbridgeable distance that remains beween the Father and Jesus in his human existence: God, and God alone, is the absolute mystery and, as such, is at the source, at the heart and at the center of all reality. While it is true that Jesus the man is uniquely the Son of God, it is equally true that God stands beyond Jesus. When Jesus Christ is said to be at the center of the Christian mystery, this is not to be understood in an absolute

---

15. DUPUIS, *Toward a Christian Theology* (n. 2), pp. 203-384 (part II).

sense but in the order of the economy of God's freely undertaken dealings with humankind in history.

The pneumatic aspect of the mystery of Jesus Christ needs to be stressed, even more than the Godward orientation of his person and work. A trinitarian Christology will have to express clearly Jesus' relatedness to the Spirit. A Spirit-Christology is required that would show the influence of the Spirit throughout the earthly life of Jesus, from his conception through the power of the Spirit down to his resurrection at the hands of God by the power of the same Spirit. Such a Christology would, furthermore, extend beyond the resurrection to illustrate the relationship between the action of the risen Lord and the economy of the Holy Spirit[16]. While an "integral Christology" requires the Spirit-component in all situations, the same requirement is equally binding where the aim is to build up a Christian theology of religious pluralism. In such a theology the universal presence and action of the Spirit in human history and in the world will not only need to be affirmed; they will also have to serve as guiding threads and principles.

We have already pointed out that Christology and pneumatology cannot be construed into two distinct and separate economies of God's personal dealings with humankind. Nevertheless, the "hypostatic distinction" between the Word and the Spirit as well as the specific influence of each in the Trinitarian rhythm of all divine-human relationships, individual and collective, serve as a hermeneutical key for the real differentiation and plurality obtaining in the concrete realization of the divine-human relationships in diverse situations and circumstances. While it is true that "[t]he Spirit is the Spirit of Christ and where the Spirit of Christ is, there is Christ"[17], the reverse is also true: Christology does not exist without pneumatology; it cannot be allowed to develop into a Christomonism. A well-poised theological account of the relationship between Christology and pneumatology must combine various elements: on the one hand, the roles of both the Son and the Spirit must not be confused but must remain distinct, even as their hypostatic identities are distinct; on the other hand, there exists between them a "relationship of order" which, without implying any subordination of one to the other, translates into the divine economy the order of eternal relationships of hypostatic origination in the intrinsic mystery of the Godhead.

---

16. DUPUIS, *Who Do You Say I Am? Introduction to Christology*, Maryknoll, NY, Orbis Books, 1994, p. 169.

17. J. COBB, *The Christian Reason for Being Progressive*, in *Theology Today* 51 (1995) 548-562; see p. 560.

Thus, while the functions of the Son and the Spirit need to be kept clearly distinct, there is no dichotomy between them. There is total complementarity in one divine economy of salvation: only the Son became human, but the fruit of his redemptive incarnation is the outpouring of the Spirit symbolized at Pentecost. The Christ-event is at the center of the historical unfolding of the divine economy, but the punctual event of Jesus Christ is actuated and becomes operative throughout time and space in the work of the Spirit.

It follows that a theology of religions elaborated on the foundation of the Trinitarian economy will have to combine and to hold in constructive tension the central character of the punctual historical event of Jesus Christ and the universal action and dynamic influence of the Spirit of God. It will thus be able to account for God's self-manifestation and self-gift in human cultures and religious traditions outside the orbit of influence of the Christian message. However, it will do this without construing Christology and pneumatology into two distinct economies of divine-human relationships, one for Christians and another for the members of other traditions.

III. The Historical Particularity of the Jesus-Christ-Event and the Universal Economy of the Word and the Spirit

I have suggested elsewhere that the constitutive uniqueness of Jesus Christ as universal Saviour must be made to rest on his personal identity as the Son of God[18]. No other consideration seems to provide an adequate theological foundation for this uniqueness. The "Gospel" values which Jesus upholds, the Reign of God which he announces, the human project or "program" which he puts forward, his option for the poor and the marginalized, his denunciation of injustice, his message of universal love: all these, no doubt, contribute to the difference and specificity of Jesus' personality; none of them, however, would be decisive for making him or recognizing him as "constitutively unique" for human salvation[19].

Neither can a "Spirit-Christology", according to which the Spirit of God is preeminently and from the first moment of his existence present in the human person of Jesus, serve as an adequate foundation for his

18. Dupuis, *Jesus Christ* (n. 1), pp. 192-197.
19. The weakness of H. Küng's book *On Being a Christian* (New York, Doubleday, 1977) lies in his attempt to establish on these values Jesus' uniqueness, while failing to assert unambiguously the ontological sonship. See the discussion in Dupuis, *Jesus Christ* (n. 1), pp. 193-196.

constitutive universality as Savior of humankind[20]. According to such a Christology Jesus would simply be a man preeminently filled with the Spirit of God; he would not be a divine subject become an actor in human history through the human existence he has made his own. I have already stressed the keenly-felt need to develop a Spirit-Christology which would put in full relief the universal presence and action of the Spirit of God in the human existence of Jesus, the Son of God made human, as well as the outpouring of the same Spirit by the risen Christ, symbolized in Pentecost. No Spirit-Christology can, however, substitute for the Logos-Christology or the Christology of God's "only Son" (Jn 1,18) who "became flesh and dwelt among us" (Jn 1,14); nor can it stand without it. Were this the case, Jesus Christ would be reduced to a man, among others, in whom and through whom God is present and active; he would not be the Son of God in whom God stands revealed and communicated. Nor could he be the constitutive and universal Saviour of humankind. To be complete, a pneumatic Christology must show that Christocentrism and pneumatology belong together in the same economy of salvation.

The universality of Jesus-the-Christ cannot, however, be allowed to overshadow the particularity of Jesus of Nazareth. It is true that Jesus' human existence, once transformed by his resurrection and glorification, has reached beyond time and space and become "transhistorical"; but it is the historical Jesus who has become that. The universality of the Christ who, "being made perfect", became "the source of eternal salvation" (Heb 5,9) does not cancel out the particularity of Jesus, "made like his brothers and sisters in every respect" (Heb 2,17). A universal Christ, severed from the particular Jesus, would no longer be the Christ of Christian revelation[21]. The stress on the historical particularity of Jesus is not, in fact, without bearing on an open theology of religions. Nor is it indifferent in a context of interreligious dialogue[22].

---

20. R. HAIGHT, *The Case of Spirit-Christology*, in *Theological Studies* 53 (1992) 257-287 is of opinion that only such a Christology can leave room for the saving value of other paths proposed by the various religious traditions. See the response by J.H. WRIGHT, *Roger Haight's Spirit Christology*, in *Theological Studies* 53 (1992) 729-735, who, on the foundation of R. Haight's own methodological criteria, shows his reductionist Christology to be inacceptable.

21. See the discussion on the personal identity between the historical Jesus and the Christ of faith in the context of the theology of religions, in DUPUIS, *Jesus Christ* (n. 1), pp. 178-190.

22. See J.B. REID, *Jesus: God's Emptiness, God's Fullness. The Christology of St. Paul*, Mahwah, NY, Paulist Press, 1990; also J. PERKINSON, *Soteriological Humility: The Christological Significance of the Humanity of Jesus in the Encounter of Religions*, in *Journal of Ecumenical Studies* 31 (1994) 1-26.

The historical particularity of Jesus imposes upon the Christ-event irremediable limitations. This is necessarily part of the incarnational economy willed by God. While the human existence of the man Jesus is truly that of the Son of God, it necessarily shares with all humanity the limitations of historical human existence. There follows that the human consciousness of Jesus as Son could not, by nature, exhaust the mystery of God, and, therefore, left his revelation of God incomplete. There likewise follows that the Christ-event itself does not and cannot exhaust God's saving power. God remains beyond the man Jesus as the ultimate source of both revelation and salvation. Jesus' revelation of God is a human transposition of God's mystery; his salvific action is the channel, the efficacious sign or sacrament, of God's salvific will. The personal identity of Jesus as the Son of God in his human existence notwithstanding, a distance continues to exist between God (the Father), the ultimate source, and he who is God's human icon. Jesus is no substitute for God[23].

If this is true, it will also be seen that, while the Christ-event is the universal sacrament of God's will to save humankind, it need not therefore be the only possible expression of that will. God's saving power is not exclusively bound by the universal sign God has designed for his saving action. In terms of a Trinitarian Christology, this means that the saving action of God through the nonincarnate Logos (*Logos asarkos*), of whom the Prologue of John's Gospel speaks (Jn 1,9), endures after the incarnation of the Logos (Jn 1,14). The mystery of the incarnation is unique; only the individual human existence of Jesus is asssumed by the Son of God. But, while he alone is thus constituted the "image of God", other saving figures may be "enlightened" by the Word to become pointers to salvation for their followers, in accordance with God's overall design for humankind.

Admittedly, in the mystery of Jesus-the-Christ, the Word cannot be separated from the flesh it has assumed. But, inseparable as the divine Word and Jesus' human existence may be, they nevertheless remain distinct. While, then, the human action of the *Logos ensarkos* is the universal sacrament of God's saving action, it does not exhaust the action of the Logos. A distinct action of the *Logos asarkos* endures – not, to be sure, as constituting a distinct economy of salvation, parallel to that realized in the flesh of Christ, but as the expression of God's superabundant graciousness and absolute freedom.

---

23. See C. Duquoc, *Messianisme de Jésus et discrétion de Dieu*, Genève, Labor et Fides, 1984.

The particularity of the Jesus-Christ-event in relation to the universality of God's saving plan opens new inroads for a theology of religious pluralism that would make room for diverse "paths" to salvation.

Similar observations are called for where the abiding, universal, and active presence of the Spirit is concerned. Trinitarian Christology shows that the particularity of the Christ-event leaves space for the action of the *Logos asarkos*; likewise, Spirit-Christology helps us to see that the Spirit of God is universally present and active, before and after the event. The Christ-event is as much the goal of the working of the Spirit in the world as it is its origin; between one and the other there exists a "mutually conditioning relationship", by virtue of which the Spirit can rightly be called, throughout salvation history, "the Spirit of Christ"[24].

However, just as the action of the Logos cannot be constrained by the particularity of the incarnational event, similarly the universal influence of the Spirit cannot be limited to his effusion upon the world by the glorified humanity of the risen Christ. The Spirit of Christ is, independently of the incarnation of the Logos, he who "originates" from the Father through his Logos. Prior to being the Spirit of Christ, then, he is the Spirit of the Father and the Son and as such his universal presence to human history cannot be circumscribed by his presence and action through the sacrament of Jesus' humanity. God's saving economy is and remains one, of which the Christ-event is at once the culminating point in history and the universal sacrament; but the God who acts is "three", each being personally distinct and remaining distinctly active. God saves with "two hands". It follows that, just as saving figures in other religious traditions can be "enlightened" by the Word of God, similarly they can be "inspired" and enlivened by the Spirit of God, and become pointers to salvation for their followers in accordance with God's design for humankind.

IV. CONVERGENT PATHS IN ONE DIVINE ECONOMY OF SALVATION

A Trinitarian Christology is thus able to show that God's saving action, which always operates within the framework of a unified plan, is one and, at the same time, multifaceted. It never prescinds from the Christ-event, in which it finds its highest historical density. Yet the

24. See J.H. WONG, *Anonymous Christianity: Karl Rahner's Pneumato-Christocentrism and the East-West Dialogue*, in *Theological Studies* 55 (1994) 609-637; K. RAHNER, *Jesus Christ in the Non-Christian Religions*, in *Theological Investigations*, Vol. 17, London, Darton, Longman and Todd, 1981, 39-50; see p. 46.

action of the Word of God is not constrained by his becoming human historically in Jesus Christ; nor is the Spirit's work in history limited to its outpouring upon the world by the risen and the exalted Christ. The mediation of God's saving grace to humanity takes on different dimensions which need to be combined and integrated. Three elements need to be considered: (1) the inclusive presence in history of the mystery of Jesus Christ; (2) the universal power of the Logos; (3) the universal action of the Spirit.

1. The Inclusive Presence of the Mystery of Christ

That the historical event of Jesus Christ, which culminates in the paschal mystery of his death-resurrection, has universal significance needs little elaboration once it is recognized that, in his incarnate Son, God has contracted "once for all" an irreversible bond of union with the human race. The Jesus-Christ-event is God's deepest and unsurpassable involvement with humankind in history. What, on the contrary, needs to be accounted for, is how its saving power reaches out to the members of other religious traditions. Are these traditions channels of Christ's saving power, and in what sense? Do they lend visibility and a social character to the power of Christ as it reaches out to their members? Are they signs of his saving activity?

To see that they are, it is of primary importance to stress the worldly and social character of the human person. The human person, as an incarnate spirit, is a 'becoming' which expresses itself in time and space, in the history of the world. It is also essentially a social being, who becomes oneself in virtue of his or her interpersonal relationships with other human beings. If this is true, the conclusion must follow that the religious traditions contain, in their institutions and social practices, traces of the encounter with divine grace which is implied in the authentic experience of God made by their founders and leaders, their sages and their prophets. The religious traditions contain "supernatural, grace-filled elements"[25]. No dichotomy can be erected between human beings' subjective religious life and the religion they profess, between their personal religious experience and the historico-social religious phenomenon (or religious tradition composed of sacred books and practices of worship) to which they adhere.

In order to show how the various religious traditions can serve their members as a mediation of the mystery of salvation, we must begin with

---

25. See K. RAHNER, *Christianity and the Non-Christian Religions*, in *Theological Investigations*, Vol. 5, London, Darton, Longman and Todd, 1966, 115-134; see pp. 121, 130.

the mystery of Christ himself and then proceed to consider the presence of Christ to human beings. In Christ, God enters into a personal relationship with human beings; God becomes present to them. Can the religious traditions contain and signify, in some way, this presence of God to human beings in Jesus Christ? Does God become present to them in the very practice of their religion? It is necessary to admit this, if, as has been explained, it is theologically unrealistic and impractical to separate a person's religious life from the religious tradition in which he or she lives it. Indeed, the sincere religious practice of the members of the religious traditions is the reality that gives expression to, supports, bears, and contains, as it were, their encounter with God in Jesus Christ. Accordingly, the religious traditions are indeed for them ways and means of salvation[26].

2. The Universal Action of the Logos and the Spirit

It needs to be borne in mind that the Christ-event, however inclusively present, does not exhaust the power of the Word of God, who became flesh in Jesus Christ. The Word was present and active in history from the beginning. The transcendent, illuminating power of the divine Logos, operative throughout human history, accounts for the salvation of human beings even before the manifestation of the Logos in the flesh. As the early apologists had already seen[27], people could be "enlightened" by the Logos, who is the one source of divine light. Here, too, however, the worldly and social character of the human being must be kept in mind. Not only could individual persons – Socrates, the Buddha, and so on – receive divine truth from the Logos; but human undertakings also – Greek philosophy and wisdom, as well as Asian wisdom – were the channels through which divine light reached persons. The religious traditions of humankind contain elements of "truth and grace" (*Ad gentes*, 9), sown in them by the Logos, through which his enlightening and saving power is operative. Moreover, the divine Logos continues, even today, to sow his seeds among peoples and in their traditions: revealed truth and divine grace are present in them through the agency of the Logos.

Similar observations are called for where the Spirit of God is concerned. The universal presence of the Spirit has been progressively

---

26. For further elaboration of the inclusive presence of the mystery of Christ in the other religious traditions, see DUPUIS, *Jesus Christ* (n. 1), pp. 125-151; also ID., *Toward a Christian Theology* (n. 2), pp. 316-319.

27. See DUPUIS, *Toward a Christian Theology* (n. 2), pp. 53-83.

stressed by the Church magisterium's[28] in recent times – without, however, the implications of such presence for the theology of religions being necessarily adequately brought out. The Holy Spirit is seen as present not only in persons but in cultures and religions. To quote but one text:

> The Spirit's presence and activity affect not only individuals but also society and history, peoples, cultures, and religions. Indeed, the Spirit is at the origin of the noble ideals and undertakings which benefit humanity on its journey through history.... Again, it is the Spirit who sows the "seeds of the Word" present in various customs and cultures, preparing them for full maturity in Christ (*Redemptoris Missio*, n. 28).

Elements of "truth and grace" (*Ad gentes*, 9) are thus present in the human cultures and religions, throughout human history, due to the combined action of God's Word and of his Spirit. This combined action constitutes the saving figures of the religious traditions as pointers to salvation for their followers. The same twofold action of the Word of God and his Spirit accounts for the mediatory function of the religious traditions themselves: on the one hand, they convey to their adherents God's offer of grace and salvation; on the other hand, they give expression to the positive response of their members to God's gracious gift of self. The Word and the Spirit, the "two hands" of God, combine through their universal action in endowing the religious life of persons with truth and grace and in impressing "saving values" upon the religious traditions to which they belong.

It is, of course, important to preserve the unity of the divine plan of salvation for humankind, which embraces the whole of human history. The becoming-human of the Word of God in Jesus Christ, his human life, death, and resurrection, is the culminating point of the process of divine self-communication, the hinge upon which the process holds together, its interpretative key. The reason is that the Word's "humanization" marks the unsurpassed – and unsurpassable – depth of God's self-communication to human beings, the supreme mode of immanence of his being with them[29]. However, the centrality of the incarnational dimension of God's economy of salvation must not be allowed to obscure the universal abiding presence and action of the divine Word and the Spirit. The "enlightening" power of the Logos and the "inspiring", enlivening action of the Spirit, are not circumscribed by the particularity of the historical event.

---

28. See DUPUIS, *Jesus Christ* (n. 1), pp. 157-165; also ID., *Toward a Christian Theology* (n. 2), pp. 173-177.

29. See DUPUIS, *Jesus Christ* (n. 1), pp. 94-101; ID., *Who Do You Say I Am?* (n. 16), pp. 144-150.

They transcend all boundaries of time and space. Through the transcendent saving power of the Logos and the Spirit, Trinitarian Christology is able to account for the mediatory function of religious traditions in the order of salvation, thus laying the foundation for the due recognition of pluralism in God's ways of dealing with humankind.

V. CONCLUSION

The problematic in the theology of religions has shifted repeatedly in recent years. Since the time surrounding the Second Vatican Council, the problematic has moved from the traditional question of the possibility of salvation outside the Church to a more positive approach in which the mediatory function of the religious traditions as "channels" and "paths" to divine salvation is recognized and affirmed. The recent past has witnessed a further shift in the problematic. The question which is now being asked is no longer whether and in what sense the religious traditions may be said to be channels of divine salvation; theologians further inquire whether the religious pluralism in which we find ourselves today has, in the plan of God for humankind, a positive meaning intended by God. In other words, is the plurality of religious traditions today simply a fact of life to be reckoned with, or a positive factor to be welcomed as a gift of God? Or again: Are we dealing with a pluralism of fact (*de facto*) or of principle (*de iure*)?

Without presuming to fathom God's plan for humankind, a Trinitarian Christology is able to provide a foundation for a pluralism *de iure* of religious traditions. Religions have their original source in a divine self-manifestation to human beings; religious plurality rests therefore primarily on the superabundant richness and diversity of God's self-manifestions to humankind. The divine plan for humanity is one, but multifaceted. It belongs to the nature of the overflowing communication of the Triune God to humankind to prolong outside the divine life the plural communication intrinsic to that life itself.

In accordance with the mainline Christian tradition, the constitutive uniqueness and universality of the Jesus-Christ-event must be maintained. Such uniqueness must not, however, be construed as absolute; what is absolute is God's saving will. Neither absolute nor relative, Jesus' uniqueness is "constitutive" and "relational". In what sense can it be described as "relational"? The answer is, in the sense that the singularly unique event of Jesus Christ is inscribed in the overall ambit of God's personal dealings with humankind in history, and, therefore, related to all other divine manifestations to people in the one history of salvation.

In this way, it is possible to go beyond not only the exclusivist paradigm but the inclusivist as well, without, however, resorting to the "pluralistic" paradigm in so far as this is based on the negation of Jesus Christ as constitutive Saviour of humankind. The model drawn from Trinitarian Christology makes it possible to discover in other saving figures and traditions truth and grace not brought out explicitly in God's revelation and manifestation in Jesus Christ. These represent additional and autonomous benefits on the part of God; more divine truth and grace are found operative in the entire history of God's dealings with humankind than are available simply in the Christian tradition.

It is therefore legitimate to speak of complementarity and convergence between Christianity and the religious traditions. "Complementarity" is not intended here unilaterally, as though values found outside were destined to be one-sidedly "fulfilled" by Christian values and to be merely "integrated" into Christianity. It is a question of a mutual complementarity, in which a dynamic interaction between those traditions and Christianity results in mutual enrichment. Mutual complementarity in turn makes a reciprocal convergence possible. It is the task of interreligious dialogue to turn the potential convergence inherent in the religious traditions into a concrete reality.

If the perspective to which a Trinitarian Christology is leading needs to be expressed in terms of the models that have become familiar in the theology of religions, the most appropriate term would seem to be that of an "inclusivist pluralism" that holds together the constitutive and universal character of the Christ-event in the order of human salvation and the salvific significance of religious traditions in a *de iure* plurality of religious traditions within the one manifold plan of God for humankind.

Pontifical Gregorian University   Jacques DUPUIS
4 Piazza della Pilotta
00187 Rome
Italy

JESUS OF NAZARETH, HISTORY OF GOD, GOD OF HISTORY.

Trinitarian Christology in a Pluralistic Age

Why is Jesus not merely interesting, but indeed absolutely important for the Christian faith? Is the claim of absoluteness inseparable from this faith, bound as it is to the conviction that the Crucified and Risen Lord is the norm and measure of history in a definitive and absolute way? Do not the words of John 14,6 – "I am the way, and the truth, and the life" – immediately followed by "No one comes to the Father except through me", come across as the evident expression of an absolute claim? Is it not true, according to these Gospel statements, that the human being is given no other place to cross the threshold towards the abyss, no other door where the silence of God, mystery of the world, becomes accessible? In the answer to these questions Christian identity either stands or falls, and the universal missionary thrust of the Church is either founded or swept away.

The question becomes even more topical in our postmodern age, characterized as it is by the crisis of the adult reason: with reference to a pluralistic world, is it still possible to think that the way, the truth and the life are in the One Crucified on Good Friday? Also at stake in the same question are the consistency and specificity of Christianity with respect to other religions and the "human condition" in general. How is it possible to imagine that a Christian, firmly convinced that Jesus Christ is the way, the truth and the life, can truly dialogue with people of a different belief? What room is there in the Christian self-consciousness and in its presumption of possessing the Truth, for the other person, for his or her dignity? Here lies the very heart of the question concerning the singularity of Christ in a pluralistic age. The following reflections entail a short analysis of the challenge of the present, postmodern, pluralistic age and a reconsideration of the interpretative models of the universal claim asserted by the Christian faith in history ("the myriad Christ"). The overall aim is to propose a radical theological rethinking of that claim, one that is able to promote a Christian self-consciousness which, while in no way denying faith in the absoluteness of the Trinitarian revelation, can better conjugate it with respect for otherness and diversity[1].

---

1. For more developments and documentation about the following reflections see B. Forte, *Gesù di Nazaret, storia di Dio, Dio della storia. Saggio di una cristologia*

I. THE CHALLENGE OF A PLURALISTIC AGE

The parabola of the "second Modernity" starts with the triumph of all
– embracing reason at the end of the 18th century, the age of Enlightenment (*le siècle des lumières*). The speculative shift to the subject
effected by Descartes prepared both the striking task of the bourgeoisie
in the French Revolution and the celebration of the power of reason in
the idealistic system of Hegel. In all these steps the "order of reason"
(*l'ordre de la raison*) tends to embrace the whole of reality. Everything
has to be brought back to the norm and the measure of the spirit (*Geist*),
so that the slightest shadow might be dispersed and all resistance to the
process of emancipation overcome. The speculative equation between
"ideal" and "real" reflects the aim of making the human person the only
subject of historical processes and the yardstick of the world, including
all its relationships. Similarly, it represents the ambition for crystal-clear
thought, where everything is transparent, with nothing remaining outside, and no sense of beyond. In this way, Modernity implies a thirst for
totality which, by its very constitution, is absolute and violent. A world
explained conceptually tolerates no resistance, puts up with no interruption, and seeks only to exorcize all singularity, and any surprise arising
from difference. Totality, embraced in thought, will not take long to convert itself into totalitarianism, a hard and violent historicity, reaching out
to adapt reality, however intransigent or obtuse, to the progressive and
enlightened ideal.

The parabola of modern ideologies highlights this frightening causality:
devoid of attention to concrete reality and closed to the surprises of what
is not planned, ideological worlds immediately issue in terrible boredom
and a high human, social and ecological cost. The crisis of the "adult reason" – the so-called "Dialectic of Enlightenment" – springs from the
painful consciousness that "the fully enlightened earth radiates disaster triumphant"[2]. Ideology does not free human beings from the toil of living.
The horizons of meaning offered by ideological totality collapse: a need

---

come storia, Milano, Edizioni San Paolo, 1994[7] (Spanish: Madrid, Ediciones Paulinas,
1989[2]; German: Mainz, Matthias-Grünewald-Verlag, 1984; French: Paris, Cerf, 1984;
Portuguese: Saô Paulo, Ediçôes Paulinas, 1985); *Trinità come storia. Saggio sul Dio
cristiano*, Milano, Edizioni San Paolo, 1993[5] (Portuguese: Sâo Paulo, Ediçôes Paulinas,
1987; Spanish: Salamanca, Ediciones Sìgueme, 1988; German: Mainz, Matthias-
Grünewald- Verlag, 1989; English: New York, Alba House, 1989; French: Paris, Nouvelle Cité, 1989); *Teologia della storia. Saggio sulla rivelazione, l'inizio e il compimento*,
Milano, Edizioni San Paolo, 1991 (Portuguese: Sâo Paulo, Paulus, 1995; Spanish: Salamanca, Ediciones SíGueme, 1995).

2. See M. HORKHEIMER & T.W. ADORNO, *Dialectic of Enlightenment*, New York, NY,
Herder & Herder, 1972, p. 3.

for difference breaks the closed circle born of adult reason. The future reappears with surprising rashness: it is not something programmed or simply deduced from the present, as in the case of ideology, but something darker, worrying, something not easily available[3]. Beyond the second Modernity, age of Enlightenment and ideologies, the so-called "postmodern" age arrives as unease, crisis and farewell to all security. The pluralistic character of this age is, first of all, a rejection of the satiated totality and the planned and all-embracing unity of ideologies. This process leads to a broad experience of fragmentation. Whereas modern reason had clear and obvious solutions, worked out within the context of an all-comprehensive, transparent and unifying meaning, the postmodern age rediscovers the dark recalcitrance of life with respect to any ideal reconciliation. The so-called "weak thought" – which justifies every kind of relativism and absolute pluralism – is the result of the farewell to being and to basics, which stems from the crisis of the totalizing answers of modern reason[4].

Therefore, the crisis of meaning seems to become the specific characteristic of postmodern unrest. While, for the adult reason, everything had meaning, for the weakened reason of the postmodern condition, nothing seems to have meaning anymore. Everything is in a state of shipwreck and decline. It is the situation pictured by Dietrich Bonhoeffer as the age of *décadence*[5]. *Décadence* is not the simple abandonment of values or the rejection of any unifying horizon: *décadence* means depriving people of the passion for truth. It takes away all desire to fight for a higher goal. *Décadence* involves the attempt to persuade people that there is no need to stand firm against the negative, because one can agree with everything and everybody to affirm oneself. The great sickness of the modern "global village", that is to say, the world under the power of the "media" and the economic forces behind the media, would seem to be precisely the lack of a passion for the truth. In the climate of *décadence* everything conspires to prevent people from thinking, to encourage their flight from any desire, and any sacrifice, for the truth, and to promote their dependence on the immediately accessible 'benefits' of the consumer society. It is the triumph of the mask at the expense of the truth. The strong reason, expression of ideology, is itself fragmented into many streams. There is a lack of common goals, a poverty of great

---

3. See E. BLOCH, *Das Prinzip Hoffnung*, Frankfurt am Main, Suhrkamp, 1978[5].

4. See G. VATTIMO & P.A. ROVATTI (eds.), *Il pensiero debole*, Milano, Feltrinelli, 1986[4].

5. "Das ist die einzigartige Situation unserer Zeit, und es ist echter Verfall": D. BONHOEFFER, *Ethik*, E. BETHGE (ed.), München, Kaiser Verlag, 1966, pp. 114f.

hopes. Everyone seems to be closed within his/her own particular aims. We all are sick from a lack of hope.

Of course, our analysis cannot exclude some of the more positive signs of this pluralistic age. The modern ideal of emancipation – understood as the bringing back of the whole world and of all human relationships to the human person itself[6] – inspired the great cultural and social emancipatory processes of the modern age, including those involving the so-called "Third World" as well as the exploited classes, and those involving both oppressed races and women. It is precisely the consciousness of the emancipation which has not been achieved that produces the persistent longing "for perfect and consummated justice" (Max Horkheimer), which can be recognized within the unrest of the present crisis as a *pursuit for lost meaning*. What is at stake here is not "une recherche du temps perdu", a kind of nostalgia. Instead, what is at stake is the attempt to recognize an ultimate horizon from which to renew hope and to assess the progress already made. Connected with this pursuit for meaning there is a kind of "rediscovery of the other". With Emmanuel Levinas it is possible to recognize that the "face" of the other, in its bareness and its specificity, in the simple turning of its gaze towards us, becomes the unfounded measure for the sum total of all of the "ego's" pretensions. Neighbors, by the sole fact of their existence, challenge us to live an unconditional going out of ourselves and to find the meaning of life in the commitment to others. The growing awareness of the demands of solidarity can be seen as an expression of this search for lost meaning. In the same way there are signs of the rediscovery of the longing for the Totally Other (Max Horkheimer), a kind of *rediscovering of the ultimate One*. Again it is Levinas who recognizes in the face of the other the traces of the absolute Other, and who establishes the supremacy of the call to ethics with respect to all metaphysical abstraction and all nihilist renunciation. This revives the need which, generically, could be defined as religious. It is the need of a foundation, of a global meaning, of an ultimate basis and of a final homeland, which is not that of a manipulative and violent ideology. To start again with God is no longer the exclusive concern of believers. It is a challenge for all.

The Other, which is the ultimate foundation for living and for living together is, therefore, the open question of the crisis of our age. Now, according to Christian faith, it is in Jesus Christ that the transcendent and sovereign Other has spoken. Hence, it is necessary to turn to Him in

6. K. MARX, *Zur Judenfrage,* in S. LANDSHUT (ed.), *Die Frühschriften*, Stuttgart, Kroner, 1971, p. 199.

order to find our way as believers in the crisis of our pluralistic age. The prophecy of Zechariah (12,10), as recaptured by John (19,37), is valuable for us as well: "They will look on the one whom they have pierced".

II. THE MYRIAD CHRIST
PORTRAYALS OF THE LORD AND SAVIOR IN HISTORY

The portrayals of Christ which have been developed in the history of christological investigation reflect the shifting attempts to answer the question concerning the singularity of the Lord Jesus. They sketch "the myriad Christ": this provocative formula depicts not only the variety of the interpretative patterns of the absoluteness of Christianity, but also the parabola of glory and failure that characterizes most of them. Three patterns need to be considered: the "cosmic Christology" of the Fathers; the "anthropological christology" of modernity; and the "historical christology" of our days.

1. Cosmic Christology

Up until the major developments of the patristic era, the early Christian writers reasoned within a mental framework based on the unifying principle of Christ's exclusive sufficiency. The core idea was that what is offered in the Lord Jesus is the universal Logos, where all truth may be both sought and discovered. Therefore, the "jealousy" of Christianity and its exclusivism are sufficiently motivated. They find expression, especially at the beginning of Christianity and also at the time of its osmosis with the culture of the ancient world by virtue of the pax Constantiniana, in the conviction so clearly asserted in the letter to Diognetus: "All that is beautiful pertains to us Christians". This idea was to attain its fulfilment in the Augustinian theology of Christus totus.

Insofar as this totality is contained in the Scriptures, christological sufficiency was identified with biblical sufficiency, and Christians were, therefore, to engage in intense scrutiny of the Scriptures. The rise of allegory and symbolism in the theological thought of the Fathers is understandable from this viewpoint. These were used as instruments to delve deeply into the Scriptures and to go beyond the letter, in order to penetrate into the depths of the mystery. And accordingly, since the Scriptures are embodied in the reality of Christ's ecclesial body, the Fathers understood the Church as the place where all truth dwells (extra

Ecclesiam nulla salus). Christological, biblical and ecclesial sufficiency
all express the same profound conviction, namely, that the entire universe is an order of signs where everything is symbol, related to the
divine depth which in Christ was revealed. All that exists is to be experienced in the unity of a progressive inclusion by an elevation (*ana-
gogia*) towards the beyond of everything. *Universa pertingens, universa
pertransiens*! Cosmic christology is therefore the answer given by
ancient Christianity to the question about the singularity of Jesus Christ
in the face of the unifying horizon of Greek *paideia* and pagan wisdom.
This kind of answer was to return in new transpositions, identified with
the ever-living Christian soul which considered the experience of the living Lord also as the experience of the deep truth of everything which
exists.

2. Anthropological Christology

The christological reflection of the modern age expresses the response
of Christian faith to the modern question concerning the uniqueness of
Jesus Christ. Characteristic of modern culture is the awareness of subjectivity, where totality is grasped on the basis of the subject and no
longer on the basis of a horizon considered to be objective. In dialogue
with this culture the absoluteness of Christianity was conceived in a different way. The new outlook was formulated within an "anthropological
christology": the subject was read as an open question (or "self-transcendence", according to Karl Rahner's terminology), while Christ was
seen as the only adequate response to this transcendental openness.
Christ is the only true offering of meaning and fullness of life to the infinite self-transcendence of human subjectivity. Therefore, Jesus Christ is
not so much the abstract truth of the world, but rather the truth of
humankind, the meaning of human existence, the absolute bearer of salvation (*der absolute Heilsbringer*). He does not upset this world's logic.
Rather, he is the supreme fulfilment of the expectations of human reason. According to Friedrich Schleiermacher – the father of that "liberal
Protestantism" which was the outcome of the encounter between Christian faith and modern rationalism – religion is a "province of the spirit",
a mere dimension of subjectivity, a result of the sentiment of infinite
dependence, which finds its exemplary form in Jesus Christ. In the
Romantic christologies, Jesus becomes the model of the beautiful soul
which has been able to realize both absolute dependence on God and
unconditional dedication to the neighbor, "the ideal of humanity pleasing to God" (Immanuel Kant).

Here, too, there is a claim to totality: Christ is no longer the "all" of the cosmos but he is certainly the "all" of human being, in whom the subject attains complete fulfilment. It is easy to understand how this approach was to turn out to be extremely weak, since it confused Christian absoluteness with the totalitarianism of the ideological worlds produced by modern reason. The liberal or revolutionary reduction of Christianity reveals its fragility precisely when faced with the incompleteness and the violent nature of ideologies, based on the self-celebration of the power of human reason. Christology reduced to anthropology is simply unable to criticize the limits of historical subjects and of their plans to change the world and life.

3. Historical Christology

The crisis of modernity, the so-called "dialectic of Enlightenment", challenges in a new way the Christian claim to absoluteness. The "historical christology" of our age recognizes in Jesus Christ the living encounter of human history *(exodus)* and divine revelation (advent). He is seen neither as the universal Logos of the cosmos, nor as the response to human self-transcendence, but first of all as the horizon of sense for the whole development of world and life. In Christ is to be found the meaning of history. Here, one can recognize the attempt to justify the singularity of Jesus in the context of emerging "historical consciousness". And yet, if the resurrection of Christ is the anticipation of the end, the *prolepsis* of the eschatological hour, which reveals the final goal of everything in history, then the destiny of humankind and of historical development seems swept away and the interplay of human liberty appears to be obfuscated. The "not yet" of the promise is resolved in the splendor of the "already"[7].

In this way, the tension between the first and the second advent of the Son of God is eliminated, as if consumed in advance by the already manifested lordship of Jesus Christ. But the hard core of real history, with its countless contradictions, precludes this ideal reconciliation. As long as pain and death are present, any vision of the absoluteness of Christianity which claims that the scandal they arouse has already been resolved, will necessarily appear as an ideological masking of the drama revealed in the passion and death of the Redeemer of the world. Therefore, the "historical christologies" run the risk of being as ideological as the visions of the world and history proposed by modern reason (*Weltanschauungen*).

7. Cf. W. PANNENBERG, *Grundzuge der Christologie*, Gütersloh, Mohn, 1964.

The interpretative patterns thus far described have a common denominator: the claim to totality. In the horizon of patristic thought, inspired as it was by the passion for objectivity, and in the perspective of modern culture, marked as it is by the triumph of subjectivity, as well as within the horizon of the interplay between historical "subject – object", Christ becomes but a component of the whole, albeit the loftiest and the greatest one. He is no longer a challenge, the Word through which the eternal Silence of the "beyond" of everything offers itself to historical reality. Therefore, every effort to explain Jesus as absolute truth with respect to a totalizing horizon is inevitably destined to failure in our pluralistic and postmodern age, an age characterized by the general decline of all-embracing visions of the world and of life.

From the side of God (*ex parte Dei*), it is easy to acknowledge that if Christ is the fulfilment of everything we can know and realize, then there is nothing scandalous and new in his person and work. On the contrary, his "newness" would actually belong to the horizon of this world; it would by no means be the divine newness, beauty "*tam antiqua et tam nova*", but merely an answer to the outstanding question of human being in history. The christological *novum* would be lost and the scandal of God as totally Other would be eliminated. The true question of meaning resides not in the encounter with what is a part of this world or of the horizons of human reason, but in the "impossible possibility" of God (Karl Barth: "*die unmögliche Möglichkeit Gottes*") to let Himself be known and experienced as the mystery of the world, the mystery that is beyond everything and cannot be caught by our understanding. A Christ already included in the possibilities of our expectations does not say anything really new.

From the side of humankind (*ex parte hominis*) it must be admitted that any interpretation of Christ as the answer to our expectations risks belying the complexity of world and life. History is not made up of totalizing and unifying horizons, but of an intricate complexity of discontinuous and broken pathways ("*Holzwege*": Martin Heidegger). After the collapse of the ingenuous presumptions of ideological reason it is necessary to discover anew the courage of discontinuance, the dignity of fragments, even the value of the incompleteness of meaning. We ought to "restore death" ("*restituer la mort*": Ghislain Lafont). This challenge, – characteristic of our pluralistic age – impacts in a profound way on the theological self-consciousness of believers, because the presentation of "Christ as the answer" is quite reassuring. This is the foundation of every kind of Christian "fundamentalism", justifying the presumption that one has attained certainty about everything. But, conversely, it is also allows for the "secular" reduction of Jesus which absorbs his new-ness into the human commitment for justice and peace.

The shortcomings of these interpretations of Christ's uniqueness drive theological investigation towards new attempts, which seek to take up the challenge of the crisis and the downfall of ideological, all-embracing horizons. What can Jesus truly say about the beyond of all being and the meaning of human life and history, without eliminating their complex-ity? How can the words of John 14,6 be interpreted in a way which respects the dignity of different cultural and religious worlds, without falling into a totalizing, reassuring interpretation, reminiscent of the ide-ological patterns which have so shockingly collapsed?

III. THE THREEFOLD "EXODUS" OF JESUS

The anti-ideological character of Christological faith has been evident since New Testament times. Actually, God's revelation in Christ pierces any all-enveloping system, produced by human reason, because the com-ing of the Kingdom – preached and realized by the Lord Jesus in his per-son – signifies the sovereign imminence of the ultimate reality, which bursts into the penultimate one. Christ crucified and risen is the place in which the transcendent Other has come to speak in fullness to us. That is why the encounter with the Word of the Cross is able to liberate and to change our heart and our lives. Christ before Pilate testifies that the truth is not a logical system or a castle of well constructed ideas. Truth is the Innocent one who reaches out to us with the discretion of his pres-ence of love. Truth is not something that one possesses, but Someone who possesses us in the communion of His faithful people. In order to recognize the face of the Other, who is the only one who can overcome the crisis of fragmentation of modern culture without restoring the power of an ideological system, it is necessary today more than in other age of Christian history to return to the witness of the New Testament. Christological renewal depends on the biblical renewal, which has char-acterized the Christian theology of the twentieth century and the spring-time of Vatican II.

According to the New Testament, the identity and the mission of Christ are to be understood within the double movement of his coming from the Father and his return to the Father in the Spirit of resurrection. In the language of the Fathers and of the Scholastics these two move-ments were called *exitus a Deo* and *reditus ad Deum*. The Son made flesh oversteps the double threshold from God to history and from time to eternity: he oversteps the limits and makes it possible for human beings to know and to share God's life. A kind of "transgression" marks the beginning and at the end of "the days of his flesh" (Heb 5,7). But the continuous dynamic of his life is also a permanent "exodus" from himself. Jesus is free for the Father and for the neighbors, free from himself, up to and including the laying down of his own life for his friends. From the Father to the world, from himself to others, from this world to the Father: Jesus' life and mission are marked by this threefold "exodus". That is why he does not allow himself to be captured by static definitions: he is the truth precisely in so far as he is the way and the life (cf. Jn 14,6).

a) First of all Jesus offers himself as "the Word which proceeds from the divine Silence", the coming out of God from himself for our sake, the Son made flesh who opens to us the way to search the mystery of the trinitarian God. His "exodus" from the Father makes the divine life accessible to us, even if its depths exceed any human understanding. In modern western, and especially German, theology, this decisive aspect has been obscured due to a semantic slip of great importance. God's self-communication in history, expressed by the Greek word ἀποκάλυψις and by the Latin re-velatio, was translated by the German word Offenbarung. These terms were erroneously regarded as equivalent. In fact, they are very different. The Greek and Latin terms suppose a dialectic of openness and hiddenness, signified by the composition of the verb velare (= to veil) and καλύπτειν (= to hide) with the prefix re (meaning at the same time "repetition" and "change") and ἀπό (of analogous, dialectical value). Revelatio – like the Greek word – means a falling away of the veil's coverage and at the same time a further intensification of it. Therefore, in the two main languages of the ancient and medieval Church, the term 'revelation' means the contemporaneous self-manifestation and self-withdrawal of the divine mystery, the unveiling of what is hidden and the veiling of what is revealed. This dialectical interplay has been lost in German, where the word Offenbarung (from offen = open, and bären = to carry in the womb and to give birth to) is evocative only of a self-opening.

Where re-velatio has been understood as Offenbarung and then as God's total manifestation, the hidden depth of the divine mystery has been resolved into an openness without reserve and the way has been opened to the triumph of ideology. The eloquent example of this process is offered by Hegel's idealistic system: he considers himself the great exegete of Christianity, just as he understands it as the religion of the

Offenbarung, the religion of openness and not of secrets, of manifestation and not of closeness[8]. But it is precisely this logic-centered presumption, where everything is included, that generated the totalitarian vision of the world, matrix for all possible violence against others.

The God of Jesus Christ is completely different from this God of the *Offenbarung,* compelled to a total and indiscreet self-manifestation. Jesus' Father is the God of the *re-velatio,* who resists being turned into ideological formulas that attempt to explain everything. That is why the New Testament insists on the faith of Jesus, "the pioneer and perfecter of our faith" (Heb 12,2), who does not know "the day and the hour" (Mk 13,32) and lives in a constant climate of prayer and commends his spirit into the hands of the Father at the supreme moment of the Cross (cf. Lk 23,46). The faith of the Son Incarnate is the radical negation of every ideological, logic-centered reduction of Christianity, which would presume to explain all things. If Christianity is the religion of the *revelatio,* by which God communicates God-self without eliminating the excess of the divine mystery in relation to human reason and history, then no all-embracing formulas, either ideological, political or even moral must be smuggled into it. Neither should it be cheapened by being turned into some support for one or other of the powers of history, whatever be the secondary effects which one wishes to propose. Faith in Christ's revelation of the trinitarian God nourishes a permanent critical vigilance.

b) Jesus of Nazareth reveals the Father and offers reconciliation with him by means of a further double "exodus": his going out from himself even to the abandonment of the Cross, and his going out from this world to the Father in the power of the Spirit of resurrection and life. By accepting to exist for the Father and for the others, Jesus is free in an unconditional way. In him, the experience of otherness corresponds to the freedom to love. The existence of the Son in the flesh is entirely received from the Father and given to others. For this reason the Gospels emphasize that a constant characteristic of the Prophet of Galilee was his freedom. His public life begins and ends with two great struggles for freedom, the agony of the temptation and the agony of Gethsemane. In both cases Jesus is faced

---

8. "Die christliche Religion ist die Religion der Offenbarung. In ihr ist es offenbar, was Gott ist, daß er gewußt werde, wie er ist, nicht historisch oder sonst auf eine Weise wie in anderen Religionen, sondern die offenbare Manifestation ist ihre Bestimmung und Inhalt selbst, nämlich Offenbarung, Manifestation, Sein für das Bewußtsein, und zwar für das Bewußtsein, dab es selbst Geist ist, d.h. also Bewußtsein und für das Bewußtsein": G.W.F. HEGEL, *Vorlesungen über die Philosophie der Religion,* ed. G. LASSON, Hamburg, Meiner Verlag, 1974, II/2, p. 32.

with the radical alternative which demands the fully free choice expressed
by the powerful formula of Augustine: "The love of self even to the forgetting of God or the love of God even to the forgetting of self"[9]. Jesus
makes the radical choice for God. He is free from himself, free to exist for
the Father and for others. This freedom reaches the depth of an unconditional self-giving on the Cross, when the abandoned Son cries to the divine
Silence: "My God, my God, why have you forsaken me?" (Mk 15,34).

Christological reflection must verify itself vis à vis this mystery of
Jesus' abandonment (*derelictio Jesu*), which reveals at the same time the
freedom of the Prophet of Galilee and his relation to the hidden God:
"*In humilitate et ignominia crucis revelatur Deus*" – "*Crux probat
omnia*" (Luther)! The Cross of the abandonment is the revelation of the
Trinity of the Christian God: "In this is love, not that we loved God but
that he loved us and sent his Son to be the atoning sacrifice for our
sins… So we have known and believe the love that God has for us. God
is love" (1 John 4,10. 16). The Cross reveals the Father who gives up
the beloved Son for all of us (cf. Rom 8,32), the Son who gives himself
for our sake (cf. Gal 2,20), and the Spirit, whom Jesus gives up on the
Cross (cf. Jn 19,30: the Greek verb in all these quotations is *paradí-
domi*[10]), by "offering himself without blemish to God" (Heb 9,14).
Therefore, Jesus' freedom to love to the end (cf. Jn 13,1) reveals God's
freedom to love: the Cross is the revelation of the Trinity, the event of
the death in God, freely assumed for our sake. The scene of the *Trinitas
in Cruce* means that the supreme revelation of God's love for us concerns each one of the three divine Persons in the unfathomable unity of
their love, without confusion and without separation. God's Trinity as
revealed on the Cross is eternal freedom to love, the unique and undi-
vided love of the eternal Lover, the Father, of the eternal Beloved One,
the Son, and of the eternal Spirit, Love that unites and sets free the
divine life. The historical event of Good Friday reveals the Trinity as the
eternal history of love, that enters our history to assume it into the living
relations of the Three. One could say, therefore, that the Cross is the narration of the Trinity and the Trinity is the concept of the Cross: not the
ideological, atheistic death of God, but the trinitarian death in God, revelation of God's infinite love, is the Christian good news. The *exodus* of
the Son Jesus from himself breaks any ideological circle and prevents
any reassuring capture of the divine mystery in worldly horizons.

9. AUGUSTINUS, *De Civitate Dei* XIV,28 (CCSL, 48), Turnhout, Brepols, 1955, p. 451.
10. See S.W. POPKES, *Christus traditus. Eine Untersuchung zum Begriff der
Dahingabe im Neuen Testament* (ATANT, 49), Zürich, 1967.

c) Jesus is "the Christ", "the Risen One", "the Lord of life", who goes out from this world to the Father. By this *reditus* to the glory from which he has come Christ becomes the living witness of God's otherness with respect to this world and of the primacy of the ultimate reality with respect to what is penultimate. In the resurrection he receives from the Father the Spirit of life (cf. Rom 1,4), that he had given up on the Cross, and becomes the giver of the Spirit. "Logos-christology" and "Spirit-christology" mirror the two aspects of the same dynamism of redemption: if, through the "exodus" from the Father, Jesus enters into the human condition of receiver of the Spirit, then, through the resurrection – his powerful "exodus" from death to the Father – the risen Christ becomes the source of the living water that gushes from the eternal spring. By this gift of the Spirit the Lord Jesus brings into history the eternal life of God and leads human beings, whose weakness he had assumed to the ultimate experience of suffering and death, to share the glory of Him who will be all in all (cf. 1 Cor 15,28). This means that Christianity is not the religion of the negative, but it is and remains the religion of meaning and hope. To believe in the risen Lord – even in a world that has lost the desire to pose the question about meaning after the collapse of ideological securities – means to hope against any hope, to bear witness to the greater horizon opened by God's promises. In the midst of the unrest which stems from the lack of meaning of post-modern nihilism, christological faith implies the joyful proclamation of the ultimate hope disclosed by Christ's resurrection as a basis which motivates life and death, solidarity and self-commitment. Nevertheless this meaning has nothing to do with all-embracing ideologies, because the hope of faith does not dissolve the unfathomable transcendence of God and the abysmal Silence, from which the Word has come into history.

If Jesus, the Word that comes from the Silence, founds Christianity as radically opposed to any ideology and if his freedom calls on charity as the unconditional going out from oneself that can overcome all ideological violence, the risen Christ calls on believers to bear witness to the ultimate goal of life and history, which gives meaning to human days and works.

IV. THE TRINITARIAN STRUCTURE OF REVELATION

The content of revelation – which is inseparably christological and trinitarian – also characterizes its form: in God's self-communication each one of the divine Persons acts according to their distinctiveness. It was an undoubted merit of Hegel's philosophy of religion to affirm the full correspondence of subject and object of revelation[11]: in the "absolute religion", which is the Christian one, the historical self-communication of God corresponds to the eternal process of the divine self-knowledge[12]. By becoming object to be known by himself, the divine Subject lives eternally a dialectic of self-distinction and self-identification, which are respectively the generation of the Son and the procession of the Spirit. Incarnation, Cross and Resurrection are the historical manifestation of the eternal divine self-distinction, just as Pentecost manifests historically God's eternal self-identification. In this way, Hegel's philosophy of religion challenges Christian theology to think of God not as a dead object, but as a living Subject: for this reason one could say that the question of the living God – raised by Hegel's thought – has marked all modern attempts at Christology. The fundamental axiom of trinitarian theology (*"Grundaxiom"*) formulated by Karl Rahner takes up Hegel's challenge: "The economic Trinity is the immanent Trinity, and vice-versa"[13]. What God reveals in history corresponds to what God is in the depth of the divine mystery, because God is faithful. That is why no other way is given to us to know God properly than revelation: only a biblical Christology opens to our knowledge the abyss of the Trinity!

The risk of Hegel's philosophy of religion is to put such a stress on the correspondence between the revealed God and the hidden God, that the excess of divine transcendence is lost and the eternal process of the trinitarian life and the historical dialectic of revelation are simply identified. Actually this equation is the very basis of the whole idealistic system and therefore of the many different ideologies derived from it, rightist or

---

11. "Gott ist also hier offenbar, wie er ist; er ist so da, wie er an sich ist; er ist da, als Geist. Gott ist allein im reinen spekulativen Wissen erreichbar, und ist nur in ihm und ist nur es selbst, denn er ist der Geist; und dieses spekulative Wissen ist das Wissen der offenbaren Religion": G.W.F. HEGEL, *Phänomenologie des Geistes*, J. HOFFMEISTER (ed.), Hamburg, Meiner Verlag, 1952⁶, p. 530.

12. "Gott offenbart sich. Offenbaren heißt... dies Umschlagen der unendlichen Subjektivität, dies Urteil der unendlichen Form, ihr sich Bestimmen, für ein anderes zu sein; dies sich Manifestieren gehört zum Wesen des Geistes selbst. Ein Geist, der nicht offenbar ist, ist nicht Geist... Gott ist als Geist wesentlich dies, für ein anderes zu sein, sich zu offenbaren... Diese Religion also ist die offenbare; denn sie ist Geist für den Geist. Sie ist Religion des Geistes und nicht des Geheime, nicht verschlossen, sondern offenbar und bestimmt, für ein anderes zu sein, das nur momentan ein anderes ist. Gott setzt das andere und hebt es auf in seiner ewigen Bewegung. Der Geist ist dies, sich selbst zu erscheinen": Hegel, Vorlesungen über die Philosophie der Religion (n. 8), p. 35.

13. "Die 'ökonomische' Trinität ist die 'immanente' Trinität und umgekehrt": K. RAHNER, *Der dreifaltige Gott als transzendenter Urgrund der Heilsgeschichte*, in *Mysterium Salutis* II, Einsiedeln – Zürich – Köln, Benziger Verlag, 1967, p. 328.

leftist. Even in Rahner's axiom, the "vice-versa" runs the risk of completely exhausting the immanent Trinity into the economic Trinity, so that the self-mediation of God as Spirit is the all-embracing key of divine life and human history[14]. God's mystery is greater than any horizon of this world, even when, through a free act of love, God decides to reveal the trinitarian depth of divine life to human beings. To prevent ourselves from falling into ideological traps it is necessary to mark clearly the difference between immanent and economic Trinity. The dialectic between God and history must be maintained: here Barth's reaction against liberal theology and Hegel's idealism retains its permanent value. God must not be reduced to this world, and this world must not be annihilated by the divine, buried by the fire of God's truth.

To respect the dialectic of revelation – where openness does not exclude concealment and God's self-communication does not abolish the excess and the transcendence of the divine mystery – we ought to overcome the modern conception of *Offenbarung* as full self-manifestation of the absolute Spirit and go back to the original idea of *re-velatio*, which implies the trinitarian structure of the divine self-revealing. When God speaks to us through the Word, there is and remains, beyond this Word made flesh which is true self-communication of the divine mystery, a greater divine Silence. This Silence is the eternal Origin, from which the Word proceeds and with which the Word *is* eternally. Since the beginning of Christological reflection, the Father has been conceived as the living God who "revealed himself through his Son Jesus Christ, who is his Word proceeding from the Silence"[15]. Just as the Son is one with the Father, even if he is distinguished from him, so the Word is one with the divine Silence, even if the Word is distinguished from it. If the Word would not be one with its silent Origin, the Word would not be the self-communication of God; however, if it were not distinguished from the eternal Silence as the Word eternally pronounced and made flesh in time, the divine Origin and the worldly destination would be confused. Divine Word and human Word are united in the Person of the Incarnate Son without confusion or change, but also without division or separation[16].

---

14. Cf. G. LAFONT, *Peut-on connaître Dieu en Jésus-Christ?*, Paris, Cerf, 1969, pp. 220-226; G. GRESHAKE, *Der dreieine Gott*, Freiburg – Basel – Wien, Herder, 1997, pp. 141-145.

15. IGNATIUS OF ANTIOCH, *Ad Magnesios* 8,2, in K. BIHLMEIER & F.X. VON FUNK (eds.), *Die Apostolischen Väter*, Tübingen, Mohr, 1924, vol. 1, p. 236 (in PG 5,669s the text is based on Codices, influenced by anti-Gnostic traditions).

16. According to the formula of the Council of Chalcedon (451): *DS* 302.

The Word comes out from the Silence and resounds in the Silence: just as there is a provenience of the Word (*Herkunft des Wortes*) from the silent Origin, there is also a destination of the Word, in the fashion of a "future" (*Zukunft*) as the eternal place of the coming (*Ankunft*) of the Word[17]. This "*Zukunft des Wortes*", this destiny and welcoming of the Word in the divine life and in time, is called in the New Testament, Holy Spirit, the Spirit of truth (cf. Jn 16,7.13). The Spirit, too, is, therefore, a kind of Silence: he follows the Word, just as the Word follows the first Silence. However, the Spirit is not the Silence of the Origin, but the Silence of the destination and of the ultimate homeland. Through the Spirit the Word made flesh meets the depths of the human being and the whole of history, today in the time of pilgrimage, tomorrow in the fulfilment of God's promises: "The one who really has the word of Jesus can perceive his silence, too, so that he/she may be perfect and may behave through the things of which he/she speaks and may be recognized through those about which he/she keeps silent"[18]. The trinitarian theology of the *re-velatio*, therefore, listens to the Word within two Silences, the Silence of the Origin and the Silence of the Spirit: these *altissima silentia Dei* are the place where any Christological discourse is at home. We have to speak about Christ by being silent and to be silent by putting into words the living experience of his Spirit in us[19].

If the structure of revelation implies this dialectic of Word and Silence, the response to the divine self-communication cannot be one of ideological arrogance: the Trinity does not allow itself to be possessed as a dead object, but rather welcomes and receives in itself those who correspond "through faith for faith" (Rom 1,17) to the revealed Word. This attitude is defined in the New Testament "ὑπ-ακοή πίστεως", "obedience of faith" (cf. Rom 1,5). The terms "*ob-audire*", "ὑπ-ακόυειν" mean to listen to what is underneath, below, beyond, or hidden with respect to the immediately audible words. Then, the response to revelation is an adhering to the Word by corresponding to the Silence from which it comes. The Word is like a door that enables us to enter into the abyss of the divine Mystery. This is because the encounter with Christ in the obedience of faith calls us to transcend the Word itself towards the eternal Silence which it opens for us. One obeys the Word listening to the Silence: "One Word spake the Father, which Word was

---

17. See E. JÜNGEL, *Gott als Geheimnis der Welt*, Tübingen, Mohr, 1978³, §25, 2c.
18. IGNATIUS ANTIOCHENUS, *Ad Ephesios*, J.-P. MIGNE (ed.) (PG, 5), Paris, 1894, 15,1-2; pp. 657.
19. See what D. Bonhoeffer writes in his lectures of 1933: *Christologie-Vorlesung*, E. BETHGE (ed.), München, 1981.

His Son, and this Word He speaks even in eternal silence, and in silence must it be heard by the soul"[20]. "Whoever receives me receives him who sent me" (Jn 13,20). The Trinitarian understanding of revelation shows that the final goal of the faith which receives revelation is not the Person of the Verb, acting in it, but – through the Word and in obedience to it – the Person of the Father, God hidden in silence, who made himself accessible through the incarnation of the Son[21].

In the course of this dynamic obedience the Spirit guides the believers into all the truth (cf. Jn 16,13): the Spirit is the living and powerful memory of God: "The Advocate, the Holy Spirit, whom the Father will send in my name, will teach you everything, and remind you of all that I have said to you" (Jn 14,26). If the Word made flesh is the exegete of the Father (cf. Jn 1,18), the Spirit is the exegete of the Son, Spirit of truth, who will speak whatever he hears and will declare the things that are to come (cf. Jn 16,13f.). To receive the Word, by listening to the divine Silence hidden in it, is "ecstasy", coming out from ourselves to go towards God's depths, from where we are attracted by the pure Source of the Light, the Father of the eternal Word. The "ecstatic" love of God, because of which God goes out from the eternal silence through the Word of creation and redemption, provokes a correspondence, which is similarly "ecstatic", because it goes out from the closed limits of our world to walk on the endless path of the divine Silence. This is the fruit of the event of revelation. "No one can come to me unless drawn by the Father who sent me" (Jn 6,44).

However, all of this does not mean that the mediation of the Incarnate Word may be by-passed: the concealed God (*Deus absconditus*) only allows himself to be reached through the revealed God (*Deus revelatus*): "No one comes to the Father except through me" (Jn 14,6b). The dialectic of revelation, the inseparable unity of God's self-communication and God's self-withdrawal in Jesus Christ, totally depends on the scandal of the christological *concretissimum* of the Word, where the unutterable divine depth becomes accessible without being absorbed into the measures of human reason. This dialectical structure corresponds to the idea of *revelatio Dei sub contraria specie*, which is central to Luther's theological hermeneutics, but which is also present in, for example, Hans

20. *Joannes a croce, entences* C.H. LONG and J.M. KITAGAWA, n. 21.

21. Cf. B. FORTE, *Im Hören der Stille. Philosophischer Glaube und Offenbarungsglaube*, in W. BEINERT e.a. (eds.), *Unterwegs zum einen Glauben. FS Lothar Ullrich* (ETS, 74), Leipzig, Benno, 1997, pp. 74-81, and *"Offenbarung" oder "re-velatio"? Offenbarung, Hermeneutik und Theologie*, in E. SCHOCKENHOFF & P. WALTER (eds.), *Dogma und Glaube: Bausteine für eine theologische Erkenntnislehre. Festschrift für Bischof Walter Kasper*, Mainz, Matthias-Grünewald, 1993, pp. 193-212.

Urs von Balthasar's theological aesthetics, based as they are on the "perception of the form" (*die Schau der Gestalt*) made possible in Christ, who is the visible form of the invisible God. The God who comes is Trinitarian both in the depth of his mystery and in the way he communicates himself to human beings.

V. TRINITARIAN CHRISTOLOGY AND THE QUEST FOR UNITY

What are the possible consequences of this idea of revelation for the theological understanding of the singularity of Jesus Christ and of the absoluteness of Christianity in a pluralistic world? Does the dialectic of revelation justify a "myriad Christ", where every possible portrayal of Jesus is authorized in name of the unfathomable profundity of the divine mystery, revealed through him? Does this exclude any quest for unity? Or are there in the *revelatio Dei sub contraria specie* decisive and unifying criteria, which cannot be eliminated or by-passed?

In fact, the awareness that the divine mystery goes beyond its historical mediation through the Word made flesh will enable Christian theology to recognize the salvific value that can be found in other religions. It will thus be possible to overcome any form of exclusivism (K. Barth), which denies all meaning to other religious worlds with respect to the knowledge of God and the salvation made possible in Jesus Christ[22]. On the other hand, the no less decisive necessity of the mediation of the incarnate Word to reach the hidden depths of the Trinity ought to preclude that relativistic pluralism (J. Hick, P. Knitter) which would exhaust the newness and the scandal of the Cross[23]. The dialectic of *revelatio* provides a basis for an inclusiveness, which not only recognizes the values of other religions in the light of the Christological criterion (J. Daniélou, H. de Lubac, H. U. von Balthasar), but also acknowledges that the religions could have in themselves a value of salvific mediation. Although God's self-mediation is realized in fullness by Jesus Christ, this does not imply that the divine mystery is adequately manifested by human words and therefore that any participation in God's life is absent elsewhere. Why should we not recognize a certain sacramentality of other religions, as proposed by Yves Congar and Edward Schillebeeckx? Or,

22. Cf. about the radical Christocentrism of God's election K. BARTH, *Die Kirchliche Dogmatik*, II/2, *Die Lehre von Gott*, Zürich, TVZ, 1959⁴, §33.

23. Cf. J. HICK & P.F. KNITTER (eds.),*The Myth of Christian Uniqueness: Toward a Pluralistic Theology of Religions*, Maryknoll, NY, Orbis Books, 1987, and the response G. D'COSTA (ed.), *Christian Uniqueness Reconsidered.:The Myth of a Pluralistic Theology of Religions*, Maryknoll, NY, Orbis Books, 1997.

again, why should it not be possible to distinguish between the particular and the general history of salvation, as Karl Rahner or Heinz Robert Schlette sought to do[24]?

The inclusivistic understanding of Christ's uniqueness seems to respect both the pluralistic character of our postmodern age and the quest for unity, which can be discerned in it as a kind of pursuit for lost meaning. However, the Christological inclusivism based on both the trinitarian content and the trinitarian structure of revelation, must be understood in a no less trinitarian way. This means that in relation to the Incarnate Son, central object and necessary mediation of God's self-communication, we always ought to keep in mind the scandal that is Christ; in relation to the Spirit, who "blows where it chooses" (Jn 3,8), we have to respect, always and in everyone, the place of human liberty; in relation to God the Father we must stress the dialogic structure of faith, made of calling and response, of challenge and decision.

In the pure proclamation of Jesus Christ, he is and remains for ever a "stumbling block". So it is in the New Testament; so must it be in every Christological discourse. A Christian theology which lost the scandalous dimension of its object, irreducible to any all-embracing comprehension, would reduce revelation to a world-bound ideology and would be unavoidably alienated from its true identity (this was the *solvere Christum* which the Fathers accused the heresies of perpetrating). Where *the challenge of the scandal* is no longer present, the newness of the revelation is also absent, as well as the salvific power of the faith. Christ is "the sign of the scandal and yet the object of faith" (Soeren Kierkegaard), precisely because he is the living Word of the transcendent Silence, the *revelatio Dei sub contraria specie* in his own Person of Incarnate Son. The scandal is first and foremost the original one of God revealing himself in the shame of the Cross: "*In humilitate et ignominia Crucis revelatur Deus*" (Luther). Actually, God's weakness and folly are scandalous because it is in them that there emerges God's pure otherness with respect to each and every human measure. The beyond and the new are expressed in a fragment, which human reason would have never dared to imagine as the place of God's revelation.

Hence, where the *stultitia Crucis* is lost, Christian identity is also lost. In this sense, Christ is not the answer to human expectations, but first of

24. Cf. on these different interpretations C. MÉNARD, *Jésus le Christ est-il l'unique sauveur?*, in J.-C. PETIT & C. BRETON (eds.), *Jésus: Christ universel? Interprétations anciennes et appropriations contemporaines de la figure de Jésus*, Québec, Fides, 1990, pp. 55-78, and A. AMATO, *The Unique Mediation of Christ as Lord and Savior*, in *Pro Dialogo: Bulletin of the Pontificium Consilium Pro Dialogo inter Religiones*, 1994/1 (Special Issue of the Theological Colloquium of Pune, India, August 1993), pp. 15-39.

all their subversion, the crisis that challenges us to take a decision and which is able to free us from ideological captivity. After an age like the modern one, which seemed to promise to humankind the fulfilment of every need and wish, and after the dramatic collapse of all these promises, Jesus' subversion can be proclaimed with new efficacy. Therefore, it is not a surprise that, especially in our post-ideological age, the Cross seems to generate an interest which was unthinkable at the time of the triumph of ideologies. Karl Barth has the merit of having understood this long before the collapse of ideological presumptions: "The scandal which in one way or another we all receive in Christ is not what is blasphemous; what is blasphemous is the opinion that something can be done with him or that something can be said or heard about him without scandal"[25]. Without this "criterion of scandal"[26] any Christological reflection risks losing the obedience of faith on which it depends!

A second element of the "paradoxical" understanding of Christ's uniqueness, based on the dialectic of Trinitarian revelation, is the absolute *respect for liberty* it invokes: liberty is the measure of the scandal. The Silence of the Spirit is the condition for listening to the Word made flesh and for receiving it by corresponding to the divine Silence of the Origin. And the Spirit is freedom: "The Lord is the Spirit, and where the Spirit of the Lord is, there is freedom" (2 Cor 3,17). The risk of freedom belongs to the possibilities of faith, as the disturbing question voiced in Luke 18,8 implies: "And yet, when the Son of Man comes, will he find faith on earth?". In the history of salvation nothing is taken for granted. The God of biblical revelation is not only the God of "suspension bridges", that is to say, of peaceful certainties about the mystery, but also the God of a "broken span" gaping above the abyss, that is to say, the God of the silent and incomprehensible withdrawal, the God of the "exile of the Word"[27]. This God, silent and mysterious, always leaves open for the human partner of the covenant the possibility of refusal. The awareness of the difficulties inherent in self-abandonment into the hands of the silent Father, who calls through the scandal of the Son, given up on the Cross and abandoned to death, must make Christian theological awareness continuously open to the possibility that

25. K. BARTH, *Der Römerbrief*, Zürich, Evangelischer Verlag, 1954⁹, p. 263: "Blasphemie ist nicht das Ärgernis, das wir alle an esus nehmen, der eine hier, der andere dort, wohl aber die Meinung, ohne Ärgernis zu nehmen mit ihm auskommen, von ihm reden und hören zu können".

26. *Ibid.*, p. 261.

27. See A. NEHER, *L'exil de la parole. Du silence biblique au silence d'Auschwitz*, Paris, Seuil, 1970.

people may turn their backs on Christ's proclamation. The same awareness also founds the need for the highest possible respect for this refusal,
as in the case of any other human religious or philosophical conviction.
Christ cannot be imposed on anyone, he can only be proposed. In the
power of the Spirit, Jesus summons everyone to the audacity of freedom.
The structure of revelation confirms this call to liberty: the hidden God
appeals to the free obedience of faith; the revealed God calls everybody,
but compels nobody.

All this means that, with respect to Christ's uniqueness, human beings
have and will always retain the power of decision before God, the
Father. The Kingdom of God, which is so decisive in Jesus' preaching,
is offered, never imposed. After the collapse of the violent kingdom of
the adult reason, we do not need a new all-embracing prison. God's
kingdom embraces everyone who freely accepts being reached and
transformed by God's mercy and grace. Just as there is an excess of the
divine mystery in the revelation of the Word, because the Silence of the
Father remains hidden as the source and the goal of the whole life of the
Trinity and of the whole history of the world, so there is an excess of
salvation, which cannot be reduced to the visible ways of Christian
proclamation. Of course, this excess of God's kingdom does not mean
that salvation is a matter of a private and purely subjective choice, made
exclusively between the soul and God. The Christological mediation is
and remains necessary: the respect of the mysterious way of the Kingdom does not exclude, for Christian faith, the duty and the urgency to
proclaim the Gospel. Dialogue and proclamation are both necessary
within the perspective of a Trinitarian inclusivism, just as God's excess
and Christ's unique mediation both belong to the structure of divine self-
communication to us.

The interplay of these elements marks the objective character of the
human decision before the God of Jesus' preaching. "How are they to
believe in one of whom they have never heard? And how are they to
hear without someone to proclaim him? And how are they to proclaim
him unless they are sent?" (Rom 10,14-15). The decision one is invited
to take is always grounded in an *extra nos*, that is to say, in an objective
element coming from without. The call to faith is not one of already
given human possibilities, but the challenge that reaches a free person in
a credible way and invites that person to transform their heart and life by
opening them to God's "impossible possibility" ("*die unmögliche
Möglichkeit Gottes*": Karl Barth). By this free decision before the event
of the free self-communication of the living God, historically transmitted
by witness to witness in the living tradition of the faith of the Church,

the empty instant of human time becomes the καιρός, the time for God, qualified by his presence and action in the power of the Spirit. Therefore, the decision for Christ always passes through the mediation of others and attains its full realization only in faith and love shared with others and related to them. In the economy of God's kingdom this decision might not always be completely explicit and conscious, something which is reflected in the doctrine of baptism by desire (*votum baptismatis*). But even in this case one cannot speak of a pure internal decision, because the mediation of God's self-communication always reaches one through others, by means of the language and signs that are objective communicative systems.

In this perspective, the specific task of the Church is understandable, but so too is the possible participation of other religious mediations in the unique mediation of the incarnate Word. To discern the forms and the degrees of this participation is the true challenge of interreligious dialogue for Christian faith and theology. The non-ideological proclamation of the uniqueness of Christ's mediation, in line with the Trinitarian dialectic of revelation, constitutes the challenge which needs to be confronted by the partners to this dialogue. In this way, pluralism and the quest for unity are not opposed to one another. Our pluralistic age urgently requires their dialectical synthesis, in order to overcome the fragmentation which followed upon the collapse of ideological worlds and to give reasons for hope and life to those who are prepared to commit themselves to the decisive pursuit for lost meaning, the signs of which signs are undeniable at the end of this century and this millennium.

Pontificia Facoltà dell' Italia Meridionale   Bruno FORTE
Via Petrarca 115
80122 Naples
Italy

CHRIST AND THE SPIRIT

Towards A Bifocal Christian Theology Of Religions

My suggestion in this paper will be that the confession of Jesus as the Christ of God, essential as it may be in expressing Christian identity, still remains a stumbling block in interreligious dialogue, unless it is complemented by the confession of the Spirit as a power from God working within but also beyond the boundaries of the Christian tradition. This suggestion will be elaborated in four steps: (1) the problem of Christology in interreligious dialogue; (2) Christology and pluralism; (3) Christology and Trinitarian theology, and (4) a bifocal Christian theology of religions.

I. The Problem of Christology in interreligious dialogue

This first step sounds like an oversimplification: confessing Jesus of Nazareth as the Christ of God is not always a problem. Many people make this confession and act as good neighbours to people with other religious beliefs. They may be good neighbors precisely because they are good Christians. On the other hand, many people are actively involved in interreligious dialogue without ever mentioning the name of Christ at all. The problems of theologians sometimes seem to be quite remote from the 'dialogue of life' which is the kind of dialogue that really matters because it is done at the grassroots level[1]. Nevertheless, some of the Christian participants in a dialogue with Muslims, organized by the Friars Minor in my hometown, said that the greatest differences between them and their Muslim partners did precisely concern the person of Christ as Savior[2].

The Council of Churches in the Netherlands has had the same experience over the past years. As a member of the Faith and Order committee of this Council, I came across this problem because the Council did not

---

1. On these levels of dialogue, see the SECRETARIATUS PRO NON CHRISTIANIS, *Notae quaedam de Ecclesiae rationibus ad asseclas aliarum religionum*, in *Acta Apostolicae Sedis* 76 (1984) 816-828 (Italian text). An English version in *Bulletin secretariatus pro non-christianis* 56 (1984) 126-141.

2. See *Waar je mee omgaat, raak je mee besmet: ervaringen van moslims en christenen in dialoog*, Utrecht, Franciscaanse samenwerking, 1996.

know how to respond to a number of proposals by its committee on Interreligious Encounter. The department concerned with 'interreligious encounter' started from specific problems, as experienced in the actual practice of such encounters. In this way, it sought to develop theological reflection on, for instance, marriages between Christian and Hindu partners, highlighting the many common characteristics between the religions concerned. This type of reflection, however, was not acceptable to all members of the Council of Churches. Some of them even raised severe objections against what they considered to be a form of syncretism, while stating that Christianity is unique as a religion because it confesses Christ as the Savior of humankind. The Council thought it necessary to deepen the theological perspectives on the relationship between Christian identity in Christ and the dialogues with other religions. Over the past two years, members of the committees on Faith and Order and on Interreligious Encounter have cooperated in a project on 'Christology and Dialogue'. It is in this context that we, after some long discussions, were convinced that a Christological perspective is not sufficient in expressing the real nature of a Christian identity which does not hinder, but rather promotes interreligious dialogue.

II. Christology and Pluralism

Christian identity has never been affirmed in a cultural or religious vacuum. In an apologetic and sometimes polemical fashion, the Christian tradition has posited its unique relationship to God by means of Christ, in opposition to the Jews, the pagans, and, incidentally, the Saracens. The modern awareness of global cultural and religious plurality, however, has challenged this old affirmation of uniqueness. Very broadly speaking, the old exclusivist position in Christian self-awareness, as characterized by the famous dictum, *extra Ecclesiam nulla salus*[3] has given way to several new perspectives. One of these is called an inclusivist position; it is the one underlying the *Nostra Aetate* declaration of the Second Vatican Council on the relationship between the Roman Catholic Church and people of other faiths. Its roots are rather old, because it goes back to the Church Fathers and their idea of the *Logos spermatikos*: the Word of God is present in all cultures, but it is clearly visible in the Church. The third position calls itself pluralistic, because it affirms a plurality of valid human approaches to God. While

3. Cf. W. KERN, *Ausserhalb der Kirch kein Heil?*, Freiburg-Basel-Wien, Herder, 1979.

Christ, as the incarnated Word of God, remains normative, according to the inclusivist position, He is seen as only one of the ways leading to the ultimate Reality, according to the pluralistic position[4].

If Christology is a problem in interreligious dialogue, the pluralistic position seems to be the solution to this problem, because it offers a manner of speaking about Christ which may be acceptable for persons of other religions. John Hick, one of the prominent spokespersons for this pluralistic point of view, says that expressions such as 'Jesus was God the Son incarnate' should be interpreted as metaphorical, instead of metaphysical, expressions[5]. This interpretation, however, is at odds with the manner in which most Christians understand their faith in Jesus Christ. Hick's Christology looks just a bit too much like the liberal *Leben Jesu Forschung* in the nineteenth century, as he himself admits[6].

Generally speaking, the pluralistic hypothesis seems to fail in giving Christians (or people of other religious affiliations, for that matter) the idea that it expresses their religious identity sufficiently. What it gains in expanse, it loses in depth. It conveys a very abstract and lofty idea of the ultimate goal of human life, but it does not succeed in making the connection with the concrete ways of envisioning this ultimate goal as embedded in religious traditions[7].

In a recent publication, Paul Knitter tries to respond to these criticisms by formulating a Christology that is faithful to the New Testament witness about Jesus. He reaffirms the uniqueness of Christ as follows: God was *truly* in Christ, but this does not mean that God was *only* in Christ.

---

4. The tripartition in exclusivist, inclusivist and pluralistic points of view is rather common in recent surveys of the theology of religions, but it is not the only one. See, for instance, P.F. KNITTER, *No Other Name? A Critical Survey of Christian Attitudes Toward the World Religions*, Maryknoll, NY, Orbis, 1985; J. VAN LIN, *Modellen voor een theologie van de godsdiensten*, in A. CAMPS, et al. (ed.), *Oecumenische inleiding in de missiologie: teksten en konteksten van het wereldchristendom*, Kampen, Kok, 1988, pp. 186-202. While opponents of the pluralistic viewpoint are rather sceptical of this tripartition (see J.A. DI NOIA, *The Diversity of Religions: A Christian Perspective*, Washington DC, Catholic University of America Press, 1992; S.M. HEIM, *Salvations: Truth and Difference in Religion*, Maryknoll, NY, Orbis, 1995), P. SCHMIDT-LEUKEL defends this tripartition in *Die religionstheologische Grundmodelle: Exklusivismus, Inklusivismus, Pluralismus*, in A. PETER (ed.), *Christlicher Glaube in multireligiöser Gesellschaft: Erfahrungen, theologische Reflexionen, missionarische Perspektiven*, Immensee, Neue Zeitschrift für Missionswissenschaft (supplementa, vol. 44) 1996, pp. 227-248.

5. See J. HICK, *Jesus and the World Religions*, in ID. (ed.), *The Myth of God Incarnate*, London, SCM Press, 1977; *The Non-Absoluteness of Christianity*, in ID., P. KNITTER (eds.), *The Myth of Christian Uniqueness*, Maryknoll, NY, Orbis, 1987; *The Metaphor of God Incarnate*, London, SCM Press, 1993.

6. HICK, *The Metaphor of God Incarnate*, p. 18. See also his *The Rainbow of Faiths: Critical Dialogues on Religious Pluralism*, London, SCM Press, 1995.

7. See the publications by di Noia and Heim (footnote 4).

The revelation of God in Jesus is universal, decisive and indispensable, but not full, definitive or unsurpassable. This means that Jesus is unique, but in the manner of a relational uniqueness: He is the way that is open to other ways[8]. Referring to Edward Schillebeeckx, Knitter now admits the normativeness of Jesus Christ for the Christian faith. But as to the contents of this norm, he only refers to the Reign of God as the center of Jesus' life. Just like Hick, he refers to Jesus as a Prophet filled by the Spirit[9]. Again, this is true but it is not enough. It does not tie in with some of the basic tenets of Christian faith, and, moreover, it does not avail itself of the opportunities of a Trinitarian theology of religions.

III. CHRISTOLOGY AND TRINITARIAN THEOLOGY

If the pluralistic option within the Christian theology of religions does not give a real answer to the problem of Christology, and if the exclusivist option is no longer a plausible alternative because of the fact of religious plurality, is the inclusivist option then the only available alternative?

Some authors do think so. Jacques Dupuis and Gavin D'Costa, for instance, say that inclusivism is the only point of view that is able to hold together these two basic expressions of Christian faith – Christ the Savior is unique, and His salvation is universal[10]. While I do agree with these authors, I also must say that I have some problems with inclusivism. In most of its traditional forms, it says that all forms of salvation in other religions are salvific because of their relatedness to Christ. There are two dangers here. The first is that we incorporate other religions in the salvific influence of Christianity. This is, of course, a form of presumptuousness that has haunted the history of Christianity. The second danger is that we loosen the connection between the Word of God that is present in other religions as well, and the contingent history

8. P. KNITTER, *Jesus and the Other Names: Christian Mission and Global Responsibility*, Marknoll, NY, Orbis, 1996, pp. 61-83.

9. HICK, *The Metaphor of God Incarnate*, pp. 108-110; KNITTER, *Jesus and the Other Names*, p. 92.

10. J. DUPUIS, S.J., *Jésus-Christ à la rencontre des religions*, Paris, Desclée, 1989. English edition: *Jesus Christ at the Encounter of World Religions*, Maryknoll, NY, Orbis, 1991. G. D'COSTA, *Christ, the Trinity, and Religious Plurality*, in ID. (ed.), *Christian Uniqueness Reconsidered: the Myth of a Pluralistic Theology of Religions*, Maryknoll, NY, Orbis, 1990, 16-29; ID., *Toward a Trinitarian Theology of Religions*, in C. CORNILLE, V. NECKEBROUCK (eds.), *A Universal Faith? Peoples, Cultures, Religions, and the Christ*. FS F. De Graeve (Louvain Theological & Pastoral Monographs, vol. 9), Louvain, Peeters, 1992, 139-154.

of the man Jesus Christ[11]. As the missiologist Dupuis notes, this is the danger of some of the recent Christologies formulated in an Indian context[12].

As to the first danger, this is summarized in Karl Rahner's much-discussed phrase 'anonymous Christianity'. Although these words sound imperialistic, they may contain some truth. As Christians, we always derive our criteria about what is salvific from Christ. Christ remains our norm for evaluating other religious phenomena, and that is the basis of the inclusivist position. As Diana Eck puts it: "Christians cannot help but be inclusivists in Christology"[13].

But again, this is not enough. While the inclusivist option safeguards the uniqueness of Christ, it does not do justice to the universality of the salvation made visible in Christ. That is why D'Costa urges a Trinitarian form of inclusivism:

> Broadly speaking I believe that the Trinitarian doctrine of God facilitates an authentically Christian response to the world religions because it takes the *particularities* of history entirely seriously as well as the *universality* of God's action. This is so because the doctrine seeks to affirm that God has disclosed himself unreservedly and irreversibly in the contingencies and particularity of the person Jesus. But within Trinitarian thinking, we are also able to affirm, in the action of the third person, that God is constantly revealing himself through history by means of the Holy Spirit[14].

In the fourth and final step of this paper, I want to develop these ideas by Gavin D'Costa (and Karl Rahner, and Raimun Panikkar, and Jacques Dupuis) beyond the category of inclusivism. Because of the double focus of Christology and Pneumatology, this Christian theology of religions will be both inclusivist and pluralistic[15].

---

11. See W. LOGISTER, *In the Name of Jesus Christ: Christology and the Interreligious Dialogue,* in *A Universal Faith* (n. 11), pp. 155-181; ID., *Het zwaard van Damocles boven de christologie-van-beneden,* in N. SCHREURS, H. VAN DE SANDT (eds.), *De ene Jezus en de vele culturen: christologie en contextualiteit,* Tilburg, Tilburg University Press, 1992, pp. 61-79.

12. DUPUIS, *Jesus Christ at the Encounter of World Religions* (n. 11), pp. 178-190.

13. D.L. KECK, *Encountering God: A Spiritual Journey from Bozeman to Banaras,* Boston, Beacon Press, 1993, p. 86.

14. G. D'COSTA, *Toward a Trinitarian Theology of Religions* (n. 11), p. 147 (italics his).

15. See HEIM, *Salvations* (n. 5) on the pluralism of certain inclusivist positions, as well as the exclusiveness of certain pluralistic positions. Each interreligious encounter, if it is taken seriously, requires a threefold attitude in both partners: an exclusivist attitude ('I have something of my own'), an inclusivist attitude ('You have something which I also have') and a pluralistic attitude ('You have something of your own').

IV. A BIFOCAL CHRISTIAN THEOLOGY OF RELIGIONS

Let me begin by explaining why I talk about a 'bifocal' theology of religions. My suggestion is that the theological language about Christ and the theological language about the Spirit may be compared to a pair of glasses with a double focus. Theological language about Christ as the second person of the Trinity, who was sent to become a human being, helps us to focus on ourselves, and on what is nearby and very concrete in our faith. This is evoked in the unique position of Jesus Christ as the incarnation of God. Theological language about the Spirit as the third person of the Trinity, who was sent to speak through the Prophets, helps us to focus on others and on what is farther away and sometimes only dimly visible from the viewpoint of our faith. This is evoked through the idea of the breathing of the Spirit as the inspiration of God in every creature[16]. The Trinitarian formula behind this metaphor is the twofold mission or self-communication of God to human beings. The Trinity sends the Word into history as a human being; it sends the Spirit into the world as an empowering gift. According to Karl Rahner, the sending of the Word results in an 'incarnational singularity', which is different in various religions. The singularity of Christ as the Word of God in Christianity corresponds to the singularity of the Qur'ân in Islam, and to the singularity of the Covenant (or the Torah) in Judaism. The sending of the Spirit does not result in a singularity but rather in a general human characteristic which is openness for the grace of God[17]. Both the incarnation and the inspiration are really divine, since the *missiones* of Word and Spirit are extensions of the *processiones,* or relations between the so-called persons of the Trinity. In this manner, Rahner defends the Trinity as a radical form of monotheism.

But how does this bifocal theology of religions solve the problem of Christology in interreligious dialogue? In my opinion, it preserves Christian identity through the nearby focus on the uniqueness of Jesus Christ, and it promotes interreligious dialogue through the distant focus on the breathing of the Spirit in all human cultures and religions. Moreover, it relates both focuses dialectically, because the Spirit is the Spirit of Christ, but S/He is also working beyond the boundaries of Christian

16. This double focus is related both to contents (Christ – the Spirit) and to manners of perception (of self – of others). My point is that there is an analogy between contents and perception.

17. See K. RAHNER, *Einzigkeit und Dreifaltigkeit Gottes*, in A. BSTEH (ed.), *Der Gott des Christentums und des Islam* (Beiträge zur Religionstheologie, 2), Mödling, St. Gabriel, 1978, pp. 119-136.

faith as well[18]. In doing this, the bifocal perspective relates the inclusivist and the pluralistic viewpoint in the same manner. Christ remains normative for Christians, but the Spirit yields its own gifts that may be recognized in the old monastic practice of *discretio spirituum*[19]. It is quite difficult to keep both focuses in balance. If myopia dominates, as is usually the case in the Western tradition of Christianity, the Spirit is neglected or looked upon with distrust. The controversial addition of the word *Filioque* in the Creed by the Western Church is a case in point. If, on the other hand, the distant focus predominates, the threat of relativism or anarchy is easily evoked[20].

Apart from this, both focuses are different in kind. While the nearby focus tends to be clear and sharp, the distant focus tends to be vague and soft. In theological language, we speak of 'Christocentrism', but there is no such 'Pneumatocentrism'. There are, however, some excellent reasons to pay more attention to this underdeveloped distant focus. In the first place, according to the New Testament, it is the Spirit who guides us into the full truth (John 16,13). If it is true that nobody comes to the Father except by the Son (John 14,6), it is equally true that no one can say "Jesus is Lord", except under the influence of the Holy Spirit (1 Cor 12,3). In the second place, the Christian tradition contains some indications that may help to focus the distant lens. Apart from the gifts of the Spirit, discussed above, the Creed contains a passage about the Spirit who "has spoken through the Prophets"[21]. While these words refer to the prophets of the Old Testament and the prophets in the Christian communities in the first place, the Fathers of the Church thought about Virgil and the Sibylline books as well. I think that it is a matter of fairness nowadays to take the Qur'ân into consideration, in spite of the theological problems relating to Islam as a post-Christian religion[22].

---

18. S. SAMARTHA, *Between Two Cultures: Ecumenical Ministry in a Pluralist World*, Geneva, WCC, 1996, p. 194.

19. Cf. DR. FR. DINGJAN O.S.B., *Discretio: les origines patristiques et monastiques de la doctrine sur la prudence chez saint Thomas d'Aquin*, Assen, van Gorcum, 1967.

20. This is one of the main points in Y. CONGAR, *La Parole et le Souffle*, Paris, Desclée, 1983.

21. Cf. J. DUPUIS, *Jesus Christ at the Encounter of World Religions* (n. 11), pp. 152-177; P. SCHOONENBERG, *Gods Geest in de heilsgeschiedenis*, in *Communio* 11 (1986) 5-18; ID., *De Geest, het Woord en de Zoon: theologische overdenkingen over Geest-christologie, Logos-christologie en drieëenheidsleer*, Averbode, Altiora; Kampen, Kok, 1991.

22. See R. LEUZE, *Christentum und Islam*, Tübingen, Mohr, 1994, pp. 21-39 (on Muhammad as a Prophet), and 56-71 (on the Qur'ân). Cf. H.M. VROOM, *Geen andere goden: christelijk geloof in gesprek met boeddhisme, hindoeïsme en islam*, Kampen, Kok, 1993, pp. 100-110. On Islam as a post-Christian religion, see *Tijdschrift voor Theologie* 37 (1997) no. 1.

This brings me to my last point. A bifocal Christian theology of religions is, in my opinion, able to give a balanced idea of the relationship between Christianity and other religions. In the final chapter of his book on religions and the truth[23], Henk Vroom presents some models of the relationship between different religions. The first model which he presents, is a pluralistic one. It suggests that all religions lead to the same ultimate truth, and that the differences between religions are inessential and thus, to be placed on the outside border of a big circle[24]. The second model is an exclusivist one. This says that one religion is totally different from all other religions, so that there are no points in common between them. The third model is an inclusivist one, and this tries to do justice to both the singularity of each religion and the common features between them. It is presented by Vroom as a wreath of ellipses with two focuses. The religions have one focus in common, the Transcendent, and another focus (for instance, Jesus Christ) of their own. My bifocal model would look like this third 'bi-centered' model in Vroom's book[25], but it would have the appearance of a daisy, in which the common core is bigger than the petals. In this manner, it combines the advantages of the inclusivist and pluralistic models. The petals are the 'incarnational singularities' of each religion, according to the model I have borrowed from Rahner. But the common core would refer rather to the Spirit breathing in each religion, while the Transcendent – in Trinitarian terms: the Father as origin of both Word and Spirit – would be the source from which the flower originated, and which keeps it alive.

Of course, this comparison falls short[26]. The real relationships between religions are much more complicated, because the distance between them may vary according to the cultural circumstances, or according to the point at issue. As regards the Roman Catholic Church, *Nostra Aetate* gives a general analysis of the extent of compatibility between this Church and other religions[27]. A bifocal theology of religions could proceed in the

---

23. H.M. VROOM, *Religies en de waarheid*, Kampen, Kok, 1988, pp. 286-296. English translation: *Religions and the Truth: Philosophical Perspectives and Reflections*, Amsterdam – Atlanta, GA – Grand Rapids, MI, Rodopi, 1990.

24. On this model, cf. my *Christ and the Other Ways*, in T. v.d. HOOGEN, H. KÜNG, J.-P. WILS (eds.), *Die widerspenstige Religion*. FS H. Häring, Kampen, Kok Pharos, 1997, pp. 377-396.

25. Vroom himself opts for a fourth, 'multi-centered', model.

26. Mainly because it does not do justice to the role of the Father as source of the Trinitarian *processiones*, and of the Trinitarian *missiones* of Word and Spirit.

27. Cf. M. RUOKANEN, *The Catholic Doctrine of Non-Christian Religions According to the Second Vatican Council* (Studies in Christian Mission, 7), Leiden – New York – Köln, E.J. Brill, 1992; J. ZEHNER, *Der notwendige Dialog: die Weltreligionen in katholischer und evangelischer Sicht* (Studien zum Verstehen fremder Religionen), Gütersloh, Mohn, 1992..

same manner, carefully distinguishing the signs of the Spirit in other religions. Both historically and systematically speaking, Christians are closely connected with Jews, and Muslims are closely connected with both Jews and Christians. Important as the connections with the followers of other religions may be in several parts of the world, the Jewishness of Jesus of Nazareth remains a singularity that relates the uniqueness of Christ and the universality of the Spirit in a particular way. This historical fact warns us about forgetting the particular bonds between Christianity and Judaism[28]. While Christians are gradually learning to do this, respecting Judaism both as their older sister and as a different religion, they still have to learn to do the same thing with respect to their younger sister, Islam. Difficult as this may be, such a respect should not diminish their respect for other religions. But, in my opinion, Christians still have a lot to learn from Jews and Muslims, precisely because they are both so familiar and so different. Because the common features of Judaism, Christianity and Islam as the three religions of the 'children of Abraham' are so prominent, the nearness leads to mutual recognition, but also to disastrous violence, as the history of European culture abundantly teaches[29]. Maybe the middle distance between the nearness of the intra-Christian ecumenism and the farness of very different religions is the most difficult distance to master with bifocal lenses.

Katholieke Universiteit Nijmegen   W.G.B.M. VALKENBERG
Postbus 9103
6500 HD Nijmegen
The Netherlands

28. This is particularly emphasized in some feminist theological reflections on Christology. See M. KALSKY, *Elkaar tot spreken horen*, in M. KALSKY, Th. WITVLIET (eds.), *De gewonde genezer: christologie vanuit het perspectief van vrouwen in verschillende culturen*, Baarn, Ten Have, 1991, 169-197; M. DE HAARDT, *Het kwetsbare voorbeeld: Jezus in feministische theologieën*, in *De ene Jezus en de vele culturen* (n. 12), pp. 81-118; E. SCHÜSSLER FIORENZA, *Jesus: Miriam's Child, Sophia's Prophet: Critical Issues in Feminist Christology*, New York, NY, Continuum, 1994.

29. See K.-J. KUSCHEL, *Streit um Abraham: was Juden, Christen und Muslime trennt – und was sie eint*, München-Zürich, Piper, 1994; cf. also P. VALKENBERG, *The Myth of a Dialogue Between Equals: Who Needs Interreligious Dialogue in Western Europe?*, in W.G.B.M. VALKENBERG, F.J.S. WIJSEN (eds.), *The Polemical Dialogue: Research into Dialogue, Truth, and Truthfulness* (Nijmegen Studies in Development and Cultural Change, 24), Saarbrücken, Verlag für Entwicklungspolitik, 1997, pp. 85-104. See also H. HÄRING, *Ploegscharen omgesmeed tot zwaarden (Joël 4,10): de wortels van het geweld in de religie*, in: *Tijdschrift voor Theologie* 37 (1997) 265-290.

II

THE MYRIAD CHRIST

BIBLICAL AND PATRISTIC PERSPECTIVES

THE MONOTHEISTIC BACKGROUND OF NEW TESTAMENT CHRISTOLOGY

CRITICAL REFLECTIONS ON PLURALIST THEOLOGIES OF RELIGIONS

In recent pluralist theologies of religions[1], there seems to be a double development at work. A first development could be called a tendency to reduce the number of fields where a Christian claim of uniqueness can be situated. The Catholic theologian Paul Knitter gives the following description of a theological framework for a pluralistic view of religions: "One way of grounding and justifying this new view is to see it as the most recent stage of a *'natural' evolution* in Catholic theology of religions *from ecclesiocentrism* (Christ/Church against the religions) *to christocentrism* (Christ within or above) *and now to theocentrism*. No longer the Church (as necessary for salvation), nor Christ (as normative for salvation) but God as the divine Mystery is the centre of salvation history and the starting point for interreligious dialogue"[2]. He even goes a step further by pleading for a next move beyond theocentrism to *soteriocentrism*. The reason for this is "that in urging God as the common basis for dialogue, Christians are implicitly but still imperialistically imposing their notions of Deity on other religions which (like Buddhism) may not even wish to speak of God or Transcendence"[3]. Therefore a theological assessment of other religions as to their capacity to promote salvation, i.e., the well-being of humanity, is needed.

A second model which is common to proponents of the pluralist theology of religions is that there is an irreversible movement from exclusivism through inclusivism to pluralism. Exclusivism is no longer defensible in today's world. Inclusivism, defended by notable scholars like

---

1. For a general description, see J. HICK & P. KNITTER (eds.), *The Myth of Christian Uniqueness. Toward a Pluralistic Theology of Religions*, New York, 1987; J. HICK, *The Rainbow of Faiths. Critical Dialogues on Religious Pluralism*, London, 1995 (bibliography on pp. 151-156); T. MERRIGAN, *The Challenge of the Pluralist Theology of Religions and the Christian Rediscovery of Judaism*, in D. POLLEFEYT (ed.), *Jews and Christians: Rivals or Partners for the Kingdom of God? In Search of an Alternative for the Theology of Substitution* (Louvain Theological and Pastoral Monographs, 21), Leuven, 1977, pp. 95-132; L. SWIDLER & P. MOIZES (eds.), *The Uniqueness of Jesus. A Dialogue with Paul F. Knitter* (Orbis Books), Maryknoll, NY, 1997.

2. P. KNITTER, *Catholic Theology of Religions at a Crossroads*, in *Concilium* 183 (1986) 99-107, esp. p. 104.

3. *Ibid.*, p. 105.

K. Rahner, H. Küng and many others, and accepted in a certain sense by
Vatican II, can only be a transitory position. From a logical point of
view inclusivism necessarily leads to pluralism. This crossing of a theological Rubicon (Knitter), or this Copernican turn of thought (J. Hick) is
provoked by the new situation in which we find ourselves today: the
modern awareness of religious pluralism, the co-existence of various
religions in the world in which we live. Three main arguments for this
paradigm shift are given[4]: (i) every particular system of belief is culturally conditioned and cannot therefore claim to express the whole truth or
to pronounce a universally valid judgment on other religions; (ii) the
"Ultimate Reality" of God cannot be known definitively; it transcends
all images of God that are culturally conditioned; (iii) any claim to
absolute or final normativity is unethical and oppressive: to posit the
uniqueness of Christianity leads to a depreciation of other religions. In
short, historical-cultural relativity, the impossibility of knowing the mystery of the 'ultimate reality', and the requirement of justice in interreligious dialogue are the keywords used to justify the enterprise of pluralist theology.

Nobody can deny that interreligious dialogue is an urgent, unavoidable task for religions and churches today. It is a main point on the
agenda of Christian theology on the threshold of the Third Millennium. To be sure, for the interreligious encounter to become a real
dialogue, each partner involved should be respected in its identity and
otherness. When the divergent positions of the dialogue partners are
reduced to a common denominator before the exchange is even
started, a real dialogue between real religions has no chance of success. Before anything else, the interreligious dialogue is a dialogue
between world communities, not between individuals. Individual theologians indeed have an indispensable contribution to make to the
dialogue, but only insofar as they truly represent the full richness of
the religious tradition in which they stand, can their contribution be
valuable. Therefore, for Christian theologians a constant reference to
the foundational Scriptures of their religion is a must. Our own modest contribution to this discussion will be a critical reflection upon the
project of a pluralist theology of religions from a biblical point of
view. Christian biblical scholars take for granted the fundamental
unity of the Old and New Testament books collected in what the

---

4. K.W. BREWER, *The Uniqueness of Christ and the Challenge of the Pluralistic Theology of Religion*, in H. HÄRING & K.-J. KUSCHEL (eds.), *Hans Küng. New Horizons for
Faith and Thought*, London, 1993, pp. 198-215, esp. p. 201.

Christian Tradition considers to be the canon of the Bible. The ideas we would like to develop can be summarized in five theses[5]:

(i) The biblical concept of "salvation" cannot be separated from the biblical notion of God, Jesus Christ and God's people/church and receives its specific content from this relationship. The central theme of the Bible is the reality of God and his relationship to the world. The biblical concept of God determines the characteristic features of the salvation which God offers to his people and to humankind through his Son Jesus Christ. The pluralists are right when they say that "God" should be the central theme of interreligious dialogue.

(ii) The God of the Bible is not an abstract, philosophical concept, a common denominator of all possible representations of the "Absolute", the "Ultimate Reality", but a personal God who reveals himself to humankind and can therefore be known in a real way by men and women.

(iii) According to the Bible, Yahweh, the God of Israel, is the true, living God, the one and only God, incomparable with other deities. That means not only that He is the Creator of heaven and earth, the Savior of all humankind, but also that He alone may be worshipped. "Judaism was unique among the religions of the Roman world in demanding the *exclusive* worship of God"[6]. In other words, biblical monotheism comprises at the same time a notion of exclusivism and universalism, within a context of religious pluralism. Although the religious pluralism of our time presents itself in a cultural context different from the Graeco-Roman world, neither this phenomenon nor the pluralist reaction to it is radically new.

(iv) Early-Christian claims about the uniqueness of Jesus Christ can only be properly understood against the background of the Jewish concept of the uniqueness of Yahweh. They are always linked to assertions about the uniqueness of God. Because of his divine status, Jesus, the Son of God, shares in the unique characteristics of the only, true God, and receives divine worship from his followers. From the very beginning, "Christians held to exclusive monotheism as tenaciously as they did to the worship of Jesus"[7]. Christianity's exclusive claims are not for Christianity but for God and for Jesus Christ.

---

5. This develops an approach which we employed earlier in a Dutch periodical: *"Bij niemand anders is er redding" (Hand. 4,12). De uniciteit van Jezus Christus volgens het Nieuwe Testament*, in *Tijdschrift voor Theologie* 28 (1988) 228-246; *Eén God, één Heer. Over de joodse wortels van de christelijke visie op Jezus' uniciteit*, in *Tijdschrift voor Theologie* 29 (1989) 369-378.

6. Cf. R. BAUCKHAM, *The Worship of Jesus*, in *ABD* 3 (1992) 812-819, esp. p. 816.

7. *Ibid.*, p. 816.

(v) The dialogue between Christians and other world religions can only be a dialogue of defenseless love, a *martyria* eventually at the cost of their own lives, because Christians "preach Christ crucified" (1 Cor 1,23). Jesus Christ offered God's salvation to his people in a free way, without external pressure or violence. He is their only model on their journey to other believers.

I will not develop these points one after another, but rather focus on two of them, namely, points three and four.

I. THE INCOMPARABLE GOD OF THE JEWISH RELIGION

The worship of the one, exclusive, and only God is the center of the religion of Israel. Yet, before such an explicit statement of faith developed, such as is expressed, for example, in Deuteronomy or Deutero-Isaiah, it took a long way of several hundred years to move from the "God of the Fathers", who was worshipped as the supreme God El (2000-1700), to Yahweh, the God of Moses and the people of the exodus and the conquest (ca. 1300-1050), and then, finally, to the "one God" of the exilic period (587-539).

The way the Deuteronomist interprets the history of the people of Israel suggests that the tribes intruding into the land of the Canaanites from outside, who finally took possession of the land of Palestine, had, from the very beginning, a clear monotheistic vision which was radically discontinuous with the polytheist convictions of the native Canaanites. But, in the course of its history, Israel showed itself to be an unfaithful partner who continually broke the covenant which Yahweh, its sovereign Lord, had made with Israel. Again and again, it turned to Baal and served foreign gods[8].

But recent archeological work has cast doubts upon this traditional understanding of Israel's history. A new paradigm is now suggested, namely, that "Israel emerged in the highlands of Palestine in Iron Age I in a peaceful and internal process that took centuries to accomplish. This, in turn implies that the social and intellectual connections between so-called Canaanite and so-called Israelite culture were very great, especially in the early formative years". Therefore, biblical "scholars are sensing an equally great continuity between pre-exilic Israelite religion and Canaanite religion"[9]. From a historical point of view, one might see

8. Cf. M. NOTH, *The Deuteronomistic History* (JSOT SS, 15), Sheffield, 1981.
9. Cf. R.K. GNUSE, *No Other Gods. Emergent Monotheism in Israel* (JSNT, 241), Sheffield, 1997, p. 346. For a survey of the discussion of the history of premonarchic

Yahwism as a mutation from Western Asian religion, just as Christianity was a mutation from Judaism.

However, biblical authors see this process not merely as a natural development of human religious insights. The biblical view is rather that the ultimate purpose of God's particular action in the history of Israel (i.e., the calling of Abram) is that "God, as the saving and covenant God Yahweh, should be known fully and worshipped exclusively by those who as yet imperfectly know him as El"[10]. Notwithstanding the resemblances between the Canaanite religion and Yahwism, the end result of what God began to do with Abram had far-reaching consequences for the way worshippers of Yahweh looked at the Canaanite religion and finally rejected it. To be sure, in the pre-exilic era, biblical religion represented the beliefs of only a minority of people, the 'Yahweh-aloneists' as some call them. "Biblical religion is truly an exilic or post-exilic phenomena. Israelites moved toward monotheism over a six century process until its culmination or breakthrough in the Babylonian exile"[11].

It is, of course, impossible to give even a superficial survey of the whole process of this emerging monotheism[12]. Nevertheless, a first insight

Israel, see N.K. Gottwald, *Recent Studies of the Social World of Premonarchic Israel*, in *CR:BS* 1 (1993) 163-189; N.P. Lemche, *Early Israel Revisited*, in *CR:BS* 4 (1996) 9-34; W.G. Dever, *Revisionist Israel Revisited: A Rejoinder to Niels Peter Lemche*, in *CR:BS* 4 (1996) 35-40.

10. Cf. J.E. Goldingay & C.J.H. Wright, *'Yahweh our God Yahweh One': The Old Testament and Religious Pluralism*, in A.D. Clarke & B.C. Winter (eds.), *One God, One Lord. Christianity in a World of Religious Pluralism*, Grand Rapids, MI, ²1993, pp. 34-52, esp. 39.

11. R. Gnuse, *No Other Gods* (n. 9), p. 347. The author adds that "Significant crises or socio-historical developments in the pre-exilic period fueled this advance, so that monotheism appears to emerge as a culmination of several intellectual 'jumps' with a final breakthrough in the exile. Authors, therefore, see this movement as both evolutionary and revolutionary in its advance. It is evolutionary in that it takes centuries to emerge. However, it is revolutionary in that the process really occurs in a relatively short period of time compared to the greater scope of human history, and the final breakthrough in the exile to radical monotheism was not the inevitable result of the gradual process, but rather it was a quantum leap prepared for by many previous smaller revolutions" (p. 347).

12. For the growth and nature of biblical monotheism, see D.V. Edelman (ed.), *The Triumph of Elohim: From Yahwisms to Judaisms*, Grand Rapids, MI, 1996; D. Faivre, *L'idée de Dieu chez les Hébreux nomades. Une monolâtrie sur fond de polydémonisme*, Paris/Montréal, 1996; E. Haag (ed.), *Gott, der Einzige. Zur Entstehung des Monotheismus in Israel* (Quaestiones disputatae, 104), Freiburg, 1985; O. Keel (ed.), *Monotheismus im Alten Israel und seiner Umwelt* (BibB, 14), Freiburg, 1980; H. Lang (ed.), *Der Einzige Gott*, München, 1981; J. de Moor, *The Rise of Yahwism. The Roots of Israelite Monotheism* (BETL, 91), Leuven, 1990; D. Patrick, *The Rendering of God in the Old Testament* (OBT, 10), Philadelphia, PA, 1981; J.J. Scullion, *God in the OT*, in *ABD* 2 (1992) 1041-1048; M.S. Smith, *The Early History of God. Yahweh and the Other Deities in Ancient Israel*, New York, NY, 1990; E. Zenger, *Der Gott der Bibel*, Stuttgart, 1979; J.-M. van Cangh, *Les origines d'Israël et de la foi monothéiste. Apports de l'archéologie et de la critique littéraire*, in *RTL* 22 (1991) 305-326.457-487.

may be derived from the observations made above which may have some impact on interreligious dialogue. When religions discuss the different ways they express their ideas about the reality of God, it should be clear that it cannot be simply a comparison of concepts which were once and for all fixed at a certain moment of their history. The way religions perceive the reality God is a complex, never-ending historical process. At the same time, it is a result of reciprocal exchange and influence. By its very nature, interreligious dialogue itself will challenge religions to rethink their vision on the "ultimate reality". However, no particular religion can give up what it sees as the moment of truth in its specific approach. But, at the same time, it will be enriched and maybe partly modified by the encounter with other specific religious "theological" traditions.

What is the specific nature of biblical monotheism? Let us look at three significant texts.

2 Samuel 7,22-24

After the prophet Nathan has told David of Yahweh's promise that He will make firm forever his house and his throne (2 Sam 7,1-16), David says a prayer of thanks (7,18-29). One fragment of this provides a summary of Jewish monotheism (2 Sam 7,22-24; cp. 1 Sam 2,2; 1 Chron 17,20-23):

22 How great you are, O Yahweh God!
    For there is no one like you, and there is no God but you,
    (*kî 'ên kamôka we'ên 'elohîm zûlateka*)
    according to all that we have heard with our ears.
23 And who is like your people, like Israel,
    (*ûmî ke'ameka kîyisra'el*)
    the one nation on earth (*gôy 'ehad ba'ares*)
    that God went out to redeem as a people for himself;
    and to make a name for himself
    to perform great and awesome wonders
    by driving out nations and their gods from before your people,
    whom you redeemed from Egypt?
24 You have established your people Israel as your very own forever,
    and you, O Yahweh, have become their God. (NIV)

This text contains all the essential aspects of the Jewish faith in the one and only God. The concept of uniqueness refers to both Yahweh ánd his people. On the one hand, Yahweh, Israel's God, is incomparable with other gods ("there is no one like you"[13]) and unique ("there is no

---

13. The idea of the incomparability of Yahweh is expressed in the form of a negation: "The is none like Me/Yahweh our God/God/Thee" (Ex 8,6; 9,14; Deut 33,26; 1 Sam 2,2; 2 Sam 7,22; 1 Kgs 8,23; 2 Chron 14,10; 20,6; Ps 86,8; Jer 10,6.7) or of a rhetorical

god except you"[14]). As in other texts, the incomparability and the uniqueness of Yahweh are here clearly juxtaposed (cp. Deut 4,34-35; 32,12; 1 Sam 2,2; Ps 86,8-10; Is 43,10-13; 44,7; 46,9). On the other hand, Israel is incomparable ("who is like your people Israel?"), a unique nation on earth among the other nations ("the one nation on earth"), because God has done for Israel what he has done for no other nation: he redeemed it from the slavery in Egypt and made it his own people. The contrast between the "one nation" and the many "nations" corresponds to that between the one God and the many gods. Verse 24 refers to the Covenant on Mount Sinai (Ex 6,7; Dt 7,26; 26,17; 29,12), which is the basis and the sign of a monogamous, exclusive relationship between God and his people. In contrast to philosophy, which derives the uniqueness of God from his perfection[15], the Bible understands the uniqueness of God in a relational and soteriological sense. Yahweh is the only redeemer of Israel (cp. Dt 32,12). Therefore, He is a jealous God, who does not accept that Israel worships other gods (cf. Ex 20,5; 34,14). He asks for the exclusive worship of Him alone (cf. Dt 5,6-8).

Deuteronomy 6,4-5

This conception finds its classical expression in Deut 6,4-5 which, at least from the end of the first century A.D., formed the opening words of the *Shema'*, a prayer recited twice a day containing Deut 6,4-9; 11,13-21 and Num 15,37-41[16]:

question "who is like thee/Yahweh?" in Ps 35,10; 89,9; 113,5; Ex 15,11; Micah 7,18, Ps 77,14, or "who is like me?" (Yahweh speaking) in Jer 49,19 (= 50,44) and Is 44,7.

14. The idea of the uniqueness of Yahweh is noted by the expression "there is none/no God besides/except thee" or "there is no god besides/except me" (e.g. Deut 4,35; 32,39; 1 Sam 2,2; 7,22; 22,32; 1 Chron 17,20; Judith 9,14; Ps 18(17),32; Is 26,13; 44,6; 45,5.21; 64,4; Hos 13,4). Within the notion of uniqueness, one should at least distinguish three different meanings: (i) singularity or particularity (in that sense each individual or collective reality is unique: e.g., every religion is unique); (ii) perfection, excellence, or incomparability (e.g., among the many religions, Christianity represents the highest form of religion; Zeus is the highest god among the many gods; Yahweh is incomparable with other gods); and (iii) numerical uniqueness (e.g., there is no god except Yahweh: i.e., only Yahweh fulfils the conditions of the notion "God"). The first two meanings refer to the essence (answering the question 'What is it'), the third meaning refers to the existence (answering the question 'Is it?'); see S. BRETON, *Unicité et monothéisme* (Cogitatio fidei, 106), Paris, 1981, p. 11-13.

15. Cf. S. BRETON, *Unicité et monothéisme* (n. 14), pp. 59-60: "Si l'on excepte la preuve par l'ordre du monde qui conclut de la multiplicité ordonnée à l'unicité du principe d'ordre, la justification de l'unicité divine s'appuie presque toujours, en dépit de la diversité des métaphysiques, soit sur l'infinité de la perfection divine soit sur l'identité en Dieu de l'essence et de l'existence soit sur son absolue simplicité".

16. For a discussion of the translation and the meaning of Deut 6,4-5, see S.D. McBRIDE, *The Yoke of the Kingdom*, in *Interpretation* 27 (1973) 273-306, esp.

Hear, O Israel!
Our God is Yahweh, Yahweh alone! (*YHWH 'elohênû YHWH 'ehad*)
You shall love Yahweh your God with all your heart,
and with all your soul, and with all your strength.

Within the context of Deuteronomy, the point of these verses is to
ensure the exclusive allegiance of Israel towards its zealous God Yahweh. There is indeed a constant danger that Israel rebels against its
divine suzerain and follows after other gods. In that context, the uniqueness of Yahweh, compared with other gods, is explicitly stated and the
exclusive love of his people is required. Of course, Israelites were aware
that other nations worshipped their own gods. Yet, when Yahweh is the
true God, El Most High, Creator of heaven and earth, then one could
even suggest that the worship of other deities by non-Israelites is ordered
by God himself (Deut 4,19; 32,8-9; cf. 29,26). On the other hand, there
is the expectation that all peoples will finally come to acknowledge Yahweh as the Lord of all the world (as is expressed several times in the
Psalms). So the provisional acceptance of these foreign forms of worship
should be interpreted in the light of God's ultimate purpose. To the
extent that Yahweh's self-revelation brings Israel to a fuller knowledge
of God, the way is open to critique other gods and religions[17].

Deutero-Isaiah (43,10-12)

Deutero-Isaiah represents the culmination of monotheistic belief. The
uniqueness and incomparability of Yahweh is stressed by several synonymous and characteristic expressions[18]. It is striking how they are
concentrated in the oracle of Is 45,18-25[19]. Let us quote another eloquent
example, Isaiah 43,10-12:

> 10   "You are my witnesses", declares Yahweh,
>   and my servant whom I have chosen,
>   so that you may know and believe me

pp. 291-293, where he argues that the declaration of Deut 6,4 is an answer, not to the
implied question "Who is Yahweh?" but to the question "Who is our god?". We accept
his translation.

17. Cf. GOLDINGAY & WRIGHT, *'Yahweh our God Yahweh alone'* (n. 10), p. 41-42.

18. Cf. Is 40,18.25; 43,10.11.13; 44,6.7.8; 45,5.6.14.18.21.22; 46,5.9; cp. 64,3. See
also the expression *'anî hû'* ("I (am) he") in 41,4; 43,10.13.25; 46,4; 18,12 (cf. 52,6);
elsewhere Dt 32,39; Ps 102,28. For a discussion of the expressions which denote Yahweh's incomparability, see C.J. LABUSCHAGNE, *The Incomparability of Yahweh in the Old
Testament* (Pretoria Oriental Series, 5), Leiden, 1966, pp. 8-30.

19. See v. 18: He says: 'I am the Lord *('anî YHWH*), and there is no other' (*we'ên
'ôd*); v. 21: And there is no God apart from me (*we'ên 'ôd 'elohîm mibbale'aday*), a
righteous God and a Savior, there is none but me (*'ayin zûlatî*); v. 22: Turn to me and be
saved, all you ends of the earth; for I am God, and there is no other (*'anî 'el we'ên 'ôd*).

and understand that I am he (*'anî hû'*).
Before me no God was formed (*lepanî lo' nôsar 'el*),
nor will there be one after me (*we'aharî lo' yihyeh*).
11 I, even I, am Yahweh (*anôkî, anôkî YHWH*),
and apart from me there is no savior (*we'ên mibbale'adî môsîa'*).
12 I have revealed and saved and proclaimed-
I, and not some foreign god among you.
"You are my witnesses", declares Yahweh, that I am God. (NIV)

What is the exact meaning and the content of the incomparability of Yahweh? Should we say, with G.E. Wright, that the language used to express Yahweh's incomparability is only hyperbolic, that these comparative expressions are really nothing more than 'honorific ascriptions to God' or 'exclamations of praise' borrowed from a pagan context and used of Yahweh[20]? There is, of course, abundant evidence that in neighboring religions, such as those of Assyro-Babylon and Egypt, expressions of incomparability referring to god were quite common, especially in hymns adressed to their gods[21]. In that perspective, it would seem acceptable, at first sight, that the religious language of Israel was not radically different from other metaphorical or mythical usages of religious language. However, the intended meaning of these comparative expressions depends to a large extent on the global religious belief system in which they function. In the light of the polytheistic world view of the surrounding religions, it is obvious that the expressions of incomparability lost their comparative notion and became nothing but standard exclamations of praise, which could be simultaneously applied to different gods within the pantheon of the same religion[22]. This was clearly not the case with Israel. In the Old Testament there can be no doubt that in many of these expressions a definite comparison is made between Yahweh and the pagan

---

20. So G.E. WRIGHT, *The Old Testament against its Environment*, in *Studies in Biblical Theology* 2 (1951), p. 34, n. 49.

21. Cf. LABUSCHAGNE, *Incomparability* (n. 18), p. 31-63.

22. K. KEYSSNER, *Gottesvorstellung und Lebensauffassung im griechischen Hymnus* (Würzburger Studien zur Altertumswissenschaft, 2), Stuttgart, 1932, pp. 79-82 speaks of the "hyperbolic style" of the hymns adressed to the gods. Especially in Orphic hymns henotheistic predicates were interchangeable: creation of the world and exclusive power are ascribed to several gods. See also R. BRUCKNER, *'Christushymnen' oder 'epideiktische Passagen'? Studien zum Stilwechsel im Neuen Testament und seiner Umwelt* (FRLANT, 176), Göttingen, 1997, p. 44: "Für die Ausdruckweise der Hymnen ist besonders der Hang zu überschwenglichen und superlativischen Aussagen characteristisch. Diese weisen insgesamt einen henotheistischen Zug auf, wirken aber gerade deshalb etwas übertrieben – lassen sich doch mit denselben exklusiven Zuschreibungen (sogar innerhalb einer Hymnensammlung) mehrere Götter gleichermassen preisen. Eine deutliche Zunahme dieses Stils ist seit der hellenistischen Zeit zu verzeichnen".

gods (or the heavenly beings)[23]. Israel's confession "you alone are God" (2 Kgs 19,15; Ps 86,10; Is 37,16.20) is not a hyperbolic utterance belonging to mythical language, but is meant to express something real about God[24]. Yahweh is not said to be unique in the same sense that all other particular gods are unique.

One may even ask whether it was not the intention of Deutero-Isaiah to polemize against the conception of the people in the pagan environment that Yahweh was nothing but one god among the many gods. For the prophet, it may have been essential to stress emphatically the incomparability of Yahweh[25]. He also takes a polemical stance against the Babylonian gods Bel and Nebo, the equivalents of El and Baal. He excludes any possibility of seeing Bel as the name under which the Babylonians worship the one God. That was entirely out of the question: Yahweh alone is God, no other god. In his strong emphasis on "mono-Yawhism" and on Yahweh's commitment to Israel, the author of Deutero-Isaiah seems to be one of the most exclusivist and even nationalist writers of the Hebrew Bible. Yet, at the same time, he has a strong universalist view when he stresses the significance of Yahweh's relationship with Israel for the whole world. Israel's history is designed to embrace all peoples. It is God's dream that, in the end, all nations will come to learn from Yahweh in Jerusalem (cp. Is 2,2-4; 45,4.6)[26].

23. Labuschagne (*Incomparability* [n. 18], pp. 67-89) refers to Ex 8,6; 9,14; 15,11; Deut 3,24; 4,7.34; 32,1-43; 2 Chron 14,10; 20,6; Is 40,18.25; 44,7; 46,5.9; Jer 10,2-16 and to the Pss 35,10; 40,6; 71,19; 77,14; 86,8; 89,7-9; 113,5f. and in hymnic sections or passages fallung under other *Gattungen*, such as Deut 33,26; 1 Sam 2,2; 1 Ki 8,23; Jer 10,6; Micah 7,18; Job 36,22.

24. Cf. G. DELLING, ΜΟΝΟΣ ΘΕΟΣ, in *TLZ* 77 (1952) 469-476 (= ID., *Studien zum Neuen Testament und zum hellenistischen Judentum. Gesammelte Aufsatze 1950-1968*, Göttingen, 1970, pp. 391-400), p. 396: "Die jüdischen Aussagen von dem ΜΟΝΟΣ schlechthin stehen im Eigentlichen jenseits von griechisch-hellenistischer Frommigkeit und Philosophie, trotz gewisser Verbindungslinien... nun wird sofort ein wesentlicher Unterschied sichtbar: man kann auf die Überschwenglichkeiten verzichten – gerade deshalb, weil man wirklich nur dem Einzigen dient, weil der Gott, den man bekennt, der Schlechthinnige ist. Und die höchsten Aussagen wirken echt, weil dahinter der Glaube an den wirklich Einzigen steht". Compare L.W. HURTADO, *What Do We Mean by "First-Century Jewish Monotheism"?*, in *SBL 1993 Seminar Papers*, pp. 348-368, esp. pp. 356-357: "...monotheistic rhetoric, e.g. the use of *heis* and *monos* formulae in references to the divine, can be found in non-Jewish sources of the Greco-Roman period as well, as Erik Peterson has shown. But in religious practice, this pagan "monotheism" amounted to the recognition of all gods as expressions of one common divine essence or as valid second-order gods under a (often unknowable) high god, and, as such, as worthy of worship. This was categorically different from the exclusivist monotheism of Jews who rejected the worship of all beings other than the one God of the Bible".

25. Cf. LABUSCHAGNE, *Incomparability* (n. 18), p. 74, who refers to B.J. VAN DER MERWE, *Pentateuchtradities in die Prediking van Deuterojesaja*, Groningen, 1955, pp. 16f.

26. Cf. GOLDINGAY & WRIGHT, *art. cit.* (n. 10), p. 45.50; J.D. LEVENSON, *The Universal Horizon of Biblical Particularism*, in M.G. BRETT, *Ethnicity and the Bible* (Biblical

What are the aspects and qualities that make Yahweh totally different from other gods[27]? (a) The dominating characteristic is Yahweh's redeeming intervention in history, which is shown in the power with which he delivered Israel from slavery in Egypt (cf. Deut 5,6-7; 2 Sam 7,23)[28]. It is Yahweh alone who saves; He is the only Savior of Israel, and even of the nations (Is 43,3.11; 45,15.17.21.22). The other gods are wooden idols who are nothing (Is 45,14), powerless, not able to save (Is 45,20; 46,7). In this context, John Goldingay and Christopher Wright rightly remark: "The question, therefore, of whether there is salvation in other religions, is in Old Testament terms a non-question. There is salvation in *no* religion because religions don't save. Not even Israel's *religion* saved them. It was at best a response to Yahweh, the living God who had saved them"[29]. It should be added that, although in the Old Testament there is a strong emphasis on the this-wordly nature of salvation (God delivers his people from slavery), the spiritual and the eschatological dimension are not at all absent[30]. (b) Another aspect displaying Yahweh's incomparability is his activity as Creator of heaven and earth (1 Sam 2,8; Ps 89,10ff.; Jer 10,16 and Is 40,12-31, esp. vv. 18.25; 45,18). This aspect is intimately connected with the preceding one, and is even secondary to it. "The Creator-God is the same God as the 'portion of Jacob', the Redeemer-God" (cp. Jer 10,16)[31]. (c) Still another

Interpretation Series, 19), Leiden, 1996, 143-169, argues that there is a duality in the Bible's concept of election: the choice of Israel is partly grounded in passion (the mystery of Yahweh singling out Israel among the peoples; self-sufficency) and partly in universals (the chosen people exercices a special office: to be particular witnesses of a universal God and Savior; instrumentality). "The purposes do not override the chosenness, and chosenness cannot be reduced merely to the commitment to certain values. The specialness of Israel is neither altogether self-sufficient not altogether instrumental" (p. 156); "For Jews in the post-Enlightenment West, where ideas of human equality and democratic government hold sway, there is a powerful temptation to stress the instrumental dimension of Jewish chosenness and to deny or ignore the self-sufficient dimension" (p. 157).

27. For an elaborate answer to this question, see Chapter Four of C.J. LABUSCHAGNE, *Incomparability* (n. 18), pp. 64-123.

28. The notion of God as Redeemer is of course linked with and expressed by a number of other qualifications: "The intervention of Yahweh in history as the redeeming God, the fighting God, who revealed Himself as the Living, Great, Mighty, Holy and Terrible God, the God of justice, who on the one hand renders help to the oppressed, the wronged and the weak, and who on the other and judges the self-sufficient and the haughty, the God of the Covenant, the Ruler and the wise Conductor of history, was utterly new and unique in the religious world of that time" (LABUSCHAGNE, *Incomparability* [n. 18], p. 136).

29. GOLDINGAY & WRIGHT, *'Yahweh our God Yahweh One'* (n. 10), p. 42-43.

30. Cf. G.G. O'COLLINS, *Salvation*, in *ABD* 5 (1992) 907-914, esp. p. 908: "It would be false to contrast an OT, very earthly salvation with a NT, spiritual and thoroughly other-wordly salvation"; he then describes the three aspects in both the Old and the New Testament (pp. 908-909.911-912).

31. LABUSCHAGNE, *Incomparability* (n. 18), p. 111.

aspect of Yahweh's incomparability is his teachership (cp. Job 36,22b) and his unquestionable wisdom. Yahweh, as opposed to other deities, is the only one who knows the things to come and what is yet to be (Is 44,7; 46,9f.; cp. Jer 10,7). According to Deutero-Isaiah, a great trial between Yahweh and the gods, Israel and the nations, takes place (41,1-42,9). Israel is to be God's "witness" to the nations of Yahweh's sole sovereignty by its reemergence as a people as it returns to its homeland (the new Exodus-Conquest) (43,9-44,5). There lies the significance of Israelite religion, not in itself or in some distinctive features in comparison with other religions. "Written in the context of overbearing religious pluralism, the prophet did not encourage Israel to compare their religion with the Babylonians' and feel superior. He directed their thoughts to the mighty saving acts of Yahweh in their actual history and tells them, 'You are my witnesses'"[32].

Our short investigation of a number of Old Testament texts makes clear that the biblical notion of the one, living God (monotheism) does not start from an abstract idea of God, a reflection about God, but from a relationship with God, who demands an exclusive worship and service of him alone (*monolatreia*). By this essential feature, biblical monotheism distinguished itself from philosophical monotheism, which started from the (implicit) search for the One that might explain the existence of the plural; but this idea of pure oneness cannot be the object of worship or devotion[33].

A recent study of Larry W. Hurtado confirms these observations[34]. First-century Jewish monotheism, he says, is in some sense comparable with the prevalent belief-structure of the ancient world, involving a

---

32. GOLDINGAY & WRIGHT, *'Yahweh our God Yahweh One'* (n. 10), p. 44. On p. 45 they continue: "There is no salvation in them (= the other religions), not because they are somehow inferior as religions to the religion of Christianity, but because they are not witnesses to the deeds of the God who saves. One might add that to stress this role of Israel and Christians as witnesses to what God has done is part of the answer to the charge of religious arrogance. The gospel is not something we invented or can take any credit for. We merely bear witness, as messengers and stewards, to what God has done in the whole biblical story, culminating in Christ himself. We do not so much say 'We have the gospel', as 'There is a gospel'".

33. Cf. Y. AMIR, *Die Begegnung des biblischen und des philosophischen Monotheismus als Grundthema des judischen Hellenismus*, in *EvTh* 38 (1978) 2-19. S. Breton (*Unicité et monothéisme* [n. 15], p. 29) quotes the "théorème célèbre de Proclus: 'toute multiplicité participe de quelque manière à l'un'"; cp. G. DELLING (ΜΟΝΟΣ ΘΕΟΣ [n. 24] p. 391): "Die ΜΟΝΟΣ-ΘΕΟΣ-Aussagen der antiken Welt können unter drei Gesichtspunkten betrachtet werden...Zu unterscheiden sind: 1. die superlativischen Wendungen der polytheistischen Frommigkeit; 2. die Sätze der Philosophie; 3. die Prädikationen der monotheistischen Religion".

34. L.W. HURTADO, *"First-Century Monotheism"* (n. 24), pp. 348-368.

"high god" who presides over other deities[35]. Yahweh also presides over a court of heavenly beings who are likened to him, but there are distinguishing features of Graeco-Roman Jewish monotheism: whereas the high god in pagan versions was posited but not really known (in philosophical traditions it was even emphasized that he cannot be known)[36], the "El" or "High God" of Israel, Yahweh, has in fact revealed himself in history and in Scripture. As such He is known and can be characterised[37]. He can and even must be addressed in prayer and worship. Moreover, whereas worship of a high god in the surrounding pagan religions did not exclude worship of other gods, Jewish religious practice restricted worship to the one God and prohibited devotion to other gods, even God's own glorious angelic ministers. "First-century Jewish monotheism was, thus, an exclusivist, monarchial view of God, manifested particularly in 'orthopraxy' in cultic/liturgical matters"[38]. We think pluralist theologians are right in considering the reality of God as the main point on the agenda of interreligious dialogue. But this starting point and criterion should be the living experience of God in the history of the various religious traditions, not one or another concept of God in some philosophical system or some preconceived religio-historical theory. It is only at a second level that philosophical and other methods of reflection can eventually be applied[39].

---

35. M.P. NILSSON, *The High God and the Mediator*, in *HTR* 56 (1963) 101-120.

36. In the great Leiden Hymn to Amon we read: "God is too great to be worshipped, too powerful to be known" (cf. J. BERGMAN, *yada'*, in *TDOT* 5 [1986], p. 455).

37. See e.g. G.J. BOTTERWECK, *yada'*, in *TDOT* 5 (1986) 468-481, on the expression "and you will/shall know that I am Yahweh" (71 times in Ez!), which is almost always preceded by a statement about an act of Yahweh (p. 471-472); "The expression 'know that Yahweh is God' appears in the Deuteronomistic history to emphasize the uniqueness of Yahweh or his name. Solomon, for instance, prays that Yahweh will maintain the cause of Israel 'that all peoples of the earth may know (*lema'an da'at kol-'ammê*) that Yahweh is God; there is no other'" (p. 474). Compare the way Paul addresses the Galatians who converted to Christianity: "Formerly, when you did not know God, you were slaves to those who by nature are not gods. But now that you know God – or rather are known by God – how is it that you are turning back to those weak and miserable principles" (Gal 4,8-9). It should be added that even in the Old Testament not every non-Israelite was thought to be deprived of the knowledge of the God of Israel: "Yahweh is near to all who call upon him, to all who call upon him in truth" (Ps 145,18). "Quite apart from the specific selfdisclosure of God to Israel, then, the Bible assumes a natural knowledge of God available to all humanity. The technical term for this universally available religion is *yir'at 'elohim* or *yir'at YHWH*, 'the fear of God' or 'the fear of the Lord,' and is associated with moral rectitude" (cf. J.D. LEVENSON, *art. cit.* [n. 26], p.149). The same conviction lies behind Paul's letter to the Romans 1,18-32.

38. L.W. HURTADO, *First-Century Monotheism* (n. 24), p. 368.

39. A good example of second level philosophical reflections on the Jewish-Christian religious tradition is S. BRETON, *Unicité et monothéisme* (n. 15).

II. EARLY CHRISTIAN CLAIMS ABOUT JESUS, THE ONLY LORD AND SAVIOR

In New Testament times, Deut 6,4 was quite common in Jewish liturgy. From the Jewish religion, Early Christianity has consciously inherited the monotheistic formula 'God is one' (εἷς θεός). In different places of the New Testament this confession is quoted or alluded to: in Pauline and deutero-Pauline letters[40], in the Gospels[41], and in Jewish-Christian circles[42]. The number of references or allusions to Deut 6,4 is greater in the New Testament than in the Old Testament (Zech 14,9 is one of the few examples). The New Testament use of the adjective 'alone' (μόνος) to qualify God[43], often in doxologies and confession formulas, is dependent upon Old Testament or intertestamental monotheistic statements. In their own self-understanding, early Christians were convinced monotheists, even when fellow Jews had doubts about that. When pagans became Christians, they had first to "turn to God from idols to serve the living and true God" (1 Thess 1,9). Throughout its history, Christianity has tried to be faithful to this commitment to the one, living God. In the first centuries of the Christian era the monotheistic commitment of the Christian religion took place in a context of religious pluralism[44], which sometimes provoked reactions that are quite similar to those of modern pluralists. In the fourth century, the senator Symmachus wrote to the emperor Theodosius with this reflection: "Whatever god all human beings worship, it amounts to the same. We all see the same stars: heaven is common to all; we are all in the same world. What is beyond that? About this matter everybody searches for his truth according to his proper wisdom. One cannot arrive at such a great mystery by one way only"[45].

40. Rom 3,30; 1 Cor 8,4.6; Gal 3,20; cp. 1 Thess 1,9; 1 Cor 12,2; Gal 4,8 and Eph 4,6; 1 Tim 2,5. See C. DEMKE, *Ein Gott und viele Herren. Die Verkündigung des einen Gottes in den Briefen des Paulus*, in *EvTh* 36 (1976) 473-484; C.H. GIBLIN, *Three Monotheistic Texts in Paul*, in *CBQ* 37 (1975) 527-547; R. SCROGGS, *The Theocentrism of Paul*, in ID. (ed.), *The Text and The Times. New Testament Essays for Today*, Minneapolis, MN, 1993, pp. 184-191.
41. Mk 12,29.32 presents Jesus explicitly quoting Deut 6,4-5; see also Mk 2,7; 10,18 par.; Mt 23,9; Jn 8,41.
42. James 2,19; cp. 4,12; PsClem Hom. 13,15; Ep Petri 2,1.
43. Cp. Mt 4,10 par. Lk 4,8; 5,21; Jn 5,44; 17,3; Rom 16,27; 1 Tim 1,17; cp. 6,15; Jud 25.
44. Cf. R.M. GRANT, *Gods and the one God: Christian Theology in the Graeco-Roman World*, London, 1986; C. WINTER, *In Public and in Private: Early Christian Interactions with Religious Pluralism*, in A.D. CLARKE & B.C. WINTER (eds.), *One God, One Lord. Christianity in a World of Religious Pluralism*, Grand Rapids, MI, 21993, pp. 112-134.
45. Quoted in A. VERGOTE, *"Tu aimeras le Seigneur ton Dieu..."*. *L'identité chrétienne*, Paris/Montréal, 1997, p. 25-26. Original text in *Monumenta Germaniae historica*, vol. VI,1, Berlin, 1961, p. 282.

The theo-logical problem of how to witness to the one God in a pluralist world is common to the three monotheistic religions. Christianity
as well as Islam are inheritors of the Jewish religion. Over against the
relativism of Eastern religions (every particular god is an epiphany of
the unfathomable Mystery of Life) and of the Enlightenment (the Divine
can never coincide with a historical-contingent image of god, and certainly not with a historical-contingent person), the three monotheistic
religions have to give a common witness.

However, the Christian religion gave and continues to give witness to
something more. Early Christians confessed that "Jesus Christ is the one
Lord" (cf. 1 Cor 8,6) and that "salvation is found in no-one else" than in
his name (Acts 4,12)[46]. Moreover, aside from this christological rhetoric,
there also emerged a liturgical practice focused on Jesus Christ. Very
soon Jewish Christians, whose religious background placed great emphasis upon the uniqueness of God, began to develop a cultic veneration of
Jesus Christ as a divine figure, which in their eyes did not diminish their
loyalty to the one God of their Fathers[47]. From the very beginning the
Christian religion seems to have focused on christological statements and
to have underlined the centrality of Jesus Christ. And very soon pagan
observers and critics centered Christian identity on the divine worship of
Jesus[48]. In a letter to Trajan, Pliny the Younger, governer of Bithynia,

46. Cf. M. SAEBO, *"Kein anderer Name". Sieben Thesen zur christologischen Auss-
chliesslichkeitsforderung aus dem Horizont des alttestamentlichen Gottesglaubens*, in
Kerygma und Dogma 22 (1976) 181-190.

47. See R. BAUCKHAM, *Worship of Jesus* (n. 6). A excellent description of the origin
of the worship of Jesus and its Jewish presuppositions can be found in L.W. HURTADO,
One God, One Lord. Early Christian Devotion and Ancient Jewish Monotheism, Philadelphia, 1988, esp. p. 11: "... within the first two decades of Christianity, Jewish Christians
gathered in Jesus' name for worship, prayed to him and sang hymns to him, regarded him
as exalted to a position of heavenly rule above all angelic orders, appropriated to him
titles and Old Testament passages originally referring to God, sought to bring fellow Jews
as well as Gentiles to embrace him as the divinely appointed redeemer, and in general
redefined their devotion to the God of their fathers so as to include the veneration of
Jesus. And apparently they regarded this redefinition not only as legitimate but, indeed, as
something demanded of him". Hurtado examines six features in New Testament texts
dealing with early Christian religious devotion, which indicate this Jesus oriented mutatu-
tion in the Jewish monotheistic tradition: (1) hymnic practices, (2) prayer and related
practices, (3) use of the name of Christ, (4) the Lord's Supper, (5) confession of faith in
Jesus, and (6) prophetic pronouncements of the risen Christ" (pp. 100-114).

48. Cp. R. BAUCKHAM, *Worship of Jesus* (n. 6), p. 815-816: "Most 2d- and 3d-century
pagan writers who discuss Christianity emphasize the worship of Jesus (Pliny Ep.
10.96.7; Lucian Peregrinus 13; Celsus ap. Or Cels. 8.12, 14, 15; Porph. ap. Aug. civ. Dei
19:23; cf. Mart. Pol. 17:2). Also the 3d-century anti-Christian graffito from the Palatine
hill depicts a man in prayer before a crucified man with the head of a donkey, and the
inscription: "Alexamenos worships [his] God" (*Alexamenos sebete theon*; cf. Min. Fel.
Oct. 9:4; Tert. *Apol.* 16; *Ad Nat.* 1.14)".

writes that Christians gather together 'on a certain day before sunrise in order to sing an antiphonic hymn to Christ, as though he were their God (*carmenque Christo quasi deo dicere secum invicem*)[49].

Yet in view of the interreligious dialogue, it is extremely important to stress the fact that New Testament christological language ultimately always points to the reality of God. New Testament christology is at heart a description of what God has done for the world. Christology is theology, or at least the Christian variant of theology. Both Paul and John are *theo*centric, even when christology is predominant in their writings[50]. When the first Christian writers reflect on what the one God has done in and through Jesus Christ, they describe Jesus' identity and activities in relation to God. An important process takes place when a whole range of titles, qualities and activities which, up until that time were reserved for God alone, are now transfered to Jesus[51]. The more Jesus Christ is aligned at the side of God or his divine status is perceived[52], the more his uniqueness is affirmed. He participates as it were in the uniqueness of the only God. Let us look at some New Testament texts in which

---

49. Plinius, *Epist.* 10.96.7. See A.N. SHERWIN-WHITE, *The Letters of Pliny*, Oxford, 31985, pp. 702-710, esp. 704.

50. Cf. R. SCROGGS, *Theocentrism of Paul* (n. 40); M. DE JONGE, *Monotheism and Christology*, in J. BARCLAY & J. SWEET (eds.), *Early Christian Thought in its Jewish Context*. FS M.D. Hooker, Cambridge, 1996, pp. 225-237, esp. p. 235: "Johannine christology, with all its statements about Jesus' unity with God, remains theocentric".

51. C.J. DAVIS, *The Name and Way of the Lord. Old Testament Themes, New Testament Christology* (JSNT SS, 129), Sheffield, 1996, p. 182: Appendix: *(Old Testament) Citations and Allusions about the Divine applied to Christ*. On the origins of New Testament Christology, see W. BOUSSET, *Kyrios Christos: A History of the Belief in Christ from the Beginnings of Christianity to Irenaeus*, Translated by J.E. Steely, Nashville, 1970; R.E. BROWN, *An Introduction to New Testament Christology*, London, 1994; P.M. CASEY, *From Jewish Prophet to Gentile God: The Origins and Development of New Testament Christology*, Louisville/Cambridge, 1991; R.H. FULLER, *The Foundations of New Testament Christology*, New York/London, 1965; M. DE JONGE, *Christology in Context. The Earliest Christian Response to Jesus*, Philadelphia, PA, 1988; I.H. MARSHALL, *The Origins of New Testament Christology*, Downers Grove, IL, 1976; updated ed., 1990; C.F.D. MOULE, *The Origin of Christology*, Cambridge, 1977; P. POKORNÝ, *The Genesis of Christology. Foundations for a Theology of the New Testament*, Cambridge, 1987. See also notes 47, 61 and 71.

52. For the question whether Jesus' divinity is attested in the N.T., see R. BROWN, *Does the New Testament Call Jesus God?*, in *Theological Studies* 26 (1965) 545-573 (= ID., *Jesus God and Man: Modern Biblical Reflections*, Milwaukee, WI, 1967, pp. 1-38): "In three clear instances [Heb 1,8-9; Jn 1,1; 20,18] and in five instances that have a certain probability [Jn 1,18; Rom 9,5; Tit 2,13; 2 Petr 1,1; 1 Jn 5,20] Jesus is called God in the New Testament.... This does not mean that we can take a naïve view about the development that took place in the New Testament use of "God" for Jesus (nor, for that matter, in the gradual development in the understanding of Jesus' divinity)" (pp. 28-29); M.J. HARRIS, *Jesus as God: the New Testament Use of Theos in Reference to Jesus*, Grand Rapids, MI, 1992.

christological statements, implying the idea of Jesus' uniqueness, are linked very closely to statements about the unity and uniqueness of God.

Pauline tradition

1 Thessalonians 1,9-10

Paul's letters show the oldest traces of a christological reflection on the "newness" which appeared in Christ and which had to be integrated in the traditional belief in the one, true God. One example is 1 Thess 1,9-10. There is discussion among scholars whether this text is pre-Pauline or not[53]. But whatever the solution to this debate, Paul reminds his readers of the early Christian kerygma as it was preached to pagans and as he himself had presumably preached:

9b I how you turned to God from idols
             to serve the living and true God,
10 II and to wait for his Son from heaven
             whom he raised from the dead,
                   Jesus who delivers us from the wrath to come.

The tradition contains a theological (Θεός) and a christological dimension ('Iησοῦς). It mentions the two steps which pagan converts to Christianity have to make. First, pagans who become Christians should accept the essence of the Jewish religion: leave polytheism to serve the one and only God. This requirement alludes to the fundamental monotheistic creed of the Jewish people. The second requirement is more specifically Christian: they should wait for the parousia of Jesus, the risen and glorified Son. Jesus receives a soteriological function which properly belongs to God alone: deliverance from the eschatological judgment and so bringing the faithful to God. In this he deals so to speak in one of God's exclusive qualities. The salvation envisaged in this text is primarily of an eschatological nature as in many other texts. Yet it should be added that the New Testament version of salvation also includes an earthly and a spiritual dimension[54]. When pluralist theologians contend

53. Cf. T. Holz, *Der erste Brief an die Thessalonicher* (EKK, XIII), Zürich/Neukirchen, 1986, pp. 54-62.
54. Cf. G.G. O'Collins, *Salvation*, in *ABD* 5 (1992) 907-914, esp. p. 911: the NT concept of salvation includes "a practical concern here and now for needy people (Rom 12:8; 1 Cor 13:3; Heb 13:16; 1 John 3:17; Jas 1:27; 2:14-17)" (earthly dimension), and "it brings a new freedom from sin (Rom 6:1-23), from the law (Rom 7:4; Gal 2:15-21), from death (Rom 6:21), and from the cosmic powers (Gal 4:8-10; Col 2:16-23). Salvation means life 'in Christ' (Rom 8:1; 16,7; 1 Cor:22), the gift of the Holy Spirit (Rom 5:5; 8:9,11), 'peace with God' (Rom 5:1), 'justification' (Rom 4:25), being a 'new creation' (2 Cor 5:17), and enjoying 'reconciliation' (Rom 5:10-11; 2 Cor 5:18 + 20) and existence as 'adopted' sons and daughters of God (Gal 4:4-7)" (spiritual dimension).

that the theological assessment of religions ultimately lies in their capacity to promote the welfare of humanity, they sometimes overlook the rich biblical understanding of the divine origin and the spiritual and eschatological dimensions of "salvation".

1 Corinthians 8,4-6

Whithin the framework of a discussion about eating food offered to idols Paul brings in a text where the uniqueness of Christ's Lordship is linked explicitly to the uniqueness of God (1 Cor 8,4-6)[55]:

```
4a   Hence, concerning the eating of food offered to idols,
b    we know:     I    an idol in the world is "nothing",
c                 and: II   there is no God but one.
5a   I'           For although there may be so-called gods
b                             whether in heaven or on earth
c                 A           - as indeed there are many "gods"
d                 B           and many "lords" -
6a   II' yet for us
                  A'          there is one God, the Father,
b                             from whom (come) all things and to whom we (go),
c                 B'          and one Lord, Jesus Christ,
d                             through whom (come) all things
                                      and through whom we (go to the Father).
```

In verse 4 Paul declares his agreement with the monotheistic faith of the "strong" members of the Church in Corinth, even when he does not agree with all of the practical consequences they draw from it. He even seems to quote their confessional formulas, which sound well-known because they are borrowed from Jewish tradition.

Verse 5 is a concessive sentence: in principle there are no idols because there is only one God (v. 4b), nevertheless, the so-called "gods" and "lords" are a reality for many people. This is true not only for pagans, but even for some Christians, the "weak", who until now are accustomed to idols and who think they behave wrongly when eating sacrificial meat. This verse points to Paul's realism. Although he proclaims God's exclusive uniqueness, he is aware of living in a pluralist world where this one God has rivals, even within the community. Although these "gods" are not real (they are merely λεγόμενοι), yet for those who believe in them they are still a reality.

---

55. We summarise here a more detailed analysis in our study: *Theology and Christology in 1 Corinthians 8,4-6. A Contextual-Redactional Reading*, in R. BIERINGER (ed.), *The Corinthian Correspondence* (BETL, 125), Leuven, 1996, pp. 593-606. See also B.W. WINTER, *Theological and Ethical Responses to Religious Pluralism – 1 Corinthians 8-10*, in *Tyndale Bulletin* 41 (1990) 209-226.

Verse 6 contains, in the form of a perfect parallelism[56], a theological (6ab) and a christological statement (6cd) very closely linked to each other. It forms an antithesis to v. 5 (many gods vs. one God; many lords vs. one Lord): in contrast to the polytheism of the surrounding pagan culture, Paul formulates a Christian version of monotheistic confession, such as he would like his fellow Christians of Corinth to accept. There has been much discussion about the origin of the "baptismal acclamation" of v. 6. D.R. de Lacey has made a plausible plea for the possibility that in v. 6 Paul presents a 'Christianizing' of the shema (Dt 6,4: Ἄκουε Ἰσραήλ, Κύριος ὁ Θεὸς ἡμῶν, Κύριος εἷς ἐστι): "Just as his contemporaries saw a dual function in the confession, so Paul sees a dual referent in kyrios and theos, glossing the latter with pater ('father') and the former with Jesous Christos"[57].

In the first part (6ab) Paul points to the uniqueness of the "one God" in contrast to the "many gods" (5c). The qualification of God as Father probably suggests a reference to his role in creation. In Hellenistic Judaism God could be called "Father of all men and Creator of all things"[58] or "Father and origin of all things"[59]. Here, the contrast with v. 5 points to a similar meaning: the powers "in heaven and on earth" (i.e. in the whole universe) may be called "gods" and "lords", but they are not, because "all things" (i.e. the whole universe again) derive from the only God[60]. For us, Christians, God is "the Father from whom

---

56. The two parts of v. 6 are in perfect parallel. The formulae "one God" and "one Lord" are qualified by "the father" and "Jesus Christ", and each is followed by a set of prepositional phrases. The effect of this parallelization is a strong association, if not a Gleichsetzung of the one Lord Jesus Christ with the one God the Father. Cf. J.A. FITZMYER, *The Semitic Background of the New Testament Kyrios-Title*, in ID., *A Wandering Aramean. Collected Aramaic Essays* (SBL Monogr. Ser., 25), Missoula, MT, 1979, pp. 115-142, spec. p. 130: "...early Christians regarded Jesus as sharing in some sense in the transcendence of Yahweh, that he was somehow on a par with him. This, however, is meant in an egalitarian sense, not in an identifying sense, since Jesus was never hailed as אבא. It involved a *Gleichsetzung*, but not an *Identifizierung*".

57. Cf. D.R. DE LACEY, *'One Lord' in Pauline Christology*, in H.H. ROWDON (ed.), *Christ the Lord: Studies in Christology Presented to Donald Guthrie*, Leicester, 1982, pp. 191-203, esp. p. 200. On p. 196 he refers to the linking of Dt 6,4 with Zech 14,9 which was seen as the eschatological fulfilment of the second reference "the Lord (is) one": "At an early stage the rabbis put these two passages together, so that 'The Lord our God' referred to the present relationship between God and his people Israel, while the second part of the affirmation, 'the Lord (is) one', referred to the coming universal rule of God over all the nations".

58. PHILO, Op. 89; Decal., 64; Spec. Leg. I,96; II,6; Eb. 81.

59. JOSEPHUS, Ant. VII, 380.

60. W. THÜSING, *Per Christum in Deum. Studien zum Verhältnis von Christozentrik und Theozentrik in den paulinischen Hauptbriefen* (NTAb, n.F., 1), Aschendorff, 1965, pp. 225-232, esp. p. 227.

(come) all things". As Father, God is also the goal of the Christian community: "and we (go) to Him". The uniqueness of God is thus manifested in his role in creation and salvation.

The second part (6cd) contains, in the light of the parallelism with v. 6ab, a strong christological affirmation. (a) Through the correspondence of the formulae "one God" "one Lord", Paul expresses the conviction that Jesus Christ somehow partakes of the uniqueness of the One God. God's uniqueness is shared in a certain sense with Christ. He receives a role which is unique, yet subordinated to that of the Father. The twofold use of the preposition διά situates this role in the field of mediation. (b) The formula "all things (came) through him" ascribes to Christ a unique instrumental role in creation, and implies his pre-existence[61]. (c) The formula "we through him" ascribes to Jesus Christ a soteriological mediation: through him the Christians go to the Father. In Paul's thinking the last affirmation was the starting point from which he arrived at the bolder statement about Jesus' role in creation[62]. This strong assimilation of Jesus into the work and the person of the One God has, for its conceptual formulation, been prepared by the Jewish-Hellenistic language about a divine agent under the one God and by the experiences of the historical Jesus and the risen Christ[63].

1 Timothy 2,5-6

Christ's unique function of mediator in the realisation of God's salvific will for all human beings is expressed in the first (deuteropauline) letter to Timothy 2,5-6. These verses were probably extracts from a catechetical or liturgical formula, already familiar to the readers. The formula is imbedded in an instruction on worship. The readers are

---

61. Cf. M. HENGEL, *Christology and New Testament Chronology. A Problem in the History of Earliest Christianity*, in ID. *Between Jesus and Paul*, London, 1983, pp. 30-47, esp. p. 40: "Philippians 2.6ff.; I Cor. 8.6; Gal. 4.4; Rom. 8.3 and I Cor. 2.7 already bear witness to the pre-existence and divine nature of Jesus and his mediation in creation. The subordination which is clear in I Cor. 15.23-28 does not tell against this; in its way it only demonstrates the unique connection between the Son and the Father which is quite unparalleled".

62. Cf. A. FEUILLET, *La profession de la foi monothéiste de 1 Cor. VIII,4-6*, in *Stud.Bibl.Franc.Lib.Annus* 13 (1962/63) 7-32, esp. p. 29: "de la conviction qu'il n'est de salut pour les hommes que par le moyen du Christ crucifié, l'Apotre est passé tout naturellement à cette autre conviction que c'est également par le Christ, Sagesse de Dieu, que Dieu a créé le monde".

63. For a full description of this important development see L.W. HURTADO, *One God, One Lord* (n. 47). See the review article of Hurtado's book by P.A. RAINBOW (*Jewish Monotheism as the Matrix for New Testament Christology: A Review Article*, in *NovT* 33 [1991] 78-91). Unfortunately we could not consult the dissertation of P.A. RAINBOW (*Monotheism and Christology in 1 Corinthians 8:4-6* [Doct. Phil. diss.], Oxford, 1987).

asked not to limit their intercessions to the community of believers, but to pray for all men and women, kings and authorities included (v. 1-2a). Two reasons are advanced for such an inclusive, universal attitude to prayer. First, as a beneficial result, Christians may expect to lead a quiet and peaceful life in all godliness and holiness (v. 2b). Then, the author comes to a second, more theological reason (v. 3-4), which is enhanced by the statements of the liturgical formula (vv. 5-6); it is this last fragment which asks for our attention here:

3   This is good and acceptable to God our Savior,
4a   who wants all human beings to be saved
b   and to come to the knowledge of truth.
5a   For there is one God
b   and one mediator between God and human beings,
c   the human being Christ Jesus,
6a   who gave himself as a ransom for all-
b   the testimony given in its proper time.

In this text the notion of the uniqueness of the mediator Jesus Christ is also linked very closely to the εἷς θεός-formula. At first sight, the mediating role of Jesus Christ seems to be exclusive: it is only through him that human beings can receive God's salvation[64] and come to the knowledge of truth. The way he fulfils this role is through death on the cross, interpreted here as giving himself as a ransom "for all (human beings)". His mediation covers the whole of humankind (cp. Col 1,18-20; Eph 2,11-22), excluding other possible candidate mediators such as demonic powers, angels (Col 2,18; Hebr 2,2), even Moses (Gal 3,19; Hebr 3,1-7). His role characterises the new religion of Christianity (in Hebr 8,6; 9,15; 12,24, Jesus is called "mediator of a new covenant")[65]. However, this exclusive mediating role ascribed to Christ (in v. 5), stands in tension with the inclusive force of the preceding verse where the universality of God's saving will is stressed. This has embarrassed some Church Fathers who tried to limit the universal scope of "all human beings" in v. 4 in relation to the necessity of Jesus' unique mediation

---

64. 1 Tim 2,3 reminds us of the traditional title of "God, the Savior". "The NT applies the term 'Savior' to God 8 times (for example, Luke 1:47; 1 Tim 1:1) and to Jesus 16 times (for example, Luke 2:11; John 4:42; Acts 13:23; Phil 3:20). No one else is called 'savior'. It is the same with *ruomai* ('to rescue' or 'deliver'): when the agent of deliverance is named, it is always God (for example, Matt 27:43; 2 Cor 1:10; Col 1:13; 2 Petr 2:7) or Jesus (1 Thess 1:10)" (cf. G.G. O'COLLINS, *Salvation*, in *ABD* 5 [1992] 907-914, esp. p.910).

65. Christian tradition has understood this mediation as proceding in two directions: from God to men and from men to God; cf. B. SESBOÜÉ, *Jésus-Christ l'unique médiateur. Essai sur la rédemption et le Salut* (coll. "Jésus et Jésus-Christ", 33), Paris, 1988, pp. 88-103.

affirmed in v. 5[66]. Yet, the context stresses the human side of the process of salvation[67]. It looks as if the author foresees that the gospel of salvation through Jesus, which has already transcended the borders of Israel, is going to spread to the ends of the inhabited world. In order to realise that purpose, the human nature of Jesus becomes important: in using such a mediator God can reach every individual and all people. But at the same time this accomplishment is still hoped for in the future. The author exhorts his readers to 'pray' for all, because God 'wants' all to be saved. This gives an eschatological connotation to the unique mediation of Christ[68]. At the same time it leaves some space for the historical circumstances in which God's salvific will reaches humankind and, maybe, it makes us suspicious of identifying Christ's unique mediation too easily with a particular realisation thereof at a particular moment of history.

The Q-community and John's Christology

After having looked at the Pauline tradition, let us now move to the other end of the New Testament spectrum, the christology of John. His Gospel is an obvious example of extreme christological concentration. In fact, John even expresses in a certain way the notion of Jesus' divinity. At two well chosen places of his Gospel he calls Jesus divine (anarthrous θεός), viz. at the beginning (1,1) and at the end (20,28)[69]. In several places, the title "Son of God" also contains the connotation of the divinity of Jesus (5,18!). The author takes the risk of ascribing to Jesus a kind of "equality" with the Father with regard to the divine being. Yet at the same time he emphasizes the total subordination and dependence of the Son on the Father (e.g. 5,19-30), and thus respects the

66. Cf. J.N.D. KELLY, *The Pastoral Epistles* (Black's New Testament Commentary), London, 1963, p. 62-63: "The truth is that all the profound questions which later theology was to raise were remote from the Apostle's mind. In affirming the universal scope of God's will to save he was probably conscious of taking issue with (a) the Jewish belief that God willed the destruction of sinners and the salvation of the righteous alone, and (b) the Gnostic theory that salvation belonged to the spiritual élite alone".

67. The author exhorts to intercession "for all human beings"; God "wants all men to be saved"; one is "the mediator between God and men: the man... who gave himself...for all men".

68. Cf. D. CERBELAUD, *Les versets "exclusivistes" du Nouveau Testament. Essai de lecture*, in *Théophilyon* 2 (1997) 243-256, esp. p. 249-250.

69. In the prologue (Jn 1,1) the pre-existent Logos is described as θεός in 1,18 the Logos made flesh is called the "unique Son, God" (μονογενὴς θεός) (this reading is to be preferred to variant reading μονογενὴς υἱός: cp. B.M. METZGER, *A Textual Commentary on the Greek New Testament*, Stuttgart, 21994, p. 169-170), and in Thomas' confession (Jn 20,28) the risen Jesus is confessed as "my Lord and my God" (cp. 1 Jn 5,20). One feels John's hesitation: he never calls Jesus "God" (ὁ θεός because his monotheism (only Yahweh is "the God") forbids it.

uniqueness that Jewish monotheism attributes to God. Jesus' divine Sonship, taken in the strongest sense of the word, gives us the key to reading the Fourth Gospel[70].

Elsewhere, we have put forward the hypothesis that John has heard or read somewhere the Q-saying Mt 11,27 par. Lk 10,22 (most probably in the Matthean of Lukan form, or maybe elsewhere[71]). With its well-balanced and bold formulation, it profoundly influenced John's mind, because it partly met his own way of thinking about Jesus Christ. The saying has in a certain sense been seminal for John's christology. He has developed it in many directions, in the light of his own central christological conviction: Jesus' divine Sonship. In that sense, the saying (Mt 11,27) could be considered as a summary of John's christology:

a   All things have been delivered to me by my Father
b   and no one knows the Son but the Father,
c   neither does anyone know the Father but the Son
d   and he to whom the Son may choose to reveal him.

The first clause points more to a transmission of divine power (including the power of revelation), than to a handing on of teaching. This theme is omnipresent in the Fourth Gospel. Twenty-seven (or 28) times John uses the verb δίδωμι with God or the Father as subject of the act of giving and the Son as the beneficiary or receiver of what has been given[72]. The formula "the Father gives something to the Son" seems to be concentrated in the sections where the Father/Son relation is reflected upon explicitly: i.e., in 5,19-30 and especially in the prayer of 17,1-24. John 5,19-30 presents a meditation on the Sonship of Jesus. This section comes just after the accusation of the Jews that Jesus makes himself equal with God (5,18). It shows what kind of ἐξουσία the Father is conferring on his Son: the works (cp. 5,36; 17,4) that only God can do: the power to judge (5,22.27), and the power to give life (5,21.26).

---

70. Cf. J.D.G. DUNN, *Christology in the Making*, London, 1980, p. 59: "In short, for the first time in earliest Christianity we encounter in the Johannine writings the understanding of Jesus' divine sonship in terms of the personal pre-existence of a divine being who was sent into the world and whose ascension was simply the continuation of an intimate relationship with the Father which neither incarnation nor crucifixion interrupted or disturbed".

71. In what follows, we summarise some elements of our study: *The Q-logion Mt 11,27 / Lk 10,22 and the Gospel of John*, in A. DENAUX (ed.), *John and the Synoptics* (BETL, 101), Leuven, 1992, pp. 163-199.

72. Jn 3,34(?); 3,35; 5,22.26.27.36; 6,37.39; 10,29; 11,22; 12,49; 13,3; 14,31; 17,2(2x).4.6(2x).7.8.9.11.12.22.24(2x); 18,9.11. In 16 cases it is said that God/the Father gives disciples to Jesus/the Son: 3,35; 6,37.39; 10,29; 13,3; 17,2.6b.d.9.24; 18,9. The object that is given can be expressed in different ways, but in some cases there is a striking similarity to our saying because of the use of the demonstrative "all" (πάντα or πᾶν) (3,35; 6,37.39; 13,3; 17,2.7; cp. 10,29).

The second and the third clauses of the Q-logion (Mt 11,27bc) show several features which seem to be present in the Gospel of John in a more elaborate way: the absolute use of the titles "the Father" and "the Son"; the mutual knowledge (e.g. Jn 10,15) (and intimate exclusive relation[73]) of Father and Son; and the exclusion of all others from this knowledge (e.g. Jn 3,13; 6,46; 14,6).

The fourth clause posits the unique status of Jesus as revealer. Because only the Son knows the Father (v. 27c), only he can reveal the Father to humankind (v. 27d). The idea that Jesus is the unique revealer, also belongs to the core of John's christology, as is explicitly attested in sentences such as Jn 1,18 and 3,13[74].

One aspect of John's christology not mentioned in the "Johannine" Q-logion is the idea that Jesus is the unique mediator of salvation, as is expressed in Jn 3,16-18 and 1 Jn 4,9. The Johannine Jesus can say: "I am the way and the truth and the life. Nobody comes to the Father except through me" (Jn 14,6). He is the only mediator of God's salvation because he is the Son of God. His divinity is the basis of the unique character of this mediation. No one else can give to the world "eternal life", eschatological "salvation" (exclusive dimension). And at the same time he wants to bring salvation to "the world", in as much as the world accepts it in faith (intended inclusive, universal dimension).

One could summarise John's view on the unique status of Jesus Christ as follows: as unique Son of the Father, who became man, Jesus Christ

73. For the author of John, the notion of mutual knowledge between Father and Son is embodied in the broader reality of the unique reciprocity of the relation between Father and Son, which is expressed in such texts as: "The Father and I are one" (10,30); "I am in the Father and the Father is in me" (14,10.11.20); "That they all may be one...as You, Father, are in me, and I in You" (17,21). To be sure, the disciples can participate in the filial relation between Father and Son, yet there is a qualitative distinction between the relation the Son has to the Father (πατήρ/υἱός and the relation they have towards God (θεός/τέκνα) because the relation of the faithful is always a gift from above, an adoptional childhood (cp. Jn 1,12-13). For John, as Son Jesus is μονογενής, that means "unique" (1,14.18; 3,16.18; 1 Jn 4,9).

74. In 1,18 John first asserts that nobody has seen God, i.e. that no one can speak about God from a connatural knowledge. In contrast to this general statement follows the utterance that only Jesus Christ can really reveal God, because he knows him from within: "the unique Son, God (himself), who is in the bossom of the Father, he has made him known". Precisely for that reason Jesus Christ is identified in the Prologue with 'the Word' (used absolutely). In the chiastic sentence of 3,13, "No one has ever gone up into heaven, except he who has come down from heaven, the Son of Man", the formula "No one has ever gone up into heaven" stems from the sapiential literature and means that no human being is capable of knowing and communicating divine secrets (e.g. Dt 30,12; Prov 30,4; Bar 3,29; Wis 9,16; 4 Esr 4,8). The construction points to the impossibility of knowing the divine reality. When an exception is then made with respect to Jesus, the purpose is to state that only he knows the divine reality (because of his divine pre-existence) and that he has come down from heaven to reveal that reality.

stands in a special relationship with God (ontological uniqueness). Precisely for that reason only He can reveal God to humankind (uniqueness as Revealer of God) and bring humankind to God and its final destination, eternal life with God (soteriological uniqueness)[75].

Conclusion

First-century Christians had the conviction that they were commissioned to be "witnesses" of Jesus Christ to all nations (Lk 24,46-48; Acts 1,8; cp. Mt 28,19-20). Their witness continued that of God's people during the first Covenant (cp. Is 43,9-44,5). Ultimately, Christians have to witness to the one, living and saving God in and against a world serving other gods. Moreover, Christian witness has a christological focus. In the historical mission of Jesus of Nazareth God revealed himself as a redeeming God. Christians have to witness to this concrete historical experience (1 Jn 1,1-2). The content of their witness could be summarised in this way: "And this is the testimony: God has given us eternal life, and this life is in his Son" (1 Jn 5,11). The Christian witness is not based on "myths" but on historical experiences of the people of God through history. It will be contested because it is part of the "trial" between God and the world going on in the course of time. It will therefore have an apologetic dimension, seek for intelligibility, try to convince. The Christian Church(es) cannot give up that mission without giving up her (their) identity.

However, mission does not exclude dialogue with other religions. Dialogue is different from, though not unrelated to, mission. It has its own dynamic and ethos. Dialogue demands reciprocity and a kind of mutual commitment, listening and replying, trying to understand and being understood, asking questions and being questioned, readiness to communicate oneself and to trust what others say about themselves[76]. In the past the Christian Church has sometimes used methods of intolerance and violence to impose the truth of the Gospel. It has acted in contradiction to the way Jesus Christ, her "founder", has offered God's salvation to his people: freely, without pressure or violence. When the Christian Church enters into the age of dialogue, she should turn to the

75. See also D.M. BALL, 'My Lord and my God': the Implications of 'I am' Sayings for Religious Pluralism, in, in A.D. CLARKE & B.C. WINTER (eds.), One God, One Lord. Christianity in a World of Religious Pluralism, Grand Rapids, MI, ²1993, pp. 53-71.

76. Cf. PONTIFICIUM CONSILIUM AD CHRISTIANORUM UNITATEM FOVENDAM, Directory for the Application of Principles and Norms on Ecumenism, Vatican City, 1993; what is said there (in nr. 172) about interecclesial ecumenical dialogue could be applied in a certain sense to the interreligious dialogue.

only model she has: Jesus Christ, "the faithful and true witness" (Rev 3,14), "who bore witness in the same noble confession in Pontius Pilate's time" (1 Tim 6,13). The dialogue between Christians and world religions should ultimately be a dialogue of defenseless love. It sometimes will take the form of a martyria, eventually at the cost of their own lives, because Christians "preach Christ crucified: a stumbling-block to Jews and foolishness to Gentiles" (1 Cor 1,23).

Faculty of Theology   Adelbert DENAUX
Katholieke Universiteit Leuven
St. Michielsstraat 6
B-3000 Leuven

"MY KINGSHIP IS NOT OF THIS WORLD" (JOHN 18,36)
THE KINGSHIP OF JESUS AND POLITICS

A nationalistic-political outlook is one of the most widespread assumptions concerning first-century Jewish messianic expectations. The Jewish people at that time are seen to have expected the messiah as a liberator whose troops would drive the Roman occupation forces out of the country and reestablish self-government. Studies about social unrest in Palestine caused by messianic pretenders and would-be kings seem to confirm this view. The four gospels, in rare harmony, agree that Jesus was condemned to death and executed under the charge of pretending to be the messiah in this narrow nationalistic-political sense. In all four gospels, Pilate begins his interrogation of Jesus by asking, "Are you the King of the Jews?". The four gospels equally agree as to the charge against Jesus which is displayed on the cross and which presents him as the "King of the Jews". The synoptic gospels do not seem to find it necessary to contradict this accusation or to nuance its content[1]. It is, however, a characteristic of John's passion narrative that it attempts to nuance or even contradicts the accusations raised against Jesus. Since the very beginning, exegetes of the fourth gospel have been fiercely divided, however, as to the question whether the rejection of the charge against Jesus as messianic pretender left any room for a political dimension to his mission.

In this paper, we shall approach the issue of Jesus and politics from the angle of the famous word of the Johannine Jesus: "My kingship is not of this world"[2] in Jn 18,36. After situating the problem and presenting the major issues that emerge from recent studies, we shall offer our own approach.

---

1. See, for instance, M. HENGEL, *Reich Christi, Reich Gottes und Weltreich im 4. Evangelium*, in *Theologische Beiträge* 14 (1983) 201-216, p. 203: "Nach den Synoptikern besiegelt Jesus durch die bejahende Antwort und das anschließende Schweigen seinen Tod... Der römische Präfekt *mußte* im Grunde Jesus wegen seines politisch interpretierbaren messianischen Anspruchs zum Tode am Kreuz verurteilen".
2. We follow here as in the title of our study the translation of the "Revised Standard Version" (RSV). See also the "New Revised Standard Version" (NRSV) where we find the translation: "My kingdom is not from this world". In general scripture quotes in this study are taken from the "New Revised Standard Version", unless specified otherwise.

I. SITUATING THE PROBLEM

The question whether Jesus is the Messiah plays an important role in the fourth gospel. This is evident from the fact that it is the only book in the New Testament which uses the word Μεσσίας (1,41; 4,25). There are 19 uses of Χριστός in this gospel[3], two of which are found in close connection with the title Μεσσίας. Fifteen of the remaining occurrences are used in a titular way, which has led the NRSV to "translate" them in the text as "Messiah" (while the RSV used "the Christ" in these places). There are only two places in the fourth gospel (1,17 and 17,3) where Χριστός is used as part of the name Ἰησοῦς Χριστός. In view of our interest in this study, it is striking that all but one of the explicit references to Χριστός are concentrated in the first part of the gospel (chapters 1–12; cf. 20,31). In the synoptic passion narratives Χριστός enjoys a higher relative frequency than in the other parts of these gospels[4]. Moreover, other christological titles such as Son of Man and Son of God are used as well. Χριστός is completely absent from the Johannine passion narrative. Here the title "king" comes into prominence[5]. Indeed, in the Johannine passion narrative it is the only title used for Christ with the exception of "Son of God" in 19,7. There seems to be little doubt among the interpreters, past and present, that in the passion narratives "king" is used as a messianic title, and that it has nationalistic-political overtones. We conclude from these observations that, while sharing the same common ground with the synoptics, John has achieved a single-minded concentration on the royal, political dimension of messianism.

The trial before Pilate in Jn 18,28–19,16a is well-known as a "carefully structured literary unity"[6]. In seven chiastically arranged scenes[7] the drama between Jesus, the "Jews" ("highpriests") and Pilate unfolds in characteristically Johannine fashion. In comparison with the synoptic gospels where Jesus remains silent before Pilate and where the political aspect is not developed, the fourth gospel stages an elaborate dialogue

3. Mt 16x, Mk 7x, Lk 12x and John 19x. The frequency per 1,000 words of text (Mt 0.9, Mk 0.6, Lk 0.6 and John 1.2) demonstrates the relative importance of this terminology in John. For the statistics we rely on Gramcord.

4.	frequency of Χριστός	Mt	Mk	Lk	Jn
	entire gospel	16	7	12	19
	passion narrative	4	2	6	0

5. The frequency of βασιλεύς in the passion narratives of the four gospels is as follows: Mt 4x, Mk 6x, Lk 4x and John 12x.

6. D. HILL, *"My Kingdom is not of this world" (John 18.36)*, in *IBS* 9 (1987) 54-62, p. 55.

7. See *ibid.*, pp. 55-56. Cf. R. BROWN, *The Gospel According to John (xiii–xxi)* (AnB, 29A), vol. 2, Garden City, NY, Doubleday, 1970, p. 859.

between the two figures. In this conversation, the gospel contains several statements (in the mouth of Jesus and the "Jews") which are clearly of a socio-political nature: "We are not permitted to put anyone to death" (18,31). "My kingship is not of this world" (RSV) (18,36). "You would have no power over me unless it had been given you from above" (19,11). "Everyone who claims to be a king sets himself against the emperor" (19,12). "We have no king but the emperor" (19,15). This demonstrates that the fourth gospel has a special interest in the political dimension of the material which it has in common with the other gospels. In the trial narrative, and particularly in 18,36-37, John formulates a Christian response to the charge that Jesus claimed to be a nationalistic-political messiah, a charge that ultimately convinced Pilate to condemn Jesus to death. There is, however, no agreement among exegetes as to how this response must be understood. In what follows I shall give an overview of the most important positions in recent discussion with a special focus on the arguments put forward in the debate.

II. THE POLITICAL READING OF JOHN 18,36
IN THE EXEGETICAL DISCUSSION

The core of Jesus' reply to Pilate is found in 18,36 where the same statement is repeated three times with slight variations. ἡ βασιλεία ἡ ἐμὴ οὐκ ἔστιν ἐκ τοῦ κόσμου τούτου in Jn 18,36, according to W. Howard-Brook "one of the most terribly misrepresented passages in the fourth gospel"[8], has been interpreted in three ways.

1. The Spiritualistic (Spatial) Interpretation

There are a number of elements in Jn 18,36 which have been used to justify a spiritualistic or spatial interpretation. βασιλεία can mean kingdom as a specific territory, and κόσμος could be understood in the sense of the material world. The expression ἔστιν ἐκ is then read as if it was synonymous with ἔστιν ἐν. 18,36 would in this case have to be translated: "My kingdom is not in this (material) world". This is then seen as implying positively: My kingdom is internal, spiritual, and private[9]. It is

8. W. HOWARD-BROOK, *Becoming Children of God. John's Gospel and Radical Discipleship*, Maryknoll, NY, Orbis, 1994, p. 399.

9. Cf., e.g., K. KASTNER, *Jesus vor Pilatus. Ein Beitrag zur Leidensgeschichte des Herrn* (NTAbh, 4/2-3), Münster, Aschendorff, 1912, p. 90: "Der Heiland... zeigt dem Landpfleger, daß sein Königtum im geistigen Sinne verstanden werden müsse". E.E. JENSEN, *The First*

evident that such a reading amounts to an outright rejection of any political implications of Jesus' βασιλεία.

The spiritualistic interpretation is already found in the apocryphal
Acts of Pilate IV as variant reading of the version B, where ἐκ is indeed
changed into ἐν[10]. Augustine was one of the first to reject the spiritualistic interpretation. "Non ait: nunc autem regnum meum non est hic,
sed: non est hinc"[11]. In recent exegesis the spiritualistic reading has
almost universally been rejected. This is based on a more accurate linguistic analysis of the Johannine meaning of κόσμος and of ἐστιν ἐκ,
as we shall see below.

2. The Future-Eschatological (Temporal) Interpretation

The defenders of a future-eschatological interpretation are also pointing to linguistic support in our text. They read κόσμος οὗτος as 'this
transitory world' in contrast to the next, eternal world. Additional support is found in the expression νῦν in 18,36 which is understood to be
temporal. The Johannine Jesus would then be saying: My kingdom/
kingship does not exist presently in this (transitory) world. This would
imply: but it will later exist in the next (eternal) world.

Such a future-eschatological view, albeit independent of Jn 18,36, is
already found in the self-defense of relatives of Jesus before the
Emperor Domitian. This witness which was more or less contemporary
to John goes back to Hegesippus and was reported by Eusebius[12].
"Questioned about the Christ and his Kingdom... they said that it was
not worldly or on earth, but heavenly and angelic, and that it would be
established at the end of the world"[13].

Century Controversy Over Jesus as a Revolutionary Figure, in *JBL* 60 (1941) 261-272,
p. 270: "It appears that John has Pilate present Jesus to them as the king of the Jews in a
spiritual sense". Cf. also the New Jerusalem Bible translation of John 18:36f: "my kingdom does not belong here".

    10. See H. SCHLIER, *Jesus und Pilatus nach dem Johannesevangelium*, in ID., *Die Zeit
der Kirche. Exegetische Aufsätze und Vorträge*, Freiburg – Basel – Wien, Herder, 1972,
pp. 56-74, p. 62.
    11. AUGUSTINUS, *In Joh., tract.* 115, 2.
    12. EUSEBIUS, *Historia ecclesiastica*, III, 20, 4.
    13. This English translation is taken from GCS 9[1]: 234. According to BROWN, *John*
(n. 7), vol. 2, p. 852, John 18:36 "somewhat resembles" what the relatives of Jesus
answered Domitian. Brown supports this view by reminding us that "in Johannine
thought the ultimate goal of the disciples is to be withdrawn from the world" (cf. 14,2-3;
17,24). Somewhat surprisingly, SCHLIER, *Jesus und Pilatus* (n. 10), pp. 61-62, considers
what the relatives of Jesus say one-sided (to say the least). In the perspective of his study
one would expect a clearer rejection of this view.

The future-eschatological interpretation rejects any political dimension of Jesus' βασιλεία, assuring this-worldly powers that they have nothing to fear from Christians. This has frequently served an apologetic function in situations of persecution.

There are a number of exegetical problems connected with the future-eschatological interpretation which discourage most scholars from accepting it. Most importantly, most scholars see John's eschatology primarily as realized, not future. The fourth gospel does not use κόσμος as an eschatological term. "This world" may not be understood in the sense of "this age". It should also be noted that νῦν in 18,36 is more likely to have a logical than a temporal meaning.

3. The Ethical-Religious (Anthropological) Interpretaton

Scholarship of the past 50 years agrees almost unanimously on what could be called an ethical-religious interpretation. Here βασιλεία is mostly understood in the functional sense of "kingship", "dominion". The expression ἐστιν ἐκ refers to the source or the origin, and consequently the essence of a person or thing. This interpretation of ἐστιν ἐκ has found virtually universal approval. The group of representatives of the ethical-religious interpretation is nevertheless quite diverse, since there are important variations within the way the term κόσμος is interpreted. They all have in common that they see the "world" anthropologically as the sphere into which we are born. Interpretations differ as to the degree to which human sin enters into the picture. They range from the neutral understanding "earthly stage of human existence"[14] to the "sphere of darkness" which is the result of the fact that human beings reject the knowledge of their own creatureliness, i.e., that they cut themselves off from God[15]. Some authors interpret κόσμος in a somewhat narrower sense as the social-political order with its social and political values[16].

14. R. SCHNACKENBURG, *Das Johannesevangelium. Kommentar zu Kap. 13–21*, vol. 3, Freiburg – Basel – Wien, Herder, 1975, p. 285.

15. R. BULTMANN, *Das Evangelium des Johannes* (KEK), Göttingen, Vandenhoek & Ruprecht, [10]1941, [14]1956, p. 33-34. See the mediating position in J. BLANK, *Krisis. Untersuchungen zur johanneischen Christologie und Eschatologie*, Freiburg i. Br., Lambertus, 1964, pp. 186-198, p. 191: "Aber die Schöpfung wird nicht einfach durch die Tatsache, daß das Handeln des Menschen welt-konstituierend ist, zur 'Welt' mit negativem Akzent, sondern erst dadurch, daß der Mensch sich darin absolut setzt und so Welt gegen Gott konstituiert".

16. Cf. D. SENIOR, *The Passion of Jesus in the Gospel of John*, Collegeville, MN, Liturgical Press, 1991, p. 81: "The evangelist portrays two co-existing and yet ultimately conflicting 'worlds' of values and meaning".

Correspondingly Jn 18,36 would then mean: "My kingship does not have its origin in this earthly human world, but in the transcendent world of God"; "My kingship does not have its origin in this sinful human world which has cut itself off from God, but its origin is in God"; "My kingship does not have its origin in the social-political order of this world". Some authors combine this anthropological interpretation with the Johannine perspective of realized eschatology[17].

Authors readily agree that Jesus' βασιλεία does not originate in the world of humans and that this means a rejection of human action as the foundation of Jesus' kingship. But the question remains open whether the human sphere is considered insufficient for Jesus' kingship because of its humanness (finitude) or because of its sinfulness. On the other hand, 18,36 can hardly be understood as flatly denying any relationship between Jesus' kingship and this world. The precise relationship must, however, be inferred from the negative description of the βασιλεία in 18,36 and the positive description in 18,37. What is said there, leaves room for a number of different interpretations. The minimum consensus is that, even though it is not from this world, Jesus' βασιλεία is *in* this world. This conclusion is reached from the fact that Jesus who came into the world is not of the world (8,23), and that the disciples who are in the world (17,11) are not of the world (17,16). Moreover there is general agreement that "Jesus does not deny that his kingdom or kingship affects the world"[18] or impinges on the world[19]. The question is, however, whether the way Jesus' βασιλεία affects the world has political consequences or not. Those who answer in the affirmative are convinced that for those who listen to Jesus' voice (18,37) conflict with the political powers will be inevitable, precisely because the latter are of the world while they are not[20].

---

17. BULTMANN, *Johannes* (n. 15), p. 506: "sie ist – im joh. Sinne – eine eschatologische Größe". J. BLANK, *Die Verhandlung vor Pilatus Joh 18,28–19,16 im Lichte johanneischer Theologie*, in *BZ NF* 3 (1959) 60-81, p. 69: "Βασιλεία ist eschatologisch zu verstehen, freilich im Sinne der joh. Eschatologie, als jene eschatologische Größe, die ihren Anspruch in Jesu Gegenwart geltend macht". A. DAUER, *Die Passionsgeschichte im Johannesevangelium. Eine traditionsgeschichtliche und theologische Untersuchung zu Joh 18,1–19,30* (SANT, 30), München, 1972, p. 254: "Jesus spricht also nicht von seiner Herrschaft am Ende der Zeiten noch von einer 'himmlischen' Herrschaft, sondern von einer gegenwärtigen, die aber die Vorwegnahme und Gegenwärtigsetzung der eschatologischen ist".

18. BROWN, *John* (n. 7), vol. 2, pp. 868-869. Cf. BLANK, *Verhandlung* (n. 17), p. 70: "Gerade ihr nicht-welthafter Charakter ist es, durch den sie auch die politische Sphäre an ihrer Wurzel tangiert und in Frage stellt".

19. Cf. HILL, *Kingdom* (n. 6), p. 61: "our actions will impinge on the political order".

20. Since the the publication of Bultmann's commentary on John in 1941 a number of important studies dealing with Jn 18,36 have been published. Among them, SCHLIER,

Before we turn to our own approach, we summarize the result of this overview. As could be expected, the spiritualistic and the future-eschatological interpretations of 18,36 have no room for a political understanding of Jesus' βασιλεία. In their opinion, 18,36 was precisely formulated to affirm the absence of any political dimension in the kingdom/kingship of Jesus. The landscape of the ethical-religious interpretation has proved to be rather complex. Those who reject the political dimension nonetheless accept that Jesus' βασιλεία is in this world and that his βασιλεία affects the world. For Bultmann "political", like "world", is an expression for the sinful self-realization of the human person cut off from God. Thus not having its origin in the world by definition excludes a political dimension. Hengel considers the βασιλεία to be so radically different from worldly realities that the qualification "political" does not do justice to it[21]. This radical difference does, however, not mean that the kingship of Jesus does not have consequences for the worldly political powers. The disciples of Jesus, those who listen to his voice, will inevitably find themselves in conflict with the political powers. Those who accept the political dimension of Jesus' kingship accept that in 18,36 the title of king is redefined, but not in a way that removes its political dimension[22]. They are convinced that the refusal to use violence is itself a political option and not an escape into safe spiritualized or privatized areas[23].

Jesus und Pilatus (n. 10), 1941; BLANK, *Verhandlung* (n. 17), 1959; W.A. MEEKS, *The Prophet-King. Moses Traditions and the Johannine Christology* (SuppNT, 14), Leiden, Brill, 1967 and ID., *The Ethics of the Fourth Evangelist*, in R.A. CULPEPPER & C.C. BLACK (eds.), *Exploring the Gospel of John*. FS D. Moody Smith, Louisville, KY, Westminster & John Knox, 1996, pp. 317-326; D. RENSBERGER, *Johannine Faith and Liberating Community*, Philadelphia PA, 1988 (first publ. 1984); L. SCHOTTROFF, *"Mein Reich ist nicht von dieser Welt". Der johanneische Messianismus*, in J. TAUBES (ed.), *Religionstheorie und politische Theologie*, part 2: *Gnosis und Politik*, München – Paderborn – Wien – Zürich, Fink, 1984, pp. 97-108; HOWARD-BROOK, *Becoming Children of God* (n. 8), 1994, have come out explicitly in favor of a political interpretation. BULTMANN, *Johannes* (n. 15) 1941, R. SCHNACKENBURG, *Die Messiasfrage im Johannesevangelium*, in J. BLINZLER, O. KUSS & F. MUSSNER (eds.), *Neutestamentliche Aufsätze*. FS J. Schmid, Regensburg, Pustet, 1963, and ID., *Johannesevangelium* (n. 14), 1970; DAUER, *Passionsgeschichte* (n. 17), 1972; HENGEL, *Reich Christi* (n. 1), 1983, a more hesitant or even nonpolitical reading.
21. HENGEL, *Reich Christi* (n. 1), p. 204: "die radikale Andersartigkeit der Herrschaft Christi gegenüber den etablierten politischen Mächten".
22. Cf. RENSBERGER, *Johannine Faith* (n. 20).
23. HOWARD-BROOK, *Becoming Children of God* (n. 8).

III. A SOCIAL-POLITICAL READING OF JOHN 18,36-37 IN ITS CONTEXT

In 1983 M. Hengel, in a study devoted to 18,36, boldly stated: "The gospel of John is the end of all *political* theology"[24]. The context of the article demonstrates that Hengel really means "all"[25]. Interestingly enough, another leading German exegete, H. Schlier, had come to the exact opposite conclusion in a study published almost 20 years before Hengel's. I quote from Schlier:

> All the authors of the New Testament are convinced that Christ is not a private person nor is the Church a private club. That is why they reported about encounters of Jesus and his witnesses with the world of politics and the state as well as with their institutions. The one who has the most fundamental insight into this is the evangelist John. He sees the story of Jesus as a court case which the world represented by the Jews is waging against Jesus or has the illusion of waging. This trial takes on a public, judicial form before Pontius Pilate, the representative of the Roman State and the holder of political power[26].

J.B. Metz quotes Schlier's text to illustrate one of the two goals of political theology: "Political theology intends to reclaim for present-day theology the awareness of the ongoing trial between Jesus' eschatological message and socio-political reality"[27]. This is the critical, liberating task of theology. The other goal of political theology is to deprivatize religion, i.e., to restore a social-historical, a community-oriented and structure-conscious dimension to theology. While acknowledging with Metz[28] that "political theology" is a misunderstandable and an historically loaded term, I shall use "political" in this two-fold meaning: social-critical (with regard to the individual, history, community and structures) and eschatological-critical (cf. the "eschatological reserve" which calls for ongoing reevaluation, since any state of affairs is provisional and prone to the effects of sin). Starting from this understanding of the term "political", I shall offer a political reading of Jn 18,36 in its Johannine and contemporary contexts.

24. M. HENGEL, *Reich Christi*, p. 214: "Das Johannesevangelium bedeutet das Ende aller *politischen* Theologie".
25. See *ibid.*, p. 203, where he speaks in a disapproving way about "political theology" and adds: "was immer darunter gemeint sein mag".
26. H. SCHLIER, *Besinnung auf das Neue Testament. Exegetische Aufsätze und Vorträge*, Freiburg i. Br., Herder, 1964, p. 193. The English text is my own translation of the German text.
27. J.B. METZ, *Zur Theologie der Welt*, Mainz – München, Grünewald – Kaiser, 1968, ²1969, p. 105.
28. *Ibid.*, p. 99.

1. The Justification of a Political Reading in Johannine Perspective

For many people, including biblical exegetes, John's gospel has been a spiritual or mystical gospel[29]. It has been considered to be full of "symbolism" and lacking in reliable historical data. As a consequence the interpretation of this gospel has been characterized by a focus on its spiritual theology. Most interpreters have assumed that the concrete socio-historical situation of the author and the addressees has left but a few traces in this gospel. While this view of the fourth gospel is still prevalent in many circles, it has been termed "outdated" by W.A. Meeks no less than 30 years ago[30]. Historical, archeological and topographical studies of the second half of this century have contributed greatly to a new, more historically grounded reading of the fourth gospel. J.L. Martyn[31] in North America and later K. Wengst[32] in Europe have tried to link the gospel to a concrete historical situation of a real community at the end of the first century. Nevertheless centuries of unhistorical and spiritualist readings are still lurking, and a lot of work still needs to be done to come to a consistent, new reading. The present effort sees itself in that line.

One characteristic feature of the fourth gospel that has encouraged the spiritualist readings is Johannine dualism: God – Satan, heaven – world, above – below, flesh – spirit, life – death, truth – lie, light – darkness, faith – unbelief, love – hatred. The question arises whether we have to understand this dualism in a temporal (two aeons), spatial (two realms) or in an ethical-religious sense (two value-systems)[33]. Recent scholarship has largely opted for the latter. In this case, John uses dualist expressions to confront people with a choice between two fundamental values[34]. As is seen in L. Schottroff's interpretation of Jn 18,36, the ethical-religious

---

29. In about the year 200 C.E., Clement of Alexandria used the term "spiritual gospel" to characterize John. This term has had an effective history which is hard to overestimate.

30. MEEKS, *The Prophet-King* (n. 20), p. 64, n. 1: "the prevalent but outdated notion that Jn. is a 'spiritual' or 'mystical' gospel". Cf. ID., *Ethics* (n. 20), p. 326: "Traditionally, the way of correcting the one-sidedness of the Johannine voice has been by treating its imagery as 'mystical' and 'spiritual', in the warm and foggy sense that alone is left to these words in our degenerate speech. To domesticate the Fourth Gospel in this fuzzy way, however, simultaneously robs it of its power".

31. J.L. MARTYN, *History and Theology in the Fourth Gospel*, rev. ed., Nashville, TN, Abingdon, ²1979.

32. K. WENGST, *Bedrängte Gemeinde und verherrlichter Christus. Der historische Ort des Johannesevangeliums als Schlüssel seiner Interpretation* (Biblisch-theologische Studien, 5), Neukirchen/Vluyn, Neukirchener, 1981.

33. See R. KYSAR, *John. The Maverick Gospel*, rev. ed., Louisville, KY, Westminster & John Knox, 1993, pp. 58-67.

34. Cf. the German expression *Entscheidungsdualismus*.

interpretation of Johannine dualism has important implications for a political reading[35].

A characteristic of the gospel that can both work in favor or against spiritualization is "realized eschatology". Salvation is for the most part seen as already present despite concrete experiences to the opposite. While interpreting 18,36 we need to keep in mind that this verse is most probably written in the perspective of realized eschatology[36].

2. The Literary Context of 18,36

John's passion narrative can be subdivided into five parts: 1. The arrest (18,1-11); 2. The interrogation before Annas and the denial of Peter (18,12-27); 3. The trial before Pilate (18,28–19,16a); 4. The execution of Jesus (19,16b-30); 5. The burial of Jesus (19,31-42). Among these the trial before Pilate is the most extensive and the most dramatically developed. Scholars generally agree that 18,28–19,16a can be subdivided into seven scenes which form a chiasm. The drama develops between three actors, the "Jews" (more specifically "the highpriests and the police" in 19,6 and "the highpriests" in 19,15) who are outside the praetorium, Jesus who is inside, and Pilate who goes back and forth between the two. 18,36 is part of the second scene (18,33-38a) which contains the first interrogation of Jesus by Pilate. In the concentric structure this scene is parallel with the sixth scene (19,9-11), the second interrogation.

18,33-38a begins and ends with a question of Pilate. After setting the scene by naming the actors and the place, Pilate asks Jesus: "Are you the King of the Jews?". This question which is identical in all four gospel accounts comes somewhat surprisingly since the "Jews" had just refused to inform Pilate of the accusation that they bring against Jesus. In Mt 27,11 and Mk 15,2 the question is equally unmotivated. Only Lk 23,2 lists the charges brought against Jesus before Pilate which culminate in his "saying that he himself is the Messiah, a king". In the three synoptic gospels Jesus' answer is: σὺ λέγεις, "you say so" which is usually understood as an answer in the affirmative[37]. In John, literally the same reply is found later in the conversation. Between the question and the answer that are identical with the synoptics, the fourth gospel

---

35. SCHOTTROFF, *Mein Reich* (n. 20), pp. 103-107.
36. See above, n. 17.
37. See, for instance, J. GNILKA, *Das Matthäusevangelium. Kommentar zu Kap. 14,1–28,20 und Einleitungsfragen* (HTK, I/2), vol. 2, Freiburg – Basel – Wien, Herder, 1988, p. 455: "Die Antwort Jesu 'Du sagst es' kann nur im Sinn eines Ja aufgefaßt werden".

has a conversation (18,34-37c) that is clearly intended to nuance the meaning of the terminology used. In 18,34 the Johannine Jesus raises the question that is on the mind of the reader: How does Pilate come to ask Jesus, "Are you the King of the Jews?"? Pilate's answer leaves no doubt that the accusation originates with Jesus' nation and the highpriest (18,35).

3. Interpretation of 18,36-37 in Political Perspective

To facilitate communication we first quote the text of Jn 18:33-38 (RSV) in a sense-line presentation:

33a Pilate entered the praetorium again
33b and called Jesus,
33c and said to him,
33d "Are you the **King of the Jews**?"
34a Jesus answered,
34b "Do you say this of your own accord,
34c or did others say it to you about me?"
35a Pilate answered,
35b "Am I a Jew?
35c Your own nation and the chief priests have handed you over to me;
35d what have you done?"
36a Jesus answered,
36b "**My kingship is not of this world**;
36c if **my kingship were of this world**,
36d *my servants would fight*,
36e that I might not be handed over to the Jews;
36f but **my kingship is not from the world**."
37a Pilate said to him,
37b "So you are a **king**?"
37c Jesus answered,
37d "You say
37e that I am a **king**.
37f For this I was born,
37g and for this I have come into the world,
37h *to bear witness to the truth*.
37i Every one who is of the truth hears my voice."
38a Pilate said to him,
38b "What is truth?"

After clarifying whose accusation he is responding to, Jesus is willing to talk to Pilate (18,36). In the five lines of his reply, he repeats the same idea, viz. "My kingship is not of this world", three times with only slight variations. This already underlines the importance which the fourth evangelist attributes to this statement. In view of the original question, six aspects of the response are striking: 1. Jesus shifts the focus from his being king to his βασιλεία. 2. Jesus broadens the perspective from "the Jews" to "this world". 3. Instead of giving a positive answer, Jesus says what his βασιλεία is not. 4. Instead of identifying with a suggested role, Jesus speaks about the origin and essence of his βασιλεία. 5. At this point the question remains open whether Jesus' βασιλεία is in this world or intersects with kingships in this world, as the βασιλεία of the King of the Jews presumably would (in Pilate's mind). 6. Thus Jesus does not answer Pilates' question, but presupposes the question: Where is your βασιλεία from? What is its essence?

We should keep in mind that in 18,36 there is no positive description of Jesus' kingship. Even the illustration of the meaning of "My kingship is not of this world" in the conditional clause ("my servants would fight" in 18,36cde) is contrary to fact and thus implicitly negated. At this point the text is silent about the origin and the essence of the βασιλεία. There is still more than one way of making that silence speak. We have to wait until 18,37 for a positive description.

a) Kingship

In order to gain a better understanding of what Jesus disclaims we need to investigate the meaning of βασιλεία and κόσμος. We have already pointed out that there is an almost exclusive concentration on royal terminology in Jn 18–19. The other references to βασιλεύς and βασιλεία are found in Jn 1–12, in 1,49; 6,15; 12,13.15 and 3,3.5 respectively. We see that, true to its overall christology, the fourth gospel is focused on the person of Jesus as king, while the synoptics are concentrating on the Kingdom of God (Heaven). In John there is a contrast between "King of Israel" in the first part of the gospel and "King of the Jews" in the passion narrative. The two expressions have in common that they are talking about the Messiah as a king. As P.J. Tomson has demonstrated "Israel" is the "inner-Jewish self-designation", while "Jew" is used by non-Jews with reference to Jews or "a self-designation of Jews used in communication with non-Jews"[38]. Consequently "Israel" has a more religious connotation than "Jew". This could imply that H. Schlier[39] is correct when he considers "King of the Jews" to be the political version of the messianic religious "King of Israel". It is important to note that in both contexts where "King of Israel" is applied to Jesus, the title is supplemented (though not refused) by the expression

38. P.J. TOMSON, *The Names of Israel and Jew in Ancient Judaism and in the New Testament*, in *Bijdr* 47 (1986) 120-140, p. 140.
39. H. SCHLIER, *Jesus und Pilatus* (n. 10), p. 60.

'the Son of Man who has to be glorified' (on the cross) in 1,51 and in 12,23-24 (cf. 12,31-34).

The only other context where βασιλεία is used in John is in 3,3.5. We agree with scholars like Hengel who are convinced that in Johannine theological perspective there is no difference between the βασιλεία of Jesus and the βασιλεία of God[40]. In 3,3.5 it is clear that seeing or entering the βασιλεία of God presupposes a birth "from above"[41]. This is a clear parallel to "not of this world" in 18,36. When addressed to the highly political figure Nicodemus, "a leader of the Jews", the invitation into the βασιλεία of God might involve a change from one political order and value-system to another. In 18,36 Jesus confronts the βασιλεία of the Jews with his own. By using the possessive adjective emphatically three times, a clear contrast is expressed. We should not overlook the fact that, already here, Jesus accepts that he is a king. This explains why Pilate, in 18,37b repeats his original question, saying, "So you are a king?". For a brief moment it seems as if Pilate was going to understand that Jesus claims a βασιλεία different from that of the Jews. But, as the inscription "King of the Jews" which Pilate has put on the cross (19,19) demonstrates, Pilate ultimately remains closed to the religious dimension of Jesus' person and message. While the βασιλεία of "the Jews" obviously has its origin in this world, Jesus' βασιλεία does not.

b) The world

In order to understand this better, a few words about κόσμος are in place. This is a clearly Johannine term with a specifically Johannine meaning. It refers to the created world with special emphasis on the human world. At the risk of using an anachronistic term, "world" seems to refer to what modern sociologists call 'socially constructed reality', the space into which one is born which is constituted by human action[42]. This includes the political order, but is not limited to it. Against Bultmann and with Blank[43], we insist that social construction of reality is not by definition sin, but

40. HENGEL, Reich Christi (n. 1), p. 212.
41. The Greek word ἄνωθεν means both "anew" and "from above". According to R. BROWN, The Gospel According to John (i–xii) (AnB, 29), vol. 1, Garden City, NY, Doubleday, 1966, p. 130, "the double meaning is used here as part of the technique of misunderstanding". While Nicodemus understands the meaning "anew", Jesus intended the meaning "from above", as is obvious from 3,5 (cf. 3,31; 19,11.23). R. SCHNACKEN-BURG, Das Johannesevangelium. Einleitung und Kommentar zu Kap. 1–4 (HTK, IV/1), Freiburg – Basel – Wien, Herder, ³1972, p. 381, considers "from above" to be the only legitimate translation.
42. BLANK, Krisis (n. 15), p. 191.
43. See above, n. 15.

rather that this process is marred by sin which, however, does not completely control it. The world is the reality into which Jesus came as light,
prophet, Χριστός, Son of God, where he was sent as Son. Jesus is in the
world, but he is not of the world (8,23). Jesus is the lamb of God who takes
away the sin of the world, and he is the light of the world. He has not come
to judge but to save the world. God's love for the world is such that God
gives the son to save the world (3,16). The world does not receive Jesus,
hates Jesus and the disciples. Jesus has overcome the world (16,33). This
limited overview demonstrates that, when using "world", sometimes
John's focus is on the term in its neutral, sometimes in its utterly sinful
character, and perhaps mostly on both together without special focus. In
18,37g "and for this I have come into the world" the term is used in its
comprehensive meaning. It is most likely to be the same in 18,36. Jesus'
βασιλεία is different from this world in all its aspects. The fact that "from
this world" is taken up by "from here" seems to confirm this.

c) "My servants would fight"

Nevertheless in what follows in 18,36d the focus is on a sinful aspect
of the world from the political arena, viz. that the kings of this world
have servants/soldiers who have to fight for them to defend them against
the attacks of others. John's use of ἀγωνίζομαι is different from the
other five uses of this verb in the NT and is parallel with two of the three
LXX usages. In 2 Macc 8,16 and 13,14 this verb unmistakably refers to
the violent military fighting of soldiers under the leadership of Judas
Maccabeus. This parallel hardly seems accidental in a context where
Jesus is accused of pretending to be a political liberator from the Roman
occupation forces. The biblically-trained ear can hear Jesus say implicitly, 'Unlike Judas Maccabeus I do not have soldiers to fight for me, not
even when my life is in danger, when I am in danger of being handed
over to the Jews', which happens indeed in 19,16. If there are no soldiers
to defend Jesus, it is even less likely that he has any soldiers who would
fight against the Romans. In that sense it might not be exaggerated to see
in Jesus' words a rejection of insurrection and armed struggle for liberation[44]. Authors who make this point too easily jump to the conclusion that
by pleading for nonviolence Jesus rejects any political dimension to his
mission. So far we have seen that Jesus accepts kingship, but he rejects
explicitly using people to fight for his own liberation[45]. He obviously

---

44. HOWARD-BROOK, *Becoming Children of God* (n. 8), pp. 400-401, overlooks this
point. He sees in ἀγωνίζομαι the nuance of "endless competitive striving".
45. Cf. Mk 10:41-45.

accepts a basic political dimension, but he rejects a certain way of using political power[46].

Messianic pretenders or freedom fighters of the first century had followers who would fight and frequently die for them. In Jesus' case it is the other way around. What Jesus says in 18,36d is consistent with the other parts of the passion narrative. In 18,8 Jesus negotiates free passage for his disciples and in 18,10 he tells Peter not to use his sword to keep Jesus from being arrested.

In parallel with 1,49 and 12,13.15 the Johannine Jesus ever so subtly reshapes the meaning of kingship in the light of his own death. This implicit reference will become clearer in 18,37 where a positive description of Jesus' kingship is added.

d) "To bear witness to the truth"

In 18,37 Jesus describes the purpose of his birth as a human being and of his coming into the world as "to bear witness to the truth". Both "to bear witness" and "truth" are typically Johannine terminology. According to Bultmann, "truth" in John is the "divine reality"[47]. J. Blank understands ἀλήθεια against the background of the Hebrew Bible, stressing the meaning of "absolute reliability" and thus bringing out its personal character[48]. Y. Ibuki interprets truth as divine reality in the relational sense: truth is the unity of Father and Son which is shared with the "world" in Jesus' testimony[49].

In 18,37 "truth" is clearly antithetical to "world". Jesus has come into the world, characterized at least partially by lies, to bear testimony to the truth. It is possible to be in the world and to be of the truth, but one cannot be of the world and of the truth at the same time. Truth clearly points to the divine reality. We propose to understand the divine reality in Jn 18,37 as the absolutely reliable love relationship between Jesus and God. It seems that, in 18,37, John has not left behind the theme of the imminent death of Jesus. Jesus' bearing witness to the truth, to his unique love relationship with God, ultimately leads him to the cross.

---

46. See also MEEKS, *Ethics*, (n. 33), p. 324: "The Johannine group may look to us like some modern survivalist sect, but this sect does not stockpile weapons. Nevertheless, Jesus' kingship has 'real' world political consequences, and the political decisions of Pilate and the Jewish leaders have 'religious' consequences".

47. R. BULTMANN, art. ἀλήθεια, in *TWNT* 1 (1935) 233-251, p. 245.

48. J. BLANK, *Der johanneische Wahrheitsbegriff*, in *BZ* 7 (1963) 163-173.

49. Y. IBUKI, *Die Wahrheit im Johannesevangelium* (BBB, 39), Bonn, Hanstein, 1972, p. 169: "Das Zeugnis erschließt die Einheit von Vater und Sohn, und wer diese göttliche Wirklichkeit nicht annehmen will, bleibt von ihr ausgeschlossen".

Here is a first indication that the political accusation of making himself king is not the only, perhaps not even the real reason for the fact that the "Jews" want to see him dead. In 5,18 and 10,33 they accuse him of making himself (equal to) God in reaction to Jesus' testimony to his special relationship with God (oneness). Both times it stirs the anger of the "Jews" and leads to attempts to kill or arrest him. In the context of the passion narrative a similar accusation is raised in 19,7: "He has made himself Son of God". Jesus insists that he has not made himself king, he rather is king. He has not ursurped a special relationship with God, but it is a reality. That is his testimony to the truth.

But the "Jews" quickly revert back to the political charges. There may, however, be an important link between the political and the religious levels of the accusation. We find traces of this throughout the passion narrative. In 18,11 the reason given for the rejection of the use of violence to defend Jesus is "The cup that the Father has given me, am I not to drink it?". Generations of Christians, including theologians, have raised the question, 'Why has the Father given this cup to Jesus?' To my mind, this question has frequently received an incorrect answer. My alternative answer in the context of 18,36-37 is, 'The Father has given this cup to Jesus, because Jesus and God in their love relationship agree that violence is not a proper means to establish the kingship of Jesus on earth'. In the context of 18,11 the focus is not on why Jesus is dying, but how the kingship is established. This interpretation is confirmed by D. Senior who says: "Jesus is determined to drink the 'cup' of his death because this act of ultimate friendship love – and not the use of violent force – is capable of revealing God's own redemptive love for the world"[50].

Jn 19,11 which is structurally parallel to 18,36 might equally call for a similar interpretation. While in 18,8.10 and 18,36 the text clarifies why Jesus' disciples did not interfere to liberate him, 19,11 like 18,11 clarifies why God did not interfere. In the same way as the kingship of Jesus and the "cup", i.e., his death, the power of Pilate to release Jesus or crucify him, is something connected with the divine reality, i.e., with the truth to which Jesus bears witness. This, however, means that the power given to Pilate is not related to the Father as an isolated unrelated being who takes solitary decisions (e.g., that Jesus must die), but rather to the unique love relationship between God and Jesus. For 19,11 this would imply that the nonviolent establishment of Jesus' kingship is the only possibility that is in keeping with the love relationship between Jesus

---

50. SENIOR, *Passion* (n. 16), p. 54.

and God. Pilate's power is only his (given to him) because he uses soldiers to reach his political ends. Jesus restricts his activity to bearing witness to the truth. He addresses his testimony also to Pilate. This nonviolent attempt at stopping Pilate from handing Jesus over to the "Jews" is permitted. But it is in vain, since Pilate is not of the truth and thus does not listen to Jesus' voice.

Summarizing the results of our investigation we paraphrase 18,36: 'The essence of my kingship is determined by my love relationship with God'. That is why a violent establishment of Jesus' kingship is excluded. Since Pilate is not of the truth, only the use of arms could stop Jesus from being executed. As Jesus on the basis of his love relationship with God rejects the use of violence, he drinks the "cup".

IV. CONCLUSION

The fourth evangelist's reply to the "Jewish" accusation of Jesus, viz. that he pretends to be the nationalistic-political Messiah-King, is varied and complex. Two things have, however, become clear in our investigation: 1) John does not simply agree with the charges which are raised against Jesus. This was to be expected. 2) The conclusion that may be more surprising is that he does not simply reject it either. In chapters 18–19, John creates an intricately interwoven network of the political and the religious dimensions of the charges. By "bearing witness to the truth", Jesus keeps reminding people of the religious dimension of his life and mission. But in doing so, he does not do away with the political dimension. He rather critiques it and reshapes it. The experience of first-century contemporaries of Jesus and John was that freedom fighters and messianic pretenders expected their followers to lay down their lives for their leaders. The Johannine Jesus does the exact opposite by laying down his life for his followers. This is stressed very much in John 5 and 10. By doing so, John does not deny the political dimension of Jesus' mission, but he rather corrects widespread first-century political practice by going back to the biblical theme of the shepherd. Jesus is the good shepherd who lays down his life for his sheep. He is the Messiah-King promised by God in the prophetic tradition.

Faculty of Theology   Reimund BIERINGER
Katholieke Universiteit Leuven
St. Michielsstraat 6
B-3000 Leuven

JESUS' EQUALITY WITH GOD
A Critical Reflection on John 5,18

The fourth gospel pays much attention to conflicts between Jesus and his Jewish opponents, referred to by John as 'the Jews'. Whereas in the Synoptic gospels representatives of the Jewish people mainly take offence at Jesus' attitude regarding the regulations of the Law, the topic of the conflicts with the Johannine Jews is the person of Jesus himself. The first confrontation between Jesus and the Johannine Jews takes place in Jerusalem (at the pool of Bethsata[1]) on the occasion of a healing on the sabbath (John 5,1-18). The conflict which follows the sabbath healing soon turns into a controversy on the identity of Jesus when he justifies his action by replying that his Father works on the sabbath and so does he (5,17). The statement stirs up the hostility and violence of 'the Jews': at first they were persecuting Jesus (5,16), now they are seeking all the more to kill him (5,18a). Their motives are that "he not only broke the sabbath, but also called God his own Father and made himself equal to God" (5,18b)[2].

By narrating that 'the Jews' accused Jesus of making himself equal to God, the fourth evangelist presents them as having immediately understood what is the implication of Jesus' saying in 5,17. This is, at least, the interpretation found amongst the great majority of exegetes[3]. They

1. Scholars still disagree about both the name and the exact location of this place. See for more information: DUPREZ, *Jésus et les dieux guérisseurs*; DAVIES, *The Gospel and the Land*, pp. 302-313; KÜCHLER, *Die 'Probatische'*, pp. 127-154; KOESTER, *Topography and Theology*, pp. 436-448.

For the full bibliographical references, see the attached bibliography. References in the footnotes are given in chronological order. Commentaries are indicated by the name of the author.

2. The translation of the biblical references is from the hand of the author, unless differently indicated.

3. Zie LÜCKE, p. 25; KLEE, p. 174; MEYER, p. 225: "Was ihm die Juden als todeswürdige (gotteslästerliche) Vermessenheit anrechneten... leugnet er nicht, sondern stellt den Sachverhalt in's rechte Licht"; MAIER, pp. 23-24; KLOFUTAR, p. 101; BURGER, p. 141; CORLUY, p. 133; KEIL, p. 222; PLUMMER, p. 136: "They fully understand the force of the parallel statements"; SCHANZ, p. 240: "Die Juden ziehen auch alsbald den Schluß aus Jesu Worten, daß er sich Gott gleich stelle... ποιῶν ist freilich von den Juden im Sinne einer Anmaßung gemeint, aber damit ist doch zugegeben, daß Jesus den Anspruch wirklich erhob"; O. HOLTZMANN, p. 218: "Seine Gleichstellung mit Gott verteidigt nun Christus in der ersten grossen Rede des Evangeliums"; H.J. HOLTZMANN, p. 121: "... dass er damit ἴσον ἑαυτὸν ποιῶν τῷ θεῷ, schliessen die Juden auch im Sinne des Evangelisten mit Recht... Sie verstehen und verneinen mit Einem Worte hier

defend that the Johannine Jews rightly heard in Jesus' statement a claim to equality with God, though the unacceptability of it incites them to seek to kill Jesus (ἐζήτουν αὐτὸν ἀποκτεῖναι). It is surprising that most of these exegetes apparently take the meaning of the expression ἴσος τῷ θεῷ as self-evident and read in 5,18 another indication of the divinity of the Johannine Jesus. In this paper, I would like to focus on the question 'What do "the Jews" actually accuse Jesus of by saying that he makes himself equal to God, ἴσος τῷ θεῷ?' Only when we have an idea of what the Johannine Jews mean by the accusation that Jesus makes himself ἴσος τῷ θεῷ, are we in the position of confirming or denying whether they understood Jesus as he is proclaimed by the Johannine community.

Tracing the commentaries and studies which have, directly or indirectly, dealt with this question resulted in (what I discern as) two different positions. After a presentation of these positions I will search for more elements which could bring clarity in the conflict between Jesus and the representatives of the Jewish people as portrayed in John 5.

wie 10,33 die spezifisch johann. Christologie"; MACRORY, p. 83; KNABENBAUER, p. 197; CEULEMANS, p. 74; BALJON, p. 90; BELSER, p. 173; WESTCOTT, p. 187; BAUER, p. 56; TILLMANN, p. 125; LAGRANGE, p. 142; MACGREGOR, p. 173: "thereby… making himself equal to God. In the last words we have the very essence of the Johannine theology, which here, as in 10:33, is vigorously disputed by the Jews"; BÜCHSEL, p. 74; KEULERS, p. 120; HOSKYNS, p. 267: "The Jews recognize the vastness of the claims that lay behind the Saying of Jesus"; BULTMANN, pp. 182-183; WIKENHAUSER, p. 142; GROSHEIDE, p. 358: "Daarom is het een goddeloos verzet, want de Joden hebben begrepen waar het om ging, en achten de waarheid Gods Godslastering"; HENDRIKSEN, p. 196: "By the words, *he also called God his own Father, making himself equal with God*, the author once more brings into clear view the purpose of his Gospel… the Jewish authorities… immediately understood that Jesus claimed for himself deity in the highest possible sense of that term. That claim was either the most wicked blasphemy, to be punished with death; or else, it was the most glorious truth, to be accepted by faith"; LIGHTFOOT, p. 139; VAN DEN BUSSCHE, p. 75; SANDERS & MASTIN, p. 164: "To John this claim was of course fully justified"; DUPREZ, *Les dieux guérisseurs*, p. 148: "C'est là une des affirmations les plus nettes de la divinité du Christ et de son égalité avec le Père. Les Juifs ne s'y sont pas trompés: le Christ… revendiquait… avec Dieu… une égalité"; SUNDBERG, *Isos To Theo Christology, passim*; MORRIS, p. 274; SCHNACKENBURG, p. 128; LINDARS, p. 219: "The evangelist… knows that the claim is true; SCHULZ, p. 85: "es ist… der Anspruch Jesu, Gott gleich zu sein, der die Juden zum Mord treibt"; MOLLAT & BRAUN, p. 107; BOISMARD & LAMOUILLE, p. 165; GNILKA, p. 40: "Die Juden sind durchaus in der Lage, den Anspruch Jesu zu begreifen, deuten ihn aber als Gotteslästerung"; ELLIS, p. 90; KYSAR, p. 79; BEASLEY-MURRAY, pp. 74-75; RIDDERBOS, p. 225; NEYREY, *An Ideology of Revolt*, pp. 1 & 9 and *passim*; LÉON-DUFOUR, pp. 38-40; MEEKS, *Equal to God*, pp. 310-311; ASHTON, *Understanding, passim*; ID., *Studying John*, pp. 71-89; CARSON, p. 249; CASEY, *From Jewish Prophet to Gentile God*, p. 23; VOIGT, p. 110; BRODIE, p. 245: "The account has an echo of tragedy, yet its final emphasis, as indicated by its closing phrase, is on the positive message of Jesus – the startling idea of a certain equality with God"; HOWARD-BROOK, p. 127; LEE, *Symbolic Narratives*, pp. 112-113; O'DAY, p. 580; WITHERINGTON III, p. 139; DE JONGE, p. 77.

Before starting, it should be stressed that the accusation of 'the Jews' reflects the evangelist's view on what is at stake in their conflict with Jesus. Since R. Alan Culpepper's *Anatomy of the Fourth Gospel*, it is generally accepted that the evangelist of the fourth gospel is an omni-scient narrator who knows the motives of his story's characters and who explains their actions by using inside views[4]. In other words, the contro-versy of John 5,1-18 and the issues that are at the center of it are the evangelist's presentation and interpretation of a conflict between Jesus and 'the Jews'. It remains a question whether John has the intention to stage here the debate of his time or whether he is using the conflict as a narrative technique to clarify the Johannine proclamation by confronting it with opposite views and misunderstandings.

Let us turn to the actual issue, 'What do "the Jews" accuse Jesus of by saying that he makes himself ἴσος τῷ θεῷ?'. A first position is taken by exegetes who defend that the Johannine Jews accused Jesus in 5,18 of claiming deity, divinity or *Wesensgleichheit* with God[5]. The statement of G. Stählin cannot be misunderstood: "ἴσος drückt in J 5,18 weder Vergleich noch Identität, sondern Würde-, Willens- und Wesensgleich-heit aus, das, wofür später mit dem Begriff ὁμοούσιος gekämpft wurde"[6]. Some exegetes argue that the accusation of 'the Jews' is based on the fact that Jesus called God ὁ πατήρ μου in 5,17. They hold that the Johannine Jews (rightly) understood that by calling God his own Father (πατέρα ἴδιον ἔλεγεν τὸν θεόν: 5,18), Jesus was claiming divine sonship and, thus, deity, divinity or *Wesensgleichheit*[7].

What provokes 'the Jews' about Jesus' (alleged) claim of equality with God is expressed by C.H. Dodd: "For a strict Jewish monotheist they [= expressions such as 'making himself equal to God'] would imply

---

4. CULPEPPER, *Anatomy of the Fourth Gospel*, pp. 21-26.

5. See MAIER, pp. 23-24: göttliche Natur und göttliche Würde; SCHANZ, p. 240: gle-iches Wesen mit Gott; BAUER, p. 56: Wesensgleichheit mit Gott; STÄHLIN, ἴσος, p. 353: Würde-, Willens- und Wesensgleichheit; KIRMIS, *Kapitel V*, p. 94: Wesensgleichheit; HENDRIKSEN, p. 196: deity; MORRIS, p. 275: he partook of the same nature as his Father; SPICQ, ἴσος, p. 359: égalité d'être ou de nature; SCHULZ, p. 85: Wesenseinheit; CARSON, p. 250: deity; CASEY, *From Jewish Prophet to Gentile God*, p. 23: divinity.

6. STÄHLIN, ἴσος, p. 353.

7. MAIER, pp. 23-24: "Der Heiland erkennt ihre Folgerung, daß er Gott im eminenten Sinne Vater nenne und sich so göttliche Natur und Würde zuschreibe, als richtig an"; BAUER, p. 56: "Die Juden verstehen richtig, was der joh. Christus meint, daß nämlich der Anspruch, Gottes Sohn zu sein, in seinem Munde nichts anderes als die Anerkennung seiner Wesensgleichheit mit Gott (1,1) fordert"; HENDRIKSEN, p. 196: "They did not try to tone down the character of Christ's sonship. They immediately understood that Jesus claimed for himself deity in the highest possible sense of that term"; MORRIS, p. 275: "He had called God 'his own Father' and this meant that he was 'making himself equal with God'".

that the person making such claims is setting himself up as a rival to the one God"[8]. But, Dodd continues, "certainly the Jew would be mistaken in supposing that He [= Jesus] is presented [by John] as a 'second God'"[9]. D.A. Carson's attempt to explain the irritation of the Johannine Jews is in line with Dodd's interpretation: "what 'the Jews' understood by 'equal with God' was not exactly what either Jesus or John meant by it.... Jesus is not equal with God as *another* God or as a *competing* God... Their understanding of Jesus' equality with God needs serious modification, for Christians will not accept di-theism or tri-theism any more than 'the Jews' themselves"[10]. In short, according to this interpretation, 'the Jews' rightly heard Jesus making a claim to divinity, deity or *Wesensgleichheit*, but from a Johannine perspective they are wrong in considering this as a threat to monotheism.

Bernhard Weiss is firm in his reaction to this interpretation of John 5,18: "Der Gedanke an Wesensgleichheit... liegt nicht einmal als unklare Vorstellung im Hintergrunde"[11]. According to him and several others, calling God his own Father is not the basis for the accusation that Jesus makes himself equal to God, as some proponents of the first position hold. They think the basis for the accusation is to be situated rather in Jesus' claim κἀγὼ ἐργάζομαι[12], and this brings us to a second position regarding the question 'what do the Johannine Jews accuse Jesus of by saying that he makes himself ἴσος τῷ θεῷ?'

In 5,17, Jesus states that God is working till now (ἕως ἄρτι), which implies 'on this sabbath day', namely the sabbath on which the healing took place. Literature contemporary to John's gospel testifies to the growing conviction that God is active on the sabbath and that this activity does not conflict with the sabbath regulations, in other words, that God is not bound by the sabbath law[13]. According to a great number of scholars, Jesus' saying "My Father is working till now" (ὁ πατήρ μου

---

8. DODD, *Interpretation*, p. 327.

9. *Ibid.*, p. 328.

10. CARSON, p. 250.

11. WEISS, p. 170.

12. WEISS, p. 170: "Denn indem er in einzigartiger Weise Gott seinen Vater nenne, mache er sich (in dem κἀγὼ ἐργάζομαι) in blasphemischer Weise Gott gleich..., indem er ein gleiches Thun wie dieser beanspruche"; see also MEYER, p. 225; DE WETTE, p. 105; KLOFUTAR, p. 101; GODET, p. 361; BURGER, p. 140; H.J. HOLTZMANN, p. 121; WESTCOTT, p. 187; ZAHN, p. 293; ODEBERG, p. 203; BLIGH, *Jesus in Jerusalem*, p. 125; DUPREZ, *Les dieux guérisseurs*, p. 147; LINDARS, p. 219.

13. Scholars have in particular referred to PHILO OF ALEXANDRIA, *Legum allegoriae*, I,5, (compare with ID., *De Cherubim*, par. 87) I,6 and I,16; ID., *De migratione Abrahami*, par. 91; and the midrashim *Exodus Rabbah* 30,9 and *Genesis Rabbah* 11,10.

ἕως ἄρτι ἐργάζεται) has to be read against this background[14]. Now, the Johannine Jesus connects with this saying about God's working on the sabbath a statement about his own working, namely κἀγὼ ἐργάζομαι. It is this statement which causes the accusation that he makes himself ἴσος τῷ θεῷ, since it can be understood (as 'the Jews' did) as if Jesus is placing his activity on the same level with God's activity[15] and is claiming the divine prerogative to work on the sabbath[16]. When the Johannine Jews accuse Jesus of making himself ἴσος τῷ θεῷ they accuse him of placing himself on an equal footing with God. What makes 'the Jews' so angry about this, according to Hugo Odeberg, is that a person who makes such a claim, claims to be independent of God and this "implies some degree of 'rebellion' against the Divine government"[17]. B. Lindars'

14. Authors who have referred to both Philo and the rabbinic midrashim: WESTCOTT, p. 186; BAUER, p. 55; STRACK & BILLERBECK, pp. 461-462; MACGREGOR, pp. 173-172; KEULERS, p. 120; BARRETT, p. 256; LOHSE, σάββαττον, p. 27; SANDERS & MASTIN, p. 163 and p. 164 n. 1; SCHNACKENBURG, p. 127; LINDARS, p. 218; BERNARD, *La guérison de Bethesda*, pp. 18-19, p. 27 and p. 29; BOISMARD & LAMOUILLE, p. 164; HAENCHEN, pp. 273-274; LÉON-DUFOUR, p. 35; NEYREY, *Ideology of Revolt*, p. 21, p. 231 n. 36 and p. 35; ENSOR, *Jesus and His 'Works'*, pp. 186-187. Authors who have referred only to the writings of Philo: H.J. HOLTZMANN, p. 121; BALJON, p. 90; LOISY, p. 208; BERNARD, p. 236; DODD, *Interpretation*, pp. 320-321; BECKER, p. 280; BLANK, p. 20; LÉON-DUFOUR, p. 35; BORGEN, *The Sabbath Controversy in John 5:1-18*, p. 214. Authors who have referred only to the rabbinic midrashim: ZAHN, p. 292 n. 36; STRACHAN, p. 169; TILL-MANN, p. 125; LAGRANGE, p. 141; ODEBERG, p. 202; BULTMANN, p. 184 n. 4; WIKEN-HAUSER, p. 141; LIGHTFOOT, p. 140; VAN DEN BUSSCHE, p. 75-76; BROWN, p. 217; MOLONEY, *The Johannine Son of Man*, p. 69 n. 12; BEASLEY-MURRAY, p. 74; CARSON, p. 247.

15. WEISS, p. 170; BELSER, p. 173; WESTCOTT, p. 187.

16. MEYER, p. 225: "*indem er* (zugleich) *auf gleiche Stufe sich selbst setzt mit Gott*, nämlich durch jenes κἀγὼ ἐργάζομαι V.17., wodurch er, als der Sohn, sich selbst die Gleichheit des Rechts und der Freiheit mit dem Vater zuschreibe"; BURGER, pp. 140-141: "Gott gleich macht Er sich durch die V. 17. ausgesprochene Zusammenstellung seines Thuns mit dem des Vaters, wonach Er eben so vom Sabbatgebot entbunden sei, wie sein Vater in seiner Thätigkeit durch dasselbe nich gehemmt werden könne"; ZAHN, p. 293: "In bezug auf sein Handeln, meinten sie, habe er sich mit Gott gleichgestellt und eine Erhabenheit über das Gesetz für sich beansprucht, die nur etwas dem göttlichen Geset-zgeber zustehen mag"; BERNARD, p. 237: "... but it was a much graver offence that He claimed to have Divine prerogatives"; ODEBERG, p. 203: "... the profanation of the Holy One which inhered in the words of J in vs. 17 consisted not in calling the Holy One his Father, but in his presuming upon a peculiar sonship in virtue of which he had the right of performing the same 'continual work' as his Father"; BLIGH, *Jesus in Jerusalem*, p. 125: "But more probably the Jews mean that Jesus is making himself equal to God by claiming to be above the sabbath law and exempt from it, just as the Father is above it and exempt from it"; BROWN, p. 217: "In claiming the right to work even as his Father worked, Jesus was claiming a divine prerogative."

17. ODEBERG, *The Fourth Gospel*, p. 203. Odeberg's interpretation has inspired BULT-MANN, pp. 182-183, who has been in his turn an inspiration for BEASLEY-MURRAY, pp. 74-75; LEE, *Symbolic Narratives*, pp. 112-113; O'DAY, p. 580, among others. Odeberg's interpretation is based on the conviction that the Greek expression ἴσον ἑαυτὸν ποιῶν τῷ θεῷ "corresponds exactly to the Rabbinic expression משוה את עצמו לאלהים which to

explanation is that "It was not only the ultimate folly to put oneself on a level with God, but absolute blasphemy"[18]. J. Bligh relates the accusation to the *hybris* of Adam and Eve: "St John may mean that the Jews regarded Jesus as repeating the original sin of Adam and Eve in attempting to set himself up as God's equal"[19]. Clearly, in all of these explanations, the notion of *Wesensgleichheit* is not the central issue.

At this point, I am in favor of the idea brought to the fore by the representatives of the second position, namely that the Johannine Jews accuse Jesus of placing himself on an equal footing with God, which is blasphemous self-exaltation. I am rather doubtful about the first interpretation which holds that Jesus is accused of claiming deity which implies that he is setting himself up as a second God. I suspect especially Stählin, who connects ἴσος with ὁμοούσιος, but also the other proponents of this position, of spontaneously applying concepts from the dogmatic tradition to the interpretation of this New Testament text. In what follows, some elements are collected which have not (or rarely) been taken into consideration but might be helpful in trying to clarify what is at stake in the conflict between Jesus and the representatives of the Jewish people as narrated in John 5.

First, dictionaries have pointed out that the adjective ἴσος is generally used to indicate "an external, objectively measurable and established likeness and correspondence", as E. Beyreuther and G. Finkenrath put it in an attempt to distinguish ἴσος-terminology from "the words connected with *homoios* [which] express more substantial, essential likeness"[20]. The term

---

a Rabbinic ear is equivalent to 'makes himself independent of God', *i.e.* by usurping for himself the Divine power and authority; the expression, implies some degree of 'rebellion' against the Divine government". By way of argumentation, he refers to a few passages (which neither C.H. DODD, [*Interpretation*, p. 326 n. 3] nor myself were able to verify) where a son who rejects the authority of his father is characterized as עצמו לאביו משוה, making himself equal to his father. He is not giving any indication of a rabbinic work where the Hebrew expression משוה את עצמו לאלהים (he makes himself equal to God) can be found. I wonder whether Odeberg really had at his disposal Rabbinic texts containing the expression which allegedly corresponds with ἴσον ἑαυτὸν ποιῶν τῷ θεῷ.Or did he perhaps apply the phrase משוה עצמו לאביו that dealt with interpersonal relationships between fathers and sons of his own accord to the relation God-humans? Besides these obscurities, one also has to take into account the limited usefulness of rabbinic materials for the study of the New Testament since they are of a rather late date (see e.g. J.C. THOMAS, *The Fourth Gospel and Rabbinic Judaism*, in *ZNW* 82 [1991] 159-182).

18. LINDARS, p. 219.

19. BLIGH, *Jesus in Jerusalem*, p. 126; compare with BROWN, p. 213: "'The Jews' are charging Jesus with rebellion and pride similar to Adam's sinful attempt to be like God (Gen iii 5-6)"; LÉON-DUFOUR, p. 39: "Jésus attribuerait la dignité divine, il aurait succombé à la parole du Tentateur: 'Vous serez comme des dieux' (Gn 3,5; cf Ph 2,6)".

20. BEYREUTHER & FINKENRATH, *Like, Equal*, pp. 496-497. It should be noticed that it is sometimes hard to draw a clear line between ἴσος- and ὁμοίος-terminology, as they

ἴσος is frequently used to denote arithmetic or geometric equality/equivalence (numbers, sizes), proportional equality, substantial equality (e.g., of the copy with its original), political and legal equality (e.g., equal rights, fairness, impartiality)[21].

Secondly, the adjective ἴσος is a *hapax legomenon* in the Gospel of John and also in the other books of the New Testament where it occurs rather rarely[22]. In John 5,18, ἴσος appears in the construction ἴσον ποιεῖν τινά τινι, which is attested in two other passages in the Greek Bible, namely in 2 Macc 9,15 and Matt 20,12. In both passages, (groups of) persons are 'made equal' to each other, although it is stressed that they have little or nothing in common with each other. 2 Macc 9,15 describes Antiochus' changing attitude towards 'the Jews': "the Jews, whom he had not considered worth burying but had planned to throw out with their children for the wild animals and for the birds to eat, he would make, all of them, equal to citizens of Athens (*NRSV*) (τοὺς δὲ Ἰουδαίους ... πάντας αὐτοὺς ἴσους ᾿Αθηναίοις ποιήσειν)". In Matthew's parable of the laborers in the vineyard, the laborers of the first hour grumbled against the landowner: "These last worked only one hour, and you have made them equal to us (ἴσους ἡμῖν αὐτοὺς ἐποίησας) who have borne the burden of the day and the scorching heat" (Mt 20,12; *NRSV*). W. Bauer translates the expression ἴσον ποιεῖν τινά τινι by "jemanden einem andern gleichstellen, gleich behandeln"[23]. Ceslas Spicq renders the expression in Mt 20,12 with the words "être mis sur le même pied"[24]. In both 2 Macc 9,15 and Mt 20,12 the expression ἴσον ποιεῖν τινά τινι refers to the equal treatement, in the case of 2 Macc 9,15 maybe even the equal rights, granted to the two groups of people who are put on an equal footing with each other.

Thirdly, the gospel of John mentions other accusations similar to the one found in 5,18, namely in 8,53; 10,33; 19,7.12. Without doubt, they can throw additional light on ἴσον ἑαυτὸν ποιῶν τῷ θεῷ. All reproaches are formulated by means of the construction ποιέω ἐμαυτόν with an attribute, although the accompanying attribute differs in every passage. In

---

can be interchangeable; cf. *ibid.*, p. 496; compare with DODD, *Interpretation*, p. 328 n. 1, referring in particular to the use of ἴσος in John 5,18.

21. *Ibid.*, p. 497; compare LIDDELL, SCOTT & JONES, *Greek-English Lexicon*, p. 839; SPICQ, ἴσος, pp. 351-352.

22. See Matt 20,12; Mark 14,56.59; Luke 6,34; Acts 11,17; Phil 2,6 and Rev 21,16.

23. BAUER & ALAND, *Griechisch-deutsches Wörterbuch*, c. 772.

24. SPICQ, ἴσος, p. 356: "Dans le parabole des ouvriers envoyés à la vigne, ceux qui furent engagés dès le point du jour se plaignent d'être 'mis sur le même pied' que les ouvriers n'ayant travaillé qu'une heure... en leur donnant le même salaire, tu les as faits pareils à nous!".

8,53 the Johannine Jews ask Jesus the question: τίνα σεαυτὸν ποιεῖς; (Who do you claim to be [*NRSV*]?) In 10,33 they declare they want to stone him because of blasphemy, οτι σὺ ἄνθρωπος ὤν ποιεῖς σεαυτὸν θεόν (because you, a human being, are making yourself God). During the trial before Pilate (19,7) 'the Jews' declare that, according to their law, Jesus has to die because he made himself the Son of God (ὅτι υἱὸν θεοῦ ἑαυτὸν ἐποίησεν). Finally, in 19,12 'the Jews' try to stop Pilate from releasing Jesus arguing that πᾶς ὁ βασιλέα ἑαυτὸν ποιῶν ἀντιλέγει τῷ Καίσαρι ("everyone who makes himself a king sets himself against the emperor" [*NRSV*]).

Strikingly, in the context of all the mentioned accusations Jesus' humanity is emphasized[25]. After Jesus said: "Whoever keeps my word will never see death", 'the Jews' challenge him in 8,53: "Are you greater than our father Abraham, who died? The prophets also died. Who do you claim to be (*NRSV*)? (τίνα σεαυτὸν ποιεῖς;)." It seems as if they were asking him: "You, mortal being, who do you think you are?" In 10,33 they explicitly say: "You, a human being, are making yourself God." Bringing Jesus, dressed with the crown of thorns and the purple robe, outside the headquarters, Pilate places him before the people while pronouncing the well-known words ἰδοῦ ὁ ἄνθρωπος. It is this human being 'the Jews' are accusing of making himself the son of God in 19,7. In the context of 5,18 too, the humanity of Jesus is brought to the fore in the question of 'the Jews' addressed to the healed man: "Who is the ἄνθρωπος who said to you, 'Take it up and walk'?" (5,12).

Combined with the emphasis on Jesus' humanity, the use of the verb ποιέω in all the mentioned accusations underlines 'the Jews'' vexation about Jesus' (alleged) claims. Their complaint seems to be that Jesus *makes himself* something (ἴσος to God, God, Son of God, king) "he *is* 'obviously' not"[26].

Considering the possible implications of the collected material for the question 'What do the Johannine Jews actually accuse Jesus of by saying that he makes himself ἴσος τῷ θεῷ?', the following observations can be made. First, the interpretation that the Johannine Jews accuse Jesus in 5,18 of placing himself on an equal footing with God since he

---

25. The references to Jesus as ἄνθρωπος in the fourth gospel are not free from irony, as has been noticed by several authors such as THOMPSON, *The Humanity of Jesus*, p. 107: "one should note the frequent, sometimes sarcastic and disparaging, sometimes innocent, but usually ironic references to Jesus as 'this man'". See also SIDEBOTTOM, *The Christ of the Fourth Gospel*, p. 96; SMALLEY, *John*, pp. 195-196; CULPEPPER, *Anatomy of the Fourth Gospel*, pp. 171-172; DUKE, *Irony*, pp. 105-107.

26. Compare for 5,18d HOWARD-BROOK, p. 127.

claimed the divine prerogative to work on the sabbath, seems to be strengthened by the fact that the adjective ἴσος is generally used to denote external likeness and correspondence such as numerical equality or equality of rights (not essential likeness). Secondly, the similarities between 5,18 and the other two biblical attestations of the construction ἴσον ποιεῖν τινά τινι point in the same direction. In these passages, groups of persons who have practically nothing in common, are put on an equal footing and the equality referred to in these passages is an external equality connected with equal treatement, in the case of 2 Macc 9,15 maybe even equal rights. Thirdly, reading 5,18 in line with the passages 10,33; 19,7.12 where the Johannine Jews accuse Jesus of *making* himself something (respectively God, Son of God and king) he *is* not, highlights the irritation of 'the Jews' about the blasphemous self-exaltation and objectionable haughtiness they hear in the sayings of the Johannine Jesus.

Nevertheless, several questions remain unanswered and call for further investigation. A first question is connected with the basis for the accusation ἴσον ἑαυτὸν ποιῶν τῷ θεῷ. Taking κἀγὼ ἐργάζομαι as a basis favors the interpretation that Jesus is accused of placing himself on an equal footing with God. On the other hand, considering (also) the reproach 'he called God his own Father' as a basis for the accusation – and this seems to be the reading with a greater grammatical support (the finite verb ἔλεγεν followed by the participle ποιῶν) – raises the question whether the Johannine Jews heard in Jesus' calling God 'my Father' (ὁ πατήρ μου) a certain claim of *Wesensgleichheit* with God. In other words, does the divine sonship of the Johannine Jesus already imply what the later tradition has called *Wesensgleichheit* with God the Father?

A second question is, what makes 'the Jews' so angry about a person who claims to be ἴσος τῷ θεῷ, though his humanity is beyond doubt? Is it only because of the blasphemous character of this claim, or do they really consider such a person as a rival to the one God? Maybe we should ask this question also on the level of the Johannine community who worships Jesus as the Messiah and the Son of God (20,31) but is confronted with the hostility of members of the Jewish people who can see Jesus only as an ordinary human being. The question becomes then: Do the Jewish opponents accuse the Johannine Christians of idolatry (worshipping a human being as a divine being) or do they consider the Christian worship as an attack on their monotheistic belief (the uniqueness of Israel's God is threatened)?

A last question deals with the content of the Johannine proclamation. At the beginning of this exposition, I mentioned that the great majority of exegetes holds that John presented 'the Jews' as having immediately understood that the Johannine Jesus is ἴσος τῷ θεῷ I hope this affirmation has in the meantime lost some of its self-evidence. Answering this question is a whole research project. It will have to take into account not only the first verse of the prologue (the Logos was God) and the confession of Thomas (20,28: My Lord and my God), which are frequently used to support an affirmative answer[27]. It will also be insufficient to refer only to Jesus' saying in 14,28 (the Father is greater than I), often used as an argument for denying Jesus' equality with God[28]. In order to answer the question whether the Johannine Jesus is ἴσος τῷ θεῷ, all the affirmations about Jesus' relationship with God will have to be taken into account.

BIBLIOGRAPHY

I. COMMENTARIES

BALJON, J.M.S., *Commentaar op het evangelie van Johannes*, Utrecht, 1902.
BARRETT, C.K., *The Gospel According to St John. An Introduction with Commentary and Notes on the Greek Text*, London, 1955, ²1978.
BAUER, W., *Johannes* (HNT, 2/2), Tübingen, 1912.
BEASLEY-MURRAY, G.R., *John* (WBC, 36), Waco, TX, 1987.
BECKER, J., *Das Evangelium nach Johannes*, deel I: *Kapitel 1–10* (ÖTK, 4/1), Würzburg, 1979, ²1985, ³1991.
BELSER, J.E., *Das Evangelium des heiligen Johannes, übersetzt und erklärt*, Freiburg i. Br., 1905.
BERNARD, J.H., *A Critical and Exegetical Commentary on the Gospel According to St. John* (ICC), vol. I, Edinburgh, 1928, ⁶1962.
BLANK, J., *Das Evangelium nach Johannes* (Geistliche Schriftlesung, 4), vol. 1b, Düsseldorf, 1981.
BOISMARD, M.-É. & A. LAMOUILLE, *Synopse des quatre évangiles en français*, vol. III: *L'Évangile de Jean. Commentaire*, Paris, 1977.
BRODIE, T.L., *The Gospel According to John. A Literary and Theological Commentary*, New York – Oxford, 1993.
BROWN, R.E., *The Gospel According to John. Introduction, Translation, and Notes*, deel I (AncB), Garden City, NY, 1966.
BÜCHSEL, F., *Das Evangelium nach Johannes übersetzt und erklärt* (NTD, 4), Göttingen, 1934, ⁴1946.

---

27. See, in connection with John 1,1: MEEKS, *Equal to God*, p. 310; HOWARD-BROOK, p. 127; WITHERINGTON III, p. 139.
28. See e.g. BERNARD, p. 238; BROWN, p. 214; NIEUWENHUIS, p. 120.

BULTMANN, R., *Das Evangelium des Johannes* (KEK, II/19), Göttingen, 1941, [10]1968.

BURGER, C.H.A., *Das Evangelium nach Johannes deutsch erklärt*, Nördlingen, 1868.

CARSON, D.A., *The Gospel According to John*, Leicester – Grand Rapids, MI, 1991.

CEULEMANS, F.C., *Commentarius in evangelium secundum Joannem cui succedit synopsis chronologica quatuor evangeliorum*, Mechelen, 1901.

CORLUY, J., *Commentarius in evangelium S. Joannis in usum praelectionum*, Gent, 1878, [3]1889.

DE JONGE, M., *Johannes. Een praktische bijbelverklaring* (Tekst en toelichting), Kampen, 1996.

DE WETTE, W.M.L., *Kurze Erklärung des Evangeliums und der Briefe Johannis* (Kurzgefasstes exegetisches Handbuch zum Neuen Testament, 3/1), Leipzig, 1837, [5]1863 (red. B. BRÜCKNER).

ELLIS, P.F., *The Genius of John. A Compositional-Critical Commentary on the Fourth Gospel*, Collegeville, MN, 1984.

GNILKA, J., *Johannesevangelium* (Neue EB), Würzburg, 1983.

GODET, F., *Commentaire sur l'Évangile de Saint Jean* (Bibliothèque théologique), vol. II: *Explication des chapitres I-VII*, Neuchâtel, 1866, [4]1903.

GROSHEIDE, F.W., *Het Heilig Evangelie volgens Johannes* (Kommentaar op het Nieuwe Testament, 4), vol. I: *Hoofdstukken 1-7*, Amsterdam, 1950.

HAENCHEN, E., *Das Johannesevangelium. Ein Kommentar aus den nachgelassenen Manuskripten herausgegeben von Ulrich Busse*, Tübingen, 1980.

HENDRIKSEN, W., *Exposition of the Gospel According to John* (New Testament Commentary), vol. I & II, Grand Rapids, MI, 1953; 1954.

HOLTZMANN, H.J., *Evangelium des Johannes* (HCNT, 4/1), Tübingen, 1891, [3]1908, ed. W. BAUER.

HOLTZMANN, O., *Das Johannesevangelium untersucht und erklärt*, Darmstadt, 1887.

HOSKYNS, E.C., *The Fourth Gospel*, (ed. F.N. DAVEY), London, 1940.

HOWARD-BROOK, W., *Becoming Children of God. John's Gospel and Radical Discipleship* (The Bible & Liberation Series), Maryknoll, NY, 1994.

KEIL, C.F., *Commentar über das Evangelium des Johannes*, Leipzig, 1881.

KEULERS, J., *Het evangelie van Joannes vertaald en uitgelegd* (De boeken van het Nieuwe Testament), Roermond – Maaseik, 1936.

KLEE, H., *Commentar über das Evangelium nach Johannes*, Mainz, 1829.

KLOFUTAR, L., *Commentarius in evangelium sancti Joannis*, Vienna, 1862.

KNABENBAUER, I., *Commentarius in quatuor s. evangelia Domini N. Iesu Christi* (CSS), vol. IV: *Evangelium secundum Ioannem. Cum approbatione Superiorum*, Paris, 1898.

KYSAR, R., *John* (Augsburg Commentary on the New Testament), Minneapolis, MN, 1986.

LAGRANGE, P.-J., *Évangile selon saint Jean* (ÉBib), Paris, 1925, [7]1947.

LÉON-DUFOUR, X., *Lecture de l'Évangile selon Jean* (Parole de Dieu), vol. II: *Chapitres 5-12*, Paris, 1990.

LIGHTFOOT, R.H., *St. John's Gospel. A Commentary*, Oxford, 1956.

LINDARS, B., *The Gospel of John* (NCeB), London, 1972.

LOISY, A., *Le quatrième Évangile. Les Épîtres dites de Jean*, Paris, 1903, ²1921.

LÜCKE, F., *Commentar über das Evangelium des Johannes* (Commentar über die Schriften des Evangelisten Johannes), vol. II: *Auslegung von Kap. V-XXI*, Bonn, 1824, ²1833; ²1834.

MACGREGOR, G.H.C., *The Gospel of John* (The Moffat New Testament Commentary), 1928, ¹⁰1949.

MACRORY, J., *The Gospel of St. John. With Notes Critical and Explanatory*, Dublin, 1897, ⁶1924.

MAIER, A., *Commentar über das Evangelium des Johannes*, vol. II: *Auslegung von Kap. V-XXI*, Freiburg, 1845.

MEYER, H.A.W., *Kritisch exegetisches Handbuch über das Evangelium des Johannes* (KEK, 12), Göttingen, 1834, ⁵1869.

MOLLAT, D. & F.-M. BRAUN, *L'Évangile et les épîtres de saint Jean* (La Sainte Bible), Paris, 1973.

MORRIS, L., *The Gospel According to John* (NICNT), 1971, ²1995.

NIEUWENHUIS, J., *Het laatste evangelie. Een goed bericht van Johannes voor de gemeente van nu*, vol. I, Kampen, 1995.

O'DAY, G.R., *The Gospel of John. Introduction, Commentary, and Reflections* (NIB, 9), Nashville, TN, 1995.

ODEBERG, H., *The Fourth Gospel. Interpreted in its Relation to Contemporaneous Religious Currents in Palestine and the Hellenistic-Oriental World*, Amsterdam, 1929, repr. 1968.

PLUMMER, A., *The Gospel According to St. John* (The Cambridge Bible for Schools and Colleges), Cambridge, 1882, repr. (Thornapple Commentaries) 1981.

RIDDERBOS, H.N., *Het evangelie naar Johannes. Proeve van een theologische exegese*, vol. I: *Hoofdstuk 1-10*, Kampen, 1987.

SANDERS, J.N. & B.A. MASTIN, *A Commentary on the Gospel According to St John* (BNTC), London, 1968.

SCHANZ, P., *Commentar über das Evangelium des heiligen Johannes*, Tübingen, 1885.

SCHNACKENBURG, R., *Das Johannesevangelium* (HThK, IV), vol. II: *Kommentar zu Kap. 5-12*, Freiburg – Basel – Wien, 1965; 1971.

SCHULZ, S., *Das Evangelium nach Johannes übersetzt und erklärt* (NTD, 4), Göttingen, 1972.

STRACHAN, R.H., *The Fourth Gospel. Its Significance and Environment*, London, 1917, ³1955.

STRACK, H.L. & P. BILLERBECK, *Kommentar zum Neuen Testament aus Talmud und Midrasch*, vol. II: *Das Evangelium nach Markus, Lukas und Johannes und die Apostelgeschichte erläutert aus Talmud und Midrasch*, München, 1922, ⁴1965.

TILLMANN, F., *Das Johannesevangelium übersetzt und erklärt* (HSNT, 3), Bonn, 1921, ⁴1931.

VAN DEN BUSSCHE, H., *Het vierde evangelie* (Woord en beleving), vol. II: *Het boek der werken. Verklaring van Johannes 5-12*, Tielt – Den Haag, 1960.

VOIGT, G., *Licht – Liebe – Leben. Das Evangelium nach Johannes*, Göttingen, 1991.

WEISS, B., *Das Johannes-Evangelium* (KEK, 2), Göttingen, ⁶1880, ⁹1902.

WESTCOTT, B.F., *The Gospel According to St. John. The Greek Text with Intro-duction and Notes*, 1908, repr. (Thornapple Commentaries) Ann Arbor, MI, 1980.

WIKENHAUSER, A., *Das Evangelium nach Johannes übersetzt und erklärt* (RNT, 4), Regensburg, 1948, ³1961.

WITHERINGTON III, B., *John's Wisdom. A Commentary on the Fourth Gospel*, Cambridge, 1995.

ZAHN, T., *Das Evangelium des Johannes* (KNT, 4), Leipzig – Erlangen, 1908, ⁵⁻⁶1921.

II. STUDIES

ASHTON, J., *Understanding the Fourth Gospel*, Oxford, 1991 (chapter 4: *Religious Dissent*, pp. 124-159).

—, *Studying John. Approaches to the Fourth Gospel*, Oxford, 1994, (chapter 3: *Bridging Ambiguities*, pp. 71-89).

BAUER, W., *Griechisch-deutsches Wörterbuch zu den Schriften des Neuen Testaments und der frühchristlichen Literatur*, Berlin – New York, 1924, ²1928, ³1937, ⁴1952, ⁵1958, ⁶1988 (eds. K. ALAND & B. ALAND).

BERNARD, J., *La guérison de Bethesda. Harmoniques judéo-hellénistiques d'un récit de miracle un jour de sabbat*, in *Mélanges de science religieuse* 33 (1976) 3-34; 34 (1977) 13-44.

BEYREUTHER, E. & G. FINKENRATH, Art. *Like, Equal*, in *NIDNTT* 2 (1976) 496-505.

BLIGH, J., *Jesus in Jerusalem*, in *HeyJ* 4 (1963) 115-134.

BORGEN, P., *John and the Synoptics*, in D.L. DUNGAN (ed.), *The Interrelations of the Gospels. A Symposium led by M.- É. Boismard – W.R. Farmer – F. Neirynck, Jerusalem 1984*, Leuven, 1990, pp. 408-437.

BORGEN, P., *The Sabbath Controversy in John 5:1-18 and Analogous Controversy Reflected in Philo's Writings*, in D.T. RUNIA (ed.), *The Studia Philonica Annual. Studies in Hellenistic Judaism*, vol. III, Atlanta, GA, 1991, pp. 209-221.

CASEY, P.M., *From Jewish Prophet to Gentile God. The Origins and Development of New Testament Christology. The Edward Cadbury Lectures at the University of Birmingham, 1985-86*, Cambridge – Louisville, KY, 1991 (chapter 3: *God Incarnate – Jesus in the Johannine Community*, pp. 23-40).

CULPEPPER, R.A., *Anatomy of the Fourth Gospel. A Study in Literary Design* (New Testament Foundations and Facets), Philadelphia, PA, 1983.

DAVIES, W.D., *The Gospel and the Land: Early Christianity and Jewish Territorial Doctrine*, Berkeley, CA, 1974, pp. 302-313.

DODD, C.H., *The Interpretation of the Fourth Gospel*, Cambridge, 1953.

DUKE, P.D., *Irony in the Fourth Gospel*, Atlanta, GA, 1985.

DUPREZ, A., *Jésus et les dieux guérisseurs, à propos de Jean V* (CahRB, 12), Paris, 1970.

ENSOR, P.W., *Jesus and His 'Works'. The Johannine Sayings in Historical Perspective* (WUNT, 2/85), Tübingen, 1996.

KIRMIS, F., *Kapitel V des Johannesevangeliums mit einer Ausführung über die Dauer der öffentlichen Wirksamkeit Jesu, den Bethesdateich und die Stellung von c. 5 zu c. 6*, Breslau, 1940.

KOESTER, C.R., *Topography and Theology in the Gospel of John*, in A.B. BECK (ed.), *Fortunate the Eyes that See*. FS D.N. FREEDMAN, Grand Rapids, MI, 1995, pp. 436-448.

KÜCHLER, M., *Die 'Probatische' und Bethesda mit den fünf ΣΤΟΑΙ* (Joh 5,2), in A. KESSLER, T. RICKLIN & G. WURST (eds.), *Peregrina Curiositas. Eine Reise durch den orbis antiquus* (NTOA, 27). FS D. Van Damme, Freiburg-Göttingen, 1994, pp. 127-154.

LEE, D.A., *The Symbolic Narratives of the Fourth Gospel. The Interplay of Form and Meaning* (JSNT SS, 95), Sheffield, 1994 (on John 5, see pp. 98-125).

LIDDELL, H.G. & R. SCOTT, *A Greek-English Lexicon With a Supplement*, revised and augmented by H.S. JONES, Oxford, 1968.

LOHSE, E., Art. σάββαττον, in *ThWNT* 7 (1964) 1-34.

MEEKS, W.A., *Equal to God*, in R.T. FORTNA & B.R. GAVENTA (eds.), *Studies in Paul & John. The Conversation Continues*. FS J.L. Martyn, Nashville, TN, 1990, pp. 309-321, pp. 310-311;

MOLONEY, F.J., *The Johannine Son of Man* (Biblioteca di scienze religiose, 14), Roma, 1976, ²1978.

NEIRYNCK, F., *John and the Synoptics. Response to P. Borgen*, in D.L. DUNGAN (ed.), *The Interrelations of the Gospels. A Symposium led by M.- É. Boismard – W.R. Farmer – F. Neirynck, Jerusalem 1984*, Leuven, 1990, pp. 438-450.

NEYREY, J.H., *An Ideology of Revolt. John's Christology in Social-Science Perspective*, Philadelphia, PA, 1988.

SIDEBOTTOM, E.M., *The Christ of the Fourth Gospel in the Light of First-Century Thought*, London, 1961.

SMALLEY, S.S., *John: Evangelist and Interpreter*, Exeter, 1978.

SPICQ, C., Art. ἴσος, ἰσότης, ἰσότιμος, in ID., *Notes de lexicographie néo-testamentaire. Supplément* (OBO, 22/3), Fribourg-Göttingen, 1982, pp. 351-360.

STÄHLIN, G., Art. ἴσος, ἰσότης, ἰσότιμος, in *TWNT* 3 (1938) 343-356.

SUNDBERG, A.C., *Isos To Theo Christology in John 5.17-30*, in *Biblical Research* 15 (1970) 19-31.

THOMAS, J.C., *The Fourth Gospel and Rabbinic Judaism*, in *ZNW* 82 (1991) 159-182.

THOMPSON, M.M., *The Humanity of Jesus in the Fourth Gospel*, Philadelphia, PA, 1988 = *The Incarnate Word. Perspectives on Jesus in the Fourth Gospel*, Peabody, MA, 1993.

Faculty of Theology
Katholieke Universiteit Leuven
St. Michielsstraat 6
B-3000 Leuven

Bianca LATAIRE
Research Assistant of the Fund
for Scientific Research –
Flanders (Belgium)

CHRISTOLOGY AND CREATION

TOWARDS AN HERMENEUTIC OF PATRISTIC CHRISTOLOGY

I. INTRODUCTION

Any trained theologian these days should be able to give a standard account of the so-called development of Christology as established by the historical approach to patristic texts. True, critical orthodoxy is a moving target and there is debate over details; still the general point holds. But the question is: what then does the theologian do with it?

One common response is simply to accept the traditional formulae, however they were arrived at, so as to remain orthodox. Another is to offer a critique and risk deviating from the tradition in the interests of creating a more plausible Christology in the modern, or perhaps we should say postmodern, context. The word 'hermeneutic' in my title is meant to signal a different approach. It recognises, on the one hand, that an act of interpretation is involved in giving any account of patristic theology, and on the other, that theology has an interest not merely in historical reconstruction but in the question of appropriation – for Christian identity is not unlike personal identity in being something recognisable over time.

My first aim, then, is to offer an interpretation of patristic Christology which is not simply a developmental account but seeks key features of its underlying structure: in other words neither origins nor end-product will determine the assessment. My second will be briefly to suggest connections and areas of dialogue which might enable us to appropriate the thinking of the past in a new context, and could bear fruit in relation to the subject of this conference, namely the pluralist context in which the Christological question now has to addressed.

II. INTERPRETATION

A number of observations, which may not immediately seem to cohere, will contribute to the interpretation I offer. Each will be explored in its own right, and the ultimate construction will eventually emerge.

1. My first observation is that there are a couple of theological puzzles which are rarely faced directly, the common answer to which alerts us to the fact that early on there was no problem of Christology as such and at the same time uncovers the reasons for this.

The first puzzle is why Paul and the earliest Christians were apparently unaware that their confessions concerning Christ were a threat to monotheism. From our standpoint, and indeed that of the later debates about the relationship between God and Logos, or Father and Son, it seems extraordinary that New Testament authors and other early Christian writers apparently perceived no threat in their Christological affirmations to their loyalty to the one true God of the scriptures. That they did not surely demands explanation.

The second puzzle is this: why do the various systems of the second-third centuries, whether philosophical, syncretistic, gnostic, Jewish or Christian, bear such a distinct, and perhaps disturbing, family likeness? Now that question may well surprise you because it presupposes an observation that few are ready to make in so explicit and stark a form. But to my mind it is inescapable.

From this distance, it looks as though the structure of the universe underlying the argument between Origen and Celsus is much the same, even though they contest many details. So is the structure of Valentinian Gnosticism and other systems. And, surprising though it may seem, so is the structure of Judaism. All presuppose a hierarchy, with one God at the apex, and a ladder of descending beings, divine, angelic, spiritual, cosmic, and earthly. The bones of contention lie around two questions: the evaluation of the material and carnal side of existence, and the proper object of worship. Thus, to illustrate briefly the latter point, Celsus, and later a neo-Platonist like Porphyry, would argue that the supreme transcendent God is worshipped by pursuing the traditional polytheistic rituals – you honour the ultimate source of all Being through honouring the local gods and daemons that are more accessible; whereas Origen, like the Jews, would argue that only the one true God is to be worshipped, even though there are many angelic beings which are God's servants. And as for the former issue, the Gnostics would regard themselves as belonging to the transcendent divine world, awaiting redemption from material existence; Irenaeus would affirm the goodness of God's material creation; Origen would try to have it both ways.

My point is this: though there were areas of contention, they all belonged to a hierarchically conceived universe, and where Christ, or the Logos, was important, he took his place within the hierarchy. Exactly what that place was might be contested, between Gnostics and Christians, between a critic like Celsus and his Christian respondent, even between different groups claiming to be Christian. But that he had a place in a hierarchy of beings would be simply assumed.

So why did Paul and the earliest Christians not see their confessions concerning Christ as a threat to monotheism? And why do the various systems of the second-third centuries, whether philosophical, syncretistic, gnostic, Jewish or Christian, bear such a family likeness? The answer to both questions is the same: there was at this stage a common fuzziness about the distinction between God and everything else. Divinity was not clearly distinct from other orders of being. Gods might emerge through the apotheosis of human heroes and divine rulers – that was the well-known Euhemeran theory of religion, and Celsus and Origen threw it at each other, *mutatis mutandis*. Souls were eternal and in their own way divine. God's immanence, even in Judaism, was mediated through angels who had names deriving from divine attributes, and through human prophets and righteous men who were God's sons, embodying God's Word, Wisdom or Spirit; indeed Enoch was assumed to heaven like any other 'divine man'. The hierarchical structure of belief meant a common blurring of the line between the one God at the apex and the rest, between the divine and the human; or rather a failure to perceive that such a line might be there at all. Only when that line was clarified was there any real Christological problem as such.

2. My second observation is this: the first contested issue in Christian theology was what we would call the doctrine of creation.

It is often assumed that the notion of creation *ex nihilo* was inherited by the Christian church from its Jewish matrix. But there are serious problems with that assumption, as an increasing number of scholars are recognising[1]. It was only in confrontation with Greek cosmological theories that the doctrine emerged explicitly within Judaism, and there was little interest in it before the Middle Ages. Christians of the second century were as unclear as is scripture itself, Justin Martyr, for example, presupposing that God created out of formless matter; as indeed the Jewish philosopher, Philo, seems to have assumed before him, despite the ambiguity of some of his language. Both simply followed a set of Platonist assumptions without question.

---

1. Cf. J.R. LYMAN, *Christology and Cosmology: Models of Divine Activity in Origen, Eusebius, and Athanasius*, Oxford, Clarendon, 1993; G. MAY, *Creatio ex nihilo: The Doctrine of 'Creation out of Nothing' in Early Christian Thought*, Edinburgh, T. & T. Clark, 1994; F. YOUNG, *'Creation ex Nihilo': A Context for the Emergence of the Christian Doctrine of Creation*, in *Scottish Journal of Theology* 44 (1991) 139-151.

Retrospective light is thrown on the second century by the clearest statement we have of the possible alternatives, namely that of Tertullian. Against Hermogenes, a fellow-Christian whose views Tertullian lambasts, he affirms that God did not create out of the divine self, nor out of eternal co-existing matter; if it was neither out of God's self nor out of something else, it must have been out of nothing. The same options had apparently been reviewed by Hermogenes himself, and he had given good reasons for adopting the Platonist answer of Philo and Justin.

It is worth taking a moment or two to consider how what I have called the 'Platonist' view was reached. Plato believed in the eternity of the universe. Reality was an eternal interaction between Mind, Matter and Form. Matter was the somewhat recalcitrant medium, or receptacle, of the form or idea which gave it shape and thus brought something into being. The *Timaeus* expressed this by means of a myth which represented Mind as the Demiurge, the cosmic craftsman, who acted like a sculptor giving shape to a block of stone. Taken literally this myth was interpreted by Platonists from a Jewish or Christian background as an account of beginnings commensurate with that in the book of Genesis. Instead of being eternal, the universe came into being through the will and act of the Creator, the Demiurge. It is notable that the term 'Demiurge' is used consistently in early Christian literature when reference is made to God as Creator – it was not, as some textbooks almost seem to imply, a specially Gnostic term.

In the Gnostic systems, of course, the term is used for the fallen God who created the material universe. For them matter was a disaster. The recalcitrant medium, often treated in rather negative terms in Platonism, has become evil, a prison from which salvation is escape. In Platonism itself formless matter was in a sense notional – it was 'infinite' in the sense of 'indefinite', and therefore 'non-existent' in the sense that there was nothing there in particular; unformed matter could be called 'non-being'. Yet there was something. Typical is the view of Plutarch:

> For creation does not take place out of what does not exist at all but rather out of what is in an improper or unfulfilled state, as in the case of a house or a garment or a statue. For the state that things were in before the creation of the ordered may be characterised as 'lack of order' (akosmia); and this 'lack of order' was not something incorporeal or immobile or soul-less, but rather it possessed a corporeal nature which was formless and inconstant, and a power of motion which was frantic and irrational. (*On the Creation of the Soul in the Timaeus* 1014B.)

Thus everything came from something. 'Nothing comes from nothing' was a Greek commonplace, and implied that anything coming from nothing was a sham!

Now it has been argued that that indeed was the view of early Christians who adopted the *ex nihilo* idea: they were awaiting the end of the world, and all, especially the martyrs, looked to another world as more real. Some Christians in the second century no doubt did take what we might call a docetic view of the world; and certainly some Gnostics may have thought in such terms – Basilides has been claimed as the originator of the *ex nihilo* doctrine by at least one scholar. But the argument of Tertullian already outlined, and second-century precedents to which we will turn, suggest that this was by no means the intention of those who argued that God created out of nothing; far from the unreality of the world lying behind the doctrine of creation 'out of nothing', the main motive was to affirm the power and sovereignty of the one true God who was to be identified as Creator of all.

Theophilus of Antioch is the author whose work clarifies this for us. In *Ad Autolycum* II.4 we read as follows:

> Plato and his followers acknowledge that God is uncreated, the Father and Maker of the universe; next they assume that uncreated matter is also God, and say that matter was coeval with God. But if God is uncreated and matter is uncreated, then according to the Platonists God is not the Maker of the universe, and as far as they are concerned the unique sovereignty (*monarchia*) of God is not established.

This term *monarchia* is significant. It meant sovereignty, but also implied the sole first principle – the only *arche*, source or beginning. Theophilus goes on to ask:

> What would be remarkable if God made the world out of pre- existent matter? Even a human artisan, when he obtains material from someone, makes whatever he wishes out of it. But the power of God is revealed by his making whatever he wishes out of the non-existent, just as the ability to give life and motion belongs to no-one but God alone.

In other words, God is greater than a human craftsman in not needing wood or stone or whatever to work with. Furthermore God alone can bestow life on his artefacts. Thus God is more powerful than man, as in making something endowed with reason, life and sensation, so also in making

> the existent out of the non-existent; he made whatever he wished in whatever way he wished.

Evidently Theophilus is directly confronting Platonism, possibly even the same Hermogenes as Tertullian. The denial of the existence of eternal matter was an explicit rejection of the Platonist assumption, and its grounds lay in the need to affirm the absolute priority of God. You could not have two eternal first principles without having two divine beings of some sort. So everything had to be contingent upon the will of the one true God who was the sole first principle. That was the only way of staying true to the tradition of scripture when confronted with Platonist presuppositions.

That then is one side of the debate, and the conclusion was that God could not have created out of pre-existent matter. The other side concerned the notion that God might have created out of the divine self. Emanation from the divine seems to have been a common notion, and it is certainly reflected in the Gnostic systems. The whole spiritual *pleroma* emerges from the ultimate Bythos or Depth which is the Forefather of all the aeons, or eternal beings. Such a system implies that everything is in a sense divine – monism rather than monotheism. It then has to explain why everything falls short of the divine nature, and in particular why what is inherently divine has apparently got trapped in material existence. Hence the Gnostic myths of pre-cosmic fall, and their tendency to welcome a docetic view of the material universe. Creation out of the divine self lay at the heart of those systems which Irenaeus and others had exposed as deeply antipathetic to scripture and tradition. For Tertullian, as indeed for Hermogenes, it was an impossible option because it implied partition of the indivisible divine nature. Creation 'out of nothing', with all its difficulties and potential for misunderstanding, was the only viable conclusion.

The struggle of the second century, then, revolved around the doctrine of creation. But the full consequences of the adoption of the formula *creatio ex nihilo* would take a long time to work out. Origen, Platonist though he was, accepted the doctrine. But he argued that if God was Creator and God was unchangeable, God must always have been Creator and therefore creation must be as eternal as the One who created it; he used the same argument, of course, to establish the eternal generation of the Son from the Father. He conceived an eternal hierarchy, as we noted earlier. The material creation came into being out of nothing with time, and was God's answer to the problem of disobedience in the eternal spiritual creation. So far the principal outcome of challenging prevailing assumptions with the notion of God's power to create out of nothing was to establish the goodness of the material creation; for creation was grounded in God's providential will. Further consequences, such as the radical difference between the Creator and every creature, whether spiritual or material, angelic or human, would take more time to emerge.

The most important point to note from this, my second, observation is this: the doctrine of creation out of nothing expressed, in terms that related to contemporary Greek philosophical discussions about origins, a fundamental element in the Christian view of God. In those little letters attributed to Paul which we know as the Pastorals, right through the works we refer to as the Apostolic Fathers, and on into the second-century apologetic literature, God is presented as having universal oversight of all that goes on, even in the mind and heart, as the one who will ultimately judge all according to the divine laws of justice and righteousness God himself has established, as the sovereign of all who not only brought all things into being originally but will again bring everything into being at the resurrection when everyone will answer for what they have done. Such a God could not in the end be

> conceived as ontologically intertwined with the world, as he was in Stoicism, in Pseudo-Aristotle's *De Mundo*, and most contemporary cosmologies. Nor was he simply the active principle in relation to a passive principle. God became independent of the world as its sole *arche*, its 'sovereign' as well as its 'beginning'. Furthermore, God was not subject to necessity but free, and that was a better and more biblical grounding for his transcendence and impassibility than a mere adoption of Platonic axioms. He was conceived as containing all things while not being himself contained: thus even before Plotinus, indeed in Irenaeus, the concept of God's infinity began to be grasped[2].

3. My third observation is this: Logos-theology was less about a claim to uniqueness than a claim to belong to the universal.

Now this observation is clearly related to those that have gone before; for both the emphasis on one God, the source of all, and the blurring of distinctions between what is divine and what is not are evident in this doctrine. The Logos easily came to be conceived as *a* being within the hierarchy. My argument would be that this undermined the structure of the doctrine, which was not about *a particular being at all*. Ultimately this becomes apparent when the two features already discussed came into collision with one another, as they were bound to do. But that is to anticipate my fourth observation.

Before developing that, we must examine more carefully the universalist thrust of the Logos-doctrine. The whole point about the arguments of the second-century Apologists is that they have knowledge of the one true God who is the sole source and sovereign of the entire universe – so what they have to say has universal applicability. Furthermore they have access to what this God has revealed for the benefit of all humankind. The instrument of this revelation is God's own Logos. This Logos is

---

2. YOUNG, *'Creation ex nihilo': A Context for the Emergence of the Christian Doctrine of Creation*, pp. 150-151.

universal – indeed is in a sense divine immanence in the creation, present in all human rationality, known to Socrates, spoken through the prophets, incarnate in Jesus who is thus the embodiment of all truth and goodness, not so much exclusively as inclusively.

In other words, there are two inseparable aspects of the Logos as conceived by Justin, Theophilus and others. On the one hand, the Logos is the very Reason and Mind of God, God being conceived as a transcendent rational being who, as we have seen, is the supreme sovereign. Since everything in all creation comes under God's purview, there is nothing that escapes divine notice; and everything is universally directed by divine providential purpose, which is naturally a function of the divine Mind. The oversight of the Logos must be universal since that is the way things are, and it was according to the ideas and plans in God's Mind that everything was brought into being in the first place. Everything is ordered according to the Wisdom of the Creator. On the other hand, that Wisdom is built into everything God made. Both the rational order underlying the cosmos as a whole and the rationality in rational creatures derives its being from divine rationality. Logos-theology was therefore about the immanence of the divine. True this was subject to distortion because of the disobedience and folly that had afflicted humanity, so generating falsehood, irrationality, idolatry and wickedness. Nevertheless, wherever there was truth and goodness, it ultimately came from the immanent Logos of God, and anticipated the full revelation of the Logos in Jesus Christ.

As already noted, this was inclusive not exclusive. That it was understood to be inclusive is, I think, proven by what we find later in the theology of Athanasius. A passage from the *Contra Gentes* shows that the Logos is universal in both the senses I have indicated – it is because particulars participate in the Logos as universal principle of wisdom, rationality, life and holiness that they have those attributes. The universal principle (or Platonic absolute) is not just another instance of these things; as the principle which makes possible the participation of other entities in itself, it is essentially different. In other words it is both universal and inclusive precisely because it is impossible to separate out its immanence in creation and its transcendence as God's own Wisdom and Word. I quote:

> Being with [God] as wisdom, and as Word seeing the Father, he created the universe, formed it, and ordered it; and being the power of the Father, he gave all things the strength to come into existence... His holy disciples teach that everything was created through him and for him, and that being the good offspring of a good Father and true Son, he is the power of the

> Father and his wisdom and Word, not by participation... but he is absolute wisdom, very Word, and himself the Father's own power, absolute light, absolute truth, absolute justice, absolute virtue, and indeed stamp, effulgence and image. In short, he is the supremely perfect issue of the Father, and is alone Son, the express image of the Father.....[H]e is the Word and wisdom of the Father, and at the same time condescends to created beings; to give them knowledge and an idea of [the Father], he is absolute holiness and absolute life, he is door, shepherd and way, king, guide and saviour for all, life-giver and light and universal providence (*Contra Gentes* ii. 46-7).

In the end for Athanasius the universality of the Logos is the lynch-pin of his soteriology. The humanity of Christ is itself universal, and it was the universal restoration of the Logos to humanity in Christ which enabled the participation of particular human beings in this new creation. The absolute Son and Heir makes possible particular sons and heirs (of both genders!). Logos-theology, I suggest, always had an inclusivist thrust. (I would myself argue for an exegesis of John's Gospel which takes the Logos as comprehensively embracing all in human culture and experience that speaks of God, and therefore refuses to interpret the claim that Jesus is the way, the truth and the life in an exclusivist way.)

But there is another feature of Patristic texts that also confirms the universalist ring of the Logos-doctrine, and links directly with the theme of this conference, *The Myriad Christ*. Maybe you noted in the quotation from Athanasius the many different epithets given to the Logos: he was designated not just Word and Wisdom, but Power, Light, Truth, Justice, Virtue, Holiness, Life, Door, Shepherd, Way, King, Guide, Saviour. This multiplicity of 'names' is clearly derived from scripture, not least the Gospel of John, and it is characteristic of homiletic material over many centuries. There the assembly of metaphors and their allegorical interpretation is often striking and extraordinary.

But here let me just remind you of the first book of Origen's *Commentary on John*. For Origen the exposition of the Gospel's prologue, and therefore of the meaning of *logos*, requires a survey of all the *epinoiai* attributed to Christ. His list includes all those we noted in Athanasius together with Son of God, Righteousness, Propitiation, First-born of the dead, Physician, Healer, Redemption, Resurrection, Messiah, Christ, Lord, Vine, Bread of Life, the Living One, Alpha and Omega – First and Last, Beginning and End, Lion of Judah, Jacob/Israel, Rod, Flower, Stone, a Chosen Shaft, Sword, Servant of God, Light of the Gentiles, Lamb of God, Paraclete, Sanctification, High-Priest. Each is given elaborate exegesis. For Origen all these 'names' are taken 'for our sakes', and you cannot say that the Saviour is metaphorically a Stone and literally Word. All have meaningful content. Christ is whatever he needs to be so as to relate to the multiplicity of creatures.

And that is what is fundamentally important: for underlying Origen's discussion there seems to be the philosophical struggle to understand how 'the Many' could be derived from 'the One', and the Logos for Origen is the required missing link, the being which is both One and Many, a complex unity which shares Oneness with God and multiplicity with the creation. This Logos is therefore universal by being 'myriad'.

4. But the moment has come to pick up the point anticipated a while ago, and move to my fourth observation. What the Arian controversy did was to expose the inconsistencies and problems inherent in the three elements we have already explored. The evolutionary model which posits 'development of doctrine' is inadequate, because post-Nicene theology had to be innovative, but it was innovative precisely in taking account of the consequences of elements in Christian theology perceived to be key to its structure. Let me explain what I mean.

Creatio ex nihilo meant a radical distinction between what is divine and what is creaturely. But pre-Nicene Logos-theology worked precisely by avoiding such a distinction. It was the very role of the Logos to be a mediator between different levels in a hierarchy of Beings, a continuous ladder of existence with no break point, a universe in which there was the kind of blurring between the divine and the creaturely we first explored. There is a sense in which the question where you draw the line between Creator and created was never explicitly put by either side in the Arian controversy and historians may argue about whether it was implicit in Arius' challenge or Athanasius' reply. But my observation is more systematic than historical. The issue between Arius and Athanasius was whether the Logos incarnate in Jesus belongs to the divine or created order, a question which was bound to shatter the traditional Logos-theology and create what we know as the Christological problem.

Rather than giving yet another account of the theological and Christological struggles of the fourth and fifth centuries, let me give an example of the theology of mediation that emerged as a result. The position sketched is certainly that of the Cappadocians, but their work is voluminous and wordy. So instead I turn to the more economical presentation that we find in the poems of Ephrem the Syrian. Perhaps the poetic medium itself is significant, for it earths theological abstraction in the language of reverence and worship. It also demonstrates the way in which continuities with the old Logos theology were maintained in a new and vibrant grasp of what incarnation really meant – you will recognise Origen's 'myriad Christ'.

(a) In the case of the Godhead, what created being is able to investigate Him?
For there is a great chasm between him and the Creator.
(On Faith 69.11; Brock, 1985, p.49)

(b) Who is so stupid and stubborn as to suppose, even just a little,
that because human beings have been called by names that belong to God,
that the nature of man and of God is consequently one,
or that, because the Lord has also been called by a name appropriate to his servants,
that we should weigh with a single comparison both what is made and its Maker.
When God called us 'king', using the name appropriate to Himself,
the true use remains with Him, the likeness applies to us.
But when again He called himself by a name appropriate to his servants,
the natural usage lies with us, but the appellation with Him.
The true name needs to be recognized and the borrowed name needs to be recognized,
both in His case and in ours.
Accordingly, in His mercy, He provided for the discerning among His creatures
His various names – not to be investigated, but to be savoured and enjoyed.
So, brethren, let prying dry up and let us multiply prayers,
for though He is not related to us, He is as though of our race,
and though He is utterly separate, yet He is over all and in all.
(On Faith 63. 9-11; Brock, 1985, p. 47)

(c) God has names that are perfect and exact,
and He has names that are borrowed and transient.
(On Faith 44. 2; Brock, 1985, p. 45)

(d) Let us give thanks to God who clothed Himself in the names of the body's various parts:
Scripture referes to His 'ears', to teach us that He listens to us;
it speaks of His 'eyes', to show that He sees us.
It was just the names of such things that He put on,
and, although in His true Being there is no wrath or regret,
yet He put on these names too because of our weakness.

Refrain:
Blessed is He who has appeared to our human race under so many metaphors.
We should realize that, had He not put on the names
of such things, it would not have been possible for Him
to speak with us humans. By means of what belongs to us did He draw close to us:
He clothed Himself in our language, so that He might clothe us
in His mode of life. He asked for our form and put this on,
and then, as a father with his children, He spoke with our childish state.
It is our metaphors that He put on – though he did not literally do so;

> He then took them off – without actually doing so: when wearing
> them, He was at the same time stripped of them.
> He puts one on when it is beneficial, then strips it off in exchange for
> another;
> The fact that He strips off and puts on all sorts of metaphors
> tells us that the metaphor does not apply to His true Being:
> because that Being is hidden, He has depicted it by means of what is
> visible.
>
> (*On Faith* 31. 1-3)[3]

The gulf between God and the created order is now fundamental, and the bridging of that gulf has to be an act of the divine will issuing from divine condescension and love. The person and work of Christ has to be re-conceived within such a framework. But all along that issue had been implicit though unrecognised – that is why I claimed not to offer an interpretation shaped by origins or ends.

So did the Logos incarnate in Jesus belong to the divine or created order? The Arian answer that he was the first and greatest of the creatures was firmly ruled out: for the Logos was God's own Mind and Reason and to posit another creaturely Logos was to end up with two Logoi. But at the same time, it was humanity which was renewed and recreated by being re-endowed with the Logos, and that humanity belongs firmly among the creatures called into being out of nothing. Mediation and incarnation now had to involve the marrying of apparent incompatibles, the union without confusion of two natures. Yet for all its problems, only such a paradoxical Christology could do justice to key elements in the structure of Christian theology. The incarnate Logos somehow belonged both to the divine and the created order.

5. So pulling all this together my final observation is this: structurally patristic Christology is the resolution of the question how the Creator relates to the creation.

God is and is not present everywhere in the created order. Indeed it may be argued that the absence and presence of God are both necessary for the universe to exist – for the infinite God could only create by withdrawing and so allowing something other than the divine self to come into being out of nothing. Simone Weil spoke of the act of creation as an act of abandonment. And when Jesus cries out on the cross, 'My God, my God, why hast thou forsaken me?', do we not most dramatically find ourselves confronted with the paradoxically simultaneous absence and presence of God?

3. S. BROCK, *The Luminous Eye: The Spiritual World Vision of St. Ephrem*, Placid Lectures, Rome, C.I.I.S., 1985, pp. 43-44.

Within the structure of Christian theology Christology is the lynchpin. Christ is, and is not, God. The words of men in scripture are not, and yet are, the Word of God. The bread and wine of the eucharist is bread and wine, and yet also the Body and Blood of Christ. The church is the Body of Christ and yet a flawed human institution. The two natures may never be confused; yet they interpenetrate in ways beyond human analysis.

Now all this means that Christology constitutes an affirmation of Christian monotheism and not the threat it is so often perceived to be. It is the divine Creator, not some other divine being, who is immanent in the creaturely human being, realising the image of God in humanity. It is humanity which is divinised in Christ, thus enabling particular humans to become fellow-heirs with Christ. This Christ can and must have universal significance: for he is identified as Creator and identified with the human creature which God intended, the universal in whom human particulars may find their ultimate destiny.

Footnote: What I have just said presupposes the doctrine of the Trinity. It offers a challenge to social or tritheistic forms of that doctrine, while acknowledging also the inadequacies of Modalism. Trinitarianism cannot be divorced from Christology, but to deal with that too must lie outside the scope of this paper.

III. TOWARDS APPROPRIATION

My agenda included an attempt to appropriate this, to draw out connections or suggest areas of dialogue between the subject of this conference and the interpretation I was to offer. Clearly all I can do in conclusion is to throw out some hints as to possible lines of exploration.

1. Within the plurality of religions in the modern world Christology is usually perceived as a rock of offense because of the claim to Christ's uniqueness. But comprehensiveness was fundamental to Logos-theology and is implied in claims to the universal significance of the incarnation for humanity. Doesn't that comprehensiveness demand of Christian theology a greater openness than it is often prepared to admit?

2. Discussion of the figure of Christ which is simply conducted at the level of parallel prophets, holy men, gurus, is not without precedent. The Euhemeran theory of religion went both ways in ancient argument; and the earliest Christologies certainly blurred the distinction between the divine and human as have many philosophies and religions of ancient and modern times. But what does it mean for modern inter-religious dialogue that such lines of thought came to a dead end?

It certainly challenges Christian participants to avoid getting hung-up on rival claims about Christ or Mohammed being the final prophet, or wrangles about Jesus Christ being the Son of God in the ambiguous, and implicitly hierarchical, sense of early (and most popular) Christianity. For it is a reduction of what Christology is about to let such issues dominate the discussion. In fact there is a sense in which the person of Christ and the status of this particular historical individual known as Jesus is only part of the issue.

3. The real issue concerns God and the universe – on the one hand, the uniqueness of God in the sense of the divine Oneness and utter Otherness, on the other hand, the contingency of the created order, which is creaturely and not divine except by participation or adoption.

That the universe is created must either be the case or not. There are many who do not share such a view of the cosmos, both non-religious and religious people. Creation may be a fundamental tenet Christians share with Jews and Moslems, but when it comes to other faiths such as Hinduism and Buddhism, this is the crucial divide. The problem with all monotheisms is their tendency towards monism, their difficulties with diversity. Pluralism challenges this directly and profoundly. Is there a universe, let alone a God who created it?

Christology is but an element in that much bigger issue. Focussing on Christology without setting it in its structural context within Christian theology as a whole can distort the issues – as if the figure of Christ could simply be reassessed, or Chalcedon straightforwardly challenged or reaffirmed, without attending to the consequences for the whole structure of Christian belief from beginning to end.

If the claims of Jews, Christians and Moslems are true, then the whole diverse and pluralist society of the globe is somehow God's, whether others recognise it or not. If those claims are not true, then monotheisms will surely die as the Greek myths did. The key theological issue remains the question how we maintain belief in one God and one universe while also embracing the reality of pluralism. We are back with the problem of the One and the Many.

So maybe patristic Christology provides us with a model to work with after all. Of course those who do not accept the monotheistic hermeneutic of the world, or who seek to resolve its problems within other traditions, are not likely to be convinced; but what we seek is a way forward that both respects the other as other and does justice to our own tradition. What our own tradition affirms is that, in the person of Jesus Christ, the one God who created the universe in all its diversity and plurality has, in freedom and by grace, entered into costly and loving engagement with creatures contingent upon the divine will.

University of Birmingham   Frances YOUNG
Edgbaston, Birmingham
B15 2TT
United Kingdom

"GOD BECAME HUMAN IN ORDER THAT HUMANS MIGHT BECOME GOD"
A REFLECTION ON THE SOTERIOLOGICAL DOCTRINE OF DIVINIZATION

I. INTRODUCTION

The soteriological doctrine of divinization can best be summarized in the aphoristic expression that "(in Christ) God became human in order that humans might become God"[1]. The idea is deeply rooted in both Greek and Latin patristic theology[2]. It is also present in the later theological traditions of both East and West[3]. In the Orthodox Churches today it is still both a lived reality and an important part of theology. And as the literature cited in this article indicates, it has received much attention in recent literature. The foundation of this doctrine is christological: our salvation is warranted, or guaranteed by Christ's becoming human. This salvific process is conceived of as 'becoming divine', as divinization. It is essentially Christian, since it is founded on the Incarnation of Christ, who is understood to be our Savior. Nevertheless, it could be argued that the idea of salvation, as a process of becoming "divine" by receiving divine grace, is an experience founded on a more

---

1. We find the expression for the first time in IRENAEUS, *Adversus Haereses*, V, preface, ed. A. ROUSSEAU (SC, 153), Paris, Cerf, 1969, pp. 14-15. Later we find it also *inter alia* in ATHANASIUS, *De Incarnatione Verbi* 54, ed. R.W. THOMSON, *Contra Gentes and De Incarnatione* (Oxford Early Christian Texts), Oxford, Clarendon, 1971, pp. 268-269 and in GREGORY OF NAZIANZE, *Poema Dogmatica* 10, 5-9 (ed. *PG* 37, col. 465); GREGORY OF NYSSA, *Oratio Catechetica Magna* 25; (ed. *PG* 45, col. 65).

2. I.-H. DALMAIS, art. *Divinisation. II. Patristique grecque*, in *DSpir* 3 (1954), col. 1376-1389; 1376; B. STUDER, art. *Divinization*, in A. DI BERARDINO (ed.), *Encyclopedia of the Early Church*, Cambridge, J. Clarke 1992, vol. I, pp. 242-243, p. 242; M. GEORGE, *Vergöttlichung des Menschen. Von der platonischen Philosophie zur Soteriologie der griechischen Kirchenväter*, in D. WYRWA – B. ALAND – C. SCHÄUBLIN (eds.), *Die Weltlichkeit des Glaubens in der Alten Kirche. FS U. Wickert* (BZNW, 85), Berlin – New York, De Gruyter, 1997, 115-157.

3. On Maximus Confessor see J.C. LARCHET, *La divinisation de l'homme selon saint Maxime le Confesseur* (Cogitatio Fidei, 194), Paris, Cerf, 1996; for Thomas Aquinas see the article by A.N. WILLIAMS, *Deification in the* Summa Theologiae*: A Structural Interpretation of the Prima Pars*, in *The Thomist* 61 (1997) 219-255. References to Luther and other authors of the Reformation in F.W. NORRIS, *Deification: Consensual and Cogent*, in *SJT* 49 (1996) 411-428. See for Luther also K. BAKKEN, *Holy Spirit and Theosis: Towards a Lutheran Theology of Healing*, in *St. Vladimir's Theological Quarterly* 38 (1994) 409-423.

general human experience of life, and that it is therefore open to, and relevant for, non-Christians as well.

Before this proposal can be investigated, some preliminary remarks concerning terminology ought to be made. From the time of Clement of Alexandria, the most commonly used term was *theopoièsis*. It was only with Pseudo-Dionysius[4] that the term *theosis* became more important. The equivalent Latin terms, *deificare* and *deificatio*, obtained only a rather modest importance from the fifth century onwards[5]. As a translation the synonyms "deification" and "divinization" are both possible[6]. However, there are two reasons to recommend the term divinization: (1) it denotes a more gradual process than deification, which sounds rather magical; (2) the term, deification, could be read as abolishing the distance between God and humanity, while all Eastern theologians, both ancient and modern, firmly reject any hint of pantheism in the interpretation of the concept of divinization. Whatever transformation this divinization brings about, humanity does not lose its human nature. So *theosis* or *theopoiesis* leads to a genuine union with God, while men and women retain their human nature. The distance between God and humanity is respected and not done away with.

We shall begin with the Scriptural basis for the idea of divinization. Then we shall discuss the place divinization held in the theology of Athanasius, for whom it was a very important concept. By way of conclusion, we shall provide an evaluation of the doctrine and an assessment of its relevance for people anno 2000. Can divinization be a meaningful answer for someone asking what it means to confess Jesus as their Lord and Savior?

II. The Scriptural Basis for the Concept of Divinization

The explicit Scriptural basis for the concept of divinization is very limited[7]. The most important and best known text is probably 2 Pe 1,3-4:

4. G.W.H. Lampe, *A Patristic Greek Lexicon*, Oxford, Clarendon, 1968, col. 630; 649.

5. B. Studer, art. *Divinization*, in A. Di Berardino (ed.), *Encyclopedia of the Early Church*, vol. I, p. 242. One example to illustrate this: in the entire corpus of Augustine's writings, *deificare, deificatio* and the like occur only fifteen times and in some of these cases not in relation to the doctrine of divinization (cf. G. Bonner, *Augustine's Conception of Deification*, in *JTS* 37 [1986] 369-386, p. 369).

6. In what follows we will use the translation divinization rather than deification, though these are synonyms (J. E. Simpson – E.S.C. Weiner (eds.), *The Oxford English Dictionary*, vol. IV, Oxford, Clarendon, 1989², p. 403 (s.v. 'deification') and p. 895 (s.v. divinization').

7. For a survey of the Scriptural basis of theosis, see D.B. Clendenin, *Partakers of Divinity: The Orthodox Doctrine of Theosis*, in *JETS* 37 (1994) 365-379, pp. 369-371;

"God's divine power has bestowed on us everything that makes for life and true religion, through our knowledge of him who called us by his own glory and goodness. In this way He has given us his promises, great beyond price, so that through them you may escape the corruption with which lust has infected the world, and may come to *share in the very being of God*"[8]. One might also refer to Ps 82,6-7 (though it is clear that v. 7 is problematic): "(v. 6) This is my sentence: 'Though *You are gods*, and all of you are sons of the Most High, (v. 7) yet you shall die as mortals die, and fall as any prince does'". (Another more or less direct text is Wisd 2,23 ("But God created man imperishable and made him the image of his own eternal self")). Being gods, or being partakers of the divine nature would appear to be scriptural content of the notion of divinization. But, of course, the textual support is obviously quite limited.

However, in the process of developing the doctrine, the patristic tradition adduced many other scriptural texts to buttress the theologoumenon of divinization. These included: man as the Image of God (Gen. 1, 26-27); divine sonship (Gal. 3,26; 4,5; Rom. 8,15); imitation of God (Mt. 5,44-48) and Christ (Phil. 2,5-11). Texts presenting the new life of Christians as a pledge and anticipation of future glory were also considered in this light (1 Cor. 13,12; 2 Cor. 3,18; 1 John 3,1-3)[9]. Later Orthodox theology extended this array of texts on divinization to include Moses' transfiguration on Sinai (Ex 34,30) or Peter's on Mount Tabor (Mt. 17,4). Another text which was often invoked to in the discussion of divinization, understood as unification or becoming one with God, is Paul's prohibition of fornication in 1 Cor 6,16-17: "You surely know that anyone who joins himself to a prostitute becomes physically one with her, for Scripture says: 'The two shall become one flesh'. *But anyone who joins*

---

for a critical reflection regarding the weakness of the explicit Scriptural basis of the doctrine of theosis, see B. DREWERY, *Deification*, in P. BROOKS (ed.), *Christian Spirituality. Essays in Honour of Gordon Rupp*, London, SCM, 1975, pp. 35-62.

8. This and other translations are from *The Revised English Bible with the Apocrypha*, Oxford – Cambridge, Oxford University Press – Cambridge University Press, 1989.

9. "At present we see only puzzling reflections in a mirror, but one day we will see face to face. My knowledge now is partial, then it will be whole, like God's knowledge of me" (1 Cor. 13,12); "And because for us there is no veil over the face, we all see as in a mirror the glory of the Lord, and we are being transformed into his likeness with ever increasing glory, through the power of the Lord who is the Spirit" (2 Cor. 3,18); "Consider how great is the love which the Father has bestowed on us in calling us his children! For that is what we are. The reason why the world does not recognize us is that it has not known him. Dear friends, we are now God's children; what we shall be has not yet been disclosed, but we know that when Christ appears we shall be like him, because we shall see him as he is. As he is pure, everyone who has grasped this hope makes himself pure" (1 John 3,1-3).

himself to the Lord is one with him spiritually". One final text which deserves to be mentioned is Gal 3,28: "There is no such thing as Jew and Greek, slave and freeman, male and female; for you are all one person in Jesus Christ". It is precisely by attaining divine likeness through divinization that we transcend these and other differences.

It can then be argued that the doctrine of divinization is not unscriptural though, strictly speaking, its biblical foundations are weak. In view of this weak biblical foundation, some authors downplay its value[10]. However, it can be argued that the weaving of adjacent themes into the concept of divinization enriched reflection on the topic and contributed to making it a richer, multifaceted doctrine.

An author for whom divinization was an important theological theme, and who exercised a profound influence on its later development, was Athanasius of Alexandria. He deserves separate treatment.

III. DIVINIZATION IN THE THEOLOGY OF ATHANASIUS OF ALEXANDRIA

Athanasius became bishop of Alexandria in 328 after a much disputed election. Despite five "exiles" – periods during which he was forced to leave his see temporarily and was not able to govern his diocese – he held this see until his death in 373. Athanasius is most often portrayed as the defender of the *homoousios*, of the consubstantiality of the Father and the Son. This portrayal is essentially correct, though *homoousios* did not really become his catchword until after 350. However, it would be unfair to narrow down his theology to this tenet alone. A full exposition of his life, works and theology is beyond the scope of this paper[11]. We

---

10. B. DREWERY, *Deification* (n.7).

11. The last decade has see the publication of a number of good biographical accounts. Regarding Athanasius' activity on the stage of international ecclesiastical affairs, see A. RIALL, *Athanasius of Alexandria: The Politics of Spirituality*, unpublished dissertation, Univ. of Cincinatti; T.D. BARNES, *Athanasius and Constantius. Theology and Politics in the Constantinian Empire*, Cambridge (Mass.) – London, Harvard University Press, 1993. Other studies focus on Athanasius as the leader of Egyptian Christianity and his dealings with the various forms of ascetic life: A. MARTIN, *Athanase d'Alexandrie et l'Église de l'Égypte en IVᵉ siècle* (Collection de l'École Française de Rome, 216), Paris – Rome, Boccard – Bretschneider, 1996; C.BADGER, *The New Man Created in God. Christology, Congregation and Asceticism in Athanasius of Alexandria*, unpublished dissertation Duke University, 1990; D. BRAKKE, *Athanasius and the Politics of Asceticism* (Oxford Early Christian Studies), Oxford, Oxford University Press, 1995. Good surveys of Athanasius' theology are A. PETTERSEN, *Athanasius* (Outstanding Christian Thinkers), London, Chapman, 1995 and K. ANATOLIOS, *Athanasius: The Coherence of His Thought* (Routledge Early Church Monographs), London-New York, Routledge, 1998. See also the bibliography by C. BUTTERWECK, *Athanasius von Alexandrien. Bibliographie*

must limit ourselves to highlighting the place of the "doctrine" of divinization in his theology and explaining why it was important to him, although it will become clear that the concept as such was not sharply defined in his works.

The background for Athanasius' salvation theology, as it is sketched in the double work *Contra Gentes-De Incarnatione Verbi*, his first great dogmatic writing[12], can be summarized as follows. According to Athanasius there exists an unbridgeable gap between the divine realm and the created realm. In contrast to the divine realm, the world of created beings is characterized by corruptibility, changeability, instability, imperfection, mortality and so forth. Humankind was created in the image of the Logos (who himself is the image of the Father), in contemplative union with God and with the gifts of immortality and incorruption. On the level of their nature they remained corruptible but, as created in the divine image, this original nature was, so to speak, not changed but superseded. However, humanity transgressed the divine law and, as a consequence of this sin, became corruptible again. In view of this situation, the Logos assumed a human body and came into the world to save fallen humanity. By the Incarnation itself, the Logos, both fully human and fully divine, confers upon humankind the potential for restoration in his image[13].

To understand fully the pivotal role of the Incarnation in Athanasius' soteriology, one must take into account that Athanasius worked with a concept of humanity very different from ours. In the Alexandrian tradition, being human primarily meant being receptive to the divine. Human agency, moral responsibility, personal identity etc., was not their first concern. Athanasius presents Christ's human receptivity as a climax in the economy of God's giving of grace. This economy of grace is a real communication of the divine with the human, which takes place in and through the Logos Incarnate. The giving of grace belongs to the divine realm, the receiving to the created realm. Both are completely different, but the Logos Incarnate unites the two in his person: in his divinity he

---

(Abhandlungen der Nordrhein-Westfälischen Akademie der Wissenschaften, 90), Opladen, Westdeutscher Verlag, 1995.

12. For the status quaestionis of the ongoing debate on the date of this work, see J. LEEMANS, *Thirteen Years of Research on Athanasius (1985-1999): a Survey and a Bibliography*, in *Sacris Erudiri* 40 (2000), forthcoming.

13. L. SCHEFFCZYK, *Urstand, Fall und Erbsünde. Von der Schrift bis Augustin* (Handbuch der Dogmengeschichte II 3a), Freiburg-Basel-Wien, Herder, 1981, pp. 124-130; E. CONTRERAS, *Elementos di antropologia teologica cristiana en el "De Incarnatione Verbi" de San Atanasio*, in *Stromata* 46 (1990) 361-395; M. STAVROU, *L'anthropologie de saint Athanase d' Alexandrie dans le De Incarnatione et les Discours contre les Ariens*, in *Contacts* 44 (1992) 187-207.

mediates divine grace and in his human nature he receives it on our behalf. And by virtue of his divinity he receives it in a perfect way. This grace is the Holy Spirit and thus the Incarnation of the Logos provides the foundation for our salvation[14].

However, the Incarnation should not be stressed too much as a soteriological act in itself. It is not by the act of Christ's taking a human body alone, but by his entire life, death and resurrection[15] that He reopened the path to salvation, a path which humanity had closed to itself by the Fall. Athanasius does not mean to say that humanity is hereby restored to its prelapsarian state. This would include the ever-present possibility of a new Fall. In Athanasius' view, the effects of the Incarnation are more definitive. One can distinguish two effects of the Incarnation that are keysoteriological themes in Athanasius' theology, namely, the manifestation of knowledge about God (relating to the mind) and the reversal of corporeal corruption (relating to the body). In the double work *Contra Gentes – De Incarnatione Verbi*, Athanasius characterizes the achievement of Christ as "the two ways God had compassion on us". In the *Contra Arianos* the accent is on the body of Christ. The salvific functioning of Christ's assumption of a human body is highlighted under two aspects. The Incarnation *in se*, like a kind of automatic infusion of divine essence into dissipated humanity, is only the *structure* of the saving act. It is through the progressive history of the Incarnated Word's achievements, including the cross, resurrection and ascension, that grace is established in the assumed body. This assumed body, with its accumulated grace, so to speak, becomes the medium and the conduit for human salvation[16]. Through participation in the Logos' assumed body, we can partake of this divine grace and become deified. Thanks to the double nature of the Logos, we are able to participate in the giving and receiving of divine grace which takes place in him, and so become "similar to Christ". Christ has restored for us the gateway to the heavenly feast, but we still must travel the road towards it.

In this process of becoming divinized, the Incarnated Logos is our warrant and foundation. What the Son is by nature, people must become by grace. We are brought into a holy communion with God and with one another, through the grace secured in and through Christ's assumed humanity. In this process, people, as fallible and mortal creatures, are transformed. It is a gradual process, which begins when a person accepts

14. K. ANATOLIOS, *The Soteriological Significance of Christ's Humanity in St. Athanasius*, in *St. Vladimir's Theological Quarterly* 40 (1996) 265-287.
15. G. BEBAWI, *St. Athanasios: The Dynamics of Salvation*, in *Sobornost* 8 (1986) 24-41.
16. C. BADGER, *The New Man Created in God* (n. 11).

Christ as His Lord and becomes a member of the Church by baptism. The process continues throughout one's lifetime and is perfected in the life to come. In this process, the Spirit, as Paraclete and inspiration, acts to guide and inspire. Athanasius felt that it was his duty, as a bishop, to guide his flock in this process and to encourage them to persevere. He sought to relate the gradual process of divinization, understood as a response to the divine offer of grace, to the concrete reality of daily life.

Athanasius' communication with his flock regarding the process of divinization, of becoming "similar to Christ", takes place on two different wavelengths, so to speak, and was directed to two different audiences: on the one hand, to "ordinary Christians", and, on the other, to "professional ascetics". In his yearly *Festal Letter*[17], Athanasius translated these soteriological and christological themes into a pastoral program for the ordinary Christian. He outlined how the celebration of the feast of Easter should be seen as a process, an event by which the believer lays hold of grace. It is a key medium both for the individual believer and the community to "advance" in the Christian, i.e., the ascetic life. In his *Festal Letters* he encouraged Christians to imitate the saints and to struggle in their progress towards the heavenly feast. Everyone can appropriate the benefits achieved in Jesus' incarnate ministry. The imitation of the saints is firmly rooted in Christ's own achievement. In the *Festal Letters* we find a pastoral program with noetic (meditation, the study of Scripture) as well as corporeal (ascetic discipline) elements. These elements are translated into concrete pastoral exhortations, into Athanasius' conception of the "easy" and "secure" way to the heavenly feast.

The other type of audience to which Athanasius directs his message is the participants in the various ascetic movements in Egypt and Alexandria. Badger has shown that the same christological framework lies behind Athanasius' approach to this public. His pastoral aim is to give ascetics confidence in their calling, but through the christological formation of this confidence he reformulates the basis for holiness and its power. There is a tendency to criticize radical models of holiness which come to expression in extreme withdrawal, in favor of a socially integrated ascetic striving. The latter finds its theological basis in the Incarnate Christ whose "triumphs"

---

17. At least from the middle of the third century, Athanasius sent out brief, yearly notifications concerning the precise date of Easter during the forthcoming year. The Easter date of these notifications was then confirmed in an annual letter that was send out later. These letters were, for the Egyptian bishops, an ideal medium for the direct exhortation, encouragement and instruction of their flock. For a thorough study of Athanasius' *Festal Letters* see A. CAMPLANI, *Le lettere festali di Atanasio di Alessandria. Studio storico-critico* (Unione Accademica Nazionale. Corpus dei Manoscitti Copti Letterari), Rome, Centro Italiano Microfiches, 1989.

the believer appropriates. Brakke has highlighted the unifying effect of this message: by sketching a model of ascetic living, grounded in the example of the ministry of the Incarnate Christ, and trying to impose it, the Alexandrian bishop made an effort to bring the various existing ascetic movements under the umbrella of the hierarchy of the Church, of which he was the head. His *Letters to the Virgins* and his *Vita Antonii* must be read and understood in this light[18].

As regards his understanding of the lifelong practice of divinization, and the images he uses to discuss it, Athanasius is in line with what was said above about the tradition in general. The limited scriptural basis is colored and enriched by related models. Consider, for example, Athanasius' use of the term *theopoièsis*. He rarely uses the term, divinization, stricto sensu, as a description of the state of the redeemed after they have been offered the grace of the Incarnation[19]. Divinization is but one of a set of several, closely-related, soteriological models which together form part of the tapestry of Athanasius' multifaceted soteriology. The other models include renewal of creation / new creation; partaking of God, of the Logos, of the divine nature; being united to the Logos, to God; being Sons of God; and being exalted or sanctified or perfected in Christ[20]. Hence, divinization *stricto sensu* is certainly not the central soteriological theme in Athanasius' theology[21]. However, the idea of divinization, of becoming partakers of the divine nature, of participation in the divine nature, of being renewed, of being renovated is prominently present to express the changed state of fallen humanity after the Incarnation.

In conclusion, then, we can say the following of Athanasius' concept of divinization:

(1) It is a gradual process of growth towards similarity with Christ, which takes place within the community of believers.

18. D. BRAKKE, *Athanasius and the Politics of Asceticism* (n. 11).

19. *De Incarnatione Verbi* 54.3, ed. R.W. THOMSON, *Athanasius. Contra Gentes and de Incarnatione* (n. 1), pp. 268-269; *Contra Arianos* I, 39 (ed. *PG* 26, col 92); *Contra Arianos* I, 42, ed. *PG* 26, col. 97-100; *Contra Arianos* I, 45, ed. *PG* 26, col. 104-105; *Contra Arianos* II, 59, ed. *PG* 26, col 275; *Contra Arianos* II,70, ed. *PG* 26, col. 296; *Epistula ad Maximum* 2, ed. *PG* 26, col. 1088; *De Synodis*, 51, ed. H.G. OPITZ, *Athanasius' Werke. II. Die Apologien*, Berlin-Leipzig, 1939, pp. 274-275; *Epistula ad Serapionem* I, 25 (ed. *PG* 26, col. 589. Cf. H. HESS, *The Place of Divinization in Athanasian Soteriology*, in *Studia Patristica* 26 (1993) 369-375, p. 371.

20. See H. HESS, *The Place of Divinization* (n. 19), pp. 371-372.

21. G.R. STRANGE, *Athanasius on Divinization*, in *Studia Patristica* XVI/2 (Texte und Untersuchungen, 129), Berlin, 1985, 342-346; H. HESS, *Salvation Theology in the Festal Letters of St Athanasius of Alexandria*, in A. CHIROVSKY (ed.), *Following the Star from the East. Essays in Honour of Archimandrite Boniface Luykx*, Ottawa – Chicago, Sheptytsky Institute Saint Paul University, 1992, 229-242; ID., *The Place of Divinization* (n. 19), pp. 369-375.

(2) The goal of the process is participation in the Logos for which the Incarnation has created the possibility and of which it is the warrant.

(3) This process is the individual Christian's answer to the divine offer of grace through the life and works of the Incarnate Logos.

(4) Divinization *stricto sensu* is but one term indicating the same theologoumenon. In line with Scripture, Athanasius uses many other images.

IV. EVALUATION:
FROM IMAGE TO LIKENESS – A LIFE-GIVING EXPERIENCE

The question that remains to be asked is whether Athanasius still has something to say to contemporary men and women. A cautious "yes" would seem to be the appropriate answer to this question. In what follows, I would like to point out the positive elements in the theology of the great Alexandrian bishop, and to reflect briefly on three points which call for more attention.

One positive feature in Athanasius' presentation of the idea of divinization, of unification with God, is the opportunity it could provide for dialogue with people of other faiths. Indeed, this image is found among other religions, though it operates there within a different constellation. The notion, in some strands of Hinduism and Buddhism, that, after death, the soul is absorbed into a universal Spirit or into God, in the fashion of a drop in the ocean, shows clear parallels. Shankara, an influential Indian philosopher from the ninth century, developed such a notion. On the Christian side, Paul Tillich moved along similar lines in developing his recapitulation theory[22]. The idea of divinization might even appeal to those who profess no religious affiliation.

A second positive feature of Athanasius' presentation is his appreciation of the gradual character of divinization. Divinization is a life-long process, one involving setbacks. It is akin to the struggle to forge one's own identity. As such, it is an all-encompassing process which permeates every dimension of our development.

A third feature of Athanasius' presentation is its practical character. Athanasius situates the process squarely in daily life, as a process of divine action and human response. The Christian lays hold of grace by a variety of means, including intellectual exercises such as meditation on the

---

22. C. CORNILLE, *De wereldgodsdiensten over schepping, verlossing en leven na de dood*, Leuven, Davidsfonds, 1997, p. 109.

Scriptures or sermons, and ascetic practices such as fasting. Athanasius reminds us that both are important and challenges us to develop our liturgy so that it might become a more "holistic experience", touching participants in both their senses and their mind. In this regard, too, it is worth recalling that Athanasius invited both the "professional ascetics" and "ordinary Christians" to engage in the quest for divinization.

Of course, from the perspective of today, Athanasius' proposal is not without its deficiencies. In the first place, it might be described as narrowly ecclesiastical. In our age, it would seem advisable to broaden the experience of divine nearness, understood as a divine calling or a divine offer of grace, to include those depth-moments of human existence which Schillebeeckx, among others, has treated?[23]. Athanasius' proposal might also be criticized as excessively individualistic. The pastoral program he envisages seems to be geared primarily to the individual, though it is always pursued within the broader community. Finally, one must ask whether Athanasius' 'essentialist' understanding of the Incarnation is suited to our day. An alternative might be to conceive the believer's participation in the Logos as a *sequela Jesu*, or an *imitatio Christi*. This would involve immersing oneself in the words and deeds of Christ and taking them as a source of life, as an example and an inspiration. Christ would then become the norm for our own lives. To accept this norm is to share in the journey which Christ himself undertook, the journey from God to humankind and back. In the words of Stavropoulos:

> In the Holy Scriptures, where God Himself speaks, we read of a unique call directed to us. God speaks to us human beings clearly and directly and he says: "I said, 'You are gods, sons of the most high – all of you'" (Ps. 82:6 and John 10:34). Do we hear that voice? Do we understand the meaning of this calling? Do we accept that we in fact should be on a journey, a road which leads to Theosis? As human beings we each have this one, unique calling, to achieve Theosis. In other words, we are each destined to become a god; to be like God Himself, to be united with Him. The Apostle Peter describes with total clarity the purpose of life: we are to "become partakers of the divine nature"(2 Pe 1:4). This is the purpose of your life; that you be a participant, a sharer in the nature of God and in the life of Christ, a communicant of divine energy – to become just like God, a true God[24].

Faculty of Theology   Johan LEEMANS
Katholieke Universiteit Leuven   Research-Assistant
St. Michielsstraat 6
B-3000 Leuven

23. E. SCHILLEBEECKX, *Mensen als verhaal van God*, Baarn, Nelissen, 1990, pp. 34-47.
24. C. STAVROPOULOS, *Partakers of Divine Nature*, Fortress Press, Minneapolis, 1976, 17-18; quoted in D.B. CLENDENIN, *Partakers of Divinity* (n. 7), p. 365.

III

THE MYRIAD CHRIST

AND THE PLURALITY OF RELIGIONS
AND CULTURES

JESUS CHRIST IN THE MIDST OF RELIGIONS.
AN INDIAN PERSPECTIVE

The significance of Jesus Christ for us can be spelt out in many ways. In India we have a tradition of praising and glorifying God with a thousand and one names, recalling God's qualities and mighty deeds. Following this tradition we can give many names to Jesus that highlight his excellence or his significance for us. We see such names in the New Testament: the Good Shepherd, the true Lamb of God, the Messiah, the Son of God, the High Priest, the way, the truth and the life, the living water, the light of the world and so on. Continuing this tradition Jesus has been given many names in India: the true *Guru*, the supreme *Satyagrahi* (fighting for truth/justice), the *Jivanmukta* (the realized person), the *Yogi*, the Mother, the cosmic Dancer, etc. These names do point to various ways in which Jesus can bring meaning to our lives. Jesus can have other such names in other cultures: the great Ancestor in Africa or the Way in Japan or the Sage in China. The myriad Christ can indeed have a thousand and one names. Giving such names is a non-controversial activity, though it can be a very fruitful exercise. But this is not the approach I am taking here.

India is the cradle of great world religions like Hinduism and Buddhism and host to others like Christianity and Islam. All religions claim to mediate salvation/liberation. Christians affirm that Jesus Christ is the only mediator of salvation. How do we reconcile these two claims? Before I proceed to answer this question from an Indian perspective, let me try to specify the exact context in which I am trying to answer the question.

1.

We should not confuse the uniqueness of Christ with the uniqueness of Christianity. I think that the affirmation of the uniqueness of Christ is often a hidden affirmation of the uniqueness of Christianity. We no longer affirm that there is no salvation outside the Church. On the contrary we do affirm, with the Second Vatican Council, that "the Holy Spirit offers to all the possibility of being made partners, in a way known to God, in the paschal mystery"[1]. One could discuss whether this

---

1. *Gaudium et Spes*, 22.

action of God should relate to the Church as a visible community and, if so, how. This question comes from a particular idea of the Church and I am not going to pursue it here. An Indian theologian has even suggested that it is an European problem that does not find much echo in a religiously pluralistic situation like that of India[2]. Any way, I am talking here of Jesus Christ, not of Christianity.

I am not engaged either in a comparative study of religions as ways of salvation. One often hears of the paradigms of exclusivism, inclusivism and pluralism. I find that this is an abstract, *a priori*, approach that does not clarify the problem. Religions do not save. Salvation comes from God or the Ultimate. God is sovereignly free to choose any way. Comparing and contrasting religions without considering the basic relationship in which God is offering salvation and humans are responding in faith is a useless exercise. Such comparison imposes an abstract uniformity of concepts which do not exist in experience. Salvation does not have the same meaning in the different religions.

The role of Jesus Christ in Christianity is very different from that of Mohammed in Islam, the Buddha in Buddhism and Krishna in Hinduism. To speak of them all as mediators is a misuse of the term. Speaking of Jesus Christ as the only mediator is to set him in the context of many mediators, when many of these persons do not claim to be mediators at all. I would request you therefore not to seek to fit what I am going to say into any *a priori* scheme.

2.

My quest starts from an experiential context of religious pluralism. This experience is not simply a recognition that people among whom I live follow many religions. It implies also an acknowledgment that my neighbors of other religions do have an authentic and salvific experience of God or of the Ultimate in their religions. I take them and their experience seriously, as befits their dignity as humans. My own experience of Jesus Christ makes me feel that he has a relevance not only for me but for every one, for the whole world. I am trying to understand and spell out this universal significance of Jesus. Universality is not the same thing as uniqueness. While the language of uniqueness excludes, the language of universality can reach out to the other without excluding the

2. F. WILFRED, *The Language of Christian Uniqueness,* in *From the Dusty Soil,* Madras, Department of Christian Studies, University of Madras, 1995, pp. 176-200.

identity of the other. I am not trying to offer an explanation that would be understood and accepted by all my neighbors of other faiths. I am only trying to make sense of my own experience in a religiously pluralistic context.

I can now reformulate my original question. I believe that Jesus Christ is the universal savior. How do I understand this affirmation in the context of my experience of other believers and my acceptance of the legitimacy of their experience of God.

3.

Before I go on to develop the Indian answer, I would like to mention two others and say why I do not find them satisfactory. The first answer was proposed by Karl Rahner and is adopted by many others. This consists in the *a priori*, transcendental affirmation of the role of Jesus Christ in the mystery of salvation. The conclusion is that every one is saved in and by Christ, even if they are not aware of it. Rahner makes it clear that this is a faith affirmation when he agrees that a sincere Buddhist must consider every other believer an anonymous Buddhist[3]. While this respects the alterity of the other, it does not really take account of and respect the plurality of experience. I am not ready to look upon my Hindu and Buddhist friends as anonymous Christians.

A second answer accepts the presence and action of God in other religions, but attributes it, not to Jesus Christ, but to the Holy Spirit. But this solution is not a solution since one often adds immediately that the Spirit is the Spirit of Christ. So one is really talking of two ways in which Christ can be active, either openly and directly or in a hidden manner through the Spirit. I am not sure that it is wise to use the distinction of persons in the Trinity to solve the problem of pluralism. All actions *ad extra* are of the Trinity as a whole: where the Spirit is, the Father and the Son are also.

4.

The answer that most Indians would give to the question is rather simple. Jesus Christ mediates for us God-experience so that we experience

---

3. K. RAHNER, *Theological Investigations*. Vol. 16, London, Darton, Longman and Todd, 1979, p. 219.

him also as divine. This means that he is experienced wherever God is
experienced. This is possible because Jesus is the historical manifestation
of the mystery of the Son of God which is universal. The Indians often use
the term cosmic Christ to indicate this mystery and to distinguish it from
the historical Jesus. I, however, prefer to talk about the Mysteric Christ,
since the term 'cosmic' refers to the cosmos and so may be confusing.
While the Christians relate to the mystery of Christ in and through the
Jesus of history, the other believers relate to the same divine mystery
through other symbols and manifestations. The 'what' and the 'how' of
these will have to be discerned through experience and dialogue.

5.

A similar answer was first given, though theological precision is lacking,
by Keshub Chunder Sen (1838-1884) who never joined any Christian
Church, but wanted to establish a new universal religion that would integrate
all religions. In one of his lectures on the Trinity, delivered in 1882, he says:

> The one ideal Christ manifests in multiform concrete little Christs. Sum up
> all that is true and good and beautiful in the life of humanity, and you have
> the grand Logos of the early Christians, the Christ of Universal Theism.
> Thus all reason in man is Christ-reason, all love is Christ-love, all power is
> Christ-power [...] I commend to you not the little Christ of little Christian
> sects, but the grand Christ of universal humanity, the perfect man, the ideal
> Son, that was, is, and shall continue to be[4].

He claimed that Christ was a true Asian, a Hindu, an authentic Yogi and a
Bhakta, who has been misunderstood by the West[5]. Quotations can be multi-
plied. Sen discovers in his own experience of Christ the universal nature of
his mystery which cannot be limited to one of its particular manifestations.

6.

We shall skip many other witnesses and travel more than a hundred
years to hear Raimon Panikkar, who speaks of the *cosmic, transhistorical Christ*[6]. He characterizes him as

---

4. D.C. Scott (ed.), *Keshub Chunder Sen,* Madras, The Christian Literature Society,
1979, p. 238.
5. *Ibid.,* pp. 215-216.
6. R. Panikkar, *A Dwelling Place for Wisdom,* Louisville, KY, Westminster/John
Knox Press, 1993, p. 152.

the mystery which is the beginning and will be the end; [...] the light shining upon all creatures; the word contained in every authentic word; [...] that which we are – and are supposed to be – and which we have been; this symbol of all reality, not just as it used to be or is now but also as it will continue to be freely, even through our cooperation; that mystery, I believe is Christ.

With such a view of Christ I am not avoiding the *skandalon* of the Incarnation and the process of salvation [...] The point is simply that I am not worshiping history as if it were God, and I am not limiting reality to history – not even to human history – and not to the history of abrahamic lineage [...] Every creature is a *christophany*[7].

I have quoted Panikkar as a type who represents what many other Indian theologians have said over the years. Many Indian theologians today will agree with this perspective, though they may not express it as forcefully. Let me now try to explain, and even defend, this perspective.

7.

A common objection to this perspective and particularly to the term 'mysteric Christ' is that it reduces the importance of the historical Jesus. One reason for this is that the distinction 'mysteric Christ – historical Jesus' is often confused with 'Christ of faith – Jesus of history'. The mysteric Christ is not presented as the product of our faith, but as our discovery of his mysterical, divine dimension as we contemplate the historical Jesus. In this we follow the example of Paul and John. Paul's meditation on Jesus leads him to see in Jesus the mystery – the divine plan – which reveals the Christ in whom every thing was created and in whom every thing will be gathered together. (Eph 1,3-10) Similarly, contemplating Jesus, John discovers the *Logos* in and through whom every thing is created, who enlightens every one coming into the world and who becomes flesh at the opportune time. (Jn 1,1-14)

In the West, history is opposed to myth. Myth is unreal, while history is real. Therefore there is a lot of insistence on history. The other religions and their revelations are considered mythical and set in contrast with the Christian revelation which is historical. The Indians distinguish history not from myth, but from mystery. In humans, as spirit-bodies, the historical actions of the body find their full meaning only at the level of the spirit. The meaning includes and transcends the discrete historical events, though it can find expression only in history. But the history

7. *Ibid.*, p. 153.

does not exhaust the mystery. Human love finds expression in a succession of events and yet transcends them. Love cannot be reduced to its varied expressions. At the same time human love cannot remain unexpressed. What is true of the human world is much more true of the divine world in relation to the human. God's mystery or divine plan finds expression in history, which involves materiality, corporeity and time. And yet the mystery transcends history: it should not be reduced to history. History points to mystery: it symbolizes mystery. History is real; but its reality is relative to the mystery of which it is the expression. This symbolic structure is true also of the sacraments. Though they guarantee, in faith, God's action, God acts through symbol.

The history of Jesus is important. But it should lead us, as it did Paul and John, to contemplate the mystery of which it is the symbol. The experience of the pluralism of religions is the discovery that the divine mystery has also been present and active beyond the limits of the visible Church. This obviously relativize its history. God alone is absolute. Every historical, human expression of God can only be conditioned by humanity, its culture and history. This is true even of the Incarnation, which is, moreover, a *kenotic* manifestation of the divine mystery. This is not the relativity of a subject that is limited and conditioned in its capacity of knowledge, though this need not be excluded, but the relativity and relatedness of the expression of any experience or reality in human, historical and symbolic terms.

The affirmation of the mysteric Christ is therefore the recognition that the mystery of Christ transcends its historical manifestation in Jesus. Some would object to the use of the word 'Christ' in this context and suggest that one should speak rather of the 'Word' or the 'Logos'. But since the Logos has entered human history as Jesus Christ, the term 'mysteric Christ' recognizes the necessary association of the Logos with the Jesus of history. It is Jesus who leads us to the Logos. The term 'Christ' recognizes and affirms this relationship. St. Thomas says that the term 'Christ' can signify both natures, as by it "are to be understood both *anointing divinity* and *anointed humanity*"[8]. So it can be used also to refer to the divine nature.

8.

What is the mystery that the history of Jesus points to? It is the divine plan to "gather up all things" in Christ (Eph 1,10), to "reconcile

---

8. St. Thomas Aquinas, *Summa Theologiae, III, 16, 5, R,* in *Summa Theologiae, vol. 50,* London, Eyre and Spottiswoode, 1975, p. 23.

to himself all things, whether on earth or in heaven", (Col 1,20) so that "God may be all in all" (1Cor 15,28). The vision of salvation as presented by Paul is not merely of individual souls saved from a wicked world, but of a new world in which the cosmos too is integrated (Rom 8,21). John too has a similar vision when he speaks of "a new heaven and a new earth" when God will make "all things new" (Rev 21,1.5).

Keeping this vision in mind we can re-image the whole of salvation history. The mystery of God manifests itself in a multiplicity of ways in the course of history in the lives and cultures of different peoples. Such manifestations have led to the foundation and growth of different religions. One traditional view of salvation history sees these different manifestations as developments from less to more perfect along a single historical line, so that Jesus will come as the most perfect, ultimate, word. With our present experience of other religions we can hardly maintain this picture of a single historical line. It is not a question of opposing a Greek-Christian linear to an Indian circular view of history. It is rather an attempt to see history as having multiple strands and multiple levels. Since God, being One, has only one plan for the universe, these strands have to be inter-weaving. Similarly, the mystery is working itself out in history in various ways, but transcends and, at the same time, unifies them.

Such a view of history as made up of different strands does not mean that all the strands have the same significance or value. Much less does it mean that all are the same. But no strand is dispensable, because each is willed by God. In this sense each strand has a unique significance. They all represent aspects of divine-human encounter in history. They embody the freedom of God's self-communication and the freedom of human response in community. Therefore they deserve our respect. Their significance will have to be spelt out not only in themselves, but also in terms of their relationship to one another. This relationship can be clarified, not in the abstract, but only in the concrete, in the course of a common, intertwined history, through dialogue.

9.

What is the specificity of the history of Jesus in this universal history of salvation? Salvation as divine-human encounter is taking place in mysterious ways, unknown to us, for every human person. But salvation also has a cosmic purpose of gathering all things together. In Jesus, God enters human history by becoming a human being through incarnation.

Jesus lives and symbolizes in himself in an exemplary manner the universal salvific mystery of divine-human encounter, especially in the paschal mystery of his death and resurrection. Jesus lives it as a manifestation of love in total self-gift, even unto death on the cross.

But by entering history, Jesus also gets involved in the ongoing struggle between God and Mammon. Jesus proclaims the coming of God's Kingdom. But it will not simply be God's gift, but also the fruit of human struggle. The quest for the Kingdom becomes a historical movement. George Soares-Prabhu has expressed this well.

> When the revelation of God's love (the Kingdom) meets its appropriate response in man's [humanity's] trusting acceptance of this love (repentance), there begins a mighty movement of personal and societal liberation which sweeps through human history. The movement brings *freedom* inasmuch as it liberates each individual from the inadequacies and obsessions that shackle him. It fosters *fellowship*, because it empowers free individuals to exercise their concern for each other in genuine community. And it leads on to *justice*, because it impels every true community to adopt the just societal structures which alone make freedom and fellowship possible [...]
>
> The vision of Jesus [...] does not present us with a static pre-fabricated model to be imitated, but invites us to a continual refashioning of societal structures in an attempt to realize as completely as possible in our times the values of the Kingdom [...] Lying on the horizons of human history and yet part of it, offered to us as a gift yet confronting us as a challenge, Jesus' vision of a new society stands before us as an unfinished task, summoning us to permanent revolution[9].

The Church embodies this movement towards a permanent revolution launched by Jesus. This movement is focused, not merely on saving individual souls, but in recreating and reuniting the whole universe. This recreation and reunification has to happen not merely through some mysterious intervention of God, but through a historical struggle. Jesus has not only entered this struggle, but has launched a new movement in it. The disciples of Jesus, gathered in the Church, carry on this struggle of Jesus.

10.

The other Asian religions, namely Hinduism and, particularly, Buddhism, are also involved in this struggle with Mammon. Diagnosing the

---

9. G. SOARES-PRABHU, *The Kingdom of God: Jesus' Vision of a New Society*, in D.S. AMALORPAVADASS (ed.), *The Indian Church in the Struggle for a New Society,* Bangalore, National Biblical, Catechetical and Liturgical Centre, pp. 601, 607.

root of evil as egoism and desire, they suggest absolute renunciation of
self, symbolized by voluntary poverty. But Jesus, focusing on societal,
not only personal, transformation suggests not merely an option to *be*
poor, but also an option *for* the poor, to struggle with them on their side
and on their behalf. Aloysius Pieris spells it out in the following way:

> Jesus, both as message and person, can hardly be encountered, and much
> less proclaimed, except in terms of these two axioms; they are (1) (Jesus
> is) the irreconcilable antinomy between God and Mammon; and (2) (Jesus
> is) the irrevocable covenant between God and the poor [...]
> The spirituality of discipleship revealed in the first axiom is the common
> denominator between Christianity and all nonbiblical religions in Asia;
> whereas the mission given to us in the second axiom is conspicuously
> absent in the Scriptures of other religions [...]
> Interreligious solidarity, then, is not optional, but the obligation of the
> whole Church to stand together with non-Christians, on the common plat-
> form of evangelical poverty, that is, the renunciation of Mammon; for only
> from that platform can the Church announce with authority, the specific
> message entrusted to her: "Jesus is the covenant between YHWH and the
> nonpersons of this world"[10].

Though I think that the contrast between Christianity and other Asian
religions seems overstressed in the light of recent liberation movements
and reflection in them, the figure of Jesus on the cross, condemned to die
as responsible for public unrest, does underline the specificity of Jesus'
option for the poor, which expressed, not merely compassion for, but
solidarity with them.

11.

One way of underlining the specificity of Jesus in the context of the
pluralism of religions is to look on him as the final word or the fulfillment of all that went before him. This vision depends on a unilinear
view of history. God's plan is certainly leading the world to its fulfillment in Christ. But this fulfillment is in the future when Christ himself
will reach his fullness – *pleroma* –, when all things will be gathered in
him and God will be all in all. In the meantime the Kingdom is an inspiring vision in course of realization. The Church is called to be the symbol and servant of this Kingdom. Unfortunately the Church is also a pil-
grim and is only growing towards this goal. The other manifestations of
God also contribute to this fullness. They are not just preparations for

10. A. PIERIS, *Fire and Water. Basic Issues in Asian Buddhism and Christianity*,
Maryknoll, NY, Orbis, 1996, pp.150-151.

Christ or partial manifestations. They are authentic experiences of God
and manifestations of God's mystery. They will all be assumed – nothing will be lost – in the final fullness.

God, God's Word and Spirit are actively engaged in realizing God's plan
and in building up the Kingdom in and through history in many mysterious
ways unknown to us. We are called to be servants of this mystery, discerning God's presence and action in history and collaborating with it. Sometimes we think and act as if we are the plenipotentiary agents of God in the
world. The way of Jesus in mission is a way of humility and service.

12.

I can now briefly summarize the vision that I have outlined. God's
salvific plan for the universe is to gather all things in Christ. God is leading
the universe towards this goal through a multiplicity of divine manifestations in history. History itself is seen as the struggle between God and
Mammon, symbolized of course by the humans. God's incarnation is a special, unique divine intervention which is at the service of the divine plan. It
is not simply a visibility of a mystery that is active everywhere and always.
Jesus is not simply one of the many names given to the same mystery. In
Jesus God is entering history to launch a movement towards the realization
of God's plan. In the context of the ongoing struggle between God and
Mammon Jesus is taking the side of the poor. God does this freely. But the
movement has to be carried on by us in history by being at the service of
God's action in the world manifested in the people belonging to various
religions. All humans are called to the Kingdom and the collaboration of all
is required for its realization. Dialogue seems an essential activity to
achieve and actualize such collaboration.

In the context of this global vision, I have to clarify two more points:
the meaning and relevance of the paschal mystery, and the significance
of the person of Jesus.

13.

We believe that the paschal mystery of Jesus' passion, death and resurrection has universal significance. How do we understand this in the
context of the preceding vision of history? Most people who explore the
theology of religions hardly attend to this question. The various theories
of redemption or atonement can be grouped into two classes. Some

would give the paschal mystery of Jesus a transcendental significance so that the whole of humanity is some how saved in Jesus. Other think that Jesus has made infinite satisfaction for the sins of humankind and the merits of his action are applied to every one. The second theory is individualist. The first is somehow a-historical. Neither of these theories demands, on the part of humans, a conscious relationship to Jesus in faith.

I think that we must look at redemption in a new way. The mystery of divine-human encounter starts from creation. The paschal mystery starts a new stage in that story when God enters into human history. Salvation acquires a new historical visibility and depth. History becomes in a new way the sacrament of mystery. The risen Jesus is the 'first fruits' of a new thrust given to the ongoing divine-human encounter in history. The salvific act in its totality is a process that demands human collaboration and this collaboration can take various forms. It is not merely individualist, spiritual and 'other worldly'. It works itself out in history. What is crucial is to love the other, particularly the poor (Mat 25).

The vision of salvation I have outlined above offers a new dimension. The entrance of the Word of God into history to start a movement towards its consummation automatically gives it a universal significance. We cannot think any more of human history without God being part of it. While in the past we have had the tendency to arrogate to ourselves this specificity, today we are happy to affirm it as present and active everywhere and to be its witnesses and servants.

14.

One of the objections to the discourse concerning the cosmic Christ is that the distinction between the mysteric Christ and the historical Jesus does not preserve the personal unity of Jesus Christ. Jesus Christ is two natures in one person. This makes possible a *communicatio idiomatum* so that whatever we can say of Jesus can be said of the Word and vice versa. The talk about the mysteric Christ as distinguished from the historical Jesus seems to question this unity.

I think that, in affirming the unity of the person of Christ, some do not consider seriously the distinction between the two natures which, according to the Council of Chalcedon, should neither be confused nor be separated. This tendency has led popular piety and even theological reflection to a practical monophysitism. In any case our experience of the presence of God in other religions and of the many manifestations

of the Word in history may lead us, not to deny any of the clarifica-
tions achieved by the early Councils, but to develop new insights into
the mystery. I think that the concern of the Fathers of the early Councils was to affirm that Jesus was divine. Jesus could not have communicated God's life to us if he were not God. Therefore, whatever Jesus
did, God – the Second Person of the Blessed Trinity – did. One can
therefore say that God suffered and died on the cross, though, for precision, we must add that the Second Person of the Blessed Trinity
died in his human nature. Even with this precision, to be able to say
that God suffered and died is a mystery that we cannot easily fathom.

But I wonder whether in the name of the unity of the person this
relationship between the divine and the human nature in Jesus can be
simply reversed. Can we say that whatever the Second person of the
Blessed Trinity did Jesus did? Can we ascribe to Jesus whatever the
Word does? The two natures in Christ are two separate centers of
activity, though ascribed to a single person. Jesus' human nature is
assumed by the divine person of the Word. The divine person can
claim all that is done by the human nature. But this does not mean that
the human nature loses its human, historical and cultural limitations,
even without bringing in the dimension of the *kenosis* involved in the
incarnation. The human Jesus does not know everything concerning
the plan of God; he grows in knowledge, experience and wisdom like
other humans; he experiences weakness and fear before the vision of
his impending sufferings; he feels the absence of God on the cross.
The human nature of Jesus does not have a personality of its own to
which we can ascribe the actions of the divine nature. Therefore it
seems that the relationship between the human and divine natures in
Jesus is not reversible. It is the divine person who assumes the human
nature, not vice versa.

15.

In a talk to some Indian Bishops in October 1986, Cardinal Ratzinger
refers to this and says that the denial of simple reversibility "is correct
in so far as the two natures, the divine and the human, remain distinct".
But he continues:

> Nevertheless, in the incarnation, the eternal Logos has so bound Himself to
> Jesus such that the reversibility of the formulae results from His *person* [...]
> Whoever comes into contact with the Logos touches Jesus of Nazareth.

Jesus is more than the sacrament of the Logos. He is the Logos Himself who in the man Jesus is an historical subject[11].

The question then is whether, in becoming an historical subject, the Logos also takes on human and historical conditioning. Does the human nature cease to be such and become divine in the process? Does the unity of the person cancel out the difference of natures? The Second Vatican Council says in its Document on the Church in the Modern World: "By his incarnation, he, the Son of God, has in a certain way united himself with each man"[12]. One can say this of the Logos. The phrase "in a certain way" qualifies the relationship. Can we say this also about his human nature? What would that mean at the level of history and conscious awareness?

We can keep discussing these questions. But whatever happens in the mysterious realm of the Logos – and Indian theologians are open to it since they speak about the cosmic Christ – in the realm of religions we are talking about people relating to God in conscious, human ways in history. The majority of people today are not relating to Jesus in this manner. Their relationship to God is actually mediated through other divine manifestations. Attempts to ascribe them to the Spirit acknowledges this difference.

Sometimes it is suggested that the humanity of Jesus becomes mysteric and universal after his resurrection. We do not know what a resurrected human nature is. The risen humanity of Jesus does not become divine. Even if it is freed from spatial and temporal conditionings it cannot escape the limitations of being human (and not divine), if it remains really human even after the resurrection.

16.

St. Thomas Aquinas asks the question whether one divine person can assume two human natures. Let us look at his answer.

Whatever has power for one thing and nothing else has a power limited to that. The power of a Divine Person is infinite, nor limitable in regard to anything created. So, then, we should not state that a divine person assumes a human nature in such a way that he is powerless to take up another[13].

11. Cardinal J. RATZINGER, *Report* at the Meeting with the Bishops of India, 21-24 October 1996, p. 10. (Unpublished Manuscript)

12. *Gaudium et Spes*, 22.

13. St. THOMAS AQUINAS, *Summa Theologiae, III, 3, 7, R*, in *Summa Theologiae, vol. 48*, London, Eyre and Spottiswoode, 1975, p.107.

Answering one of the objections which suggests that this is not possible because, as Damascene says, Christ is "perfect God and perfect man, wholly God and wholly man", Thomas continues:

> The divine and human nature are not referred uniformly to the divine person. The divine nature has precedence in being one with the divine person from eternity. The human nature, however, is related to the divine person secondarily as assumed in time, and not in such a way that the nature should be the person, but that the person subsist in the nature. The Son of God *is* his divinity, but is not his humanity[14].

I am not interested here in affirming the possibility of many incarnations. The question is hypothetical. But the possibility of many incarnations questions a perfect fit between the divine and the human in Christ and makes space for statements about the divine and the human in him that are not reversible. Besides, the incarnation does not exclude other manifestations of the Word in history. These manifestations can express aspects or dimensions of divine nature and action that are really different from those manifested by the incarnation, especially if the incarnation chooses to be kenotic. All that we can expect is that the different manifestations of the Word are not contradictory to each other, but rather converge towards a harmony through dialogue. Contradictions, however, should not be assumed too easily, since the manifestations may be two poles of a dialectic that will remain dynamically in tension rather than find an easy formula of reconciliation.

17.

I would like to suggest, therefore, that the Indian discourse about the mysteric Christ and the historical Jesus seeks, on the one hand, to affirm the unity of the divine action in the world in and through the Word (and the Spirit) and, on the other, the historical diversity through which God's action is being worked out in history. By becoming incarnate in history the Word has not sought to escape the conditionings of history. On the contrary, he is taking the process of history seriously and he is contributing, through his own action and through the lives and actions of his disciples, to the transformation of the world in history, through historical means. These include respect for, and dialogue and collaboration

---

14. *Ibid.*, *Ad 3*, p. 109.

with, other believers and all people of good will in the ongoing struggle with Mammon, trusting that God is coordinating everything and leading all things to final harmony.

Vidyajyoti College of Theology   Michael AMALADOSS
23 Raj Niwas Marg
110054 Delhi
India

CHRISTIAN VEDANTA:
AN ABSURDITY OR AN OPPORTUNITY?

Vedanta is the name given to a set of schools of Indian religious thought, all of which have in common the fact that they base their teachings on a particular text, the 'Vedanta Sutras' of Badarayana. These Sutras in turn form an extremely cryptic commentary on the Upanishads, which are usually taken as revealed and inerrant scriptures. There are many different ways of interpreting the Upanishads and Badarayana's commentary on them, ranging from the non-dualistic system of Sankara to the wholly dualistic system of Madhva. The sheer range of diverse doctrines, even in this one strand of Indian thought, is bewildering. Even a cursory knowledge of them makes it quite clear that one cannot characterise Indian religious thought as 'monistic' or 'pantheistic', as holding that the world is an illusion or as being somehow world denying. All these views can be found within Vedanta, but so can their opposites, so it is better not to try to generalise too much.

One has a whole set of differing views, but they do all claim to be reasonable interpretations of the Upanishads, and they do all accept the general Upanishadic conceptual framework of one spiritual basis of reality, and the development of an appropriate human relation to that supreme Spirit by a long process of individual spiritual training, probably over many lives, leading to ultimate release from the chains of rebirth, desire and suffering.

The Vedantic view can be put in a way which makes it sharply contrast with most understandings of Christianity. It might be said, for instance, that Brahman, the supreme reality, necessarily emanates worlds without beginning or end, and the cycles of existence repeat themselves again and again by a sort of inner necessity. Human liberation must be achieved individually by human effort alone, by a long process of renunciation and meditation. The world is a realm of desire and suffering, and each soul is born into the world an almost uncountable number of times, in all forms of animal and human life. The world has no positive goal or purpose, and the aim of the religious life is to obtain release from the cycle of reincarnation, so that there will be no more rebirth. When liberation is achieved, individual existence comes to an end, and one is finally absorbed in the undifferentiated unity of Brahman.

Put in that way, there does not seem much hope of achieving any sort of unity of Christianity and Vedanta, and there does not seem much point in trying. There are Vedantins who hold all the views just mentioned, just as there are Christians who believe that the vast majority of humans will suffer endlessly in Hell, that God has the power to will anything he pleases, without being limited by logical or moral principles, that only those who explicitly confess Jesus as their Lord and Saviour will be saved from Hell, and that Jesus will return to earth at any moment and the redeemed will receive their bodies back again to live for ever in a vegetarian Paradise.

It should be obvious that it would be a travesty to claim that Christians have to, or even normally do, believe all those things. In the same way, it is a travesty to claim that Vedantins would normally all accept the very limited views I have outlined for them. Among the vast range of options open to Vedantins, the following represents a rather different possibility.

In Vedanta, the one spiritual basis of reality is construed as Brahman, the one and only self-existent reality whose nature is supreme wisdom and bliss[1]. Brahman unfolds itself into an infinity of worlds, in such a way that each of these worlds, or universes, expresses something of the nature of Brahman, actualising its inner potentialities in many forms of finite being, without beginning or end[2]. One need not speak of eternal recurrence, however, and in fact such a notion comes to grief with acceptance that liberated souls are not reborn in this sort of universe – which entails that precisely the same universe will never recur. Rather, one may speak of endlessly new worlds expressing the play, or *lila,* of the Supreme Lord, all of which express new ways of manifesting divine love and compassion[3].

It is true that worlds seem to emanate from Brahman by necessity, and to be explications of potentialities immanent in Brahman. But it is also true that such emanation is often seen as willed by Brahman, and is not just some sort of unwilled 'overflow' of being[4]. This is an intelligible concept of creation, in that each world is wholly dependent on Brahman for its existence, and Brahman intends that it should, as a whole, exist.

1. *Brihadaranyaka Upanisad*, 3, 9, 28, in P. OLIVELLE (trans.), *Upanisads,* Oxford, University Press, 1996, p. 52.
2. 'I alone am the creation, for I created all this', *Brihadaranyaka Upanisad*, 1, 4, 5, in *ibid.,* p. 14.
3. 'Who alone... in whom the universe comes together at the beginning and dissolves in the end', *Svetasvatara Upanisad*, 4, 1, in *ibid.,* p. 259.
4. 'He [*brahman*] had this desire': Let me multiply myself. Let me produce offspring' *Taittiriya Upanisad* 2, 6, in *ibid.,* p. 187.

The idea that some creation is necessary is not wholly foreign to Christian thought, especially if one takes the view that God's essential nature as love can only be properly expressed by the creation of others to whom God can relate in love. And it may be a positively helpful thought, when considering the existence of suffering and evil, to suppose that there are internal necessities in the being of the creator which limit the sorts of worlds that come into existence, making it impossible to produce a world without suffering which will instantiate the sorts of goodness this world does instantiate.

The Vedantic notion of causality (*satkaryavada*) is that effects pre-exist in their causes, and are not distinct from them, so that Brahman is said to 'become' the world. This sounds quite different from the typical Christian notion of causality, which tends to distinguish effects from causes, and therefore say that the world as the effect of God's willing is different from the creator. I suspect, however, that this is largely a verbal difference, a matter of different conceptual backgrounds, rather than a substantive disagreement. For while Brahman is said to be the 'material cause' of the world, this does not entail that everything in the world, including suffering and evil, is part of what Brahman essentially is. Brahman creates without changing in its essential being. It is 'the changeless among the changing'[5] so it does not just 'turn into' a finite universe. Indeed, since the world is in some sense a fall into illusion, it is actually as different from Brahman, the wholly real and perfectly blissful, as anything could be.

The substantive point is rather that nothing in the world is ever separated from Brahman. It exists solely by the support of Brahman, and Brahman is present to it at its heart. But the Christian doctrine of God also holds that view, since God is omnipresent and every finite thing depends wholly for its existence on God. Moreover, for theologians like Thomas Aquinas, all effects pre-exist in God 'in a higher manner'[6]. The doctrine of *creatio ex nihilo* primarily states that there is nothing other than God out of which the universe is formed. The Vedantic view agrees wholly with this, and it seems to me that the well-known view of the Upanishads that 'all this is Brahman' is reasonably interpretable as just another way of stating the Christian view of divine omnipresence and sole ultimate causality.

Since Brahman is the only self-existent reality, it is true that all finite beings have no independent being, but are in some sense 'parts' of

---

5. *Svetasvatara Upanisad* 6, 13, in *ibid.*, p. 264.
6. AQUINAS, *Summa Theologiae*, 1a, 4, 2, trans. Thomas Gilby, Blackfriars, 1964, p. 52.

Brahman. Yet their identification with Brahman is far from simple. Finite souls are prey to greed and the delusion of separate independent existence. It is certainly not the case that, in all their greed and hatred, their suffering and despair, they express what Brahman essentially is. Within Vedanta, there are many different ways of construing the sense in which Brahman is identical with the finite soul or *jiva*.

One main option, represented by Ramanuja, is to see all finite souls as constituting the body of Brahman. Like the cells of a human body, they may have a certain autonomy. They may become sick. They may frustrate the overall will of the body. But insofar as the body functions as it should, they will co-operate in expressing the reality of the supreme self. There is no question of individuality being absorbed into some impersonal reality. Each soul exists eternally, and its destiny is to exist in conscious loving relation to *Isvara*, the supreme Lord, not to be transmuted into some supra-personal unity[7]. Moreover, if all liberated souls form the body of the Lord, they will live in a community of perfect harmony, of justice and peace. Both individuality and community are preserved and fulfilled in this form of Vedanta.

This world is a realm of suffering and conflict, in which souls are bound by desire and egoism. There are forms of Vedanta which do seem to take an unduly negative view of the finite world, to regard it as simply something to be escaped from. But Ramanuja and Madhva, together with most twentieth century Vedantins, insist on a much more positive view. After all, if 'all this is Brahman', it can hardly be wholly negative and pointless. In some sense, it may be seen as at least potentially divine. Consequently, while one may look for release from suffering and selfish desire, one may hope for a fulfilment of truly personal life in other forms of being beyond this one[8].

In this form of space-time the body of Brahman is to some extent diseased. The desirable goal of human life is to obtain release from the sickness caused by egoistic desire, but it is not simply to end individual life. Rather, it is to enter a more glorious realm in which the body of Brahman can function as it should, to express the wisdom and joy of Brahman itself in many finite ways. In the tradition, there are three main ways of obtaining such release or liberation. There is the way of *jnyana*

---

7. 'Souls, matter and the Lord are essentially distinct', RAMANUJA, *The Vedanta Sutras,* trans. George Thibaut, Delhi, Motilal Banarsidass, 1962, in *Sacred Books of the East,* ed. Max Muller, vol. 48, p. 102.

8. 'The released soul... abides in its true essential nature... and may have experience of different worlds created by the Lord engaged in playful sport' (RAMANUJA, *The Vedanta Sutras,* p. 764).

yoga, of renunciation and meditation, by which the mind is withdrawn from the world of sensual desire and focusses one-pointedly on the reality of the Supreme Self which lies within, in the 'cave of the heart'. There is the way of *bhakti yoga,* of devotion, by which one learns to love selflessly some particular expression of the Supreme Self, and thus transcend egoistic desire. And there is the way of *karma yoga,* of obedience and works, by which one seeks to obey the revealed will of the gods, and to practice compassion by service of others.

In each of these ways, the emphasis is on overcoming the sense of ego and achieving an awareness of the presence of the Supreme Self in all things, and of all things in the Supreme Self[9]. Such overcoming is usually thought to involve a long progress, before greed, hatred and delusion can be transformed fully into non-possessiveness, compassion and knowledge of the Supreme Self. There are, however, many schools for which the grace *(prasada)* of the Lord may instantaneously deliver one from egoism into a loving relationship with the Supreme. While there is a stress on the teaching that each soul must reap the consequences of its own acts, in many forms of embodiment, there is also a strong element of the compassionate grace of the Lord, which ensures that a strictly retributive notion of justice may be transcended by the forgiving compassion of a Lord of love. It is simply untrue that Vedantins preach a gospel of salvation by works, and not of grace.

Most Vedantin schools accept the general Indian religious cosmology of rebirth and karmic law, such that souls will be reborn on earth in many different bodies. But the deepest emphasis is on the necessity of progressing in goodness and insight, in forms of being beyond this earthly life. Rebirths may thus take place in lower (Hell) or higher (Heaven) worlds, as each soul follows its own path of enmeshment in desire and its consequences, or of liberation from desire and an infinite journey into Brahman. Belief in reincarnation on earth is not essential to Vedanta. What it is concerned to teach is that each individual life will, by its acts, shape its own future, in many forms of being which are subsequent to existence on this planet and in this form of space and time. There is no idea that anyone is condemned to Hell for ever, just because of their acts in one short earthly life, or that one may go directly to the presence of God, without the need for any further spiritual progress. Souls are bound to births involving suffering and loss, until, by their transcendence of the egoistic self, they achieve conscious union with the Supreme Self. Then they can continue an endless progress through infinite forms of

---

9. *Isa Upanisad,* 6 in OLIVELLE, *Upanisads,* p. 249.

knowledge and love. Such a view is virtually identical with that of Gregory of Nyssa, and it undermines any very radical opposition between the theories of reincarnation and of resurrection.

If Christians follow the teaching of 1 Corinthians 15, they will look for resurrection in very different bodily forms – glorious and incorruptible – and in a very different form of space-time, where the laws of entropy have ceased to operate[10]. In that case, the resurrection world will be a different realm of embodiment, virtually a form of rebirth. If, in that world, there are places where unresolved human desires can work themselves out (a sort of Purgatory or intermediate state), and if there is opportunity for growing in the knowledge and love of God, one has a concept of many afterlife worlds in which human souls can learn and progress which is not radically different from the Vedantic idea of forms of rebirth in which one's *karma*, the consequences of one's acts in this life, can be worked out.

It should be clear that there are many possibilities of bringing Vedanta and Christianity together and allowing them to influence one another in creative ways. In speaking of a 'Christian Vedanta', I am speaking of the beliefs of a person who accepts the general Vedantic teaching about the nature of the supreme reality, of the final human goal, and of the ways that lead to the attainment of the goal. The many schools of Vedanta share these core concepts, while giving various interpretations of them, and they share a veneration for the Upanishads as inspired writings, conveying deep spiritual truths of great importance to human understanding. A Christian Vedantin would accept Jesus as one who, from the very different Jewish religious tradition, shows in a distinctive way the nature of the supreme Spirit of which the Upanishads teach, and who opens, or even constitutes, a way of spiritual progress which leads to final release from egoism and union with the Supreme Self.

Put in this broad way, it may seem obvious that one can be a Christian Vedantin. Surely all Christians believe that Jesus shows the nature of the supreme Spirit, God, and that he releases people, or will eventually release them, from egoism and enable them to be united with God in fellowship and love. There is nothing provocative about that. This very fact establishes one important truth: that the conceptual worlds of Vedanta and Christianity are not locked into separate, incommensurable compartments. They are inter-translatable, and indeed are talking about recognisably similar topics. At least in this case, there is the possibility of a common religious discourse, and of a good degree of mutual understanding and agreement.

10. 1 Cor 15,42-44.

Sometimes the personal theism of Christianity has been contrasted with what is called the 'impersonal monism' of Hinduism. As I have indicated, any alleged contrast made in these terms simply overlooks the richness of both Christian and Indian concepts of God. The Thomist idea that God is his own existence (*Deus est suum esse*)[11] is about as impersonal as one could get, and the 'dualistic' Vedanta of Madhva distinguishes finite souls and matter quite as sharply from God as any Christian could wish. Brahman, though in some schools it is regarded as wholly without qualities and as beyond any description, also has a strongly personal aspect. If it has the nature of consciousness and bliss, then it has some characteristics of a personal being, possessing at least analogies to understanding and feeling. So the gulf between Vedanta and classical Christian theism is not so great after all.

Nevertheless, there are differences of tone between an Upanishad-based notion of Brahman and a Bible-based idea of God. In the Upanishads there is a continued interest in the nature of ultimate reality, and in the way to attain knowledge of it. There is a central concern with the true understanding of existence, or with a knowledge of the Supreme which will liberate one from ignorance and illusion. Consistently with this emphasis, the religious path is primarily one of sitting alone in meditation, aiming to withdraw the mind from sensory desires and achieve awareness of the inner nature of the self. This is a way of intuitive knowledge, and the Upanishads constantly teach that, beneath the multiplicity and suffering of the world there is one being of bliss, which is the inner reality of all things, which can be known in human experience.

The Hebrew Bible, by contrast, has almost no interest in speculation about the true nature of reality. It speaks of a God who is active to liberate Israel from slavery and oppression, and who makes a covenant of mutual loyalty and trust with human beings. This God gives a moral law, and if humans obey that law, God will grant them happiness and fulfilment.

For the Upanishads the Supreme is the inner reality of all things, to be known by the calming of passions and concentration of mind. For the Bible the Supreme is a demanding moral will, to be feared and loved as a subject who stands over against every human will. Thus the central symbols of the divine in the Upanishads and in the Bible, symbols of the Universal Self and the Moral Will, are distinctive and different. They are not, however, incompatible, and a richer view of the divine may be obtained if the main insights of both traditions are accepted.

11. AQUINAS, *Summa Theologiae,* 1a, 3, 4, Blackfriars ed., p. 30.

Many criticisms have been made of the Biblical idea, pointing out its incipiently authoritarian and paternalistic character. God may be seen as a heteronomous tyrant, who is to be unquestioningly obeyed, and whose commands and purposes are arbitrary and inscrutable. This is a caricature, no doubt, but there have been enough authoritarian and paternalistic religious leaders to have given the caricature social embodiment in church institutions. The negative aspect of Biblical theism is its tendency to authoritarian intolerance. But its positive aspect is the importance it gives to morality, to the inescapable demand for social justice and personal compassion. The Bible unequivocally portrays the will of God as commanding justice and the development of a community of peace on earth. The faith of the ancient Israelites is not an otherworldly tradition in any sense, and it binds religion, personal morality and social justice together in a way quite distinctive among the religious cults of its time.

A similar tension of negative and positive aspects is characteristic of the Upanishadic traditions. Negatively, there have been constant criticisms, largely from Indian traditions themselves, that a stress on the sole reality of Brahman devalues the individual and leads to a lack of concern with social justice. Indeed, the widespread belief in reincarnation may give rise to the thought that people deserve whatever happens to them because of past-life wrong actions. When the *sanyassin* leaves his family and goes into the forest to seek liberation, this can be seen as a form of callous self-absorption, and the Upanishads have often been criticised for giving support to the caste system, which builds a permanent and inescapable inequality into social structures.

The positive aspect of Upanishadic thought is its stress that the religious life is a seeking for non-attachment, non-violence, universal compassion and inner calm and bliss. The way of liberation is a way of escape from egoism, and the teaching of the unity and omnipresence of the Supreme Self forbids the characterisation of others as damned or rejected by a judgmental God. All souls are parts of Brahman, and enlightenment is possible for them, if they will practice renunciation. There is here a pronounced sense of personal responsibility for one's own destiny, together with a sense that one is never truly estranged from the Supreme Self.

If the Vedantin and Biblical views could be taken together, one might have a commitment to social justice together with a personal search for wisdom, compassion and bliss. It may seem that they could not be taken together, since for Vedanta the universe is part of Brahman, while the Biblical God always stands over against creation. However, I have suggested that this is an over-simple contrast. It is at this point that the Christian doctrine of incarnation begins to bridge the seeming gulf between the *prima facie* Hebrew doctrine of the utter transcendence of God and the *prima facie* Vedantin doctrine of the immanence of the divine in the universe. A God who 'becomes flesh' cannot exclude all finite reality from itself. Indeed, the Pauline letters go much further than this, and speak of the church as 'the body of Christ', an extension of the incarnation, so that at least parts of this universe are one with God, as the body of the eternal Word. The letters speak of the destiny of the universe as being that all things, in heaven and on earth, should be united 'in Christ'[12], and thus they propound a vision of the participation of all the universe in God. The Christian God does not stand over against creation, but in the person of the Word, enters into creation, unites it to the divine, and raises it to share in the divine glory. If, for Christians, the whole world is not now the body of God, it is, Paul's letters suggest, meant to be and it eventually, if only in a 'new creation', will be.

On the other side, Vedanta does not simply identify everything in the universe with God, as though it expressed the inner nature of Brahman just as it is. On the contrary, finite souls are seen to be ensnared in greed, hatred and delusion[13]. To them, the divine self must appear as infinitely other and greater, a being of pure wisdom, compassion and bliss[14]. There is here a proper otherness of Brahman, and each soul must progress far beyond its present individuality before it can realise the true form of its unity with the Supreme Self.

In most schools of Vedanta (especially those of Ramanuja and Madhva) individual souls will always remain distinct, and will be parts of Brahman by being related in loving service and devotion to the Supreme Self, and being vehicles of the joyful play of Brahman in creation. This is perhaps most closely paralleled in Christian tradition by the doctrine of the Holy Spirit, who works within each finite soul to transform it into an image of wisdom, compassion and joy, and bring it into loving relationship with the glorified Jesus, who is the human form of God. The Vedantin looks within to find the Self of all, and learns to see all finite things as held within the Supreme Self. So the Christian looks within to find that ultimate mystery, 'Christ in you, the hope of glory'[15], and

12. Eph 1,10.
13. "The individual self is like a lame man, weighed down by fetters made up of the fruits of good and evil deeds", *Maitri Upanisad* 4, 2, in R.C. ZAEHNER (trans.), *Hindu Scriptures*, J.M. Dent, 1966, p. 225.
14. "This is the immense and unborn self, unageing, undying, immortal, free from fear", *Brihadaranyaka Upanisad* 4, 4, 25, in OLIVELLE, *Upanisads,* p. 68.
15. Col 1,27.

learns to see all finite things as held together in Christ. The Christian is then called to live as a member of the body of Christ, following the pattern of Jesus' actions in the world, healing, forgiving and reconciling, living as the servant of all to bring in the kingdom of God, the community of justice and love.

In this sense, Christ forms a bridge between the Biblical and the Vedantic traditions. He unites what Friedrich Heiler called the prophetic and mystical aspects of religion in himself[16] – or, more guardedly, many of his early followers in the churches laid the groundwork for doing so. Of course there was no link made with the thought of Vedanta in early Christianity. The new faith was worked out with the help of concepts drawn from Greek philosophy, which had already been employed in Hellenistic Judaism to provide a speculative background to the prophetic tradition. It is only in this century that the Indian tradition of Vedanta has been renewed and reinvigorated sufficiently to offer a new set of interpretative concepts for contemporary Christian thought. There have been many explorers of these new possibilities, most notably, perhaps, Abishiktananda, Bede Griffiths, Raimundo Pannikaar and C. F. Andrews, Christians in India who have tried to develop Indian interpretations of the Christian tradition. This is not just a matter of what is sometimes called 'indiginisation', as though it was a means of putting unchanging Christian ideas into words that Indians will more readily appreciate. It is a matter of bringing together two major religious traditions, the Indian and the semitic, to form a broader understanding of what Christianity is.

Jesus obviously stood in the Biblical tradition, and in some respects he speaks as a prophet, declaring judgment on Israel and a promise of renewal for those who obey God. But he was interpreted by his followers, if one takes the gospels as a reliable guide, as shattering the prophetic mould. Obedience to Torah was replaced, in the community of his disciples, by the guiding of the Spirit who was experienced as the power of the living Christ[17]. The decisive Judgment was seen as having been vicariously accepted by Jesus himself, so that God's forgiving mercy was freely offered to all who trusted his word. The promise of peace was transferred from the political realm to the resurrection world, to a future beyond this historical time in which all suffering and conflict would be ended. But that eschatological future was also experienced in the church, as the disciples found a new life in Christ and were bound

16. F. HEILER, *Erscheinungformen und Wesen der Religion*, Stuttgart, W. Kohlhammer, 1961.

17. 'The law of the Spirit of life in Christ Jesus has set me free from the law of sin and death' (Rom 8,2).

together as the body of the eternal Word of God, nourished by the life of Christ within them.

All these elements derive from the Jewish tradition, though they introduce a much more unitive view of the relation of creator and creation. God not only creates and judges, but also enters into creation to participate in its joys and sorrows. God not only inspires the prophets, but also unites human lives to the divine life, as they seek to become a servant community of reconciliation in the world, empowered by the Spirit of God. God not only promises a future just society, or a share in the world to come, but also raises creation, through Christ, to share in the being of God and be transfigured into the life of Christ.

From the very first, the mission of Jesus was understood in a cosmic context. Even in the most down to earth gospel of Mark, Jesus is portrayed as the Son of Man who will come in the glory of God to unite humans to himself and bring this world-order to an end. In John's gospel, Jesus explicitly embodies the eternal Word, in whom humans are to be united, fulfilled and made one with the creator of all. One sees within the New Testament a development of understanding about the cosmic role of Jesus, and his place in God's purpose for humanity. Such development continued, through much debate and discussion, in the early church, until the Chalcedonian definition provided a normative statement of the relation of Jesus to the eternal Word of God.

Chalcedon is, however, more like the statement of a research proposal than like a completed piece of work. Jesus Christ may be a normative disclosure of God for Christians, but there is still much that we have to learn about what the Christ is. In the modern world, there are two main resources for extending our understanding of Christ. One is the development of the sciences, including especially evolutionary cosmology and biology, and the other is an increased awareness and knowledge of the global dimension of religious belief. It is the latter with which I am concerned here. If revelation is to occur, it is necessary that it should occur at particular times and in particular contexts. But it is impossible to think that a God of universal love would not give some revelation of the divine nature and the ultimate human goal to people in many different cultures. The Indian complex of religious traditions is one major cultural source of religious beliefs, and it seems reasonable to expect that there will be genuine disclosures of the divine in those traditions.

As one examines various traditions of revelation, however, it becomes obvious that they contain cultural features which are partly restricting of vision, though also partly complementary to one another. It does not seem rational to make a wholly privileged exception in one's own case, and so one is led to see one's own tradition as containing a genuine disclosure of the divine, but as also containing many cultural and conceptual limitations, and so as standing in need of complementary insights from other cultures. One main reason for speaking of a Christian Vedanta lies in the belief that a meeting of two great complementary traditions may enable some of one's own cultural restrictions to become clear, and may transform the understanding of both traditions in a wider, though to be sure still limited, perspective.

A Christian Vedanta will provide a distinctive interpretation of the Indian tradition, by stressing the way in which God enters into a particular history to act in new and creative ways. It will stress the particularity and the importance of events in history in a way which the vast cosmological perspectives of Vedanta may overlook. It will stress the absolute moral demands for justice and compassion that God makes, but also the suffering and serving form of the love of God, which will forgive and reconcile those who confess their failure to meet those demands and turn to God for help. It will stress the features of personal relationship and community which do sometimes get overlaid in Vedanta by more introspective and individualistic patterns of spirituality.

On the other side, an understanding of Vedanta can help Christians to see that God is not only the severe Judge who condemns humans as miserable sinners, but the Self of all, with whom all sentient beings are united indivisibly at the very heart of their being. It can help Christians to see that there are many paths to God, and that those paths must be evaluated by their capacity to lead to non-attachment, wisdom and compassion, not simply by their conformity to some doctrinally correct formula. And it can help Christians to see how persons are pursuing a spiritual path in which each is responsible for their own liberation or bondage, under the forgiving and guiding love of God.

To speak of Christian Vedanta is to speak of crossing of the gulf between Abrahamic and Indian traditions, a crossing which, once it is made, can seem entirely natural and even inevitable. In such a crossing, Jesus would not be wholly subsumed either into the ideal Abrahamic or Indian type. He would not be simply a prophet, inspired by the spirit of God. He would not be an avatar, one of many who manifest the divine life in the appearance of a human form. He would be a fully human person, manifesting the divine life in time in a historically unique way, by the unhampered power of the spirit of God. Just as reflection on his life led to a breaking of the boundaries of Judaism, so it might now lead to a breaking of the boundary between Abrahamic and Indian religious traditions.

Vedanta and Christianity are only two of the world's many religious traditions, and what I have sketched is just part of a many-sided conversation which the modern world offers to the Christian believer. But, if I may end on a personal note, I myself have always been attracted by the writings of Ramanuja, Aurobindo, and Radhakrishnan, by the Upanishads and the Bhagvad-Gita, and by Indian traditions of meditation and discipleship. I have found that they have extended what might otherwise have been, on my part, a rather exclusive and narrow Christian view. They illuminate parts of the New Testament tradition (about the unity of all things in Christ, for example) that seem to have been strangely overlooked in much Christian writing. And they offer practices of meditation which complement the rather unduly verbal traditions of prayer I had encountered. So I have no difficulty in thinking of myself as a Christian Vedantin, able to draw on the resources of two great spiritual traditions, a disciple of Jesus Christ who seeks a more adequate understanding of his role in human history by beginning to see him in the world view of the Upanishads, and ultimately in a global religious perspective. This is a picture which may have at least a small place in the gallery of portrayals of the myriad Christ.

Christ Church College
University of Oxford
Oxford OX1 1DP
United Kingdom

Keith WARD

BUDDHIST VIEWS OF CHRIST
AND THE QUESTION OF UNIQUENESS

One of the main christological problems of our times is that of the uniqueness of Christ. It is a problem which is often regarded as a uniquely Christian one, since none of the other religions seems to make the same claim for the unique ontological nature and soteriological role of their respective founder. It has come to be regarded as a stumbling block in the openness toward, and the dialogue with, other religions, and has led to a strong polarization within the field of the theology of religions. Some theologians insist on the traditional understanding of the uniqueness of Jesus while others have come to reinterpret this uniqueness in a variety of ways so as to allow for the possibility of salvation through other religious traditions. The latter have been labeled pluralists, while the former are called exclusivists or inclusivists, depending on whether or not divine grace is believed to be operative in other religious traditions.

While the question of the uniqueness of Jesus Christ may be regarded as one internal to Christian dogmatic theology, it has also become one of the crucial issues in the attempts at inculturation and interreligious dialogue. Inculturation is not merely a matter of adaptation, but it includes dialogue with the religious tradition which traditionally has given shape to that culture. Both inculturation and interreligious dialogue involve a re-thinking of traditional Christian categories from a radically different hermeneutical horizon, based on the idea that a truly universalistic religion should transcend the limited historical and philosophical context in which it took shape, and be capable of reformulation in categories belonging to different traditions. Thus, while the understanding of Jesus Christ in Africa is often in terms of a spiritual healer or great ancestor, in India, Jesus Christ has come to be understood through the Hindu categories of *guru* or *avatar*.

While most attempts at inculturation and dialogue may question the traditional Christian understanding of the uniqueness of Jesus Christ, it is predominantly the encounter with the religious traditions of Asia, more particularly Hinduism and Buddhism, which has posed the most direct challenge. This may be illustrated, for example, by the writings of the French Benedictine monk Henri Le Saux, who after a lifetime of reinterpreting the Christian experience in Hindu terms came to understand the uniqueness of Jesus in purely mystical, relational or symbolic terms:

> The divinity of Jesus is not separated from the "divinity" of every created being. It is its summit, its total accomplishment[1].

> The only thing important: that Christ be Everything for me. That there be nothing held back in me with regard to him. That every human being be unique, my everything to whom I give myself wholly. In This I shall have the experience of the Unique[2].

> Why do we want to compare Jesus, make him enter into the crowd of gurus, make of him a guru apart? My guru is unique just as I am unique[3].

These reflections set the tone for the Asian understanding of the uniqueness of Jesus. In this paper, however, I shall focus on a Buddhist understanding of the figure of Jesus Christ and its implications for the Christian idea of uniqueness. Buddhism lends itself probably better than any other world religion to the rethinking of christology from a different hermeneutical horizon. Like Christianity, Buddhism is a universalistic religion, based on a historical founder to whom an absolute status and soteriological powers have been attributed.

Within the Buddhist tradition, various schools developed with very different conceptions of the nature and role of the Buddha or savior. Whereas the original Theravada school focused mainly on the historical Shakyamuni Buddha, other schools place more emphasis on the transcendent Buddha-principle, while the later, Mahayana tradition of Buddhism came to believe in heavenly Buddhas such as Amida Buddha or the more universal ideal of the *Bodhisattva*. Each of these categories has been used to rethink the figure of Jesus Christ from a Buddhist point of view.

This rethinking does not necessarily imply the need or even the possibility of adopting Buddhist hermeneutics within the Christian tradition. As John Keenan points out in his *Mahayana christology*, the fact that Christianity has used existing philosophical concepts and traditions in the articulation of its faith "does not mean that all philosophies are amenable to the articulation of Christian faith"[4]. What the use of a radically different hermeneutical tradition may offer Christianity is, therefore, first, a sharper understanding of the constituent elements of the traditional understanding

---

1. H. LE SAUX, *La montée au fond du cœur. Le journal intime du moine Chrétien – Sannyasi Hindou 1948-1973*, Paris, 1986 (1954), p. 125.
2. *Ibid.*, p. 455 (1973).
3. *Ibid.*, p. 421, (1972).
4. J. KEENAN, *The Meaning of Christ. A Mahayana Theology*, Maryknoll, NY, 1989, p. 187.

of the uniqueness of Jesus Christ and, second, an invitation to experiment with the traditional limits of orthodoxy. In other words, it serves to bring about a critical dialogue between the essence of Christian faith and the new ways which present themselves for expressing it.

I. JESUS CHRIST AS A BUDDHA

The term Buddha, literally "one who has awakened" or "enlightened one" was not exclusively and probably not originally attributed to the founder of Buddhism, Siddhartha Gautama, also called Shakyamuni (ca. 566-486). The title belongs within the Indian world which developed around 800 B.C.E. and which regarded life and time from the perspective of radical transience and eternal return or repetition (*samsara*), and enlightenment as a state or an experience of liberation from samsara. Various spiritual masters or founders of religious traditions such as Jainism were regarded by their followers as the embodiment of that experience and called Buddha.

While most of the life of Siddhartha Gautama is shrouded in myths which developed in the first six centuries of the Buddhist tradition, the oldest sources, the Sutras of the Pali Canon, do recount in detail the experience of "supreme and perfect enlightenment" (*bodhi*), which gradually led to his identification with the title of "the Buddha". It came to refer not only to the state of full enlightenment or mental liberation, but also to the ability to understand the cause of suffering and to lead others to the same state of liberation. In the Theravada canon it is explained as "a name, derived from the final liberation of the Enlightened Ones, the Blessed Ones, together with the omniscient knowledge at the root of the Enlightenment Tree; this name 'Buddha' is a designation based on realization"[5].

From the early scriptures, it is clear that the Buddha regarded himself as no more than a path-finder and a teacher or guide, rather than as a savior. To the Brahmin Moggalana, he said "There is a Nirvana and a path which leads to Nirvana, and I am here as adviser. However, among the disciples whom I exhort and instruct in this way, some attend the supreme goal, Nirvana, others do not attain it. What can I do in this matter, O Brahmin? The Tathagata, O Brahmin, is merely a shower of the path"[6]. The Buddha

---

5. From the *Patisambhida* of Buddhaghosa (trans. NYANAMOLI), *The Path of Purification, Visuddhimagga*, Colombo, 1964, p. 213.

6. *Majjhima Nikaya*, II, p. 6, quoted by E. LAMOTTE, *History of Indian Buddhism*, Leuven, 1988 (original French edition 1958), p. 644.

guided disciples for about 45 years, recruiting many to his monastic order (*sangha*) and leading a large number of disciples to the state of liberation or *nirvana*. At the age of 80, in approximately the year 486 B.C.E[7]., he died in Kusinagara from eating a bad dish of pork, offered to him by the smith Cunda. Unlike Jesus Christ, whose sudden and violent death cried for meaning, the Buddha thus died at an old age from a rather trivial cause. At the time of his death, the Buddha is said to have admonished his disciples, saying: "Behold now, brethren, I exhort you saying, 'Decay is inherent in all component things! Work out your salvation with diligence'"[8]. These last words of the Buddha both refer to his own mortality, or radical finitude, and call attention to the ultimate self-reliance of his disciples. In a further meditation on these words, Brahma Sahampati states:

> They all, all beings that have life, shall lay
> Aside their complex form – that aggregation
> Of mental and material qualities,
> That gives them, or in heaven or on earth,
> Their fleeting individuality!
> E'en as the teacher – being such a one,
> Unequaled among all the men that are,
> Successor to the prophets of old time,
> Mighty in wisdom, and in insight clear, Hath died![9]

Buddhist soteriology is based on the idea that underlying the mental and material qualities or aggregates which form the human person, there is no permanent and unchanging Self. This is the teaching of *anatman*, or "no self". The departed Buddha is thus regarded as the "thus gone" or the *tathagata*, and no divine or eternal person thus remains to be worshiped, invoked or expected to return. While the Buddha is thus regarded as a plain human being, his death, like his birth, is surrounded by mythical events: "When the Blessed One died there arose, at the moment of his passing out of existence, a mighty earthquake, terrible and awe-inspiring, and the thunders of heaven burst forth"[10].

In the course of the Buddha's teaching, many of his disciples came to realize enlightenment. While the Buddha's path to liberation was regarded as unique in the sense of new and absolutely reliable, discipleship of the Buddha was never regarded as the only way to nirvana.

---

7. This is according to the chronology of E. LAMOTTE, *History of Indian Buddhism*, p. 16.

8. *Maha-parinibbana-sutta*, 6.10 (trans. T.W. RHYS DAVIS), *Sacred Books of the East*, vol XI, p. 114.

9. *Ibid.*, 6.15, vol. XI, pp. 116-117.

10. *Ibid.*, 6.14, vol. XI, p. 115.

Besides the *sramanas* (or ascetics) who followed the Buddha, the tradition acknowledged the existence of *pratyeka-Buddhas*, ("individual Buddhas"), or people who have reached the state of enlightenment without the help of the Buddha. (It is here that Buddhism situates the origin of its tolerance toward all other religions.) The texts, however, reserve the title of Buddha for Shakyamuni, while disciples and others who realized enlightenment or *nirvana* were called *arhat*, "worthy one". The Buddhist tradition thus did develop a certain sense of the unique role of the Buddha in history. While the Buddha was not the first or the last living Buddha, he was regarded as the only one in our world age or *kalpa*. Some texts mention the existence of six (others 24) Buddhas prior to Shakyamuni, and only a few centuries after the death of the Buddha, there emerged a belief in the future Buddha Maitreya, who is presently in the Tulsita heaven, awaiting his descent in the coming age. While every age has its Buddha, humans thus have only a limited chance to meet and follow a Buddha. The biographies of the Buddhas which appear in the early scriptures thus came to answer to certain stereotypical and superhuman motives. A Buddha is one who in the course of countless incarnations has acquired sufficient merit to be reborn in the Tulsita heaven, where he awaits his final rebirth as a Buddha. Both the conception and the birth of a Buddha are recounted as miraculous events, the conception being virginal or purely conceptual, and the birth accompanied by various natural phenomena such as earthquakes, flowers falling from the sky, etc. A Buddha is born with thirty-two marks of a "great being", and in a state of full consciousness. In time, the unique and divine characteristics of the Buddha were further developed and reinforced through various glorifying titles and epithets which were attributed to him such as "Lord of the Cosmos" (*lokanatha*), "Knower of the world" (*lokavidu*), "Universal monarch" (*cakravartin*), "Lord" (*bhagavan*). All kinds of miraculous powers were also attributed to the Buddha. It is said that upon seeing him, "the blind see, the deaf hear, the dumb speak, the mad recover their reason, nakedness is covered, hunger and thirst are appeased, the sick cured, the infirm regain their wholeness"[11]. Based on his study of the epithets in the *Mahaparinirvanasutra*, Andre Bareau compares the later conception of the Buddha to that of any other divine savior:

> Perfect in all points, superior through distance from all beings, unique, the Beatific had evidently taken, in the thought of his followers, the place

---

11. *Lalitavistara* (pp. 278-9), quoted by E. LAMOTTE, *History of Indian Buddhism*, pp. 645-646.

which the devotees of the great religions attributed to the great God whom
they adored[12].

Etienne Lamotte attributes this process of divinization of the Buddha
to the input of popular or lay religiosity:

> If monks, devoted to a life of study and meditation, are able to resign them-
> selves to regarding their founder only as a sage who had entered Nirvana,
> lay followers, who are exposed to the difficulties of their times, require
> something other than a "dead god" of whom only the "remains" could be
> revered. They want a living god, a "god superior to the gods" (*devatideva*)
> who will continue his beneficial activity among them, who can predict the
> future, perform wonders, and whose worship will be something more than
> mere recollection[13].

While popular feeling may have attributed explicitly divine characteristics to the historical person of the Buddha, the monastic tradition
developed its own process of absolutization, not of the Buddha himself,
but of his teaching, or *dharma*. The Buddha came to be identified with
his teaching, which was elevated to an absolute and ultimate principle
called the *dharmakaya*, the "dharma-body", or "body of truth". With
this, the historical Buddha, or the physical body (*rupakaya*) of the Buddha came to be regarded as a mere manifestation or apparition of the
dharmakaya, and thus of lesser importance. Within certain schools of
ancient Buddhism such as the Lokottaravadins, this developed into a
form of Buddhist docetism. Buddhas were regarded as otherworldly,
perfect and pure.

While this approach was rejected in other schools, the emphasis
remained upon the transcendent essence of the Buddha or the *dharmakaya*,
and the historical Shakyamuni Buddha came to be referred to as the phan-
tom-body (*nirmanakaya*) of the Buddha. This led to a greater freedom and
flexibility in recognizing incarnations of the *dharmakaya* in various historical figures who were recognized as Buddhas. With this, however, the
uniqueness of historical Buddhas also came to be downplayed.

It is within this context that some Buddhists also recognize the figure
of Jesus Christ as a Buddha. For example, D.T. Suzuki, a famous Zen
master and one of the pioneers of the Buddhist-Christian dialogue, states
that for him Jesus Christ is "a manifestation of the Dharmakaya in
human form. He is a Buddha and as such not essentially different from
Shakyamuni"[14].

---

12. *Myths and Symbols* (eds. C.H. LONG and J.M. KITAGAWA), Chicago, IL, 1969,
pp. 19-20.
13. E. LAMOTTE, *History of Indian Buddhism*, p. 645.
14. D.T. SUZUKI, *Outlines of Mahayana Buddhism*, New York, 1963, p. 259.

The understanding of Jesus as a Buddha focuses exclusively on the life of Jesus a religious revolutionary who was brought to a new experience of the absolute reality as expressed in the words "I and the Father are one" (John 10,30) and who led his disciples to the same experience. In this Buddhist view of the figure of Jesus Christ, no particular soteriological meaning is attached to the suffering, death and resurrection of Jesus. On the contrary, the death of Christ is often regarded as shocking and repulsive, as reflected in the words of Suzuki:

> The crucified Christ is a terrible sight and I cannot help associating it with the sadistic impulse of a physically affected brain. Christians would say that crucifixion means crucifying the self or the flesh, since without subduing the self we cannot attain moral perfection. This is where Buddhism differs from Christianity. Buddhism declares that there is from the very beginning no self to crucify. To think that there is the self is the start of all errors and evils. Ignorance is at the root of all things that go wrong. As there is no self, no crucifixion is needed, no sadism is to be practiced, no shocking sight to be displayed by the road-side[15].

From a Buddhist perspective, suffering has at most a didactic and not a soteriological function. In viewing Jesus Christ as a Buddha, Jesus then becomes one of many wisdom teachers.

II. JESUS CHRIST AS AMIDA

In some of the schools of the later Mahayana tradition of Buddhism, the emphasis came to lie not so much on the historical Buddha or his teaching as model or example, but on a heavenly Buddha as savior. The belief in heavenly Buddhas developed as part of a new cosmology which located an infinite number of heavenly worlds outside of this world, with some of them presided over by a heavenly or a cosmic Buddha. In addition to the figure of Shakyamuni, the four main celestial Buddhas were Amida, presiding over the Western paradise or Pure Land, Akshobhya, presiding over the Pure Land of the East, Amoghasiddhi, the Buddha of the Northern Pure Land, and Ratnasambhava, Buddha of the Pure Land of the South. Furthermore, other heavenly Buddhas were recognized with very specific functions, including Bhaisagyabuddha, who is regarded as the medicine Buddha. While in some Mahayana Sutras all these Buddhas were seen as various forms or manifestations of Shakyamuni, each acquired its own attributes, mythology and forms of devotion. The veneration of these heavenly Buddhas may be regarded as a

---

15. D.T. SUZUKI, *Mysticism Christian and Buddhist*, London, 1957, p. 99.

Buddhist rendering of the devotion to Hindu Gods, and as an answer to popular devotion.

Buddhologically, these heavenly Buddhas were regarded as an emanation from the *dharmakaya*, and called *sambhogakaya*, "body of bliss" or "enjoyment body" of the Buddha. While the sambhogakaya came to occupy a central place in the devotion of many Buddhists, the various heavenly Buddhas were not regarded as permanent and ultimate realities, but as dependent upon the *dharmakaya*.

The most famous heavenly Buddha in the Mahayana tradition is the figure of Amida Buddha (derived from the Sanskrit Aithabha "infinite light" or Amitayus "infinite life"). The origin of devotion to this Buddha may be found in the Pure Land Sutras, or the *Sukhavativyuha* Sutras, which are dated around the beginning of the Common Era. The Sutras tell the story of a monk called Dharmakara who, contemplating the suffering of the world, vowed not to enter Nirvana until he had accumulated sufficient merit to create a world which would be free from suffering – a world from which there would be no rebirth in this world, and where the Buddhist dharma would be heard without effort. Among the 46 (or 48, according to some sources) different vows of Amida, the most important ones are vows 19 and 20, stating that those who believe in Amida and sincerely wish to be reborn in his Pure Land or Western Paradise need only hear or repeat the name of the Buddha, or think of him in order to be reborn there. For Pure Land Buddhism, liberation thus comes about through the grace and power of Amida, much more than through one's own effort. The Pure Land school of Buddhism became very popular, first in China, beginning around the sixth century, and later in Japan. In Japan, different schools developed within the Pure Land tradition, based on the question of the relation between works and grace. Honen (1133-1212), founder of the Japanese Jodo-school, believed that both works and grace were instrumental in the proses of salvation, and that the recitation of the name of Amida was a form of religious discipline which would bring about the saving grace of Amida. His disciple Shinran (1173-1262), on the other hand, permeated by the sense of human sinfulness and limitations, believed that human beings could do nothing to bring about their own salvation, and that the very act of surrender and devotion to Amida was an expression of the fact that one was already saved rather than a means to bring it about. He became the founder of the *Jodo-shinshu* or the "true Pure-Land" school of Buddhism.

In the Buddhist-Christian dialogue, comparisons have often been made between the figures of Shinran and Luther, and between the conceptions of Amida and Christ. In his *Beyond Dialogue*, John Cobb tries to rethink the figure of Jesus Christ through the category of Amida and vice versa. Both Christ and Amida are represented in their respective traditions as a transcendent source of saving grace, and it is the response to this grace by an act of total self-surrender which leads to salvation. But while the risen Christ is regarded as absolute and as ontologically real in the Christian tradition, Amida is to be understood as a reality which ultimately needs to be internalized. Since there is only one ultimate reality which is understood as the formless and unqualified *dharmakaya*, heavenly Buddhas might be understood as a concession to human weakness, which must ultimately lead to a more spiritually mature understanding of reality. For Pure Land Buddhism, faith or surrender to Amida ultimately represents a state of consciousness, rather than a permanent interpersonal relationship. Or, as John Cobb puts it, "although in the initial presentation and acceptance the accent falls on relation to the Other Power, the deepening of the understanding leads toward an identity of that Other with the state of being which it promises and bestows"[16]. The understanding of Christ as Amida thus leads to a radical internalization of the reality of Jesus Christ. Insisting that the Pure Land faith in Amida is ultimately the same as the Christian faith in Jesus Christ, Cobb states that:

> The grace that works faith in our hearts is at once the Other and the Other's presence. Our faith is not only a relation to the source of grace but also the believing heart which that grace affects by its presence. In the deepening of faith the imagery often shifts from that of I and Thou to that of the indwelling of Christ or the Holy Spirit. Though there is no final identity of self and Other, the Other is constitutive of the self[17].

For Cobb, a Buddhist conception of Christ as Amida may help Christian faith to overcome its attachment or clinging to a particular image of Jesus Christ, thus coming to a more open faith. However, with the internalization of the reality of Jesus Christ, the unique ontological status and function of the risen Christ is dissolved. Even though Christ or Amida may be experienced as unique and ultimate in the faith of the believer, in the end the uniqueness involved is understood to be no more than functional and subjective. Jesus Christ then becomes, at most, a symbol of absolute reality which brings about absolute surrender. But even as symbol, Jesus Christ would not be regarded as unique from a Buddhist point of view. There are many heavenly Buddhas who may be regarded

---

16. J. COBB, *Beyond Dialogue: Toward a Mutual Transformation of Christianity and Buddhism*, Philadelphia, PA, 1982, p. 103.

17. *Ibid.*, p. 103.

as various forms of Shakyamuni or of Christ, but all are ultimately subordinate to the absolute reality or the *dharmakaya*.

III. Jesus Christ as Bodhisattva

Besides heavenly Buddhas, the Mahayana tradition came to focus
on the figure of the *Bodhisattva* as a mediator of salvation. The term
Bodhisattva was originally used to refer to the Buddha in the course
of his many lives leading up to the experience of liberation. These
lives were mainly characterized by deeds of total selflessness and
compassion. When in the Mahayana tradition, Buddhahood came to
be regarded as accessible to all, the *Bodhisattva* became the general
ideal, and the term came to refer to those who are aiming for full Buddhahood for the benefit of all. Within Mahayana cosmology, both
human and heavenly *Bodhisattva*s were recognized and the difference
between a fully enlightened Buddha and a *Bodhisattva* was not always
clear.

While a *Bodhisattva* is characterized by six virtues (giving, morality,
patience, vigor, meditation and wisdom), the distinctive characteristic of
a *Bodhisattva* is the element of compassion. This is reflected in one of
the oldest Mahayana texts, the *Prajnaparamita Sutras*:

> Great compassion [...] takes hold of him. He surveys countless beings with
> his heavenly eye, and what he sees fills him with great agitation [...] And
> he attends to them with the thought that: "I shall become the savior of
> those beings, I shall release them from all their sufferings"!. But he does
> not make either this, nor anything else, into a sign to which he becomes
> partial. This also is the great light of a *Bodhisattva*'s wisdom, which allows
> him to know full enlightenment[18].

The category of the *Bodhisattva* belongs within a Mahayana philosophy which conceives of ultimate reality as emptiness or *shunyata*, referring to an absence of any permanent essence of substance in things. Liberation, from this point of view, consists of the insight into the emptiness
of reality resulting in a state of freedom from worldly attachments and
commitment to the liberation of others. This is possible because within a
Mahayana worldlier "Emptiness is Form" and "Form is Emptiness". A
Bodhisattva is thus one who has become completely selfless, free from
attachments, conventional norms and distinctions, and transparent to
absolute reality.

---

18. From the *Asta* (trans. E. Conze), *The Perfection of Wisdom in Eight Thousand
Lines and its Verse Summary*, Bolinas, 1973, pp. 238-239.

It is in the context of the inculturation of Christianity in East-Asia and the dialogue with Mahayana Buddhism, that attempts have been made to understand the figure of Jesus Christ through the notion of the *Bodhisattva* and the category of *shunyata*. While acknowledging the theological and philosophical differences between Christianity and Mahayana Buddhism, Hee-Sung Keel, in his article on Jesus as *Bodhisattva*, points to the similarities between the qualities of a *Bodhisattva* and those which characterize the life and person of Jesus. Like that of a *Bodhisattva*, the life of Jesus was characterized by freedom: "Freedom from the world, freedom from religious attachment, and freedom from self"[19]. For both Jesus and the *Bodhisattva*, this freedom involves total and unconditional love and compassion for all living beings. "Undoubtedly", Keel submits, "the *Bodhisattva*'s great compassion and Jesus' unconditional love are embedded in different religio-cultural backgrounds and find different expressions in practice. Yet both are based on the freedom arising from a transcendent wisdom, and both embody pure and absolute love, which challenges our conventional worldly ethics. Ultimately, both are grounded on a deeper reality called emptiness and God's love"[20].

While Jesus Christ may be regarded from a Christian point of view as "the one who revealed most concretely and powerfully the image of the *Bodhisattva*"[21], there is no ground in the Mahayana worldlier for affirming the ontological uniqueness of Jesus. The ultimate state of emptiness allows for no distinctions or gradations. This is implicitly acknowledged in John Keenan's Mahayana christology, when he states that "the Christ preached by the church is definitive because ultimate and not because Christ's historical contingency was better than any other historical contingency"[22].

The focus of Keenan is, however, not no much on the *Bodhisattva* as a model for reinterpreting Jesus Christ as on the category of *shunyata* as a corrective against all ideological clinging to any one christological theory or truth. This is done by means of the theory of Two Truths which has been developed in the Mahayana tradition to express the difference between a direct mystical awareness, on one hand, and its articulation in conventional categories, on the other. While conventional truth has its own relative validity, it must be recognized as such, and ultimately overcome in a direct experience of absolute reality. As far as a Mahayana

---

19. HEE-SUNG KEEL, *Jesus the Bodhisattva: Christology from a Buddhist Perspective*, in *Buddhist-Christian Studies* 16 (1996), p. 176.

20. *Ibid.*, p. 179.

21. *Ibid.*, p. 185.

22. KEENAN, *The Meaning of Christ*, p. 239.

understanding of Jesus Christ is concerned, Keenan points out that the idea of dependent origination, which is the corollary of the notion of emptiness, allows for a full recognition of the humanity of Jesus, his radical commitment to the establishment of the kingdom of God, and his intimate relationship to the Father. At the same time, the notion of emptiness reflects Jesus' state of complete transparency to ultimate reality. Emptiness and dependent origination thus form the basis, according to Keenan, of the Mahayana understanding of the divinity and the humanity of Jesus: "Jesus as empty of any essence whatsoever is an ineffable outflow from the ultimate realm. But as emptiness is identical with dependent co-arising, so Jesus is enmeshed in the web of the constantly flowing and changing events of his time. He is ultimate and absolute inasmuch as he is totally empty, and human and relative inasmuch as he is totally interrelated with the world"[23]. The ultimacy or divinity of Jesus thus implies the impossibility of capturing the essence of Jesus in any christological formula:

> A Mahayana christology sees Jesus not in terms of any essence or dual nature. The notions of essence and nature are, within this philosophical culture, branded as illusions and seen as projections of a deluded consciousness that has failed to gain insight into the reality of life just as it is. Emptiness and dependent co-arising are coextensive, both describing the suchness of human experience[24].

IV. CONCLUSION

The application of Buddhist hermeneutics to the understanding of Jesus Christ rules out a traditional Christian understanding of the uniqueness of Jesus Christ. This is because, first, the concept of a once and for all redemptive and eschatological event in history has no meaning or ground within the cyclical worldlier of Hinduism and Buddhism. Secondly, Buddhism has no concept of a personal Creator-God who is also the source of grace and salvation. While a variety of human and divine mediators of salvation or liberation have appeared in Buddhist history, liberation or *nirvana* is ultimately the result of personal realization. And, thirdly, the Buddhist notion of *karma*, which may be regarded as analogous to the Christian idea of sin, is a matter of individual responsibility while the Christian notion of original sin is anterior to human responsibility. While various schools of Buddhism also developed the

23. *Ibid.*, p. 237.
24. *Ibid.*, p. 232.

belief in transcendent mediators of grace, based on the sense of impossibility of overcoming one's own karma, the savior figure was not regarded as ontologically real or as unique. The Christian idea of the uniqueness of Jesus is thus based on the combined belief in a personal Creator-God, on a linear and eschatological understanding of history, and on the idea of the fundamental human sinfulness, beliefs which are not part of Buddhist worldlier and soteriology.

Nevertheless, the idea of the uniqueness of the founder or of various mediators of salvation is not completely absent in Buddhism. Even though Shakyanumi, the founder of Buddhism, regarded himself merely as a path-finder and teacher, a variety of miraculous and soteriological powers were attributed to him. However, it was ultimately the transcendent idea of the Buddha-essence or *dharmakaya*, rather than the historical Buddha, which acquired unique attributes. In the later school of Pure Land Buddhism, the idea of uniqueness comes to lie in the relationship of total self-surrender to Amida, rather than in the ontological uniqueness of the heavenly Buddha. And with the development of the ideal of the *Bodhisattva*, uniqueness consists in a life of complete self-effacement and transparency to absolute reality, rather than in any personal or historical characteristics. Each of these Buddhist understandings of uniqueness is reminiscent of Christian attempts to rethink the uniqueness of Jesus Christ from a more pluralist point of view. The understanding of the uniqueness of the Buddha as *dharmakaya*, for example, reminds one of Raimundo Panikkar's attempt to shift the focus of the uniqueness of Jesus Christ from the historical Jesus to the transcendent or Cosmic Christ, allowing for the possible manifestation of Christ in other religious traditions. The idea of uniqueness as an act of faith and complete self-surrender is also found in Paul Knitter's subjective and relational, rather than ontological understanding of the uniqueness of Jesus Christ. And the conception of uniqueness as that of complete transparency to absolute reality, but without necessarily exhausting it, may be found in the christology of someone like as John Hick. Buddhist christologies thus rejoin certain forms of pluralist christologies.

But seen on their own, the different forms of Buddhist christology also correspond to various forms of Christian heresy. The representation of Jesus Christ as a Buddha, for example, leads to the heresy of docetism in as far as the historical manifestations of the *dharmakaya* come to be regarded as mere phantom-bodies of the ultimate reality. Though generally open to the challenges of Buddhist philosophy for Christianity, Joseph O'Leary also insists on "the irreducibility to Buddhist categories of the incarnational covenant between a transcendent God and human finitude"[25]. While Buddhism focuses on reality as such, Christian thought emphasizes the difference between the finite and the infinite, between immanence and transcendence, and preserves the tension between them.

While the notion of Amida as a divine or transcendent source of grace may allow for the possibility of thinking the Christian belief in the continued saving activity of the risen Christ from a Buddhist perspective, theologically, a Buddhist hermeneutics would lead to a form of subordinationism. As John Cobb observes, Amida is not equal to the *dharmakaya*, but a temporary and limited manifestation of it:

> This is because the Dharmakaya, ultimate reality as such, is beyond and above the other manifestations of the Buddha body. Amida as the Sambhogakaya still has a distinct character, the character of wisdom and compassion [...] Ultimate reality assumes the form of Sambhogakaya for the sake of those who cannot realize ultimate reality as such, but this is a concession to human weakness and should not be taken as the ultimate truth[26].

From the point of view of Pure Land Buddhism, Christ would thus be a temporary reality and subordinate to God. The focus on Christ as *Bodhisattva*, finally, may be regarded as a form of Arianism in that it focuses entirely on the humanity of Jesus Christ as a manifestation of the highest human potential.

Buddhist christology may thus point to the possible heresies which pluralist christologies and the attempt at inculturation of christology in a Buddhist (or Asian) context might also entail. But it may also challenge traditional christology to reflect anew on the presuppositions of its traditional understanding of the uniqueness of Jesus Christ so as to determine whether or not these presuppositions really do belong to the heart or the essence of the teaching and the person of Jesus Christ.

Faculty of Theology   Catherine CORNILLE
Katholieke Universiteit Leuven
St. Michielsstraat 6
B-3000 Leuven

25. Joseph O'LEARY, *Religious Pluralism and Christian Truth*, Edinburgh, 1996, p. 257.
26. *Ibid.*, p. 125.

THE CHALLENGE OF MOHAMMED
TO THE PLACE OF JESUS CHRIST

Theology is directed by two trends. The first involves what the religious tradition has expressed and professed in the past. The second involves the sentiments of the pious heart here and now. These two trends sometimes fit together harmoniously. However, there are times when they are in tension with one another. Such times are the matter of this matter. Since the promulgation of *Nostra Aetate*, there has been a widespread desire among all ranks in the church for a new relationship with Islam and increased respect for Mohammed. This desire is perhaps now greater than at any previous period in Christian history. The name of Mohammed no longer causes the fear it has generated since the battle at Poitiers (732) or, even more so, since the battle of Lepanto (1571).

It would appear, however, that this positive and sympathetic attitude is utterly opposed to the classical profession, that in the person and the life, death and resurrection of Jesus God has revealed himself absolutely and in eschatological definitiveness. Accordingly, there seems to be hardly any room left for a revelation to Mohammed. Consequently, it remains to be seen whether the sincere wish to enter into a new relationship with Moslems will be nipped in the bud. Or does the profession that Jesus is the Christ and the Son of God, offer more openings and more space than we have been previously suspected? This suggestion is an aspect of the present-day sentiment with respect to Islam. Perhaps the Spirit is blowing in the direction of our delivery from narrow-mindedness where Islam is concerned.

The sympathetic attitude with regard to Islam is of recent date. It has got hold of us like a kind of Pentecost fire. Or is it one of the many ambiguous signs of our time? At any rate, it is not the result of lengthy theological reflection, as is the case with other new sentiments in the church. Here theology appears only latterly. Can it account for this sentiment with regard to the tradition? It is obvious that the last word on this issue remains to be said. For the time being, it can only be a matter of hypotheses, about which thorough discussions will have to be held. It is a matter of trial and error. This is equally true of this article. In a series of circles I shall attempt to discern what the challenge of Mohammed holds[1].

---

1. The name of Mohammed is intended here to include his convictions, as they are recorded in the Koran and understood in Muslim tradition.

I. A SERIOUS CHALLENGE

Mohammed and the Koran pose a question to Christians: How do you account for monotheism, in view of the position you attribute to Jesus? Have you listened sufficiently to Abraham, Moses and Jesus himself? Are you fully aware of what you are doing, when you call Jesus "homoousios tooi patri"[2]?

It is not easy to comprehend the seriousness and profundity of Mohammed's question. To do this, we would have to know much more about Islamic religious experience and spirituality. For the point is, that this is not a theoretical question, which can be expressed in purely intellectual terms. There is more required than scientific-theological tools. Great sympathy is demanded. We have not yet come that far. We still know too little about what ultimately motivates Moslems, and how it motivates them. We have hardly yet outgrown our defensive-apologetic attitude. However, we cannot postpone Mohammed's christological questions, until we have fully grasped his Anliegen proper. In his opinion it is precisely our christology which blocks this. We are not able to listen well, in view of our own preoccupations. Self-analysis regarding our profession of Christ, and listening to Islam, belong together and are, properly speaking, part and parcel of each other. Therefore, when, in the conclusion to this paper, I focus exclusively on christology, this cannot be the final word, neither about Christian christology nor about Mohammed's question. It is merely an initial exploration of the issue.

Mohammed puts his question in connection with his own religious experience of God. This experience also developed within him in the light of his confrontation with the religious experience of Jews and Christians, and with the disputes in which they were involved. This gave him a shock, it raised questions, resulting in a new understanding of God's concern for human beings. That God cares for humankind and reveals himself to them, is not at issue. What matters is the position granted to humankind in view of God's charity. Mohammed opts for the position granted to Abraham. For him, Abraham is the prototype: Abraham became the friend of God after God first made himself known as his friend. In terms of Old Testament theology, this is a firm covenant between two utterly unequal partners. In Mohammed's judgement, the respect for the peculiar texture of this covenant is the criterion for any true religious experience and theology. In virtue of this, he censures the

---

2. Cf. G. RISSE, *Gott ist Christus, der Sohn der Maria. Eine Studie zum Christusbild im Koran*, Bonn, 1989; H. GODDARD, *Muslim Perceptions of Christianity*, London, 1996.

christology of the Christians. There is too little respect for the basic difference between God and humankind. They assume too high a position for themselves and therefore for Jesus; they display great arrogance. That is the source of all evil.

Although the same words and terms are used, there is in fact a great difference between the monotheism of Christians and Moslems. According to Mohammed, Christians, properly speaking, throw monotheism overboard, whatever they maintain. And they do this in spite of Abraham, Moses and Jesus. Mohammed wants to return to these great prophets.

That is a provocative attitude. The Reformation of the sixteenth century is nothing in comparison with this. The reformers did think that the church and especially the church authorities had illegitimately appropriated divine rights, but they stuck to classical christology. And this is precisely Mohammed's target. According to him the source of all evil among Christians is to be found here. And Mohammed was convinced that Christians are, and remain, deaf to his critical voice.

During the last few decades we have come to realize that the Reformation rightly poses questions to the Roman Catholic Church. At long last, a dialogue has been started between Reformation and Counter-Reformation. We have also acknowledged that we ought to listen to the criticism formulated by non-religious humanism. The latter may not be simple, but is also not hopeless, since this humanism is itself an outcome of the Wirkungsgeschichte of Christianity. Mohammed, on the other hand, seems to be a complete outsider. Even though he claims not to teach anything that runs counter to Jesus, he is in fact a stranger, someone outside the ecumenism of the Christian Churches, and the founder of a separate religion.

The dialogue with Islam would seem to be foredoomed to failure, if we go on regarding Mohammed merely in this way. Up until now, Christian theology has mainly concerned itself with Mohammed's misapprehensions. He was not well informed, or relied on extremely heretical groups within Christendom. He did not consider the subtle nuances in Christian theology. To a certain extent that may be so. But is it not the case that does indeed Mohammed put a serious christological question? And do we not obscure that question by criticism of its details? The fact that Mohammed did not attend to every aspect and nuance of christology does not invalidate his challenge. Approached with critical sympathy, Mohammed reminds Christians who are concerned with the question of revelation of a limit beyond which they must not go, namely, the absolute sovereignty of God. Does he not, in this way, belong to the

Wirkungsgeschichte of the Old Testament and perhaps also of the New Testament?

In mainstream Christian theology, the mystery of Jesus, as confessed at Chalcedon and as understood in the Council of Constantinople (553), is "the principle of understanding, the yardstick by which the data of other religious traditions would be measured"[3]. But how incontestable is this yardstick, when the meeting with Mohammed begins? He puts questions about our yardstick. It is not only in the margins that we will be "enriched by contact with specific elements of other religious and theological traditions"[4]. In my opinion, there is more gunpowder here than we have acknowledged. Dupuis calls other traditions "a word through which God speaks to Christians themselves, even though in Jesus Christ God has spoken the decisive divine Word to the world"[5]. The "even though" must not be allowed to detract from the claim which precedes it. To claim that Jesus is the only one through whom we can be saved (Acts 4,12), does not prevent others from posing serious questions about the contents and purport of the claim, or about our understanding of it. What does Mohammed wish to say?

II. BETWEEN JESUS AND OUR PROFESSION OF HIM

The question Mohammed poses to our profession of Christ reads as follows: Do you genuinely bear in mind the distinction between God and humanity? Do you not corrupt Jesus' status as a prophet by deifying him? Do you not forget that the unity between God and humankind can only mean that we consent to the word God speaks to us, but that no creature – not even a human being – can ever become a unity with the essence of God? These questions can also be expressed in the fashion of the following directives: You should once again subject the route which lead to the christological profession to critical examination. At a certain moment you have made a wrong turn. And this has become so self-evident that you no longer consider the issue.

Mohammed can go quite a long way with Christianity in the elevation of Jesus, provided he remains absolutely a creature, provided he is not deified. Perhaps Mohammed, as "the seal of the prophets", leaves open a position for Jesus which is even higher than the one he now possesses.

---

3. J. DUPUIS, *Jesus Christ at the Encounter of World Religions*, Maryknoll, 1991, p. 242.
4. *Ibid.*, p. 243.
5. *Ibid.*, p. 244.

According to the Koran, Jesus was born of a virgin, thanks to a striking operation of the creative Spirit of God; the Angel Gabriel protects him from the voice of Satan; he was without sin and had the power to cure sick people; God has not given death power over him. Does this not rise above Mohammed? Is Mohammed perhaps the seal of the prophets in this way, that he begs the followers of Moses and Jesus to listen to them at long last? Doesn't the seed of Tora and Gospels come to full bloom thanks to Mohammed? In nay case, there is no tendency in the Islamic tradition to compare Mohammed with Jesus. By urgently imploring his followers not to do this, and therefore not to pursue the deification of himself or of any other human being, Mohammed is the very seal of the prophets.

So Mohammed takes his stand in between Jesus and our profession that Christ is "homoousios tooi patri". This is a critical position, one comparable to the position of the Old Testament prophets within Israel. And just as their prophetic-critical voice still expresses a question about aspects of our lives and our way of thinking as believers, do does Mohammed. He, too, wishes to be a prophet for Christian people. Is that possible? Are we willing to allow it? Can we look upon him as one sent by God, who questions us about our christocentric religious experience, about our notions of deification, about our view of the link between God's hiddenness and God's love for humankind?

The issue, in brief, is whether our christology does justice to the nature and the context of revelation. For Mohammed, revelation is not "Selbstoffenbarung Gottes", but a sincere word of God to humankind. This word does not reveal God's eternal nature. God will be a Mystery for ever. For Mohammed, Jesus is clearly in accord with this. When Mohammed refers to Jesus, it is not the Jesus that our century calls "the earthly and human Jesus". No doubt, for many theologians the quest for the *ipsissima intentio Jesu* is related to a critical consideration of what I abbreviate as 'Chalcedon'. But in this critical consideration, the classical Christian approach to the relationship between God and humanity is largely maintained. For some, Jesus is precisely the great exception to the distinction between God and humanity; for others, it is in Jesus that God very obviously becomes a dimension of earthly and human reality, one which is to be in some way incarnated in all people.

In other words, the interweaving of the divine and the human nature is in fact not at issue. Certainly not with Jesus, and perhaps not with other people. More than ever, God appears to live in human beings, and a kind of pantheism or at least panentheism dawns, especially (though not exclusively) in the West. Feuerbach's critique of religion and his non-religious

humanism ought perhaps (at least partly) to be regarded as a consequence of the fact that Christianity brings God and humankind so close
together. It is true that there has been a revival of negative theology, of
the acknowledgment that God is hidden. However, it remains to be seen
whether this is sufficient to do justice to Mohammed's criticism. In his
eyes, Christian negative theology starts too late.

Let me approach the issue in a different way. The new aspect in Pannenberg's christology, from 1964 onwards, is the emphasis on two
points: firstly, that the christology of elevation is the framework of the
theology of incarnation, and, secondly, that Jesus did not have a relationship with the eternal Son, but with the Father[6]. These two views,
however, are so quickly and so strongly joined to the category "Selbstoffenbarung Gottes", that their critical capacity can hardly be developed. The power of the classical paradigm still stands. This is even more
so in Catholic theology, with Vatican II's preference for "sese revelavit"
(*Dei Verbum*) above the "facta revelata" of Vatican I.

The question which Mohammed poses from his monotheistic awareness, has everything to do with this. Perhaps he would be able to go a
long way with a christology of elevation, provided justice were done to
the "inconfuse" of Chalcedon, and provided the "indivise" is not all-
important. However, for the monophysitic trend, that was dominate in
Council of Constantinople (553), precisely this "indivise" was the main
focus. It is perhaps not without reason that, in Rome, great objections
were initially made against this christology! However, within a few
years, Rome, too, understood Chalcedon in the light of the Council of
553. Was Mohammed articulating the initial doubts of Rome? Or was
Rome only concerned about the real human life of Jesus, God's own Son
and, apart from that, fully in accord with the Council?

Something striking is taking place. At present, just as western culture
inclines more and more to either agnosticism or pantheism, Jesus'
humanity, and his "verba et facta", are increasingly enveloped in mag-
nificent aureoles. (This is certainly an element of the Wirkungsgeschichte
of the classical paradigm). For some, Jesus is an absolute hero, not unlike
the heroes in the work of Albert Camus. For others, his words and acts
are seen as the absolute presence of God himself in his eternal nature.
There is apparently no third way alongside either the reduction of Jesus
to "a man like us" (cf. the tendency of leveling in modern biographies
of Jesus), or the ideologizing of Jesus to "God in our midst". The bar-
riers with regard to Islam have certainly not been lowered by these

---

6. W. PANNENBERG, *Grundzüge der Christologie*, Gütersloh, 1964.

developments. Mohammed would censure the fading away of Jesus, no less than he would the Jewish approach to Jesus. And he would still fear the glorification of Jesus, the human being, because of the Christian urge to reduce the distance between God and humankind. In discussions with Islam, a low christology is often no less an obstacle than a high christology!

III. How to React?

Which ways of thought and experience could we turn to, if we wish to take Mohammed's questions seriously? From the beginning, Christological apologetics vis à vis Islam have involved rational arguments and the criticism of Mohammed's way of life[7]. In the changing ecumenical situation of our days, there have been less apologetic attempts to integrate Mohammed's criticism, in one way or another, into Christian theology[8].

In the first place, we should realize that classical christology is not without aporias. In recent discussions between Chalcedonian and non-Chalcedonian churches it has become clear that every church is struggling with terms and conceptions, when it seeks to put into words the impact of everything that Jesus stood for. Perhaps all of them wish to bring to the fore the same Anliegen or perspective. However, when they begin to speak or sing about it, such striking differences arise that it almost becomes understandable that, in former times, each branded the other a heretic. Obviously, that Jesus Christ is a person, a human being and God, remains an aporia. Isn't this the aporia which struck Mohammed?

Secondly, although Docetism and the Jewish-Christian christology of adoption are very different, they agree with one another in one respect: one must neither deify what is human nor humanize what is divine. We might say that this was the Anliegen proper of Nestorius. Here, too, begins Mohammed's point.

Thirdly and most importantly, perhaps we can consider the development of the doctrine of Trinity as an endeavor to account for the fact that God is, on the one hand, incomparably the Other and the Greater One, and, on the other hand, that He is, in Himself and out of Himself, the

---

7. Cf. the survey of H. BODZIN, *Islam und Christentum 7.-19. Jahrhundert*, in *TRE* 16 (1987) 336-349.

8. Cf. H. ZIRKNER, *Islam. Theologische und gesellschaftliche Herausforderungen*, Düsseldorf 1993; R. LEUZE, *Christentum und Islam*, Tübingen 1994; R. LEUZE, *Dezelfde ene God. Christenen en Gods openbaring aan Mohammed*, in *TvT* 37 (1997) 24-40.

potentiality of being close to human beings with merciful compassion, and of getting along with them on the same intimate terms as a father gets along with his son. Christians endeavor to probe the potentialities of God's love more profoundly than Jews and Moslems do. The latter accept this fact as a mystery which we cannot probe any further, and whose foundation is hidden from us. It is very important that the confession of the Trinity be understood not as a way of grasping God but as a doxology, as thanksgiving and praise, that it be understood not in the sense of "securitas" but of "certitudo" (Luther).

The fact that Christians probe further here, is partly due to Jesus himself, who stressed the penetrating and elevating nature of God's love and who not only testified to it through his word, but considered his life and death as an expression or sacrament of this love. The intensity of Jesus' relationship with God suggests that the category of "friend" is not completely adequate. Moreover, God not only legitimated Jesus' deeds and words in the resurrection, but put his name and his countenance in the heavens or on his right hand.

This is why the narrative of Jesus' life and death is given ample space in the Christian gospels – whereas the Koran contains almost no stories about Mohammed, his person and his life. And the stories about Abraham, Jacob, Moses, Samuel or David in the Old Testament serve as illustrations, and context, of the message, but are not the message itself. Jesus, however, with his person and his history penetrates into the heart of the Gospel. All kinds of christological titles and trains of thought are perhaps exchangeable, but the letter or the fact of Jesus' life, death and resurrection may not be obscured in an allegorical or spiritual way. The crucified and risen One has in a very specific way a place near God: on His right hand, as the one beloved son, as Word originating from God Himself. He is not merely one of the prophets, or one who encouraged humankind to a strong commitment to God and His will.

Here Christianity and Islam clearly go different ways. What Islam knows about Jesus is in reality christology in the sense of testimony about humanity's unconditional submission to God's will. For Moslems Jesus does not reveal what God commands of, and demands from, men and women. That Jesus is identified as "homoousios with the Father" only after he has passed through utter self-renunciation and death and after he has withdrawn from our sight, cannot conceal the fact, according to Mohammed, that a limit has been overstepped, a limit beyond which one must not go. Evidently, even a christology of adoption runs up against absolute objections in Mohammed's view, where adoption means that Jesus, after his death, becomes the Son of God himself. This is also true as regards Nestorius; despite his desire to keep the human and the divine aspects separate, he nevertheless blends them in the end.

IV. CONCLUSION

For human beings, however holy they may be, there is at most a place in the created height of heaven, at an unbridgeable distance from God. That belongs for Mohammed to the heart of any true monotheism. For Christians, however, as we read in Dante's *Divine Comedy*, in Jesus "the image of man" has been taken up in the heaven of God Himself. In Jesus the qualitative difference between God and humankind is transcended. In the eyes of Mohammed, the fences have been broken down at this point. The boundary has been crossed. In the end, the result will be either the deification of all men and women and of the whole world, or the renunciation of God in modern atheism. Both are fruits of the same tree.

Perhaps Mohammed did not have a real sense of all the implications of Christian experience and reflection. There is a real difference in the way Christians and Moslems connect monotheism and revelation. Do they complete each other, or do they exclude each other? In Christian monotheism, human beings, as the image of God, get closer to God than is the case in Islam. This does not exclude the awareness that God is hidden. The human person retains his name: human. God remains the Greater One. In his prophetic role, Mohammed calls for sensibility to the proportions of the relationship between God and humankind.

Mohammed urges us to rethink the New Testament's terminology, that Jesus is not "ho theos", but "theos". He is not God in His monotheistic idiosyncrasy. Surely, he is the person who, without any sin and in the deepest possible way, expresses what God wants to say to humankind. God reveals him as the sacrament of His own philanthropy. Is the outcome of this view, that we can only speak of a moral unity of the human being, Jesus, with God? Is the outcome an "Arius redevivus"? I do not think so, for the philanthropy of God is unquestionable. We can hardly consider God's solidarity with humankind, as found in Jesus, intense enough. Provided we maintain God's sovereignty or the "inconfuse" of Chalcedon, we have to stress the "indivise" as strongly as possible! Or, in doing this, are we doing an injustice to the unicity of

Jesus, as Chalcedon sought to confess it, and doing an injustice to Mohammed's point as well?

Theologische Faculteit   Wiel LOGISTER
Katholieke Universiteit Brabant
TFT, Postbus 9130
5000 HC Tilburg
The Netherlands

THE RATIONAL DEFENSE OF CHRISTOLOGY
WITHIN THE CONTEXT OF ISLAMIC MONOTHEISM

I. JESUS IN THE QURAN

Islam stands in the tradition of the Biblical religions, Judaism and Christianity. It shares with them not only the monotheistic faith, but also a common font of historical records. The Muslims venerate the women and men from the Old and the New Testament. Besides such important saints as Noah, Abraham and Moses, Jesus Christ also figures among the most prominent persons in the Quran. The Quran not only narrates the biblical stories of holy men, but gives its own interpretation of these biblical stories. They are shaped in such a way that they fit into the overwhelming quranic concept of strict monotheism. This strict monotheistic view is the reference point against which the whole Quran has to be interpreted.

Thus the quranic Jesus differs clearly from the biblical or dogmatic Jesus Christ, even when titles are used in the Quran which we find also in the New Testament or in Christian theology. It is not possible to present here the whole picture of the quranic Jesus nor to mention all the titles which the Quran attributes to him.

Jesus is called the son of Mary. His mother was chosen by God in a special manner (S 3,33). Her conception of Jesus was the result of a divine creation (S 619,20f) or of the inspiration of the Spirit (S 19,22). The infant Jesus protests publicly against the accusation that Mary has given birth to an illegitimate child and he loudly proclaims his divine mission: As a servant of God he received the book and was made a prophet (S 19,30; cf. 4,156; 21,91; 66,12). But his miraculous birth is not understood in the Quran as an indication of his divinity. In the quranic view Jesus remains a simple servant or man. The creation of Jesus by God was understood to have taken place according to the example of Adam's creation and this creation was at least as marvelous as that of Jesus (S 3,52).

Jesus is called a Prophet (S 19,31) or Envoy (S 4,156.169; 61,6). He was sent to a specific people with a divine mission like all prophets. He proved his mission through miracles (cf. S 2,254.81, 3,43; 5,110; 43,63; 61,6). To mention some of his signs: Jesus spoke in the cradle with the authority of a grown-up man (S 3,41; 19,30); he made small clay models of birds and breathed life into them (S 3,43); he cured both a man who was blind from birth and a leper (S 5,110); he raised up the dead, but always "with God's permission" (S 3,43; 5,110); and at the request of the Apostles he made a "Prepared Table" descend from the sky (S 5). His mission consisted especially in the proclamation of the Gospel, as Moses had proclaimed the Torah and Muhammad was to proclaim the Quran.

The Quran attributes also the title messiah to Jesus, though only in those suras which originate in the Medina period (cf. 3,45; 4,171s; S, 17.72.75). This title derives from the Judeo-Christian tradition, and the Quran gives no interpretation whatsoever to this title. Only much later Muslim commentaries give a number of different interpretations, but always respecting the strict monotheistic view of the Islamic faith.

Jesus is also called the Word of God (S 3,39-45; 4,171). And again, even if the terminology comes from the Christian tradition, it has to be understood in the light of the Quranic context: like all creatures Jesus is called into life by the word of God and as a prophet and an envoy he proclaims the word of God. He is also called the word of God because he spoke on behalf of God and thus directed men onto the right way. Jesus also is a word of God because, in his own person, he himself is "good tidings". The characterization of Jesus as the Spirit of God (S 4,171; 21,91; 66,12) is to be understood in the same way.

Jesus is called the servant of God ('Abd, literally slave). In theological terms this title means "creature". Like all men Jesus also is the "servant" of God and his "property". This title then decries all attempts to make Jesus into God (cf. S 42,59). The first word he uttered was in recognition of his character to be truly a servant, so as to make stronger the argument against anyone who might claim that he was God.

The logic of the Quran does not allow that Jesus, a prophet and a man of God, could be crucified. It is God's practice to let faith ultimately triumph over evil and adversary forces (cf. S 22,49; 44,5s). The crucifixion of Jesus would have meant that his enemies had triumphed and God would never allow that. What happened to Jesus after he escaped crucifixion is not related in the Quran, but reference is made to Jesus' ascension to God and his purification (S 3,484). According to the Quran, Jesus will not assist God in the Judgment at the end of times, but on the day of the resurrection Jesus will witness against the Christians, accusing them of having regarded him and his mother as equals to God (S 5,116). The Quran accuses the Christians of saying that God is one in three and proclaims very loudly that there is no God beside God (S 5,73). Even if the Quran makes false accusations against the Christians and misunderstands the Christian Trinity as a tritheism of God, Mary and Jesus, the strict monotheistic Islamic faith also seems to exclude the orthodox faith of the Trinity. The Quran does not use the word "Ibn" for "son" as the Christians do, but rather the word "walid" which terminologically infers a biological implication, viz. giving birth to a child. And such a biological element cannot be attributed to God (S 112,1-3)[1].

II. THE ISLAMIC CONTEXT OF THE CHRISTIAN APOLOGISTS

The foregoing was a very brief synopsis of the Islamic teachings concerning Jesus, with which Christian apologists and theologians were confronted after the Islamic Conquest of the Middle East. This religion was not just a new Christian heresy as John Damascene assumed[2], but indeed a new religion. Consequently, Christians could not treat the Muslims like they treated heretics in the past. On the religious level they had no scripture in common with the Muslims, which could serve as basis for a discussion regarding the faith. Whatever common religious tradition there was, was interpreted differently in the respective Holy Scriptures. Neither the New nor the Old Testament were accepted as authoritative by the Muslims who held the opinion that the holy books of the Christians were subject to changes[3]. Thus they do not transmit the authentic Word of God. On the other hand, Christians did not accept the Quran as a religious authority. As both sides were not able to present a common written text as an accepted authority, only reason could be the common basis for dispute. Particularly in the first centuries of the Abbasid period the Greek and Hellenistic philosophy, and especially Aristotle's philosophy, were invoked by the Muslims in their theological reasoning[4]. During this time the *ilm al-kalām* "the intellectual discipline that is devoted to the reasoned justification of the truths of the divine revelation and to the exploration of the implications of revealed truth for human thought in general"[5] acquired its

1. For literature on Jesus in the Quran and Islam see the bibliography of the article G.C. ANAWATI, *'Isā*, in *EI²* 4, Leiden 1978, 81-86.

2. *De Haeresibus* Chap. 101, in *PG* 94, 764-773.

3. Cf. Jean-Marie GAUDEL, Robert CASPAR, *Textes de la Tradition musulmane concernant le taḥrīf (Falsification) des Écritures (Présentations textes arabes et traduction française annotée)*, in *Islamochristiana* 6 (1980) 61-104.

4. Cf. Tilman NAGEL, *Geschichte der islamischen Theologie. Von Muhammad bis zur Gegenwart*, München, 1994, 95-135; W. Montgomery WATT, *The Formative Period of Islamic Thought*, Edinburgh, 1973.

5. S.H. GRIFFITH, *Faith and Reason in Christian Kalām: Theodore Abū Qurrah on Discerning the True Religion*, in Samir KHALIL SAMIR – Jørgen NIELSEN (eds.), *Christian Arabic Apologetics During the Abbasid Period (750-1258)*, Leiden, 1994, pp. 1-43, here 1.

definitive shape. Discussions on religious matters, as they took place in Christian academic centers, may have stood model in the beginning for this Islamic science. The latter rapidly developed into a kind of speculative reasoning on religious matters within the Islamic intellectual milieu with grammatical theories and philosophy as a basis. It was rather a discourse regulated by reason and logic, which in the mind of those who practiced this science was considered as the decisive authority regarding truth or falsehood in a religious dispute.

Defending their faith in Jesus Christ in this context, Christians could only argue on the basis of reason. Biblical citations could only show that the Christians were faithful to their traditions, but they could not prove the veracity of their faith. In response to objections to their faith on the part of the Muslims they too had to apply the very method of the *ilm al-kalām*. The agenda was thus set by the Muslims[6] and the principal topics were always the unity of God, the Trinity of the persons in the one God and the Incarnation of the Word of God, which is a reflection of the main objections on the part of the Quran regarding the Christian concept of God. Other topics concerning Christian life and practices might also be included. Though the Christian *mutakallimun*[7] were following the Muslim agenda, they seemingly were not trying to convert or convince the Muslims, but their main aim was to reassure their Christian brothers against Muslim attacks. In due course the Christian *mutakallimun* distanced themselves from an apologetic attitude and their way of reasoning about their faith became a way of presenting that very faith in the new context, where the Islamic idiom, not merely the Arabic idiom, became evermore dominant. The traditional teaching of the Church was now being expressed in a hitherto unexplored way, a process we call today inculturation.

III. The Christian Arabic Polemics and Apologetics

The Defense of the Trinity

The most basic point in debating Christology was obviously the possible proof that Jesus Christ could have a divine nature and be one of the persons of the Trinity, which is not the same as Tritheism. The Trinity had to be understood as a logical consequence of God's unity.

---

6. Christian texts are often quoting first a Muslim objection or question before developing their arguments or they are responses to a Muslim letter.
7. A theologian reasoning in the way of *ilm al-kalām*.

Abū Rā íṭah at-Takrītī (at the beginning of the 9th century)[8] and Yaḥyā Ibn ʿAdī (893-974)[9], as well as Paul of Būš[10] (1170/5- ~1250) affirm that God is substantially one in essence. But immediately they also address the question what kind of oneness is this. And in line with the philosophy of Aristotle[11] they offer three possibilities: the first being the oneness of gender, the second of species and the third of number[12]. But as soon as they have posed the question, they indicate that none of these three possibilities can be correctly applied to God. The solution is that God has to be viewed as being one in one aspect and multiple in another[13]. And herein lies the first step towards the rational demonstration of the Christian faith. The authors believe that they have proved that the oneness of God necessarily implies multiplicity under another aspect. A next step is to show under which aspect God is one and under which aspect God is multiple.

To demonstrate God's concurrent oneness and multiplicity his attributes formed part of major discussions. Christians as well as Muslims ascribe a number of attributes to God: being, living, knowing, seeing, hearing, creator, powerful, unlimited and so on[14]. These attributes can be divided into two categories: attributes which belong to the essence of God, and attributes which God comes by through an act, e.g. creator. The first category are attributes which are essential to God and God could never be without them. From eternity God must have been living and knowing. There cannot have been a moment that God was not living or knowing[15]. Other authors mention other attributes which are deemed to be essential, e.g., goodness, power and wisdom[16], or living

---

8. Harald SUERMANN, *Der Begriff ṣifah bei Abū Rā íṭah,* in: Samir KHALIL SAMIR, Jørgen NIELSEN (eds.), *Christian Arabic Apologetics During the Abbasid Period (750-1258),* Leiden 1994, 157-171, here 159.

9. Cf. *Le traité de l'Unité de Yaḥyā ibn ʿAdī (893-974)* (étude et édition critique par KHALIL SAMIR) (Patrimoine Arabe Chrétien, 2), Jounieh, Roma, 1980, 197-203.

10. *Traité de Paul de Būš sur l'Unité et la Trinité, l'Incarnation et la Verité du Christianisme* (étude, édition critique et index exhaustif par KHALIL SAMIR) (Patrimoine Arabe Chrétien, 4), Zouk Mikhaël, Liban, 1983.

11. Aristotle, *Topic* VII,1; *Metaphysic* V,9 (1018a); *Petits traités apologétiques de Yaḥyā ben ʿAdī* (édité et traduit par Augustin PÉRIER), Paris, 1920, 124-127; *Yaḥyā ibn ʿAdī* (KHALIL SAMIR), 203.

12. Yaḥyā ibn ʿAdī speaks of six manners of being one: gender, species, relation, continuity, definition and indivisibility.

13. *Die Schriften des Jacobiten Ḥabīb ibn Hidma Abū Rā íṭah* (übersetzt von Georg GRAF) (CSCO, 131; Script. Arab., 15), Louvain, 1951, 5; *Die Schriften des Jacobiten Ḥabīb ibn Hidma Abū Rā íṭah* (übersetzt von Georg GRAF) (CSCO, 130; Script. Arab., 14), Louvain, 1951, 5; *Yaḥyā ibn ʿAdī* (KHALIL SAMIR) 209-221.

14. Abū Rā íṭah (Georg GRAF) 3f.; 3.

15. Paul de Būš (KHALIL SAMIR) 141-147, *Abū Rā íṭah* (Georg GRAF) 10;11.

16. *Yaḥyā ibn ʿAdī* (KHALIL SAMIR) 248-264.

and speaking[17]. Each of these essential attributes supposes that there is
an entity which is eternal without being the same as the essence of God.
If it would be the same, the attributes would have no meaning. If a distinction is to be made between the essence and the attribute, then there
must exist at least two eternal entities. This demonstrates once again, so
the reasoning, that God is one in essence but multiple in attributes.
These attributes are regarded as corresponding to the persons in the theology of the Trinity. However, Muslims would answer that, if this way
of reasoning is logically pursued, then there were also to exist an unlimited number of attributes of God and consequently also an unlimited
number of persons of God. Therefore the Christians had to show that
three essential attributes are necessary and that all other essential attributes can be reduced to these three. The argumentation for three basic
attributes is however very weak as it lacks a proper rationale. Thus the
authors are forced to use images and analogies in order to demonstrate
the unity of the Trinity. One of the most common analogies is that of the
fire with its heat and its light[18], or that of intelligence, intelligent and
intelligible[19]. In discussing the attributes the second person of the Trinity is often identified with the attribute of speaking or knowing or with
one element of the analogy like intelligent or light. Using the concept of
attributes in order to explain the Trinity was one step towards inculturation in the Islamic context. First of all, the Muslims themselves were
induced to discuss how God's attributes had to be understood, and moreover an Arabic translation of Syriac or Greek terms regarding the theology of the Trinity, which had unwanted connotations in the Islamic context, could thus be avoided.

The Incarnation

Having demonstrated that God is Trinitarian, the next step for the
Christians was to demonstrate that one of these persons became human.

One of the first questions that had to be addressed concerned the issue
whether, if God is Trinitarian, all three persons have become human. Of

17. Paul de Būš (KHALIL SAMIR) 152-154; 'Ammār al-Baṣri, Apologie et Controverses (par Michel HAYEK), 46-56.

18. Paul de Būš (KHALIL SAMIR); cf. Bénedicte LANDRON, Chrétiens et musulmans en Irak: Attitudes Nestoriennes vis-à-vis de l'Islam (Études Chrétiennes Arabes), Paris, 1994, 169.

19. LANDRON, Chrétiens, 172-177; Emilio PLATTI, Yaḥyā b. 'Adī and his refutation of al-Warrāq's Treatise on the Trinity in Relation to his other works, in Samir KHALIL SAMIR and Jørgen NIELSEN (eds.), Christian Arabic Apologetics During the Abbasid Period (750-1258), Leiden, 1994, pp. 172-191 here 188-189.

course, the answer was that only one of the three persons became human, not God as the Trinity, but that the one person who became human was truly God[20]. Abū Rā ītah argued as follows: "Our opponents say: 'Provide us with information about the person who became flesh as you understand it! Is he God or is he man?' Our answer is: According to our teaching he who became flesh is God having become man.' They may answer: 'If he who became flesh is according to your teachings God and you affirmed in the beginning of your treatise, that God is several persons, then he who became flesh is all three persons. But what reasons do you have to think that he who became flesh is only one of three persons and not all three?' Our answers will be: For us the name God has at the same time a general and a special meaning[21]. We only wanted to make clear that he who became flesh is God, i.e., one of the persons, the son who is the living Word of God, is eternally god, not three persons.'" And in the very same way the next part of Abū Rā ītah's demonstration follows the same way of reasoning: the issue touches on the question whether the incarnation is an activity or a part of God. Abū Rā ītah answers: "You are asking about the one who became flesh. Therefore you are asking about an essence who became flesh, of which both body and incarnation are necessarily part. For it is not possible to speak of someone becoming flesh without an incarnation and without a body. But how does this happen? You are asking us: is the one who became incarnated an activity or a part? Thus you are saying about the body of the one who became flesh, that is about the incarnation: is this a part or an activity? However we are saying: the incarnation of he who became flesh is on his part distinct from both activity or part, for it is rather a way towards activity. When, in the use of the word incarnation, you are foremost thinking about the body and then ask, whether that body is a part or an act of him who has become flesh, we have to ask you: Are you affirming that the body is part of the incarnated substance or do you only refer to a part of him who is intrinsically united with the incarnated substance? If you ask then, whether he is part, that is a part of the divine substance, we have to deny that the body is part of the divine substance; because the latter cannot be divided or separated. But if you are asking: is he part of the union of God's substance and the body? Then we agree with you that he is both part and activity"[22].

20. Cf. Paul de Būš (KHALIL SAMIR) 197-201.

21. Cf. Emilio PLATTI, Yaḥyā ibn ʿAdī. Théologien Chrétien et philosophe Arabe. Sa théologie de l'Incarnation (Orientalia Lovaniensia Analecta, 14), Leuven, 1983, 102-103.

22. Abū Rā ītah (Georg GRAF) 37-38; 27-28.

These passages are very indicative of how arguments were being framed. First, a Muslim asks a question, thus setting the agenda. Abū Rā ítah then analyses the question in order to detect the conditions under which an answer can be given. After he has framed the question more precisely, he gives the answer. The content is not new, but the way of presenting it to his audience differs from traditional Christology. The aim is to show that dogma does not run counter to logic and that logic is to reason according to the philosophy of Aristotle.

Abū Rā ítah is only one among many Christians who presented Christology to an audience which seemed to be primarily Muslim. Others were using more or less the same technique. The two foregoing short passages demonstrate the way in which the Christian faith was being argued and defended in a Muslim context.

In answer to the question who is the agent of incarnation, the Christian *mutakallimun* start to analyze the very notion of an act and the consequences of an act. They make the distinction that the act of creation and its volition are acts of the Trinity as such, but the act of manifestation and revelation is always an act of one of the three persons in accordance with the proprieties of each one. So the incarnation as an act of volition is an act of the three persons, but as a manifestation, i.e., as the execution of the common volition, it is the act of one person according to his propriety[23]. To the question whether anyone of the three persons could be incarnated, Yaḥyā Ibn ʿAdī answers that only the Word could become incarnated in view of its specific place within the Trinity. His explanation refers to the analogy of the pure intellect, which represents the Father, the intelligible of a pure intellection, which represents the Spirit and the intelligent of a pure intellection, which represents the Son. Man can neither be a pure intellect nor an intelligible of a pure intellection, but he knows his creator by his intelligence and he may be the intelligent of an intellection. Because God's Son and man can be or are intelligent, only the Word can become incarnated and become man, and not the Father and the Spirit[24].

The answer to the question how God can be incarnated in a woman created by himself or how divinity and humanity can be united, is

23. *Abū Rā ítah* (Georg GRAF) 39; 28; Paul de Buš (KHALIL SAMIR) 197-201; Hans PUTMAN *L'Église et l'Islam sous Timothée I (780-823). Étude sur l'Église nestorienne au temps des premiers ʿAbbāsides avec nouvelle édition et traduction du dialogue entre Timothée et al-Mahdi* (Recherches, Nouvelle Série B. Orient Chrétien III), Beyrouth, 1975, 229.18.

24. *Yaḥyā ibn ʿAdī* (Emilio PLATTI) §8, cf. Rachid HADDAD, *La trinité divine chez les théologiens arabes 750-1050)*, Paris, 1985, 222-233; LANDRON, *Chrétiens*, 204.

normally not a philosophical discourse. Christian apologetics gave the hint that God had been also in the burning bush and man is much more noble[25] so that it is normal that God became incarnated as man. Others evoke the quranic verse that God is sitting on a throne[26] and argue that God consequently is confined by his incarnation in a human being[27]. Again others describe the incarnation, the union of the two natures, in imagery like comparing it to oxymel (a mixture of honey and vinegar)[28], an image which is rejected by the Nestorians, or they use the image of the fire present in the red-hot iron[29], or of the word which is used to express something in a letter[30], or of a thought and of the sound of the voice or of a written expression[31]. Images evoking the light of the sun reflected by a shining surface describe the manifestation of God through the humanity of Christ. These images and analogies are in relation with the Trinitarian representation of the divine Word as the light of the sun[32]. Quite common is the analogy of the body and the soul forming one man[33]. Other images and analogies can be enumerated, and they often have a pre-Islamic origin. The choice of images and analogies employed depend on the Christology of each church, and in turn is again a source of division between the different churches[34]. Against the objection that divinity and humanity, the limited and the unlimited, cannot join, ʿAbdīšūʿ of Nisibis refers to the fact that man's soul is regarded by the pre-Socratic philosophers as divine and immortal. He points to the Bible where it is said that Adam was created in the image of God. In this way there exists a likeness between the human essence and the divine essence which makes it possible that the divine and the human can be joined[35]. Abū Rā ítah rejects the Muslim affirmation that the incarnation added something to the essence of God. He argues that increase can only affect

25. Paul de Būš (KHALIL SAMIR) 193-196.
26. Quran 7,53.
27. *Le Dialogue d'Abraham de Tibériade avec ʿAbd al-Rahmān al-Hāšimī à Jérusalem vers 820* (études, édition critique et traduction annotée par Giacinto BULUS MARCUZZO) (Textes et études sur l'Orient Chrétien, 3), Rome, 1986, 374,375; cf. Timothée (ed. PUTMAN) 62.; Abū Rā ítah (Georg GRAF), 58-59; 45-46.
28. *Muḥyī al-Dīn al-Isfahānī, Épître sur l'Unité et la Trinité, Traité sur l'intellect, Fragment sur l'âme* (édité, traduit et annoté par M. ALLARD, G. TROUPEAU) 26.44.
29. LANDRON, *Chrétiens*, 191; vgl. *Abū Rā ítah* (Georg GRAF), 4147; 30-35; Paul KHOURY, *Paul d'Antioche, évêque melkite de Sidon (XIIe s.)* (Recherches, 24), Beyrouth, 1964, 201s.100; cf. *ʿAmmār al-Baṣri* (Michel HAYEK) 179-180.
30. Paul d'Antioche (KHOURY) 201.100; Timothée (PUTMAN) 229.18.
31. Timothée (PUTMAN) 229.18.
32. LANDRON, *Chrétiens*, 192.
33. *Ibid.*, 191.
34. *Ibid.*, 191-193.
35. *Ibid.*, 193.

bodies, and as God is total perfection, there is no increase possible. And bodies can only be increased where it concerns weight, length, space or quantity. As God is immaterial, he cannot increase in so far as it concerns the first three dimensions. But in so far as it concerns the number, the Logos has been one before the incarnation and after the incarnation. There is no increase in like manner as there is no increase with man, for the spirit adds nothing to the body and neither does the body add anything to the Spirit[36].

Yaḥyā ibn ʿAdi demonstrates very comprehensively how it is possible that both divinity and humanity are united in Christ who is essentially one. Platti has shown this reasoning process very clearly in his excellent work on the doctrine of incarnation of Yaḥyā ibn ʿAdī. Of course the demonstration concerns the Monophysite doctrine, as the Nestorians have another concept of Christ and consequently have to argue differently. The question is whether the union in Christ is hypostatic, substantial, personal or only nominal or voluntary. Only in the first case is there a real unity. The whole polemic between Yaḥyā ibn ʿAdī and his adversaries is about the difference between God and Man. Is it impossible to profess that Christ is at the same time eternal and created? Yaḥyā ibn ʿAdī states that conditions concerning a contradiction must relate to the very terms. Where it concerns a composite, an affirmation or a contradiction must deal with the same part and reality. The two parts of a contradiction must be present at the same time and in the same state. According to Yaḥyā ibn ʿAdī, the conditions for a contradiction are not given in the case of Christ, because the attributes eternal and created do not concern the same aspect of the subject. The hypostatic Christ is eternal according to one aspect and created according to the other. Yaḥyā ibn ʿAdī develops this argument in many steps and he looks at it from different sides. But the question is still whether Christ is one person having at the same time a divine substance and a human substance and yet uniting both in himself, or whether Christ possesses two substances without actually being two substances. Yaḥyā ibn ʿAdī must reject the affirmation of his adversaries when they refer to the philosophy of Aristotle that the only definition of substance is what exists in itself. For a creature or a thing there exists only one definition. If one considers the components of Christ and their intrinsic differences, is it possible to speak about one Christ in terms of a real unity? Yaḥyā ibn ʿAdī affirms the unity of the components even if it cannot be accepted by his adversaries and then applies the principle that

---

36. *Abū Rā ītah* (Georg GRAF), 56-58; 43-44.

the totality is different from its parts and consequently the definition of the whole is essentially different from each component taken separately. There is only one sole definition concerning Christ as far as he is one. But as far as he is composed there are two definitions. He pleads with his adversaries that they must accept this exception. Yaḥyā ibn ʿAdī then applies this rule to different aspects of the christological dogma, like the united nature of Christ[37].

Not only the possibility of incarnation has to be proved but also the reality. According to the Jacobite Maḥyī ad-Dīn al-Iṣfahānī a rational proof of the incarnation is not possible, because the union comes from the divine power and belongs to the faith outside of which no proof is possible. But other authors like the one of Madal or ʿAbdallah ibn aṭ-Ṭaiyib and ʿAbdīšūʿ of Nisibis tried to prove in a rational way the incarnation or at least to show that the incarnation is within the line of rational logic. The starting point of the argumentation is the goodness and the generosity of God[38] or the union of divinity and humanity as being the greatest gift to men such that God in his infinite goodness is not able to refuse this gift to men[39]. ʿAbdallah ibn aṭ-Ṭaiyib speaks of the necessity of the incarnation. Starting from the point that divine goodness is essentially communicative, he argues that perfect goodness must spread to other beings and God must possess this perfection. On account of his goodness God was compelled to create the world in order to communicate his goodness. The necessity of the incarnation consistently derives from the necessity of creation: he who was at one time good must be good again. God's goodness began only with creation and is accomplished in the union of humanity and divinity[40]. Many other authors do not admit that God was compelled to create and to take on flesh. But according to them God created Adam simply because he was good and generous, and that, without any compulsion, the Word itself took on flesh for goodness' sake towards creation, thereby bringing salvation[41].

Incarnation was the ultimate response to the human desire to see God. ʿAmmār al-Baṣrī said that man always aspires after more knowledge both in natural and in spiritual matters. To see the creator is the supreme joy for man. On account of his goodness God, who is essentially

---

37. *Yaḥyā ibn ʿAdī* (Emilio PLATTI) 99-106.
38. LANDRON, *Chrétiens*, 193.205-206; Paul de Būš (KHALIL SAMIR) 205-207; *Abū Rā ítah* (Georg GRAF), *47-48; 35-37.*
39. LANDRON, *Chrétiens*, 193.
40. *Ibid.*, 205.
41. Paul de Būš (KHALIL SAMIR) 205-207.

inaccessible to the human senses, wants to respond to the aspiration of man and thus became visible in the form of a man[42].

According to Bénédicte Landron the Nestorians put great emphasis on the idea of God's manifestation, the theophany, at the expense of the idea of ransom. Specifically the idea that satisfaction has been rendered to God for human sins through Christ's sacrifice recedes into the background. The glory of the theophany in the person of Christ is central[43]. In the total process which starts with creation and ends with incarnation, God wanted to reveal himself to man who at the beginning had no natural knowledge of God, in the opinion of ʿAmmār al-Baṣrī[44]. Other authors see in the carnal condition of man, prisoner of his sensual passions, the obstacle to knowledge of God[45]. God who is inaccessible to men revealed himself first by speaking in certain places, then through holy men and finally through the incarnation, revealing himself without intermediary[46].

It was necessary that the Word brought salvation, because only the Word could restore man, who had lost eternal life, to his original state. As no creature is master over eternal life, only God, the Word, could renew man's eternal life[47]. But God cannot communicate, directly and divinely, eternal life to men, because man does not share in the divine substance. That is the reason why God himself became man and gave eternal life to the body of man united with him. As incarnated person he accepted the suffering and passion, which men deserved, in order to save their souls. This was an act of justice. Through his resurrection he became the prince of life and the collateral of our resurrection. In this way God saved his image through his image[48].

Christians also disputed with Muslims on the titles given to Christ. The Quran affirms that Jesus was the servant (ʿAbd) of God and Muslims knew that the passages of Isaiah on the suffering servant are applied to Jesus Christ. Christians could have affirmed the quranic title of servant as applied to Jesus if this title had not been interpreted differently in the Islamic context. Servant (ʿAbd) stands opposed to Master (Rabb). Hence, applying the title servant to Jesus did imply a denial of his divinity. Timothy and ʿAmmar al-Baṣri discussed this problem with Muslims,

42. ʿAmmār al-Baṣri (Michel HAYEK) 66-70. 215.
43. LANDRON, Attitudes Nestoriennes, 206.
44. M. HAYEK, Ammar al-Baṣri, Apologie et Controverses 64-65 (arab).
45. LANDRON, Chrétiens, 206.
46. Ibid., 107.
47. Paul de Buš (KHALIL SAMIR) 208-214.
48. Ibid., 215-219.

when they were asked why they did not give the title of servant to Jesus Christ, though the prophets themselves had referred to Jesus as servant. After citing other examples in which the prophets had also called Jesus Christ the Son and God, they affirmed that not all titles in the Scriptures expressed the real nature of the Christ, as they are very often only images like stone, door, way[49]. The Nestorians affirmed that all divine attributes are given to Christ on account of his divine nature and all human attributes on account of his human nature. However, it is not good to insist on the human attributes, since it is best that Christ should be spoken of in terms of his divine attributes. In order to affirm this point concretely, Timothy points to the fact that Ismael is considered a free man on account of his father Abraham and not a servant on account of his mother Hagar. ʿAbdallah ibn aṭ-Ṭaiyib insisted that the aim of the incarnation was the glorification of human nature and not the humiliation of the divine nature. That is why human attributes are not transferred to the divine nature, but only divine attributes to human nature[50].

CONCLUSION

Within the context of Islam, then, Christians not only had to grapple with quranic affirmations concerning Christ, but also with the way of reasoning which developed in the Muslim milieu. This way of reasoning was determined by the philosophy of Aristotle and other classical philosophers. In disputing with Muslims they had to accept certain rules if they wanted to propose their faith in a convincing manner: the doctrine had to be evident by itself or had to be proven by argumentation or demonstration, or on the basis of principles which were accepted as valid by the adversary. The common ground was philosophy and logic. Secondly they had to translate their faith in a new language which soon became their own colloquial language. This new idiom was not simply a new language into which the presentation of the faith had to be translated, but this new language was coined by the new religion of Islam which challenged the Christian faith in its own monotheistic conception. Certain terms and concepts could not be used to render dogma and thus new ones had to be found. Neither Arab Christology nor the whole of theology can be understood simply as a translation from Syriac and

---

49. ʿAmmār al-Baṣri (Michel HAYEK) 259-261.
50. LANDRON, Chrétiens, 201-203.

Greek into Arabic, but must be seen as an attempt to formulate anew the faith in a new religious context.

Platanenweg 21 Harald SUERMANN
52249 Eschweiler
Germany

JESUS OF AFRICA:
VOICES OF CONTEMPORARY AFRICAN CHRISTOLOGY

O great and powerful Jesus, incomparable Diviner,
the sun and moon are Your **batakari** [robe]
it sparkles like the morning star.
Sekyere Buruku, the tall mountain,
all the nations see Your glory[1].
The mountains of Jerusalem surround us
We are in the midst
of the mountains of Zion.
Satan, your bullets can't touch us.
If Satan says he will rise up against us
we are still the people of Jesus.
If Satan troubles us,
Jesus Christ,
You who are the Lion of the grasslands,
You whose claws are sharp,
will tear out his entrails
and leave them on the ground
for the flies to eat[2].
Jesus, Saviour of the poor,
who brightens our faces!
Damfo-Adu [lit. Great Friend, Dependable Friend]
we rely on you as the tongue relies on the mouth[3].

Striking images of Christ are voiced by an illiterate Ghanaian woman, Afua Kuma, one who works her fields, serves as village midwife, and worships in the Church of the Pentecost. In the vivid language, proverbs and poetry of the Akan people, she expresses the reality and significance of Jesus in her everyday life and that of her community. The recent recording and publishing of her prayers and praises illustrates an important point; namely, that African Christians have understood and responded to Jesus in light of received biblical teaching *and* their own cultural heritage. Indeed, perceptions of Christ "through African eyes" have been operative among indigenous believers for as long as Christianity has been on the continent.

In the last few decades, however, African theologians south of the Sahara have identified a "christological crisis"; that is, a lack of critical

---

1. A. KUMA, *Jesus of the Deep Forest – Praises and Prayers of Afua Kuma*, tr. J. Kirby, Accra, Asempa, 1981, p. 6.
    2. *Ibid.*, p. 46.
    3. *Ibid.*, p. 5.

and systematic reflection on Jesus Christ by Africans in light of their own cultural inheritance and identity, including ontology, cosmology and epistemology, in order to articulate an *African christology* in keeping with the needs of African Christians. For example, an early pioneer of contemporary African theology, John Mbiti, claimed that "African concepts of Christology do not exist"[4]. Yet he then proceeded to delineate those aspects of Jesus which do indeed correspond to an African conceptualisation of the world. The need for such endemic expression was recognised even earlier, for in 1963 John V. Taylor spoke passionately of "a sense of urgency in the search for the true meeting-place where Christ is conversing with the soul of Africa"[5]. Elaborating on the significance of Christianity being perceived in Africa as a "white man's religion", Taylor pinpointed the heart of the problem in a most penetrating way:

> Christ has been presented as the answer to the questions a white man would ask, the solution to the needs that Western man would feel, the Saviour of the world of the European world-view, the object of adoration and prayer of historic Christendom. But if Christ were to appear as the answer to the questions that Africans are asking, what would he look like? If he came into the world of African cosmology to redeem Man as Africans understand him, would he be recognizable to the rest of the Church Universal? And if Africa offered him the praises and petitions of her total, uninhibited humanity, would they be acceptable[6]?

In the decades since Taylor voiced his diagnosis of the theological malaise, an increasing number of African theologians have likewise expressed the need for African Christians to perceive and respond to Jesus in a way that is meaningful and relevant to the African mentality and experience. The fact that this felt need continues to the present time is reflected in recent publications. For example, Anselme Sanon, citing Ernest Sambou, emphasises that "in most African countries, the prime theological urgency consists in discovering the true face of Jesus Christ, that Christians may have the living experience of that face, in depth and according to their own genius"[7]. Or perhaps even more poignant is the charge from Efoé Julien Pénoukou:

4. J.S. MBITI, *Some African Concepts of Christology*, in G.F. VICEDOM (ed.), *Christ and the Younger Churches*, London, SPCK, 1972, p. 51.

5. J.V. TAYLOR, *The Primal Vision: Christian Presence amid African Religion*, London, SCM, 1963, p. 7.

6. *Ibid.*, 16. Where non-inclusive language occurs in quoted material, here and elsewhere, the author's original language has been maintained in recognition of different conventions employed in other times and cultures.

7. E. SAMBOU, *Une voie réaliste pour l'ecclésiologie*, in *Lumière et Vie* 159, p. 32; quoted in A.T. SANON, *Jesus, Master of Initiation*, in R.J. SCHREITER (ed.), *Faces of Jesus in Africa*, Maryknoll, NY, Orbis, 1991, p. 85.

The spiritual torment – or to put it positively, the profound hope – of Christians of Africa in our day recalls Jesus' challenge to his disciples: 'And you – who do you say that I am?' ...

... We shall constantly have to reread or evaluate our intuitions and elaborations regarding the data revealed by the Son of God, in order to better know ourselves in him and to better recognize him in ourselves. What appear here are paths of christology, paths to an ever deepening reappropriation of our faith in Christ, for a new outlook on the spiritual and human expectations of the African[8].

What "paths of christology", what new trails for seeking Jesus are currently being blazed across Africa? And where do such new paths lead? What is their import in terms of the wider context of global christologies? Or, in the words of two leading theologians from East Africa, what is "the specific significance of Christ as seen by Africans, particularly by African Christians, at the present stage of their appropriation, understanding and appreciation of Him and faith in Him"[9]? In order to explore such questions, a brief overview of the sources and methods of African christology will set the context for highlighting selected voices of contemporary African theologians.

I. SOURCES AND METHODS OF AFRICAN CHRISTOLOGY

First, a few introductory definitions are in order. Although the term "African theology" is widely recognised as a legitimate discipline, clarification of its precise meaning may be salutary. "Critical African theology" is stated succinctly to be "the organized faith-reflection of an authentically African Christianity"[10]. Or, more elaborately, African theology has been defined in its broad sense as "the understanding and expression of the Christian faith in accordance with African needs and mentality", and in its narrow sense as "the systematic and scientific presentation or elaboration of the Christian faith according to the needs and mentality of the African peoples"[11]. In the same way, African christology has been

---

8. E.J. PÉNOUKOU, *Christology in the Village*, in R.J. SCHREITER (ed.), *Faces of Jesus in Africa* (n. 7), p. 37.

9. J.N.K. MUGAMBI and L. MAGESA, *Introduction*, in J.N.K. MUGAMBI and L. MAGESA (eds.), *Jesus in African Christianity: Experimentation and Diversity in African Christianity*, Nairobi, Initiatives, 1989, xi.

10. R. GIBELLINI, *Introduction: African Theologians Wonder ... and Make Some Proposals*, in R. GIBELLINI (ed.), *Paths of African Theology*, London, SCM, 1994, p. 6.

11. C. NYAMITI, *Contemporary African Christologies: Assessment and Practical Suggestions*, in R. GIBELLINI (ed.), *Paths of African Theology* (n. 10), p. 63.

defined as "discourse on Christ in accordance with the mentality and needs of the people in the black continent"[12].

The sources for christological discourse were clearly delineated from the outset of African theology in recent decades. In the same essay cited above in which John Mbiti lamented the lack of African concepts of Christ, he likewise stated that the African Church was "without a theology, without theologians, and without theological concern"[13]. He therefore urged his fellow Africans to develop theological reflection on the basis of four rich sources of material. The first of these "four pillars" was the Bible, which he asserted to be the final authority on religious matters. The second was the theology of the older churches, referring especially to the scholarship and tradition of the Church in Europe. The third pillar was the traditional African world, which he insisted must be taken seriously since "[i]t is within the traditional thought-forms and religious concerns that our peoples live and try to assimilate Christian teaching. These traditional thought-forms strongly colour much of their understanding of the Christian message"[14]. Finally, the living experience of the Church was to be an important source of theological reflection. In this regard, Mbiti showed openness to further investigation of the African Independent Churches as an authentic expression of African Christianity.

Looking back over the development of African theology since Mbiti's appeal, it is evident that these four pillars have indeed supported the theological endeavours of Africans thus far. While the relative weight given to each source will differ among theologians, the potential for drawing upon all categories has certainly been tapped. A clear indication of wider assent regarding these sources is set forth in the "Final Communiqué" of the 1977 Pan-African Conference of Third World Theologians, held in Accra, Ghana. Like Mbiti before them, these theologians point to *the Bible and Christian heritage* as the first source, emphasising that "[t]he Bible is the basic source of African theology, because it is the primary witness of God's revelation in Jesus Christ. No theology can retain its Christian identity apart from Scripture"[15]. Second, they point to *African anthropology* and include cosmology in addition, stressing that the salvation of the human person is inextricably bound to that of the cosmos. Third, *African traditional religions* are appealed to on the basis of the

12. *Ibid.*
13. MBITI, *Some African Concepts of Christology* (n. 4), p. 51.
14. *Ibid.*, p. 52.
15. Pan-African Conference of Third World Theologians, December 17-23, 1977, Accra, Ghana, *Final Communiqué*, in K. APPIAH-KUBI and S. TORRES (eds.) *African Theology en Route*, Maryknoll, NY, Orbis, 1979, p. 192.

fundamental premise that "[t]he God of history speaks to all peoples in particular ways. In Africa the traditional religions are a major source for the study of the African experience of God. The beliefs and practices of the traditional religions in Africa can enrich Christian theology and spirituality"[16]. The fourth source identified is the *African independent churches*, and the final one is *other African realities*, a broad category covering everything from cultural forms of life and arts, to family and communal life, to the struggles against racism, sexism, and any other form of economic, political, social, and cultural oppression.

Depending upon the sources favoured and the methods employed, it has become customary to distinguish two broad schools of African theology: "African" or "cultural" theology, and "Black" or "liberation" theology[17]. More recently, the former school has generally adopted the term "inculturation" theology[18]. The latter category has been further subdivided into South African Black theology, arising out of the particular context of apartheid in that country, and African Liberation theology, found throughout independent sub-Saharan Africa and broader in scope. Its intention is summarised as follows:

> Liberation theology in independent Africa endeavors to integrate the theme of liberation in the rest of the African cultural background. Liberation is not confined to modern socioeconomic and political levels but includes emancipation from other forms of oppression such as disease, poverty, hunger, ignorance, and the subjugation of women[19].

While the broad classifications of inculturation and liberation theologies may serve their purpose in distinguishing the various contexts and approaches of African theology, there is also the danger of erecting or promoting false dichotomies between the two strands. Consequently, there is currently a move towards diminishing the boundaries between them. As John Parratt explains,

> While they represent differing emphases, which result largely from historical factors, there is a unity in the theological task throughout Africa that derives from its common concern and its common sources. Its concern is to relate the Christian faith to contemporary life; its common sources lie in

---

16. *Ibid.*, p. 193.

17. E.g. D.M. Tutu, *Black Theology and African Theology – Soulmates or Antagonists?"* in J. Parratt (ed.) *A Reader in African Christian Theology*, London, SPCK, 1987, pp. 46-57.

18. The reasons for the change in terminology lie beyond the scope of the present paper. However, a brief survey of the development may be found in J. Baur, *2000 Years of Christianity in Africa: An African History 62-1992*, Nairobi, Paulines Publications Africa, 1994, pp. 295-297.

19. Nyamiti, *Contemporary African Christologies*, in R. Gibellini (ed.), *Paths of African Theology* (n. 10), p. 66.

the Bible and Christian tradition on the one hand, and in the African heritage and present experience, in its widest sense, on the other. The use that theologians make of these sources, their assumptions as to their usefulness and authority, the relative weight they attribute to each – these factors will clearly affect both the method and the final result. In essence, however, there is no disagreement as to the fundamental sources that lie at the base of the task of theology in Africa[20].

Concerning the sources and methods of African christologies more specifically, a brief outline will be provided here and then illustrated further in the next section. Perhaps the simplest and most lucid typology, which clarifies the complex subject of christological methodology, is that of Charles Nyamiti[21]. He suggests two broad categories: christologies of inculturation and christologies of liberation. Dealing first with the christologies of inculturation, which he defines as an effort "to incarnate the Gospel message in the African cultures on the theological level"[22], Nyamiti maintains that this is the most common and developed approach which encompasses most African christologies. He then outlines two methods undertaken by theologians: (1) starting from the biblical material about Christ and moving to the African cultural context to discern relevant christological themes, and (2) drawing upon the African cultural background as the point of departure for christological elaboration.

John Mbiti stands out as an example of the movement from the biblical teaching to the African reality. In his early explorations in African christology, he surveyed the New Testament (NT) materials of christological interest and summarised the evidence in terms of the most significant events of Jesus' life: his birth, triumphal entry, death and resurrection. Of these, his resurrection is deemed to be the dominant interest and also the one that appeals most to African Christians. Mbiti therefore highlights Jesus as the *Christus Victor*, explaining his significance to Africa as follows: "The greatest need among African peoples, is to see,

20. J. PARRATT, *Reinventing Christianity: African Theology Today*, Grand Rapids, MI, Eerdmans, 1995, pp. 193-194.

21. C. NYAMITI, *African Christologies Today*, in R.J. SCHREITER (ed.), *Faces of Jesus in Africa* (n. 7), pp. 3-14; cf. *Contemporary African Christologies*, in R. GIBELLINI (ed.), *Paths of African Theology* (n. 10), pp. 64-73. For an alternative typology which is also instructive, see J.S. UKPONG, *Christology and Inculturation: A New Testament Perspective*, in R. GIBELLINI (ed.), *Paths of African Theology* (n. 10), pp. 41-45. Ukpong outlines five different approaches, namely the *incarnational approach*, the *Logos Spermatikos (Seeds of the Word)*, the *functional analogy*, the *paschal mystery*, and the *biblical* approach. While he claims to take a different approach himself, his method does not differ markedly from the biblical approach.

22. NYAMITI, *African Christologies Today*, in R.J. SCHREITER (ed.), *Faces of Jesus in Africa* (n. 7), p. 3.

to know, and to experience Jesus Christ as the victor over the powers and forces from which Africa knows no means of deliverance"[23]. He also notes that the birth, baptism, and death of Jesus are of special interest to the Aladura Church and likely to other African Christians as well. He accounts for this observation in terms of the crucial importance of *rites de passage* among African societies, and suggests that these events in the life of Christ are especially meaningful to African peoples since they demonstrate that Jesus is "a perfect man" and "one who fulfils everything which constitutes a complete, corporate member of society"[24]. While the NT christological titles are said to lack meaning for Africans, other aspects of NT teaching provide fruitful contact with traditional concepts, such as solidarity in Christ's Body and the sacraments, especially baptism. He then concludes,

> If the Gospel is to make sense to African peoples it can happen only through their picture and experience of Jesus. It is only by understanding who he is, by experiencing who he is, and by participating in him as he is, that they will be transposed from traditional solidarity, or any other solidarity, to the solidarity of Christ[25].

> Thus Mbiti is among those theologians who demonstrate the methodological movement from the biblical sources to the present reality.

Most frequently, however, theologians move in the other direction from the African reality to christology. Nyamiti explains, "In this approach, the author examines the mystery of Christ from either the perspective of the African worldview, or from the angle of some particular theme taken from within the African worldview"[26]. It is in this category, known as the "thematic" or "functional analogy" approach, that African christologies have flourished. Since this method will be demonstrated in greater detail below, only brief descriptions will suffice at present to introduce the array of creative christologies which have recently emerged. For example, Harry Sawyerr begins with the assertion of Dr. Bengt Sundkler that "theology in Africa has to interpret ... Christ in terms that are relevant and essential to African existence"; therefore it "must needs start with the fundamental facts of the African interpretation of existence and the universe"[27]. While

---

23. MBITI, *Some African Concepts of Christology* (n. 4), p. 55.
24. *Ibid.*, p. 56.
25. *Ibid.*, p. 62.
26. NYAMITI, *African Christologies Today*, in R.J. SCHREITER (ed.), *Faces of Jesus in Africa* (n. 7), p. 4.
27. B. SUNDKLER, *The Christian Ministry in Africa*, London, SCM, 1962, p. 281; quoted in H. SAWYERR, *The Basis of Theology for Africa*, in J. PARRATT (ed.), *The*

objecting to an earlier proposal of Jesus Christ as "Chief"[28], Sawyerr suggests instead that he be represented as the "First-born" among many brethren who form the Church "in keeping with African notions"[29].

John Pobee questions, "Why should an Akan relate to Jesus of Nazareth, who does not belong to his clan, family, tribe or nation?"[30]. He then seeks to explicate Christ's divinity and humanity according to the Akan understanding, and portrays Jesus as the "Great Ancestor (*Nana*)" who is superior to all ancestors and spirits. Several other African theologians favour the term "Ancestor" for Christ, including Kwame Bediako[31], Charles Nyamiti[32], François Kabasélé[33], and Bénézet Bujo[34] who will be considered further below. Christ as "Healer" is another symbol discussed, for example, by Aylward Shorter[35] and Césé Kolié[36]. Closely related is Matthew Schoffeleers' proposal of the *Nganga* ("the medicine person") paradigm for understanding Christ at the level of folk theology[37]. Moreover, Anselme Sanon develops the theme of Jesus as the "Head and Master of Initiation"[38], a status gained by his passing

Practice of Presence: Shorter Writings of Harry Sawyerr, Grand Rapids, MI, Eerdmans, 1996, p. 100.

28. Made by Paul Fueter, for example. See SAWYERR, *The Basis of Theology for Africa*, in J. PARRATT (ed.), *The Practice of Presence: Shorter Writings of Harry Sawyerr* (n. 27), pp. 104-105, for the reasons he objects to the term. Cf. F. KABASÉLÉ, *Christ as Chief*, in R.J. SCHREITER (ed.), *Faces of Jesus in Africa* (n. 7), pp. 103-115, for a recent restatement of the christological symbol of chiefship.

29. SAWYERR, *The Basis of Theology for Africa*, in J. PARRATT (ed.), *The Practice of Presence: Shorter Writings of Harry Sawyerr* (n. 27), p. 105.

30. J.S. POBEE, *Toward an African Theology,* Nashville, TN, Abingdon, 1979, p. 81.

31. K. BEDIAKO, *Biblical Christologies in the Context of African Traditional Religions*, in V. SAMUEL and C. SUGDEN (eds.), *Sharing Jesus in the Two Thirds World*, Bangalore, Partnership in Mission-Asia, 1983, pp. 115-175; *Jesus in African Culture – A Ghanaian Perspective,* Accra, Asempa, 1990.

32. C. NYAMITI, *African Christologies Today* (n. 21); *Christ as Our Ancestor: Christology from an African Perspective*, Gweru, Mambo Press, 1984.

33. F. KABASÉLÉ, *Christ as Ancestor and Elder Brother*, in R.J. SCHREITER (ed.), *Faces of Jesus in Africa* (n. 7), pp. 116-127.

34. B. BUJO, *African Theology in its Social Context*, tr. J. O'Donohue, Nairobi, St. Paul Publications – Africa, 1992.

35. A. SHORTER, *Jesus and the Witchdoctor: An Approach to Healing and Wholeness*, London, Chapman, 1985.

36. C. KOLIÉ, *Christ as Healer?* In R.J. SCHREITER (ed.), *Faces of Jesus in Africa* (n. 7), pp. 128-150.

37. M. SCHOFFELEERS, *Christ in African Folk Theology: The Nganga Paradigm*, in T.D. BLAKELY, W.E.A. VAN BEEK, and D.L. THOMSON (eds.), *Religion in Africa: Experience and Expression*, London, James Currey, 1994, pp. 73-88.

38. A.T. SANON, *Jesus, Master of Initiation*, in R. SCHREITER (ed.), *Faces of Jesus in Africa* (n. 7), pp. 85-102.

through the human stages of initiation, climaxing in his death and resurrection. As the "Master" who himself endured and triumphed over
the pain, he now acts as guardian and guide to all those who obey him.

Christologies of liberation form a second major division, since
Christ as "Liberator" is increasingly resounding across sub-Saharan
Africa as evidenced in the two forms of liberation theologies mentioned above. Points of departure are found in both a "christology
from below", beginning with the man, Jesus of Nazareth, and highlighting the liberating dimensions of his ministry, and in the contemporary context as the locus for theological formulation. For example,
Laurenti Magesa describes his task of discerning a liberating christology in Africa as follows:

> [W]e have to commit ourselves to what we know is the way and action of
> Jesus Christ the Liberator on [sic] this historical experience. It is by doing
> this that we shall be true to our calling as Christians.
> Drawing on the experience of the general mass of the African peoples, and
> also on the work of the various social sciences which have analyzed the
> codified experience, a theological examination of the socio-economic and
> political situation prevalent in Africa brings to the fore numerous ethical
> and moral questions. ... All of these are questions of suffering, issues of
> lack of freedom in its various aspects. Further problems to be seen all over
> the continent – problems of ignorance and preventable disease, of famine
> and ethnic wars, of class antagonisms and racial persecutions – are the
> direct consequence of ignoring this basic question of 'unfreedom.' They
> are a result of not confronting it in time with the active, liberating word of
> God[39].

Thus an initial survey of the sources and methods of African theology
brings to light the enormous complexities of contemporary life in Africa
and the wide range of christologies which have arisen in response to
such complexities. Schreiter rightly questions where Jesus Christ is in
the midst of all this, and wisely notes that in many ways the understanding of who Jesus is mirrors the challenges that Africa faces today[40]. This
observation will become further evident through a brief introduction to
selected voices of contemporary christology, summarised under three
central themes.

---

39. L. MAGESA, *Christ the Liberator and Africa Today*, in R. SCHREITER (ed.), *Faces of Jesus in Africa* (n. 7), pp. 151-163.

40. R.J. SCHREITER, *Introduction: Jesus Christ in Africa Today*, in R.J. SCHREITER (ed.), *Faces of Jesus in Africa* (n. 7), p. ix.

II. Voices of Contemporary African Christology

1. Christ as Ancestor

Bénézet Bujo

Bénézet Bujo, a Roman Catholic priest from the Democratic Republic of Congo (formerly Zaire) and presently Professor of Moral Theology at the University of Fribourg, Switzerland, is gaining increased recognition as a creative and respected theologian. In his most substantial work thus far, *African Theology in its Social Context*, he emerges as one who blurs the boundary between "inculturation" and "liberation" theologies, as indicated above. He denounces the theology of inculturation in scathing terms as "a pompous irrelevance, truly an ideological superstructure at the service of the bourgeoisie"[41]. He clearly sides with the goal of liberation theologies in seeking the emancipation of men and women, yet he qualifies his position as follows: "I am not speaking of some sociopolitical liberation to be achieved through revolution, but of liberation in all its aspects, personal as well as social. People should enjoy fullness of life at every level"[42]. The means to achieve such liberation, however, require a serious reconsideration of the traditional cultures of Africa. Responding to the inadequacies of both inculturation and liberation theologies, he asserts,

> In all of this, the problem of culture cannot be ignored. The Black African must rediscover his roots so that the ancestral tradition may enrich post-colonial men and make them adopt a critical attitude towards modern society. Then Africa will be able to breathe with a new life which neither idealizes the past, simply because one is black, nor treats the past as an idol. What is needed is a new synthesis. It is not a question of replacing the God of the Africans but rather of enthroning the God of Jesus Christ, not as the rival of the God of the ancestors, but as identical with him[43].

It is precisely such a synthesis which Bujo attempts in urging the rediscovery and reappropriation of the traditional African heritage in a way that will further the cause of liberation from all forms of present day oppression.

The central question Bujo poses is as follows: "*In which way can Jesus Christ be an African among the Africans according to their own religious experience?*"[44]. To address this challenge, he develops an

---

41. BUJO, *African Theology in its Social Context* (n. 34), p. 71.
42. *Ibid.*, p. 130.
43. *Ibid.*, pp. 15-16.
44. *Ibid.*, p. 9; emphasis original.

ancestral theology on the presupposition that "[t]here is no African tribe which does not revere its ancestors"[45]. While a full explanation of his ancestral theology cannot be undertaken at present, it must be introduced as the framework for his christological formulation. In this respect, the most significant factors include the eschatological and salvific dimensions inherent in communion with the ancestors, according to traditional belief. These crucial components are summarised as follows:

> Here we begin to understand the supreme importance of the past for the African: for the secret of life is to be found above all in the hallowed attitudes and practices of the ancestors. In their wisdom is to be found the key to a better and fuller life, and it is therefore crucial that the rites, actions, words and laws which the ancestors have bequeathed to their descendants be scrupulously observed: they are the indispensable instruments of salvation. The way a person treats this inheritance is decisive, for life or for death. The ancestral traditions are gifts of God, they have a truly sacramental character. The life-giving traditions of the past must determine the present and the future since in them alone is salvation to be found[46].

Having outlined the ancestral cult in terms of its pervasiveness and significance, Bujo then proceeds to relate this cultural heritage to biblical revelation and Church tradition. He states his sources and methods clearly in this way:

> What the Church needs to do today is to uncover the vital elements of African culture which are stamped on the African soul. Once the African heritage has been clearly understood, then it can be placed alongside the biblical and patristic traditions, and progress will be possible. Our guide in the construction of an African theology must be, apart from African tradition, the Bible and the Fathers of the Church[47].

He acknowledges the need to distinguish between those traditions which truly continue and those which have died, and also to be discriminating about which traditions should be maintained. The task requires not only theology, but also other disciplines such as depth psychology, cultural anthropology, popular art, and sociology. Every available resource is to be utilised "to promote a real understanding of the kingdom of God in which Africans can be truly themselves"[48].

In order to relate the African heritage to the biblical material, Bujo draws a striking parallel between the ancestral cult and "narrative theology". In other words, he likens the African perspective of remembering

45. *Ibid.*, p. 120.
46. *Ibid.*, p. 27; see pp. 23-29 for further detail.
47. *Ibid.*, p. 68.
48. *Ibid.*, p. 70.

and re-enacting the past as a means of guaranteeing prosperity for the
future to the biblical tradition of "Exodus theology"[49]. He stresses that

> [i]n making their acts of pious remembrance, Africans are seeking more
> than earthly prosperity; they are seeking salvation in its fullness. ... In
> other words, the remembering and re-enactment of the deeds of ancestors
> and elders is a memorial-narrative act of salvation designed to secure total
> community, both before and after death, with all good and benevolent
> ancestors[50].

It is on this basis, therefore, that Bujo suggests the title for Jesus as
the "Ancestor Par Excellence" or the "Proto-Ancestor". He recognises the importance of a "christology from below" for the African
context, and interprets Jesus' earthly ministry in terms of those qualities and virtues which Africans seek to attribute to their ancestors. He
explains,

> If we look back on the historical Jesus of Nazareth, we can see in him, not
> only one who lived the African ancestor-ideal in the highest degree, but
> one who brought that ideal to an altogether new fulfilment. Jesus worked
> miracles, healing the sick, opening the eyes of the blind, raising the dead to
> life. In short, he brought life, and life-force, in its fullness[51].

Bujo goes on to explain that in identifying himself with humanity in
this way, Jesus encompasses all the history and religious aspirations of
the ancestors, so that he himself becomes "the privileged locus for a full
understanding of the ancestors"[52]. That is to say, the African can now
understand the mystery of the Incarnation,

> for after God had spoken to us at various times and in various places,
> including our ancestors, in these last days he speaks to us through his Son,
> whom he has established as unique Ancestor, as Proto-Ancestor, from
> whom all life flows for His descendants (cf. Heb 1,1-2). From him derive
> all those longed-for prerogatives which constitute Him as Ancestor. The
> African ancestors are in this way forerunners, or images, of the Proto-
> Ancestor, Jesus Christ[53].

Thus Jesus becomes the Saviour whose passion, death, and resurrection must be remembered and retold down the generations, for he is the
one who opens up the future which the ancestors had sought to secure.
Interpreting Christ in this way, insists Bujo, will be far more meaningful
to Africans than titles such as *logos* (Word) and *kyrios* (Lord). Hence he
concludes,

49. *Ibid.*, pp. 29-30.
50. *Ibid.*, p. 78.
51. *Ibid.*, p. 79.
52. *Ibid.*, p. 83.
53. *Ibid.*

It is important that Christianity show the Africans that being truly Christian and being truly African are not opposed to each other, because to be a true Christian means to be a true human being, since it was Jesus himself who was truly human and who humanised the world. Once however we have established that the legitimate yearnings of the African ancestors are not only taken up in Jesus Christ, but are also transcended in him, can we not use the concept of Proto-Ancestor as the starting-point of a Christology for which the enthusiasm of the African will be more than a passing fashion[54]?

So although Bujo prefaces his work by stating that it is not to be viewed as a treatise on christology, he nonetheless introduces some profound reflections on Christ which are firmly rooted in African ancestral practice and directly relevant to Christian belief and practice today. Before concluding his work by spelling out such implications, he summarises his basic conviction as follows: "I believe that a truly dynamic Christianity will only be possible in Africa when the foundation of the African's whole life is built on Jesus Christ, conceived in specifically African categories"[55].

2. Christ as Liberator

Jean-Marc Éla

Another contemporary theologian who has received widespread acclaim is Jean-Marc Éla, a Camerounian priest. Like Bujo, Éla claims not to write a theological treatise, but to respond to the urgent requests arising from his decade of ministry to the Kirdi people of north Cameroun. Hence he writes a highly contextualized theology in that his experience of living among village peasants, whom he refers to as those "rejected by history"[56], continually informs his reflections on the faith. Yet his theology is not restricted to this particular context; rather, he draws upon their common experience of suffering injustice and oppression to address the broader concerns of independent, sub-Saharan Africa. Again like Bujo, Éla blurs the distinction between inculturation and liberation theologies in his central thesis that "liberation of the oppressed must be the primary condition for any authentic inculturation of the Christian message"[57]. And further like Bujo, he seeks to address the central question of the Christian faith: "Jesus of Nazareth asks us:

54. *Ibid.*, p. 84.
55. *Ibid.*, p. 91.
56. J.-M. ÉLA, *My Faith as an African*, tr. J. Pairman and S. Perry, Maryknoll, NY, Orbis, 1988, p. xviii.
57. *Ibid.*, p. xvi; emphasis original.

'Africans, who do you say I am?' and we must answer from our world of today"[58].

Indeed, it is his prophetic perception of and response to the "world of today" which lends such power and distinctive focus to Éla's writing. He finds clear rationale for his approach in recent directives of the Roman Catholic Church[59] as well as in the conclusions of the 1977 Pan-African Conference of Third World Theologians in Accra. Éla asserts that the Final Communiqué from this conference is a landmark in that it not only acknowledges the new challenge for African theology to manifest "the liberation of our people from a cultural captivity", but also admits that oppression extends beyond culture to political, economic, and social structures. Hence Accra confirmed that "African theology must also be liberation theology"[60]. Given such freedom and necessity, Éla launches into full-scale attack on the deplorable conditions across contemporary Africa. Space does not allow for recounting the litany of ills suffered by the continent, but it is in such expression that Éla's writing is at its most incisive. Nor does the Church escape his scorching critique, as one example will suffice to show:

> In our environment, our faith does not ask questions about the sex of the angels or the infallibility of the pope; instead we question the lack of any genuine application of the critical function inherent in the Christian faith. How can we show that the African church is blocked by an ecclesiastical praxis that is, in fact, a kind of museum of a narrow moralism,

58. *Ibid.*, p. 148.

59. E.g. those articulated by the Symposium of the Episcopal Conferences of Africa and Madagascar (SECAM) at Accra in 1977, the African bishops meeting in Yaoundé in 1981, and various statements from Pope John Paul II. See, e.g., J.-M. ÉLA, *Christianity and Liberation in Africa*, in R. GIBELLINI (ed.), *Paths of African Theology* (n. 10), pp. 136-139.

60. This section of the Final Communiqué is worth citing in full in view of its significance for the development of liberation theology in Africa. The document records,

Because oppression is found not only in culture but also in political and economic structures and the dominant mass media, African theology must also be *liberation* theology. The focus on liberation in African theology connects it with other Third World theologies. Like black theologians in North America, we cannot ignore racism as a distortion of the human person. Like Latin American and Asian theologians, we see the need to be liberated from socio-economic exploitation. A related but different form of oppression is often found in the roles set aside for women in the churches. There is the oppression of Africans by white colonialism, but there is also the oppression of blacks by blacks. We stand against oppression in any form because the Gospel of Jesus Christ demands our participation in the struggle to free people from all forms of dehumanization. African theology concerns itself with bringing about the solidarity of Africans with black Americans, Asians, and Latin Americans who are also struggling for the realization of human communities in which the men and women of our time become the architects of their own destiny. See *Final Communiqué*, in K. APPIAH-KUBI and S. TORRES (eds.), *African Theology en Route* (n. 15), p. 194.

a ritualistic sacramentalism, a disembodied spirituality, and a withering dogmatics[61]?

From this context of what Éla perceives to be "a form of decaying Christianity, bound up in its doctrine and discipline"[62], he proposes what he calls "shade-tree theology – a theology that, far from the libraries and the offices, develops among brothers and sisters searching shoulder to shoulder with unlettered peasants for the sense of the word of God in situations in which this word touches them"[63]. Once again, an examination of his theology cannot be undertaken at present other than a brief consideration of his method and christological reflections.

It comes as no surprise, then, that Éla finds his point of departure for theology in the present context. He writes, "These urgent problems of contemporary Africa become the obligatory locus of theological research. ...[I]t is no longer enough to pose the questions of faith on the level of culture alone. We must also pay attention to the mechanisms and structures of oppression at work"[64]. His overriding concern is to testify to the gospel message in terms of incarnation, which entails far more than merely adopting African words and African rhythms to speak of God and sing his praise. With eyes fully fixed on the plight of the poor and oppressed, Éla calls for the *"pedagogy of the discovery of situations of sin and oppression* – situations that rear their heads in contradiction with the project of the salvation and liberation in Jesus Christ"[65]. This includes promoting a mentality of active solidarity among the suffering people, and making an inventory of the factors or mechanisms of injustice. Then, in addition to exposing such sin in the contemporary world, the church must submit itself to a critical analysis to reveal its *"radical incompatibility with God's plan for the world"*[66]. From here, leaders must arise as prophetic voices within the community, and together the community must seek transformation so that they might experience more of the justice and peace intended by God[67].

As a liberation theologian, Éla also works from the fundamental premise that *"God is not neutral.* God is revealed as the one who brings

---

61. ÉLA, *My Faith as an African* (n. 56), p. 153.
62. *Ibid.*, p. 5.
63. J.-M. ÉLA, *African Cry*, tr. R.R. Barr, Maryknoll, NY, Orbis, 1986, p. vi.
64. J.-M. ÉLA, *Christianity and Liberation in Africa*, in R. GIBELLINI (ed.), *Paths of African Theology* (n. 10), p. 140.
65. *Ibid.*, p. 143; emphasis original.
66. *Ibid.*; emphasis original.
67. For summary statements of Éla's method, cf. *African Cry* (n. 63), p. 28, and *My Faith as an African* (n. 56), p. xvi.

justice to the oppressed (Ps. 146:7-9)"[68]. Consequently, the ministry of Jesus is interpreted in the same terms: "God's revelation through the incarnation obliges us to unmask the ultimate scandal of our faith: Jesus Christ made a radical choice in favor of those considered to be the dregs of the world"[69]. Éla then contrasts this reality with the dominant theology of the rich, which normally reigns and which is said to spiritualize Jesus to such an extent that his humanity, with all its tensions and conflicts, is forgotten. Hence he emphasises,

> The incarnation is the supreme event of our faith – God's final word to us (John 1:14; Heb. 1:1-2). It is difficult to realize its full significance unless we grasp it through the world of poverty and oppression. The real world of the gospel is one of hunger, wealth and injustice, sickness, rejection, slavery, and death. It is precisely through the structures of such a world that God is revealed. God is present through Jesus of Nazareth, who, in the incarnation, reveals God's omnipotence in weakness and establishes a form of conspiracy between God and the downtrodden[70].

Jesus' ministry is then expounded in terms of his announcing the good news, beginning with an option for the poor, and his central act of proclaiming the Kingdom of God for the sake of the poor. His actions are rooted in the prophetic tradition of protest against injustice and oppression. It must therefore be noted, according to Éla, that Christianity begins with a criticism of religion, which is essentially a criticism of all society, of human relationships, and of power (Mt 20:25). However, the real issue Jesus confronted was the oppressive laws which assured the prosperity of some at the cost and exclusion of others. He summarises his interpretation as follows:

> In the end, the gospel confronts a strategy of domination leading to hunger, set in a world structure where the administration of the wealth of the earth is monopolized by those who control the economic and political apparatus. Jesus reveals God and his option for the poor and the little ones – in the heart of a society built for ideological and religious reasons on the basis of marginalization, misery, and oppression[71].

Thus, concludes Éla, Jesus constantly sides with the poor and defenceless against the rich and powerful, and the Kingdom of God means the liberation of the oppressed.

This perspective on the life and ministry of Jesus also shapes the way in which his death and resurrection are perceived. Since his life was one of solidarity with the poor, this forms the key to a credible interpretation

---

68. ÉLA, *My Faith as an African* (n. 56), p. 104; emphasis original.
69. *Ibid.*, p. 105.
70. *Ibid.*
71. *Ibid.*, p. 107.

of his death in the contemporary context. Jesus, as a victim of repressive violence, is said to pay for the boldness of his subversive ideas with his life. Hence today his death is to be understood in terms of God's presence amidst actions that break away from the dominant religion and society. Éla explains,

> Jesus' death is the result of his option for the poor and oppressed. The contemporary society, in turn, condemns Jesus as a blasphemer for having shown the God of the exodus to the poor.
> ... Jesus died so that people can stand upright – that is the center of the gospel message.... To 'follow Jesus' is to live out his subversive plan, his stance for the poor against situations of misery and oppression. The presence of misery and oppression is a basic form of the 'sin of the world' that contradicts the kingdom of justice and freedom inaugurated by Jesus of Nazareth. ... For Christians and the church, the liberation of the poor, then, is the basic issue at stake in the death of Jesus[72].

Similarly, the resurrection of Jesus is acknowledged to be the summit of revelation, and the means by which he has conquered death and inaugurated a new world. Éla immediately questions, however,

But how can we celebrate the resurrection where millions of men and women live in suffering and oppression? How can the resurrection of Jesus become an historical experience in the struggle for life itself by those who are weak and without power? How does the resurrection of the humiliated begin today[73]?

Such questions lead to the heart of the biblical message and Christian faith today, for in Éla's view, Africans are presently living out the passion of Jesus in history. Hence he questions, "If the poor and oppressed are the presence of the crucified God, can we read the Bible apart from contemporary situations of poverty and oppression?"[74] On this basis he urges the questioning of everything that traditional theology has taught about the meaning of Jesus' death and resurrection, voicing doubt that it has any real meaning at all today. Instead, he asserts the following interpretation:

If we view the cross of Jesus Christ as the cross of the Third World, the very existence of the Third World shows us what sin is and how it is structured in history. The Third World carries within itself the hidden Christ. It is the historic body of Jesus Christ today.

We must go and rediscover Christ in the slums, in places of misery and domination, among the majority of the poor and the oppressed people. It

---

72. *Ibid.*, p. 109.
73. *Ibid.*, p. 110.
74. *Ibid.*

is the Third World that allows the church to make salvation in Jesus Christ visible[75].

With this view of ministering the gospel, Éla reflects the centrality of Jesus of Nazareth to his own thought and action. He comments, "Certain events force me to turn back to the Nazareth experience, to go to the heart of that time and to live it again, not as a time of pre-mission, but as the mission itself. That is not easy"[76]. Yet his primary conviction is that salvation in Jesus Christ means liberation from every form of slavery, and the Church must demonstrate this salvation concretely by creating conditions that liberate humans and allow them to grow. He states,

> The church must adopt the practice of Jesus himself. Jesus did not limit his mission to preaching an inner conversion. His concern was precisely for the liberation of the poor and oppressed (Luke 4:16-21). In Jesus, God is glimpsed in the gesture of shared bread and in the act of the person who rises up and walks. The practice and message of the good news will be translated by acts of liberating people from legalism and ritualism[77].

Thus, according to Éla, "Only through an active but humble involvement in the dynamics of African society will they [Christians] be able to live and proclaim Jesus Christ as the ultimate Liberator"[78].

3. Christ at the Well: Views of African Women Theologians

Jesus' encounter with the woman at the well (Jn 4) may be seen as a portrait, or a paradigm, of what is presently occurring in African women's christologies. Just as Jesus cut through deep prejudices of race, religion, gender and class to make meaningful contact with the Samaritan woman in her own context of suffering, so Christian women in Africa today relate how Christ meets them directly in their various contexts of suffering, especially those caused by oppressive structures in male-dominated societies. Hence Jesus' solidarity with those who are marginalized becomes a main motif for these women theologians, as expressed by Thérèsa Souga from Cameroun: "There seems to be a deep bond, even a complicity, between Jesus of Nazareth and African women, a bond due to the fact that the women are among those who are most marginalized in our society"[79]. Likewise his message of liberation and

---

75. *Ibid.*, p. 99.
76. *Ibid.*, p. 7.
77. *Ibid.*, p. 142.
78. ÉLA, *African Cry* (n. 63), p. 87.
79. T. SOUGA, *The Christ-Event from the Viewpoint of African Women: I. A Catholic Perspective*, in V. FABELLA and M. ODUYOYE (eds.), *With Passion and Compassion: Third World Women Doing Theology*, Maryknoll, NY, Orbis, 1988, pp. 26-27.

life becomes central to their understanding and expression of what Jesus means to them in their situations of suffering. Consequently, these theologians assert that African women's experience in church and society must be taken into account in formulating relevant christology. Before hearing from selected women, however, it is beneficial to note the common ground which they share with male African theologians.

Like their male counterparts, African women theologians draw upon the sources and methods considered most relevant to contemporary christological reflection. For example, Mercy Oduyoye from Ghana, acknowledged as a leading woman theologian in Africa today, devotes a chapter to christology in one of her main publications, *Hearing and Knowing: Theological Reflections on Christianity in Africa*. In addressing the topic of salvation, she begins by citing the contemporary realities which provide the context for Africans seeking salvation. She then turns to the Bible and, taking the approach of a word study, explains her method and its import as follows:

> If one studies the Old Testament with the knowledge of the primal worldview of Africa and an awareness of the political and sociological realities that are shaping Africa as part of one's critical equipment, many similarities surface. The primal cry for salvation (*yeshuah*) is taken up in the New Testament and salvation is declared by Christianity to be in Christ. This I believe is the reason for the continued attraction of Christianity to Africans, in spite of the negative burdens associated with its carriers. The Christ of Christianity touches human needs at all levels, and Africans are but ordinary members of the human race feeling the need for salvation[80].

Likewise, Oduyoye writes an essay on christology with Ghanaian theologian Elizabeth Amoah. Together they work not only from Christian Scripture but also from the "unwritten Scriptures" of the Fante of Ghana[81], and speak graphically of "the need to rewrap Christology in African leaves"[82].

Furthermore, these women theologians share similar concerns to the male writers concerning the content of contemporary African christology. Amoah and Oduyoye provide incisive critique concerning the main christologies which Africa inherited from the modern missionary enterprise, such as the problems surrounding the "royal Christology" and

---

80. M. ODUYOYE, *Hearing and Knowing: Theological Reflections on Christianity in Africa*, Maryknoll, NY, Orbis, 1986, pp. 98-99.

81. A. AMOAH and M. ODUYOYE, *The Christ for African Women*, in V. FABELLA and M. ODUYOYE (eds.), *With Passion and Compassion: Third World Women Doing Theology* (n. 79), p. 35.

82. *Ibid.*, p. 37.

those related to eschatology[83]. In doing so, they reflect similar views regarding inculturation and liberation christologies as those articulated by male African theologians.

For the present purpose, however, attention will be focused on the emergence of the feminist paradigm in contemporary African christological reflection. First, these authors lament the fact that until recent decades, most written theology was produced by men and from a male perspective. Not only was the female perspective left unarticulated, but also "The theology on the person of Jesus tended to be much more philosophical and abstract than that of the existential Jesus of the Gospels who calls people as individuals and as a community to authentic human existence"[84]. Ann Nasimiyu-Wasike, a Catholic theologian from Kenya, traces the origin of the problem to the early church era when christological formulations were being forged in the context of Jewish and Hellenistic categories of thought. As a result of the patriarchal realities of the time, theological references to Christ became heavily androcentric, reinforcing the assumption that God was male. Therefore, only male metaphors were considered appropriate to speak of God; moreover, "Christ had to be male in order to reveal a male God, and this was taken literally"[85]. While man was understood to be made in the image of God, woman was only seen as the image of man and only saved through man. Such concepts about God and Christ in relation to man and woman coloured the development of theology in Europe for centuries, and consequently tainted perceptions of Christ brought by modern European missionaries to Africa. Nasimiyu-Wasike summarises the problem as follows:

> The African church has inherited the misinterpretation of woman and her relation to God and Jesus from the European church. Therefore, the African woman, in addition to being under her cultural bondage and oppression, also experiences the socio-economic oppression of neo-colonialists in the church[86].

Given this historical backdrop, it is not surprising that African women theologians today are raising new questions in their exploration of christology. For example, Amoah and Oduyoye ask, "What have women to do with the concept of Christology? What do women say about Christology?

83. *Ibid.*, pp. 36-38.
84. A. NASIMIYU-WASIKE, *Christology and an African Woman's Experience*, in J.N.K. MUGAMBI and L. MAGESA (eds.), *Jesus in African Christianity: Experimentation and Diversity in African Christology* (n. 9), p. 123.
85. *Ibid.*, p. 129.
86. *Ibid.*, pp. 129-130.

Is there such a thing as a women's Christology? Do the traditional statements of Christology take into account women's experience of life?"[87] Likewise Souga questions,

> Is this Jesus whom we find to be full of concern for the women of his own time also today standing with African women in their particular context? Can African women understand Jesus Christ and understand themselves in relation to Jesus of Nazareth? Doesn't the concrete historic situation of African women challenge the theology that we would like to live in the churches of Africa[88]?

In similar fashion, Louise Tappa, also from Cameroun, voices what she considers to be the fundamental question as follows: "In the sociopolitical, socioeconomic, sociocultural, and socioreligious context of Third World countries in general and of Africa in particular, what does confessing Christ mean for the African woman?"[89]

Once again, new paths of christology emerge in response to such questions. Women theologians are quick to point out that despite the paucity of written christologies by African women, reflections on Christ do exist even if they are virtually unknown. For example, Amoah and Oduyoye mention Afua Kuma, cited above in the introduction, whose prayers and praises to Jesus have only recently been translated and published for wider access. Or, Nasimiyu-Wasike, recognising the shortage of written materials, conducted interviews with a variety of African Christian women concerning the central question, "Who is Jesus Christ in your life?"[90]

On the basis of such explorations, these women theologians attest to the fact that African women's christologies tend to reflect primarily *the interplay of faith and life*. Amoah and Oduyoye point out that the men and women of Africa share the same traditions and present realities, and they learned their Christianity "from the same Western, male-centered, clerically minded missionaries". They then claim that "African women, however, have a different experience and interpretation of this common reality and of lived Christianity", explained as follows:

87. AMOAH and ODUYOYE, *The Christ for African Women*, in V. FABELLA and M. ODUYOYE (eds.), *With Passion and Compassion* (n. 79), p. 35.

88. SOUGA, *The Christ-Event from the Viewpoint of African Women: I. A Catholic Perspective*, in V. FABELLA and M. ODUYOYE (eds.), *With Passion and Compassion* (n. 79), p. 25.

89. L. TAPPA, *The Christ-Event from the Viewpoint of African Women: II. A Protestant Perspective*, in V. FABELLA and M. ODUYOYE (eds.), *With Passion and Compassion* (n. 79), p. 31.

90. NASIMIYU-WASIKE, *Christology and an African Woman's Experience*, in J.N.K. MUGAMBI and L. MAGESA (eds.), *Jesus in African Christianity: Experimentation and Diversity in African Christology* (n. 9), p. 125.

Though, in general, the women affirm the Christological position of the African men, at times they go beyond it or contradict it altogether. This can be gleaned not so much from the writings of African women as from the way they live and from their Christianity – their very spirituality, their witness to what Christ means for their lives[91].

For example, while affirming the recognition of Christ as liberator, they offer their perspective on what this means for African women:

This Christ is the liberator from the burden of disease and the ostracism of a society riddled with blood-taboos and theories of inauspiciousness arising out of women's blood. Christ liberated women by being born of Mary, demanding that the woman bent double with gynecological disorders should stand up straight. The practice of making women become silent 'beasts' of societies' burdens, bent double under racism, poverty, and lack of appreciation of what fullness of womanhood should be, has been annulled and countered by Christ. Christ transcends and transforms culture and has liberated us to do the same[92].

Moreover, they object to the ruler-image of Christ the King as developed by John Pobee, on the basis that human experience of hierarchies, which are usually patriarchal structures, does not commend itself to those being alienated and oppressed. They stress, "Patriarchal/hierarchical structures have little room for the participation and inclusiveness that those whose humanity is being trampled upon yearn for"[93].

Instead, Amoah and Oduyoye affirm Jesus in their understanding and experience as the true companion, friend, and teacher, and

the true 'Child of Women' – 'Child of Women' truly because in Christ the fullness of all that we know of perfect womanhood is revealed. He is the caring, compassionate nurturer of all. Jesus nurtures not just by parables but by miracles of feeding. With his own hands he cooked that others might eat; he was known in the breaking of the bread. Jesus is Christ – truly woman (human) yet truly divine, for only God is the truly Compassionate One[94].

Finally, their main conclusion is worth quoting at length, to capture the voices of these women in their contemporary christological reflection:

An African woman perceives and accepts Christ as a woman and as an African. The commitment that flows from this faith is commitment to full womanhood (humanity), to the survival of human communities, to the 'birthing,' nurturing, and maintenance of life, and to loving relations and life that is motivated by love.

91. AMOAH and ODUYOYE, *The Christ for African Women* in V. FABELLA and M. ODUYOYE (eds.), *With Passion and Compassion* (n. 79), p. 43.
    92. *Ibid.*
    93. *Ibid.*, p. 41.
    94. *Ibid.*, p. 44.

Having accepted Christ as refugee and guest of Africa, the woman seeks to make Christ at home and to order life in such a way as to enable the whole household to feel at home with Christ. The woman sees the whole space of Africa as a realm to be ordered, as a place where Christ has truly 'tabernacled.' Fears are not swept under the beds and mats but are brought out to be dealt with by the presence of Christ. Christ becomes truly friend and companion, liberating women from assumptions of patriarchal societies, and honoring, accepting, and sanctifying the single life as well as the married life, parenthood as well as the absence of progeny. The Christ of the women of Africa upholds not only motherhood, but all who, like Jesus of Nazareth, perform 'mothering' roles of bringing out the best in all around them. This is the Christ, high priest, advocate, and just judge in whose kingdom we pray to be[95].

Nasimiyu-Wasike provides further insight into African women's christologies. First, she points out that most African women work sixteen to eighteen hours daily to provide the basic necessities for their families. Hence she observes, along with her theological colleagues from West Africa, that

[t]hey have very little time to seriously reflect on their relationship with other people and with God. Nevertheless, these women believe that their lives are lived in union with God; their theology is not one which is written and articulated but one which is lived and practised in everyday activities and experiences[96].

Working from the context of African women's experience, Nasimiyu-Wasike notes that their main struggles are against those forces which deny them control over their own destiny and which prevent them from fulfilling their God-given potential. Severe hardships include the physical labour demanded of them, particularly in the rural areas, as well as ongoing cultural oppression. Nasimiyu-Wasike sums up, "Despite their nurturing, maintaining, and serving life for the survival of human communities, women are always marginalized and given an inferior status"[97].

Having considered the contemporary context, Nasimiyu-Wasike proceeds by analysing her personal interviews with women as mentioned above. From her findings, she discerns the actual role which Jesus plays in their lives, such as protector from evil powers and provider of strength, comfort, courage, and hope midst the hardships within home, church, and society. She also examines the gospel materials concerning

95. *Ibid.*, pp. 44-45.
96. NASIMIYU-WASIKE, *Christology and an African Woman's Experience*, in J.N.K. MUGAMBI and L. MAGESA (eds.), *Jesus in African Christianity: Experimentation and Diversity in African Christology* (n. 9), p. 130.
97. *Ibid.*, p. 124.

Jesus and women, and asserts that Jesus' attitude to women was "revolutionary" and "countercultural"[98]. Hence she concludes that despite the inferior status of women in Jewish society, "Jesus esteemed them and gave them equal status to men. The original relationship between women and men first established by God at creation was restored in Jesus Christ"[99]. She then reviews several christological models in contemporary theological discussion, adding a feminist perspective to the eschatological, anthropological, liberational, and cosmological models[100].

Particularly noteworthy is Nasimiyu-Wasike's proposal of Jesus as "mother". Elsewhere she expands on this theme as follows:

> In Jesus' life we see him take on the qualities of a mother. He is a nurturer of life, especially that of the weak. Jesus' motherhood is characterized by nourishment, protection, and care for the poor and marginalized. The way Jesus related to people and especially the disciples, showed warm tenderness, affection, receptivity and a readiness to restore life to wholeness. ... All the followers of Christ, especially those in Africa, are called today to be mothers that nurture life in all its different dimensions[101].

She further highlights Christ the healer as being especially relevant to the African reality. Finally, she summarises her reflection on christology as follows:

> The African woman's experience calls for a christology that is based on a holistic view of life. She needs the Christ who affects the whole of her life, whose presence is felt in every corner of the village and who participates in everything and everybody's daily life. She needs the Christ who relates to God, the God who can be reached through the spirits and the living dead or through direct intercession. This God, the Christ, is the one who takes on the conditions of the African woman – the conditions of weakness, misery, injustice, and oppression.
> ... He continues to empower and enable the African woman today so that she passes from unauthentic to authentic human existence, and so that she discovers her true identity of being made in the image and likeness of God[102].

Thus it becomes evident that African women's experiences of Christ provide new perspectives on current christological inquiry. In their

---

98. *Ibid.*, pp. 126, 130.
99. *Ibid.* p. 126.
100. *Ibid.*, pp. 131-134.
101. A. NASIMIYU-WASIKE, *Witnesses to Jesus Christ in the African Context at the Dawn of a New Millenium*, [photocopy, unpublished manuscript of a lecture delivered in Assisi, Italy, June 1997, made available by the author], p. 7.
102. NASIMIYU-WASIKE, *Christology and an African Woman's Experience*, in J.N.K. MUGAMBI and L. MAGESA (eds.), *Jesus in African Christianity: Experimentation and Diversity in African Christology* (n. 9), pp. 130-131.

reflections upon biblical and African traditions and the contemporary context, these female theologians seem especially concerned to grapple with the reality and significance of Jesus to the everyday existence of African women. Perhaps it is this interplay of faith and life exemplified by women across the continent that will comprise their lasting contribution to contemporary African christology, for as Amoah and Oduyoyue stress,

> Christology down the ages, though derived from the experiences of the early companions of Jesus of Nazareth and those of their immediate associates, has been formulated in response to the actual historical realities of each age and place. Persons have contributed by the way each perceives and experiences Christ. 'Christ' has *been explained* through imagery, cosmology, and historical events by both 'speakers' and 'listeners.' This process continues in Africa. One thing is certain: whatever the age or place, the most articulate Christology is that silently performed in the drama of everyday living[103].

III. CONCLUSION

If indeed the centre of gravity of world Christianity has shifted to the southern hemisphere, as it is increasingly recognised, then Africa warrants careful consideration in any dialogue concerning current developments in theology. This introductory exploration of new paths of African christology, however brief and selective, has attempted to highlight certain voices that are representative of the creative christologies presently flourishing across the continent. What, then, is the significance of these christologies, both within Africa and within the wider context of global christologies?

African Christian theologians express optimism at the progress which has been made from the initial declaration of need for African christology to be formulated, to the actual proliferation of such christological expressions in recent decades[104]. Despite the ongoing needs and challenges, a plurality of christological reflections is in fact emerging from the African context. Nor should such a plurality of christologies be considered a theological novelty, since the critical question of Jesus, "Who do you say I am?" (Mk 8:29) is understood by Christians to be addressed to every individual and generation in every context. As John Pobee explains, christology pertains to

---

103. AMOAH and ODUYOYE, *The Christ for African Women*, in V. FABELLA and M. ODUYOYE (eds.), *With Passion and Compassion* (n. 79), p. 45; emphasis original.

104. E.g., NYAMITI, *Contemporary African Christologies: Assessment and Practical Suggestions*, in R. GIBELLINI (ed.), *Paths of African Christology* (n. 10), p. 70.

people's attempt to articulate and portray the Christ who confronts them or whom they have experienced or met on a Damascus Road. And they do that articulation from their being and as they are. So one ... can expect different and varying emphases in that articulation, differences determined by one's experience, by one's heritage, by one's gender, by one's race. The encounter on the Emmaus road is not identical with the encounter on the Damascus road[105].

The very existence of this plurality of African christologies reflects a crucial observation, that Jesus Christ has indeed nudged his way into the spiritual universe of the African. No longer need he be regarded as a "white man's god", a stranger, or a guest, as he may have been viewed in the past. Instead, these African theologians have articulated how African Christians may understand and respond to Jesus not only as Lord and Christ, Saviour and Shepherd, but also as "Ancestor", "Elder Brother", "*Nganga*" ("the medicine person"), and "Master of the Initiation". Even more significantly, in understanding and appropriating Jesus according to their own cultural inheritance and identity, these African Christians clearly evidence the universality of the gospel message. Ghanaian theologian Kwame Bediako notes, "For Christianity is, among all religions, the most culturally translatable, hence the most truly universal, being able to be at home in every cultural context without injury to its essential character"[106]. He further emphasises that once this discovery is made,

the important question is no longer: why should we relate to Jesus of Nazareth who does not belong to our clan, family, tribe and nation? Rather the question becomes: how may we understand more fully this Jesus Christ who in fact relates to us most meaningfully and most profoundly in our clan, family, tribe and nation[107]?

As Jesus becomes more deeply rooted in various African families, clans, and nations, with the concomitant plurality of African christologies, further theological significance emerges for the wider context of global theologies. Yusufu Obaje points out,

As the Lord of life, no one or no particular group of persons in any given period of life can exhaust the full meaning of who he is and the implications of his life for either the individual, the Church, or the world as a whole. This must be the case, for there is always the known, the not-yet-disclosed or the unknown dimension of the one 'who is and who was and who is to come, the Almighty' (Revelation 1:8b)[108].

---

105. J.S. POBEE, *In Search of Christology in Africa: Some Considerations for Today*, in J.S. POBEE (ed.), *Exploring Afro-Christology*, Frankfurt, Peter Lang, 1992, pp. 9-10.
106. BEDIAKO, *Jesus in African Culture: A Ghanaian Perspective* (n. 31), p. 43.
107. *Ibid.*
108. Y.A. OBAJE, *Theocentric Christology*, in J.S. POBEE (ed.), *Exploring Afro-Christology* (n. 105), p. 43.

No single context of Christianity, then, can claim a monopoly on christological reflection. Rather, as Andrew Walls has ably demonstrated through biblical and historical investigation, the perception and experience of Jesus by different cultures throughout history has in fact expanded our corporate understanding of Christ. Examining what occurred in the apostolic church as Christ was communicated across cultural boundaries, he explains:

> And the process was hugely enriching; it proved to be a discovery of the Christ. As Paul and his fellow missionaries explain and translate the significance of the Christ in a world that is Gentile and Hellenistic, that significance is seen to be greater than anyone had realized before. It is as though Christ himself actually grows through the work of mission – and indeed, there is more than a hint of this in one New Testament image (Eph. 4:13). As he enters new areas of thought and life, he fills the picture (the Pleroma dwells in him). It is surely right to see the process as being repeated in subsequent transmission of the faith across cultural lines[109].

Given such biblical and historical precedents, there is every reason to believe that contemporary African theologians are extending this very process in their efforts to articulate African christologies. This would seem to be at the heart of Éla's appeal when he states, "The Risen One exposes faith to an inexhaustible realm of possibilities. That is why we are searching for a form of speech that will bring the voices of Africa to the life of the world-wide church"[110]. May we therefore welcome the voices of those men and women who bring the Jesus of Africa to our attention, for "It is a delightful paradox that the more Christ is translated into the various thought forms and life systems which form our various national identities, the richer all of us will be in our common Christian identity"[111].

The University of Edinburgh   Diane STINTON
New College, Mound Place
Edinburgh EH1 2LX
Scotland

109. A.F. WALLS, *The Missionary Movement in Christian History: Studies in the Transmission of the Faith*, Maryknoll, NY, Orbis, 1996, p. xvii.
110. ÉLA, *My Faith as an African* (n. 56), p. 143.
111. WALLS, *The Missionary Movement in Christian History* (n. 109), 54.

THE NATIVE AMERICAN CHRIST

The purpose of this short essay is to present a christological reflection from a Native American perspective. This research is based on testimonies which I gathered in field studies among the First Nations Peoples of Canada between 1982 and 1992. Since I have already published the main results of this research in my book *Christ is a Native American*[1], I will center my attention in this paper not directly on the content of this Native American christology, but rather on its socio-cultural context and the theological process it represents. How do Native Americans theologize? How do they visualize Christ? What is the impact of the gospel on their life? In answering these questions, my concern will not be to show how Native Americans have integrated the western Christ images of the missionary churches, but to understand the specific contributions they are making to a deeper and larger vision of the Christ mystery.

I. The Native American Socio-Cultural Context

One of the most fascinating aspects of Canada's multicultural reality is the renaissance of its aboriginal peoples. Those who, only fifty years ago, were rightfully described as "vanishing peoples" have made, since the 1970s, a remarkable return to the central stage of Canadian public life[2]. We are no longer dealing with vague, weak or vanishing groups of individuals who are on the verge of total assimilation into our political, economic, social and religious structures, but with members of distinct societies who strongly desire to maintain their cultural identity and to be recognized as nations by Canada's other peoples and political leaders.

---

1. A. PEELMAN, *Christ is a Native American*, Maryknoll, NY, Orbis 1995 – Ottawa, Novalis, 1995; *Le Christ est amérindien. Une réflexion théologique sur l'inculturation du Christ parmi les Amérindiens du Canada*, Ottawa, Novalis, 1992.
2. Compare the two works by the native (Cree) author H. CARDINAL, *The Unjust Society: The Tragedy of Canada's Indians*, Edmonton, M.G. Hurtig Ltd., 1969, and *The Rebirth of Canada's Indians*, Edmonton, Hurtig Publishers, 1977. For an overview of the situation see T. LEMAIRE and F. WOJCIECHOWSKI (eds.), *Terugkeer van een verdwijnend volk. Indiaans en Inuit activisme nu*, Nijmegen, Instituut voor culturele en sociale anthropologie, Katholieke Universiteit, 1985.

By way of a "nation to nation dialogue"[3], Canada's First Nations want to become once again the makers of their own history and contribute to the well-being of the other peoples who now share their land.

It is important to note that, notwithstanding its socio-political implications, this native revitalization is above all a spiritual movement. In the Native American mind there is a close connection between the land, culture and religion. Emma Laroque, a native historian, wrote as early as 1975: "If there is any Indian renaissance today, it is in the world of religion. Young people are coming to the elders for spiritual guidance and the elders are once again sharing their secrets"[4]. In the course of my field studies I met a considerable number of native women and men who had been travelling across North America in search of spiritual guides who could help them reconstruct their personal life and revivify their communities. Spirituality remains the quintessence of the Native American reality. Although most western observers of the native scene see only the political and economic dimensions of the "Indian problem", more attention ought to be paid to the astonishing vitality of the Native American spiritual traditions. All over Canada these ancestral religions are developing new forms of visibility. This revalorisation of ancestral spirituality appears to be an essential dimension of the development of peoples whose history is marked by a long period of political, cultural and religious oppression. Insofar as the suppression of their traditional religions by governments and churches was one of the factors that contributed to their social collapse, the revitalization of these primal religious traditions, in the wake of the growing pressures of secularization and technology, has become an indispensable element in their new quest for cultural identity and integrity[5]. In the third part of this paper I will directly deal with the implications of this phenomenon for the Christian churches.

Notwithstanding the fact that, as a result of their cultural revitalization, Canada's First Nations Peoples have gradually taken over responsibility and jurisdiction for the education of their children as well as essential social services, especially child welfare, their social situation

3. This is the guiding theme of the Report presented by the Royal Commission on Aboriginal Peoples in November 1996. The result of almost six years of widespread consultations and research, this impressive Report (3537 pages in 5 volumes) calls for urgent and major reforms in all sectors of Canadian public life.

4. E. LAROQUE, *Defeathering the Indian*, Agincourt, The Book Society of Canada, 1975, p. 27. See also B. CLEARY, *L'enfant de 7000 ans. Le long portage vers la délivrance*, Sillery, Les Éditions du Pélican/Septentrion, 1989.

5. V. COSMAO, *Changing the World: An Agenda for the Churches*, Maryknoll, NY, Orbis, 1984, pp. 46-49.

remains extremely fragile. Many native communities have been broken by successive waves of violence. Their social and psychological conditions are worse than in any other segment of Canadian society. Recent statistics demonstrate, for example, that in the areas of child protection, infant mortality, education, unemployment, criminality, alcohol and substance abuse, violent deaths and suicides, the native situation remains disastrous. We cannot assess this situation without referring in a particular way to the social condition of numerous native women and children. Canada's native population is young: 56,2% are less than 25 years, compared to 34% of the general Canadian population. In 1990, only 43% of the native population above 15 years found work compared to 61% of the general Canadian population. Many natives (45% of the total native population) have moved to the Canadian cities often out of desperate economic needs. This forced migration results in the creation of ghettos instead of fostering a positive rapport between the natives and other city dwellers. The urbanization of Canada's natives is a complex phenomenon in terms of human adaptation, the loss of cultural identity, and the danger of social conflicts[6].

The history behind all these statistics is rather disconcerting. It is the history of oppressed peoples trying to cope with the disastrous consequences of many years of forced acculturation. In fact, we must recognize that most of the violence in the native communities can be interpreted as the dramatic reaction by which the native population manifests its opposition to the western politics of assimilation and to the western obsession with having all peoples conform to its viewpoint and ways of thinking. It is the almost fatal result of what Doctor Wolfgang Jilek has called a situation of "anomic depression", which causes the socio-cultural disintegration of individuals and the cultural confusion of their communities[7]. This syndrome has affected numerous native persons who find themselves in conflicting situations with respect to the dominant society. They are perceived as irresponsible when not acculturated to mainstream interpretations of time, land-ownership, work, juridical procedures, etc., of the hegemonic Canadian society. Due to their aggressive marginalization by the economic, political, and religious mainstream, they have become dependent, desperate, and powerless[8].

6. See L. Krotz, *Urban Indians: The Strangers in Canada's Cities*, Edmonton, Hurtig, 1980; B. Richardson (ed.), *Drumbeat: Anger and Renewal in Indian Country*, Toronto, Summerhill Press – The Assembly of First Nations, 1989; L. Krotz, *Indian Country. Inside Another Canada*, Toronto, Mclelland & Stewart, 1990.

7. W. Jilek, *Indian Healing: Shamanic Ceremonialism in the Pacific Northwest Today*, Surrey – Washington, Hannock House, 1982.

8. G. Young, *The Dispossessed: Life and Death in Native Canada*, Toronto, Lester & Orpen Dennys, 1989.

Unfortunately, the media have made most Canadians familiar with only this negative side of the Native American reality. They end up believing that the Indians are the members of a "culture of poverty" or, even worse, that they have no culture at all. It is therefore important to remind ourselves that the basic differences between the First Nations Peoples and the other Canadian peoples is not a matter of pathologies! These differences are truly cultural differences deeply rooted in the past. The North American native peoples have mastered the art of survival in a unique way. Historians who are acquainted with the great cultural developments of humankind consider this instinct of survival as a quality of peoples who live close to the earth. These peoples do not draw their energies from their social or political achievements, but from the spiritual quality of their existence[9]. Over the centuries, the North American native peoples have developed a unique type of relationship with the land. The close-to-the-earth mysticism which constitues the very centre of their spirituality remains for many of them a deep well of extraordinary vitality.

Christological Reflections I: The Historical Jesus

The majority of christological testimonies I was able to record during my field study are straightforward answers to the question: "But who do you say I am?" (Mk 8,29). What characterizes these answers in the first place is their contextual nature. They reveal a deep concern for the many problems faced by the native communities today: the development of the Native American identity within the multicultural Canadian society, the struggle for political and economic self-determination, and, above all, the revival of traditional spirituality and its relationship to Christianity. The christology which can be deduced from these testimonies is profoundly experiential. Its dramatic and aesthetic dimensions cannot be ignored. It bears the mark of the practical, participatory mode of learning (learning-by-doing) which is so typical of the Native American cultures. In these cultures, to know is to have experienced by personally participating or performing. Native Americans will not share their vision of Christ unless they have met, heard or personally experienced him in their lives. It will always be difficult to evaluate this type of christology in dogmatic terms and even from the point of view of its content. What

9. T. Berry, *The Indian Future*, in *CC* 26 (1967) 133-142. See also P. Beck & A. Walters, *The Sacred: Ways of Knowledge: Sources of Life*, Tsaile (Navajo Nation), The Navajo Community College Press, 1977; J. Highwater, *The Primal Mind: Vision and Reality in Indian America*, New York, NY, Harper & Row, 1981; J.E. Brown, *The Spiritual Legacy of the American Indian*, New York, NY, Crossroad, 1982.

counts here, in the first place, is not the content, but the process: the journey of the Native American mind to the Christ figure and the concrete native appropriations of the gospel message. For most native persons I have met this journey is a profoundly mystical journey. When reading the gospels, Native Americans manifest an almost spontaneous capacity to enter into the story, to identify with figures in Jesus' entourage, and to become contemporary to the events experienced by Jesus without ever questioning their historical nature[10]. They become, so to speak, part of the concrete Jesus *Gestalt* which unfolds in the gospel stories. This mystical approach allows them also to bring this Jesus *Gestalt* out of the gospels back into their own contemporary context. They see the suffering Jesus in the abused persons they take care of. They feel his energy at work in their community-building efforts. They experience his presence in their own traditional healing rituals.

Given the fact that Canada's First Nations Peoples belong to the so-called "Fourth World"[11], a world of oppression and struggle for liberation, their contextual and mystical appropriation of the gospel message focuses on specific aspects of the Christ figure which can be gathered under the common denominator of search for integrity and identity. They appreciate Jesus' own efforts to integrate and to challenge the religious and cultural traditions of his own Jewish people. They admire his openness to and acceptance of the others, the foreigners. Jesus is perceived by them not only as a powerful healer but as the most powerful of all "medicines"[12], especially because he is a truly spiritual being with tremendous shamanic powers. What impresses them most is his compassion for those who suffer and the way he dominates evil. He is welcomed as the "Son of the Creator, our older brother". He is perceived as a real example of humanity and as someone who would have been a "good Indian"[13]. Although the focus of many of these gospel appropriations is

10. Like many Christians in the Third World countries, Native Americans, even those who have an academic and theological formation, manifest little or no interest in the western disputes concerning the relationship between the historical Jesus and the kerygmatic Christ.

11. The term "Fourth World" has been created by George Manuel, a well-known Shuswap chief (British Columbia), to describe the dispossessed peoples which have become the internal colonies of nation-states in the western hemisphere. See G. MANUAL & M. WATKINS, *The Fourth World: An Indian Reality*, Don Mills, Collier-Macmillan Canada, 1974; J. MILLER, *Skyscrapers Hide the Heavens: A History of Indian-White Relations in Canada*, rev. ed., Toronto, University of Toronto Press, 1989, pp. 233, 266, 281.

12. In the Native American world the term "medicine" is often the equivalent of religion or spirituality.

13. See A. PEELMAN, *Christ Is a Native American*, pp. 99-132 for a detailed presentation of these testimonies.

on the healing ministry of Jesus, it should be noted that Native American theologians seem reluctant to apply the dynamics of Latin America's liberation theologies to their own context. This is most probably due to the fact that Native American theology and ethics are not directly rooted in history but in spatiality[14].

II. CHRISTIANITY AND NATIVE AMERICAN SPIRITUALITY

In the second part of this essay I will focus directly on the spiritual dimension of the contemporary Native American renaissance and on its christological ramifications. Notwithstanding the tremendous impact of western culture and Christianity on the aboriginal communities, their ancestral spirituality is alive and well in contemporary native North America. Even though their native languages do not possess technical terms to designate what we call theology, philosophy, religion or church, Canada's First Nations Peoples define themselves, basically as "spiritual peoples". In 1983, while visiting a remote Dene Tha community in northwestern Alberta, a middle-aged woman who had received a western and Christian education told me: "The most important thing about our native way is that it is a spiritual way. We are a spiritual people. No one can take this spirituality away from us". Statements like this one can be heard all over Canada and the United States. They illustrate the deep rootedness of the aboriginal peoples in their spiritual traditions, while reflecting at the same time serious concerns and tensions. Because of the negative attitudes of the missionary churches vis-à-vis the traditional Indian religions, many contemporary natives continue to struggle with the question: Is it possible to be both native and Christian in any meaningful way[15]? Some have made a decisive return to their traditional religion, while others continue to move rather spontaneously from one religious system to the other according to the concrete circumstances of

14. V. DELORIA, A Native American Perspective on Liberation, in G. ANDERSON & T. STRANSKY (eds.), Mission Trends No 4: Liberation Theologies in North America and Europe, New York, NY, Paulist Press, 1989, pp. 261-270; R.A. WARRIOR, Cannanites, Cowboys and Indians: Deliverance, Conquest and Liberation Theologies Today, in Christianity and Crisis, September 11, 1989, pp. 261-265 (Reproduced in J. TREAT (ed.), Native and Christian: Indigenous Voices on Religious Identity in the United States and Canada, New York, NY – London, Routledge, 1996, pp. 93-104); W. BALDRIDGE, Native American Theology: A Biblical Basis, in Christianity and Culture, May 28, 1990, pp. 17-18; A. PEELMAN, Les Droits Autochtones et la Théologie de la Libération au Canada, in TJT 8 (1992) 261-286.

15. See the various testimonies collected by J. TREAT (ed.), Native and Christian. Indigenous Voices on Religious Identity in the United States and Canada.

their lives. The simultaneous practice of native religion and Christianity is a widespread phenomenon in Canada and the United States. I have also met a considerable number of persons who, profoundly committed to the integration of the two spiritual traditions, are elaborating personal forms of dialogue between their native spirituality and Christiany, mostly outside the boundaries of the institutional churches and yet in continuity with the creative responses given by their ancestors to the Christian invasion of their land[16].

I will abstain here from entering into the debate on the scientific status of the Native American spiritual traditions as primal religions and their relationship to the so-called great world religions[17]. Native Americans themselves often describe their spiritual traditions as a "way of life" more than as a religion[18], as a "metaphysic of nature"[19], and even more commonly as a spiritual journey, a religious process or a state of consciousness with a performative and immediate (mystical) rapport with the Great Mystery[20]. In many native communities across Canada, even in those whose members consider themselves Christian, traditional native spirituality continues to be an important factor of social and cultural integration[21]. Because of the historical and contemporary interactions between Christianity and Native American spirituality the question then arises almost spontaneously: Is there room for Christ in this traditional spiritual journey or religious process?

16. A. PEELMAN, *Christ Is a Native American*, pp. 61-96 (Amerindian Responses to Christianity). Various interpretations of these native attitudes can be found in H. HERTZBERG, *The Search for an American Indian Identity: Modern Pan-Indian Movements*, Syracuse, NY, Syracuse University Press, 1971; W. STOLZMAN, *The Pipe and Christ: A Christian-Sioux Dialogue*, Chamberlain, SD, Tipi Press, 1986; C. VECSEY, *Imagine Ourselves Richly: Mythic Narratives of North American Indians*, New York, NY, Crossroad, 1988; P. STEINMETZ, *Pipe, Bible and Peyote Among the Oglala Lakota: A Study in Religious Identity*, Knoxville, TN, The University of Tennessee Press, 1990.

17. See J.L. COX, *The Classification 'Primal Religions' as a Non-Empirical Christian Theological Concept*, in *SWC* 2 (1996) 55-76; D.H. TURNER, *Aboriginal Religion as World Religion: an Assessment*, in *SWC* 2 (1996) 77-96; J.Z. SMITH, *A Matter of Class: Taxonomies of Religion*, in *HTR* 89:4 (1996) 387-403.

18. G. TINKER, *Spirituality, Native American Personhood, Sovereignty and Solidarity*, in *ER* 44 (1992) 312-324. Reprinted in J. TREAT (ed.), *Native and Christian*, pp. 115-131.

19. J.E. BROWN, *The Spiritual Legacy of the American Indian*, pp. 64, 71, 110.

20. A. HULTKRANTZ, *Native Religions in North America. The Power of Visions and Fertility*, San Francisco, CA, Harper & Row, 1987; S. GILL, *Native American Religious Action: A Performance Approach to Religion*, Columbia, SD, University of South Dakota Press, 1987; C. ALBANESE, *Nature Religion in America: From the Algonkian Indians to the New Age*, Chicago, IL, The University of Chicago Press, 1990, pp. 16-46.

21. A. PEELMAN, *L'actualité des religions amérindiennes au Canada*, in *RIAC/IRCD* 26/66 (1991), pp. 111-128.

Christological Reflections II: The Cosmic Christ

Although the term "Cosmic Christ" seemed unfamiliar to most natives I have met, various elements of a cosmic or creation-centered christology can be detected in their prayers or rituals. Well-known chief John Snow of the Stoney People (Alberta) offers a short commentary on Jn 3,16 that captures the essence of this cosmic christology: "When *we* read 'For God so loved the world that he gave his only Son', the native interpretation is that God so loved the waters, the trees, and the animals." Since Christ died for all of them, therefore we as Christians must respect all creatures. Chief Snow affirms what Native Americans innately believe: that God's spirit is in everything, not just in humankind. They are certain that the day is coming when the dominant society will turn to the native culture to help revive nature. Snow advocates that if we integrated Jn 3,16 into a greater perspective, we would not be running into the vast ecological and economic crises of today. Christians are thus invited to learn respect for the native interpretations[22]. There is a notable cosmic dimension to Jesus' death as a saving event. Native American elders like John Snow often compare their natural environment with the bible. For them, the order of creation or the cosmos itself is part of God's personal manifestation. This is very much in continuity with the cosmic christologies of Justin, Irenaeus, and Maximus Confessor! Also commenting on Jn 3,16, Adam Cutland, a Native American Anglican priest, affirms: "Western man does not access or realize the real truth of the statement – the key word being *world* which in the original Greek was *Kosmos*, when properly translated, means the Universe and everything in it – the earth, mountains, rocks, stones, trees, birds, animals, plants, insects and all other living things"[23]. Native Americans view the universe as a sacred (*wakan*) and animated universe: the habitat of spiritual powers associated with the Great Mystery (*Wakan Tanka*).

For many Native Americans, however, the question concerning the place and role of Christ among the spiritual powers associated with *Wakan Tanka* remains very delicate[24]. Designations of Jesus such as "Son of the Creator, our elder brother" are understood as a confession of faith in the uniqueness of Jesus as Christ while introducing him at the same time into the mysterious world of the ancestors and the spiritual

22. A. PEELMAN, *Christ Is a Native American*, p. 131.
23. A. CUTLAND, *A Native Anglican Priest Speaks*, in *Interculture* 15, No. 1, Cahier 74 (1982), p. 38.
24. See, for example, W. STOLZMAN, *The Pipe and Christ*, pp. 116-130.

powers. But when answering the question about the relationship between Christ and these powers, most Native Americans limit themselves to stating that Christ is the most powerful of all medicines and that he offers them protection against bad medicine and the obscure elements which threaten their existence. They are not particularly concerned with defining the ontological status or the exact nature of these powers and of Christ. Their approach is more soteriological than ontological. While situating Christ among the powers, they may recognize that, like these powers, he is personally involved in the drama of human existence. This is very much in line with the general orientation of Native American spirituality. Strictly speaking, traditional Native Americans do not believe in God where believing is taken to mean assent to doctrinal propositions or a deposit of faith. They *know* the Great Mystery through personal or collective experiences and they vizualize this mystery as the very core of their own being and of the entire universe. They are convinced that no human person can achieve anything in life without the "supernatural" assistance of the Great Mystery and its surrounding powers. Yet the ritual search for this assistance is not aimed at establishing a personal relationship with the supreme being, but to become attentive to its presence, when and where it manifests itself. The Native American religious experience, with all its ascetical and mystical orientations, its dreams, visions and rituals, is a sustained and repeated effort to connect with the Great Mystery in order to receive the vision which determines one's unique place in a universe where all things are interrelated. It comes as no surprise that the christologies or soteriologies which emerge in this spiritual context are more experiential than dogmatic, more cosmological than historical. During my field study I encountered an interesting illustration of this in the commentary made by a young Anishnabe man on the Prologue of the Fourth Gospel, a text he had been meditating time and time again. The Prologue places the Logos at the very beginning of creation. He compared this Logos with the Dream which in many Native American creation stories gives birth to the universe. John 1,1 might thus be translated: "In the beginning was the Dream, and the Dream was with God, and the Dream was God...". There was no doubt in his mind that Christ the Logos-Dream has been journeying with his people from their very beginning.

The cosmic dimension of the Christ mystery also finds a unique expression in contemporary Native American art. The painting *Tree of Life*, a work by Anishnabe artist Blake Debassige, produced in 1983 for the Jesuit Anishnabe Centre in Anderson Lake (Ontario) is a profound illustration of the cosmic meaning of Jesus' death[25]. The tree is a cedar, known and respected by the people for its medicinal qualities. The naked Christ is totally incorporated into the tree. He is male and female – symbol of the fullness of life. The entire painting is a celebration of life. But the owl, which is set atop the tree, reminds us that we are mortal. Death is part of our living. In my book *Christ Is a Native American*, I have compared this painting with another one, entitled *Christ on the Tree of Life*, a work by the Italian artist Pacino De Bonaguido (beginning of the fourteenth century)[26]. By their common Tree of life symbol, these two paintings represent two specific appropriations of the Myriad Christ. Pacio De Bonaguido's painting, which is inpired by Bonaventure's *Lignum Vitae*, a work dealing with the origin, passion and glorification of Christ, illustrates a specifically western and historical approach to the Christic mystery. On the contrary, Blake Debassige's painting, profoundly influenced by the traditional Anishnabe Midewiwin religion, connects the cross with the ancestral Anishnabe world. The two paintings focus on the universal meaning of the Christ event. They celebrate the universal Christ mediated in diverse cultures. But Blake Debassige's painting reminds western society, dominated by its mystique of anthropocentric redemption and its obsession with linear progress, about the need for a cosmology that views the universe as a living organism and as the meeting place with the Great Mystery.

Similar elements of a cosmic christology can be found in Anishnabe painter Leland Bell's *Stations of the Cross*, produced for the Catholic church in West Bay (Manitoulin Island). Each of these stations is like a Byzantine icon. With its vivid colors and elongated figures, each station leaves us with the impression of a unique movement. We see the figures walk in a sacred (*wakan*) manner as actors in a cosmic drama of which the Creator himself is the choreographer and the main actor[27].

Throughout my field study I was able to observe that Christ has found its place in many of the traditional rituals in which I was invited to participate. Most of these rituals are performed in the intimate circle of family and clan. Their concrete performance is often influenced by the dreams and visions of their presiders, mostly medicine persons, elders or shamans. When these women and men bring the Christ figure into their ritual this is not the result of any kind of theological reflection but of the

25. Reproduced in A. PEELMAN, *Christ Is a Native American*, p. 194.
26. Reproduced in R. COOK, *The Tree of Life, Image of the Cosmos*, London, Thames and Hudson, 1974.
27. G.P. LEACH & G.J. HUMBERT, *Beedahbun: First Light of Dawn*. Featuring the paintings of Leland Bell, North Bay, Tomiko Publications, 1989.

visions they received. It is important to note that there are almost no written accounts of Christ's "integration" into the native spiritual universe. Personal participation in the experience is often the only access to the emerging Native American christology[28]. Personal participation in Vision Quests, Sweat-lodge and Sacred Pipe rituals has allowed me to witness evocations of Christ as healer, shaman, ancestor or spiritual power. The native focus on these particular dimensions of the Christ mystery is significant given the fact that most rituals are healing or reconciliation rituals with elaborate cosmic symbolism. In this context, the natives vizualise both the historical and the cosmic dimensions of Jesus' paschal journey. They understand that the healing of their own brokenness is closely connected with the well-being of the entire universe[29].

Similar christological interpretations have been observed during the celebration of the Sun Dance which represents for the traditional Native Americans what Holy Week means for the Christians: the very center of their sacred space and time. Joseph Epes Brown writes: "The annual sun dance ceremonies of the Plains Indians of North America give to these peoples – as indeed to all peoples, today as in the past – a message through example affirming the power of suffering sacrifice, revealing in rich detail the mystery of the sacred in its operations, in all life, and through creation. Where there is no longer affirmation or means of sacrifice, of 'making sacred,' where the individual loses the sense of the centre, the very energy of the world, it is believed, will run out"[30]. All the symbols implied in the annual Sun Dance celebration suggest a dramatization of the cyclical rebirth of the world. It is both a celebration of thanksgiving and a ritual of personal and collective purification. It is a ritual effort to restore the universal order of things by means of the sacrifice which dancers accept for themselves and for others so that their community may again become whole and holy. It has been reported that for some dancers the central pole of the lodge represents Christ or the cross as Tree of Life[31]. It may be noted that the Tree of Life symbol also occupied a central place in the spiritual journey of the well-known Oglala prophet Nicholas Black Elk who received a vision of the Lakota

---

28. A. PEELMAN, *Christianisme et cultures amérindiennes. Présentation et analyse d'une démarche théologique interculturelle*, in *ET* 22 (1991) 131-156.

29. A. PEELMAN, *Christ Is a Native American*, pp. 133-162 (The Sacred Pipe and Christ); pp. 163-193 (The Indian Road to Salvation).

30. J.E. BROWN, *The Spiritual Legacy of the North American Indian*, p. 101.

31. P. STEINMETZ, *Pipe, Bible and Peyote*, pp. 30-39; S. LAVOIE, *Worship Without Walls*, in *Kerygma* 23 (1989).147-151.

Christ[32]. One of the traditional motivations of the dancers is to assume personal sacrifices for the healing of others, to obtain spiritual powers for others or to fast and dance for the well-being of the entire community. Since 1982, I have met with persons who explicitly assume this dimension of the Sun Dance in communion with Christ who carried his cross for the salvation of the world.

Carl Starkloff, a theologian who has worked among the Arapaho people (a western Algonquian tribe), reports identifications between their trickster figure or cultural hero and Jesus-Christ as transformer of history. He considers the fact that many native leaders have incorporated the Christ-mystery within rituals of personal and social healing as a promising christological development for both the Native American peoples and the universal church[33].

III. Concluding Observations

Canadian historian John Webster Grant succinctly summarized the missionary epic in Canada by stating: "If the measure of success is that most Indians have become Christian, the measure of failure is that Christianity has not become Indian"[34]. This conclusion seems obvious when we look at this missionary epic from the vantage point of the churches. Notwithstanding large numbers of native conversions in the past, truly Native American Christian communities have not yet seen the light of day. It is as if no cultural transfer ever took place between the Native American cultures and Christianity. Grant's conclusion is less self-evident when we look upon the same missionary epic from the vantage point of the Native American peoples themselves. Contemporary ethno-historical studies clearly demonstrate that the Native Peoples ought to be considered co-actors in this missionary epic and that they were able to develop native forms of Christianity mostly outside the official boundaries of the Christian churches they adopted[35]. The prophetic movements which emerged among the

32. See particularly P. STEINMETZ, *Pipe, Bible and Peyote*; M. STELTENKAMP, *Black Elk, Holy Man of the Oglala*, Norman, OK and London, University of Oklahoma Press, 1993; C. HOLLER, *Black Elk's Religion: The Sun Dance and Lakota Catholicism*, Syracuse NY, Syracuse University Press, 1995.

33. C.F. STARKLOFF, *Aboriginal Cultures and the Christ*, in *TS* 53 (1992) 289-312.

34. J.W. GRANT, *Moon of Wintertime: Missionaries and the Indians of Canada in Encounter Since 1543*, Toronto, University of Toronto Press, 1984, p.262.

35. A. PEELMAN, *Christ Is a Native American*, pp. 61-96 (Amerindian Responses to Christianity).

Native Peoples in the nineteenth century and the later development of the *Native American Church of North America* (the Peyote religion) are clear examples of cultural interactions between North America's primal religions and Christianity. They illustrate the Native Peoples' own theological creativity[36]. The same thing can be said about the contemporary native appropriations of the Christ figure. These particular manifestations of the Myriad Christ challenge the Canadian churches to engage in the development of culturally contextualized and sensitive soteriologies and to do this in real partnership with Canada's First Nations Peoples. This presupposes of course that the Canadian churches openly recognize the validity and the authenticity of the traditional Native American spirituality and engage in dialogue with it, something which they have failed to do till now.

Conclusion

During his 1984 visit to Canada, Pope John Paul II declared: "Not only is Christianity relevant to the Indian peoples, but *Christ, in the members of his Body, is himself Indian*". One of the main purposes of my field study was to let Canada's First Nations Peoples themselves tell us who this Native American Christ truly is. In this essay I have evoked the socio-cultural and spiritual climate of their contemporary appropriations of the Christ figure. The situation of this emerging Native American christology is unique. It is not yet supported by truly native Christian communities and liturgies such as we may find them in many African countries. It is far from having the impact and the scope of the liberation christologies of Latin America and the christologies which are developing in the Asian context of interreligious dialogue. In fact, this Native American christology finds itself in a sort of theological "no man's land", largely because of the ecclesial and socio-political marginalization of its actors. The Native American Christ reflects this double marginalization. At present, there is no home for him except in the hearts of the native women and men who have welcomed his gospel and still count on his presence. Yet, their theological contributions are significant. They reveal one of the most beautiful aspects of the Native American cultures: their mystical capacity. The Native American cultural languages are the integrating

36. See, for example, A. WALLACE, *The Death and Rebirth of the Seneca*, Toronto, Random House, 1972; J. MOONEY, *The Ghost Dance Religion and the Sioux Outbreak of 1890*, Chicago, IL, The University of Chicago Press, 1965 (Original edition, 1896); O. STEWART, *Peyote Religion: A History*, Norman, OK, University of Oklahoma Press, 1987.

languages of the intuitive heart, the aesthetic mind, and the moving body in unison. Therefore, they are also a truly universal language, a language that can help the entire Christian community to develop a larger and deeper vision of the Christ mystery[37].

Saint Paul University   Achiel PEELMAN
Main Street 223
Ottawa ON Canada
K1S 1C4

37. Financial assistance for this research was provided by The Professor Henry Herbert Glasmacher Fund of Saint Paul University, Ottawa.

IV

THE MYRIAD CHRIST

IN THEOLOGICAL REFLECTION

FRIARS IN NEGATIVE CHRISTOLOGY:
THOMAS AQUINAS AND LUIS DE LEÓN

One of the questions inevitably raised in dealing with the myriad Christ, the many faces, the many names of Christ, is the very question: why? Why are there so many names, in Scripture itself, in tradition, in present-day religious communication and theology? Do we have to charge human intellectual and emotional weakness with it, or does it somehow belong to the reality of Jesus Christ himself? If the latter is the case, can we rightly speak not only of *Theologia negativa* but also of *Christologia negativa*? And moreover, is such a question as to why there are so many names a relatively new question, or can one say that it belongs to the perennial problems of christology?

In my contribution I will employ a well-defined concept of negative christology, and will argue for three theses.

The definition of negative or apophatic christology is such: a reflection on the person and work of Jesus Christ that endorses, not in a superficial way or out of misplaced spiritual modesty, the view that Christ is a mystery and that no name can capture the profound totality of his being.

The three theses are the following:

1) Negative christology is not merely a modern or even postmodern phenomenon, but belongs to the very tradition of christology.
2) This is rightly so, because the reality of Christ himself necessitates such a christological approach.
3) A christology that develops an apophatic awareness meets a number of modern challenges in an appropriate way.

My contribution will consist of three parts. First I will give some elements of an apophatic christology that are based in Scripture. Second I will call upon two major witnesses in the tradition of theology, i.e., Thomas Aquinas and Fray Luis de León. Third and last, I will mention some examples of the relevance of negative christology[1].

1. I would like to thank Harm J.M.J. Goris, University of Notre Dame IN, for his commentary on an earlier draft of this paper.

I. Elements from Scripture

A careful reading of Scripture yields a number of peculiarities that are relevant for our topic. I will mention only three.

1) The kingdom of God, focal point of Christ's preaching and thus focal point of his personhood, is never described, let alone defined. On the contrary, it is approached in parables, it is intimated by certain courses of action, and it is expressly stated that one cannot say that the kingdom of God is here or there (Lk 17,20). Apparently, the kingdom of God is an open affair, not to be claimed to be essentially so and so, a reality that invites and is not presented in a definitive way.

One is reminded of Augustine's notion of the *Totus Christus*[2]. The whole Christ includes his relationship to his followers, to the Church, to all those to whom his offer of salvation is extended. Such a view of Christ therefore includes the view that the whole Christ is still under way, is yet reaching for completion and fulfilment, in other words: is fundamentally an eschatological reality. It is only in the eschatological congregation of the elect that the *Christus integer* will be revealed[3].

2) Another peculiarity of Scripture, especially the Synoptics, is the absence of definitive statements of Christ about himself, about his own person. We are all familiar with the extremely complicated research into the titles of Christ, into Christ's self-knowledge. However, there seems to be a consensus among scholars that Christ never spoke about himself

2. Relevant texts of Augustine are contained in his *Enarrationes in Psalmos* (CC SL 38-40), Turnholti, Brepols, 1956: *in Ps.* 30, II, serm. 1,3; *in Ps.* 58, serm. 1,2; *in Ps.* 90, serm. 2,1; *in Ps.* 138, 2 and passim; *Sermo* 341, 9 (11) and 10 (12), PL 39, 1499-1500. Cf. T.J. Van Bavel, *Augustinus. Van liefde en vriendschap*, Utrecht, 1977, Chapter VII "De totale Christus", pp. 93-111.

3. This touches upon the discussion of how the Kingdom of God is brought about. Kasper for instance proposes a dialogical model in which there is a cooperation of Christ with his body: "Geschichte ereignet sich vielmehr im Dialog zwischen Gott und dem Menschen (...) Gottes Herrschaft kommt also nicht am Glauben des Menschen vorbei, sondern sie kommt dort, wo Gott tatsächlich im Glauben als Herr anerkannt wird". W. Kasper, *Jesus der Christus*, Mainz, Matthias Grünewald Verlag, 1992[11], p. 91.

Schillebeeckx draws attention to the fact that the author of the Revelation to John explicitly underlines the eschatological nature of naming Christ. Having discussed all the honorary titles that are mentioned, Schillebeeckx says that according to Revelation the proper name of Christ will appear only at the end of time: "I will inscribe on it the name of my God and the name of the city of my God, the new Jerusalem which is coming down from my God in heaven, and my new name as well" (Rev 3,12). The name itself is not mentioned, apparently it is yet unknown: "the name written on him was known only to himself" (Rev 19,12). Schillebeeckx says: "Let us stay modest; not out of minimalism (for the author suggests something greater than even the most splendid honorary titles), but out of religious awe and especially because God's revelation is only definitive at the parousia" [my translation – hs]. E. Schillebeeckx, *Gerechtigheid en liefde. Genade en bevrijding*, Baarn, H. Nelissen, 1977[2], p. 406.

as 'Son of God', or 'Messiah'. And even whether he talked about himself as 'Son of Man', although in the Synoptics it is only Christ that employs that name, is doubtful. One should add that even if we were to establish as a historical fact Christ's self-reference as Son of Man, the fundamental problem would not yet be solved. It would shift our attention to an even greater puzzle, trying to determine the meaning of the title 'Son of Man' in its specific application to Christ. If one is prepared to accept the incarnation as an unprecedented and singular event, as the Christian faith holds, all names and titles receive a meaning that can only be construed, in the end, on the basis of an interpretation of the singular relation between the names and the actual person of Christ. To put it semantically, the connotation of any name for Christ is not independent of its denotation. In all cases where denotation is unique, i.e., as regards the singular person of Christ, the connotation can only be intimated from the context of the event of Christ itself[4].

3) A third peculiarity of Scripture in this respect are two significant features of the stories about Christ's resurrection and his appearances. First there is the fact that nowhere in the gospels is an account, a description, provided of Christ's resurrection. There are only stories that lead up to it, or stories that attempt to approach the reality of the risen Christ. The second feature, concerning his appearances, is even more telling. Each and every appearance is described as a hidden appearance. Whether it is the disciples of Emmaus, Mary Magdalen, or the Apostles themselves, at first all of them do not recognize the risen Christ. Moreover, Luke explicitly states that when the risen Christ took on eucharistic shape, breaking the bread, "their eyes were opened and they recognised him; but he had vanished from their sight" (Lk 24,31). Now why would Luke add that Christ vanished, if not to stress this inherent aspect of the hiddenness of the risen Christ?

It seems to me that if we compare the above-mentioned to the definition of the council of Chalcedon (451), this definition stands on solid

---

4. An elaboration of this, i.e., the relation between common predicate-terms and their meaning when applied to Christ, can be found in B. MARSHALL, *Christology in Conflict: The Identity of a Saviour in Rahner and Barth*, Oxford/New York, 1987. Especially the introduction of Strawson's 'logical primitive predicate' in order to understand Aquinas is most helpful: there are, in christology, predicates that 'precede' other predicates, and Aquinas considers *incarnatus* and *Deus* to be such predicates. It is God who is the subject of the history of Jesus Christ, and therefore any application of predicates that are not logically primitive, is to be verified, concerning their signification, according to this specific predication to Jesus Christ. The signification of concepts applied to Christ is not all set before the actual predication takes place: Christ himself determines the meaning of being, for example, saviour.

Scriptural ground in stressing the ineffable union of both natures in one person. Chalcedon is mostly understood to give some sort of a description of the 'essence' of the person of Jesus Christ, but in my view it is better taken as a rule for speech about Christ. Divine immanence and transcendence on the one hand, and humanity on the other, are never to be regarded as simply contrasted or as simply mixed, but mysteriously one and mysteriously two[5]. All names given to Christ, in Scripture and tradition, where 'names' should be conceived as involving enunciations as well, share in this mystery, and are to be regarded as analogical. They can never be regarded as mere descriptions, because analogical as they are, they involve the one speaking or interpreting him- or herself, by way of reasonable and responsible judgment (Lonergan), and at the same time are always greater than the one speaking or interpreting. The nature of knowing a person is more than simply knowing *about* someone, and the nature of (divine) mystery is never simply 'out there' but always engaging, inviting, challenging and sharing participation.

II. WITNESSES FROM THE TRADITION OF THEOLOGY

Let me now turn to two theologians in the history of theology, who have shown more than average interest in the subject of naming Christ, and in what we today would call apophatic or negative christology. The ones I have in mind are Thomas Aquinas, and the Spanish Augustinian Friar Luis de León.

1. Thomas Aquinas (1224/5-1274)

It is well-known that in his most influential work, the *Summa Theologiae*, Thomas Aquinas placed christology near the very end. I will not go into detail regarding the discussion about theological method and outlook that this order has resulted in. One of its side-effects, however, has been that hardly any interpretation has given attention to the question whether Aquinas' early treatment of the divine names has any bearing on his later treatment of christology[6]. It is my view, however, that

---

5. What is developed here in the area of christology, Kathryn Tanner has developed in the area of the theology of creation, i.e. calling for an astute understanding of the relationship between divine immanence and transcendence, that does not allow for a simple identification or a simple contrast of the two. K. TANNER, *God and Creation in Christian Theology: Tyranny or Empowerment?*, Oxford/New York, 1988.

6. Exemplary is G. LAFONT, *Structures et méthode dans la "Somme théologique de saint Thomas d'Aquin*, Paris, Les Éditions du Cerf, 1996 (reprint of 1960). This is the

Aquinas intended his treatise on the divine names to be an hermeneutical entry not only to the doctrine of the one God, but also to the doctrine of God Triune and God the Redeemer, i.e., it was meant to be relevant to naming Christ as well. For, Aquinas' views on the analogical usage of language *in divinis* obtain in the area of christology as well. What else could be the case concerning a christology introduced as dealing with *De Deo Salvatore*[7]. The same thing holds, by consequence, for his distinction between substantial and relational names, and for his distinction between substantial names and names that directly or indirectly signify a relation of God with creation. To the latter belongs the name *Salvator*[8]. This treatment of the divine names flows forth from the treatment of divine simplicity and consequent "attributes" of what God is not[9]. The meaning of ascribing simplicity to God, i.e., stating the identity of being and essence in God, turns out not to describe God as simple, but to show the ultimate otherness of God vis-à-vis created reality, to show his profound ineffability[10]. Human language reflects in its grammatical and syntactic structure the metaphysics of created being, and therefore this language is inept for the metaphysics of uncreated, i.e., divine being[11]. One could say that the isomorphism that exists between human language and created being is lacking when humans talk about God. Now, this isomorphism plays an important role in Aquinas' christology. Not only does he devote attention to concrete, mostly Scriptural names of Christ, but he mentions more than 100 of them in his *Tertia Pars*. Not only does he analyze them along the lines set at the very beginning of the *Summa*, but he also invests his knowledge of simplicity and isomorphism into the area of naming Christ. The very treatment of the hypostatic union is carried through on the basis of the same distinction that underlies his treatment of divine simplicity and naming the divine, i.e., the distinction between signification and supposition. This distinction, as I have shown

more puzzling, since the author, when dealing with the hypostatic union, stresses the analogical character of the attribution of created composition to Christ (pp. 329-330).

7. THOMAS AQUINAS, *Summa Theologiae* (*ST*), III, prologue. If no edition of a work by Aquinas is mentioned, the edition of the *Commissio Leonina, S. Thomae Aquinatis doctoris angelici Opera Omnia iussu impensaque Leonis XIII P.M. edita*, Romae 1882-, is employed.

8. *ST* I, q. 13, a. 7, corpus.

9. *ST* I, qq. 3-11.

10. Cf. W.J. HOYE, "Die Unerkennbarkeit Gottes als die letzte Erkenntnis nach Thomas von Aquin", in: *Miscellanea Mediaevalia* 19, Berlin/New York, 1988, 117-139, who interprets Aquinas as stating divine incomprehensibility as the core of faith instead of one of the features of its mode of knowing. See also the work of D. BURRELL CSC, especially *Knowing the Unknowable God: Ibn-Sina, Maimonides, Aquinas*, Notre Dame, 1986.

11. *ST* I, q. 13, a. 1, ad 2 and ad 3; q. 13, a. 12.

elsewhere, is the linguistic variant of the distinction between essence and being[12]. Aquinas makes sense of the traditional doctrine of the hypostatic union, i.e., the theory of two natures and one person, by appealing to two different faculties in human semantics, one being signification, nowadays called connotation, and one being supposition, nowadays called denotation. Supposition regards the being, the person of Christ, signification both natures[13]. The hypostatic union must be a created union, and therefore the basic structure of human naming applies: there is in any sentence a subject-term and a predicate-term. The subject-term primarily denotes the being of the thing meant, whereas the predicateterm primarily connotes the essence or nature that the one indicated shares in.

In two respects, however, the mystery of Christ is at odds with the structure of ordinary language. One is the simplicity of divine nature and divine person that obtains in Christ, which is not reflected in a normal sentence composed of subject-term and predicate-term. The other is the togetherness of human nature, calling for predication and thus for composed sentences, with a divine person, calling for a subject-term which, when it reflects divine metaphysics, does not agree with any predicate whatsoever. Thus, the composition in any sentence, for instance *Deus est homo*, a key enunciation in Aquinas' explanation of his understanding of the theory of the *communicatio idiomatum*[14], both does and does not reflect the identity of Christ. Inasmuch as it does, it forms a highly formal grammatical analogy for the identity of Christ, expressed in saying that there are two natures in Christ (signification, predicate-term) and one *suppositum* (supposition, subject-term).

What consequences do these remarks on christological metaphysics and semantics have? It shows for one thing how substantial and structural Aquinas' awareness of the ineffability of the reality of Christ in

12. On the medieval theory of supposition see L.M. DE RIJK, *Logica Modernorum. A Contribution to the history of early terminist logic*, Assen, 1962-1967; ID., "The origins of the theory of the properties of terms", in *Cambridge History of Later Medieval Philosophy*, Norman Kretzmann, Anthony Kenny, Jan Pinborg (eds.), Cambridge etc., 1982, 161-173; P.V. SPADE, "The Semantics of Terms", in: *Cambridge History of Later Medieval Philosophy*, pp. 188-196. On supposition and signification in Aquinas see my "Aquinas and supposition: the possibilities and limitations of logic *in divinis*", in *Vivarium* XXXI,2 (1993) 193-225. Highly relevant for Aquinas' position considering the other major semantic current in the high middle ages, i.e. that of the *Modistae* is: I. ROSIER, "Signes et sacrements. Thomas d'Aquin et la grammaire spéculative", in *RSPT* 74 (1990) 392-436.

13. Cf. *ST* III, qq. 16-17; I, q. 13, a. 12.

14. Cf. *ST* III, q. 16. On the compositeness of human knowing and naming the person of Christ, cf. *ST* III, q. 2, a. 4.

fact is. These are no cheap or misplaced disclaimers at the start. Incomprehensibility and ineffability are part and parcel of any intellectual dealing with Christ[15]. Moreover, the naming of Christ, and Christ himself being a 'name', a manifestation of the divine, are at the core of Aquinas' position[16]. He not only expresses this on the level of christological metaphysics, but he also has a kind of language at his disposal that is more explicitly related to Scripture.

Aquinas' prologue to his commentary on the letters of Saint Paul is strikingly beautiful and attests to Aquinas' keenness in naming Christ. For, as he says, the one and only subject of all these letters of Paul is the name of Christ. All of the letters originate from the apostle's life which is aimed at only one thing: the knowledge, love and conduct filled with the name of Jesus, which means compassion and salvation. Paul, Aquinas says, was chosen by God to proclaim the name of Christ to the gentiles. He has knowledge of this name, he loves the name and lives a life of the name, through suffering, preaching and writing letters. The letters explain the hidden meaning of Scripture, which is the name of Christ[17].

Let me finally draw attention to Aquinas' commentary on Isaiah. In the book of Isaiah Aquinas identifies about ninety names as names of Christ. They are the result either of a spiritual reading of Scripture or of the application of prophecy to the person of Christ[18]. Of these ninety names over forty are not mentioned in the New Testament, e.g., Flower, Stream, Mountain, Fruit of the Earth, Covenant.

An example of the nature of Aquinas' commentary is his commentary on IX, 5. The Vulgate translation contains six names: the Wondrous

---

15. Cf. *ST* I, q. 12; *Super Evangelium Johannis* I, l. 13 (ed. Marietti, Taurini/Romae, 1952); *Scriptum super Sententiis* III, d. 24, q. 2, qu. 3 (ed. M.F. Moos, Paris, 1933). See also the first chapter of my *Christ the 'Name' of God: Thomas Aquinas on Naming Christ* (Publications of the Thomas Instituut Utrecht, Vol. I), Louvain, Peeters Publishers, 1993, concerning the word *Mysterium*. The only perfect representation of God is his Word, which entails that all names used to signify the word fall short of representing the Word itself: *Sed si esset aliqua res perfecte repraesentans Deum, non esset nisi una tantum, quia uno modo repraesentaret, et secundum unam formam; et ideo non est ibi nisi unus Filius, qui est perfecta imago Patris. Similiter etiam intellectus noster secundum diversas conceptiones repraesentat divinam perfectionem, quia unaquaeque imperfecta est; si enim perfecta esset, esset una tantum, sicut est unum tantum Verbum intellectus divini, Quaestiones Disputatae De Veritate*, q. 2, a. 1.

16. *In Isaiam* XXX, *Super Evangelium Johannis* XII, l. 5.

17. *Super Epistolam ad Romanos*, prologue.

18. The spiritual reading of passages in Isaiah concern the hidden signification that for instance Cyrus or Eljakim, the son of Isaiah, can have, in prefiguring Christ. The names that literally signify Cyrus or Eljakim, are thus interpreted to apply to Christ as well, be it in a hidden, spiritual way.

One (*Admirabilis*), Counsellor (*Consiliarius*), God (*Deus*), The Strong One (*Fortis*), Father of the age to come (*Pater futuri saeculi*) and Prince of Peace (*Princeps Pacis*). All of these, Aquinas states, are names of Christ. Some concern his divine nature, and others his human nature. Christ is called the Wondrous One, since the personal union of both natures expresses God's incomprehensible knowledge and wisdom in an eminent way. He is called the Strong or Powerful One, and he is called God, since the power of Christ is both the power of his virtuousness, and the power of the true hidden God, hidden in Christ. The other two names highlight Christ's final causality, his eschatological stature, for they express Christ's goodness in mediating and leading us into glory[19].

Thus Isaiah is understood to speak about divine and human wisdom, and about the power and goodness that in Christ are ineffably one.

Aquinas' commentaries on Peter of Lombard and on the treatise on the divine names by Pseudo-Dionysius contain much more that could be adduced to corroborate my interpretation[20]. For now it must suffice to say that for Aquinas a reflection on naming Christ goes hand in glove with an apophatic awareness, and that both constitute a very important aspect of his christology.

2. Fray Luis de León (1527-1591)

We will shift attention now to Fray Luis de León. There are two reasons for adducing Fray Luis here. First, Fray Luis published, at the end of the Spanish Golden Age, a three-volume *De los nombres de Cristo* in which he deals with the fourteen, according to his views, major names of Christ[21]. Second, and less known is the fact that in his early academic years, Fray Luis was an independent but faithful interpreter of the thought of Thomas Aquinas. He commented upon (parts of) Aquinas'

19. *In Isaiam* IX. Cf. Luis de León's use of the same passage in his commentary on Aquinas' christology: *Et denique ad alias res venit, quas longum esset explicare, quarum multas complexus est Esaias, capite IX, dum Christu tribuit varia nomina, propter varietatem rerum ab eo gerendarum, ut "Pater futuri saeculi, Princeps pacis", etcaetera, Opera* VII (note 22), pp. 244-245.

20. Cf. SCHOOT, *Christ the 'Name' of God* (note 15), pp. 90-95 and 95-103.

21. The ones treated are Bud, Face of God, Way, Shepherd, Mountain, Everlasting Father, Arm of God, King of God, Prince of Peace, Husband, Son of God, Lamb, Beloved, Jesus. The most recent edition of the text is to be found in Fray LUIS DE LEON, *De los nombres de Cristo*, Cristóbal Cuevas (ed.), Madrid, Catedra, 1977. Translations are from Fray LUIS DE LEON, *The Names of Christ*, Translation and introduction by Manuel Durán and William Kluback, New York etc., Paulist Press, 1984. For a historical overview of the tradition of the theology of naming Christ, cf. W. REPGES, *Philologische Untersuchungen zu den Gesprächen über die Namen Christi von Fray Luis de León*, Münster, 1959.

christology, and on Durandus' commentary on the christology of Peter of Lombard, in which commentary (that of Fray Luis) Aquinas plays a dominant role[22]. We can therefore hypothetically assume that the views of both of these theologians, in spite of vast historical and hermeneutical differences, bear a certain family resemblance.

And indeed, in the general treatise on divine names which prefaces the entire monograph[23], Fray Luis appears to develop a similar outlook. Metaphorical language, according to Fray Luis, is a very special and highly valuable human phenomenon. A common word may receive some other than its proper meaning because both the proper and the metaphorical referent of the word are created by God, and have their common source in the creator. Thus, God is the source of all success of the ordinary metaphor. But God himself uses metaphor as well, in order to make his truth and salvation known, and he does so in Scripture. Therefore metaphorical language has a dominant position in theology, because the divine means for descending are the human means for ascending to the divine, as is the case not only in the Bible, but in the Incarnation of Christ itself as well[24]. Christ himself may be understood to be a metaphor of the divine.

To this theological semantics also belongs the view that words used to signify, should conform to the thing signified, a thought very dear to Thomas Aquinas himself. In our age we have lost this sense of the symbolical function of (theological) language, because of all the good reasons for adopting a view on signification that is built on the idea of convention, instead of the natural similarity between words and the signified. But Fray Luis, who was a famous poet as well, sees a basic similarity between Christ the Word of God, and all words used to approach this Word. I will not dwell on the basic features of Fray Luis'

---

22. The latin commentaries are contained in *Opera omnia latina: Divinorum Librorum primi apud Salmanticenses interpretes. Opera nunc primum ex mss. ejusdem omnibus P. Augustiniensium studio edita*, Salamancae, Episcopali Calatravae Collegio, sub Rodriguez Typ. ductu, 1891-1895, 7 vols. On the historical and literary background see H.J.M. SCHOOT, "Christologia recepta. Fray Luis de León, Deel 1" (with summary in English), in *Jaarboek 1996 Thomas Instituut te Utrecht*, Utrecht, 1997, pp. 91-119.

23. Fray LUIS DE LEON, *The Names of Christ* (note 21), pp. 42-53.

24. "If metaphor properly understood could be for Fray Luis a means of ascent towards God, then the language of the Bible and all its figures of speech would show the corresponding process, the divine descent to humanity. (...) Biblical language is itself a kind of incarnation." and "Perhaps, most significantly of all, we have begun to understand how language itself is a theological phenomenon for him. Its metaphors can be a means of ascending towards the truth of God, which in the Bible itself descends covered in human words which are witnesses ultimately to the Word made flesh", Colin P. THOMPSON, *The Strife of Tongues: Fray Luis de León and the Golden Age of Spain*, Cambridge, CUP, 1988, p. 27 and 35.

technique here, since it would take too much space[25]. But it is important
to note this vast hermeneutical difference between Luis and modern concerns for the names of Christ. Fray Luis is closer to considering names
as parts of divine praise, than as potential pieces of information, closer
to names as vehicles of the divine, than to names as sole products of the
human intellect, closer to names as part of divine ineffability, than
names as a means to leave the divine mystery behind.

The names that Fray Luis deals with, and the order in which he does
so, are to be interpreted as a congenial alternative for the usual scholastic approach in dogmatics. The names of Christ are put in the order of
salvation history itself, reaching from creation to the eschaton, i.e., from
names that signify Christ's central position in creation and sustenance,
like 'Bud', and revelation, like 'Face of God', 'Way', and 'Shepherd', to
the names that are concerned with Christ's work of salvation and his
eschatological position, like 'Son of God', 'Lamb', 'Beloved' and
finally 'Jesus'. This fact alone, and there are many more indications of it
in his work, already attests to an essential christocentrism in Fray Luis'
theological approach[26]. It is through Christ that the world is created and
receives its final destiny. It is through Christ that sin and greed and
injustice and conflict are uncovered and judged[27]. It is through Christ

25. Cf. *The Names of Christ* (note 21), pp. 46-50. An example is given in note 28. It
seems that Fray Luis limits this analysis to proper (individual) names, but his text is
somewhat ambiguous: "In the same way there are words and names which apply broadly
and are called common names and others which are fitting for one object. We are now
speaking of these last ones" (*ibid.*, p. 46), but somewhat further on he nevertheless seems
to include the Hebrew names given by Adam to each thing (*ibid.*, p. 46).

26. Cf. the treatise on the first name of Christ in *De Los Nombres de Cristo*, 'pim-
pollo' or 'bud', especially this passage: "As Christ is a source or rather is an ocean which
holds in itself all that is sweet and meaningful that belongs to man, in the same way the
study of His person, the revelation of the treasure, is the most meaningful and dearest of
all knowledge. With good logic this knowledge is at the base of all other notions and
knowledge because it is the foundation and the goal at which all the actions and thoughts
of the Christian aim", p. 39. Muñoz Iglesias says: "Si se nos preguntara cuál es a nuestro
parecer la nota predominante en la Teología de Fr. Luis, responderíamos sin titubeos: Su
visión cristocéntrica del mundo natural y sobrenatural. (...) Dios predestinó, redimió, jus-
tifica y salva a los hombres por Cristo y para gloria de Cristo", S. Muñoz Iglesias, *Fray
Luis de León, teólogo. Personalidad teológica y actuación en los "Preludios de las Con-
troversiis De Auxiliis"*, Madrid, Ed. CSIC, 1950, pp. 101-102.

27. As might be expected, Fray Luis, in the traditional scholastic issue concerning the
motif for the incarnation, follows Scotus instead of Aquinas, endorsing his view that there
would have been an incarnation of Christ even without there having been sin. Cf. *Com-
mentaria in Tertiam Partem Divi Thomae*, in *Opera Omnia* (see n. 22), vol. VII, pp. 244-
273. Thompson, *Strife of Tongues* (note 24), p. 180: "God created all that is, seen and
unseen, in order to make this blessed and wondrous union, which means that the purpose
for which all the variety and beauty of the world was formed was to bring to light this
compound of God and man, or rather, this one who is God and man together, Jesus
Christ."

that the name of God can be pronounced, for the name 'Jesus' adds two consonants to the totally spiritual and unsayable Tetragrammaton, for the latter consists only of vowels. And yet silence is as important as speech[28]. *De los nombres de Cristo* consists of a dialogue between three persons, but *y calló* is said many times in the book, "and he fell silent"[29].

In the view of Fray Luis, God "is so present to us that, paradoxically, in this life His presence never appears to us" (p. 51)[30]. God is close to our being but we never have a clear vision or knowledge of him. We are obliged to give him a name. Not names that we fabricate ourselves, but that God gave to us. When God created Adam, it became necessary that God be named. And, says Fray Luis, "as God had decided that He would become man afterward, as soon as man appeared He wanted to become more human by naming himself" (p. 52). However, although there are

28. "The Hebrew word for Jesus is 'Jehosuah,' as has been mentioned before. And in it we find all the letters that go into the name of God in Hebrew, the so-called 'four letter name of God' or 'Tetragrammaton,' plus two letters more. As you know, the name of God with four letters is a name that is not uttered, because vowels are not pronounced, because we do not know what their real sound should be, or because of the respect due to God, or else, as I have suspected sometimes, because it is like the mumbling sounds that a dumb person utters as an expression of friendship, affection, love: without a clear pattern, shapeless, as if God wanted us men to use a word to express His infinite being a clumsy word or sound that would make us understand that God is too large to be embraced or expressed in any clear way by our understanding and our tongue: Pronouncing such a name is tantamount to admitting that we are limited and dumb when we come face to face with God. Our confusion and mumbling are a hymn of praise, as David declared; the name of God is ineffable and unutterable. And yet in Jesus' name two letters have been added and the name can indeed be pronounced and said out loud with clear meaning. What happened with Christ also happened with Christ's name: It is the clear portrait of God. In Christ we see God joined to a man's soul and body. God's name, which could not be said, now has two more letters and it can be said, mysteries can be revealed, made visible, can be talked about. Christ is Jesus, that is to say, a combination of God and man, of a name that cannot be uttered and a name that can" (p. 349).

29. Cf. THOMPSON, *Strife of Tongues* (note 24), pp. 14-15. One cannot resist the temptation of drawing a parallel between this feature of Fray Luis' work, and Aquinas' falling silent at the end of his life, not because of immanent death but because of having had some kind of experience causing him to state in private to his secretary and *socius* Reginald of Piperno that anything he had written was but straw in comparison with what he had experienced, after which he indeed stopped writing.

30. Fray Luis, at the very beginning of his treatment of the names in general, does exactly what Aquinas does, taking his starting-point in Divine Simplicity: "... It is like the image of simplicity that, on the one hand, there is in God, and, on the other, He has an infinite multitude of perfections, because He is altogether a great perfection and His simplicity encompasses all His perfections. If we speak with propriety God's wisdom is not different from His infinite justice, nor His justice from His greatness, nor His greatness from His mercy and His power, and in Him power, love, and knowledge are one. In each one of these perfections, however they may drift apart from each other, they are all together and from whatever part one regards it, they are all one and the same thing" (p. 50).

proper names, proper names are not the same as perfect names. "To be proper is one thing; to be equal or perfect is another. (...) Thus words cannot attain what the understanding has not attained, and thus we could never give God a complete and adequate name" (p. 52). And Christ, in his turn, is given very many names "because of His limitless greatness and the treasury of His very rich perfections and with them the host of functions and other benefits which are born in Him and spread over us. Just as they cannot be embraced by the soul's vision, so much less can a single word name them. It is as he who spills water into some glass with a narrow and long neck, and distributes it drop by drop, so the Holy Spirit which knows the narrowness and poverty of our understanding does not give us that greatness all at once, but offers it to us in drops, telling us, at times, something under one name, and some other thing, at other times, under another name" (pp. 52-53).

Fray Luis gives us both an interesting theology of the names of Christ, and an interpretation of Aquinas' christology. Even though Fray Luis is very familiar with the scholastic method and language, he does not use them in this book. He does not even employ Latin, but Spanish, thus substantially contributing to the development of the Spanish language. He employs the genre of dialogue, instead of scholastic questions and answers. His style is not detached, but involved, not technical, but accessible. Apparently this approach is Fray Luis' answer to the question in what way in his days theology should be communicated[31].

Let me finally give one example of the way in which *De los nombres de Cristo* can be thought to give a faithful interpretation of Aquinas in a totally different form. I mentioned already the discussion regarding the structure of the *Summa Theologiae*, which in fact is a discussion on theological method. The *ST* first deals with the divine names, and considers them in general, and assumes that the ones left untreated, i.e., the names

---

31. There are, of course, not only similarities between Fray Luis and Aquinas, but also dissimilarities. One dissimilarity concerns their views on metaphor in theology. Aquinas draws a sharp distinction between proper common names (which can be put to analogous usage *in divinis*) and metaphorical common names, because the latter, simply speaking, usually signify something corporeal, whereas the former do not (*ST* I, q. 13, a. 1). Consequently, saying that some words are predicated metaphorically and not properly of Christ, such as 'drinking' and 'eating', amounts to heresy for Aquinas (*Summa contra Gentiles* IV, c. 32, n. 11) Fray Luis, on the other hand, seems to work without such a distinction. Aquinas would never indistinctly list names like lion, lamb and door, together with names such as salvation, life and truth (*Names of Christ*, p. 53). It should be mentioned that, and having read Thompson this may come as a surprise, Fray Luis does not even mention the word 'metaphor' (nor 'analogy', for that matter) in the general treatise prefacing his book, which entails that any 'theory' of his on this subject cannot but be deduced from his actual semantic analysis.

given to Christ because of his humanity, belong to the third part. Fray Luis expressly states what the structure of the *ST* at best only intimates. He says that there is only one kind of name of Christ that he discusses, i.e., those that "belong to Christ as a man, conforming to the rich treasures of righteousness which encompass the humaneness and to the works which God operates and has operated in us" (p. 53). There are other names of Christ, those that are "fitting for His divinity, some related to His person and others common to the Trinity," but these "belong appropriately to the names of God" (*ibid.*). This remark of his must be understood as saying that these belong appropriately to *the treatise* of the names of God, since Fray Luis knows very well that all names of Christ are names of God, due to the *communicatio idiomatum*, for which reason he writes "the works which *God* operates etc." Scholastic theology is in the back of his mind when he writes this.

One could ask whether, for both Aquinas and Fray Luis, it is the case that the names given to Christ according to his human nature, are also the subject of a negative or apophatic approach. Should not one at least expect that these names are as clear to us as when they are used in talk about other human beings? In fact, the answer to this question has just been given. The reason for this approach is the fact that the 'human' names are predicated of God, of the Son, and that this predication cannot be true unless it accounts for the fact that predication of the divine influences even names that in themselves signify a human reality[32]. True language not only consists of signification, but of supposition as well. True language about Christ not only consists of names, but of the predication of names, of sentences as well. Two natures are ineffably united in one person, Chalcedon says, and such is the mystery that constitutes the very dynamism of any reflection on language about Christ[33].

III. NEGATIVE CHRISTOLOGY AND MODERN INTERESTS

Finally, these are not only views that a part of the tradition of theology holds. Recently Gerald O'Collins presented a "Christology" in

32. This is the point where Aquinas' distinction between metaphor and analogy becomes important. Even when one employs a more modern and thus broader conception of metaphor, it is hardly admissible to consider 'Christ is a human being' to be a metaphorical statement, but it is admissible to consider it as an analogous one.

33. In his commentary on the *Sentences* Aquinas even admits that *homo*, predicated of Christ, is a divine name, since it implicitly signifies the relation that the hypostatic union is, and the work of the entire Godhead that brought the incarnation about. Cf. *Scriptum super Sententiis* I, d. 30, q. 1, qu. 2 and d. 22, q. 1, qu. 4. See also above, n. 4.

which the elements just described are distinctly present[34]. Perhaps one can say that apophatic or negative christology is even gaining ground in recent years, despite the apparent paradox that it contains. The paradox is that the one whom faith declares as the one in whom God has revealed himself, the one in whom God has come near to humanity, is also the one who shares as much in divine ineffability as Father or Spirit. Perhaps even more so, because of the twofold mystery that the definition of Chalcedon implies. This paradox is present only to those who regard negative christology as a part of faith seeking understanding. For, generally speaking, there are two kinds of negative theology[35]. The first takes its starting-point in the present-day experience of divine absence, in the absence of names for the divine, regardless of faith, in short: in present-day "Gottesfinsternis". The other kind speaks from the angle of the overwhelming richness which is hidden in Christ (Col 2,3). Hiddenness is then not so much a new modern or postmodern phenomenon, but one that is biblical in origin and of all ages. It seems to me that both approaches are valid, but need to be distinguished in order to avoid unnecessary difficulties and illegitimate expectations. It will be recognized that my approach is the second one, the one that starts not from scratch but from hidden treasures. And yet this approach is not irrelevant to our modern understanding and to modern problems.

Let me mention two of these: the identity of the priest, and the position of Christ in interreligious dialogue.

As we all know, the identity of the priesthood is an issue that is subject to many developments and debates, and one can even call it a contested subject. In the Netherlands, the mere presence of lay pastoral ministers in the parishes, who most of the time enjoy an all-round pastoral mission from their bishop, with only restrictions regarding the administering of most of the sacraments, poses a challenge to priestly identity. There is a strong current responding to this challenge by once again educating students for the priesthood in an isolated environment, apart from those educated for lay ministry, and by once again introducing what I would call a kind of fundamentalism in matters concerning the priesthood. Formulating and implementing a necessary distinction, however, should not entail formulating

34. Gerald O'COLLINS S.J., *Christology: A Biblical, Historical, and Systematic Study of Jesus*, Oxford, OUP, 1995, esp. pp. 13-14 and 47-50.
35. Developed by J. WISSINK, "Enkele theologische reflecties over de negatieve theologie, toegelicht aan de hand van Thomas van Aquino", in I.N. BULHOF and L. TEN KATE (eds.), *Ons ontbreken heilige namen. Negatieve theologie in de hedendaagse cultuurfilosofie*, Kampen, 1992, pp. 46-65 (English translation forthcoming).

and implementing a separation. For what makes a pastor a priest? A priest represents Christ, which means that for his identity the identity of Christ is the primary fountain-head. Now, what happens to priestly identity, if the identity of Christ is coloured by its ineffability, by the hiddenness of God in Christ, by the hiddenness of ultimate humanity in Christ? Would such an approach enhance the practice of once again introducing a hierarchical separation of ordained and lay persons, in this case lay ministers, or would it for instance highlight the eschatological reality of celibacy? Would it enhance the preaching of unchangeable truths, or would it enhance a mystagogical pastoral style? Would it exclude lay ministers from the representation of Christ, or would it try to device distinct kinds of representation that are grounded in the mystery of God in Christ?

The other relevancy of negative christology that I would like to mention is the one for interreligious dialogue. Negative or apophatic christology is a necessary ingredient for any theology that wants to engage in interreligious dialogue. The negativity concerned, to be quite clear, is not playing down fundamental claims concerning Christ being the full and final manifestation of the divine and the salvation he, exclusively or inclusively, has brought about. It may be the case that genuine interreligious dialogue needs a christology that considers the normativity of Jesus Christ as essentially an open question, to be answered in the very dialogue itself, as Knitter claims[36]. However, I find it more convincing that partners in dialogue cherish the fullness of their tradition instead of taking an extreme liberal point of view. Besides, when Christians say that their ultimate norm is the person of Jesus Christ himself, they must be understood to express their helplessness or weakness regarding the subject, since no Christian can fully translate the person of Christ into a norm, without losing most of what he wants to hold on to. The confession of Christ, for instance, as the one mediator, is not only or primarily critical to non-Christian approaches of divinity and salvation, but primarily critical to those who share in this confession. To be under the critique, however, of *Deus semper major*, is what makes all men and women equal, since any mediation of the divine, in any tradition is first and foremost particular, since the divine "is always encountered through a mediator – a symbol, a sacrament, an incarnation"[37]. Even when Christians

36. P.F. KNITTER, *No Other Name? A Critical Survey of Christian Attitudes Toward the World Religions*, London, SCM Press, 1985, p. 230.
37. *Ibid.*, p. 202; Knitter also states that "The more the community realizes that its savior *really* does make God known, the more it realizes that this God is a mystery ever more than what has been made known – the *Deus semper major*, the God ever beyond. In

state the identity of this Mediator with the Mediated, the Mediated does not come about as comprehensible or directly available.

Precisely this is what negative or apophatic christology stresses. In his *The Analogical Imagination*, David Tracy has rightly called attention to this essential feature of God-talk which is indispensable for any theology interested in dialogue. Inasmuch as Christians regard, for instance, their major credal formulations as analogical, they are not relativizing their religious truth-claims, but instead consider themselves invited to prolong their analogical imagination in dialogue with other religious traditions[38]. Even mild or radical christocentric theologies, like those of Thomas Aquinas or Luis de León, can be understood to contribute to this dialogue, since both put forward the essentially analogical character of major truth-claims concerning Christ[39].

other words, the more the particular mediator's efficacy is realized, the particular mediator's efficacy is realized, the more its relativity is recognized", *ibid*. Knitter seems to forget however that the Christian tradition not only holds that Christ is a symbol of the divine, but the symbolized itself as well.

38. "So too the theological emphasis (...) will focus upon the similarities-in-difference in the extraordinary variety of reality. (...) Yet to interpret these theological traditions, the interpreter must note that the likenesses discovered in variety (...) are produced by the presence of those moments of intensity, the necessary negations: similarity-in-difference, the negation of any univocity, the manifestation in the event of sheer giftedness, the concealment in every disclosure, the absence in every presence, the incomprehensibility in every moment of genuine comprehensibility, the radical mystery empowering all intelligibility. Where analogical theologies lose that sense for the negative, that dialectical sense within analogy itself, they produce not a believable harmony among various likenesses in all reality but the theological equivalent of "cheap grace": boredom, sterility and an atheological vision of a deadening univocity". D. TRACY, *The Analogical Imagination. Christian Theology and the Culture of Pluralism*, New York, 1987, p. 413.

39. To interpret Christian religious language as essentially analogical, is quite different than interpreting it as something accidental and not substantial, as something which belongs to the medium and not to the core message of the New Testament, as Knitter holds (*No Other Name?*, see note 36, p. 182). To reduce early christology to ecclesiology is uncalled for and is in my view disrespectful to history ("Its purpose was more to define identity and membership within the community than to define the person of Jesus for all time", p. 184). In the light of the positions of Aquinas and Fray Luis, the appeal to the rise of historical awareness in order to state christological pluralism, is put into perspective. The mere presence of different names or titles for Christ, irrespective of their historical evolution, suffices to claim the *Christus semper major*. It may even be argued that their position, inasmuch as they respect the outcome of an equally historical process in, for instance, patristic theology and early christian dogmas, is more faithful to history than those who want to 'jump' from present-day challenges to experiences underlying the gospels, and vice versa.

'One and only'-qualifiers, even though they may be understood to signify exclusivity, primarily state God's and Christ's incomprehensibility, and the (analogical) gap between other revelation and salvation within the 'language-game' that is used to approach this mystery, be it Judeo-Christian or Hellenic Christian. For the theological assimilation of these fundamental Wittgensteinian insights, see G.A. LINDBECK, *The Nature of Doctrine: Religion and Theology in a Postliberal Age*, Philadelphia, 1984.

CONCLUSION

a) It seems to me that the person and work of Christ himself indicate the need for a kind of christology that may be called apophatic or negative. It is not only due to our lack of understanding and naming regarding the divine, that we need to stress the mystery that Christ is. It is an essential feature of his presentation of the Kingdom of God, of his presentation of himself, and of the biblical stories about the resurrection and the appearances of the hidden Christ.

b) In the tradition of theology, Thomas Aquinas and Fray Luis de León have endorsed this approach, so apophatic or negative christology is not merely something that needs to be developed in view of the present-day erosion of the contents of Christian belief; it follows from the overwhelming presence of all the treasures that are hidden in Christ.

c) Nevertheless, this approach is highly relevant to problems that are posed in modernity, of which I have mentioned two.

More important perhaps than any *use* that negative christology may have in dealing with modern problems, is what I would like to call its doxological heart. An apophatic christology lives from the liturgical and eucharistic presence of Christ, and enhances an understanding of Christ which concords with the doxological experiences of anyone praying to him. Christology more than ever needs an intrinsic link with this practice of not merely studying but also celebrating the name of Christ. Negative christology provides such a link.

Heidelberglaan 2   Henk J.M. Schoot
3584 CS Utrecht   Catholic Theological University of Utrecht
The Netherlands

ERNST TROELTSCH: A MODERATE PLURALIST?

An Evaluation of His Reflections
on the Place of Christianity among the other Religions

I. The Rediscovery of Troeltsch by the Advocates of Religious Pluralism

The recognition of Ernst Troeltsch (1865-1923) as their predecessor by John Hick and Paul Knitter is to be situated in a broader movement of re-appreciation of the importance of Troeltsch as a theologian and as a philosopher, which begun since the mid-1970s[1]. During his life-time, the celebrated professor of systematic theology at the University of Heidelberg (1894-1915), who in 1915 accepted a nomination to the philosophical faculty of the University of Berlin in order to dedicate the last years of his life to the study of the more general problem of the relation between history and value[2], was considered to be *the* systematic theologian of the History-of-Religions School. An important reason for the almost general neglect of his work for nearly five decades is to be found in the harsh criticism of Troeltsch by Karl Barth, who in his *Kirchliche*

---

1. A colloquium on Troeltsch's intellectual legacy, organized in 1976 by the University of Lancaster and resulting in a publication by J.P. Clayton (ed.), *Ernst Troeltsch and the Future of Theology*, Cambridge, 1976, gave the impulse to a whole series of Troeltsch-studies, in German, English and French. In his own country we mention first of all F.W. Graf & H. Ruddies, *Ernst Troeltsch Bibliographie*, Tübingen, 1982. In the same year appeared the first volume of *Troeltsch-Studien* (Gütersloh), under the general editorship of H. Renz & F.W. Graf. For an exhaustive biography we had to wait until H. G. Drescher, *Ernst Troeltsch: Leben und Werk*, Göttingen, 1992. Very recent are the studies by J.H. Classen, *Die Jesus-Deutung von Ernst Troeltsch im Kontext der liberalen Theologie* (BHT, 99), Tübingen, 1997, N. Witsch, *Glaubensorientierung in "nachdogmatischer" Zeit: Ernst Troeltschs Überlegungen zu einer Wesensbestimmung des Christentums* (KKTS, 65), Paderborn, 1997, and B.W. Sockness, *Against False Apologetics: Wilhelm Herrmann and Ernst Troeltsch in Conflict* (BHT, 105), Tübingen, 1998. Examples of the renewed interest in Troeltsch in the French-speaking world are: P. Gisel (ed.), *Histoire et théologie chez Ernst Troeltsch* (Lieux théologiques, 22), Genève, 1992, the 1996 publication of the first volume of the "Corpus Troeltsch", Paris/Genève, and the thematic issue *Ernst Troeltsch ou la religion dans les limites de la conscience historique*, in *RHR* 214 (1997) 131-266. For the Anglo-Saxon sphere see especially S. Coakley, *Christ without Absolutes: A Study of the Christology of Ernst Troeltsch*, Oxford, 1988, and G.E. Griener, *Ernst Troeltsch and Herman Schell: Christianity and the World Religions* (Europäische Hochschulschriften, XXIII/375), Frankfurt am Main, 1990.

2. Resulting in his unfinished master-piece E. Troeltsch, *Der Historismus und seine Probleme. I: Das logische Problem der Geschichtsphilosophie* (GS III), Tübingen, 1922.

Dogmatik considered Troeltsch as an exponent of 19th century liberal Protestantism, now replaced by the movement of Dialectical Theology[3].

The most significant reference to Troeltsch by the advocates of religious pluralism is definitely the one made by John Hick in his contribution to the provocative book *The Myth of Christian Uniqueness*, of which he was the co-editor[4]. The title of his article, "The Non-Absoluteness of Christianity", is the negation of the title of Troeltsch's famous book about the relation of Christianity to other religions, *The Absoluteness of Christianity and the History of Religions*[5]. Not only by means of this title, but also in the first page of the article, the only one explicitly dealing with Troeltsch, Hick mistakenly suggests that Troeltsch is defending in his book "the unqualified absoluteness" of Christianity[6]. If only he had carefully read the English translation by von Hügel of Troeltsch's 1923 lecture, "The Place of Christianity Among the World Religions"[7], he would have known better. For the translator refers to the

---

3. K. BARTH, *Die Kirchliche Dogmatik*, IV/1, Zollikon/Zürich, 1953, pp. 423-427. See especially p. 427: "Es war aber offenkundig, daß die 'Glaubenslehre' sich bei ihm in ein uferloses und unverbindliches Gerede aufzulösen im Begriff – daß die neuprotestantische Theologie überhaupt bei ihm bei allem hohen Selbstbewußtsein ihres Gehabens in die Klippen bzw. in den Sumpf geraten war. Weil wir da nicht mehr mittun konnten, sind wir gegen Ende des zweiten Jahrzehnts unseres Jahrhunderts aus diesem Schiff ausgestiegen!".

4. J. HICK, *The Non-absoluteness of Christianity*, in J. HICK & P. KNITTER (eds.), *The Myth of Christian Uniqueness*, London, 1987, 16-36, reprinted in J. HICK, *Disputed Questions in Theology and the Philosophy of Religion*, Basingstoke, 1993, 77-101.

5. TROELTSCH, *Die Absolutheit des Christentums und die Religionsgeschichte*, Tübingen, 1902. English-speaking scholars usually refer to the translation by David Reid, *The Absoluteness of Christianity and the History of Religions*, London, 1972, who based himself on the third German edition of 1929. This edition was a mere reprint of the second edition of 1912, but in preparation of this edition Troeltsch augmented his original publication with more than 20 pages. Especially when referring to the last part of the book it is important to carefully compare the first and the second editions. From now on I shall refer to the English translation as *Absoluteness*.

6. HICK, *Non-absoluteness* (n. 4), p. 16. Compare also B. REYMOND, *Troeltsch, Schweitzer, Tillich ou les voies d'un christianisme désabsolutisé*, in *LTP* 43 (1987) 3-18, p. 8: "Le titre de son opuscule de 1902 ne doit en effet tromper personne: le thème de sa réflexion n'était pas l'absoluïté du christianisme, mais bien sa non-absoluïté". The history of the modern habit to speak in terms of 'the absoluteness of Christianity' is rendered clearly by K. LEHMANN, *Absolutheit des Christentums als philosophisches und theologisches Problem*, in W. KASPER (ed.), *Absolutheit des Christentums* (QD, 79), Freiburg – Basel – Wien, 1977, 13-38, and by R. LEUZE, *Das Christentum – Die absolute Religion? Der Begriff der Absolutheit: Ursprung und Wirkung*, in *ZMR* 68 (1984) 280-295.

7. After Troeltsch's unexpected death on February 3, 1923, von Hügel edited the lectures Troeltsch was supposed to deliver in Great Britain in spring of that year, both in English – *Christian Thought: Its History and Application*, London, 1923 – and in German – *Der Historismus und seine Überwindung*, Berlin, 1924. When referring to the fourth lecture, *The Place of Christianity Among the World Religions*, I shall use the reprint in O.C. THOMAS, *Attitudes Toward Other Religions: Some Christian Interpretations*, London, 1969, 73-91. I will refer to this essay as *Place*.

earlier 1902 book not as "The *Absoluteness* of Christianity" but as "The *Absolute Validity* of Christianity", which is a more precise rendering of Troeltsch's position.

Why then is Hick celebrating Troeltsch in his article? Because in his last reflection on the theme, in the lecture of 1923, Troeltsch is said to have completed his "intellectual journey" from ascribing an "unqualified absoluteness" to ascribing a "relative absoluteness" to Christianity. This journey, then, needs to be reiterated by all Christians. Or, to use a favourite expression of Hick, all Christians should cross the "theological Rubicon" and abandon their absolutist position[8].

Admittedly, it is true that Troeltsch by 1923 no longer considered it legitimate for Christians, speaking from a particular European cultural background, to claim that their religion constitutes a universal value-system. The recognition of its validity is ultimately the result of an individual judgement, which may never be forced upon others. In Troeltsch's own words:

> This experience is undoubtedly the criterion of its validity, but, be it noted, only of its validity for us. It is God's countenance as revealed to us; it is the way in which, being what we are, we receive, and react to, the revelation of God. It is binding upon us, and it brings us deliverance. It is final and unconditional for us, because we have nothing else, and because in what we have we can recognise the accents of the divine voice. But this does not preclude the possibility that other racial groups, living under entirely different cultural conditions, may experience their contact with the Divine Life in quite a different way, and may themselves also possess a religion which has grown up with them, and from which they cannot sever themselves so long as they remain what they are. And they may quite sincerely regard this as absolute valid for them, and give expression to this absolute validity according to the demands of their own religious feeling[9].

However, the contrast between Troeltsch's 1923 lecture and the position he defended in 1902 should not be exaggerated, as Hick seems to do. Why would Troeltsch otherwise use the first half of his speech to "explain the position I adopted in my little book"[10] and conclude his summary by stating that: "From the practical standpoint at least, it contains nothing that I wish to withdraw"[11]?

Paul Knitter, for his part, offers in his doctoral dissertation on Paul Althaus as well as in his classical work on religious pluralism, *No Other*

---

8. HICK, *Non-absoluteness* (n. 4), p.16.
9. *Place*, p. 86. Hick quotes this passage in the book in which he gives for the first time an account of his pluralist position, *God and the Universe of Faiths*, Basingstoke, 1973, p. 174.
10. *Place*, p. 74.
11. *Place*, p. 83.

Name?, a more detailed exposition of Troeltsch's opinions on this matter[12]. However, it soon becomes clear that, as a religious pluralist, he, together with Hick, can only be proud about the Troeltsch of the 1923 lecture. Therefore, he calls Troeltsch's assessment of how Christianity relates to the other religions in *The Absoluteness of Christianity* a "rather confusing procedure"[13], because, on the one hand, the radical historicity of Christian religion, and, on the other hand, its superiority over the other religions is stressed. But, could Troeltsch have done otherwise, if he, as Knitter himself admits, "found himself wrestling mainly with the clash between the historical consciousness of his age and the need, which he recognised in himself and in all persons, for solid religious commitment and values"[14]? Secondly, and again similarly to John Hick, Knitter only pays attention to that part of *The Place of Christianity* in which Troeltsch altered his view with regard to *The Absoluteness of Christianity*. To state that Troeltsch "toward the end of his life had to change his stance and admit that he had been wrong"[15] is therefore only a partial truth.

My rather critical account of Hick's and Knitter's assessment of Troeltsch is certainly not meant to deny the fact that Troeltsch can reliably be presented as a forerunner of religious pluralism. In fact, at the end of this article, I shall argue that some important convictions of theologians like Hick and Knitter, such as the view that Christians need to overcome their Christo-centrism by a Theo-centrism, and that the incarnation of Christ is a mythological expression, are in some way anticipated in the writings of Ernst Troeltsch (V). This conclusion, however, needs to be preceded by a presentation of the central argumentation of *The Absoluteness of Christianity* and of *The Place of Christianity*[16] (II,III), and by some remarks on the context and background of both works (IV).

II. The Absoluteness of Christianity and the History of Religions (1902)

Before Troeltsch is able to proclaim the creed of the 'History-of-Religions School', namely, that Christianity is an historical reality, comparable

---

12. P. KNITTER, *Towards a Protestant Theology of Religions: A Case Study of Paul Althaus and Contemporary Attitudes* (MarTS, 11), Marburg, 1974, pp. 5-19, and *No Other Name? A Critical Survey of Christian Attitudes Toward the World Religions*, Maryknoll, NY, 1985, pp. 23-36.
13. KNITTER, *No Other Name?* (n. 12), p. 27.
14. *Ibid.*, p. 24.
15. *Ibid.*, p. 27.
16. Direct quotations of these works will be indicated by arabic numbers in the text.

with all other historical phenomena, and that it therefore should be studied by means of the historical-critical method, he must reject two ways of presenting Christianity as the absolute religion, the one arguing on the basis of "the form in which religious truths arise", the other on the basis of "the religious content of the manifestation" (52-53).

The first is the "orthodox, supernatural apologetic" (*orthodox-supernaturalistische Apologetik*) (51), the classical method to present Christianity as a normative truth. The only reliable evidence for a true revelation, it is argued there, consists in clear signs of its supernatural origin. In Troeltsch's time, when external miracles had become highly problematic, one relied especially on "the psychological miracle of conversion" (52). Christianity could thus be proved to be the only revelation, whereas the other religions were considered to be "a homogeneous mass of human error" (47). According to Troeltsch, however, it has become impossible to "isolate Christianity from the rest of history and then, on the basis of this isolation and its formal signs, define it as an absolute norm" (48).

Through the influence of Hegel this classical type of apologetics has become more and more replaced in theology by "the modern evolutionary apologetic" (*moderne evolutionistische Apologetik*) (51). According to this type of apologetics there is only one religion, or one "principle" (*Begriff*) or "essence" (*Wesen*) of religion, which is gradually reaching its perfect state in the course of history. Christianity is held to be "the absolute religion", or "the complete and exhaustive realisation of its principle" (49), compared to which the other religions are merely "relative truths". Of course, Christianity does not provide the "absolute knowledge of God", but in this religion human knowledge of God reaches its highest stage (54).

Troeltsch's critique envisages first of all the concept of 'essence of religion'. "The modern idea of history knows no universal principle on the basis of which the content and sequence of events might be deduced. It knows only concrete, individual phenomena, always conditioned by their context and yet, at bottom, underivable and simply existent phenomena" (66). It is impossible to formulate an essence of religion that fits all the historical forms of religion. What happens in most cases is that the so-called essence of religion is in fact a "watered-down version of Christianity" in order to make the theory that Christianity is "the ideal religion toward which all things tend" sound well (68). Second, the history of religions teaches that the great religions are not related to each other "in a stage-by-stage causal process" (*in einem kausalen Stufenverhältnis*), but that they are mostly "parallel" realities (*im Verhältnis eines*

Nebeneinander) (69). Third, Christianity is in its concrete existence certainly not an absolute religion, but a genuinely historical phenomenon. Therefore, efforts by contemporary theologians to distinguish between the absolute "kernel" (*der Kern*) and the relative "husk" (*die Schale*) are criticised as well[17]. To illustrate how Christianity has been deeply conditioned by its historical situation and environment, Troeltsch points to the fact that the radicalism of Jesus' moral preaching can be understood in view of the expectation of an imminent end of the world, whereas, from the moment that Christianity underwent the influence of the Hellenistic philosophical schools, earthly values were no longer negated (70-71). Troeltsch's last criticism pertains to the concept of evolutionary development. He dismisses it as a speculative construction, which, "when viewed from the perspective of the modern idea of history, stands in utter contradiction to real events" (73).

Troeltsch admits that it is the same thing to state that Christianity is a historical phenomenon, and, that it is "a relative phenomenon" (*eine relative Erscheinung*) (85), but he wants to get rid of the negative connotations connected with the term 'relativity', for they relate only to "an unlimited relativism" (*unbegrenzte Relativismus*) (86). "Relativity does not mean denial of the values that appear in individual configurations" (89), Troeltsch emphasises. The nucleus of his own "philosophy of history" (*Geschichtsphilosophie*) consists of the conviction that it is highly important to transcend the false dilemma between relativism and absolutism in order "to discern, in the relative, tendencies toward the absolute goal" (90)[18].

> As applied to religion, what is suggested is not a 'principle' of religion as a humanly realisable and exhaustible idea, but the concept of a goal discernible in outline and general direction. What is suggested is the concept of a goal that always remains transcendent (*ein immer transzendentes Ziel*) as far as the sum total of its content is concerned, a goal that can be apprehended within history only in individually conditioned ways. In psychological and epistemological perspective, what is normative and universally valid thus appears as the concept of a goal toward which mankind is

17. *Absoluteness*, p. 71: "Yet the result of these various attempts is that the actual absoluteness of the kernel always absolutizes the husk as well, while the actual relativity of the husk always relativizes the kernel in turn". We may presume that Troeltsch had especially in mind the famous book of A. VON HARNACK, *Das Wesen des Christentums*, Leipzig, 1900. See further TROELTSCH, *Was heißt "Wesen des Christentums"*, in *CW* 17 (1903) 443-446, 483-488, 532-536, 578-584, 650-654, 678-683, and the thoroughly revised reedition in *GS* II,386-451.

18. This celebrated sentence – only present in the 1912 version – deserves to be rendered in Troeltsch's original words: "Nicht das Entweder-Oder von Relativismus und Absolutismus, sondern die Mischung von beidem, das Herauswachsen der Richtungen auf absolute Ziele aus dem Relativen ist das Problem der Geschichte".

directed. The goal itself, however, is simply set before man as a higher reality, a creative personal reality that breaks forth out of the human spirit and has its basis in the unconditioned worth of the inner man. It is this reality that provides the creative force at work in man's conception of a goal, his forward-driving restlessness and yearning, his resistance to the merely natural world. This idea requires a turn to the metaphysical (*die metaphysische Wendung*), a retracing of all man's goals and orientations to a transcendent force that actuates our deepest strivings and is connected with the creative core of reality (100).

That said, however, Troeltsch is acutely aware of the danger of falling back to Hegelian categories and of not providing a real alternative to evolutionary apologetics. Accordingly, he insists, first, that the normative goal itself lies "beyond earthly history" (*jenseits der irdischen Geschichte*), so that, "what is required is a definitive disclosure of its main direction but not an absolute realisation" (99), and, second, that it is only by means of an historical, comparative study that the degree of closeness of these religions towards this absolute goal can be determined.

In view of the realisation of this comparison, Troeltsch makes a number of presuppositions, which contemporary experts in the study of comparative religions will no longer allow to be made[19]. Attention must only be paid to "the major forms of religious orientation" (*die großen Haupttypen geistigen Lebens*) (91), to "the great world religions with their clearly suprasensual world of absolutely transcendent religious values" (109)[20], because, according to Troeltsch, "polytheism and the numerous religions of uncivilised peoples are irrelevant to the problem of highest religious values" (92). Great religions are, therefore, those "who posit a higher world in antithesis to the merely given world of physical and psychological nature" (92). Which list does he have in mind?

> The ones to be taken into consideration here are, on the one hand, the religions that sprang from a common stock – Judaism, Christianity, and Islam – and, on the other, the great religions of the East, namely Hinduism and especially Buddhism. Also important are the philosophical attempts to sever every connection with history and create a purely rational religion in terms of monistic pantheism, dualistic mysticism, or moralistic theism (92-93).

By means of which criteria will these religions or worldviews be classified? Troeltsch wants to postpone the answer to this delicate question

---

19. A similar judgment is formulated by M. PYE, *Ernst Troeltsch and the End of the Problem about 'Other' Religions*, in CLAYTON, *Troeltsch* (n. 1), 172-195, p. 177.

20. The remark that immediately follows obviously has been written before the first and second World War: "It is these religions that free themselves from the natural confinement of religion to state, blood, and soil, and from the entanglement of divinity in the powers and phenomena of nature".

as long as possible with the relativizing remark that the determination of the criterion is, ultimately, "a matter of personal conviction (*Sache der persönlichen Überzeugung*) and is in the last analysis admittedly subjective", not, however, without an "objective basis in a scrupulous survey of the major religious orientations, in unprejudiced hypothetical empathy, and in conscientious evaluation" (96-97)[21].

The most important distinction in the history of religions is, according to Troeltsch, the one between "the religions of law" (*Gesetzesreligionen*) – Judaism and Islam – and "the religions of redemption" (*Erlösungsreligionen*) – Christianity and the Indian religions (109-111). In the former category, the other world is not really "other", because admission to it depends completely on personal efforts. Among the latter religions – "the ones that consummate this distinction between the two worlds" (109) – the Indian religions differ from Christianity in that "redemption means the annulment of the world process and the obliteration of everything personal in pure being", and in that "the redeeming divinity always remains a thing-like being that lacks the vital, activating power needed to tear men away from the world and return them, transformed, to confront the world again" (110). Christians, on the other hand, are characterised by a double attitude towards the world: insofar as it contains sinful, nature-bound elements, the world is rejected; insofar as it is God's creation and the way back to Him, it is affirmed. Since in Christianity God is conceived as a personal being, redemption means then "faithful, trusting participation in the person-like character of God" (112)[22]. The outcome of Troeltsch's comparison is as follows:

> Among the great religions, Christianity is in actuality the strongest and most concentrated revelation of personalistic religious apprehension (111)[23].

Troeltsch, however, also pays attention to a second method of comparing the great religions. He wants to assess how they have integrated the most important ideas, shared by all higher religions, namely "God,

---

21. GRIENER, *Troeltsch* (n. 1), p. 74, remarks: "There is some ambiguity on this point. (...) At issue seems to be the alleged opposition between 'objective' and 'subjective', the argument that a 'subjective judgment' has relinquished its right to be considered 'objective' and true. Troeltsch is proposing a theory of 'objectivity' based on what might be called 'authentic subjectivity'".

22. Although this idea of salvation as participating in God's personal being, is only present in the second edition (1912², p. 87), in the first edition eternal life is qualified as a "personal life" (*persönliches Leben*) as well (1902, p. 78, 1912², p. 86).

23. In the German original this important evaluation appears thus: "Das Christentum ist in der Tat unter den großen Religionen die stärkste und gesammeltste Offenbarung der [1902: religiösen Kraft] personalistischen Religiosität" (1902, p. 77, 1912², p. 86).

the world, the soul, and the higher life beyond this world" (113). Without much proof, Troeltsch concludes:

> Thus Christianity must be understood not only as the culmination point but also as the convergence point of all the developmental tendencies that can be discerned in religion (114)[24].

But Christian revelation, as Troeltsch untiringly repeats, remains a limited, historical reality. "It cannot be proved with absolute certainty that Christianity will always remain the final culmination point, that it will never be surpassed. (...) At this point proofs come to an end. Here there is simply the self-confident faith that absolutely nothing can make a new and higher religion likely for us" (114). The "absoluteness" Troeltsch still wants to predicate to Christianity is that of possessing "the highest value discernible in history" (*die Höchstgeltung*) (118)[25].

In the fifth chapter Troeltsch drops the scientific discourse for a while in order to treat the more 'pastoral' question, whether "our clergymen and theologians" will still be able to convince "ordinary devout people", when they are no longer able to present Christianity as the "absolute" religion, but as a religion that can only be "normative" for a person at a given time (121). It is clear that religious persons need to be certain that, "within the Christian orientation of life there is an authentic revelation of God and that nowhere is a greater revelation to be found" (123). But this remains, epistemologically speaking, "a statement of probability" (121). Religious persons need indeed to have access to "the absolute", in other words, to God, but this is never possible "in an absolute way" (122). Knowledge that this absolute goal exists, and that Christianity is a reliable way towards it, is sufficient. Christians must learn to live with the reality of a plurality of paths to God and do not need to construct an apologetics that "deprives everything outside Christianity of godly life and power in order to confer them in some absolute or supernatural way upon Christianity" (127). Their best teacher in this respect is Jesus himself, who was able to confirm to his audience that "the will and promise of the Father are disclosed in their fullness in what he proclaimed" (124), but who expected "complete deliverance, perfect knowledge, and permanent victory" (123) only to become reality in the world to come. Troeltsch is not able to reconcile these insights from the historical life of Jesus with the apologetical habit, already visible in the

24. See also the similar reflection on p. 127: "Indeed, it has become Christianity's distinctive task to make itself the crystallization point (*Kristallisationspunkt*) for the highest and best that has been discovered in the human spiritual world, its fitness for this task of attracting and sustaining such values being due to its superior power".

25. This precision is only present from the second edition onwards.

primitive church, of "snuffing out all other lights in order to let the light of Jesus shine alone" (124) and of "locating the complete deliverance of the future in his passion and death in order to bind everything in an absolute way to faith in Jesus" (127). Notwithstanding his harsh criticism of every christology that connect revelation and redemption exclusively to the person of Jesus, Troeltsch has no doubts about the unsurpassibility of Christ and Christianity.

> Christianity remains the great revelation of God to men, though the other religions, with all the power they possess for lifting men above guilt, grief, and earthly life, are likewise revelations of God, and though no theory can rule out the abstract possibility of further revelations. Christianity remains the deliverance, even though the power over the natural man and his cravings which is at work in every religion is also genuine deliverance, and even though Christianity's deliverance takes a step forward in history whenever faith in God is planted in weak and sinful hearts. Above all, Christianity remains the work of Jesus, having its greatest strength in its relationship to him and drawing its confidence from the authentic and living guarantee of the grace of God in his personality. Even though we discern the power and activity of God in other heroes and prophets of religion, it is in Christianity, more profoundly than anywhere else, that faith in God is bound up with the vision of the life and passion of him who reveals and guarantees that faith. Even though we cannot disprove the possibility that Jesus might someday be surpassed, the fact remains that we are all too weak to detect any higher power of God in our hearts. Instead, we gain peace and joy only through submission to him and his Kingdom (126)[26].

The essay ends with a reflection on two types of absoluteness. It belongs to the identity of the initial stage of the religious conviction that it, "quite naturally and as a matter of course regards itself as absolute" (132). But cultural behaviour requires that the believer frees herself from this "naïve absoluteness" (*naive Absolutheit*) to a more tolerant and open-minded worldview. A new overview of the religious traditions of the world brings Troeltsch to the conclusion that there is a progression noticeable from absolutizing the local or national deities in tribal religions or in polytheistic traditions, to absolutizing the one divine ruler – be it that he has still national sympathies as in Judaism or that he is characterised by arbitrariness as in Islam –, and finally to the "purely inward absoluteness" (*die rein innerliche Absolutheit*) in Jesus' preaching of God's Kingdom (144-145). Therefore, in the comparison of the different claims of naïve absoluteness, the superiority of Christianity again becomes clear. "The

---

26. Troeltsch speaks here in the first place as a believer and a religious person. See about his "mystical-spiritualistic religiosity" K.-E. APFELBACHER, *Frömmigkeit und Wissenschaft: Ernst Troeltsch und sein theologisches Programm* (BökTh, 18), München – Paderborn – Wien, 1978, pp. 43-53.

highest religion is the one that has the freest and most inwardly oriented claim to absoluteness, and it will stand by this claim as long as no trace of higher religious life appears anywhere else" (146).

With Jesus' naïve presentation of God's challenge and promise as absolute, modern Christianity would have been able to cope. This is, however, no longer the case with the "artificial, apologetic absolute-ness" (*künstliche, apologetische Absolutheit*) (149), which arose in the post-Easter Church, where the absoluteness was transferred from the Kingdom of God to "the person of the Messiah and Lord" (148). Further characteristics of this absoluteness were that it considered Christianity as the only supernatural revelation, and that it developed a rational theory in which other religions were considered as preparatory stages of Christian revelation (151-152)[27]. When this type of apologetics could no longer be defended against the attacks arising out of the scientific worldview, a new defence of Christianity's uniqueness arose under the form of "evolutionary absoluteness" (*evolutionistische Absolutheit*) (157). Christianity, as we know, was now celebrated as the realisation of the idea of religion. But the artificial nature of this second type of apologetics has been definitively unmasked by the scientific study of history as well.

Does the failure of these artificial claims to absoluteness have implications for any further recognition of the validity of Christianity? In his revised version of 1912 Troeltsch firmly wants to dissociate the two problems, because the superiority of a religion is dependent upon the religious message of its founder, not upon later truth claims.

> What is decisive, therefore, is no longer the claim to absoluteness (*der Absolutheitsanspruch*) but the reality reflected in the nature and strength of the claim – the religious and ethical world of thought and life itself. The validity (*Gültigkeit*) of Christianity is verified not by arguing the nature and

---

27. The further evolution is described in a harsh way: "On every hand natural absoluteness gradually grows beyond its naïve, self-contained outlook into a doctrine of unique and miraculous expression of the divine. This doctrine is then opposed to other religions as the one and only truth, to individual deviations as orthodoxy, and to the questing intellectual life of reflection – whether exalted or profound – as the codification of divine wisdom. Sacred books, sacred dogmas, sacred laws, and materially demarcated and guaranteed means of grace everywhere circumscribe the heritage of the founding prophets. A developed theology – sometimes mythologizing, sometimes speculative – establishes a lasting relationship between this one and only truth and the manifestations of the religious life that encompass and adhere to it" (p. 154). No doubt what the culmination point of this artificial absoluteness looks like: "It leads, in Catholicism, to the Thomistic system with its practical complement in the infallibility of the Pope, and in Protestantism to a dogmatics which combines natural and supernatural illumination and finds its practical support in the inspiration of the Bible" (p. 155) (This sentence occurs only in 1912[2], p. 140).

strength of claims to revelation, redemption, and truth but by judging what lies behind the claim. But if what is substantive *(die Sache)* takes the place of the claim *(der Anspruch)*, it likewise follows that the relativity *(die Relativität)* and similarity *(Analogie)* found in the claims of the various religions cannot threaten Christianity. Indeed, one may even venture to suggest that there is a correspondence between the uniqueness of what lies behind a claim *(der Sonderart der Sache)* and a unique form of the claim to absoluteness *(eine Sonderart des Absolutheitsanspruches)*. What is essential, however, is the former, not the latter. (...) If prophetic and Christian personalism *(der prophetisch-christliche Personalismus)* is valid, then the course it follows toward the absolute is certain and its superiority over other paths is sure. Its essentially Christian character is assured, even though it is detached from older theories of revelation and redemption, of original sin and exclusive truth. By virtue of this disengagement, Christian personalism enters freely and vigorously into the perspectives of the modern understanding of the world (159-160)[28].

In both versions, however, it is insisted that Jesus' message "remains the highest and greatest we know" (160). When it is not accompanied by a denial of the salvation present in other religions, religious persons may even uphold the naïve certainty that in Jesus believers are confronted with "the highest revelation of the divine life that holds sway over us" (161).

III. THE PLACE OF CHRISTIANITY AMONG THE WORLD RELIGIONS (1923)

Our presentation of the content of this article will be much shorter, since, as we have explained in the first section, its first half is a summary of *The Absoluteness of Christianity and the History of Religions*, which

28. The opening line is a retraction of his earlier position. Compare 1902, p. 126, "Der Anspruch selbst ist bisher nirgends widerlegt und überholt worden", and 1912[2], p. 144, "Entscheidend ist darum nicht mehr der Absolutheitsanspruch, sondern nur die in Art und Stärke des Anspruchs wiedergespiegelte Sache". Troeltsch apparently wanted to end his original lecture by assessing the truth of the naïve claim of Christianity's superiority and of the significance of Jesus Christ for the salvation of every human being. He did this by a threefold paraphrase of 1 Cor 3,11, a text which he had already used as a motto in an unpublished essay by means of which he won a contest of the theological faculty of Göttingen in 1886. Compare 1902, p. 126: "... und so bleibt es dabei, dass für das Seelenheil des Menschen kein anderer Grund gelegt ist, als Jesus Christus". *Ibid.*, p. 128: "Nicht Theologie und Apologetik, sondern die einfache Stimme des von der Last der Historie befreiten Herzens wird das Paulus-Bekenntnis sprechen: Einen anderen Grund kann niemand legen, ausser dem der gelegt ist, welcher ist Jesus Christus". And the final sentence of the whole book, p. 129: "So wird auch die wissenschaftliche Ueberlegung der Religionsgeschichte das naive Bekenntnis des Paulus in einem religionsgeschichtlich erweiterten Sinne aufnehmen dürfen...: der sicherste und stärksten Grund des Heils ist Jesus Christus". Significantly, he omitted all these paraphrases in the 1912 version.

dealt, as Troeltsch now calls it, with "the clash between historical reflection and the determination of standards of truth and value" (74).

He repeats his criticism against two apologetical theories, "both of which claimed to establish the ultimate validity of the Christian revelation in opposition to the relativities revealed by the study of history" (76). The theologians of his time who still refer to the divine miracles in order to defend the privileged status of the Christian faith are usually found among the Methodists and Pietists. Whereas in their natural theology they used to refer to God only "as the ground of the interconnection of all relative things", they uphold a limited sphere where the supernatural divine activity can be felt directly, as the inward source of the Christian's conversion (77). Troeltsch's opposition is based on the difficulty to prove such an inward miracle, on the presence of analogous claims in other religions, and on the problematic status of theories of miracles in general. His refusal of the second theory, which considers the history of religions as a progressive development towards the perfect expression of religion in Christianity, is based on the results of sincere historical research, which knows of no "natural upward trend toward Christianity" of the other religions and which has great difficulties with attempts to generalise the pluriform historical reality of Christianity itself (78). The recognition of the "individuality" (*die Individualität*) of the whole sphere of history is the merit of German Romanticism, and has been shared by "most of the German theology of the nineteenth century", Troeltsch explains to his British audience (79-80). But respect for the individual character of each religion does not exclude the possibility that these religions should possess "an element of truth" (*ein Element des Gültigen*). The recognition of the truth – and *a fortiori* of the universal validity – of Christianity is first of all a matter of "personal conviction" (*persönliche Gewißheit*), of belief. But this truth, Troeltsch believed, could "be confirmed retrospectively and indirectly by its practical fruits, and by the light that it sheds upon all the problems of life" (80).

In his 1902 book he did so by comparing the 'naïve claims to absolute validity' made by the different religions, and of their conception of divine revelation. Because of the absence of "all limitation to a particular race or nation", Christianity could be said to possess "the highest claim to universality of all the religions" (82-83). And also the content of its religious ideal seemed to be outstanding, because the revelation of the personal God "within the depths of the soul" answered "the simplest, the most general, the most personal and spiritual needs of mankind". Once the results of the comparison were known, his advice for individual believers and theologians was not to trouble themselves with "the question of the measure of validity possessed by the other religions", or with "the question of the possible further development of religion itself". He summarizes the conclusion of his 1902 book as follows:

> We may content ourselves with acknowledging that Christianity possesses the highest degree of validity (*die höchste Gültigkeit*) attained among all the historical religions which we are able to examine. (...) It is the loftiest and most spiritual revelation we know at all. It has the highest validity. Let that suffice (83).

Twenty years later, Troeltsch still considers it to be legitimate that the individual believer is convinced of the absolute validity of the religion (s)he believes in. But he wants to retract his former opinion about the possibility of retrospectively evaluating the truth claims made by the different religious traditions and deciding for a qualitative superiority of Christian revelation. His major studies of the last decade, *Die Soziallehren der christlichen Kirchen und Gruppen* (1912)[29] and *Der Historismus und seine Probleme* (1922)[30], witness to his discovery that Christianity is intimately connected with European civilisation, and that all of its internal developments have to be understood as a reaction to the changing culture. Recognition of the individual character of Christian religion – but also of all other historical realities, even of science and logic – cannot, however, easily be reconciled with "the somewhat rationalistic concept of validity, and specifically of supreme validity" (85). Undoubtedly influenced by the tragic events of World War I, Troeltsch states rather pessimistically: "What was really common to mankind, and universally valid for it, seemed, in spite of a general kinship and capacity for mutual understanding, to be at bottom exceedingly little, and to belong more to the province of material goods than to the ideal values of civilisation" (84).

Troeltsch certainly does not want to minimize the enormous significance of Christianity for European culture:

> Our European conceptions of personality and its eternal, divine right, and of progress toward a kingdom of the spirit and of God, our enormous capacity for expansion and for the interconnection of spiritual and temporal, our whole social order, our science, our art – all these rest, whether we know it or not, whether we like it or not, upon the basis of this deorientalized Christianity. Its primary claim to validity is thus the fact that only through it have we become what we are, and that only in it can we preserve the religious forces that we need. Apart from it we lapse either into a self-destructive titanic attitude, or into effeminate trifling, or into crude brutality. (...) We

---

29. *GS* I, Tübingen, 1912. Translated in English in 1931 as *The Social Teaching of the Christian Churches*.
30. *GS* III (n. 2).

cannot live without a religion, yet the only religion that we can endure is Christianity, for Christianity has grown up with us and has become a part of our very being (85).

But the enormous significance of Christianity should not be exaggerated to universal proportions. Christianity possesses a "relative value", a "validity *for us*" (*seine Geltung für uns*), comparable to the manifestations of the "Divine Life" that can be experienced in other cultures (86), which have the status of "subjective validities" (*subjektiven Absolutheiten*) as well (89). The only one capable to make a final judgement about human forms of religiosity is "God Himself" (87). This discovery of the relative status of the world religions has practical consequences: first of all for the missionary activities of the great religions, which may no longer be directed at "conversion, or transformation of one into the other, but only [at] a measure of agreement and of mutual understanding" (87-88)[31], and, second, for the internal development of Christianity, which, so Troeltsch hopes, will lead to a transcendence of the denominational differences in order to better answer the spiritual needs of the "new era in the world's history", which is longing for "a new peace and a new brotherhood" (88-89).

If the 1923 essay had reached its end at this place, there would indeed be much reason to consider it as a radical breach with his earlier book, in which so much attention had been given to *a posteriori* comparisons of the great religious traditions, resulting in the recognition of the absolute validity of Christianity. But Troeltsch is not yet completely satisfied and repeats the question with which we are familiar since the 1902 book: "Can we, then, discover no common goal of religion, nothing at all that is absolute, in the objective sense of constituting a common standard for mankind?" (89). This idea of a "common goal" (*gemeinsames Ziel*) of all genuine religious aspirations, which lies, however, beyond history, is indeed very similar to *The Absoluteness of Christianity*[32]. But in this last utterance of his metaphysics of history equal attention is given to the idea of a "common ground" (*gemeinsamer Grund*), the "Divine Spirit", who is leading believers of all religious convictions towards this one goal[33].

---

31. This is not a merely theoretical remark. Troeltsch was very engaged in the *Allgemeiner Evangelisch-Protestantischer Missionsverein*, better known as *Ostasienmission*, the only institute of this kind adhering a liberal theology. For his views on mission see *Die Mission in der modernen Welt*, in *CW* 20 (1906) 8-12, 26-28, 56-59 (*GS* II, 779-804) and *Missionsmotiv, Missionsaufgabe und neuzeitliches Humanitätschristentum*, in *ZMR* 22 (1907) 129-139, 161-166.

32. See especially *Absoluteness*, pp. 98-101.

33. In *Absoluteness*, God is mostly circumscribed as "the ultimate goal of man". Only once he is called "the eternal and abiding ground (*Grund*) of all spiritual life" (*Absoluteness*, p. 103). A more important parallel is the reference to God as "the absolute ground of all things" in the early article *Metaphysik und Geschichte*. See *infra*, n. 57.

I have already drawn attention to this fact in my earlier work. I only
wish to emphasise now more strongly than I did then that this synthesis
cannot as yet be already attained in any one of the historical religions,
but that they all are tending in the same direction, and that all seem
impelled by an inner force to strive upward toward some unknown final
height, where alone the ultimate unity (*die letzte Einheit*) and the final
objective validity (*das Objektiv-Absolute*) can lie. And, as all religion
has thus a common goal in the Unknown, the Future, perchance in the
Beyond (*im Unbekannten, Zukünftigen und vielleicht Jenseitigen*), so,
too, it has a common ground in the Divine Spirit ever pressing the finite
mind onward toward further light and fuller consciousness, a Spirit
Which indwells the finite spirit, and Whose ultimate union with it is the
purpose of the whole many-sided process. Between these two poles,
however – the divine Source and the divine Goal (*dem göttlichen Grund
und dem göttlichen Ziel*) – lie all the individual differentiations of race
and civilisation, and, with them also, the individual differences of the
great, comprehensive religions (89).

Troeltsch's conviction that the true absolute is God Himself, the common goal and source of inspiration of all authentic expressions of religiosity, constitutes an important point of continuity between his two
essays on the place of Christianity among the world religions[34]. Significantly, the last words of the 1923 essay are about "the One in the
Many". "In our earthly experience the Divine Life is not One, but
Many. But to apprehend the One in the Many constitutes the special
character of love" (91).

IV. REMARKS ON THE CONTEXT AND BACKGROUND OF BOTH WORKS

1. 1893-1902: Growing preference for the historical method in theology, and first attempts to construe a metaphysics of history

The Absoluteness of Christianity is the interim conclusion of
Troeltsch's long effort to free himself from the dogmatics of his domi-
nant teacher in Göttingen, Albrecht Ritschl (1822-1889), who considered
Christian revelation as a unique event with absolute significance, and to

---

34. I agree, however, with GRIENER, who points to an important difference in
Troeltsch's reflections about the ultimate goal of history in both works. See GRIENER,
Ernst Troeltsch (n. 1), p. 111: "In the 1902 *Absoluteness of Christianity* Troeltsch had
spoken rather ambiguously about the goal of all religious striving. The goal was, on the
one hand, outside of history, a goal to which all religions are striving. Yet, at the same
time, Christianity could be regarded as the 'convergence point' of all religious striving.
Here, in his never to be delivered England lectures, there is no mention of Christianity as
a 'convergence point'. He speaks now of a synthesis which has not yet been reached, a
synthesis which nevertheless would be the desired goal of the many historical religions".

opt, together with the other members of the *Religionsgeschichtliche Schule*[35], for a historical-critical study of the Christian religion in all its aspects. His definitive farewell to the Ritschlian school is to be found in his 1909 *Rückblick auf ein halbes Jahrhundert der theologischen Wissenschaft*[36].

But already in *Die christliche Weltanschauung und die wissenschaftlichen Gegenströmungen*[37], his first publication, which he prepared during the one and a half year that he served as an extraordinary professor of systematic theology at the University of Bonn, the first traces of his attempt to construe a metaphysics of history are present[38]. Troeltsch describes how, since the end of the German Enlightenment, most historical studies reflect a philosophy of history in which the concept of 'development' (*Entwickelung*) plays a central role. In general these philosophies deal only with immanent factors responsible for progress. There seems to be almost no place for a progressive historical revelation of the Divine Being or for the idea that absolute truth could be accessible at a particular moment of the process. Although the processes of becoming may be well described within this world view, the real causes of the historical realities remain hidden. Therefore, religious persons still experience the need for a divine revelation of the truth and meaning of their human existence[39].

---

35. Among this hardly organised group of young scholars, the names of Wilhelm Bousset, Hermann Gunkel and Albert Eichhorn deserve special mentioning. They were much influenced by the theological antipode of Ritschl in Göttingen, Anton Paul de Lagarde. For recent literature on this movement see G. LÜDEMANN (ed.), *Die "Religionsgeschichtliche Schule" : Facetten eines theologischen Umbruchs* (STRS, 1), Frankfurt am Main, 1996, and M.D. CHAPMAN, *Religion, Ethics and the History of Religion School*, in *SJT* 46 (1997) 43-78.

36. TROELTSCH, *Rückblick auf ein halbes Jahrhundert der theologischen Wissenschaft*, in *ZWT* 51 (1909) 97-135, slightly revised in *GS* II, 193-226.

37. TROELTSCH, *Die christliche Weltanschauung und die wissenschaftlichen Gegenströmungen*, in *ZTK* 3 (1893) 493-528; 4 (1894) 167-231, especially pp. 198-229. Troeltsch considered his maiden article important enough to be included (not, however, without important modifications) in the second volume of his works. See *GS* II, 227-327, especially pp. 294-324.

38. He had defended the necessity of this enterprise already in one of his *Promotionsthesen* of 1891. See H. RENZ & F.W. GRAF (eds.), *Untersuchungen zur Biographie und Werkgeschichte* (Troeltsch-Studien, 1), Gütersloh, 1982, p. 300: "An jede positive Glaubenslehre schliesst sich eine religions-philosophische Metaphysik an, auch wenn man den Unterschied von Religion und Metaphysik sehr wohl begriffen hat".

39. Here and in his later works Troeltsch is much dependent upon the historian Leopold Ranke. In *GS* II, 316, he paraphrases him as follows: "Die letzten Gründe des Geschehens aber und den höchsten Gehalt desselben zeigt die Historie nicht, sie sind der Religion zu überlassen".

In this early essay Troeltsch is still convinced that the revelation of absolute religious truth can only occur in one point, from which the whole historical reality is enlightened[40]. However, he is already conscious of the temporal and spatial limits of this revelation and of the fact that non-Christian religions, in their "lower level of revelation", share an "analogous knowledge"[41]. Since exact evidence of Christianity being the ultimate divine revelation is not possible, a decision of faith is indispensable. The unicity and transcendent origin of Christian revelation can, however, be further elucidated in a comparative study of the history of religions[42]. The main difference with *The Absoluteness of Christianity* lies in the concrete implementation of this program. All other religions are catalogued among the natural religions (*Naturreligionen*), compared to which Christianity appears as something "principally new" (*ein prinzipiell Neues*)[43]. Troeltsch also emphasizes that God is to be radically distinguished from the world and that his revelation to humankind has nothing to do with innerworldly ideals, but only with "the highest and ultimate values of personalities"[44]. In the 1902 essay, on the contrary, he will argue that the Indian religions belong to the religions of redemption as well and that it is not aversion to nature which explains the unicity of Christianity, but the unique combination of recognition and rejection of the world. At the outset of his theological development, Troeltsch also believes that the messianic consciousness of Jesus is a further argument for the uniqueness of Christianity, whereas in 1902 the absoluteness is no longer ascribed to the person of Jesus, but to his incomparable message about God's kingdom[45].

During the following years a conflict with the Ritschlian theologian Julius Kaftan, made Troeltsch definitively opt for the historical, as distinguished from the dogmatic, method of doing theology. To his article on *Die Selbständigkeit der Religion*[46], in which he blamed Kaftan for considering Christianity as the only revealed religion and the non-Christian religions as merely human postulates, Kaftan reacted with *Die*

---

40. *GS* II, 311.
41. *GS* II, 312.
42. *GS* II, 318.
43. *GS* II, 319.
44. *GS* II, 320.
45. *GS* II, 321, to be compared with *Absoluteness*, p. 145: "Whatever role messianism may have played in his preaching, by and large the person of Christ retired behind this reality – the Kingdom of God. In his preaching the Kingdom is the absolute".
46. TROELTSCH, *Die Selbständigkeit der Religion*, in *ZTK* 5 (1895) 361-436; 6 (1896) 71-110, 167-218.

Selbständigkeit des Christentums[47]. Troeltsch's reaction in the article *Geschichte und Metaphysik* is immediately followed by Kaftans *Erwiederung: 1) Die Methode; 2) Der Supranaturalismus*[48]. Friedrich Niebergall, a student of Kaftan, wished to summarize both positions more clearly in an article entitled *Über die Absolutheit des Christentums*, a title Troeltsch simply took over for his own lecture one year later. Niebergall's request for an immediate reaction from professor Troeltsch led to another classical article of Troeltsch, *Über historische und dogmatische Methode in der Theologie*[49].

Troeltsch developed his peculiar combination of a metaphysical philosophy of history and a comparative approach of the history of religions for the first time in the third part of *Die Selbständigkeit der Religion*. He expresses his belief in "the teleological coherence of reality", but emphasises at the same time that the norms to judge "development" (*Entwickelung*), "progress" (*Fortschritt*) and "finality" (*Ziel*) are to be revealed by history itself[50]. Against Kant and the Neo-Kantianism of the Ritschlian school, and in critical dependence on Hegel, he refuses to treat the religions as mere products of human consciousness. In his opinion, they are a mixture of human and divine activity (*die Gottmenschlichkeit der Religionsgeschichte*)[51]. His conviction of the indispensability of metaphysics for the study of religion is brought into balance by his intention to concentrate on the developments visible in the concrete history of religions[52].

The core of his argumentation in part four, an *a posteriori* investigation of the history of religions in order to reconstruct its main tendencies, consists of the elaboration of a central thesis. In his opinion all religions are characterized by a set of basic characteristics, which he calls "the religious principle" (*das religiöse Prinzip*)[53]. These characteristics are 1) a conception of God as a unique, personal and spiritual being demanding the highest ethical efforts of his believers, 2) a conception of a disenchanted world, standing apart from but in all its suffering longing towards God, and 3) a conception of the human soul as disconnected from the

---

47. J. KAFTAN, *Die Selbständigkeit des Christentums*, in *ZTK* 6 (1896) 373-394.
48. TROELTSCH, *Geschichte und Metaphysik*, in *ZTK* 8 (1898) 1-69; KAFTAN, *Erwiederung: 1) Die Methode; 2) Der Supranaturalismus*, in *ZTK* 8 (1898) 70-96.
49. F. NIEBERGALL, *Über die Absolutheit des Christentums*, in *Theol. Arbeiten aus dem rheinischen wissenschaftlichen Prediger-Verein* 4 (1900) 46-86. TROELTSCH, *Über historische und dogmatische Methode in der Theologie, ibid.*, 87-108 and *GS* II, 729-753.
50. *ZTK* 6 (1896), p. 72, 78.
51. *ZTK* 6 (1896), p. 80, 83.
52. *ZTK* 6 (1896), pp. 92-93.
53. *ZTK* 6 (1896), p. 176. Our summary is especially based on pp. 186-218.

enjoyments of nature and greedy of the higher good. The highest religions have developed "a concept of redemption" (*Ein Begriff der Erlösung*) as the connection of the three mentioned ideas: the world is hoping for a divine good, in the realization of which the human soul plays a mediating role[54].

From this essay on, Troeltsch is aware that Neo-Platonism and Buddhism deserve to be called "religions of redemption" as well, but they represent a lesser form, since the redemption aimed at is the annihilation of human existence. The only remaining task is then to prove that Christianity represents the highest actualisation of the religious principle. Troeltsch even reiterates that Christianity is distinguished in principle from the non-Christian religions, since they are – even in the case of Neo-platonism and Buddhism –, never able to transcend the characteristics of a natural religion completely[55]. The two remarks at the end of the essay are comparable with the more 'pastoral' paragraphs of the 1902 essay: 1) it is possible to prove that Christianity is the culmination point of the history of religions, not that it is the absolute religion, but this must be enough for the believer, and 2) Christian belief requires a claim to absoluteness in order to ensure the repugnant sinner that he will be saved[56].

Troeltsch's article *Geschichte und Metaphysik* is partially meant to criticize the supernaturalistic defence of the Christian religion of his opponent, partially to refine his own position in the debate. There are at least three reasons why it is impossible to state that Christianity is exclusively the result of a supernatural revelation, Troeltsch argues. In the course of its history it has undergone the influence of the surrounding culture, in the life of its founder human and divine elements can hardly be distinguished, and there are many non-Christian religions which share important characteristics with Christianity. His own conviction that Christianity represents the highest evolution of the history of religions is the result of a metaphysical interpretation of the developments visible within that history. His main example in this enterprise is not Hegel, but Schleiermacher. Instead of a "metaphysics of the absolute" (*eine Metaphysik des Absoluten*), a

---

54. Compare *Absoluteness*, p. 113: "Universally, the higher religious life is comprised of four sets of ideas: God, the world, the soul, and the higher life beyond this world – the world of the transcendent – that is actualized in the interrelation of the first three".

55. *ZTK* 6 (1896), p. 204.

56. *ZTK* 6 (1896), p. 212. Compare, however, the inserted paragraph at the end of the revised edition of *The Absoluteness of Christianity*, in which he has become very critical of theologians who rely too heavily on the Christian claim to absoluteness. We quoted the paragraph in full on pp. 359-360.

speculative theory about God to be verified by the history of religions, he wants to construct "a metaphysics of history or of the human spirit" (*eine Metaphysik der Geschichte oder des menschlichen Geistes*). The main tendency of the history of religions or of history in general will easily be discovered once one disposes of a rule (*eine Regel*) to interpret the pluriform historical reality, and this rule is the conviction of the unity of the human spirit, whose free actions point in the direction of an ultimate goal[57].

At the end of this article Troeltsch dissociates his own vision once more from the supernaturalistic conception of belief, which is characterized as "the subjective appropriation of the redemption, available once and for all"[58]. He would describe religious experience as "a factual elevation into the redeeming community with God, which every believer has to undergo anew through faith in the promise and commandment of Jesus"[59]. Troeltsch knows that apparently the only alternative for the supernaturalistic position is that of 'historicism', which considers "the ideals of all times and of its own time as historically conditioned and would accept no belief as normative"[60]. But it needs to be corrected by a "metaphysics of history" (*eine Metaphysik der Geschichte*), a belief in the rationality of history which leads to the recognition that "the Christian truth constitutes the kernel and goal of this history"[61].

After his article on *Metaphysik und Geschichte*, Troeltsch's preference for the historical method, to be complemented, however, by a metaphysical reasoning about the main direction of that history, will undergo no major modifications. The significance of the 1900 essay, *Über historische*

57. *ZTK* 8 (1898), pp. 40-42. On p. 42 he indicates that the comprehensive development of the human spirit is oriented towards "a definitive and concluding goal" (*ein endgiltiges und abschließendes Ziel*). Another important question to treat within this metaphysical reflection is the question about "the absolute source of all things" (*der absolute Grund der Dinge*) (*ibid.*, p. 44). Already in this early article Troeltsch seems to consider God as the source and goal of all reality, an idea which he will repeat in *The Absoluteness of Christianity*, as well as in *The Place of Christianity Among the World Religions*.

58. *ZTK* 8 (1898), p. 64.

59. *ZTK* 8 (1898), p. 65.

60. *ZTK* 8 (1898), p. 68. Troeltsch's description of some of the advantages – "a (...) sympathetic co-understanding of the most different, a sinister skill to dissolute everything which is apparently solid in something fluid and becoming" – and disadvantages – "the frivolous relativism, for whom everything is something becoming and disappearing, conditional and relative" – of this 'modern' phenomenon has astonishing parallels in contemporary analyses of the postmodern mood. His remark that in his time theologians are respected only as long as they restrict themselves to historical studies, can be actualized by referring to the popularity of the mainly American representatives of the 'Third Quest' in our time.

61. *ZTK* 8 (1898), p. 69.

und dogmatische Methode der Theologie, lies in its classic summary of historical method in "three essential aspects: the habituation on principle to historical criticism (*historische Kritik*); the importance of analogy (*Analogie*); and the mutual interrelation of all historical developments (*Correlation*)"[62]. The fundamental presupposition of this method is "the similarity in principle of all historical events" (*die prinzipielle Gleichartigkeit alles historischen Geschehens*). The question whether it is possible, then, to escape the danger of an absolute relativism does not receive much emphasis, but will be the central theme of *The Absoluteness of Christianity*. The article is dominated by Troeltsch's strong plea "to apply the historical method to theology with utter, uncompromising consistency"[63]. There are only two theological issues of which he accepts that some theologians do not study them according to the principle of analogy, "Jesus' moral character and the resurrection"[64].

Only in the final part of the article, when he has to answer some objections of Pfarrer Niebergall, does Troeltsch have the occasion to clarify once more how he is able to reconcile the historical method with a metaphysics of history. The metaphysical belief "that history is not a chaos but issues from unitary forces and aspires towards a unitary goal" is a necessary presupposition for the deduction of "a scale of values" (*eine Werthscala*) out of the same history[65].

62. We will refer mainly to the English translation *Historical and Dogmatic Method in Theology*, in TROELTSCH, *Religion in History* (eds. J.L. ADAMS & W.F. BENSE), Minneapolis, 1991, 11-32, p. 13.

63. *Ibid.*, p. 19.

64. *Ibid.*, p. 14: "Actually, fewer and fewer historical 'facts' are regarded as exempt from the exigencies of the analogical principle; many would content themselves with placing Jesus' moral character and the resurrection in this category". Compare COAKLEY, *Christ* (n. 1), p. 65: "... the use of the passive verb, and the context of the article's polemic as a whole, surely dismiss the possibility that Troeltsch himself is willing to exclude 'Jesus' moral character' and 'the resurrection' from the full implication of the historical method". In TROELTSCH, *Historismus* (n. 2), pp. 190-192, on the other hand, he will warn against the excessive use of the comparative method and the appeal to analogies of whatever kind in historical studies.

65. TROELTSCH, *Historical and Dogmatic Method* (n. 63), p. 27. From the late fifties on, some theologians, mostly adherents of the 'New Quest', used this article as the classic summary of historical-critical method. See e.g. W. PANNENBERG, *Redemptive Event and History* (1959), in ID., *Basic Questions in Theology*, I, London, 1970, 15-80, and V.A. HARVEY, *The Historian and the Believer: The Morality of Historical Knowledge and Christian Belief*, London, 1967 (chapter one). Inattentive for the polemical context of the article, which makes Troeltsch's rhetorical defence of the "omnipotence of analogy" understandable, they also neglected the metaphysical counterpart to Troeltsch's enthusiasm for this method. See also, e.g., G.E. MICHALSON, *Lessing's 'Ugly Ditch': A Study of Theology and History,* University Park/London, 1985, p. 95, who is only able to write that Troeltsch's principles are "suggestive of a fundamental impasse between theology and historical inquiry", and "properly evoke the image of a ditch or divide between faith and

2. 'Personalism' as distinctive quality of Christianity: An insight developed in the course of the preparation of the second edition of *The Absoluteness of Christianity*

In the revision of *The Absoluteness of Christianity* (1912), Troeltsch left the core of his argumentation unaltered. In fact, in his article on *The Dogmatics of the 'Religionsgeschichtliche Schule'*[66], he still considers it as the first task of the dogmatician faithful to this method to prove, as the result of a comparative study of religions, that Christianity possesses the "highest validity" (*Höchstgeltung*) for our culture and time. The second task consists in a historical reflection on Christianity's "essence" (*das Wesen*), an ever-to-be-renewed interpretation and adaptation of the powerful ideas of Christianity in a changed cultural context[67]. The explication of the content of this essence is the aim of his *Glaubenslehre*[68], a term taken over from Schleiermacher to avoid the connotation of a deposit of absolute and unchangeable truths. The first part of this work deals with the significance of the historical Jesus for faith[69]; the second part with the constitutive elements of Christian faith: the Christian account of God, world and soul, the way they are interrelated in the concept of redemption, and the consequences of redemption: church and consummation[70].

---

history", because he relies exclusively on this article, more precisely on the paragraph which contains the principles of the historical method. Troeltsch is in fact only a defender of the historical method qua method. Throughout his work he shows time and again to be an adversary of the movement of historicism, where the method has become an ideology, a metaphysical belief.

66. The text was published originally in *The American Journal of Theology* (later: *JR*) 17 (1913) 1-21, but since the English is not from Troeltsch's hand, we base ourselves on the German edition in *GS* II, 500-524.

67. *GS* II, p. 511.

68. TROELTSCH, *Glaubenslehre. Nach Heidelberger Vorlesungen aus den Jahren 1911 und 1912 herausgegeben von Gertrud von le Fort*, Aalen, 1981 [= München, 1912], especially §5: *Das christliche Prinzip und die aus ihm folgende Einteilung der Glaubenslehre* (pp. 70-80). Troeltsch uses the terms 'Wesen' and 'Prinzip' interchangeably. English translation: *The Christian Faith* (Fortress Texts in Modern Theology), Philadelphia, 1991.

69. See especially TROELTSCH, *Glaubenslehre* (n. 69), pp. 81-126 and the article on *Die Bedeutung der Geschichtlichkeit Jesu für den Glauben* of 1911. Easily available is the reprint in TROELTSCH, *Die Absolutheit des Christentums und die Religionsgeschichte und zwei Schriften zur Theologie*, München – Hamburg, 1969, 132-162. English translation: *The Significance of the Historical Existence of Jesus for Faith*, in TROELTSCH, *Writings on Theology and Religion* (eds. R. MORGAN & M. PYE), London, 1977, 182-207.

70. For the content of his theological views see TROELTSCH, *Glaubenslehre* (n. 69), pp. 127-384, and the related articles in what can be called the theological encyclopaedia of the *Religionsgeschichtliche Schule*: *Die Religion in Geschichte und Gegenwart* (1909-1913). The study of the evolution of Troeltsch's conception of the "principle" or "essence" of Christianity from the early articles in *ZTK*, via his reflections on the book of Harnack until the *Glaubenslehre*, exceeds the limits of this contribution.

One typical difference with the first edition of *The Absoluteness of Christianity* is that he now clearly saw that the superiority of Christianity rests on the "personalism" of Christian revelation[71]. We can read more about this important notion in other publications of this period. In a *Diktat* of the *Glaubenslehre* Troeltsch explains that it is above all the personal character of God that distinguishes Christianity from the other religions with their "naturalistic and anti-personalistic conception of God"[72]. In *Die Zukunftsmöglichkeiten des Christentums im Verhältnis zur modernen Philosophie* it is argued that the value of Christianity lies precisely in its "principal dualism", so much disdained by contemporary monistic speculations. The personalistic God reveals the ideal characteristics of the human personality to the world – as distinguished from God – and the human personality will be perfected in the community with the divine person[73]. Even his masterpiece during this period, *Die Soziallehren der christlichen Kirchen und Gruppen*, implies the recognition of modern individualism, in the church and elsewhere. The necessary function of institutions is precisely to form and conserve this individualism[74].

3. 'History and Metaphysics' in *Der Historismus und Seine Probleme* (1922)

In our analysis of Troeltsch's undelivered Oxford lecture we discovered that he had become reluctant to defend the absolute validity of the Christian worldview and was only willing to point to its importance within a European context. On the other hand, he emphasized again the necessity of possessing a metaphysical scheme of interpretation that gives sense and meaning to the eternal flux of apparently unconnected historical events. To be able to judge whether these are indeed the central insights of his late thinking, we need to take recourse to his opus magnum, *Der Historismus und seine Probleme*, especially the second chapter, which deals with norms to evaluate historical realities and their relation to a contemporary cultural ideal under construction[75].

---

71. In the second paragraph, we pointed to two important alterations in the edition of 1912: "Among the great religions, Christianity is in actuality the strongest and most concentrated revelation of personalistic religious apprehension" (*Absoluteness,* p. 111), and "If prophetic and Christian personalism is valid, then the course it follows toward the absolute is certain and its superiority over other paths is sure" (*Absoluteness,* p. 159).

72. TROELTSCH, *Glaubenslehre* (n. 69), p. 71.

73. TROELTSCH, *Die Zukunftsmöglichkeiten des Christentums, GS* II, 837-862.

74. TROELTSCH, *Soziallehren* (n. 29).

75. TROELTSCH, *Historismus* (n. 2), pp. 111-220. References to this work will be made in Arabic numbers. Despite his criticism of the many "repetitions, obscurities and contradictions" in *Der Historismus*, of which all the chapters are revisions of lectures and classnotes,

The task to construct a new cultural synthesis was foreseen for the second part, but its presupposition, a philosophical exploration of the values and great realisations of history, is the aim of the first book, by which Troeltsch hoped to overcome the problems of historicism[76]. Although he is still convinced that the development of history follows a teleological scheme, he, however, wants to dissociate himself from those philosophers who claim to be able to describe the future stages of the universal history, out of their knowledge of the ultimate and eternal finality (112). In his opinion, the norms to evaluate facts of history are to be derived "from the fullness of historical experience and perception" itself (117). The difficult question is then how to reconcile the idea of an absolute goal of history with "the necessary relativism of genetic-historical thinking" (122).

The solutions of authors such as Kant, Hegel, Rickert, Windelband and Weber are unacceptable for Troeltsch, because they disconnect history and the search for values. But their failure has taught him that history will never reveal abstract norms that will be valid forever. In each cultural period philosophers have to discover those spontaneous, aprioristic, self-conscious but never timeless norms, that are, however, valid and absolute for that time (160). They have to subject past cultures to a twofold evaluation. In a "first degree evaluation" they have to confront the results of that period "with its own, be it a complicated essence and ideal". In an inevitably subjective "second degree evaluation" they have to compare this culture with their own cultural ideal, which is still in a process of formation by appropriating or rejecting this past culture (172, 177).

Whereas most historians of his time restrict themselves to studies of the former kind, Troeltsch, as a philosopher of history, believes in the necessity to combine both evaluations and, by concentrating on the continuities between the different cultural periods, to elaborate "a concept of universal development" (174). He is aware that this requires a "metaphysical belief in a continuity, which is active in the deepest grounds of history" (175). The cultural ideal, discovered in each time, may then be interpreted as "an expression and revelation of the divine ground of life

---

W. BODENSTEIN, *Neige des Historismus: Ernst Troeltschs Entwicklungsgang*, Gütersloh, 1959, p. 144, correctly indicates that the central theme has remained the same as in his early period, namely "Geschichte und Metaphysik".

76. About the movement of historicism, see K. NOWAK, *Historismusfrage und Theologieverständnis im Zeitalter Ernst Troeltschs*, in *DZP* 38 (1990) 1047-1063, and G.G IGGERS, *Historismus – Geschichte und Bedeutung eines Begriffs: Eine kritische Übersicht der neuesten Literatur*, in G. SCHOLTZ (ed.), *Historismus am Ende des 20. Jahrhunderts: Eine internationale Diskussion*, Berlin, 1997.

and of the internal development of this ground towards a comprehensive meaning of the world, yet unknown to us" (175). Troeltsch himself is willing to accept that this belief in a universal development of history entails a Kierkegaardean leap (178)[77].

Troeltsch is aware that his metaphysics of history presupposes the idea of God. He wants to emphasize, in continuity "with Heraclite and the prophetic-Christian worldview", the inconceivable, but "creative liveliness of the divine Will". This view of a movable and changeable God makes, on the one hand, "the changing and development of truth and of the ideal intelligible", whereas it remains, on the other hand, possible to believe in "a last truth and unity", available for God alone. As a consequence we will never absolutize any human truth or construction of an ideal, but "we retain the possibility to conceive divine life in the relative truth and the relative ideal" (184).

Moreover, Troeltsch's solution of the tension between empirical history and the construction of norms by a philosophy of culture unmasks certain popular convictions as no longer valid (186-193). 1) The rationalist demand for universal norms, supposed to be valid for the whole of humankind, is unrealistic, for our knowledge is limited to our own cultural environment and its presuppositions. "Real universality", Troeltsch holds, is "the lively force" exercised by "individual realisations" – he has especially the force of particular religious traditions in mind – on behalf of the whole or reality. This force is thought to be similar to "the fundamental orientation of the divine will" as intuitively experienced in history. 2) We no longer need the concept of development, understood as progress, which is often used as an argument not to improve the conditions of the present. In view of the absence of knowledge of the final development of humankind, each period "has to create its ideal out of its own history and out of its own participation in the divine stimulus". 3) The comparative approach will still be helpful to better understand the particular characteristics of a certain cultural environment, but comparisons with foreign cultures may not be used to destabilize the unity of its value system[78]. 4) We will be free, Troeltsch

77. See also DRESCHER, *Entwicklungsdenken und Glaubensentscheidung: Troeltschs Kierkegaardverständnis und die Kontroverse Troeltsch-Gogarten*, in *ZTK* 79 (1982) 80-106.
78. When Troeltsch remarks, *Historismus*, p. 192, that "A real comparison makes the self-understanding grow and critically constructs the own reality, whereas a false comparison destroys the uniformity and force of a life and makes its creative process, amidst a whirlpool of analogies and rootless possibilities, self-deceiving", this implies a strong relativism of his own belief in "the omnipotence of analogy", as expressed in *Historical and Dogmatic Method* (n. 63), written in 1900. I am sure Troeltsch would now no longer refer to the resurrection as problematized by the laws of analogy.

finally states, "to answer the urgent practical vital questions of our own Western cultural environment, which arose after the desintegration of the Christian and ecclesial culture since the 18th century, and for whom the religious question is ultimately decisive". The combination of a historical and a cultural-philosophical analysis of our own cultural environment will contribute to the rediscovery of its own vitality. Troeltsch, for his part, is quite optimistic about the future of a cultural environment that holds together "classical antiquity, Christianity, the Middle Ages and modern Europe".

Before moving to chapter III, Troeltsch summarizes his view about the quest for the universal in history once more. Instead of formulating universal goals that will only be realized by human beings in a perfect age, we have to restrict ourselves to the elaboration of a cultural synthesis, which will be necessarily historical and individual. Nevertheless, the possibility of a world-wide mutual understanding, and the universality of the moral "ought", are clear signs that the individual is embedded in the universal.

> This points to a common spiritual ground, from which everything comes forth, and to an ever renewed tendency towards the higher and noble. Whether this common ground and common goal can ever become visible on earth, is admittedly beyond all question. It can only be suspected and believed, it can only surround each individual cultural construction with the atmosphere of a relation with the supra-individual and the ultimate, it can only break down every exclusivistic pride and set spurs to an ever repeated gathering up of powers. But it can never be conceived as an accomplished goal on earth; and how the universal and the individual will be reconciled so to speak in a life beyond death, is as dark as everything which lies beyond death. Not the final stage of humankind on earth, but the individuals' death constitutes the boundary of each philosophy of history (199).

With this last reference to Troeltsch's belief in God as the "common ground and goal" of all relative historical tendencies[79], we hope to have

---

79. We didn't focus our attention on the precise content of Troeltsch's doctrine of God. From his emphasis that the absolute is to be met in the relative, it may be clear that God's immanence is an important theme, although he emphasizes at other instances that God remains the transcendent goal of history. His strongest avowal of God's immanence is to be read in a short polemical article against Friedrich Gogarten, his former pupil and adept of the new movement of dialectical theology, published in 1921 in *CW*. See TROELTSCH, *Ein Apfel vom Bäume Kierkegaards*, in J. MOLTMANN (ed.), *Anfänge der dialektischen Theologie. Teil II*, München, 1963, 134-140. About God's transcendence and immanence in Troeltsch's theology see further COAKLEY, *Christ* (n. 1), pp. 81-87. It was equally not possible, within the constraints of this article, to clarify how Troeltsch in *Historismus* epistemologically conceives the reciprocal relationship between the subject and "the universal consciousness" (*das Allbewußtsein*). Troeltsch does so by reinterpreting Leibniz's monadology and Malebranche's theory of participation. See especially *Historismus*, pp. 209-211 and 675-686, and the comments in BODENSTEIN, *Neige* (n. 75), pp. 169-172, APFELBACHER, *Frömmigkeit* (n. 26), pp. 151-153.

sufficiently shown that the construction of a metaphysics of history has in fact been a constant focus of attention in his works, from early articles such as *Metaphysik und Geschichte* to *The Absoluteness of Christianity* and finally *Der Historismus und seine Probleme*[80]. His teleological world-view was not affected by the insight that he was mistaken by believing that a historical comparison of the world religions could lead to the conclusion that Christianity possesses an absolute validity. The contrast between the 1902 and 1923 essays on the place of Christianity among the other religions should, therefore, not be overestimated. Troeltsch always realized that all religions and all historical realities ultimately provide from the same source and will return to the same goal.

V. ERNST TROELTSCH AND THE PLURALIST THEOLOGY OF RELIGIONS

In this concluding section we want to make a brief comparison between Troeltsch and the major representatives of the so-called 'pluralist theology of religions', and hereby try to answer the question raised in the title of our contribution.

Historically speaking, Troeltsch can hardly be called a pluralist, because "antirationalistic individualism and pluralism"[81] were precisely the characteristics of historicism, the movement he reacted against. For them the historical method had become an ideology, and they rejected all attempts to structure the historical reality by means of aprioristic philosophical constructions. In the course of his theological formation, Troeltsch had come to realize that a historical study of religions was a

---

80. We join those interpreters of Troeltsch who rather stress the unity of his oeuvre instead of focusing on the supposed rupture of his move to Berlin. See also the articles by G.W. REITSEMA, *Einheit und Zusammenhang im Denken von Ernst Troeltsch*, in *NZSTRP* 17 (1975) 1-8, and G. BECKER, *Neuzeitliches Selbstverständnis und Religionsphilosophie: Ein Versuch zur Troeltsch-Interpretation*, in *NZSTRP* 24 (1982) 21-36. Among other commentators who have considered Troeltsch's constant attention to 'history *and* metaphysics' as the unifying factor of his thought, see especially DRESCHER, *Das Problem der Geschichte bei Ernst Troeltsch*, in *ZTK* 57 (1960) 186-230, an article based on his 1957 dissertation *Glaube und Vernunft bei Ernst Troeltsch: Eine kritische Deutung seiner religionsphilosophischen Grundlegung*. But already in 1920, the German professor of metaphysics, Peter Wust, dedicated half of a chapter of his *Zur Auferstehung der Metaphysik* (*GW*, 1), Münster, 1963, to Troeltsch's metaphysical insights (*ibid.*, pp. 275-311). Immediately after World War I, a memorable conversation with Troeltsch was the occasion for Wust to write this book. Reflecting on the defeat of the Germans, Troeltsch would have said: "If you want to do something for the recovery of our people, you have to return to the ancient faith of our fathers and to plead in philosophy for a return to metaphysics against the weary scepticism of an unfruitful epistemology" (*ibid.*, p. 9).
81. *GS* III, p. 123.

necessity, and he would remain faithful to the historical method for the rest of his lifetime. But he believed that it was equally important, in order to act morally and responsibly as historical beings, to have a certain idea of the ultimate goal of history. Against Hegel, who wanted concrete history to affirm his aprioristic idea of the absolute, he believed that all values as well as the main direction of history could be derived from history itself. By the time of *The Absoluteness of Christianity* and the revision of this essay in 1912, he was still convinced that the absolute goal was the personal God of Christianity. In his later works, this identification was judged to be the expression of a European cultural hegemonism, and in *The Place of Christianity among the World Religions,* Troeltsch spoke in more abstract terms about "the Divine Life". He, however, never retracted his conviction of the necessity of a metaphysical belief. Therefore, his construction of a 'metaphysics of history' represents a middle position between the Hegelian 'metaphysics of the absolute', or, between the more classical supernaturalistic belief in the absoluteness of Christianity, and the anti-metaphysical relativism and pluralism of the movement of historicism.

On the other hand, the question may be raised whether the pluralism of pluralist theologians like Hick and Knitter is the same as the pluralism of historicism. The pluralism of the pluralist theology of religions is certainly not characterized by the absence of metaphysical interest. On the contrary, these theologians are interested in other religions because they believe that it is impossible to say something relevant about God without taking into account the religious insights and experiences of other religious traditions[82]. Therefore, Hick's hypothesis that the religious traditions are "in contact with the same ultimate reality", which is, however, experienced differently according to their respective cultures[83], sounds very similar to the late Troeltsch, who was equally convinced of the strong relation between religion and culture, but spoke at the same time about the one "divine Life" as the ultimate source and goal of all religions. Equally pregnant with metaphysics is Hick's prognosis about the future of the history of religions:

> Beyond this the ultimate unity of faiths will be an eschatological unity in which each is both fulfilled and transcended – fulfilled in so far as it is true, transcended in so far as it is less than the whole truth. And indeed even

---

82. Compare the account of the "emerging pluralist epistemology" in T. MERRIGAN, *Religious Knowledge in the Pluralist Theology of Religions*, in TS 58 (1997) 686-707, especially the first section about the "evolutionary character of religious knowledge", pp. 688-693.

83. HICK, *God and the Universe of Faiths*, Basingstoke, 1973, p. 146.

such fulfilling must be a transcending; for the function of a religion is to bring us to a right relationship with the ultimate divine reality, to awareness of our true nature and our place in the Whole, into the presence of God[84].

The second presupposition of interreligious dialogue, as formulated by Paul Knitter, also deserves to be compared with Troeltsch. "Dialogue must be based on the recognition of the possible truth in all religions; the ability to recognize this truth must be grounded in the hypothesis of a common ground and goal for all religions"[85]. This common ground and goal, for Knitter as for Troeltsch, is the ultimate reality itself, God.

Therefore, we believe that, despite Troeltsch's aversion to the pluralism of the representatives of *Der Historismus*, it is valid to compare his insights with those of the religious pluralists of our time. Perhaps the latter will then appear less original than they are sometimes believed to be. We will now point to some other similarities.

Although neither in the 1902 study, nor in his reconsideration of this essay in 1923, is the central theme Christology, there are enough indications of Troeltsch's enormous esteem for Jesus as a human person. On the other hand, however, it is clear for him that the christological doctrine of institutional Christianity has for the greater part been construed for apologetical reasons. Institutional Christianity forged these doctrines as "its first and strongest coat of armor" by which it was able to convince its adherents that Jesus Christ had offered to humankind the perfect and definitive knowledge of God[86]. Therefore, the incarnation is called by Troeltsch an "archetypal miracle"[87]. Troeltsch's criticism of the doctrine of the incarnation resonates in *The Myth of God Incarnate*, edited by J. Hick, and in *The Metaphor of God Incarnate*, a monograph by the same author[88].

Near the end of *The Absoluteness of Christianity,* Troeltsch sees the most important reason to continue considering Christianity as the highest religion to be the fact that Jesus, in his preaching, was concentrating on "the one thing that was needful", namely, the "higher world of the Kingdom of God"[89]. "Only in the complete individualization and humanization of religion – as was the case in Jesus' own faith and experience and in his challenge to the soul – and in the radical separation of the higher, eternal, and necessary world from the earthly and transitory, does there exist the

---

84. *Ibid.*, p. 147.
85. KNITTER, *No Other Name?* (n. 12), p. 208.
86. *Absoluteness*, p. 58.
87. *Ibid.*, p. 60.
88. HICK (ed.), *The Myth of God Incarnate*, London, 1977, and *The Metaphor of God Incarnate,* London, 1993.
89. *Absoluteness*, p. 145.

absoluteness which the church transformed into definite faith-propositions but which, for Jesus, was simply included in reality itself. Whatever role messianism may have played in his preaching, by and large the person of Christ retired behind this reality – the Kingdom of God"[90]. Especially in the last phrase, Hick's famous Copernical revolution from Christo-centrism to Theocentrism is clearly prefigured[91].

In *The Absoluteness of Christianity* Troeltsch not only holds that "Christianity remains *the* great revelation of God to men", but he imme-diately goes on by stating that "the other religions, with all the power they possess for lifting men above guilt, grief, and earthly life, are likewise revelations of God"[92]. And, although he acknowledges that the religious conviction is characterized by a certain "naïve absoluteness", he implores Christians not "to buttress their faith in such a way as to establish an impassible gulf between it and all other faiths or to deny the salvation that others have received". The efforts of the adherents of the pluralist theology of religions can likewise be characterized as a crusade against a modified version of the old adagium "Extra ecclesiam nulla salus".

Troeltsch's opinion with regard to the relations between Christianity and the other religions at this stage of his thinking is admittedly more inclusivistic than pluralistic. It is the task of the Christian "to lead others to the higher clarity of the salvation he knows", and to "leave to Jesus the disclosure and consummation of the salvation of the future"[93]. In *The Place of Christianity Among the World Religions*, however, there are no more traces of this inclusivism. All the great world religions have the duty "to increase in depth and purity by means of their own interior impulses", and mutual contact between Christianity and the other reli-gious traditions can be helpful in this respect, "to them as to us"[94].

A last point of comparison. At the end of *No Other Name?* Knitter makes a strong plea for "doing before knowing"[95], for accepting the challenge of the interreligious dialogue before all theoretical obstacles are removed. But this is equally the case in the works of Ernst Troeltsch. When, in *The Absoluteness of Christianity*, Troeltsch discusses the

---

90. *Ibid.*
91. Compare HICK, *God* (n. 83), chapter 9: "The Copernican Revolution in Theol-ogy". When Troeltsch, in the last chapter of *The Absoluteness of Christianity,* speaks about the transformation of naïve speaking about Christianity's absoluteness into the sci-entific one, he uses the same metaphor: "This transformation of the naïve world view into the scientific one has made the earth revolve around the sun and the sun around invis-ible galaxies" (*Absoluteness*, p. 133).
92. *Absoluteness*, p. 126.
93. *Ibid.*, p. 162.
94. *Place*, p. 88.
95. KNITTER, *No Other Name?* (n. 12), p. 205.

method of establishing a criterion according to which the different religions are to be ranked, he insists that this deliberation must not be restricted to "a few European scholars and savants". On the contrary, this activity must be effected "in ever widening circles and in actual confrontation between religions. Here judgments that seem pleasing in theory will have to prove themselves in practice"[96]. Troeltsch's views concerning the common object of genuine religious experience, the differences between Jesus' proclamation of God and the Church's proclamation of Jesus, the salvific value of all religions, and the importance of a praxis-oriented interreligious dialogue make him a forerunner of the pluralist theology of religions.

Faculty of Theology   Peter DE MEY
Katholieke Universiteit Leuven   Research Fellow N.F.S.R.
Sint-Michielsstraat 6
B-3000 Leuven

96. *Absoluteness*, p. 97.

CHRISTOLOGY AFTER THE HOLOCAUST

Some in the Christian community may find the title of my essay somewhat strange. What possible connection can there be between Christology and the Holocaust? My response in the first instance is that of Johannes Metz who has insisted, quite rightly I believe, that the Holocaust affects all theological perceptions, not only the theology of the Christian-Jewish relationship. Metz proposes three theses as indispensable for theological reflections in the post-Holocaust era: (1) "Christian theology after Auschwitz must...be guided by the insight that Christians can form and sufficiently understand their identity only in the face of Jews"; (2) "Because of Auschwitz, the statement, 'Christians can only form and appropriately understand their identity in the face of the Jews' has been sharpened as follows: 'Christians can protect their identity only in front of and together with the history of the beliefs of the Jews'"; and (3) "Christian theology after Auschwitz must stress anew the Jewish dimension in Christian beliefs and must overcome the forced blocking out of the Jewish heritage within Chrisitanity"[1].

And doing theology "in the face of the Jews" after the Holocaust, as Metz suggests, means understanding how Jews identify themselves today. There is little doubt that the Holocaust has come to serve as a central point of identity for many, if not most, Jews today despite many disagreements about its ultimate theological implications. And so a Christology developed in the light of Metz's theses cannot ignore the Holocaust as a pivotal reality.

What then might be an appropriate Christological response to the challenge of the Holocaust? I would begin negatively in a way. The first implication is that the Holocaust has made it immoral for Christians to maintain any Christology that is excessively triumphalistic or that finds the significance of the Christ Event in the displacement of the Jewish People from an ongoing covenantal relationship with God. Such "displacement Christologies", deeply rooted in the patristic tradition and dominant in the Church's Christological consciousness until Vatican II, can no longer be regarded as authentic Christology either in academic theology or as a framework for Christian liturgy. Chapter four of *Nostra*

---

1. J.B. METZ, *Facing the Jews: Christian Theology After Auschwitz*, in E. SCHÜSSLER FIORENZA and D. TRACY (eds.), *The Holocaust as Interruption* (*Concilium*, 175), Edinburgh, T. & T. Clark, 1984, pp. 43-52.

Aetate, in insisting that there exists no basis for the notion of Jewish collective responsibility for the death of Christ, totally undercut the basis of
such a Christological approach. Gregory Baum put the Holocaust's fundamental challenge to Christology very well when he wrote some years
ago that

> Auschwitz...is an altogether special sign of the times, in which God
> empowers the Church to correct its past teaching, *including its central
> dogma*, to the extent that it distorts God's action in Christ and promotes
> human destruction.... The Holocaust acted out the Church's fantasy that
> the Jews were a non-people, that they had no place before God and that
> they should have disappeared long ago by accepting Christ. The Church is
> now summoned to a radical reformulation of its faith, free of ideological
> deformation, making God's act in Christ fully and without reserve a mes-
> sage for life rather than death[2].

Another critical dimension of a post-Holocaust Christology surely
involves recapturing Jesus' Jewish roots. The "Aryanization" of Jesus
that occurred in the writings of some German biblical scholars during
the Nazi period coupled with the general theology of Jewish displacement from the covenant by the Church widespread in Christian theology
since the Patristic era clearly contributed to Christian complicity with
the Nazis. So the process begun by scholars such as Charlesworth, Sal-
darini, Thoma, Lohfink and others after the Holocaust remains a moral
imperative.

But a post-Holocaust Christology that would concentrate exclusively
on overcoming classical Christian displacement theology regarding Jews
and Judaism, while important, is ultimately insufficient. Hence my critique of scholars such as Paul van Buren who, through contributing
immensely to the rethinking of Christology in the post-Holocaust period,
cannot e considered a true post-Holocaust theologian in the final analysis. For the Holocaust was not merely the final and most ghastly chapter
in the long history of Christian anti-Semitism. Though closely connected
with that tradition in terms of popular support for the Nazi attack on the
Hews and definitely the inspiration for some of the Nazi legislation
affecting the Jewish community, the Holocaust was the result of a constellation of modern ideologies that went far beyond classical Christian
anti-Semitism.

In the final analysis, the Holocaust marked a response, albeit a highly
destructive one, to a new level of human self-awareness. The Nazis perceived that basic changes were underway in human consciousness. The

---

2. G. BAUM, *Catholic Dogma after Auschwitz*, in A. DAVIES (ed.), *Antisemitism and
the Foundations of Christianity*, New York, Paulist, 1979, p.142.

impact of the new science and technology, with their underlying assumption of freedom, was beginning to provide the human community on a mass scale with a Promethean-type experience of escape from prior moral chains. People were starting to realize, however dimly, an enhanced sense of dignity and autonomy far more extensive than most of Western Christian theology had previously conceded. Traditional theological concepts that had shaped much of the Christian moral perspective, notions such a s divine punishment, hell, divine wrath, and providence, were losing some of the hold they had exercised over moral decision making since biblical times. Christian theology had tended to accentuate the omnipotence of God which in turn intensified the impotence of the human person and the rather inconsequential role played by the human community in maintaining the sustainability of the earth. The Nazis totally rejected this previous relationship. In fact, they were literally trying to turn it on its head.

The Holocaust thus inaugurated the beginning of a new ear in human possibility over which hung the specter of either unprecedented destruction or unparalleled hope. With the rise of Nazism, the mass extermination of human life in a guiltless fashion became thinkable and technologically feasible. The door was now ajar for an era when dispassionate torture and the murder of millions could become not merely the act of a crazed despot, not just a desire for national security, not merely an irrational outbreak of xenophobic fear, but a calculated effort to reshape history supported by an intellectual argumentation from the best and brightest minds in a society. It was an attempt, Emil Fackenheim has said, to wipe out the "divine image" in history. "The murder camp", Fackenheim insists, "was not an accidental by-product of the Nazi Empire. It was its essence".

What emerges as a central reality from the study of the Holocaust is the Nazi effort to create the "superperson", to develop a truly liberated humanity, to be shared in only by a select group, namely, the Aryan race. This new humanity would be released from the moral restraints previously imposed by religious beliefs and would be capable of exerting virtually unlimited power in the shaping of the world and its inhabitants. In a somewhat indirect, though still powerful way, the Nazis had proclaimed the death of God as a guiding force in the governance of the universe. The respected Holocaust historian George Mosse confirms this dimension of Nazism when he writes:

> The comparisons between German fascism and its counterparts in other Western European nations are highly instructive, for they demonstrate that though fascism had spread throughout Europe, the German variety came to

be unique. It was unique not only in the way it managed to displace the revolutionary impetus, but also in the primacy of the ideology of the *Volk*, nature and race. The revolutionary impetus produced an ideological reaction throughout the continent, but the German crisis was *sui generis*, besides being more deeply rooted in the national fabric. Nowhere else was the ideology planted so deep or for such a long time. Nowhere else was the fascist dynamic embedded in such an effective ideology[3].

In pursuit of their objective, the Nazis became convinced that all the "dregs of humanity" had to be eliminated or at least their influence on culture and human development significantly curtailed. The Jews fell into this "dregs" category first and foremost. They were classified as "vermin". The Nazis could not envision even a minimally useful role for Jews in the new society to which they planned to give birth. In addition, there existed a "sacral" mandate for persecuting Jews which did not obtain for other victim groups. While there may be some parallels for the Gypsy community, there is still a formidable difference between the two groups in this regard. While not endorsing Richard Rubenstein's use of the term "holy war" to describe the attack on the Jews, he is nonetheless quite correct in highlighting the "sacral" dimension of the attack on the Jews as a unique element[4].

In stressing the special nature of the attack on the Jews, however, we should not lose sight of the other Nazi victims. New research is beginning to suggest a closer affinity between the Hews and other groups especially Poles, the Roma and Sinti (Gypsies), the disabled and to a degree gay victims[5]. Evidence has now surfaced that Nazi leaders such as Hitler, Himmler and General Hans Frank entertained the idea of total extermination, not merely subjugation, of Poles at some future date[6]. But

3. G.L. Mosse, *The Crisis of German Ideology*, New York, Grosset & Dunlop, 1964, p. 315.

4. Cf. B. Rogers Rubenstein and M. Berenbaum (eds.), *What Kind of God: Essays in Honor of Richard L. Rubenstein* (Studies in the Shoah, vol. 11) Lanham, MD, University Press of America, 1995. Also cf. R.L. Rubenstein, *Holy Wars and Ethnic Cleansing: Report of Research in Progress*, in H. Knight and M. Sachs Littell (eds.) *The Uses and Abuses of Knowledge*, (Studies in the Shoah, vol. 17), Lanham, MD, New York and London, University Press of America, 1997, pp. 349-378.

5. Cf. M. Berenbaum (ed.), *A Mosaic of Victims: Non-Jews Persecuted and Murdered by the Nazis*, New York and London, New York University Press, 1990; R.C. Lukas, *Forgotten Holocaust: The Poles Under German Occupation 1939-1944* (Revised Edition), New York, Hippocrene, 1997; H. Friedlander, *The Origins of Nazi Genocide: From Euthanasia to the Final Solution*, Chapel Hill, NC, University of North Carolina Press, 1995; G. Grau, *Hidden Holocaust? Gay and Lesbian Persecution in Germany, 1933-1945*, with a contribution by C. Schoppmann, London and New York, Cassell, 1995.

6. Cf. J. Gumkowski and K. Leszczynski, *Poland Under Nazi Occupation*, Warsaw, Polonia Publishing House, 1961, p.59; and K. Pospieszalski, *Polska pod Niemieckim Prawem*, Posnan, Wyoawnictwo Instytutt ackodniego, 1946, p.189.

the mass extermination of the Jews became a reality and we should not blur the distinction between fact and possibility. Nonetheless, the extermination or subjugation of the other victim groups under the rubric of humankind's ultimate purification assumes important theological significance. Regrettably the non-Jewish victims are generally ignored in most of the theological reflections on the Holocaust to date, whether by Christian or by Jewish scholars[7].

The late Uriel Tal captured as well as anyone the basic theological challenge presented by the Holocaust. In his understanding the so-called Final Solution had as its ultimate objective the total transformation of human values. Its stated intent was liberating humanity from all previous moral ideals and codes. When the liberating process was complete, humanity once and for all would be rescued from the imprisonment of a God concept and its related notions of moral responsibility, redemption, sin, an revelation. Nazi ideology sought to transform theological ideas into exclusively anthropological and political concepts. In Tal's interpretation of the Holocaust, for the Nazis, "God becomes man in a political sense as a member of the Aryan race whose highest representative on earth is the Fuhrer"[8].

Tal's research led him to conclude that this new Nazi consciousness emerged only gradually in the decades following World War I. Its roots, however, were somewhat earlier. It was undeniably related to the general process of social secularization that had been transforming Germany since the latter part of the nineteenth century. Its philosophic parents included the deists, the French encyclopedists, Feuerbach, the Young Hegelians, and the evolutionary thinkers in concert with the developing corps of scientists who through their many new discoveries were creating the impression that a triumphant material civilization was on the verge of dawning in Western Europe. In the end, Tal argued, "these intellectual and social movements struck a responsive chord in a rebellious generation, altered the traditional views of God, man, and society, and ultimately led to the pseudo-religious, pseudomessianic movement of Nazism"[9]. To Tal's list I would join Professor Rivka Schechter in adding the name of Nietzsche. Schechter writes that

7. Cf. J.T. PAWLIKOWSKI, *Uniqueness and Universality in the Holocaust: Some Ethical Reflections*, in L. BENNETT ELDER, D.L. BARR and E. STRUTHERS MALBON, (eds.), Atlanta, GA, Scholars Press, 1996, pp. 275-289.

8. U. TAL, *Forms of Pseudo-Religion in the German* Kulture-bereich *Prior to the Holocaust*, in *Immanuel* 3 (1973-74), p. 6.

9. U. TAL, *Christians and Jews in Germany: Religion, Politics and Ideology in the Second Reich 1870-1914*, Ithaca, NY, Cornell University Press, 1975, pp. 302-303.

> Nietzsche was the ideologist of the Third Reich, even though he spoke in the name of European culture. All the later German ideologists drew from Nietzsche the dormant destructive passions which were wakened by him. For them Neitzsche's master-race was concretized in the German people[10].

Michael Ryan, looking at Nazism through a more explicitly theological lens than Tal, comes to somewhat similar conclusions. Working from an analysis of *Mein Kampf*, Ryan insists that the most striking dimension of the "salvation history" found in Hitler's thought was his willingness to confine humanity in an absolute manner to a time-bound existence. In the Hitlerian perspective, humankind must resign itself to the conditions of finitude. But this resignation is accompanied by the assertion of all-pervasive power for itself within those conditions. The end result of all this was the self-deification of Hitler who proclaimed himself the new "Savior" of the German nation. It is this Hitlerian mind-set that allows us, in Ryan's judgment, to term *Mein Kampf* a "theological" treatise. In the final analysis, in Ryan's words, Hitler's worldview "amounted to the deliberate decision on the part of mass man to live within the limits of finitude without either the moral restraints or the hopes of traditional religion – in this case, Christianity"[11].

In light of the ideological dimensions of the Holocaust, including its pseudo-messianic aspects uncovered by scholars such as Tal and Ryan, the response to our original question of "Why the Holocaust" in a discussion of Christology should now be clear. If Christology involves Messianism, if Christology involves an understanding of the divine-human encounter and its implications for human responsibility, as it does, then the challenge the Holocaust presents in these areas cannot be ignored.

What then might be an appropriate Christological response to the challenge of the Holocaust? At his stage I would say that at least two responses must be considered. They can be classified as (1) a Christology of divine vulnerability and (2) a Christology of witness. These two Christological approaches, which have many particular shadings, are not, it needs emphasizing, mutually exclusive. As I shall shortly explain, it is my growing conviction that both are required responses in light of the Holocaust.

Initial efforts at reflecting on the implications of the Holocaust for Christology led some theologians to emphasize a connection between

---

10. R. SCHECHTER, *A Cosmic Enemy*, Tel Aviv, Acksav, 1979, p. 47 (in Hebrew).

11. Cf. M. RYAN, *Hitler's Challenge to the Churches: A Theological-Political Analysis of* Mein Kampf, in F.H. LITTEL and H.G. LOCKE (eds.), *The German Church Struggle and the Holocaust*, Detroit, Wayne State University Press, 1974, pp. 160-161.

Jesus' suffering on Calvary and the suffering endured by the Jewish people over the centuries, especially under the Nazis. Franklin Sherman, for example, sees in the cross of Christ "the symbol of the agonizing God". The only legitimate Christology for Sherman after the Holocaust is one rooted in a perspective that vies the Christ Event as a further enhancement of divine participation in the sufferings of a people who are in turn summoned to take part in the sufferings of God. This theological outlook, first expressed in the prophetic tradition (especially by Jeremiah) and reaffirmed in Jewish scholarship by Abraham Heschel, should make Christians the first to identify with the sufferings of the Jewish people, especially during the Holocaust. For Sherman, Christ crucified becomes the symbol of the agonizing God. Sherman laments the fact that this symbol of the cross has become such a source of division, rather than reconciliation, between Jews and Christians throughout history. For, in fact, the cross points to a very Jewish reality – suffering and martyrdom – and should serve as a source of new unity between Christians and Jews"[12].

The Israeli Catholic scholar Marcel Dubois, O.P., interprets the meaning of Christology in the face of the Holocaust in ways that parallel the thought of Sherman. Dubois is acutely aware of the difficulty Christians confront in setting the reality of the Holocaust within the context of a theology of the cross. He likewise acknowledges that such a linkage may appear as obscenity to many Jews whose sufferings during the Holocaust the Church helped to perpetrate. Yet, despite these difficulties, Dubois remains convinced it is the direction in which Christian theology is compelled to move:

> In the person of the suffering servant there appears to take place an effable change. Our vision of Jewish destiny and our understanding of the Holocaust in particular depend on our compassion; the Calvary of the Jewish people, whose summit is the Holocaust, can help us to understand a little better the mystery of the Cross[13].

Dubois also picks up on Sherman's notion of Jewish-Christian unity in light of the Holocaust. From a faith perspective, Dubois argues, the Christian can truly affirm that Jesus fulfills Israel in her destiny of Suffering Servant and that Israel, in her experience of solitude and anguish, answers and represents without knowing it the mystery of the Passion and the Cross. The challenge of the massive human annihilation which the Holocaust ushered in stands before Jews and Christians:

---

12. F.S. SHERMAN, *Speaking of God after Auschwitz*, in *Worldview* 17 (1974) 29. Also cf. Sherman's essay on the same theme in P.D. OPSAHL and M.H. TANENBAUM (eds.), *Speaking of God Today*, Philadelphia, PA, Fortress, 1974.

13. M. DUBOIS, *Christian Reflections on the Holocaust*, in *SIDIC* 7 (1974), p. 15.

They have learnt to be united in compassion; they must now learn to be united in hope, the hope of the people that believes in the victory of life and in the fidelity of God[14].

Another prominent scholar in the Christian-Jewish dialogue, Clemens Thoma, has also briefly addressed the question of Christology and the Holocaust, following a path reminiscent of Sherman and Dubois. He views the Holocaust as anchored in an anti-Semitic ideology that was at root anti-Christian as well. Hence Christian responsibility for the Holocaust cannot be argued indiscriminately, though Thoma does not hesitate to acknowledge that Christian contempt for the Jews greatly facilitated the success of the "final Solution". His equation of Jesus' suffering and that of the Jews seems even stronger than the linkage posited by Sherman and Dubois. He writes:

> ...a believing Christian should not find it so very difficult to interpret the sacrifice of the Jews during the Nazi terror. His thoughts should be turned toward Christ to whom these Jewish masses became alike, in sorrow and death. Auschwitz is the most monumental sign of our time for the intimate bond and unity between Jewish martyrs – who stand for all Jews – and the crucified Christ, even though the Jews in question could not be aware of it[15].

This note of a nexus in suffering between Jews and Christians through the Cross is sounded as well by Douglas John Hall. His reflections on the Nazi period have left him convinced that only a theology of the cross can express the thorough meaning of the Incarnation today. Only such an approach to Christology establishes the authentic divine-human link implied in the Word becoming flesh by highlighting the solidarity of God with suffering humanity. Such a Christological direction results in a soteriology of solidarity which sets up the Cross of Jesus as a point of fraternal union with the Jewish people, as well as with all who seek liberation and peace.

For Hall, as for the other theologians we have examined, Jesus becomes a potential source of union rather than exclusion between Jews and Christians in the post Holocaust era. In his view

> the faith of Israel is incomprehensible unless one sees at its heart a suffering God whose solidarity with humanity is so abysmal that the "cross in the heart of God" (H. Wheeler Robinson) must always be incarnating itself in history. Reading the words of Elie Wiesel, one knows, as a Christian, that he bears this indelible resemblance to the people of Israel[16].

14. *Ibid.*, p. 15.
15. C. THOMA, *A Christian Theology of Judaism*, New York, Paulist, 1977, p. 159; also cf. p. 3.
16. D. HALL, *Rethinking Christ*, in A.T. DAVIES (ed.), *Antisemitism and the Foundations of Christianity*, New York, Paulist Press, 1979, p. 183. Also cf. D.J. HALL, *God and*

Sherman, Dubois, Thoma and Hall must be said to have only skimmed the surface in terms of assessing the Holocaust's impact on Christology. The most substantive effort to date is to be found in the writings of Jürgen Moltmann. Moltmann's reflections on this question began after a visit to the Maidanek concentration camp near Lublin, Poland. As he started to wrestle with the implications of his visit to the camp, he found strength in the closing words of Elie Wiesel's book *Night*: "Where is God?....He hangs there from the gallows...". From there Moltmann goes on to interpret the Holocaust as the most dramatic revelation thus far of the basic meaning of the Christ Event: God can save people, including Israel, because through the Cross he participated in their very suffering. To theologize after the Holocaust would prove a futile enterprise in Moltmann's view,

> were not the *Sh'ma Israel* and the Lord's Prayer prayed in Auschwitz itself, were not God himself in Auschwitz, suffering with the martyred and murdered. Every other answer would be blasphemy. An absolute God would make us indifferent. The God of action and success would let us forget the dead, which we still cannot forget. God as nothingness would make the entire world into a concentration camp[17].

What emerges for Moltmann from the experience of the Holocaust is a "theology of divine vulnerability" which has roots in Abraham Heschel's notion of *divine pathos*. He also argues that the idea of the suffering of God as the basic divine redemptive activity is consonant with rabbinic theology of the first century:

> The God who suffers in exile with Israel preserves the people from despair and fear. The realization of God's fellow-suffering impedes apathy, maintains sympathy for God in life, and holds hope for the future of God open[18].

Moltmann adds that in rabbinic theology it is claimed that this suffering on the part of God is something he experiences at the very core of his being. God is not merely present where people are suffering; that suffering directly affects God. As Moltmann puts it, "God is not only involved in history; history is in God himself"[19].

These Christian theological efforts at linking Jesus' suffering on the Cross with that of the Jews during the Holocaust have met with critical reaction in some quarters. I myself have some questions about its

Human Suffering: An Exercise in the Theology of the Cross, Minneapolis, MN, Augsburg, 1986 and *Professing the Faith: Christian Theology in a North American Context*, Minneapolis, MN, Fortress, 1993.

17. J. MOLTMANN, *The Crucified God*, in *Theology Today* 32 (1974) 9. Also cf. *Jesus Christ for Today's World*, Minneapolis, MN, Fortress, 1993.

18. J. MOLTMANN, *The Crucified God*, in *Theology Today* 32 (1974) 13.

19. *Ibid.*, p. 13.

appropriateness as the Jews during the Holocaust have met with critical reaction in some quarters. I myself have some questions about its appropriateness as *the* Christological response to the Holocaust. For one, it tends to ignore Christian complicity in the suffering during the Holocaust. From a more theological perspective, the Cross has always been described as a voluntary act on the part of God and Christ; the Cross can be understood in a redemptive fashion when seen as the culmination and the consequence of Jesus' active ministry. The Holocaust was neither voluntary nor redemptive in any sense.

A. Roy Eckardt has been one of the strongest critics of Moltmann's Christology in light of the Holocaust. For him there is no way we can honestly assert that millions of Jews were liberated from death or from any other suffering through the Crucifixion. It approaches blasphemy to make such a claim in light of Christian involvement with Nazism. "What does it mean", he asks, "to tell the inmates of Buchenwald or Bergen-Belsen, as this Christian theologian does, that through his suffering and death, the risen Christ brings righteousness and life to the unrighteous and the dying?"[20]. For Eckardt, Moltmann simply claims too much for the sufferings of Christ. He also expresses concern that a Christology of "divine vulnerability" will lead to an exaggerated emphasis on weakness and divine protection whereas Jewish post-Holocaust theologians have emphasized the need for the judicious use of human power after the Holocaust.

Other criticisms have come from scholars such as Francis Fiorenza (who argues for a concomitant stress on Jesus' resurrection) and from Jewish scholar Eugene Borowitz. Moltmann's theology of divine vulnerability would also likely encounter some opposition from liberationist theologians, though Douglas Hall, who has sympathy for that perspective, also exhibits positive regard for Moltmann's Cross theology.

In my judgment the criticisms of Moltmann by Echardt and others are considerably overdrawn. A Christology of the Cross is a meaningful response to the Holocaust, at least in terms of the notion of divine vulnerability if it is integrated into a larger whole.

Any adequate Christology after the Holocaust must be directly related to more fundamental discussions about God in light of this experience. It must be related to the ideological and theological dimensions of the Holocaust as uncovered by scholars such as Tal and Ryan. For me, the Holocaust has destroyed simplistic notions of a "commanding", all

---

20. A.R. ECKARDT, *Christians and Jews: Along a Theological Frontier*, in *Encounter* 40 (Spring 1979) 102.

powerful God. But equally it has exposed our desperate need to retain a "compelling" God, *compelling* because we have experienced through symbolic encounter with this God a healing, a strengthening, an affirming that buries any need to assert our humanity through the destructive, even deathly, use of human power[21]. As Vaclav Havel has noted, "as soon as man began considering himself the source of everything, the world began to lose its human dimension, and man began to lose control of it"[22]. But it is a God to whom we are drawn, rather than a God who imposes on us.

Understanding the ministry of Jesus as emerging from the heightened sense of divine-human intimacy that surfaced in Second Temple Judaism[23] Christological statements made by the Church in reflection on that ministry can be seen as attempts to articulate a new sense of how profoundly humanity is imbedded in divinity. The ultimate significance of Christology so understood lies in its revelation of the grandeur of the human as a necessary corrective to the demeaning paternalism that often characterized the sense of the divine-human relationship in the past. In this sense a major component of all authentic Christology is theological anthropology. Martin Luther understood this in *The Freedom of the Christian Man*. And Gregory Baum has stressed that in his first papal encyclical Pope John Paul II presented human dignity as integral to Christological doctrine[24].

In my view the fear and paternalism associated in the past with the statement of the divine-human relationship were at least partially responsible for the attempt by the Nazis to produce a total reversal of human meaning, as Tal has described it. Incarnational Christology can help the human person understand that he or she shares in the very life and existence of God. The human person remains creature; the gulf between humanity in people and humanity in the Godhead remains formidable. But it is also clear that a direct link exists; the two humanities can touch. The human struggle for self-identity vis-à-vis the Creator God, the source of the misuse of human power in the past, has come to an end in principle, though its full realization still lies ahead. In this sense we can truly affirm that Christ continues to bring humankind salvation in it root

21. Cf. J.T. PAWLIKOWSKI, *The Holocaust: Its Impact on Christian Thought and Ethics*, in ROCHELLE L. MILLEN (ed.) *New Perspectives on the Holocaust*, New York and London, New York University Press, 1996, pp. 344-361.

22. V. HAVEL, *Disturbing the Peace: A Conversation with Karel Hvizdala*, translated with an introduction by P. Wilson, New York, Alfred A. Knopf, 1990, p. 11.

23. Cf. J.T. PAWLIKOWSKI, *Jesus and the Theology of Israel*, Wilmington, DC, Michael Glazier, 1989.

24. G. BAUM, *The First Papal Encyclical*, in *The Ecumenist* 17 (1979) 55.

meaning-inciple, though its full realization still lies ahead. In this sense we can truly affirm that Christ continues to bring humankind salvation in it root meaning-*wholeness*.

With a proper understanding of the meaning of the Christ Event men and women can be healed, they can finally overcome the primal sin, the desire to supplant the Creator in power and in status that lay at the heart of the Holocaust. Critical to this awareness is the sense of God's self-imposed limitation, God's vulnerability, manifested in the cross. This is where Moltmann's theology can make a significant contribution. The notion of "divine vulnerability" can become a powerful Christological symbol[25] to remind us that one need not exercise power, control and dominance to be "godly". It also shows that God is simply not desirous of absorbing humanity totally back into divine being, but rather affirming its eternal distinctiveness. That is the ultimate message of the resurrection, rather than the triumphalistic interpretations given the event which A. Roy Eckardt and others have rightly criticized in light of the Holocaust. Douglas Hall takes a position in the same vein when he writes that

> Whatever emphasis may be called for in the context where faith is *con*-fessed, the *pro*fession of the faith always must entail the courage to affirm the reality of that which negates while at the same time insisting upon the gracious possibility of negating the negation. The profession of faith must do this because precisely the core of that upon which the disciple community meditates is a gospel which declares that the great negation by which creaturely life is continuously threatened has been entered into and is being overcome by a God who, by personally submitting to the aboriginal Nothingness, nullifies its power over us[26].

But let me underline that if the notion of "divine vulnerability" is to serve in the above way it must be disassociated from direct linkages to Jewish sufferings above all, as well as the sufferings of other victims of the Nazis. From a theological perspective Jesus' suffering must be regarded as voluntary and redeeming. No such claim can be made in good conscience for the sufferings endured by Nazi victims. And on the human level, it is difficult to compare the depth of sufferings endured by the Gypsies, Poles, the disabled, gays, and others with that of Jesus, as painful as his sufferings no doubt were. What I am claiming is that the Holocaust represents at one and the same time the ultimate expression of

25. On Christological symbols and the Holocaust, cf. Z. AMISHAI-MAISELS, *Christological Symbolism of the Holocaust*, in *Holocaust and Genocide Studies* 3 (1988) 457-481.

26. D.J. HALL, *Professing the Faith: Christian Theology in a North American Context*, Minneapolis, MN, Fortress, 1993, p. 79.

human freedom and evil – the two are intimately linked. The ultimate assertion of human freedom from God in our time that the Holocaust represents may in fact prove the beginning of the final resolution of the conflict between freedom and evil. When humanity finally recognizes the destruction it can produce in totally rejecting dependence on its Creator, as it did in the Holocaust, when it perceives that such rejection is a perversion and not an affirmation of human freedom, a new stage in human consciousness may be dawning. We may finally be coming to grips with evil at its roots. The power of evil will wane only when humankind develops along with a profound sense of the dignity it enjoys because of its direct links to God a corresponding sense of humility occasioned by a searching encounter with the devastation it is capable of producing when left to its own wits. A sense of profound humility evoked by the experience of the healing power present in the ultimate Creator of human power – this is crucial. On this point of humility as a critical response to the Holocaust I join with Stanley Hauerwas in his reflections on the Holocaust even though we part company on several implications of the event[27].

While the relationship between post-Holocaust human consciousness and Christology remains central to the question at hand, I now recognize that it does not exhaust the issue. Here is where the beginning reflections by several Christian scholars are to the point.

David Tracy and Elizabeth Schüssler-Fiorenza have argued that, while Christian theologians in the modern period have begun to come to grips with historical consciousness, their approach remains inadequate. They insist that Christian theology cannot fully re-enter history until it faces up to the challenge of the Holocaust. Few Christian theologians measure up to this standard. Christian theologians, in their view,

> have developed a theological hermeneutics where the subject matter – the event itself – is once again allowed to rule in theological hermeneutic. They have recognized the *Sach-Kritik* that the eschatological event itself demands. Gut they have too seldom returned to history – the real, concrete thing where events like the Holocaust happen[28].

Johannes Metz is one among several Christian theologians who have taken the Tracy/Schüssler-Fiorenza challenge to heart. Metz has emphasized

27. S. HAUERWAS, *Jews and Christians Among the Nations*, in *Cross Currents* 34 (1981) 34; also cf. *Resurrection, the Holocaust, and Forgiveness: A Sermon for Eastertime*, in H.C. KEE and I.J. BOROWSKY (eds.), Philadelphia, PA, and New York, American Interfaith Institute and Crossroad, 1996, pp. 113-120.

28. E. SCHÜSSLER FIORENZA and D. TRACY, *The Holocaust as Interruption and the Cristian Return Into History*, in E. SCHÜSSLER FIORENZA and D. TRACY (eds.), *The Holocaust as Interruption* (*Concilium*, 175), Edinburgh, T. & T. Clark, 1984, p. 32.

that post-Holocaust Christology needs to have discipleship at its very core. "This kind of Christology", he says

> is not primarily formed in a subjectless concept and system, but in discipleship stories. This kind of Christology does not bear casually, but fundamentally narrative features. This Christology of discipleship stands against a Christianity which interprets itself as a bourgeois religion; it opposes the idea that Christianity is totally at home in the bourgeois world. This Christology of discipleship also stands against that kind of Christianity which considers itself as a kind of religion of victors – with a surplus of answers and a corresponding lack of passionate questions in the being-on-the-way. This Christology of discipleship makes it clear that Christianity, too, ahead of all system knowledge contains a narrative and remembrance knowledge[29].

In his volume *Christian Theology after the Shoah*, James Moore proposes a Christological path that bears similarities to that presented by Metz. He too highlights the importance of narrative Christology in light of the Holocaust. For him the central determinative theme for any authentic Christology of witness must be *resistance* within a general theology of discipleship. The rescuer becomes a prime example of true belief in the message of Christ. Any "redemptive" emphasis in Christology must always "be tied to the historical reality of any point in time, dismissing all efforts to thoroughly spiritualize the notion of redemption"[30].

Elizabeth Schüssler-Fiorenza and Rebecca Chopp, both of whom have concerned themselves with the liberating dimensions of theology, offer general reflections on post-Holocaust faith which carry implications for Christological statements. Schüssler-Fiorenza insists that we cannot speak of the suffering of the victims of the Holocaust as merely "theological metaphor" for all human suffering. Rather, we must name that suffering in its political particularity. "The ideological catchword was 'Untermensch', the less than human, the subhuman being"[31].

Nazism for Schüssler-Fiorenza represented an extreme example of the Western capitalistic form of patriarchy with origins in Aristotelian philosophy and subsequent mediation through Christian theology. The same ancient philosophical system, imported into Christian theology by Thomas Aquinas and others, that first subjugated women as people with

29. J.B. METZ, *Facing the Jews: Christian Theology After Auschwitz*, in E. SCHÜSSLER FIORENZA and D. TRACY (eds.), *The Holocaust as Interruption*, 1984, p. 32.

30. J.F. MOORE, *Christian Theology After the Shoah* (Studies in the Shoah, 7), Lanham, MD, New York and London, University Press of America, 1993, p. 146.

31. E. SCHÜSSLER FIORENZA and D. TRACY, *The Holocaust as Interruption and the Christian Return to History*, in E. SCHÜSSLER FIORENZA and D. TRACY (eds.), *The Holocaust as Interruption,* 1984, p. 86.

a "subhuman" nature combined with religiously rooted bigotry and a new bio-theology to produce the Nazi cataclysm throughout Europe. Overcoming biblical and theological anti-Judaism, so closely identified with classical Christological statements, thus becomes the first step according to Schüssler-Fiorenza in the complicated, rather wrenching process of cleansing Western society of its patriarchal basis.

Rebecca Chopp lays particular stress on the profound connection she perceives between Holocaust literature and liberation theology, a relationship she terms unique among Western religious writings. Both perspectives in her judgment create the need for a fundamental reconceptualization of Christian theology. Christianity is now forced to grapple not merely with individual suffering, but even more with suffering on a mass scale. Liberation theology and Holocaust literature both confront Christian theology with the question "who is the human subject that suffers history?"[32].

Chopp goes on to add that both liberation theology and Holocaust literature force us to understand history not merely in terms of abstract notions of evolution or process but primarily in terms of the suffering realities of that history caused by various forms of human exploitation. The history that now must be the basis of theological reflection is not abstract history, but the history of human victims. And the voices and the memories of the tortured, the forgotten, and the dead must become primary resources for Christian anthropology. And, while Chopp does not explicitly articulate this position, one could surmise that she would identify with the direction taken by Schüssler-Fiorenza, namely, that biblical anti-Judaism with its inevitable dehumanization of concrete Jewish persons opened the way for Jewish suffering in the Holocaust and for the suffering experiences under imperialist colonialism to which liberation theology has been responding.

Clearly the emphasis by Rebecca Chopp, Johannes Metz and others on person-centered theology, on a theology that directly relates to the victims of current history, is very much to the point as I now understand the significance of the Holocaust. Christology needs to become more than a theoretical affirmation of human dignity. The late Frantz Fanon's critique of abstract philosophical humanism in the midst of colonial exploitation in his preface to *The Wretched of the Earth* speaks to this in a decisive way. Pope John Paul II's plea for a Christology that affirms human dignity *in Redemptor Hominis* must become the impetus for a

---

32. R. CHOPP, *The Interruption of the Forgotten*, in E. SCHÜSSLER FIORENZA and D. TRACY (eds.), *The Holocaust as Interruption*, 1984, p. 20.

concrete manifestation of that belief through identification with, and support of, the victims of oppression through personal and political means. This will enhance the dignity not only of the victim, but also of the person who reaches out. Donald Dietrich is quite right when he argues that "the Holocaust has reemphasized the need to highlight the person as *the* central factor in the social order to counterbalance state power"[33]. Only in this way can we root out the instinctive patriarchal impulse that elevates power over mutuality in relationships, only in this way can we guarantee that the misuse of technological capacity is neutralized. In this sense there is a profound connection between the two basic forms of post-Holocaust Christology. For the new human consciousness rooted in an understanding of *divine vulnerability* will insure that a Christology of witness does not fall into the trap of service in the name of power rather than service in the name of genuine human dignity.

In this approach to Christology the emphasis on Jesus' sufferings on the cross surely has a place. But this suffering must not be seen in isolation from his public ministry. For it is the period of the public ministry where Jesus often went out of his way to identify with, and personally affirm, the social outcasts of his time that gives significance to his experience on the cross. His continual affirmation of human dignity in very concrete ways is what brought him a death sentence.

In his volume *Moralizing Cultures*[34] Vytautas Kavolis argues that while the sacred will continue to impact culture it will do so in a different way. Kavolis speaks of a movement towards the "humanization of morality". This movement involves a fundamental shift from the dominance of abstract principles requiring adherence whatever the consequences to a more directly practical concern with the reduction of human suffering and the enhancement of non-destructive capacities within humanity. For this to continue in a socially constructive way, we require moral leaders as much as, perhaps more than, abstract principles.

Applying Kavolis' perspective to Christology after the Holocaust we can say that Jesus' own ministry becomes one such example of moral leadership. But so does the witness of the countless martyrs, whether in the Holocaust itself or subsequently, who have embodied Christology in acts of concrete witness on behalf of the oppressed. In this sense the narrative of the rescuers during the Holocaust may now be seen as a central

33. D.J. DIETRICH, *God and Humanity in Auschwitz: Jewish-Christian Relations and Sanctioned Murder*, New Brunswick, NJ and London, Transaction, 1995, p. 269.
34. V. KAVOLIS, *Moralizing Cultures*, Lanham, MD, University Press of America, 1993.

Christological resource. The personal, and even communal, "cleansing" of human consciousness from the temptations towards the destructive use of enhanced human power is a necessary first step in the humanization of morality. But the process cannot stop there. If reflection on the Holocaust leaves us merely with a Christology of witness we have failed in our basic responsibility as post-Holocaust Christians.

Catholic Theological Union
5401 South Cornell Avenue
Chicago, IL 60615-6200
U.S.A.

John T. PAWLIKOWSKI

JESUS AT AUSCHWITZ?
A CRITIQUE OF POST-HOLOCAUST CHRISTOLOGIES

INTRODUCTION

The death of Viktor Frankl silenced a crucially important voice in the ongoing dialogue amongst scholars of many disciplines about the redemptive versus non-redemptive nature of suffering in conditions of extremity. Heralded as a "champion of the will" by the *New York Times*[1], Dr. Frankl was a tireless defender of the belief that the human spirit can marshal its capacities for dignified survival in the most degrading of conditions. As a survivor of Auschwitz, his view lent an instant credibility to the notion of Holocaust survival as a "triumph of the human spirit", encouraging other survivors to come forward with similar accounts of spiritual victory in the face of the overwhelming realities of concentration camp incarceration. Corrie Ten Boom's account of her ordeal entitled *The Hiding Place*[2] is but one example of a survivor narrative that demonstrates this sort of spiritual triumph. It has been eagerly embraced by scholars in spirituality[3], along with Dr. Frankl's own work, as proof positive that the human spirit's resources for dignified survival need not undergo the kind of brutal decimation that might otherwise be expected. And interestingly, the "triumph of the human spirit" motif has been extended to include the autobiographical accounts of those individuals who indeed were eventually swept away into the maelstrom of the Holocaust, but whose spiritual tenacity enabled them to see a hopeful future for themselves and the world despite their situation of grave personal danger. The journals of Anne Frank and Etty Hillesum are two such examples. As might be expected, these kinds of accounts are also eagerly embraced by those scholars in spirituality whose determination to ratify the notion that the spirit can

---

1. R.A. SHWEDER, *Read: You're Getting Very Unsleepy*, in *New York Times*, Sept. 7, 1997, section E, p. 4.

2. C. TEN BOOM, *The Hiding Place*, New York, Bantam, 1971.

3. I am making what I believe to be a much needed distinction between the post-Holocaust scholarship of theologians and that of other scholars who theorize in the realm of spirituality proper but without claiming to rely upon the conceptual underpinnings of systematic theology: psychologists of religion, some existential-phenomenological psychologists, and scholars working in the realm of spiritual direction spring immediately to mind.

indeed triumph in cases of extreme physical dis-ease has led them, I suspect, to overlook another, darker literature whose authors record a vastly different view.

And such a literature indeed exists; its voices are equally powerful if not equally embraced by the community of scholarship in spirituality. One has only to read Primo Levi's *Survival in Auschwitz*[4], Jean Amery's *At the Mind's Limits*[5], and the poetry of Paul Celan[6] – all survivors and all eventual suicides – to be forcefully confronted with the inescapable fact that death camp survival might indeed take on a much more complex character than the "triumph of the human spirit" motif communicates. Terrence Des Pres's classic study, *The Survivor*[7], and Lawrence Langer's *Holocaust Testimonies*[8] exemplify two scholars' attempts to grapple seriously with the non-edifying realities of an extreme suffering whose nature is non-redemptive. To the best of my knowledge, these texts are largely overlooked in the scholarship of spirituality precisely because they are unable to ratify the triumphant spiritual outcome that such scholars are in quest of. Worse, I am afraid that such darker accounts risk being relativized, if not altogether dismissed, as tragic examples of individuals who were just not able to muster the requisite spiritual fortitude as exemplified by a Viktor Frankl and who must therefore be relegated, regretfully to be sure, to the dustheap of spiritual failure that is by definition unworthy of theoretical consideration by scholars in spirituality.

Turning to the post-Holocaust systematic theological landscape, however, it is indeed true that many theologians of note, both Roman Catholic and Protestant, have attempted to integrate the Holocaust into their various theological projects. This is especially true in the realm of post-Holocaust Christology. In reading these theologians, be it the work of Jürgen Moltmann, Gregory Baum, or Rosemary Ruether, I have found many poignant references to Auschwitz as the very phenomenality of evil, but have yet to encounter any attempt on the part of theologians consciously and explicitly working in a post-Holocaust milieu to take up the experiences and testimonies of survivors themselves as part

4. P. LEVI, *Survival in Auschwitz*, New York, Macmillan, 1960.

5. J. AMERY, *At the Mind's Limits: Contemplations by a Survivor on Auschwitz and its Realities*, tr. S. and S.P. Rosenfeld, New York, Schocken, 1986.

6. Cf. P. CELAN, *Poems of Paul Celan*, tr. Michael Hamburger, New York, Persea Books, 1988.

7. T. DES PRES, *The Survivor: An Anatomy of Life in the Death Camps*, New York, Oxford University Press, 1976.

8. L. LANGER, *Holocaust Testimonies: The Ruins of Memory*, New Haven, Yale University Press, 1991.

of their overall theorizing. As a spiritual theologian I find this lapse to be somewhat problematic, especially given the call to return to history and experience that seemingly drives the work of such theologians. I understand that the work of systematic theologians writing explicitly in a post-Holocaust context has required the kind of generalizing abstraction of the experience of life in extremity such that the daily struggle for survival becomes subsumed under the notion of the "Awful Event"[9], to quote Gregory Baum. Although such abstraction gives rise to the inevitable flight into a necessary systematicity that accompanies such an objectivizing impulse, yet I cannot help but wonder whether the work of systematicians theologizing "in the shadow of Auschwitz"[10], to quote Jürgen Moltmann, is ultimately served by such subsumption. And so, my concern extends to the effort amongst theologians who are laboring to develop post-Holocaust Christologies in particular because, as Roger Haight rightly notes, "a contemporary Christology must respond to contemporary problems" and must also "stimulate and empower Christian life"[11], extending itself thus into the experiential realm of concrete spiritual praxis. If Christians are to take up their responsibility for the prevention of future Holocausts, I am convinced that a post-Holocaust Christology explicitly formulated in the shadow of Auschwitz must also be formulated in light of the experience and testimony of death camp survivors themselves, especially those who have generated the "darker literature" alluded to above. In this way I believe that such Christologies may exert a sober, realistic, yet responsible and hopeful influence on the spiritual praxis of Christians. This conviction lies at the heart of the essay that follows.

My paper will argue, first of all, that many survivors are unable to ratify the "triumph of the human spirit" motif as in any way applicable to their experience. Such being the case, survivors' claims about the non-redemptive nature of their suffering must be seriously attended to by those theologians whose Christologies have been explicitly formulated in a post-Holocaust milieu. Secondly, I will critique those Christologies rooted in a theology of the Cross such as those of Jürgen Moltmann and Douglas Hall in light of the fact that, unlike the Jesus presented in the Gospels, no survivor will understand him or herself to have freely chosen his or her fate, and many survivors will insist that their suffering was

---

9. G. BAUM, *Christian Theology After Auschwitz*, London, The Council of Christians and Jews, 1976, p. 7.

10. J. MOLTMANN, *The Crucified God*, tr. R.A. Wilson and J. Bowden, Minneapolis, Fortress Press, 1974, p. xi.

11. R. HAIGHT, *The Case for Spirit Christology*, in *Theological Studies* 53 (1992) 261.

and continues to be without redemptive value. Furthermore, I will raise as a question and a problem whether or not such Christologies may unintendedly promulgate spiritualities of powerlessness and excessive vulnerability that are dangerous in the extreme when applied to a death camp context. Finally, I will examine those post-Holocaust Christologies that in my estimation may respond more adequately, albeit perhaps unintendedly, to survivors' experiences and testimonies: the incarnational Christology of John Pawlikowski, and the proleptic Christology of Rosemary Ruether. More specifically, I will put various elements of these Christologies into dialogue with survivor's experiences and claims to help foster the future emergence of a post-Holocaust Christology that might address such experiences and claims with a greater degree of adequacy[12].

THE NON-REDEMPTIVE NATURE OF HOLOCAUST SUFFERING

It is perhaps interesting to note, as our initial point of departure, that Dr. Henry Krystal dedicated a collection of essays that he edited into a book entitled *Massive Psychic Trauma*[13] to "the triumph of the human spirit". The irony here is palpable, but serves to illustrate an important point: despite incontrovertible evidence to the contrary, evidence that Dr. Krystal himself helped to gather, a curious tendency persists to shy away from the overwhelming realities of incarceration in conditions of extremity by making a comforting appeal to a higher spiritual order, one that many survivors seem to have been incapable of attaining themselves to judge from the evidence provided by Dr. Krystal's editorial and authorial efforts.

Perhaps the most telling witness to the actuality of immersion in conditions of extremity is the extensive trauma that such immersion leaves in its wake. Narratives of triumphant survival notwithstanding, psychiatric evaluations of survivors such as those recounted in *Massive Psychic*

12. Let me state at the outset that I do not intend to make distinctions *between survivors* based on adherence or lack of adherence to Judaism or Christianity. Although it is clearly true that the overwhelming number of camp prisoners were Jewish, a fact which Christianity must treat with grave seriousness as it continues to grapple with the degree of its complicity, however indirect, in contributing anti-Judaic attitudes favorable to the creation of a Holocaust, it is also reasonable to assume that conditions of extremity were suffered by all those who were incarcerated, regardless of ethnicity or religious affiliation. And this essay will indeed discuss the relationship between Christianity and Judaism as that relationship becomes central to the theological project of post-Holocaust Christological formulations.

13. H. KRYSTAL, M.D. (ed.), *Massive Psychic Trauma*, New York, International Universities Press, 1968.

Trauma paint a vastly grimmer portrait: somatization of symptoms, chronic and at times suicidal degrees of depression, emotional numbness, guilt at having survived when loved ones didn't, amongst other factors[14]. Lawrence Langer's analysis of survivor oral testimonies taken from the Fortunoff Video Archive for Holocaust Testimony at Yale University reveals a most interesting finding: "several currents flow at differing depths in Holocaust testimonies,... our understanding of the event depends very much on the source and destination of the current we pursue"[15]. Langer thus posits multiple layers of memory in relation to survivors' understanding and narration of their experiences. He notes that a surface layer of intellectualizing or "common memory" that forms the stuff of what we might call "redemptive narrations" will cover over another much more anguished "deep memory" of incarceration, inscribed in the body, that is much less capable of being spoken because it defies the very conventions of language to make meaning of experiences that defy any type of contextualization within the universe of conventionally agreed upon meaning[16]. His findings support Arthur Cohen's contention that the Holocaust "has no meaning, because it denies meaning and makes mockery of meaning"[17].

The forensic findings of psychiatrists confronted with the ongoing psychic and emotional trauma of survivors, as well as Langer's discovery of multiple layers of memory informing survivors' oral testimonies such that the story told – or perhaps the story unable to be told – to interviewers will be governed by the layer of memory currently invoked, poses an immediate problem to Christologies that purport to find some degree of redemptive meaning in the phenomenality of Auschwitz. It seems, in light of such efforts, that "Auschwitz" functions in their Christological formulations as a complex symbol of the phenomenality of evil that displays an understandable inability, given the impulse to systematicity that lies at the base of its conceptualization as such, to correspond to or even "get at" the deep, excessively traumatized memory of the actual experience of incarceration. This is so, apparently, because such Christologies have chosen, rather, to take refuge in the comforting assumption that it must be possible to extract redemptive meaning from

---

14. See my article *Death Camp Survival and the Possibility of Hope: A Dialogue with Karl Rahner*, in *Philosophy and Theology* 10 (1997) 385-419, which chronicles the longterm aftereffects of death camp incarceration in much greater detail than space limitations here will permit.

15. LANGER, *Holocaust Testimonies* (n. 7), p. xi.

16. *Ibid.*, pp. 6, 8.

17. A. COHEN, *The Tremendum: A Theological Interpretation of the Holocaust*, New York, Crossroad, 1981, pp. 4-5.

the symbol "auschwitz" to the extent that the experience of incarceration can be regarded in light of Christ's own suffering on the Cross. Yet
we have just seen that such an assumption must be seriously reconsidered to the extent that it may in fact reflect the same kind of intellectualizing tendencies to be found in the "common memory" of survivors,
such memory informed by conventionally agreed upon meanings such as
"redeeming" or "salvation" that superimpose upon the experience of
extremity a grid of meanings that is not appropriate to describe it[18].
Although my critique is in no way designed to deny the very possibility
of post-Holocaust Christological formulations, it does seem to me that
theologians who attempt such formulations must scrutinize their efforts
in light of the excessive trauma that remains so very integral to some
survivor experience – let alone the violent and outrageous murder of six
million Jews – unless they too wish to relegate such trauma to the realm
of spiritual failure discussed in the Introduction to this essay. The theological concern with history and experience demands of them no less[19].

THE THEOLOGY OF THE CROSS AS THE BASIS FOR A CHRISTOLOGY IN THE SHADOW OF "AUSCHWITZ"

My concerns, articulated above, about the use of the symbol
"auschwitz" in Christological discourse are not intended to convey the

18. LANGER, *Holocaust Testimonies* (n. 7), pp. 8-9. Also, if survivors' own testimonies are to be subjected to a hermeneutics of suspicion as to whether or not survivors
are the most reliable evaluators of their own experiences of incarceration, I would suggest
that the trajectory of such a hermeneutics should take off from the starting point offered
by "common memory" narrations. I am indebted to Dr. William Thompson for his most
helpful remarks in this regard.

19. One reads, for example, Karl Rahner's comment to Rabbi Pinchas Lapide, an
enlightening example which I quote in its entirety: "I can partially understand all that, but
you must still grant me that it is hard for a modern person to realize that this entire history of suffering [of the Jewish people] generally has something positive to do with God.
I know full well that there were Jews in Auschwitz who died with their rabbis believing
and praying. Yet they also say that the majority of Jews went to the gas chambers in god-
less despair. Whether these, and how these, could have still found God is another question altogether. But whether one could experience, in historically tangible terms, an ultimate, positive sense in this passion is still an open question. As a Christian I would say
that I can discern definitive and indissoluble evidence for the meaningfulness of the entire
history of human suffering, and so also of Israel's, only in Jesus the crucified and resurrected". Karl RAHNER and Pinchas LAPIDE, *Encountering Jesus – Encountering Judaism:
A Dialogue*, tr. Davis Perkins, New York, Crossroad, 1987, p. 19. Although I persist in
my desire to treat the experience and testimony of *survivors* without regard for their religious adherence or lack thereof, the distinction between Christianity and Judaism lies at
the heart of most theological and Christological discussions held in the context of
"Auschwitz", a distinction which will figure prominently in the discussions that follow.

impression that I find no merit in such efforts. Indeed, the opposite is the case, as the work of Jürgen Moltmann and Douglas Hall, amongst others, has constituted an important and much needed effort to recontextualize Christology in the light of death camp reality. Their particular focus on the Cross has shifted Christological discussion away from an exclusive emphasis on the primacy of the Resurrection, concentrating instead on the Crucifixion and its revelatory implications for a post-Holocaust milieu. I regard this shift to be a salutary development because it seeks to undercut, perhaps but not necessarily intentionally, a Christian triumphalism that has itself been influential in helping to create a climate of anti-Judaism throughout the centuries.

The work of Jürgen Moltmann has been particularly important in the development of a Christology based on a theology of the Cross. He insists that any "theology after Auschwitz" must be rooted in the fact that there was a "theology in Auschwitz" exemplified in the praying of the *Shema* and the Lord's Prayer in Auschwitz itself[20]. Although I do not deny the truth of his assertion, it seems to me that such a statement places his Christology within the context of the "redemptive narration" alluded to above to the extent that the fact of religious observance must *of necessity* take precedence over the fact of a suffering that has been experienced as being non-redemptive. And indeed it must be located within the meaningful context of redemption if his Christological project is to elude the meaninglessness reported by many survivors[21]. Such being the case, we find that for Moltmann, taking his inspiration from Rom 8,20, the theology of the Cross "sees nothingness itself done away with in the being of God, who in the death of Jesus has revealed himself and constituted himself in nothingness"[22]. The "hells of Auschwitz", might suggest that the world is to be thought of as an "*univers concentrationnaire*" but Moltmann relegates such a characterization to the realm of "protest atheism" that is the "brother" of a theism that creates the very possibility for protest atheism by establishing its conceptual antithesis[23]. I take issue with Moltmann's description of Auschwitz as

---

20. J. MOLTMANN, *The Crucified God* (n. 9), p. 278.

21. As evidence of such meaninglessness, I offer the following remark by Elie Wiesel: "The word has deserted the meaning it was intended to convey – impossible to make them coincide. The displacement, the shift, is irrevocable. This was never more true than right after the upheaval. We all knew that we could never, never say what had to be said, that we could never express in words, coherent, intelligible words, our experience of madness on an absolute scale". Elie Wiesel as quoted by Lawrence LANGER, *Versions of Survival: The Holocaust and the Human Spirit*, Albany, SUNY Press, 1982, p. 154.

22. MOLTMANN, *The Crucified God* (n. 9), p. 218.

23. *Ibid.*, pp. 220, 221.

"hell" since its prisoners were guilty of no crime – and hence, unlike "hell", did not deserve to be its inmates – but were rather either the unfortunate victims of the National Socialist version of "ethnic cleansing", a broad category that included homosexuals, Gypsies, and the mentally and physically handicapped, or were regarded as enemies of the State because they hampered the efforts at the establishment of a "pure" Aryan society. Yet his analysis of the ways in which a traditional theism might contribute to protest atheism is indeed valuable, because of his insight that protest atheism can only conceive of a "God within history" rather than that of a "history within God"[24]. It constitutes the basis for his shift away from the theism-atheism conceptual universe of debate into a far different realm: that of the Trinitarian God as "the event of Golgotha, the event of the love of the Son and the grief of the Father from which the Spirit who opens up the future and creates life in fact derives"[25]. Conceived as such, the Trinity becomes "an eschatological process open for men on earth, which stems from the cross of Jesus Christ"[26], which process is universally all-inclusive. There is no human experience which would locate itself outside this occurrence. Anyone who "cries out to God" in the depths of his or her suffering "echoes the death-cry of the dying Christ"; God thus "cries with" such individuals in the depths of their torment[27]. One's own forsakenness is thus lifted away... in the forsakenness of Christ", thus enabling the one who suffers to "love" and "sustain death"[28].

At this point it is important to mention that Moltmann's conception of suffering is wanting in the extreme when applied to survivors' memories of unbearable suffering – their own and particularly that of those who died. Moltmann's contention that "[t]he person who can no longer love, even himself, no longer suffers, for he is without grief, without feeling and indifferent"[29] points ironically and, I would think, unintendedly to the very worst kind of suffering in the death camp, if accounts such as Primo Levi's are to be believed. I am referring explicitly to the phenomenon of the *muselmann*, in the slang of the death camp, that individual who was so debilitated physically, psychically, and emotionally that he or she was already in an advanced state of decline that was irreversible, although he or she had not yet died:

24. *Ibid.*, pp. 246-247.
25. *Ibid.*, p. 247.
26. *Ibid.*, p. 249.
27. *Ibid.*, p. 252.
28. *Ibid.*, p. 254.
29. P. LEVI, *Survival in Auschwitz* (n. 4), p. 90.

> They [the *muselmanner*] crowd my memory with their faceless presences, and if I could enclose all the evil of our time in one image, I would choose this image which is familiar to me: an emaciated man, with head dropped and shoulders curved, on whose face and in whose eyes not a trace of a thought is to be seen.
> If the drowned have no story, and single and broad is the path to perdition, the paths to salvation are many, difficult and improbable[30].

These excessively traumatized individuals inevitably succumbed either to selections, illness, or exhaustion. An intellectualizing Christology conceived on the basis of the "redemptive narrative" has no place for this person deprived, through no fault of his or her own, of even the last vestiges of humanity – the one who can no longer muster the capacities of thinking and feeling normally invoked to designate "humanness". Yet this individual who precisely, because of trauma, starvation, and exhaustion, can "no longer love, even himself", who is "without grief, without feeling and indifferent" is precisely the very worst example of the suffering served up by Auschwitz[31]. Any Christology conceived in its shadow must take up with all seriousness this example of extreme, dehumanizing suffering. It is not enough to consign it, without further comment, to an overall "history of God" in my estimation. To do so is indeed to ratify the fact that "the drowned have no story" because *we* lack the conceptual apparatus to make that story comprehensible. On the other hand, such consignment is perhaps preferable to an easy subsumption within "redemptive" conceptual categories such that the *muselmann* becomes automatically relegated to the status of "spiritual failure".

Yet it is important to point out what I consider to be Moltmann's exemplary concern with the formulation of a Christology that is rooted in God's mercy and compassion in the face of human suffering. He states, in light of Abraham Heschel's notion of the *pathos* of God, that "at the heart of the prophetic proclamation there stands the certainty that God is interested in the world to the point of suffering"[32]. Although I understand that there is some scholarly concern with the accuracy of Moltmann's use of Heschel's formulation[33], it nevertheless seems to me

---

30. P. LEVI, *Survival in Auschwitz* (n. 4), p. 90.

31. Although I understand that Moltmann is referring to a generalized malaise, an "apathy" that is "the sickness of our time" without necessarily belonging to the death camp, I also believe that any theologian explicitly theorizing in the shadow of Auschwitz must pay especially careful attention to the claims that he or she makes in relation to *any* suffering. Cf. *The Crucified God* (n. 9), p. 253.

32. MOLTMANN, *The Crucified God* (n. 9), p. 271.

33. Cf. J.T. PAWLIKOWSKI, O.S.M., *Christ In the Light of the Christian-Jewish Dialogue*, New York, Paulist Press, 1982, pp. 117-118, 143.

that any post-Holocaust Christology must foreground a God of mercy and compassion whose care for humanity extends to a participation in humanity's own suffering if this God is not to be relegated to a status of unreachable transcendence that flies in the face of Christianity's central claims. Two problems arise, however, when Moltmann contextualizes this merciful and compassionate God within his own Christological project: all suffering becomes "redemptive", survivor claims notwithstanding, and all suffering becomes meaningful only in light of the Crucifixion[34]. Moltmann works consistently, in other words, out of the symbol of "Auschwitz" that remains impervious to survivor testimony, and he makes universalist claims about the Crucifixion that can only call into question any final affirmation of Judaism's ongoing covenantal relationship with God. Yet surely it is time for Christianity to cease making any kind of supersessionist claims about its status in relation to Judaism if another Holocaust is to be avoided. Or, if Christianity persists in making such claims, then it must be prepared to acknowledge and take full responsibility for the ways in which these pronouncements contribute to effects whose historical manifestations risk becoming murderous. Even if "Auschwitz is in God"[35], as Moltmann asserts – although I confess that I have no idea what such an assertion means, Moltmann's theology of the Cross notwithstanding, or how any one who did not suffer there could make such an assertion – it is still incumbent upon Christianity to help create a theological climate that acknowledges the validity of the Hebrew covenant such that Christian supersessionism ceases to contribute, however indirectly, to any climate of anti-Judaism[36].

For Douglas Hall, the "answer" to the problem of human suffering is the steadfast presence of the "Answerer": "The answer, the only answer that we ourselves know and that we are obliged and glad to share with others, is the ongoing presence of the crucified one"[37]. He seems to posit the ultimately redemptive nature of suffering, as seen from the perspective of faith, although he is unwilling to assert that "auschwitz" functioned as an instrument through which "God had made some people

34. Cf. MOLTMANN, *The Crucified God* (n. 9), p. 275.

35. *Ibid.*, p. 278.

36. In fairness to Moltmann, it is important to point out that he seems to be quite concerned with the effects of Christian supersessionist claims in relation to Judaism. Cf. J. MOLTMANN, *Christology in the Jewish-Christian Dialogue*, in V.A. McINNES, O.P. (ed.), *New Visions: Historical and Theological Perspectives on the Jewish-Christian Dialogue*, New York, Crossroad, 1993, pp. 77-93.

37. D.J. HALL, *God and Human Suffering: An Exercise in the Theology of the Cross*, Minneapolis, Augsburg Publishing House, 1986, pp. 94, 141.

more compassionate"[38]. For Hall, the "meaninglessness" of suffering finds its ultimate, redemptive answer in the "transformation" of metaphors of power as God's primary attribute by "conforming" them to "the image of God revealed *in the crucified One*" [emphasis his][39]. Such conformity reveals a God whose primary attribute is that of love.

Let me state at the outset that I find his Christological formulations to be a ratification of Moltmann's theology of the Cross in large measure; I will therefore limit my remarks to those aspects of his thought that offer something new to the discussion. Asserting that "[h]istory is not by itself redemptive" but is nonetheless imbued with "*a capacity for being changed from within*" [emphasis his][40], Hall finds that "the incarnation" changes history by introducing a new future into the heart of a seemingly unredeemed history – that of life itself[41]. God's ongoing presence through Christ crucified functions as a participation, in vulnerability, in the suffering of humanity and as the very assuming of "'the weight of sin' that is the root cause of our suffering, and that we cannot assume in our brokenness"[42]. And so, we are called to a certain "relief in meeting the broken Christ" that signals the answer – through Christ's ongoing presence – to our suffering in the "dereliction" of our own time[43].

The question arises as to whether such relief can extend to those whose sufferings in the very worst example of "dereliction" in our time often constituted a magnitude unimaginable to the rest of us, a suffering before which all other forms of suffering pale in comparison, if Levi's account of the *Musselmanner* is to be believed. Hall's Christological claims in particular, although Moltmann's are not exempt, call forth a critical response in light of survivors' experiences of incarceration. Prescinding away from adherence or nonadherence to a specific religious tradition, how can survivors be expected to experience "relief" in meeting "the broken Christ" when their own ordeal has differed so dramatically from his? The fact remains that they did not freely choose their fate, and that they did not understand themselves to be fulfilling a divinely ordained mission that would have conferred salvific meaning upon their suffering to the extent that it would have opened up redemption to the entire world. For the most part, these were ordinary people

38. HALL, *God and Human Suffering* (n. 36). p. 166. Cf. his statement on p. 94 where he asserts: "... the *basic* point of departure for faith is heavily informed by ... redemption" [emphasis his].
39. *Ibid.*, pp. 95, 105.
40. *Ibid.*, p. 109.
41. *Ibid.*, p. 111.
42. *Ibid.*, p. 113.
43. *Ibid.*, p. 118.

trying to go about the business of living in a regime that was hostile, for a variety of reasons, to their continued existence. To subsume their suffering under the aegis of Christ's own passion constitutes to my mind a facile evasion of the outrageous enormity of the crime committed against them. For not only was Auschwitz not "hell" as discussed earlier, they were not "martyrs" as Moltmann wrongly asserts[44], since they did not willingly take up a position in relation to a cause for which they were willing to die. They were, for the most part, innocent people who had the consummate misfortune simply to be living in the wrong place at the wrong time. How can they be expected to identify themselves with, much less find "relief" in meeting, "the broken Christ"? Certainly, there are many survivors, Christians in particular, who have felt such relief, and I have no desire to call their experience into question. I refer, rather, to the voices of the darker literature alluded to earlier who *we* risk consigning to the realm of "spiritual failure" if *we* can find no evidence of redemption in their accounts. Also, I find it questionable in the extreme as to the advisability of promulgating, however unintendedly, "vulnerability" and "powerlessness" as viable theological and spiritual responses, particularly in relation to suffering inflicted from without by regimes intent upon murder on a genocidal scale. Is it not the case that those people who find themselves to be the target of genocidal intent are precisely altogether too vulnerable and powerless already? I would rather support a Christological formulation that acknowledges the "overwhelmingness" of suffering in extremity without seeking to find within it a necessarily redemptive core that some survivors themselves have not experienced, but that nevertheless posits a hope for humankind rooted in the eschatologically oriented belief that such suffering will indeed not have the final word. It is to the discussion of such a Christological formulation that I will now turn.

POST-HOLOCAUST CHRISTOLOGIES AND SURVIVOR EXPERIENCES: A DIALOGUE

John Pawlikowski's Christological project exhibits an extreme sensitivity both to the Holocaust and to the validity of the ongoing claims of Judaism, although I do not regard him to be working out of a theoretical context that gives full weight to the testimonies and claims of survivors themselves. Yet he too is unwilling to accord Auschwitz any "redemptive"

---

44. MOLTMANN, *The Crucified God* (n. 9), p. 278.

value[45], suggesting to my mind that he is cognizant of the non-redemptive claims that inform many survivors' accounts of their ordeal and that he takes such testimony seriously. His Christology is to be welcomed for that reason alone.

Pawlikowski has chosen the Incarnation as the central focus of his post-Holocaust Christology because he believes that the prior centrality of the Resurrection in Christological formulations has contributed to the kind of triumphalistic and supersessionist claims that must assume some responsibility for the promulgation of an anti-Judaic climate across the centuries[46]. He would prefer to concentrate on Jesus' central preaching that lies at the heart of Christian faith and indeed makes it possible: "And what he preached can be summarized as the notion of the Incarnation, his proclamation of the indwelling presence of God in humanity, in a measure that was hinted at in Pharisaic theology but which still did not come out in all its power and glory"[47]. It seems to me that Pawlikowski's Christology takes up an implicitly proleptic stance, if we understand the idea of prolepsis to include the present representation of a future accomplishment, since he understands "the process begun by the Incarnation" to be "incomplete" such that "resurrection becomes a statement about future promise rather than about present reality"[48]. Such a stance lends credibility to his Christological project in light of survivors' claims about the non-redemptive nature of their suffering and indeed to some theologians' claims about the impossibility of locating any definitive redemptive movement within history itself.

The thesis undergirding Pawlikowski's Christology is simple: Jesus' person and ministry brought about the recognition – and revelation – that the human person is "profoundly integral...to the self-definition of God", and that he or she "shares in the constitutive nature of God" without being the sum total of God's being[49]. To be sure, no one exhibits the intimacy with divinity that is to be found in Jesus' person, yet part of the revelation that occurs in the life and ministry of Jesus is the communication of a hitherto unrecognized *degree* of intimacy between divinity and the individual. And so, the Christ event is salvific because it restores to the human person a sense of "wholeness"[50] understood as the healing

45. PAWLIKOWSKI, *Christ in the Light of the Christian-Jewish Dialogue* (n. 32), p. 143.
46. Cf. *Ibid.*, p. 109.
47. *Ibid.*, p. 109. Pawlikowski's Christology is formulated in light of his analysis of Jesus' stance in relation to Pharisaic Judaism, a stance which Pawlikowski finds to be "linked" to yet "separated from" Pharisaic Judaism.
48. *Ibid.*, p. 109.
49. *Ibid.*, p. 114-115.
50. *Ibid.*, p. 116.

of any desire to supplant God by means of an egoic, and hence potentially violent display of pride that posits the self as a (false) god in its
own right. In brief, what Judaism accomplished at the corporate level by
way of its own valid and ongoing covenantal relation with God, the
Christ event revealed at the level of the individual.

Pawlikowski's Christology is also concerned with the articulation of a
"link between history and human consciousness"[51] that reveals to my
mind an inherently ethical thrust that remains, however, secondary in his
Christology to the Christ event's revelatory status. Yet any Christology
that exhibits such a thrust is to be regarded as an especially welcome
development in relation to the prevention of future occurrences of life in
extremity. This is so because such a Christology posits salvation as
occurring when the link between human consciousness and the humanity of God as revealed in history is such that "dehumanizing socio-political structures" are dismantled as a way of realizing greater degrees of
"communion with God and neighbor"[52]. A Christology understood in
this sense becomes an ethically enacted responsibility for the other that
enters the realm of concrete spiritual praxis at the communal level, thus
counteracting the individual pietism that seems to have resulted from so
many traditional Christological formulations.

To be sure, Pawlikowski's Christology is not without its drawbacks.
He admits that his project retains a degree of universalism in its claims,
at the same time that he insists upon the "unique and distinctive role in
the process of human salvation"[53] that Judaism continues to exert. But is
it not the case that any ongoing assertion of Christian universalism can
only continue to support, however unintendedly, those triumphalistic
and supersessionist impulses that have exerted a heavy influence upon
Christian Anti-Judaism throughout the centuries? Christianity must
insure that its claims do not impede Judaism's right to exist. Rosemary
Ruether has also accused him sharply of the "spiritualization of salvation"[54] in the sense that he has in fact ignored history in his Christological project. Indeed, I regard his insistence upon the ethical and social
thrust inherent in his Christology as a way, perhaps, of implicitly
acknowledging and responding constructively to Ruether's earlier charge.
Although I think that Pawlikowski is himself aware that his project is

51. *Ibid.*, p. 119.
52. *Ibid.*, p. 119.
53. *Ibid.*, p. 121.
54. R. Ruether as quoted in PAWLIKOWSKI, *Christ in the Light of the Christian-Jewish
Dialogue* (n. 32), p. 118. Her charge was made prior to the writing of *Christ in the Light
of the Christian-Jewish Dialogue*.

perhaps in need of further elaboration and clarification, I believe that his Christology constitutes an important attempt within mainline Roman Catholicism to keep the suffering of Holocaust victims firmly in mind, thus seeking to avoid any theological pronouncements that simply cannot be made "in the presence of the burning children"[55], to recall Irving Greenburg's formulation.

Turning to Rosemary Ruether's Christological project, it will, perhaps, be readily apparent that from the standpoint of many survivors – and potentially all victims of suffering in extremity throughout history – her consistent unwillingness to imbue history with any redemptive movement in light of the Christ event may function as the ultimate ratification of the non-redemptive nature of their ordeal. For this reason alone her Christology must be taken very seriously by those of us who wish to allow the other than redemptive narratives or the "darker literature" to have their full say. Her unwavering criticism of a "fulfilled messianism" that culminated in Christologies that "historicized" the "eschatological event" points out the "reality-denying" nature of such Christologies[56].

Although Ruether's Christological formulations occur within the context offered by her discussion of the theological roots of anti-Semitism, a context somewhat different from the present context of survivor experience and testimony of the non-redemptive nature of life in extremity, her concern with the historicizing of the eschatological event is important to *my* discussion to the extent that I too am troubled by any Christology whose effects would constitute a denial of historical reality. I suspect that the unfortunate tendency amongst scholars in spirituality, given their silence in relation to non-redemptive narratives, is to relegate them to the realm of "spiritual failure" as a result of such scholars' own implicit and unintended denial of historical reality in favor of a higher, ahistoricized spiritual order. Ruether's caution against such denial, however one might evaluate the rest of her Christological project, is an important reminder that Christology, theology in general, and the spirituality that emerges from them must remain rooted in a realistic and sober view of history that fully acknowledges its unredeemed aspects. It is then, I believe, that the non-redemptive narratives of survivors can be taken up forthrightly and can be integrated into an overall vision of spirituality that

55. I. GREENBURG, *Cloud of Smoke, Pillar of Fire*, in J. ROTH and M. BERENBAUM (eds.), *Holocaust: Religious and Philosophical Implications*, New York, Paragon House, 1989, p. 303.

56. R. RADFORD RUETHER, *Faith and Fratricide: The Theological Roots of Anti-Semitism*, New York, Seabury, 1974, pp. 238, 246.

can remain hopeful while acknowledging fully that there *are* some forms
of suffering which consume their victims entirely, without consigning
such victims to the status of spiritual failure. I would like to believe that
Christ's own example of unlimited mercy and compassion calls us to
nothing less.

And so, Ruether's characterization of Jesus as "our paradigm of hoping, aspiring man, venturing his life in expectation of the Kingdom"[57]
functions indeed as the paradigm for concrete spiritual praxis in the face
of suffering in extremity. We are called to hope – particularly in the
sense of embodying such hope in ethical responsibility – for those who
can literally no longer hope for themselves. The rescuer of Jews during
the Holocaust understood and embodied this hope most forcefully,
regardless of his or her religious adherence or lack thereof. I would also
venture to add that Ruether's characterization of the Christ "as the symbol of the fulfillment of that hope" becomes highly appropriate in this
context. Indeed, "the hope for the coming Kingdom reaches into history
as the foundation of the present struggle, and, in its power, men recognize that the status of evil has changed, even though its sway continues"[58]. In this new context, Moltmann's contention that "Auschwitz is
in God" becomes comprehensible.

In summary, I believe that Pawlikowski's Incarnational Christology
provides us with a much needed sense of the already salvific "wholeness" which the Christ event offers, in the sense that the degree of
human intimacy with God frees us from the need to take up a violent
assertion of self as divorced from God and the larger community. By
putting his Christology in dialogue with Rosemary Ruether's caution
against what I would prefer to qualify as an *undue* historicizing of the
eschatological event, we are in a position to recognize that our intimacy
with God in Christ calls for nothing less than our full engagement with
history, a point that Pawlikowski also asserts although not with
Ruether's emphasis. Such an engagement with history also requires us to
recognize the *full* range of suffering that the overwhelming tragedy of
Auschwitz has served up, instead of constituting "Auschwitz" as an
intellectualizing symbol that ironically and unintendedly looks away
from the very worst example of suffering in this century. Only in this
way, by means of this translation of Christology into the realm of concrete spiritual praxis, can we bring our wholeness in Christ that transcends egoic concern into an ethical enactment of responsibility for *all*

57. R. RADFORD RUETHER, *In What Sense Can We Say that Jesus was "The Christ"?*,
in *The Ecumenist* 10 (Jan.-Feb. 1972) 22.
58. RUETHER, *In What Sense?* (n. 57), p. 22.

suffering others whose non-redemptive experience must constitute the first locus of our merciful and compassionate action. But first of all, we must listen to them.

Duquesne University   Marie L. BAIRD
Dept. of Theology
Pittsburgh, PA 15282
U.S.A.

"JESUS MUST BE CATHOLIC"

THE UNIQUENESS AND UNIVERSALITY OF CHRIST IN THE WORK OF HANS URS VON BALTHASAR

"There is no question that the topic of 'universalism' is part of the New Testament. You can find it in different ways in nearly all the books of the New Testament, simply because the universal meaning of Jesus Christ is constitutive of the belief of the New Testament"[1] This is the way in which the German scholar Gerhard Lohfink characterizes the testimony of the Bible. And, likewise, there is the idea of an "exclusivism of salvation", the conviction "that eschatological salvation is brought about by belief and baptism, by the acceptance of the gospel of Jesus Christ, i.e., by the acceptance of salvation opened by God in Jesus Christ" – as is "stated throughout the New Testament"[2].

The history of Christianity demonstrates that this is true, notwithstanding a variety of clarifying modifications, of course. It is true not only of the New Testament, but also of Christian self-understanding throughout the centuries. In the context of modernity and its criticism of traditional Christian claims, this position was formulated, especially within Protestant theology, by means of the concept of the 'absoluteness of Christianity'[3]. Today, at the end of the 20th century the situation is even more difficult. It is not only the Christian claim to universality which is questioned, but also the universal claim of reason, characteristic of the Enlightenment. This is not only a question of theory but also a question of experience. Even in traditionally religiously-homogeneous areas one encounters different religions. In this situation it is an urgent task to safeguard peaceful and tolerant coexistence. For many people, any conviction of religious superiority seems to be dangerous. In this climate, the claim to uniqueness and universal meaning of the Church or even the person and work of Jesus Christ loses its plausibility – even for many Christians. In this context a thesis of the Enlightenment has found

---

1. G. LOHFINK, *Universalismus und Exklusivität des Heils im Neuen Testament*, in W. KASPER (ed.), *Absolutheit des Christentums* (QD, 79), Freiburg, Herder, 1977, pp. 63-82; here 63. The translations of Balthasar's works are the author's own.

2. *Ibid.* p. 66.

3. As is well known, this term derives from Hegel; for an initial survey, see K. LEHMANN, *Absolutheit des Christentums als philosophisches und theologisches Problem*, in KASPER (ed.), *Absolutheit* (n. 1), pp. 13-38.

its place within Christianity in the so-called 'pluralistic theology of religion': "All religions are equally valid or can be so. This means that their founders, their religious leaders, are equal in the same way. This would open the possibility that Jesus Christ is 'one of several' in the world of saviours and revelatory religious authors"[4].

In this essay, I would like to demonstrate how the Swiss theologian, Hans Urs von Balthasar, tries to position Christianity and the Church within the multitude of religions. He does so by using the term 'catholicity' and 'Catholic'. The central issue for proving and understanding catholicity is the interpretation of "Christ as Catholic"[5]. The presentation and analysis given in this paper refer to a number of smaller articles by Balthasar which give us a sufficiently clear idea of what he maintains. If we want to sum it up right from the beginning we could call it 'trinitarian inclusivism': The uniqueness and universality of Jesus find their foundation in the fact that his life reveals the trinitarian Gestalt (form[6]) of God communicating himself through the Son in the Holy Spirit. This Gestalt avoids the deficiencies of eastern and western religions and fulfils their justified claims. In addition, it corresponds with the understanding of the human being as a person living in history and at the same time longing for transcendence.

I. BALTHASAR'S "CONCERN FOR GENUINE CATHOLICITY"

In a short account of his works, titled *Mein Werk* (1975), Balthasar mentions not only his then already completed theological aesthetics, *The Glory of the Lord*, and his *Theodrama,* which was just in the course of being edited, but also a great number of other publications which he characterizes as the "refraction of the fundamental concern for the multitude of actual interests"[7]. In this context he mentions the "concern for genuine catholicity"[8]. According to Balthasar it is quite urgent for a Catholic to deal with this concern before beginning a dialogue with people of other

---

4. P.F. KNITTER, *Ein Gott – viele Religionen. Gegen den Absolutheitsanspruch des Christentums*, München, 1988, p. 42. With respect to the discussion, cf. R. SCHWAGER (ed.), *Christus allein? Der Streit um die pluralistische Religionstheologie* (QD, 160), Freiburg, Herder, 1996.

5. H.U. von BALTHASAR, *Katholisch* (Kriterien, 36), Einsiedeln, Johannes, ²1975, p. 17.

6. Since, for Balthasar, the German term 'Gestalt' is a technical term, I will not translate it in this essay.

7. H.U. von BALTHASAR, *Mein Werk. Durchblicke*, Einsiedeln, Johannes, 1990, p. 80.

8. *Ibid.,* p. 82.

convictions[9]. Balthasar's own "attempts during the last years have quite intentionally aimed at these presuppositions for the ecumenical dialogue and for the dialogue with all the non-christian religions and philosophies"[10]. In this way, Balthasar sought to protect Catholics against the danger "of esteeming themselves as one denomination among others and searching for a higher synthesis – an attempt in which the ecumenical dialogue often gets stuck"[11]. A Catholic does not have to take a denominational or particularistic view, but rather a universal, that is to say, a catholic one – in the pre-denominational meaning of the term, of course. Formally this claim is made visible by the "notorious 'Catholic and'"[12]; as far as the contents are concerned "Jesus is the catholic: God and man, descending to hell and ascending to heaven, living all the personal and social dimensions of humanity and giving them a new foundation by his own experience"[13].

Balthasar's short account demonstrates some important aspects of his position: through use of the term 'catholic' (and not absoluteness) Balthasar tries to determine the place of the Church and the Christian within the multitude of religions. By doing so, Balthasar refers the claim to uniqueness and universal meaning first of all to Christ and not to the Church.

In his article, "The Absoluteness of Christianity and the Catholicity of the Church" (1977)[14] Balthasar gives an impression of how the terms 'catholic' and 'absolute' can be related to each other. First of all, he maintains that the term 'absoluteness' can be freed from the system of Hegel. On the other hand, the term can be justified by referring to the revelation witnessed by the New Testament. First of all, one must hint at the "multiple usage of the expressions for fullness and fulfilment"[15]. Then one has to take into account the "usage of 'eschatos' where it denotes something definite and final"[16]; and, last but not least, one has to remember statements "which express the impossibility of surpassing divine self-revelation and self-sacrifice to the world, 'id quo maior maius cogitari nequit'"[17]. These terms and the statements using them refer to "an ultimate fullness through integration of all which is provisional and

9. *Ibid.*
10. *Ibid.*, p. 83.
11. *Ibid.*, p. 82.
12. *Ibid.*
13. *Ibid.*
14. H.U. von BALTHASAR, *Die Absolutheit des Christentums und die Katholizität der Kirche*, in KASPER (ed.), *Absolutheit* (n. 1), pp. 131-156.
15. *Ibid.*, p.. 132.
16. *Ibid.*, p. 133.
17. *Ibid.*

particular and in this sense they refer to a kind of totality"[18]. And, therefore, in a first attempt, the term 'catholicity' can be equated with the "fullness of God as communicated to the world in Christ (the crucified and risen)"[19].

II. JESUS – CATHOLIC

For Balthasar 'catholic' is an attribute which belongs, first of all, to Jesus Christ – he is "the catholic: God and man, descended to hell, risen to heaven, covering himself in all the personal and social dimensions of being man [and woman] and founding them anew on the basis of his experience"[20].

In his small book, *Catholic* (of which the second edition was published in 1975)[21], Balthasar describes the connection between the 'catholic' claim of Christianity and the Gestalt of Jesus in detail. "Jesus must be catholic; otherwise the Church could not be called catholic even though she lives in discipleship and Jesus' fullness is promised to her. Catholic means: comprising everything, omitting nothing"[22]. What is revealed in the self-proclamation of Jesus and what can be seen is not merely Jesus alone, but a trinitarian Gestalt: It is the "revelation of the other, of the Father, who is 'greater' than him, but with whom he is one"[23]. And this is possible because of the Holy Spirit "as the uniform and personal revelation and testimony of this mysterious one-ness between the Father and the Son, as the divine We, which is more than the mere I and You"[24]. And, since the "main attribute of the Spirit... is his freedom"[25], the Spirit guarantees that this kind of universality, focused in the term 'catholic', is not only an alternative to individualism, but also to totalitarianism. In this way it is quite clear that, for Balthasar, the Gestalt of Jesus Christ not only comprises the man, Jesus of Nazareth, but "can only be understood in a trinitarian way"[26].

Therefore, in the first place, catholicity is not an attribute of the Church or of a system of doctrine, but the attribute of divine self-revelation, i.e.,

18. *Ibid.,* p. 134.
19. *Ibid.,* p. 135.
20. BALTHASAR, *Werk* (n. 7), p. 82.
21. BALTHASAR, *Katholisch* (n. 5).
22. *Ibid.,* p. 17.
23. *Ibid.*
24. *Ibid.,* p. 18.
25. *Ibid.,* p. 19.
26. *Ibid.,* p. 27.

of an event which has its origin in the freedom of God. Only in this encounter, which equally respects divine and human freedom, can you see, "that the whole catholic revelation – God, Christ and the Church – was and remains the enterprise of the free love of God"[27]. The love of God is the catholic quality, it is "the unattainable greater reality, it has no other reason but itself and it originates in and attains to a greater breadth than I could ever have conceived or imagined"[28].

III. HISTORY AND TRANSCENDENCE

According to Balthasar, catholicity is primarily an attribute assigned to the trinitarian God. And God's catholicity is of special importance for humanity. Living in history and longing for transcendence humanity finds its fulfilment in the trinitarian God, whose catholicity comprises heaven and earth, transcendence and incarnation. In his *Christianity and the World Religions* (1979)[29], Balthasar points out that, in contrast to the far-eastern religions, unity with the divine does not necessarily mean that humanity has to give up its being as persons. "If a religion is to prove itself as the absolute religion, it will be necessary to show that by this religion humanity is really caught up in its temporality and its immanence in history, and even in its being addicted to death and vanity. In other words, the order of creation and the disorder of sin (even of social sin) must appear harboured in this religion"[30] But what do we mean by 'harboured'? How is it possible for a human being to find its fulfilment in the divine without losing itself to it? This problem of unity between the divine and creation is solved in Jesus Christ. "This is expressed schematically by the well-known formula of the Council of Chalcedon (451): Christ is the true divine and the true human being and still he is only a single Who"[31]. These are the dimensions which allow us to understand Jesus Christ as "the catholic"; namely "God and man, descended to hell, risen to heaven"[32].

Creation and grace, incarnation and "the process of integration of creation into the world of God"[33] – all this must not be understood as "a

27. *Ibid.*, p. 19.
28. *Ibid.*, p. 20.
29. H.U. von BALTHASAR, *Das Christentum und die Weltreligionen. Ein Durchblick* (Antworten des Glaubens, 13), Freiburg, Informationszentrum Berufe der Kirche, 1979.
30. *Ibid.*, p. 15, n. 5.
31. *Ibid.*, p. 15.
32. BALTHASAR, *Werk* (n. 7), p. 82.
33. BALTHASAR, *Katholisch* (n. 5), p. 20.

kind of overturning dialectics"[34], not as 'coincidentia oppositorum', but as a process of harbouring, as a process of "inclusion: of nature in grace, of sin in forgiving love, of all purposes in highest gratuitousness"[35]. Therefore, it must be said with respect to the revelation and self-communication of God: "All temporality has its place within eternity"[36]. And equally: "Everything which has already existed in God's plan and eternity, has to become historical within time"[37]. And all that has developed in history finds its "point of convergence"[38] in Jesus Christ. In him, it finds "fullness and integration", and it is for this reason that "there has been communication from the beginning and an 'and' between God and the world"[39]. This is not an 'and' in the sense of an endless addition, but rather this 'and' must be understood as catholic, as the "already existing fullness, which integrates all parts, because it comprehends all", a kind of fullness which exists "in order to give a finally redeemed and non-tragic place in God to all fragments and, in this sense, to all which is tragic"[40].

IV. THEODRAMATIC CATHOLICITY – THE CROSS

Being harboured, the inclusion of nature in grace and the inclusion of creation in God is not a mechanical process, but an encounter of divine and human freedom. This encounter has its typical Gestalt and, as such, is an object of Balthasar theological aesthetics. As a dramatic event it is also the topic of Balthasar's *Theodrama*[41]. Catholicity is "not a half-hearted compromise or syncretism, but the, again dramatic, force of unification of everything which appears desperately fragmentary to man"[42]. What has been hinted at up to now becomes thoroughly clear when Balthasar presents "the cross as the centre of that which is catholic"[43].

What is the meaning of the cross? Balthasar only hints at the traditional answer that, by means of his cross, Jesus has paid penance for our guilt and has reconciled us with God[44]. For Balthasar, something else

---

34. *Ibid.*, p. 21.
35. *Ibid.*
36. *Ibid.*, p. 20.
37. *Ibid.*, p. 21.
38. *Ibid.*, p. 22.
39. *Ibid.*
40. *Ibid.*
41. Cf. H.U. von BALTHASAR, *Theodramatik*. Bd. 1-4, Einsiedeln, Johannes, 1973-1983.
42. BALTHASAR, *Werk* (n. 7), p. 82.
43. BALTHASAR, *Katholisch* (n. 5), p. 23.
44. Cf. *ibid.*, p. 24.

seems to be of greater importance in this context: light can be shed upon the outrage of the cross by the fact that God created human beings as "persons with their own proper freedom" and that "these free beings collide with each other and confine each other even before this can be called guilt or sin"[45].

This not only requires an appeal to a conciliatory attitude i.e., to morality. There is also need for a definitive possibility of being, for a "status..., in which every particular point of view with its absolute particular right (and wrong) is already harboured in the comprehensiveness of that which is catholic"[46] As history since Christ tells us, it is not so much a question of abolishing confrontation, but of the reconciliation of contradictory viewpoints through that which is catholic, as allowed purely through the possibility created by the cross[47].

The cross is the most dramatic sign of a mode of being, in which the freedom of the other remains freedom without being speculatively covered up. It is for this reason that, for Balthasar, the integration can not be the matter of an absolute wisdom or of a system like that of Hegel. Jesus must bear the confrontation "in a form of suffering which is the expression of a most active readiness to stand up for every single person according to the will of the Father. In this way, he does not overpower the particular from without, but he transcends it from within, acknowledging its relative right"[48].

V. FROM THE CATHOLICITY OF JESUS TO THE CATHOLICITY OF THE CHURCH

It has already been mentioned that Balthasar understands the catholicity of Jesus to be the absolute presupposition for the catholicity of the Church: "A Church can only be catholic because God Self is catholic first, and because the catholicity of God has opened itself to the world in Jesus Christ and finally in the Holy Spirit, revealing and communicating itself at the same time"[49]. It is not difficult to see that, for Balthasar, this thought is equally valid the other way round: the catholic fullness of God proves its fullness exactly by the fact that it comprehends also the other in the creature – "the initial phenomenon is the whole: the Word

---

45. *Ibid.*
46. *Ibid.*
47. Cf. *ibid.*, p. 25.
48. *Ibid.*, p. 26.
49. *Ibid.*, p. 19.

of God and its being heard by means of the Holy Spirit, Christ together with his Church"[50]. The Church is not "a historical effect of Christ: she is his 'fullness' and his bridal 'body'. The Christian reality of the Church is Christ himself, who expresses and impresses himself in humanity through the power of the Spirit"[51].

For Balthasar, however, there remains a question. At the cross, the most important event has already happened. If this is the case, you have to ask whether a human activity like discipleship is still possible or meaningful[52]. Balthasar finds the solution to this problem within a trinitarian perspective. From this point of view, God is understood as a God in mutual sacrifice – the sacrifice of the Father to the Son and the sacrifice of the Son to the Father. In this way, "divine fullness"[53] is a special kind of fullness. It is a fullness "granting space, making itself poor and, in this way, making the Son rich with the divinity of the Father"[54]. Also at the cross this catholic fullness proves – to a certain extent *ad extra* – a "fullness granting space. Not only overflowing outwards (bonum diffusivum sui), but opening inwards, having become poor for us (2 Kor 8,9), in order to make us rich, so that we can become 'poor in the Spirit' with it and in it"[55]. In this way it is clear that the catholicity of God becomes "the origin of the catholicity of the Church, which is thus enabled to take part in the act of salvation at the cross without questioning in the least the uniqueness, the inimitability and the sufficiency of the cross of the Son"[56].

VI. JESUS CHRIST – FULFILMENT AND CORRECTION OF ALL RELIGIONS

All well-founded claims in the various religions find their fulfilment in Jesus Christ. This is Balthasar's central thesis. Although he only hints at this thesis, at central places in his work he elaborates upon it in more detail, albeit sketchily. All the deficiencies and contradictions in the different religions are corrected and surpassed in the event of Jesus Christ. In "Claim to Catholicity" (1974)[57] Balthasar makes it clear that Christianity

---

50. *Ibid.*, p. 23.
51. H.U. von BALTHASAR, *Herrlichkeit. Eine Theologische Ästhetik*, Bd. I. Einsiedeln, Johannes, 1961, pp. 579-580.
52. Cf. BALTHASAR, *Katholisch* (n. 5), p. 24.
53. *Ibid.*, p. 27.
54. *Ibid.*
55. *Ibid.*
56. *Ibid.*
57. *Anspruch auf Katholizität*, in H.U. von BALTHASAR, *Pneuma und Institution*, Einsiedeln, Johannes, 1974, pp. 61-116.

and the Church are engaged in a "competition of 'catholicities'"[58] with
Judaism and the Far-Eastern religions and that they have to maintain
their claim in this competition. Judaism (and secularised utopian thinking) look for and find the absolute – so to say – in the horizontal dimension, i.e., in the future; the Far-Eastern religions find it in the vertical
dimension, in ecstasy and inward communion with the divine. A common feature of these conceptions is the tendency "to negate the present
time of history and accordingly to destroy humanity in its meaning"[59].
This "antinomy of immanent catholicities can only be resolved in the
cross of Jesus and consequently only in a trinitarian way"[60]. Centred
round the cross and resurrection[61], Christianity not only takes into
account history and the personality of man [and woman] but allows, at
the same time, for both horizontal and vertical transcendence. Thus,
Judaism and paganism are reconciled within Christianity and at the same
time transcended by "the divine mystery of the Holy Trinity"[62].

In his essay, *Christianity and the World-Religions* (1979), Balthasar
formulates the same conviction. For Balthasar, the "dream of a single
religion of humanity"[63], in which "the relative contradictions of the...
great religions of the world could be and should be overcome"[64], is
unrealistic. He contrasts this dream – "at least briefly" – with "the *one*
religion", which "is allowed to maintain the claim that all that is positive in other religions is harboured in it and at the same time surpassingly fulfilled; it is the one which has called itself from the beginning
the 'all-embracing' (this is the meaning of the word 'the catholic')"[65].
This "catholicity"[66], this "claim to universality, has its foundation in the
unique Gestalt of Jesus Christ which is without any analogy in world
history: Jesus Christ, who fulfils all the claims of eastern religions, of
Judaism and Islam by laying claim to divine authority and communication of life"[67].

In *Epilogue* (1987), a short book intended by Balthasar to provide an
overview of his trilogy, he takes up this argument again. Because religions "form a hierarchy of meaning", one can "try to show that those
which comprehend less can be harboured in those which comprehend

58. *Ibid.*, p. 63.
59. *Ibid.*, p. 96.
60. *Ibid.*, p. 107.
61. Cf. *ibid.*, p. 99.
62. *Ibid.*, p. 102.
63. BALTHASAR, *Durchblick* (n. 29), p. 13.
64. *Ibid.*, p. 12.
65. *Ibid.*, p. 14.
66. *Ibid.*
67. *Ibid.*

more"[68]. That which is considered as specifically Christian – "Christ as
the incarnate Word of God and God as trinitarian love"[69] – corresponds,
on the one hand, to the transcendence of God and, on the other hand, to
the personal character and freedom of human beings and their longing
for redeeming divine community. Surpassingly, it gives meaning to suffering and death. The whole concept presupposes an affirmative attitude
"towards a kind of Christology as it is implicitly or explicitly developed
in the New Testament and safeguarded by the councils (of Nicea and
Chalcedon)"[70].

VII. The Claim to Catholicity
Perceptible as the Gestalt of Divine Love

The apologetics of neo-scholastic theology, up until the time of the
Second Vatican Council, argued that the claim expressed by speaking of
the absoluteness of Christianity is well-founded and credible. Within the
framework of its so-called extrinsic procedure, it is not necessary to
legitimate the contents of this claim, but rather the instances which represent this claim; first of all, Jesus Christ as the *legatus divinus* confirmed by God, and then the Church which is founded and thereby legitimated by Christ. In this case, the reconstruction of the claim coincides
with its legitimation[71].

For Balthasar this manner of argumentation is neither promising
nor desirable: arguing in this way, we find Jesus "in a battle of proofs
and refutations"[72]. "None of these proofs" put forward by believers
or theology, "remained uncontradicted"[73]. Finally, the traditional
apologetics "has to withdraw from the enemy"[74]. This kind of apologetics is not only ineffective, it is not even desirable, because arguments "are not able to 'force' a person to accept the Christian view;
in matters of faith, arguments should not hinder the free act of faith
and devotion"[75].

68. H.U. von Balthasar, *Epilog*, Einsiedeln/Trier, Johannes, 1987, p.7.
69. *Ibid.*, p. 28.
70. *Ibid.*, p. 30.
71. Cf. M. Seckler, *Fundamentaltheologie. Aufgaben und Aufbau, Begriff und
Namen*, in W. Kern, H.-J. Pottmeyer and M. Seckler (eds.), *Handbuch der Fundamentaltheologie*. Bd. 4, Freiburg, Herder, 1988, pp. 451-514; especially pp. 456-459.
72. H.U. von Balthasar, *Leuchtet Jesus ein?* in H.U. von Balthasar, *Neue
Klarstellungen,* Einsiedeln, Johannes, 1979, pp. 8-13; here p. 8.
73. *Ibid.*
74. *Ibid.*
75. Balthasar, *Epilog* (n. 68), p. 11.

Balthasar's proposal of how the claim of Christianity can be realized and legitimized corresponds with the change from an extrinsic kind of apologetics to a kind of fundamental theology which is concerned with contents of the Christian claim. In the work of Balthasar this change can easily be seen in *The Glory of the Lord*, his theological aesthetics[76]. Its point of departure is the observation that, in the New Testament, there can be found a Gestalt of revelation which makes sense to someone touched by divine grace because of the divine glory radiating from this Gestalt. It is not a legitimate authority legitimizing the contents; rather, the contents legitimize themselves. Catholicity is an attribute of the Gestalt of Christ but it "reveals itself only if we look at it with faithful openness"[77].

Recognizing and understanding the Gestalt implies a specific kind of knowledge and a specific approach to the Holy Scripture. The Scripture is taken as a symphonic testimony of faith, which opens "the possibility of a careful rational approximation to the decisive vision"[78]. In this process, the distinction between historical facts and their interpretation by faith is "theologically insignificant"[79], because whatever is divine can only be realized by faith and by means of a testimony of faith. And faith means "not to evade the phenomenon presenting itself, not to squint, but to stay there and to let oneself be affected"[80]. The truth of faith is not found in the distance of scientific neutrality, but in the correspondence between divine grace and its light working in a human being and the Gestalt radiating the glory of God. Knowledge through faith is not founded on scientific analysis and the details of exegetical work, but on the synthetic view of the believer which grasps the whole of the Gestalt in all its glory.

Seen in a formal way, catholicity manifests itself as a Gestalt. Seen in a material way, it is the "Gestalt of Jesus", which "can only be understood in a trinitarian way"[81]. The Gestalt visible through the life of Jesus and in his word, in his death and resurrection and in the mission of the Holy Spirit is the Son returning the love of the Father through his sacrifice, even to the point of the cross, and it is the Holy Spirit uniting the Father and the Son and communicated to the world. This Gestalt is characterized by the divine glory radiating from it and seizing us – and this

76. Cf. B. KÖRNER, *Fundamentaltheologie bei Hans Urs von Balthasar,* in *Zeitschrift für katholische Theologie* 109 (1987) 129–152.

77. BALTHASAR, *Katholisch* (n. 5), p. 17.

78. H.U. von BALTHASAR, *Glaubhaft ist nur Liebe*, Einsiedeln, Johannes, ⁴1975, p. 39.

79. BALTHASAR, *Katholisch* (n. 5), p. 23.

80. BALTHASAR, *Jesus* (n. 72), p. 12.

81. BALTHASAR, *Katholisch* (n. 5), p. 27.

glory is the love of God. Humanity has a kind of pre-understanding of this love, but the "plausibility of divine love is not founded in what men and women have already accepted as love, but is only founded in the Gestalt of the revelation of love interpreting itself"[82].

The decisive term which allows us to understand the life, death, and resurrection of Christ and the mission of the Holy Spirit is love. And it is love which helps us to understand this as a singular and universally meaningful event. Love is not only the essential nature of God, but also the characteristic of God's relationship to the world. God's love does not overpower humanity, but rather grants redeeming space to humanity with its freedom and history, it grants forgiveness and admission to divine life. God is "the first to be catholic" and "in Jesus Christ and finally in the Holy Spirit God's catholicity has opened itself to the world"[83]. Divine love is divine openness for everything, "the love of God is the unsurpassable greater"[84], and the Gestalt of divine love is credibility as such.

VIII. The Apologetics of Catholicity
Legitimated as the Unsurpassable Greater

Jesus Christ is the catholic as such, but he "does not need apologetics: he makes sense"[85]. But if faith is a matter of grace and unattainable through reason, is it, in this case, irrational? And, consequently, is theology, understood as a necessarily limited attempt at a reasonable understanding in the field of faith, still possible?

In accordance with the great Christian and, in particular, the Catholic, tradition, Balthasar pleads for the possibility of justifying faith in a rational way. He ascribes this task especially to his theological aesthetics, *The Glory of the Lord*. As Balthasar himself maintains, the aim of his aesthetics corresponds to what, in traditional Catholic theology, is called apologetics or fundamental theology[86]. Nevertheless, Balthasar's work

---

82. BALTHASAR, *Glaubhaft* (n. 78), p. 36.
83. BALTHASAR, *Katholisch* (n. 5), p. 19.
84. *Ibid.*, p. 20.
85. BALTHASAR, *Jesus* (n. 72), p. 12.
86. Cf. BALTHASAR, *Herrlichkeit* (n. 50), p. 9, where Balthasar maintains that in the first volume of his *Theological Aesthetics*, which is dedicated to theological knowledge, you can find many topics "which normally are treated by so-called Fundamental Theology". And, later in this volume, Balthasar says that "the central question of so-called Apologetics or Fundamental Theology is... a question of perceiving the Gestalt, an aesthetical problem" (*ibid.*, p. 166).

represents a special kind of fundamental theology in which he tries to avoid what he calls an anthropological reduction on the one hand, and extrinsicism on the other hand. Anthropological reduction tends to reduce the contents of revelation and faith to what can be proved by means of philosophical principles. Extrinsicism is the attempt to justify revelation and faith not by proving its contents but by confirming the credibility of those who present the contents of faith[87]. In contrast to these theological conceptions, Balthasar believes revelation is not to be identified from without, but "by the self-interpretation of the incarnate logos himself"[88]. And, looking on the incarnate logos, humanity discovers the "plausibility of this love of God" which is given "by the self-interpretation of the revelation-Gestalt of love itself"[89]

This new kind of apologetics not only aims at faith, but presupposes faith. It is not the anteroom of theology, but is theology[90]. It is older than the neo-scholastic kind of apologetics. For Balthasar, it is "a necessary and yet insufficient kind of apologetics"[91]. Its guideline is 'the one who sees more, is right'[92]. According to Balthasar, this kind of apologetics is also the proper method by which to prove catholicity: "Thereby an old and nearly worn-out principle of apologetics is renewed: the one who sees more is right, the one who is able to comprehend more, especially contradictory positions and tensions which elsewhere remain isolated or are considered absolute"[93].

Accordingly, the main characteristic of this kind of apologetics is "the method of increasing integration"[94]. Once more: "The one who is able to integrate more truth into his view could lay claim to the highest attainable truth"[95]. And, according to Balthasar, Christianity can claim to be able to do so because Jesus Christ "has fulfilled all the claims of the eastern religions, the Jewish religion and Islam, but he has done so by laying claim to divine authority and salvation"[96]. In "Claim to Catholicity" and in his

87. BALTHASAR, *Glaubhaft* (n. 78), pp. 8-39.
88. *Ibid.*, p. 35.
89. *Ibid.*, p. 36.
90. It is obvious that Balthasar is indebted to what his teacher Henri de Lubac already delineated in his inaugural lecture in 1929. According to de Lubac the best means to legitimate and defend faith (apologetics) is to expose the contents of it (dogmatics) – cf. B.KÖRNER, *Henri de Lubac and Fundamental Theology*, in Com XXIII (1996), n. 4, pp. 710-724.
91. BALTHASAR, *Epilog* (n. 68), p. 7.
92. Cf. *ibid.*, p. 35.
93. BALTHASAR, *Werk* (n. 7), pp. 81f. Also in this case Balthasar is indebted to Henri de Lubac – cf. KÖRNER, *Henri de Lubac* (n.90), pp. 722-724.
94. BALTHASAR, *Epilog* (n. 68), p. 12.
95. *Ibid.*, p. 11.
96. BALTHASAR, *Durchblick* (n. 29), p. 14.

Epilogue Balthasar tries to prove this assertion under the title, "Competition of catholicities"[97]. However, as regards the power of persuasion of this kind of argumentation, Balthasar himself nevertheless remains sceptical[98].

IX. BALTHASAR'S TRINITARIAN INCLUSIVISM
SUMMARY AND ASSESSMENT

The texts underlying this short investigation are more or less sketches. With a few strokes, Balthasar delineates a position, but nevertheless it becomes quite clear what he wants to affirm. At first sight at least, Balthasar's severe formulations are sometimes appalling. For example: the assertion that non-Christian religions "destroy"[99] humanity seems to be unjust to these religions. But with regard to the contents, the coherence of Balthasar's conception of catholicity suggests that his position is not to be rejected because of these formulations, but that the real or possible truth of his assertions is to be investigated. Especially in his shorter works, Balthasar seems to speak in a more aphoristic way. He delineates a programme, but he does not argue every step. Therefore, it is not difficult to find deficiencies in his argumentation and to condemn the author. But it is also possible to take into account the special character of his sketches and to understand them as a programme and an invitation to carry out what Balthasar indicates. In this way, it might be possible to test whether the argument really can perform what Balthasar intends – to investigate a way which helps a Catholic to find his place in the context of religions. This task cannot be taken up exhaustively at this point; a few hints may serve as a kind of preparation for it:

(1) Balthasar sums up the singular claim of the Church through the use of the term 'catholicity'. But this characteristic is attributed to the Church only in a derived way – or as Balthasar puts it; it is a kind of catholicity which the Church receives[100]. According to Balthasar, Jesus is the first to be called catholic, and the Gestalt of Jesus includes the revelation and self-communication of the trinitarian love of God and the Church as well.

(2) Balthasar substitutes the more traditional term 'absoluteness' with the term 'catholicity'. In doing so he avoids the misunderstanding

97. BALTHASAR, *Anspruch* (n. 57), p. 63.
98. Cf. BALTHASAR, *Katholisch* (n. 5), pp. 7-8; *Epilog* (n. 67), pp. 35-36.
99. BALTHASAR, *Anspruch* (n. 57), p. 96.
100. Cf. *ibid.*, p. 114.

that the term 'absolute' has to be understood in opposition to the term 'relative'. This would at least include the danger of understanding God as absolute because God exists without relations. But this kind of eminence without any relation is not the way in which we should think of the essence and the existence of the trinitarian God.

(3) Balthasar uses the term 'catholicity' in a consistent, but also in an oscillating way. On the one hand he uses the term in a predenominational way – as far as the Church is concerned it denotes the universal character of the Church. At the same time, Balthasar attributes the term to the Catholic Church as a denomination, because the Roman-Catholic Church "is not a Church alongside of others, but it is the source and the mouth of all the others"[101]. But the catholicity of the Catholic Church is a potential catholicity, not necessarily an actual one. According to Balthasar, "the non-Catholic positions have to remind the Catholic of what he has forgotten to integrate into his position because of guilt or carelessness"[102].

(4) By using the term 'catholicity', Balthasar indicates a kind of religious and ecumenical inclusivism. But the term 'inclusivism' is not as clear as it seems. For the present purpose, it is used in a less specific way as the idea that elements of divine truth and salvation can also be found outside the Catholic Church – even if we are convinced that the source of all truth and salvation is Jesus Christ. If we take into account how Balthasar characterises his position it might be called a trinitarian inclusivism. And if we bear in mind the last quotation, we see that 'catholicity', as it is to be understood in Balthasar's conception, does not mean the self-sufficiency of a closed system. It marks the conviction that the Church is endowed with all the divine riches and divine fullness, and that it must necessarily get involved in dialogue and competition exactly because of its catholicity. Only in the encounter, and in confrontation, with the other will the Church – understanding itself as the Catholic Church from the beginning – gradually know the real depth and width of the fullness and the riches given to her by God.

(5) Balthasar's conception of catholicity invalidates theological arguments directed against inclusivism through the theory of

---

101. BALTHASAR, *Katholisch* (n. 5), p. 85.
102. BALTHASAR, *Werk* (n. 7), p. 82.

religious pluralism. As 'catholicity' denotes the uniqueness and universality of God's love, i.e., what Balthasar calls a "fullness which creates space"[103], Christianity and the Church are obliged to allow space for other religions and philosophies. The cross of the Lord reminds the Church that she must even be ready to pay a high price for this. The claim to catholicity, understood as the catholicity of divine love, does not exclude, but includes tolerance.

(6) Nevertheless, the question remains whether such a claim to catholicity does not devalue other religions. Any attempt to answer this should bear in mind that, according to Balthasar, all religions have the right to claim catholicity for themselves. And in the same way, the Church, looking to the origin and the presence of the divine life given to her, claims that the fullness of the space-creating love of God is present in her. This catholicity does not exist in itself and it is not the result of human performance. Rather, it is a gift, it is catholicity which is 'received'. And, in reality, the Church is far from realizing it, partly out of guilt and carelessness, partly because she has not yet reached the aim of her history and her mission. Therefore, the Church knows that she is not allowed to lay her claim to catholicity in a triumphant way, but must verify it by sacrifice[104]. And in this way she takes part in the 'competition of catholicities'.

(7) There is good reason for hoping that Balthasar's trinitarian inclusivism disallows a reduction of biblical and Christian claims, and a kind of triumphalism which inclines to violence and a devaluation of the significance of other religions.

University of Graz   Bernhard KÖRNER
Kirchengasse 4
8010 Graz
Austria

103. BALTHASAR, *Katholisch* (n. 5), p. 27.
104. Cf. BALTHASAR, *Anspruch* (n. 57), p. 114.

FOUR CHRISTOLOGICAL THEMES OF THE THEOLOGY OF KARL RAHNER

In a recent essay honoring Bruno Brinkman, Philip Endean centers his attention on the Christology of Karl Rahner. Endean offers two important perspectives: first, "Rahner sets his Christology within a vision of God's gracious gift of self to the cosmos", and second, "for Rahner, grace in us and the hypostatic union in Jesus Christ, though inseparable, remains distinct"[1].

Endean's essay underscores the fact that the theology of Karl Rahner, and more specifically in this instance, his Christology, continues to challenge and enrich us with his insights, and even more with his questions. And Endean notes where these insights and questions can be found by emphasizing that "Rahner's contribution to Christology, as in so many other fields, came through provocative essays rather than systematic treatises"[2].

A second recent study on Rahner's Christology is one done by Joseph Wong[3]. In a helpful schematization, Wong proposes "the following paradigms with a particular type of Christology attached to each: [1] *Ecclesiocentric-exclusivist view* with an exclusive Christology, [2] *Christocentric-inclusivist view* with a constitutive or a normative Christology, and [3] *Theocentric-pluralist view* with a nonnormative Christology"[4]. Wong concludes that the Christocentric-inclusivist view "is currently held by the majority of theologians"[5]. And he further reasons that within this Christocentric-inclusivist view it is possible to "formulate a Rahnerian pneumatological Christocentrism. It is an inclusivist view, representative of the mainline position of Christian theologians, and, in my opinion [states Wong] the appropriate view in the theology of religions"[6]. Having identified represen-

---

1. P. ENDEAN, *Rahner, Christology and Grace*, in *Heythrop Journal* 37 (1996) 284-297, p. 285.

2. *Ibid.*, p. 285. Endean notes the following recent secondary studies of Rahner's Christology, p. 296: J. WONG, *Logos-Symbol in the Christology of Karl Rahner*, Rome, 1984; E. FARRUGIA, *Aussage und Zusage: Zur Indirektheit der Methode K. Rahners, veranschaulicht an seiner Christologie*, Rome, 1985; I. BOKWA, *Christologie als Anfang und Ende der Anthropologie*, Frankfurt, 1990; and E. MAURICE, *La Christologie de Karl Rahner*, Paris, 1995.

3. J. WONG, *Anonymous Christians: Karl Rahner's Pneuma-Christocentrism and an East-West Dialogue*, in *Theological Studies* 55 (1994) 609-637.

4. *Ibid.*, p. 611.

5. *Ibid.*, p. 612.

6. *Ibid.*, p. 610.

tative theologians of the Ecclesiocentric-exclusivist view[7] and the Theo-centric-pluralist view[8], Wong focuses on Rahner as a representative theologian of the Christocentric-inclusivist view[9]. My own focus is one that is similar to that of Wong. I also identify Rahner as a representative of the Christocentric-inclusivist view, supporting that conclusion as a result of my study of "Four Christological Themes of the Theology of Karl Rahner".

These "Four Christological Themes of the Theology of Karl Rahner" emerge primarily from a large number of these individual essays[10]. These four themes are certainly not exhaustive of all that Rahner has to say regarding Christology, but they do represent significant insights and approaches of his theology: "The Full Humanity of Christ", "Christology Within an Evolutionary View of the World", "The Meaning of the Cross" and "Christ: The One Mediator" are engaging themes in a focus on "The Myriad Christ: Plurality and the Quest for Unity in Contemporary Christology".

The central focus for Rahner in his Christological writings is the person who is, or is called to become, a believer. For those who proclaim

7. *Ibid.,* p. 611: The Ecclesiocentric-exclusivist view "represents the most restrictive position regarding the relationship of Christianity to other religions... Karl Barth may be considered as the chief exponent of an exclusivist Christology on the Protestant side". See also, B. MARSHALL, *Christology in Conflict,* Oxford, 1987, and the critique offered by P. ENDEAN, *Rahner* (n. 1), esp. pp. 292-297.

8. J. WONG, *Anonymous Christians* (n. 3), p. 616. In Wong's judgment this approach is seen in John Hick and Raimundo Panikkar. Hick "is one of the most distinctive representatives of religious pluralism... He advocates a 'Copernican revolution in theology', namely, a paradigm shift from a Christianity-centered to a God-centered model of the universe of faiths. Hick considers the world religions, including Christianity, to be so many different human responses to the one divine Reality". Wong refers [n. 34], among other works, to J. HICK, *God and the Universe of Faith,* London, 1973, and J. HICK, *God Has Many Names,* London, 1980 [p. 616]. "In [Panikkar's] long introduction to the new edition [R. PANIKKAR, *The Unknown Christ of Hinduism: Toward an Ecumenical Christophany,* Revised Edition, New York, 1981] Panikkar advocates a universal Christology. For him, Christ is more than an historical figure. As a universal principle Christ is the most powerful living symbol of the total reality which he call 'The mystery'" [p. 618].

9. J. WONG, *Anonymous Christians* (n. 3) p. 610. Wong identifies John Cobb, "a major representative of process theologians", as one whose Christology is "generally considered as normative but not constitutive". But Wong concludes that he "would argue that Cobb's Logos Christology is constitutive as well as normative" [pp. 615-616]. Wong refers [n.28, p. 615] to J. COBB, *Christ in a Pluralistic Age,* Philadelphia, 1975

10. All references are detailed in the footnotes. I make the general observation that essays judged by Rahner as particulary important were published (for the first time or following a previous publication) in *Schriften zur Theologie* (*ST*), 16 Volumes, Zürich, Einsiedeln; Köln, Benziger Verlag, 1954-1984. These volumes were translated and published in English as *Theological Investigations* (*TI*), various translators, 23 Volumes. UK publisher, Darton, Longman and Todd, 1961-1992. US publisher, Vols. 1-6 Baltimore, Helicon, Vols. 7-10, New York, Herder and Herder, Vols. 11-20, New York, Seabury Press, Vols. 21-23, New York, Crossroad.

the message of Jesus Christ, questions about Christology are not periph-
eral. Rahner notes that we are people in a situation in life in which the
message of Jesus Christ "is not simply a matter of course, but... is controversial, doubted and rejected". Therefore for believers questions of
Christology are fundamental[11].

Considerations of the pastoral importance of Christology for the
believer are, emphasizes Rahner, by their nature tied to ecclesiology.
"For it is the Church, after all, which has passed the Gospel of Jesus
Christ on to her/him in the first place"[12]. But what is it, specifically,
which the Church has passed on? This is a subject to which Rahner has
devoted a great deal of writing[13].

I. THE FULL HUMANITY OF CHRIST

Let me preface my remarks on the theme of the Full Humanity of
Christ with some important observations. John P. Galvin has noted that

11. K. RAHNER, *Christology Today?*, in *Theological Investigations* (hereafter *TI*),
Vol. 17, London, 1981, pp. 24-38, English translation (hereafter ET) of *Schriften zur Theologie* (hereafter *ST*), Bd. XII, Einsiedeln, 1975, pp. 353-369), a previously unpublished
lecture given in December 1973 at the University of Saarbrücken, p. 24. See, also, in
regard to the personal character of belief in Jesus Christ; K. RAHNER, *Foundations of
Christian Faith* (hereafter *FCF*), London, 1978, (ET of: *Grundkurs des Glaubens* (hereafter *GdG*), Freiberg im Breisgau, 1976), pp. 305-307, in which Rahner declares the need
for an "existentiell" Christology. "In its real and essential being Christianity really
understands itself as an existentiell process, and this process is precisely what we are calling a personal relationship to Jesus Christ" (p. 306). (However, Rahner cautions that this
need must allow for "an implicit and anonymous" process. In this regard, see, below, n.
44.) And this personal relationship is "always present as something which a person still
has to realize and bring to radical actualization in the living out of her/his whole existence
throughout the whole length and breadth and depth of her/his life" (p. 307). And see also,
K. RAHNER, *Theology and Anthropology* (hereafter *Anthropology*), in *TI*, Vol. 9, London,
1972, pp. 28-45, ET of *ST*, Bd. VIII, Einsiedeln, 1967, in which Rahner cites the example of what is necessary for a true Christology: 1), to understand the human being as one
"who is oriented towards an 'absolute Savior' both a priori and in actuality (his essence
having been elevated and set in this direction supernaturally by grace)"; and 2), that the
human being is "confronted with Jesus of Nazareth as this Savior – which cannot, of
course, be transcendentally 'deduced'" (pp. 29-30).
12. RAHNER, *Christology Today?*, p. 24.
13. One of his earliest articles dealt with the theme of Christology: K. RAHNER, *Die
protestantische Christologie der Gegenwart*, in *Theologie der Zeit* 1 (1936) 189-202. One
may also note his theological doctoral dissertation, unpublished, which he defended in
1936. *E Latere Christi: Der Ursprung der Kirche als zweiter Eva aus der Seite Christi
des Zweiten Adam. Eine Untersuchung über den typologischen Sinn von Jo 19,34* (hereafter *E Latere Christi*). See the analysis offered by J. WONG, *Logos-Symbol in the Christology of Karl Rahner* (hereafter *Logos-Symbol*), Rome, 1984, pp. 40-45: "In this dissertation various aspects of New Testament typology are studied which foreshadow
Rahner's later technical concept Realsymbol" (p. 41).

"during the first two-thirds of the twentieth century... many prominent Catholic theologians urged increased emphasis on the humanity of Christ as a means of overcoming excessive stress on Christ's divinity and of presenting Christ as a model for Christian life"[14]. He then goes on to say that "during the past two decades the situation has changed dramaticaly. Such works by Catholic systematic theologians as... Karl Rahner's *Foundations of Christian Faith*" illustrate that "the earlier emphasis on Christ's human nature (in the conceptual pairing divinity/humanity) has yielded to a new focus on the historical Jesus (in the conceptual pairing historical Jesus/Christ of faith)"[15].

As a systematic theologian, Rahner builds upon his writings from earlier periods. He often assumes that the reader is familiar with themes that he has developed previously. I believe that this emphasis by Rahner in his later writings on the Jesus of history in no way is meant to be a replacement for his reflections on the humanity of Christ. We are dealing with two related but distinct issues[16]. In my judgment this newer

14. J. GALVIN, *From the Humanity of Christ to the Jesus of History: A Paradigm Shift in Catholic Christology*, in *Theological Studies* 55 (1994) 252-273, p. 252.

15. *Ibid.*, p. 255.

16. As Galvin himself suggests, there are two principal reasons for what he calls a "paradigm shift necessitated by engagement with a new set of issues and distinctions" [p. 256]. A first reason is that systematic theologians are more recently attempting "to examine the basis of Christian faith in Jesus" and this demands "greater attention to historical questions concerning his public life". A second reason is that systematic theologians are seeking "to reexamine the meaning of basic Christological assertions" [p. 259]. Key works noted by Galvin [p. 260, n. 32] are: J. MEIER, *A Marginal Jew: Rethinking the Historical Jesus,* vol. 1, New York, 1991; J. CROSSAN, *The Historical Jesus: The Life of a Mediterranean Jewish Peasant*, San Francisco, 1991; and J. GNILKA, *Jesus von Nazaret*, Freiburg, 1990. In addition, I would also include, R. HAIGHT, *The Impact of Jesus Research on Christology*, in *Louvain Studies* 21 (1996) 216-228; and P. PHAN, *Jesus the Christ With an Asian Face*, in *Theological Studies* 57 (1996) 399-430, in which Phan presents the Christologies of 1) Aloysius Pieris, 2) Jung Lee, 3) Choan-Seng Song, and 4) Chung Hyun Kyung. With regard to these Christologies and the Jesus of history, Phan comments on the importance of 'appropriateness': 'Because they are all Christian theologies, two broad sets of criteria can be applied to assess their validity, namely adequacy and appropriateness. By the former is meant the power to speak the Christian word in the contemporary idiom in order to understand and transform the condition of the addressee. By the latter is meant the relative coherence of this message with the life and teaching of Jesus as mediated through the Bible and Christian tradition' [p. 424] And Phan offers a more specific assessment: "There is one area, however, in which Asian theologies can derive much profit from contemporary Euro-American biblical research on early Judaism... Pieris and Song present a negative portrayal of early Judaism... A careful and judicious use of contemporary scholarship on early Judaism, especially on the Pharisees, will correct the age-old bias against Jews and Judaism" [p. 429]. And see also, W. JEANROND, C. THEOBALD (eds.), *Who Do You Say That I Am (Concilium)* 1997/1, London, 1997, especially, S. FREYNE, *The Quest of the Historical Jesus: Some Theological Reflections*, in *Concilium* 1997/1, 37-51.

emphasis on the historical Jesus focuses still greater light on the Christological doctrine of the humanity of Christ.

Many would be surprised to even associate the name of Rahner with the historical dimension. But to focus on Rahner's theology as primarily or exclusively transcendental does a disservice to Rahner. Leo O'Donovan refers to a 1952 address in which Rahner stresses that a knowledge of essences (*Wesenserkenntnis*) "must rely... on a two-fold method: on a transcendental method... [and] the reflection on the historical experience humanity has of itself"[17]. And as O'Donovan himself has expressed it, "Rahner has repeatedly argued for the reciprocal interdependence of transcendental and historical reflection in theology"[18]. I believe that Rahner's reflections on the humanity of Christ exemplify in an extraordinary way this reciprocal interdependence of transcendental and historical reflection in theology.

The theme of the Full Humanity of Christ is underscored by Rahner again and again in his writings. He sees it as a necessity to affirm and to safeguard belief in Jesus as fully human. This does not mean that Rahner is suggesting abandoning belief in Jesus as fully divine. The point emphasized by Rahner is that "a vertical Christology of descent, which was the approach of classical Christology, must today no longer overlook the fact that what the Logos who descended from the glory of God desired to take upon himself was precisely the sombre facts of historical existence with its limits, dependency and baseness, without which there can be no true and full humanity"[19]. The danger that classical Christology has had to struggle with over the centuries is the danger of monophysitism: "the danger, that is, of thinking of Jesus simply as God, who merely appears on earth in a

17. L. O'DONOVAN, *Orthopraxis and Theological Method in Karl Rahner*, in L. SALM (ed.), *Catholic Theological Society of America Proceedings* 35 (1980) 47-65, p. 49. Rahner's address is published as: K. RAHNER, *The Dignity and Freedom of Man* in *TI*, Vol. 2, London, 1963, pp. 235-263, esp. pp. 236-237; ET of: *ST*, Bd. II, Einsiedeln, 1955, pp. 247-277, esp. pp. 248-249. The article originated as a presentation given 1 May 1952

18. L. O'DONOVAN, *Orthopraxis*, p. 49.

19. RAHNER, *Christology Today?*, p. 29. Christology must avoid so transfiguring Jesus "even in his earthly life that it is no longer evident that he took our human, poverty-stricken and sombre fate on himself, fully and completely, redeeming us through that very fact". See, also, K. RAHNER, *The Two Basic Types of Christology* (hereafter *Types of Christology*) in *TI*, Vol. 13, London, 1975, pp. 213-223; (ET of: *ST*, Bd. X, Einsiedeln, 1972, pp. 227-238). First presented as a lecture 16 December 1971. Rahner describes these two types of Christology as the "saving type", which is a Christology viewed from below, and the other is the "metaphysical type", which is a Christology developing downwards from above (pp. 213-214). Importantly, Rahner notes tht it would be a rash conclusion to identify the classical Christology of Chalcedon with the metaphysical type in an exclusive way; "it appears on closer examination that what we have in this classic Christology is rather a mixed type" (p. 214).

human livery"[20]. And this concern has been repeated by Rahner often[21]. The end result of monophysitism is that Christology becomes mythology[22]. And consequently those who are or remain "believers" may be viewed with suspicion, and those who are "non-believers" may not be moved to a belief that is evidently "mythological". Therefore, Rahner sees it as essential that Christology affirms and supports a belief in the full humanity of Jesus Christ[23].

20. RAHNER, *Christology Today?*, p. 31. "Every concept of the incarnation which views Jesus' humanity, either overtly or implicitly, merely as the guise (*Verkleidung*) God takes upon himself in order to signalise his speaking presence (*redende Anwesenheit*), is and remains a heresy" (p. 38; *ST*, Bd. XII, p. 369). And also: "We can and still must confess with the Council of Chalcedon that the specific reality which meets us is Jesus… was and ultimately remains true man and true God in a unique and incomprehensible unity; so that we can and must talk about this one reality as being really and truly divine and human, without intermixture and division (*unvermischt und ungetrennt*), in spite of the unmixed different elements that constitute it" (*ST*, Bd. XII, p. 356).

21. Rahner himself indicates this in saying: "The present author has already complained of this in a number of earlier essays", in RAHNER, *Christology Today?*, p. 28, n. 4. See, for example, K. RAHNER, *Current Problems in Christology* (hereafter *Current Problems*) in *TI*, Vol. 1, London, 1965 (Second Edition), pp. 149-200, esp. pp. 156-157, n. 2, and pp. 159 ff. (ET of: *ST*, Bd. I, Einsiedeln, 1954, pp. 169-222.) This was published the same year, 1954, as K. RAHNER, *Chalkedon – Ende oder Anfang* in A. GRILLMEIER, H. BACHT, (eds.), *Das Konzil von Chalkedon* III Bd., Würzburg, 1954, pp. 3-49. In this article, Rahner clearly affirms the importance of fully accepting the Chalcedonian formula. "It cannot be denied that in the ordinary religious act of the Christian, when it is not referred precisely to the historical life of Jesus by way of meditation, Christ finds a place only as God. We see here the mysterious monophysite undercurrent in ordinary Christology and a tendency to let the creaturely be overwhelmed in face of the Absolute, as though God were to become greater and more real by the devaluation of cancellation of the creature" (p. 188). "Can the 'average Christian' only get on by allowing the συγ-χύτως to slip into the backround of her/his consciousness in faith in favor of the διαιρέτως, by tacitly thinking in a slightly monophysite way, to this extent at least, that the humanity becomes something merely operated and managed by the divinity, the signal put up to show that the divinity is present in the world – a world which is only concerned with the divinity and where the signal is put up pretty well for our sakes alone; because we wouldn't otherwise notice the bare divinity? Must it be an inevitable feature of our everyday religious life and practice that the Chalcedonian formula should be tacitly cut short like this, so that – here we must weigh up the matter for ourselves honestly – the 'average' non-Christian feels called upon to protest in her/his unbelief, refusing to admit that God has become a human being 'like this' and thus believing that s/he must reject the Christian doctrine of the Incarnation as a myth?" (pp. 179-180).

22. See, RAHNER, *Current Problems*, p. 156, n. 1, where Rahner defines mythology in this connection: "The representation of god's becoming human (*Menschenwerden eines Gottes*) is mythological, when the 'human' element is merely the clothing, the livery, of which the god makes use in order to draw attention to his presence here with us, while it is not the case that the human element acquires its supreme initiative and control over its own actions by the very fact of being assumed by God" (*ST*, Bd. I, pp. 176-177, n. 3).

23. RAHNER, *Current Problems*, p. 185: "The less we merely think of this humanity as something added on to God, and the more we understand it as God's very presence in the world (= *Je mehr man sich diese Menschheit nicht bloß zu Gott dazu-denkt, sondern sie als Anwesenheit Gottes selbst in der Welt begreift*) and hence (*darin*) (not, all the

This concern of Rahner's is shown throughout a study of his Christological writings. The theme of the humanity of Jesus was treated early
on by Rahner[24]. In an early article he specifically ties his reflections
about the humanity of Jesus to the Heart of Jesus which is the "original
source" of the saving actions of Christ[25]. This joining together by Rahner of his considerations on the humanity of Jesus with the Heart of
Jesus has particular significance for his sacramental theology. In fact,
the very title of Rahner's theology doctoral dissertation, itself presented
about twenty years earlier, indicates the attention he gives to this
theme[26]. For Rahner, the Heart of Jesus means "the original centre
(ursprüngliche Mitte) of the human reality of the Son of God"[27]. It is
possible, says Rahner, for one to be a Christian "without ever having
heard anything in human words about the Sacred Heart of Jesus. But one
cannot be a Christian without continually passing, by a movement of the
spirit supported by the Holy Ghost, through the humanity of Christ and,
in that humanity, through its unifying center which we call the heart"[28].

same) (*nicht trotzdem*; better translated: 'not in spite of') see it in a true, spontaneous
vitality and freedom before God, the more intelligible does the abiding mystery of our
faith become, and also (*auch*; better translated: 'specifically') an expression of our very
own existence" (= *eine Aussage unseres eigenen Daseins*) (*ST*, Bd. I, pp. 205-206).

24. K. RAHNER, *The Eternal Significance of the Humanity of Jesus for our Relationship with God* (hereafter *Humanity of Jesus*), in *TI*, Vol. 3, London, 1967, pp. 35-46. (ET
of: *ST*, Bd. III, Einsiedeln, 1959 (Third Edition), pp. 47-60.) First published in *Geist und
Leben* (hereafter *GuL*) 26 (1953) 279-288.

25. RAHNER, *Humanity of Jesus*, p. 35, "original source" = *ursprüngliche Quelle*. The
approach that Rahner takes is to comment on: 1), "the relationship between created
(numinous) realities and God in general", and 2), "the same sort of reflection on the
humanity of Christ and his human heart in particular" (p. 40). Original: *Es handelt sich
um zwei Überlegungen: eine allgemeine und grundsätzliche über das Verhältnis geschaf-
fener (numinoser) Wirklichkeiten überhaupt zu Gott; und eine solche über die Menschheit Christi und sein menschliches Herz im besonderen* (*ST*, Bd. III, pp. 52-53).

26. See also the affirmation by Rahner, written in December 1983, that the concept of
Symbol first played an important role for his theological reflections in his considerations
about devotion to the Sacred Heart, in *Foreword* to J. WONG, *Logos-Symbol*, pp. 6-7: *und
den Begriff Symbol, der zunächst in meinen Überlegungen zur Herz-Jesu-Verehrung eine
Rolle gespielt hatte.* Also, the example that Rahner presents of the Heart of Christ points
to the religious-spiritual background for his (Rahner's) reflections on symbol. See J.
WONG, *Logos-Symbol*, p. 32, who believes that religious experience is more basic to Rahner's insight into Symbol than his philosophical presuppositions. Wong identifies this
religious experience particularly in terms of Ignatian spirituality and Sacred Heart devotion, and he gives a bibliography for this religious-spiritual background of Rahner (p. 46,
n. 40).

27. RAHNER, *Humanity of Jesus*, p. 46.

28. *Ibid.*, p. 46. The original, beginning from "But one cannot...: *Aber man kann
nicht Christ sein, ohne dauernd in der Bewegung des Geistes im Hl. Geist durch die
Menschheit Christi hindurchzugehen und darin durch deren einigende Mitte, die wir das
Herz nennen*" (*ST*, Bd. III, p. 60). A translation that may be more faithful to the original:
"One cannot be a Christian without always, in the movement of the spirit in the Holy

The humanity of Christ, and consequently says Rahner, the Heart of Christ, is significant for us as human beings because it is the way for us to God. But this appreciation of the theme of Christ as mediator is best realized by studying in a subsequent section what Rahner has more specifically written on this subject.

In regard to the humanity of Jesus, the fundamental question for the theologian, in Rahner's view, is whether one has "a theology in which the Word – by the fact that he is a human being and in so far as he is this – is the necessary and permanent mediation of all salvation, not merely at some time in the past but now and for all eternity"[29]. Yet, in the context of one particular article, Rahner declares that he himself cannot be expected to completely work out such a theology. His intention is to indicate "that there can and ought to be such a theology"[30].

Spirit, passing through the humanity of Christ, and hence through its unifying center, which we call the heart".

29. *Ibid.*, p. 45: "This incarnational structure of the religious act in general does not mean, of course, that this must always be something explicitly conscious or that, given the confined area of our earthly consciousness, it would be possible, beneficial and necessary to strive for such an explicit consciousness of passing through the Incarnate Word always and in every act".

30. *Ibid.*, p. 46. In point of fact, in his later writings, Rahner does much more than indicate what "ought to be". See, what is viewed as a more systematic presentation of his Christology, K. RAHNER, *Jesus Christ IV. History of Dogma and Theology* in K. RAHNER et al. (eds.) *Sacramentum Mundi. An Encyclopedia of Theology* (hereafter *SM*), Vol. 3, New York, 1969, pp. 192-209. (ET of: *Jesus Christus II. Fundamental-theologische Überlegungen* in K. RAHNER et al. (eds.), *Sacramentum Mundi. Theologisches Lexikon für Die Praxis*, Bd. II, Freiburg, 1968, cc. 920-957. J. WONG, *Logos-Symbol*, p. 35, identifies this as Rahner's "first major systematic presentation of the topic". A few years later, Rahner published a joint work, K. RAHNER, W. THÜSING, *Christologie – systematisch und exegetisch* (hereafter *Christologie*) (QD, 55), Freiburg, 1972. Rahner's contribution consists of pp. 17-78, Thüsing's, pp. 79-303. According to J. WONG, *Logos-Symbol*, p. 30, n. 12, this work "presents the collaboration between systematic and New Testament Christology; given as lectures during the Winter Semester (1970-1971) at the Catholic Theology Faculty, University of Münster". Rahner himself notes the fruitfulness of his study with Thüsing when Rahner is giving a lecture a year later, 16 December 1971, subsequently published as RAHNER, *Types of Christology*, p. 216, n. 3. Wong also indicates, J. WONG, *Logos-Symbol*, p. 30, n. 13, that "the whole of Rahner's contribution to *Christologie* and nearly the whole article *Jesus Christ IV* in *SM* are incorporated in chapter six in *FCF*". Specifically, Rahner's contribution from *Christologie* (though, at times, revised and/or expanded) is found in *FCF*, pp. 203-212 and 228-311. However, for English-speaking readers, it must be noted that RAHNER, W. THÜSING, *Christologie*, was published in English as K. RAHNER, W. THÜSING, *A New Christology*, New York, 1980. Yet Rahner's contribution to *Christologie* is not represented in *A New Christology*. Instead, *A New Christology* contains three articles by Rahner that appear in English in *TI*, Vol. 18, and Vol. 19. Unfortunately, P. IMHOF, E. MEUSER, *Bibliographie Karl Rahner 1979-1984* (hereafter *Bibliographie 1979-1984*) in E. KLINGER, K. WITTSTADT (eds.), *Glaube im Prozess*, Freiburg, 1984 (Second Edition), p. 859, entry n. 3643, indicate (wrongly) that *A New Christology* is an English translation of *Christologie*, entry n. 2603, found in R. BLEISTEIN, *Bibliographie Karl Rahner 1969-1974* (hereafter *Bibliographie 1969-*

Rahner continues his focus on the humanity of Jesus in his reflections on the Incarnation[31]. What, he asks, does it mean to speak of God becoming a human being? He points out that when one reflects on the relationship between God and the world, it is correct and proper to recognize the world as the work of God, that is, a work distinct from God. But, God becoming a human being means that the world, that which is other than God, is not only God's work, but also is God's own reality[32]. The human being, for his or her part, says Rahner, is "defined" as the one whose "limits" are the unlimited reference to the infinite fullness of

1974), Freiburg, 1974, p. 32. The following, then, notes the original source for this material in *A New Christology*: K. RAHNER, *What Does it Mean Today to Believe in Jesus Christ* (hereafter *What Does it Mean*) in *TI*, Vol. 18, London, 1984, pp. 143-156; (ET of: *ST*, Bd. XIII, Einsiedeln, 1978, pp. 172-187); originally a lecture given 18 May 1976, = *A New Christology*, pp. 3-17. K. RAHNER, *The Church's Redemptive Historical Provenance for the Death and Resurrection of Jesus* (hereafter *Church's Provenance*) in *TI*, Vol. 19, London, 1984, pp. 24-38; (ET of: *ST*, Bd. XIV, Einsiedeln, 1979, pp. 73-90); originally a lecture given 12 November 1976 in St. Poltem, and was first published in J. REIKERSTORFER (ed.), *Zeit des Geistes*, Vienna, 1977, pp. 11-26, = *A New Christology*, pp. 18-31. And K. RAHNER, *The Death of Jesus and the Closure of Revelation* (hereafter *Death of Jesus*) in *TI*, Vol. 18, London, 1984, pp. 132-142; (ET of: *ST*, Bd. XIII, Einsiedeln, 1978, pp. 159-171); originally a lecture given October 1975, = *A New Christology*, pp. 32-41. In regard to Rahner's basic approach in the Christology section of *FCF*, he says in K. RAHNER, *Foundations of Christian Faith* (hereafter *Foundations*) in *TI*, Vol. 19, London, 1984, pp. 3-15; ET of: *ST*, Bd. XIV, Einsiedeln, 1980, pp. 48-62, especially p. 11: "... the basic thesis of the book (*FCF*) is that Jesus proclaims that in him – in his person and his teaching – the kingdom of God (that is, God's gracious self-communication) is not merely always present as an offer to the human being's freedom, but has reached us victoriously and irreversibly, has been actually victoriously established by God, and that the last, definitive word of grace has been irrevocably spoken in history: a word that in Jesus' resurrection, where he is definitively accepted in his solidarity with other human beings, has become the unsurpassable and definitive work of God in history".

31. K. RAHNER, *On the Theology of the Incarnation* (hereafter *Incarnation*) in *TI*, Vol. 4, London, 1966, pp. 105-120. (ET of: *ST*, Bd. IV, Einsiedeln, 1960, pp. 137-155.) First published in *Catholica* 12 (1958) 1-16. Later this article was wholly incorporated into *FCF*, pp. 212-228, indicating a confirmation and reaffirmation by Rahner of what he had written earlier.

32. RAHNER, *Incarnation*, pp. 106-107. "God's own reality" = *seine eigene Wirklichkeit*. See, also, K. RAHNER, *'I Believe in Jesus Christ'. Interpreting an article of faith* (hereafter *I Believe*) in *TI*, Vol. 9, London, 1972, pp. 165-168. (ET of: *ST*, Bd. VIII, Einsiedeln, 1967, pp. 213-217. (This is identified in R. BLEISTEIN, E. KLINGER, *Bibliographie Karl Rahner 1924-1969* (hereafter *Bibliographie 1924-1969*), Freiburg, 1969, p. 80, entry n. 1637, and should be distinguished from entry n. 1943, on p. 93, which has the same title and published a year later in 1968.) In RAHNER, *I Believe*, p. 166, Rahner states that if "we say 'God is made man'...we either think automatically of God being changed into a human being or else we understand the content of the word 'human being' in this context as an outer garment... But both interpretations of this statement are nonsensical and contrary to what Christian dogma really intends to say. For God remains God and does not change, and Jesus is a real, genuine, and finite human being with his own experiences, in adoration before the incomprehensibility of God, a free and obedient human being, like us in all things".

the mystery. So when God becomes a human being, the human being arrives "at the point to which it always strives by virtue of its essence"[33]. Consequently, Rahner emphasizes the Incarnation of God as "the unique, supreme case of the total actualization of human reality, which consists of the fact that a human being is in so far as s/he gives up her/himself"[34]. This notion of giving up oneself is an important one for understanding the meaning of the Incarnation. And it highlights a reality which Rahner says a "purely rational ontology might perhaps never suspect": namely that "the one who is the Absolute, has, in the pure freedom of his infinite and abiding unrelatedness, the possibility of God's self becoming the other thing, the finite"[35]. Rahner emphatically states that the starting point for an appreciation of the Incarnation is not that God assumes a human nature, but that God empties God's self, and that this is a self-emptying on the part of God[36]. This self-emptying on the part of God is a possiblity and not a necessity. And so it is not a reality that can be arrived at in an a priori way. It is a revealed truth that it has happened, and the fact that it has happened requires that this reality can only be termed love. Seen in this way, God as creator is only a "derivative, restricted and secondary possibility" which God is able to realize. That which is primary among all the possibilites that exist for God is God's ability to subject God's self to history[37]. It is important to recognize,

---

33. RAHNER, *Incarnation*, p. 109. See, also, K. RAHNER, *The Unity of Spirit and Matter in the Christian Understanding of Faith* (hereafter *Spirit and Matter*) in *TI*, Vol. 6, London, 1969, pp. 153-177; (ET of: *ST*, Bd. VI, Einsiedeln, 1965, pp. 185-214). This article originated as a lecture in 1963. "The climax of salvation history is not the detachment from the world of human beings as a spirit in order to come to God, but the descending and irreversible entrance of God into the world, the coming of the divine Logos in the flesh, the taking on of the material so that it itself becomes a permanent reality of God in which God in his Logos expresses himself to us for ever". (p. 160).

34. RAHNER, *Incarnation*, p. 110, "total actualization" = *Wesensvollzugs*. "The finite can only be surpassed by moving out into the unfathomable fullness of God" (p. 111). The same idea is formulated in RAHNER, *FCF*, p. 218: "The human being is insofar as s/he abandons her/himself to the absolute mystery whom we call God".

35. RAHNER, *Incarnation*, p. 114.

36. *Ibid*. The scriptural terminology that Rahner refers to is that of the kenosis and the genesis of God, "who can come to be by becoming another thing, derivative, in the act of constituting it, without having to change in his own proper reality which is the unoriginated origin".

37. RAHNER, *Incarnation*, p. 115. The direct quotation is: "his power of subjecting himself to history is primary among his free possibilities". The original: *weil das Selbst-Geschichtlich- werden-Können seine freie Urmöglichkeit... ist* (*ST*, Bd. IV, p. 148). In other words, the incarnation is the basis from which the ontological possibility of creation can be derived. See, also, K. RAHNER, *Nature and Grace* (hereafter *Nature and Grace 4*) in *TI*, Vol. 4, London, 1966, pp. 165-188. (ET of: *ST*, Bd. IV, Einsiedeln, 1960, pp. 209-236.) First published as *Natur und Gnade nach der Lehre der Katholischen Kirche* in L. REINISCH (ed.) *Theologie heute*, Munich, 1960, pp. 89-102, p. 176: In this view, "the

therefore, that the humanity of Jesus does not have a pre-existence. "It is something that comes to be and is constituted in essence (*Wesen*) and existence (*Dasein*) when and in so far as the Logos empties the Logos' self"[38]. This, then, has consequences in regard to one's view of redemption; for by the fact that God "pronounces as God's reality that which we are", this "constitutes and redeems our very being and history"[39]. It also has consequences with regard to one's view of creation. As Rahner puts it: "We could still say of the creator, with the Scripture of the Old Testament, that God is in heaven and we are on earth. But of the God whom we confess in Christ we must say that God is precisely where we are, and can only be found there"[40].

The conclusions which Rahner reaches through his reflections on the meaning of the Incarnation reinforce his convictions regarding the humanity of Christ. Above all is Rahner's conviction that "the humanity

---

Logos who has become part of the world is not merely the de facto mediator of grace by his merit... he is also the person who by his free Incarnation creates the order of grace and nature as his own presupposition (nature) and his milieu (the grace of the other spiritual creatures)". See also, on this same point, RAHNER, *FCF*, p. 197: "In the world as it actually is we can understand creation and Incarnation as two moments and two phases of the one process of God's self-giving and self-expression, although it is an intrinsically differentiated process. Such an understanding can appeal to a very old 'Christocentric' tradition in the history of Christian theology in which the creative Word of God which establishes the world establishes this world to begin with as the materiality which is to become his own, or to become the environment of his own materiality". See also, p. 222: "His capacity to be creator, that is, the capacity merely to establish the other without giving himself, is only a derived, delimited and secondary possibility which ultimately is grounded in this real and primordial possibility (Urmöglichkeit) of God, namely, to be able to give himself to what is not God, and thereby to have his own history in the other, but as his own history" (*GdG*, p. 220).

38. RAHNER, *Incarnation*, p. 116: "This man is, as such, the self-utterance (Selbstäußerung) of God in its self-emptying (*Selbstentäußerung*), because God expresses himself when he empties himself. He proclaims himself as love when he hides the majesty of this love and shows himself in the ordinary way of human beings" (*ST*, Bd. IV, p. 149).

39. *Ibid.*, p. 116. Rahner forcefully notes that "the unbridgeable difference" between who Jesus is and who we are as human beings is that in God's case "the 'what' is uttered as his self-expression, which it is not in our case".

40. *Ibid.*, p. 117. Rahner comments that the finite "has been given an infinite depth and is no longer a contrast to the infinite". And, "in the incarnation, the Logos creates by taking on, and takes on by emptying himself". See, also, in regard to a study of the Trinity as "the transcendent primary foundation of salvation-history", RAHNER, *The Trinity*, New York, 1974. This is a translation of K. RAHNER, *Der dreifaltige Gott als transzendenter Urgrund der Heilsgeschichte* in J. FEINER, M. LÖHRER (eds.), *Mysterium Salutis. Grundriss heilsgeschichtlicher Dogmatik* (hereafter *MS*), Bd. II, *Die Heilsgeschichte vor Christus*, Einsiedeln, 1967, pp. 317-397 (to 401 with bibliography). See, also, H. EGAN, *Book Review: M. TAYLOR, Rahner*, in *Theological Studies* (hereafter *TS*) 48 (1987) 198-199, who concludes that the "extraordinary dissertation" of M. TAYLOR, *Rahner*, in spite of Taylor's "truly creative rethinking of the Trinity has produced a metaphysical unitarianism, but only an abstract Trinity" (199).

of Christ is not the form in which God appears ('Erscheinungsform') in the sense of a vaporous and empty apparition... Since God 'goes out of' God's self, this form of his existence has the most radical validity, force and reality"[41]. Ultimately, asserts Rahner, the idea that "God disguises God's self as a human being", or that "needing to make God's self visible... makes gestures by means of a human reality which is used in such a way that it is not a real human being with independence and freedom, but a puppet on strings", this, says Rahner, must be recognized as mythology[42].

In affirming the humanity of Christ, one is truly professing belief that God has gone out of God's self. And God's "going out of God's self" has become Jesus Christ. Thus, this act on God's part is the ground or foundation of love of the other, for God has become, thus fully accepting, the other. Likewise for human beings, the way that one accepts and loves God is by accepting and loving the other, that is, the neighbor. For in loving each neighbor, God, who is always the "Nearest" (*Nächste*) but also the "Farthest" (*Fernste*), is particularly being accepted and loved[43].

II. CHRISTOLOGY WITHIN AN EVOLUTIONARY VIEW OF THE WORLD

As noted above, Rahner is fundamentally concerned with the one who is a believer, even though the believer may not always be recognized as

41. RAHNER, *Incarnation*, p. 117. The English translation is weak and can be misleading, particularly in the last part of the section quoted. The original, corresponding to "Since God himself...": *Dadurch, daß Gott selbst ek-sistiert, erhält diese seine Existenz in radikalster Weise eigene Gelgung, Macht und Wirklichkeit* (*ST*, Bd. IV, pp. 151-152). Here the original clearly emphasizes the act of God going out of himself as the very reality of God's existence, not simply as its "form".

42. RAHNER, *Incarnation*, p. 118. This view is not Church dogma, says Rahner, "even though it may be a fair description of the catechism in many Christian's heads in contrast to the printed catechism".

43. RAHNER, *Incarnation*, p. 119. The English translation is weak: "... because God himself has become this neighbor. He who is at once the nearest to us and the farthest from us is always the one person who is accepted in our nearest and dearest". The original: *weil Gott dieser Nächste selbst geworden ist und so in jedem Nächsten immer dieser eine Nächste und Fernste zumal angenommen und geliebt wird* (*ST*, Bd. IV, p. 154). The English translation breaks the sentence inappropriately and does not translate the word *zumal*. On this topic, see, K. RAHNER, *Reflections on the Unity of the Love of Neighbor and the Love of God* (hereafter *Love of Neighbor*) in *TI*, Vol. 6, London, 1969, pp. 231-249. (ET of: *ST*, Bd. VI, Einsiedeln, 1965, pp. 277-298.) First published in *GuL* 38 (1965) 168-185. Here Rahner states: "The love of neighbor, provided it is genuine and accepts its own proper incomprehensible being to the very limit, already contains the whole of Christian salvation and of Christianity" (p. 249).

such explicitly or be conscious explicitly of being a believer[44]. It is from this focus that Rahner looks to the setting, that is, to the situation "of an

44. One is directed here to the reflections by Rahner on the "Anonymous Christian". See, in this regard, K. RAHNER, *Anonymous Christians* (hereafter *Anonymous Christian 6*) in *TI*, Vol. 6, London, 1969, pp. 390-398. (ET of: *ST*, Bd. VI, Einsiedeln, 1965, pp. 545-554). Originally presented as a radio broadcast in 1964, as a review of the recent book by A. RÖPER, *Die anonymen Christen*, Mainz, 1963. Rahner's article was revised for publication in 1965. See, also, the later articles, K. RAHNER, *Anonymous Christianity and the Missionary Task of the Church* (hereafter *Anonymous Christianity 12*) in *TI*, Vol. 12, London, 1974, pp. 161-178; (ET of: *ST*, Bd. IX, Einsiedeln, 1970, pp. 498-515); and K. RAHNER, *Observations on the Problem of the 'Anonymous Christian'* (hereafter *Anonymous Christian 14*) in *TI*, Vol. 14, London, 1976, pp. 280-294; (ET of: *ST*, Bd. X, Einsiedeln, 1972, pp. 531-546); this article was first presented as a lecture 22 January 1971. Rahner explains that his purpose in developing these reflections on the theory of the anonymous Christian is one attempt to explain "how true supernatural faith in revelation can be present in an individual without any contact with the explicit preaching of the gospel. For the fact that such a thing is possible is explicitly declared in the official doctrinal statements of the Church..." (p. 291). As regards the term itself Rahner declares: "Admittedly I do regard the term 'anonymous Christian' as inescapable so long as no one suggests a better term to me" (p. 292). Rahner summarizes his view by saying: "There must be a Christian theory to account for the fact that every individual who does not in any absolute or ultimate sense act against her/his own conscience can say and does say in faith, hope, and love, Abba within her/his own spirit, and is on these grounds in all truth a sister/brother to Christians in God's sight" (p. 294). Another reference is to K. RAHNER, *Jesus Christ in the Non-Christian Religions* (hereafter *Non-Christian Religions*) in *TI*, Vol. 17, London, 1981, pp. 39-50; (ET of: *ST*, Bd. XII, Einsiedeln, 1975, pp. 370-383). This article is substantially incorporated into *FCF*, pp. 311-321. And, K. RAHNER, *Anonymous and Explicit Faith* in *TI*, Vol. 16, London, 1979, pp. 52-59; ET of: *ST*, Bd. XII, Einsiedeln, 1975, pp. 76-84; originally published in *Stimmen der Zeit* (hereafter *StdZ*) 192 (1974) 147-152. In n. 6, p. 57, Rahner states: "the author has frequently considered the question of the 'anonymous Christian' in his writings, although in a slightly different perspective to the one adopted here. The above reflections are meant to supplement these other writings from another point of view". And. see as a final reference, the comment made by Rahner in a 1979 lecture, RAHNER, *Foundations*, p. 10, in which he summarizes his position on the meaning of anonymous Christianity and anonymous Christians: "The term as such is not important. Anyone who thinks it implies a depreciation of explicit and institutionalized Christianity need not use it. The things itself, however, cannot be disputed, at least after Vatican II, since it is taught there that always and everywhere in the world anyone who is faithful to this consciousness is living in the grace of God and united to the paschal mystery of Christ. In such a view... the absolute necessity of Jesus Christ must not be obscured; but it is permissible to approach Christology from a universal pneumatology and not only to proceed in the opposite direction...". And see also the reference by P. ENDEAN, *Rahner, Christology and Grace* in *Heythrop Journal* 37 284-297, p. 296, n. 5, to the work of N. SCHWERDTFEGER, *Gnade und Welt: Zum Grundgefühe von Karl Rahners Theorie der 'anonymen Christen'*, Freiburg, 1982, pp. 164-169 "for a refutation of what was till then the standard view that Rahner had developed the concept in the famous 1950 essay, 'Concerning the Relationship between Nature and Grace' [*TI*, Vol. 1, London, 1961, pp. 297-317] and for documentation of the position I follow here. Schwerdtfeger draws on an important 1970 study of the early Rahner by the Protestant scholar Tuomo Mannermaa – unfortunately published only in Finnish, although the Karl-Rahner-Archiv in Innsbruck has a rough typescript German translation". And see also, J. WONG, *Anonymous Christians: Karl Rahner's Pneuma-Christocentrism and an*

evolutionary view of the world" in his Christological considerations. For the Incarnation is a belief which on the one hand is concerned with God, but on the other hand is concerned with "that dimension which is associated with people today as the one they are most familiar with scientifically, existentially, and affectively, namely, the dimension of the material world and of tangible history"[45].

The thesis that Rahner presents is that the Incarnation is the "necessary and permanent beginning of the divinization of the world as a whole"[46]. The "self-evident" starting point for Rahner's thesis is that "spirit and matter have more things in common (to put it this way) than things dividing them"[47]. A patently unchristian view would be to see

East-West Dialogue in Theological Studies 55 (1994) 609-637, esp. pp. 612-613: "Rahner believes that we are faced with two basic principles with regard to the question of the salvation of non-Christians. On the one hand, there is the necessity of faith in God and in Jesus Christ in order to obtain salvation. On the other hand, there is the universal salvific will of God that seriously intends to save all human beings. Rahner resolves these apparently conflicting principles by pointing out the possibility of having implicit faith in Christ. Consequently, Rahner proposes a broader concept of being related to the Church by affirming different degrees of relation to it, which would include the so-called 'anonymous Christians' as well as the explicitly professed Christians... What is of special importance is Rahner's insight that an inner unity exists among the following three realities: human transcendence, God's bestowal of grace, and the mystery of the Incarnation".

45. K. RAHNER, Christology within an Evolutionary View of the World (hereafter Evolutionary View) in TI, Vol. 5, London, 1966, pp. 157-192. (ET of: ST, Bd. V, Einsiedeln, 1964 (Second Edition), pp. 183-221.) First published in Veröffentlichungen der Paulus Gesellschaft, Frauenchiemsee, 1962, pp. 22-59. This article has been incorporated into FCF, pp. 178-203, indicating Rahner's affirmation of it in his Christology. We refer to the article as presented in FCF when it appears to be a more faithful English translation of the original as found in ST, or when the original text itself is amended or expanded in GdG.

46. RAHNER, Evolutionary View, pp. 160-161. The foundation for the divinization of the world as a whole is the Hypostatic Union, which "must not be seen as something which distinguishes Jesus our Lord from us, but rather as something which must happen once, and once only, at the point where the world begins to enter into its final phase in which it is to realize its final concentration, its final climax and its radical nearness to the absolute mystery called God" (p. 160). In addition, Rahner notes a certain similarity with his thesis and the "theorems" of Teilhard de Chardin. But he says that "if we arrive at some of the same conclusions as he does then that is all to the good. Yet we do not feel ourselves either dependent on him or obligated to him" (pp. 159-160).

47. RAHNER, Evolutionary View, p. 161. The term Gemeinsamkeit is translated in TI, p. 161, as "community", but in FCF, p. 181, as "commonality". "Commonality" is a better rendering than "community". See, also, RAHNER, Spirit and Matter, p. 154. The List of Sources in TI, Vol. 6, p. 401, notes that "the author has in certain parts of this paper (Spirit and Matter) taken over formulations from his K. RAHNER, P. OVERHAGE, Homininisation: The Evolutionary Origin of Man as a Theological Problem (QD, 13), Freiburg and London, 1965". (ET of: P. OVERHAGE, K. RAHNER, Das Problem der Hominisation. Über den biologischen Ursprung des Menschen (QD, 12-13) Freiburg, 1961; Rahner's contribution represents pp. 13-90.) Rahner states that his purpose in Spirit and Matter is twofold: 1), "to give an outline... of the immediate data of the Christian proclamation which presents us with a unity of spirit and matter"; and 2), "to

spirit as simply – or unfortunately – as utilizing "the material world as a kind of exterior stage"[48]. The clearest and most fundamental example of the unity of matter and spirit is seen in the human being. For the human being is not an "unnatural or merely temporary composite of spirit and matter, but is a unity[49]...". And this point is particularly elucidated, says Rahner, when one affirms that the consummation of all things – which means the whole reality of humanity and the cosmos – cannot eliminate materiality "as if it were a merely temporary element"[50]. Matter is rather to be seen as the condition which makes possible, among other things, "the objective other which the world and humanity (*Mensch*) are to themselves", as well as making possible "an immediate intercommunication with other spiritual existents in time and space and in history"[51].

Significantly, this affirmation of the unity of all things provides a very important foundation for Rahner's sacramental theology. For when the "relationship of reciprocal conditioning between spirit and matter" is recognized as a dynamic reality – dynamic because this relationship has a history – Rahner unhesitatingly concludes that "it is of the intrinsic nature of matter to develop towards spirit"[52]. This is because if 1), "the world is one", 2), "if as one it has a history", and 3), that "in this world not everything is already there from the beginning precisely because it is in the process of becoming, then there is no reason to deny that matter

communicate a few theological reflections which... attempt to clarify the meaning and scope of this unity of spirit and matter" (p. 154).

48. RAHNER, *Evolutionary View*, p. 161. See, also, RAHNER, *Spirit and Matter*, pp. 154-161, esp. pp. 158-159, where Rahner speaks of the existence of angels which gives rise to "the impression in the average, ordinary understanding of faith (which must not be simply identified with dogma) that there is a created kingdom of finite spirits which carries on its own history quite independently from the material world and its history". Rahner says that it is important to recognize that angels are "powers of the one and hence also material world to whose material nature they are genuinely and essentially related".

49. RAHNER, *Evolutionary View*, pp. 161-162. See, also, RAHNER, *Spirit and Matter*, p. 160: "The human being in the Old Testament writings is very undualistically and unplatonically a unity in her/his being and history, and the world is seen from the very beginning as an environment intended for human beings".

50. RAHNER, *Evolutionary View*, p. 162. This is difficult to imagine, says Rahner, because human beings may find it impossible "to form any positive image of a perfect state of materiality". See, also, RAHNER, *Spirit and Matter*, pp. 161-162. "Matter for the Christian is not a watchword for a limited period but a factor in perfection itself... Hence Christian eschatology does not know merely, or even first and foremost, the atomised salvation of each individual for her/himself in the beatitude of her/his own soul, but rather the kingdom of God, the eternal covenant, the triumphing Church, the new heaven and the new earth".

51. RAHNER, *FCF*, p. 183.

52. *Ibid.*, p. 184.

should have developed towards life and towards human beings"[53]. This development as history does not mean the "continuation of the same thing, but is precisely the coming to be of something new, of something more and not merely of something else"[54]. This recognition of the development of matter towards spirit – but not reaching some point at which matter ceases to be – is a particularly important dimension as a foundation for Rahner's sacramental theology. Rahner's starting point in presenting this picture of development is his thesis that there is a "single history of the whole of reality"[55]. This single history implies "necessarily and above all an intercommunion (*Zueinanderkommen*) among these (spiritual) subjects in each of which the whole is present to itself in its own unique way"[56]. And it is this intercommunion which constitutes the setting, the framework, in which the self-communication of God takes place. This self-communication (*Selbstmitteilung*) of God to human beings necessarily takes place as the self-communication of God to all human beings in their intercommunication (*Interkommunikation*). God's self-communication does not take place in an individualistic way. In fact, the acceptance of God's self-communication depends upon two fundamental things: 1), that God's self-communication is freely accepted; and 2), that this acceptance takes place in a common history[57]. Both of these are very important in view of Rahner's sacramentology.

53. *Ibid.*, pp. 185-186. But Rahner says that "in no way does this deny or obscure the fact that matter, life, consciousness and spirit are not the same". See, also, RAHNER, *Spirit and Matter*, pp. 162-166.

54. RAHNER, *FCF*, p. 186. See, also, RAHNER, *Spirit and Matter*, pp. 171-177, esp. p. 171: "The concept of historicity (*Geschichtlichkeit*) is a most profoundly Christian concept" (*ST*, Bd. VI, p. 206).

55. RAHNER, *FCF*, p. 186. Not to accept this thesis is to accept a "platonic dualism" such that spirit will "feel like a stranger who is on earth by chance". And then the human being will be meaningful only as the "adversary" of nature (pp. 188-189). See, also, RAHNER, *Spirit and Matter*, p. 157.

56. RAHNER, *FCF*, p. 193. See, also, for Rahner's sixth fundamental principle of symbolism regarding his view of the relationship of the individual parts to the whole: K. RAHNER, *The Theology of Symbol* (hereafter *Symbol*) in *TI*, Vol. 4, London, 1966, pp. 221-252, especially p. 247; (ET of: *ST*, Bd. IV, Einsiedeln, 1960, pp. 275-311.) First published in A. BEA, H. RAHNER, H. RONDET, F. SCHWENDIMANN (eds.), *Cor Jesu I*, Rome, 1959, pp. 461-505. A thorough analysis of this article, esp. pp. 222-235, has been made by J. WONG, *Logos-Symbol*, pp. 74-82, in which Wong presents the philosophical presuppositions of Rahner's ontology of *Realsymbol*. See also, A. LIBERATORE, *Symbols in Rahner: a note on translation* in *Louvian Studies* 18 (1993) 145-158.

57. RAHNER, *FCF*, p. 193. "We usually call self-communication only a self-communication which meets with a free and therefore beatifying acceptance. But we have always emphasized that this self-communication of God necessarily exists (the following of the original in *GdG* is missing in the English translation in *FCF*: *im Modus der Vorgegebenheit an sich und für die Freiheit* = 'in the mode of the offer in itself and in favor of freedom') either in the mode of its acceptance, which is usually called justification, or in the

These two fundamental elements form an important framework for Christology, specifically in regard to God's self-communication. Rahner offers more extensive reflections on both of these elements in one of his later articles[58]. He underscores first the fact that "the world is drawn to its spiritual fulfillment by the Spirit of God, who directs the whole history of the world in all its length and breadth towards its proper goal"[59]. It is the "whole history of the world" which is being led to salvation. God does not will anything less. Rahner notes that this truth "was not always seen with such clarity to be part of the faith of the Church as it is today"[60]. And the second element that Rahner

mode of its rejection, which is called disbelief and sin" (GdG, p. 194). See, also, RAHNER, Anonymous Christian 14, pp. 280-294, esp. p. 288: "God's universal will to save objectifies itself in that communication of God's self which we call grace. It does this effectively at all times and in all places in the form of the offering and the enabling power of acting in a way that leads to salvation". And see, also, in regard to Rahner's considerations on freedom, his earlier article, K. RAHNER, The Dignity and Freedom of Man (hereafter Dignity and Freedom) in TI, Vol. 2, London, 1963, pp. 235-263; (ET of: ST, Bd. II, Einsiedeln, 1955, pp. 247-277). This article originated as a presentation given 1 May 1952. But see, also, RAHNER, Theology of Freedom in TI, Vol. 6, London, 1969, pp. 178-196; (ET of: ST, Bd. VI, Einsiedeln, 1965, pp. 215-237). And see, also, RAHNER, Non-Christian Religions, p. 49: "... freedom is not simply the capacity continually to make new arbitrary choices; it is the capacity to decide for what is ultimate and final". And see, K. RAHNER, Grace in Freedom, London, 1969; (ET of: Gnade als Freiheit: Kleine theologische Beiträge, Freiburg, 1968). This is a collection of twenty-five selections originating from 1964-1968.

58. K. RAHNER, The One Christ and the Universality of Salvation (hereafter Universality), in TI, Vol. 16, London, 1979, pp. 199-224, (ET of: ST, Bd. XII, Einsiedeln, 1975, pp. 251-282), especially pp. 199-224. We refer to this article because, although first published in 1975, a year before GdG, the considerations found in Universality are not developed so extensively as in the later (GdG) publication. Two articles referred to above, RAHNER, Incarnation, and RAHNER, Evolutionary View, were both substantially incorporated into FCF, accordingly, pp. 178-203, and pp. 212-228. Other earlier Christological matieral was also substantially incorporated into FCF; see, above, n. 30.

59. RAHNER, Universality, p. 204. "This means that every human being, whatever her/his situation, can be saved". See, also, RAHNER, Salvation, in SM, Vol. 5, New York, 1970, p. 437: Soteriology "must be the soteriology of the one whole race of human beings as such". See, also, RAHNER, Anonymous Christian 14, p. 284: "This optimism concerning salvation appears to me to be one of the most noteworthy results of the Second Vatican Council". Rahner also notes the relationship between this total history of humanity and the history of faith: "At that stage at which this history comes explicitly to exhibit this supernatural dynamism, so that its presence is consciously recognized within the history – at that stage it is revelation history and the history of faith" p. 290.

60. RAHNER, Universality, p. 202: "The Second Vatican Council, in contrast to the previous tradition of the schools, reckons with the possibility of the saving activities of faith, hope, and love being found even in the case of atheists who remain attached to their belief. So the possibility cannot be denied to any group of human beings, whatever their externally verifiable attitudes and beliefs". Rahner recognizes that the question of "how the real and direct possibility of salvation can co-exist with a human situation which objectively ought not to be is a matter to be considered later" (in his article), p. 203. See, also, RAHNER, Spirit and Matter, pp. 160-161: "The salvation history of the individual,

emphasizes is that of freedom. He develops his reflections by considering what it means to speak of "self-redemption" as distinguished from
"redemption by another". The use of the term "self-redemption" indicates that salvation must be understood in a dynamic way. As Rahner
states: "Christian salvation can only be understood as self-redemption
in the sense that a human being does not merely receive her/his salvation in a passive manner but rather realizes it with total, and not just
partial, freedom"[61]. These two elements, therefore, that salvation is
necessarily realized both through its free acceptance by individuals and
also in a common history, must always be kept in mind in regard to
Rahner's theology.

III. THE MEANING OF THE CROSS

What meaning does the cross have for salvation which must always
be seen in the context of freedom and a common history? For Rahner,
the cross holds great significance, and is viewed in a sacramental way.

In terms of cause and effect, Rahner states that the event of the cross,
that is, that Jesus died and rose again, is the effect of God's salvific will
and not its cause[62]. Rahner outlines some of the difficulties brought
about by seeing the cross as "causing" salvation[63]. But he is still left

---

however much it means a unique personal decision in every case, always rests in the
Christian sense on the will of God for a united humanity, for the covenant, for the social
communication and tangibility of salvation both in the spatio-temporal history of the
Church and in tangible sacraments and social institutions". (The word "both" implies or
allows for a separation between "Church" and "sacraments"; the original does not
appear to justify the inclusion of the term "both": *in raumzeitlicher Geschichte der
Kirche, in greifbaren Sakramenten, in gesellschaftlichen Institutionen, ST*, Bd. VI, p. 194)
See, also, RAHNER, *Anonymous Christian 14*, p. 293: "The human being of today is first
and foremost a human being who feels her/himself at one... with humanity as a whole".

61. RAHNER, *Universality*, p. 207: "The very possibility of freedom, however, is established by God through nature and grace. To gain a proper idea of this grace one should not
conceive of the grace in which a human being achieves salvation as an external means but
rather as the innermost core of human freedom which is freely constituted by God".

62. RAHNER, *Universality*, p. 207: "God is not transformed from a God of anger and
justice into a God of mercy and love by the cross; rather God brings the event of the cross
to pass since he is possessed from the beginning of gratuitous mercy and, despite the
world's sin, shares himself with the world, so overcoming its sin".

63. *Ibid.,* p. 208. He refers specifically to the "so-called Anselmian theory of satisfaction, which in a crude or more subtle form has determined the doctrine of the redemption in western Christianity". The most difficult aspect of this theory requires that one
affirm Jesus as the "representative" (*Stellvertretung*) of human beings in a manner that is
"opposed to the correcting understanding of self-redemption" (ST, Bd. XII, p. 262). In
addition, Rahner notes that "the Pauline formula ('for us') *huper hemon* (2 Cor 5,21) is
interpreted in an unconvincing manner which forces the sense of Paul's words".

with the need to explain the fact that "it is part of the Christian confession of faith that the death of Jesus means something for the salvation of all human beings, that it was for us that he died"[64]. The resolution of this question is reached by Rahner asserting that "the cross (together with the resurrection of Jesus) has a primary sacramental causality for the salvation of all human beings, in so far as it mediates salvation to human beings by means of salvific grace which is universally operative in the world"[65]. For the cross, says Rahner, is the "primary sacramental sign of grace"[66]. But how is one to understand the cross in this way?

Rahner suggests that theological reflection upon the cross can lead one to see the cross in a way that is similar to "the sign causality of the sacraments"[67]. God wills a salvation that is complete, not partial. Thus, this offer of God's self-communication "tends toward a goal and a fulfillment of the whole of salvation history". And so, the intention, the will of God for the salvation of all seeks "an irreducible and historically tangible expression"[68]. Human beings exist only within history, so if God's own self-communication is realized in history, this can be realized by the self-communication of God to one human being. This one human being thus is the "definitive and irreversible self-gift of God to the world", that is, the full historical realization of God's offer of God's very self. Consequently, the acceptance of God's self-gift means that the salvation of the world would not be "totally lost". And this acceptance of God's self-gift is realized within history through the death of this one human being; for death marks the definitive culmination of a human being's free actions in history[69]. Therefore, Rahner indicates that this

---

64. *Ibid.*, p. 212: "The problem remains the same whether one speaks of 'causality,' 'meaning,' or 'for us'. In any event all forms of causality of a physical or moral type fail...".

65. *Ibid.*, p. 212: "primary sacramental causality" = *ursakramentale Ursächlichkeit*, (*ST*, Bd. XII, p. 267).

66. *Ibid.*, p. 212: "primary sacramental sign of grace" = *ursakramentales Zeichen von Gnade*, (*ST*, Bd. XII, p. 267). The cross "is the sign of this grace and of its victorious and irreversible activity in the world".

67. *Ibid.*, p. 212. To note Rahner's framework: "In so far as a sacrament can and should be conceived of as a 'real symbol' (*Realsymbol*), as a historical and social embodiment of grace, where grace achieves its own fullness of being and forms an irreversible gift (*opus operatum*) to this extent the sign is a cause of grace, although the sign is caused by this grace" p. 213 (*ST*, Bd. XII, p. 268).

68. *Ibid.*, p. 213.

69. See, especially, K. RAHNER, *On the Theology of Death* (hereafter *Theology of Death*), London, 1965 (Second Edition; revised by W. O'HARA), particularly, pp. 13-31, and pp. 56-80. (ET of: *Zur Theologie des Todes* (QD, 2), Freiburg, 1958.) Two articles with the same title, published, respectively, in 1949 and 1957, preceded the publication of *Zur Theologie des Todes* in 1958; see, in this regard, R. BLEISTEIN, E. KLINGER, *Bibliographie 1924-1969*, p. 17, entry n. 158, and p. 29; entry n. 449.

"historically tangible occurrence must be a sign (*Zeichen*) of the salvation of the whole world in the sense of a 'real symbol'" (*Realsymbol*), and may consequently be described as "sacramental" (*Sakramental*)[70].

But Rahner's considerations are not merely in the realm of possibility. He declares that that which is possible has been realized in Jesus. The Christian faith believes that what one may reflect on in terms of possibility, has occurred in actuality[71]. Jesus' cross and resurrection is this actual event.

Before this event of the cross and resurrection of Jesus took place, there was not a "tangible historical certainty" that there would be a positive ending to salvation history, positive with the meaning not that all human beings necessarily would be saved – for human freedom cannot be eliminated – but that all – definitively – could not be lost. This aspect of the "certainty" of salvation with respect to it being offered, being given in an irreversible way, can be appropriately described, says Rahner, by the terminology which he draws upon to speak of sacramental causality[72]. In fact, he says that to ensure that one understands the event of the cross and resurrection in an accurate way, it is necessary to use the terminology of sacramental causality. Otherwise, one may all too easily conclude that the event of the cross and resurrection is the "cause" of the divine will to save all humanity, while the opposite is true: the event of the cross and resurrection is "brought about by the prior divine will to save humankind"[73].

Rahner makes explicit the importance of the event of the cross and resurrection as a foundation for his sacramental theology. He refers to the Second Vatican Council's emphasis "that the Church is the sacrament of the world's salvation"[74]. And he says that the Council further explains this by "describing the Church as the basic sacrament (*Grundsakrament*) of salvation"[75]. Consequently, Rahner holds that "Jesus

70. RAHNER, *Universality*, p. 214; ST, Bd. XII, p. 269.
71. *Ibid.,* p. 214. The English translation misses the emphasis on the importance of understanding the cross and resurrection as one event: *Der christliche Glaube sieht in Jesus, seinem Kreuz und seiner Auferstehung ein solches Ereignis*, ST, Bd. XII, p. 270. The text in *TI* reads: "Christian faith sees in Jesus, his cross and resurrection just such an event".
72. RAHNER, *Universality*, p. 214. The (often misunderstood) notion of *opus operatum* may be in the mind of Rahner in regard to the question of the "certainty" of salvation, though he does not make this remark explicitly.
73. *Ibid.,* p. 214.
74. RAHNER, *Universality*, p. 214, n. 16. He cites *Lumen gentium* (hereafter *LG*), numbers 1,8, 48, 59; *Unitatis redintegratio* (hereafter *UR*), n. 2; *Ad gentes* (hereafter *AG*), n. 1; and *Gaudium et spes* (hereafter *GS*), n. 45.
75. *Ibid.,* p. 214, n. 17, in which he refers to K. RAHNER, *Sacraments*, London, 1977, pp. ix-xvii; (ET of: *Die siebenfaltige Gabe. Über die Sakramente der Kirche*, Munich, 1974, pp. 7-18).

Christ may be called the primary sacrament" (*Ursakrament*) since he is "the original" (*ursprünglich*), according to the Second Vatican Council, "'sign and instrument of the innermost union with God and of the unity of the whole of humankind"[76]. Now it is possible, says Rahner, to understand the term "sign" as something simply making a person aware of a particular reality. But he believes that "this form of explanation does not do full justice to the causality of Jesus and cross where salvation is concerned, or entirely explain the dogma of the redemption through the cross"[77]. The explanation that enables one to gain a true understanding of this event has as its starting point the reality of sacramental sign. A sacramental sign is such that "sign and signified are essentially one... so that the reality signified (in this case, the saving will of God and grace) comes to be in and through the sign" (that is, the cross and resurrection of Jesus)[78]. Thus, through sacramental sign, an explanation is offered, declares Rahner, that gives recognition to the fact that "the saving will of God and grace" find historical expression in the cross and resurrection of Jesus. The cross does more than make one aware of salvation in faith; it does this, but "as the universal primary sacrament of the salvation of the whole world" it says more, in fact, it says everything[79]. Nevertheless, Rahner cautions that this explanation concerning the cross that he has offered must be seen in the context of other fundamental Christological considerations. His purpose here is primarily to show how "a single historical event may be seen to possess universal meaning"[80].

---

76. RAHNER, *Universality*, pp. 214-215; ST, Bd. XII, p. 270. The reference to Vatican II is *LG*, n. 1. For a study of the meaning and relationship of Rahner's terminology *Ursakrament* and *Grundsakrament*, see my earlier work, J. FARMER, *Ministry in Community: Rahner's Vision of Ministry* (*Louvain Theological & Pastoral Monographs* 13), Leuven/Grand Rapids, 1993, especially pp. 113-119.

77. RAHNER, *Universality*, p. 215. Rahner interprets the quotation from *LG*, (see previous footnote), "sign and instrument", as "instrument because sign".

78. *Ibid.*, p. 215.

79. *Ibid.*, p. 215. Original: *aber das Kreuz Jesu als das universale Ursakrament des Heiles der ganzen Welt sagt mehr und eigentlich alles*, ST, Bd. XII, p. 271.

80. *Ibid.*, pp. 215-216. Other Christological themes explicitly mentioned by Rahner are: 1), "the solidarity of all human beings and the history of individual freedom within the totality of human history"; 2), "the connection between God's self- communication in grace and the death of Jesus"; 3), "the theology of death"; and 4), "the unity of the death and resurrection of Jesus". See, in regard to the last-noted theme of the unity of the cross and resurrection of Jesus, RAHNER, *Belief Today*, p. 17: "Cross and resurrection belong together in the authentic witness to Jesus and in genuine and responsible faith in him. The cross means the stark demand for a human being to surrender her/himself unconditionally before the mystery of her/his being which s/he can never bring under her/his control, since s/he is finite and burdened with guilt. The resurrection means the unconditional hope that in this surrender the blessing, forgiveness and ultimate acceptance of the human being takes place through this mystery".

One further question arises with regard to the cross and resurrection of Jesus. If this event, indeed, is seen as the "universal primary sacrament of the salvation of the whole world", if this event says "everything", then what is the relationship within history between this event and 1), all people who have lived before Christ; 2), non-Christians since the time of Christ; and 3), "all those who consciously and explicitly believe that they are required by their conscience to refuse to Gospel of Christ as this is presented to them"[81]. It is a question which calls to mind the extensive discussion that has been carried on about the "anonymous Christian"[82]. The question can be phrased in a more systematic way by asking why human beings for whom the possibility of salvation becomes a reality "do not merely have an unthematic, transcendent relationship to the God of the philosophers but also possess a relationship to the God who communicates himself to human beings in grace and bestows a supernatural self-revelation on human beings"[83]. The response that Rahner gives to this question is to develop some reflections on a "Christology of Quest", though a later translation, "A Searching Christology", seems more faithful to the original term[84].

What Rahner is indicating is this: "a person who is searching for something which is specific and yet unknown has a genuine existential connection, as one alert and on the watch, with whatever s/he is seeking, even if s/he has not yet found it, and so cannot develop the relation to the object of her/his quest to its full extent"[85]. This "searching" on the part of the person of good faith (*bonae fidei*) is brought about by grace, and grace "has found its historically tangible expression and its irreversible force in Jesus"[86]. Therefore, Rahner

81. RAHNER, *Universality*, p. 216. "All these groups ultimately belong to a single category, since for a variety of reasons they have not been reached by the Gospel of Jesus and yet their rejection of the Christian message does not mean an existentially serious sin".

82. See, above, n. 44, for full references to this subject. To highlight Rahner's position, one may note the following, RAHNER, *Universality*, p. 218: "It is absurd and ridiculous... to assert that supporters of this notion merely want to use it to console Church members for the diminishing numbers, both in relative and absolute terms, of those confessing explicit Christian faith... In fact, the theory arose from two facts: first, the possibility of supernatural salvation and of a corresponding faith which must be granted to non-Christians, even if they never become Christians; and secondly, that salvation cannot be gained without reference to God and Christ, since it must in its origin, history and fulfillment be a theistic and Christian salvation".

83. RAHNER, *Universality*, p. 220.

84. *Ibid.*, pp. 220-222. The original phrase is more dynamic: *suchende Christolgie, ST*, Bd. XII, p. 278. This is captured in RAHNER, *FCF*, p. 295: "A Searching Christology".

85. RAHNER, *Universality*, p. 221.

86. *Ibid.*, p. 221. The terms "expression" and "force" do not seem faithful to the original: *die ihre geschichtliche Greifbarkeit und Irreversibilität in Jesus gefunden hat, ST*, Bd. XII, p. 278. Note also the original: *aus dieser Aporie kann man wohl nur entkommen,*

concludes that a person who is searching is moved "in some measure" to the goal of Jesus Christ[87]. Rahner says that a relationship
then may best be described as a "relationship of eschatological hope
to Christ"[88]. And he suggests three "appeals" that are seen in the context of this eschatological hope[89]: 1), the appeal to an absolute love of
neighbor; 2), the appeal to readiness for death; and, 3), the appeal to
hope in the future[90].

IV. CHRIST: THE ONE MEDIATOR

As indicated above[91], Rahner consistently affirms belief in Jesus – as
fully human and fully divine – as significant for us as human beings
because Jesus is the way for us to God. But how does Rahner present
and explain this fact that Christ is Mediator? His considerations on this
aspect of Christology are of fundamental importance.

But let me first include the perspective that Joseph Wong offers with
regard to how Rahner views Christ as the One Mediator. Wong identifies Rahner's Christology as an inclusive Christology. But he notes that
an inclusive Christology can itself be further divided into "constitutive"
and "normative"[92]. Rahner, in Wong's view, presents Christ as normative. "He is the decisive and highest revelation of God and of human
existence. But the mediation of Christ is not constitutive for all. Salvation, always possible for all humanity even apart from Christ, becomes
normatively present in him"[93].

wenn für die genannten Fälle eine "suchende Christologie" als einerseits allen Men-
schen bonae fidei immer gegeben und anderseits als ausreichend betrachtet wird, ST, Bd.
XII, p. 278.

87. RAHNER, _Universality_, p. 221: "in some measure" = _gewissermaßen_.

88. _Ibid._, p. 221.

89. _Ibid._, p. 221. The original term _Appele_ may not be as faithfully translated into
English by "claim". The English translation in RAHNER, _FCF_, p. 295, uses "appeal".

90. RAHNER, _Universality_, pp. 222-224; substantially incorporated into RAHNER, _FCF_,
pp. 295-298. "We can summarize the content of these three appeals of Christology within
fundamental theology by saying that (1) the human being is searching for the absolute
savior, (2) and s/he affirms at least unthematically her/his past or future coming in every
total act of her/his existence (3) which is finalized by grace towards the immediacy of
God" _FCF_, p. 298.

91. See above, section I: "The Full Humanity of Christ".

92. J. WONG, _Anonymous Christians: Karl Rahner's Pneuma-Christocentrism and an_
East-West Dialogue in _Theological Studies_ 55 (1994) 609-637, p. 612: "According to the
former [constitutive] view, Jesus Christ is not only the decisive and normative revelation
of God, but is also constitutive of salvation. Normative Christology, on the other hand,
presents Christ as not constitutive but only normative of salvation for all people."

93. _Ibid._, p. 612.

Rahner himself first distinguishes between a consideration of the question of mediations proper to Christology, which involve the aspect of personal mediation, as contrasted with a consideration of what he calls institutional mediation[94]. A study that focuses on Rahner's reflections concerning the personal mediation of Christ prepares and lays the foundation for a subsequent study of how Rahner views institutional mediation.

Rahner notes that the Roman Catholic Church is frequently criticized as professing belief in Jesus Christ as the one and only Mediator, but as not actually living in a genuinely faithful way to this belief, in effect, accepting that there are "other" mediations of salvation besides Jesus Christ[95]. The picture emerges that Jesus Christ "is not the one who stands between us and God as sole Reconciler and Mediator, but he stands over against us on the side of God as the one with whom we have to be reconciled". And in this picture one finds the Saints, especially Mary, as many individual mediators who are needed to help "bridge the gap" between humanity and Jesus[96]. Even the Second Vatican Council uses the term "Mediatrix" in speaking of Mary. How can one reconcile the use of this terminology with the belief in the sole mediatorship of Jesus Christ[97]? Rahner's response is that the use of the term "Mediatrix" in reference to Mary, and all other references to other "mediations", are founded upon this important fact: "as a result of and by virtue of his (Christ's) mediatorship", 1), "everyone depends on everyone else", 2), "is of significance for everyone else", 3), "has a task (*Aufgabe*) subordinate to Christ (*munus subordinatum*)", and 4), "the receipt (*Empfang*) of salvation also implies the TASK of salvation" (*Heilshandelns*)[98]. The function of Mary, therefore, is one that is rooted first and foremost in the reality of the salvation-solidarity that all

94. K. RAHNER, *One Mediator and Many Mediations* (hereafter *One Mediator*) in *TI*, Vol. 9, London, 1972, pp. 169-184; (ET of: *ST*, Bd. VIII, Einsiedeln, 1967, pp. 218-235). The distinction is more clearly expressed in the original *personaler Vermittlungen and institutionellen Vermittlungen* which is (poorly) translated as "personal mediations" and "mediating institutions" (pp. 169-170, and *ST*, Bd. VIII, pp. 218-219). See, also, in regard to the mediating role of Jesus Christ, K. RAHNER, *Ich glaube an Jesus Christus*, Einsiedeln, 1968.

95. RAHNER, *One Mediator*, p. 169.

96. *Ibid.*, p. 171.

97. *Ibid.*, p. 172. The reference is to *LG*, n. 62. Rahner makes an important comment regarding the Church's dogmatic terminology. It is made up of "very different literary genres". For example, "Vatican II by no means ascribes to Mary the title and function of a mediatrix in the strict theological sense, but rather takes the freer language of pious affection…". Rahner indicates that there can be dogmatic assertions that are made in a more speculative tone, and dogmatic assertions that are made in a more devotional tone. While both have their particular danger, a devotional tone "inevitably runs the risk of giving way to excessive emotion and vague enthusiasm, undisciplined dogmatism and pious exaggeration" (pp. 172-173, n. 21).

98. K. RAHNER, *One Mediator*, p. 173; *ST*, Bd. VIII, p. 222.

the redeemed share with one another. In a style that is not infrequent with Rahner, he states that it is his intention to view these "mediations not as dependent subordinate modes of participation in the unique mediatorship of Christ, but, reversing the process... to understand the mediatorship of Christ as the eschatologically perfect and consequently the highest, the unique 'case' of human intercommunication before God and of the solidarity in salvation of all human beings"[99]. This human intercommunication and solidarity in salvation (which Rahner at one time combines in the phrase *heilssolidarische Interkommunikation*) is not abolished but fulfilled by the mediatorship of Christ, because it is both a necessary precondition as well as the effect of Christ's mediatorship[100].

For Rahner there is a fundamental question that must guide the search for the meaning of the mediatorship of Christ: "What is the transcendental horizon of understanding, and thus the hermeneutical principle, which lead to an understanding of the mediatorship of Christ which can be protected from misconceptions"[101]? What human experience provides the horizon[102]? Rahner answers that it is the human experience that a person has over and over again of always being faced by the other. There is no one or any place to which a person could withdraw and be simply alone. There is no place where one would no longer experience the need for others, that is, the need to be sustained by others. And the possibilities of needing or being needed by the other are unlimited. Now, since every human being unavoidably encounters the question of salvation in her/his existence, it follows that the reality of intercommunication is a real element of each person's existence that necessarily is involved in each person choosing for or against salvation[103]. Rahner concludes: "in the matter of salvation everyone is responsible and significant for everyone else"[104]. This element of historicity (*Geschichtlichkeit*)

---

99. RAHNER, *One Mediator*, pp. 173-174; original: *als den eschatologisch volendeten und so einmaligen höchsten "fall" einer menschlichen Interkommunikation vor Gott und einer Heilssolidarität aller*, ST, Bd. VIII, p. 223.

100. *Ibid.*, p. 174; ST, Bd. VIII, p. 223. See previous footnote for the alternate phrasing.

101. *Ibid.*, p. 175: "What and where is the unavoidable existential (*existentielle*) experience within the perspective of which we can really encounter the unique fact of the redeeming death of Jesus and find it credible"?

102. *Ibid.*, pp. 175-176. Rahner notes that "the experience of human beings' guilt does not provide this horizon. Lostness does not itself automatically give rise to a rescue, let alone lead one to understand how such a rescue is conceivable".

103. *Ibid.*, p. 176; however, relying specifically upon the original here: *gibt es also die Heilsfrage als unausweichliches Konstitutiv der menschlichen Existenz, dann ist auch die Interkommunikation ein Moment der Existenz in Heil oder Unheil*, ST; Bd. VIII, p. 226.

104. *Ibid.*, p. 176. Rahner refers to certain biblical and non-biblical concepts that presuppose intercommunicative existence: "people of God", "covenant", "Body of Christ", "pray for one another".

in salvation is on the one hand a result of the historical decisions of others, and on the other hand is both an active and a passive co-determination of each person by and of the other[105]. Rahner presents another element of the reality of intercommunicative existence, namely, that this always takes place before God (*vor Gott*)[106]. Grace and Incarnation mutually condition each other[107]. Fundamentally, this is the same point that Rahner wishes to emphasize in saying that intercommunicative existence always takes place before God. He states explicitly: "the experience of being-in-reference-to the absolute mystery we call God and the experience of intercommunication mutually determine each other"[108]. This is so because the world "is not only a world of things but the world to which the self-experiencing human being belongs: within her/himself and her/his intercommunication s/he recognizes God"[109].

Rahner recognizes that God is the one who "initiates an absolute intercommunication between God's self and human beings". And it is this very self-communication of God which establishes the possibility "of a radically serious, ultimate and secure interpersonal communication"[110]. The reality of intercommunicative existence is rooted in God's self-communication to human beings. It follows, therefore, that wherever "interpersonal communication reaches the ultimate possibility of its actual being... it is already a meeting with God"[111]. Thus it is possible to affirm that the reality of intercommunication exhibits a sacramental dimension. And this sacramental dimension itself reflects the fact that the reality of human intercommunication is not a static reality, ever unchanging, but a reality which is dynamic, which has a history of its own, because it is a history shaped by persons – "who are unique at any

---

105. *Ibid.*, p. 177. But Rahner notes that it is not always easy to determine the boundary between this active and passive co-determination. The original: *eine bestimmte Grenze läßt sich nicht festlegen, wodurch andere in der passiven oder aktiven Mitbestimmung ausgeschlossen wären, ST*, Bd. VIII, p. 227).

106. *Ibid.*, p. 178.

107. K. RAHNER, *Reflections on Methodology in Theology* (hereafter *Methodology*), in *TI*, Vol. 11, London, 1974, pp. 68-114, especially p. 109, (ET: *ST*, Bd. IX, 1970, Einsiedeln, pp. 79-126). The three lectures appear as one essay in published form and had not been published before appearing in *ST*.

108. RAHNER, *One Mediator*, p. 178.

109. *Ibid.*, p. 178.

110. *Ibid.*, p. 178.

111. *Ibid.*, p. 178. This meeting with God may not necessarily be expressly acknowledged, it may be an "unthematic" and "anonymous" meeting. Original: *wo zwischenmenschliche Interkommunikation die letzen Möglichkeiten ihres faktischen (verschwiegen von Gott und in ihm selbst gegebenen) Wesens erreicht, its sie schon Begegnung mit Gott (mag sie sich das ausdrücklich oder nicht), weil sie selbst in der Selbstmitteilung Gottes gründet, ST*, Bd. VIII, pp. 228-229.

one time" – and a history which is not cyclical, but one moving toward a goal[112]. And what is the goal toward which human intercommunicative existence is moving? Rahner answers that the "'Incarnation,' the death and the resurrection of the divine Logos" is the "eschatological meridian" (*eschatologisch Höhepunkt*) of this "history of human intercommunication and of the relationship between God and humankind"[113]. For it is precisely insofar as Jesus Christ is the "eschaton of the history of this self-communication" that one may and must call him the "Mediator of God's self-communication"[114]. Rahner underscores three reasons why Jesus must be seen as Mediator in this way: 1), "grace" (*Gnade*), "faith" (*Glaube*), "spirit" (*Geist*), and "justification" (*Rechtfertigung*) were effectual specifically before Christ and have occurred throughout all of history even where the Gospel has not been preached explicitly[115]; 2), "all salvation occurs *intuitu meritorum Christi*"[116]; and 3), "it is not the Christ-event which provides the foundation for God's will for our salvation,... the Christ-event itself is the 'effect' of the latter"[117]. It is precisely because God's self-communication in history has become irreversible in this individual Jesus that God's self-communication is seen as "eschatologically victorious". And it is precisely because each individual person is a member of this single humanity to which God's self-communication is directed that Jesus "effects God's will for the salvation of all"[118].

In addition to, but following upon, these considerations, Rahner makes the following assertions: 1), "wherever salvation occurs in the individual's salvation-history, it also (auch; better translated: 'specifically')

112. RAHNER, *One Mediator*, pp. 178-179.
113. *Ibid.*, p. 179; ST, Bd. VIII, pp. 229-230.
114. *Ibid.*, p. 179. History "takes place in reference to its fullness and its victorious end".
115. *Ibid.*, p. 180; *ST*, Bd. VIII, p. 230. He refers to two articles specifically: K. RAHNER, *The Word and the Eucharist* (hereafter *Word and Eucharist*) in *TI*, Vol. 4, London, 1966, pp. 253-286; (ET of: *ST*, Bd. IV, Einsiedeln, 1960, pp. 313-355); and K. RAHNER, *Atheism and Implicit Christianity* (hereafter *Atheism and Christianity*) in *TI*, Vol. 9, London, 1972, pp. 145-164; (ET of: *ST*, Bd. VIII, Einsiedeln, 1967, pp. 187-212). An initial shorter version of this article appeared in *Concilium* 3 (1967) 171-180.
116. RAHNER, *One Mediator*, p. 180. Rahner refers to H. DENZIGER, A. SCHÖNMETZER, *Enchiridion symbolorum: definitionum et declarationum de rebus fidei et morum. (Quod primum editit Henricus Denziger, et quod funditus retractavit, auxit, notulis ornavit Adolfus Schönmetzer* (hereafter *DS*), Barcinone, 1967 (Thirty-Fourth Edition), n. 1523, 1530, 1529, 1560.
117. RAHNER, *One Mediator*, p. 180. See, above, section III., "The Meaning of the Cross". Rahner also refers to, among others, K. RAHNER, *History of the World and Salvation-History* (hereafter *World and Salvation-History*) in *TI*, Vol. 5, London, 1966, pp. 97-114; (ET of: *ST*, Bd. V, Einsiedeln, 1964 (Second Edition), pp. 115-135.
118. RAHNER, *One Mediator*, p. 180.

mediates salvation for all others"[119]; 2), "this world of intercommunication, as history, has one apogee (*Höhepunkt*) and only one goal (*Ziel*): this is Jesus Christ, who as the God-given apogee of history, is its sole and absolute Mediator"[120]. Rahner adds two important points to these

119. *Ibid.*, p. 181; *ST*, Bd. VIII, p. 231. Rahner notes that this mediation is not to be thought of as an extraordinary or special function of a few, such as "the Saints". Rather, all believers and all the justified, as salvation is realized in them, mediate that one salvation to others. (The realization of salvation for an individual moves toward its definitive realization which can only be realized completely and unambiguously in death.) The explicit and conscious dimension of this mediation occurs as intercessory prayer and requests for intercession. See, in this regard, among others, K. RAHNER, J. METZ, *The Courage to Pray*, New York, 1981, esp. pp. 31-87, representing Rahner's contribution and entitled Prayer to the Saints; (ET of: K. RAHNER, J. METZ, *Ermutigung zum Gebet*, Freiburg, 1977). "Praying to individual saints is secondary to this general remembrance of the dead, which as a result of our hope for universal salvation, is simultaneously a commemoration of the (largely anonymous) body of all the saints. In comparison, the remembrance of a specific saint is like a request for some practical necessity (like daily bread), which is an aspect of our prayer for salvation, which is God himself" (*The Courage to Pray*, p. 87). The much earlier work, K. RAHNER, *On Prayer*, New York, 1968, (ET of: K. RAHNER, *Von der Not und dem Segen des Gebetes*, Innsbruck, 1949), does not consider explicitly the aspect of intercessory prayer. The theme of this book – in so far as a single general theme can be discovered – could be expressed in the considerations from the opening chapter: "We must find courage by facing squarely up to the fact that there can be no complete rest for the soul, but rather disillusionment and bitterness, in the things whose end is the abyss of death" (p. 19). But see, also, K. RAHNER, *The Church of the Saints* (hereafter *Church of Saints*) in *TI*, Vol. 3, London, 1967, pp. 91-104; (ET of: *ST*, Bd. III, Einsiedeln, 1959 (Third Edition), pp. 111-126); and, the very comprehensive article, K. RAHNER, *Why and How Can We Venerate the Saints* (hereafter *Venerate the Saints*) in *TI*, Vol. 7, London, 1971, pp. 3-23; (ET of: *ST*, Bd. VII, Einsiedeln, 1966, pp. 283-303); and K. RAHNER, *All Saints* in *TI*, Vol. 7, London, 1971, pp. 24-29; (ET of: *ST*, Bd. VII, Einsiedeln, 1966, pp. 304-309).

120. RAHNER, *One Mediator*, pp. 181-182; ST, Bd. VIII, p. 232. "Far from excluding the saving, intercommunicative character of the world's salvation-history, it implies it. All intercommunicative mediations of salvation are dependent upon this single goal and their eschatological consummation in Christ; but for that very reason they actually exist; they are not merely secondary, ultimately superfluous consequences of Christ's mediatorship; they are the very preconditions which Christ's mediatorship creates for itself. In other words, they constitute the condition for the possibility of such mediatorship, conditions provided, of course, by God's sovereign grace itself in and through its will towards Jesus Christ – just as, conversely, Jesus Christ is willed 'for us human beings and for our salvation'" (p. 182). It seems of crucial importance to keep this above consideration clearly in mind in order to situate and understand Rahner's comments regarding Jesus Christ as "Absolute Savior", namely, to understand "absolute" in an inclusive and not in an exclusive sense. See, for example, the section in *FCF*, The Vindication and Acceptance of Jesus' Claim to be the Absolute Savior, pp. 279-280, esp. p. 280: "(Jesus) abolishes religious and moral categories such as those touching family, marriage, nation, the laws, the temple, the sabbath and the origins of religious authority... They have now been broken through by a new and real immediacy of God coming from God himself. Consequently, they no longer have that precise function of mediating and representing God which they once correctly claimed to have". The original of the last phrase: *und somit nicht mehr genau jene Funktion der Vermittlung zu Gott, seiner Stellvertretung haben, die sie einmal mit Recht zu haben beanspruchten*, (*GdG*, p. 275).

assertions. He insists that Jesus Christ cannot be allowed to simply become an abstract idea, a Christ-principle, that would simply provide a "mythological figure unworthy of belief"[121]. So in order that Jesus Christ is not "merely another word for the incalculable sovereignty of the grace of the transcendent God", he, as a concrete, historical human being must be capable of being loved[122]. But, and this is a significant emphasis on the part of Rahner, how can the love of this concrete, historical human being, Jesus Christ, be "my salvation, if I am unable to love and be loved by other human beings, with whom I am in close, concrete proximity"[123]. This mutual loving and being loved is a human reality that does not take place apart from God. It occurs, says Rahner, "in God's Pneuma and in relation to God"[124]. For this mutual love is not simply a commandment, but this mutual love is "actually salvation"[125]. And if one is to believe this with one's whole self, then such a "living Christianity" must affirm, and not be embarrassed by, an expression of the love of God that is as real as the expression of every real human love[126].

Rahner's second point is to underline again his insistence that the mediatorship of Christ cannot be understood in a individualistic way. For Rahner will not support a view of salvation that allows or implies an individual process of salvation for a person such that it has nothing to do

121. RAHNER, *One Mediator*, p. 182.

122. *Ibid.*, p. 182. Original: *dann darf er nicht einfach nur ein anderes Wort für die unberechenbare Souveränität der Gnade des transzendenter Gottes sein* (GdG, p. 233).

123. RAHNER, *One Mediator*, p. 182.

124. *Ibid.*, p. 182. Original: in *Gottes Pneuma natürlich und auf Gott hin* (GdG, p. 233). See, also, RAHNER, *Belief Today*, p. 20: "Christians have had a basic awareness that the relation of hope and love to the incomprehensible mystery of their life which they call God can only be acknowledged, expressed and given credible form in an unconditional love of their neighbor, for this alone is capable of forcing open the hell of human self-centeredness. This love is not to be treated as self-evident, otherwise it becomes corrupted into an expression of hidden egoism. As the liberating grace of God it stretches us continually beyond our capacity and is for this reason only really possible if a human being, consciously or not, allows her/himself to surrender to the incomprehensible mystery. Then the Spirit of Jesus is at work, even if it is not explicitly acknowledged, as Mt 25 makes plain. Let us, therefore, hope tht the grace of God performs this miracle in us too (*auch*; better translated: 'specifically'); everything depends on it" (*ST*, Bd. XII, p. 38).

125. RAHNER, *One Mediator*, p. 182.

126. *Ibid.*, pp. 182-183. Rahner makes specific reference to an experience of being shocked "by the overwhelming sort of Marian devotion in which a pious Catholic rushes to Mary's bosom, loves her, entreats and importunes her in utter confidence, as if nothing in religion were so important" (p. 182). In a note Rahner comments: "However much the concrete practice of the veneration of the Saints becomes clouded over and succumbs to wrong tendencies, the fact cannot be obscured that the theological foundation is thoroughly legitimate and does not contradict the spirit of the New Testament. In their indignance at abuses, however, people have often eliminated what is essential as well" (n. 53, pp. 183-184).

with anyone else. Salvation must be concerned with unlocking and opening doors, not with slamming doors shut and seeking refuge behind locked doors. Salvation consists in living in "that single love of the Pneuma which joins all human beings together and hence makes each human being of saving importance for each other"[127]. Rahner notes how ridiculous it is to imagine that the members of the Body of Christ would be "solely concerned with the Head of the Body and have nothing to do with each other"[128]. The single most-important principle that Rahner emphasizes in regard to a study of the mediatorship of Jesus Christ is that "all 'mediation' is a mediation to the end of immediacy, and not a 'medial' something which is inserted between and thus keeps separate the objects of mediation"[129]. This principle applies both to the mediation of Jesus to God – always affirming the full humanity of Jesus, and it applies to the mediations on the part of the justified person for the other, both with respect to Jesus as well as to God. This mediation on the part of Jesus "does not destroy God's immediacy but actually constitutes it as such"[130]. Consequently, "any 'mediation' to Jesus Christ, even at the level of concepts", does not prevent one from an immediate encounter with God. Here, too, the mediation does not destroy God's immediacy, but actually constitutes it[131].

I offer these Four Christological Themes of the Theology of Karl Rahner as we draw nearer to the end of this 20th century – indeed the end of this second millennium. These themes "I) The Full Humanity of Christ, II) Christology Within an Evolutionary View of the World, III) The Meaning of the Cross, and IV) Christ: The One Mediator" so carefully and systematically developed by Rahner during the greater part of this century provide, in my judgment, a foundation for continuing reflection and discussion as we face "Plurality and the Quest for Unity in Contemporary Christology: The Myriad Christ".

Xavier University of Louisiana   Jerry T. FARMER
7325 Palmetto Street
Box 81A
New Orleans, Louisiana 70125-1098
U.S.A.

127. RAHNER, *One Mediator*, p. 183.
128. *Ibid.*, p. 183.
129. RAHNER, *One Mediator*, p. 183. Original: *daß alle Vermittlung Vermittlung zu Unmittelbarkeit ist und nicht ein Mittleres, das sich zwischen die zu vermittelnden schiebt und sie also trennt* (*ST*, Bd. VIII, p. 234).
130. *Ibid.*, p. 183.
131. *Ibid.*, p. 183.

THE CHRISTOCENTRIC SPIRITUALITY OF KARL RAHNER

I. Rahner's "existentiell" Christology

a. Introduction

One of the most polemic criticisms of Karl Rahner's Christology, indeed of his general conception of Christianity, came from no less a theologian than Hans Urs von Balthasar in his book *Cordula oder der Ernstfall*[1]. This work was essentially a reaction to Rahner's anthropologically-orientated theology, which, in von Balthasar's view, tended to reduce Christian living "to a bland and shallow humanism"[2]. In particular, von Balthasar claimed that Rahner's concept of the anonymous Christian had little to do with the message of the Gospel, and overlooked the crucial aspect or "decisive moment" (Ernstfall) of Christianity. This decisive factor for von Balthasar is the cross of Christ. The appropriate response on the part of the believer was exemplified by the early martyrs' explicit confession of Christ and their readiness for death. Von Balthasar's fear was that Rahner's notion of the anonymous Christian would inevitably lead to Christianity becoming dispensable. There would be no need for the Ernstfall, no need for prophetic witness, no need for martyrdom. If theology goes down this road, von Balthasar argued, it would ultimately become a matter of indifference whether or not one believed in God.

This is a serious criticism of Rahner and we need to ask whether it does justice to him and, in particular, to his Christology. Underlying von Balthasar's position, then, is his conviction that Rahner's transcendental method ultimately leads to a relativized Christianity. While a detailed analysis of Rahner's method is beyond our scope here, we shall endeavour to show how Rahner, far from relativizing the person and work of Christ, advocates what he terms an existentiell Christology. Further, and this is our main contention, Rahner's Christology is deeply rooted in the experience of the Spiritual Exercises of St. Ignatius

1. H. Urs von Balthasar, *Cordula oder der Ernstfall* (Kriterien, 2) Einsiedeln, 1966. ET: *The Moment of Christian Witness*, tr. by R. Beckley, San Francisco, 1969. A second edition (1967) contained an "Afterword" by von Balthasar as a response to the widespread criticism of his treatment of Rahner in the first edition.

2. von Balthasar, *The Moment of Christian Witness*, 1966, p. 126.

and this "Ignatian" influence has been largely overlooked by theological commentators[3].

b. Anthropology and Christology

If we take a representative work of Rahner's such as *Grundkurs des Glaubens*[4], which was intended as a foundational course in Christianity, we note there his reluctance to take a "too narrowly Christological approach"[5]. Simply to present Jesus Christ as the key to all existential problems of today would be too simplistic and could seem to be a kind of indoctrination. Rahner's approach, on the other hand, is to show how anthropology can issue in Christology, and how an analysis of the transcendental orientation of the human person, as a questioner, as orientated to mystery, and so on, is required first of all, before Christ and the explicit message of revelation can be proposed as the answer to humankind's searching. It is not a question of Rahner stopping short of a full acknowledgement of the significance of the person and work of Christ. Rather, God's self-communication to humanity is variously described as a "process", an "event", and a "movement", which reaches its climax in Jesus Christ. His Christology, conceived as it is within an evolutionary perspective of world history, sees in Jesus the "absolute Heilbringer", the definitive, irreversible, and eschatological revelation of God. While this claim does not come at the outset of Grundkurs, the merit of Rahner's approach, it seems to me, lies in his attempt to critically correlate the message of Christianity with the intrinsic structures of the human person. It is only by showing how the concrete, categorial events of salvation history really correspond to the basic structures of the human condition that Christianity can claim to affect

---

3. There have, of course, been exceptions to this. See, for example, the classical work of K.P. FISCHER, *Der Mensch als Geheimnis: Die Anthropologie Karl Rahners. Mit einem Brief von Karl Rahner*, Freiburg, 1974; and his *Gotteserfahrung: Mystagogie in der Theologie Karl Rahners und in der Theologie der Befreiung*, Mainz, 1986. See also H.D. EGAN, *The Spiritual Exercises and the Ignatian Mystical Horizon*. Foreword by Karl Rahner, St. Louis, The Institute of Jesuit Sources, 1976. More recent works treating of the Ignatian influence on Rahner's theology include: P. ENDEAN, *The Direct Experience of God and the Standard of Christ: A Critical and Constructive Study of Karl Rahner's Writings on the* Spiritual Exercises *of Ignatius of Loyola*. Doctoral Dissertation, University of Oxford, 1991; R. STOLINA, *Die Theologie Karl Rahners: Inkarnatorische Spiritualität: Menschwerdung Gottes und Gebet* (Innsbrucker theologische Studien, 46), Innsbruck-Wien, 1996; A. ZAHLAUER, *Karl Rahner und sein "produktives Vorbild" Ignatius von Loyola* (Innsbrucker theologische Studien, 47), Innsbruck-Wien, 1996.
4. K. RAHNER, *Grundkurs des Glaubens*: *Einführung in den Begriff des Christentums*, Freiburg, 1976. ET: *Foundations of Christian Faith: An Introduction to the Idea of Christianity*, tr. by W. Dych, London, 1978.
5. RAHNER, *Foundations of Christian Faith,* p. 13.

the human person at the ultimate level of his or her existence and subjectivity. I do not think it accurate to portray Rahner as exclusively pursuing a transcendental Christology. He was more than aware of the complicated relationship between transcendence and history and of the difficulty of keeping both these dimensions in tension[6]. In relation to Christology, he has tried to do this by showing how a Christology from below and the more classical descending Christologies are not mutually exclusive[7].

It is significant in the context of our remarks above to note that when Rahner treats of the personal relationship of a Christian to Christ in Foundations, he does so not in his chapter on Christian life, where one would normally expect such a topic to be discussed, but rather in the chapter on Jesus Christ. Rahner is advocating what he calls an "existentiell" Christology, i.e., that process of personal appropriation and actualisation of a Christian personal relationship to Jesus Christ, something which can also be spoken of in abstraction without such a personal realisation. Such an appropriation is important because the danger always exists of turning the relationship with Christ into the cult of an abstract Christ-idea. Rahner's claim, in other words, is that any understanding of the dogma about Christ only arises "subsequent to and because of a historical encounter with Jesus as the Christ"[8]. The starting-point for Rahner's Christology, is, therefore, the actual faith relationship between a believing Christian and Jesus Christ[9].

6. "...There are few philosophical, anthropological, and theological problems more difficult than the relationship between transcendentality and history. Consequently, I'm not surprised if someone wants to point out that my theology doesn't adequately handle this difficulty. ... For me transcendentality is always transcendentality that attains its goal *in* actual history that ultimately cannot be deduced a priori". K. RAHNER, *Faith in a Wintry Season: Conversations and Interviews with Karl Rahner in the Last Years of his Life*, eds. P. IMHOF and H. BIALLOWONS; tr. by H. Egan, New York, 1991, pp. 22, 26.

7. The most recent comprehensive historical and chronological survey of Rahner's Christological publications is that of E. MAURICE, *L'évolution de la pensée christologique de Karl Rahner 1934-1984*, Paris, 1995.

8. RAHNER, *Foundations of Christian Faith*, p. 203.

9. Commenting on this statement, Roman Siebenrock, manager of the Karl Rahner archives, observes: "Daher ist es nicht verwunderlich, wenn er in der ersten Zeit in Münster die denkerische Rechtfertigung eines persönlichen Christusverhältnisses in vorweihnachtlichen Betrachtungen anbietet. Jede diese denkerischen Betrachtungen endete mit einem Gebet. Dieses Ineinander von Betrachtung und Verantwortung des Dogmas, von historisch-kritischem Fragen und persönlicher Christusfrömmigkeit darf nicht gegeneinander ausgespielt werden. Ebenso gefährlich wäre es, die persönliche Christusbeziehung gegenüber der kirchlichen Glaubenslehre zu einseitig zu favorisieren". R. SIEBENROCK, *Jesus lieben – Jesus nachfolgen – Jesus Christus glauben. Zur Typologie der Christologie Karl Rahners*. Unpublished lecture given at the Gedenkakademie für Karl Rahner SJ, Studientagung 11./12.03.1994, *Zur Christologie Karl Rahners SJ. Analysen – Perspektiven*, Mainz, Erbacher Hof, 1994. I would like to acknowledge my indebtedness to Dr. Siebenrock in the preparation of this paper.

Underlying this approach is the view that "Christianity in its full and explicit form is not merely an abstract theory, Y (but) understands itself as an existentiell process, and this process is precisely what we are calling a personal relationship to Jesus Christ"[10]. Christology, then, is not primarily reflection on an idea about Jesus, but a reflection on this lived faith relationship. William Dych, the English translator of *Foundations*, captures this spiritual root and significance of Rahner's existentiell Christology well when he observes:

> "For Christian faith is not primarily a theory about Jesus, but a praxis, a way of life. It is the life of discipleship in response to his call to 'follow' himY It is by doing the truth that Jesus did that existentiell Christology acquires its concrete, experiential knowledge of Jesus of Nazareth. One sees here why Rahner accorded such importance to Ignatius Loyola and his Spiritual Exercises for his theology. Through the exercise not of the speculative intellect, but of the senses and the imagination, the Exercises are designed to put one 'in touch' with the actual Jesus and to give one a 'taste of' and a 'feel for' his life. In this encounter one does not 'grasp' something, but 'is grasped', and the faith which responds and follows is what Rahner calls the point of departure for all Christology"[11].

Prescinding from the many special questions that Rahner deals with in his Christology, our focus has been on Rahner's christological point of departure, an encounter involving the historical Jesus, and hence an "ascending Christology". It is not that Rahner believes an ascending Christology (proceeding from the human being Jesus) cannot coincide with the classical descending Christology (God becomes a human

There is a danger here of a primitive fundamentalism, against which Rahner warns: "Die Aussagen einer metaphysischen Christologie behalten natürlich ihre Gültigkeit, es ist keine Wendung zu einem primitiven Jesuanismus, aber eine gewisse Wendung zu einer schlichten Begegnung mit Jesus, mit dem Konkreten in seinem Leben". K. RAHNER, *Glaube als Mitte menschlicher Existenz. Ein Gespräch mit und über Karl Rahner aus Anlaß seines 70. Geburtstages*, in *Herder Korrespondenz* 28 (1974) 77-92, 87. [It should be pointed out that the English translation of the above quotation, based as it is on a typographical omission in the German, is incorrect. See RAHNER, *Faith in a Wintry Season*, 13-38, 29. This translation is based on K. RAHNER, *Herausforderung des Christen. Meditationen – Reflexionen – Interviews*, Freiburg, Herder, 1975, pp. 117-53, 140, rather than on the *Herder Korrespondenz* version in which the article originally appeared].

10. RAHNER, *Foundations of Christian Faith*, p. 306. See also his *Jesus Christ –The Meaning of Life*, in *Theological Investigations*, Vol. 21, tr. by H. Riley, London, 1988, pp. 208-19. [References to this series will henceforward be abbreviated to *TI* followed by volume and page number(s), thus, *TI* 21, 208-219]. A number of other Rahner publications are also significant in this context. See, for example, his *Was heißt Jesus lieben?* Freiburg, 1982 and A. Battlogg's comments on the background to the book: *Karl Rahner: Jesus Lieben? Zum Schicksal einer Veröffentlichung aus den 80er Jahren*, in *Geist und Leben* 67 (1994) 90-101. ET: *The Love of Jesus and the Love of Neighbour*, tr. by R. Barr, New York /London 1983.

11. W. DYCH, *Karl Rahner* (Outstanding Christian Thinkers Series), ed. B. DAVIES Collegeville, MN, 1992, p. 61.

being). In trying to give an account of his or her belief in Jesus Christ, a Christian will reflect first of all on the faith which they already have. In this sense, faith precedes theology. Rahner's Christological method, therefore, begins with the soteriological significance of Jesus and his fate for us, and then moves onto a consideration of "Christ in himself"[12]. In short, his Christology of ascent is one which takes history seriously[13]. Secondly, it is entirely legitimate to begin such an ascending Christology with statements about the significance of Jesus "for us" (statements which also, of course, express a reality about Jesus "in himself")[14]. In fact, Rahner is steering a middle course here: he wants both to retain the classical formulations of Christology, such as Chalcedon, while also striving to obtain new insights from the old formulations, in an attempt to bring Christology into a more positive relationship with current ways of thinking. He does this because he is aware of how traditional Chalcedonian Christology can easily fall under the suspicion of sounding "mythological" (i.e., incredible) to people of today. But far from being embarrassed about the Church's traditional two-thousand-year-old Christology, Rahner's response is to dig deeper into this christological tradition. It is a question of underscoring both the unique permanence of Christian faith while allowing for new formulations of this faith. For Rahner, this meant that the truth of traditional Christology can be stated in other ways[15].

---

12. "In describing this Christian relationship, in the first instance at least we do not have to distinguish between what Jesus is in the faith of a Christian 'in himself', and what he means 'for us'. For in their unity these two aspects cannot be completely separated from each other. For, on the one hand, we neither could nor would be concerned about Jesus if he had no 'meaning for us', and on the other hand every assertion about his meaning for us implies an assertion about something 'in itself'". RAHNER, *Foundations of Christian Faith*, p. 204.

13. RAHNER, *The Eternal Significance of the Humanity of Jesus for Our Relationship with God*, in *TI* 3, 35-46.

14. RAHNER, *Christology Today*, in *TI* 21, 223-224. Rahner also stresses this unity of Christology and soteriology in his article *Brief Observations on Systematic Christology Today*, in *TI* 21, 233-234. Rahner's preference for an ascending Christology can likewise be seen in his 1971 article *The Two Basic Types of Christology*, in *TI* 13, 213-223. Referring there to the classical descending Christology, he concludes that "in order to achieve intelligibility and to justify its own propositions, [it may] be forced to return to the quite simple experience of Jesus of Nazareth". But, he adds: "Nevertheless it is legitimate, inevitable and sanctioned by the fact that the Church, right from the earliest times down to the present day, has discovered Jesus of Nazareth precisely in these statements of a Chalcedonian christology which seem so abstractly metaphysical, almost irreligious, and strangely inquisitive in character. It has discovered him there afresh again and again" (p. 221).

15. "... Even loyalty to the faith of Chalcedon permits us and obliges us to inquire beyond these formulations of classical Christology and to search for other more original or at least equally original christological statements which are perhaps closer to Scripture..." RAHNER, *Brief Observations on Systematic Christology Today*, in *TI* 21, 232.

c. Consequences: From an Anonymous to an Explicit Spirituality

What is at issue here, and this is all we wanted to highlight in the previous section, is the importance in Rahner's spirituality of a faith encounter with Jesus, and how such an encounter forms the point of departure in his Christology. This claim is important, I believe, because of the frequent criticism of Rahner's theology by those who, like von Balthasar, find his theory of anonymous Christianity unsatisfactory. It could be asked whether Rahner's approach undermines that which is specifically Christian in spirituality. With the stress on the universal, transcendental character of religious experience, do we not run the risk of ending up with a merely vague and "anonymous" spirituality? While an analysis of Rahner's understanding of religious experience is beyond our scope here, we can say that he distinguishes between a person's ordinary, everyday experiences, and that unique, original, basic experience of self as the subject who undergoes all these particular experiences[16]. The basis for this claim lies in the transcendental reference of the human person in knowledge and freedom to the mystery of God. In other words, an experience of God is present in every human person, by virtue of one's orientation to mystery, or as Rahner sometimes puts it, by virtue of the dynamic structure of the human spirit. Each person possesses a primordial reference to God, the incomprehensible mystery. This does not mean, though, that such an experience of God or of grace is always accepted for what it really is, since the experience of God as such differs from any subsequent conceptual reflection on, or interpretation of, this original experience. Rahner has sought to show a movement or transition from an implicit, unthematic experience of God to a more explicit recognition of such an experience at the conceptual level. If, at times Rahner gives priority to the unthematic aspect of religious experience, he also underscores the importance of, and the need for, a specifically Christian spirituality, which is the making explicit of what is essentially a universally available experience of God[17].

---

16. This distinction also lies at the root of Rahner's claim that it is possible to be an "anonymous Christian". See, for example, his *Observations on the Problem of the 'Anonymous Christian'*, in *TI* 14, 287-294.

17. Rahner's clarification of the experience of God, then, is based on a twofold conviction: i) that this experience is universal (i.e., God is that which we encounter in our deepest human experience), and ii) that the God so encountered is the Father of Jesus Christ whose Spirit dwells in our hearts. See J. NORMAN KING, *The Experience of God in the Theology of Karl Rahner*, in *Thought* 53 (1978) 174-202. The relationship between spirituality and experience in Rahner is dealt with in more detail in my: *A Spirituality of Everyday Faith: A Theological Investigation of the Notion of Spirituality in Karl Rahner* (Louvain Theological and Pastoral Monographs) (forthcoming).

d. The Mystagogical Framework

Throughout his writings, Rahner stresses the importance of a *mystagogical* initiation into an experience of God, which occurs when a person "returns to him or herself" in silent reflection[18]. Such a (spiritual) exercise is an attempt to seek the unity in the multiplicity of one's activities by returning to the innermost centre ("die innerste Mitte") of one's being[19]. This turning inwards *may* then lead to an explicit act of faith. In any event, it is Rahner's belief that such a "spiritual" exercise only finds full expression *exteriorly* – in the routine of everyday life, where the summons of grace makes itself heard:

> "Have we ever kept quiet, even though we wanted to defend ourselves when we had been unfairly treated? Have we ever forgiven someone even though we got no thanks for it and our silent forgiveness was taken for granted?... Have we ever sacrificed something without receiving any thanks or recognition for it, and even without a feeling of inner satisfaction? Have we ever been absolutely lonely? Have we ever decided on some course of action purely by the innermost judgement of our conscience, deep down where one can no longer tell or explain it to anyone, where one is quite alone and knows that one is taking a decision which no one else can take in one's place and for which one will have to answer for all eternity?... Have we ever fulfilled a duty when it seemed it could be done only with a consuming sense of really betraying and obliterating oneself, when it could

18. The term mystagogy refers to that process of initiation which leads a person to an experience of mystery. In other words, it involves an initiation into the sacred. Rahner himself describes Christian mystagogy as: "the effort to mediate to oneself or, more properly, to another in as clear and as comprehensive way as possible the experience of our pre-given pneumatic existence. Christian mystagogy also refers to the attempt to render comprehensible the fact that a person's 'mystical' experience of the Spirit has been historically and irreversibly confirmed in Jesus Christ". (Translation mine). "Christliche Mystagogie ist *das Bemühen* von jemand, sich oder erst recht einem andern *eine möglichst deutliche und reflex ergriffene Erfahrung seiner vorgegebenen pneumatischen Existenz zu vermitteln*. Christliche Mystagogie ist auch der Versuch, dem konkreten Menschen verständlich zu machen, daß seine mystische Geisterfahrung ihm geschichtlich greifbar und irreversibel durch Jesus Christus zugesagt ist", P.M. ZULEHNER, *"Denn du kommst unserem Tun mit deiner Gnade zuvor..." : Zur Theologie der Seelsorge heute. Paul M. Zulehner im Gespräch mit Karl Rahner,* Düsseldorf, 1984, p. 51.

19. RAHNER, *Der Helfer-Geist,* in *Von der Not und dem Segen des Gebetes,* 37. See also his *Thoughts on the Theology of Christmas,* in *TI* 3: 24-34. Rahner's *Konzentration auf die 'Mitte' des Glaubens* is one of the most significant characteristics of his theological method: "Seine Methode, die als Methode, wie er selber sagt, sehr vieles Martin Heidegger verdankt, ist die der Konzentration der Vielfalt auf ganz wenige Grundgedanken,... auf Schlüsselbegriffe oder noch besser auf Schlüsselerlebnisse. *Der* Grundgedanke dieser Theologie oder *das* Schlüsselerlebnis ist, nachlesbar bei Rahner selber, die Erfahrung Gottes". H. VORGRIMLER, *Gotteserfahrung im Alltag: Der Beitrag Karl Rahners zu Spiritualität und Mystik,* in *Karl Rahner in Erinnerung,* ed. A. RAFFELT, Düsseldorf, 1994, p. 102. See also Vorgrimler's other article in the same volume, *Versöhnung mit der Kirche,* pp. 44-69, esp. pp. 66-69.

apparently be done only by doing something terribly stupid for which no one would thank us?"[20]

Of course, both a Christian and a non-Christian can have the experiences outlined above. But it is possible to discover in such experiences "a mute pointer in the direction of God"[21]. By silently entering into such experiences, "God allows us to become aware of his presence, if we are quiet and do not take fright and run away from the mysterious being which lives and acts in this silence"[22]. In this way, the experience of mystery (*das Geheimnis*) which is simultaneously incomprehensible *and* self-evident, comes to the fore. This experience of mystery in traditional Christian terms is called the experience of God, but it is not that Rahner is simply imposing a neat concept (God) *onto* all these various experiences in order to render them intelligible. Rather, it is the other way round: it is only from such experiences that what is meant by the term God becomes clear[23]. In other words, those who have experiences similar to those mentioned above have "also already *in fact* experienced the *supernatural*,... (if even) in a very anonymous and inexpressible manner"[24]. The encounter with God, then, takes place not normally in the form of a special divine intervention, but "anonymously" in the everyday routine of life. "Everydayness" (*Alltäglichkeit*) is a specific "existential" of human living, and one which, for Rahner, has spiritual significance: it is there in the world of the everyday that one is challenged to discover the "anonymity" or hiddenness of God[25].

Nevertheless, the examples listed above only represent, in Rahner's eyes, the "lowest step" in the experience of grace[26]. We are dealing here with a graced "root" experience. And just as the fruit is "present" in the root, so too do the different experiences of grace contain the core and source of the Christian message. Such experiences must be "developed", in that they need to be interpreted and reflected on in the light of

---

20. RAHNER, *Reflections on the Experience of Grace*, in *TI* 3:87. See also K. RAHNER, *Sendung und Gnade. Beiträge zur Pastoraltheologie*, 3rd ed., Innsbruck, 1961, p. 84.

21. RAHNER, *Thoughts on the Theology of Christmas*, in *TI* 3:26-27.

22. RAHNER, *Thoughts on the Theology of Christmas*, in *TI* 3:27.

23. See also RAHNER, *The Concept of Mystery in Catholic Theology*, in *TI* 4:48-54. We are indebted here to some perceptive remarks of N. SCHWERDTFEGER, *Gnade und Welt: Zum Grundgefüge von Karl Rahners Theorie der "anonymen Christen"* (Freiburger Theologische Studien, 123), Freiburg, 1982, pp. 363-380.

24. RAHNER, *Reflections on the Experience of Grace*, in *TI* 3:88.

25. "Also muß *in* der Welt Gott gesucht und gefunden werden, also muß der Alltag selbst Gottes Tag, die Auskehr in die Welt Einkehr in Gott, muß der Alltag 'Einkehrtag' werden. Es muß der Alltag selbst gebetet werden". RAHNER, *Gebet im Alltag*, in *Von der Not und dem Segen des Gebetes*, p. 72.

26. RAHNER, *Reflections on the Experience of Grace*, in *TI* 3:86.

the Gospel. Herein lies the "strangely ambiguous" (*Zweideutigkeit*) nature of experience[27]. This ambiguity does not remain simply at the theoretical level. The situations described above also have existential implications. They demand an openness, a renunciation, and a letting go:

> "This infinity, which silently surrounds you – does it repulse you and drive you back into your limited daily life? Does it bid you yourself to go away out of the silence in which it rules? Does it fall upon you with the merciless loneliness of death so as to make you run away from it into the more familiar sectors of your life, until it catches up with you... in death?... Or is it that which waits until you are open *to its very self* as something approaching, coming, the promised beatitude?"[28]

Rahner then develops a specifically Christian interpretation of our experiences. In Christian terms, the kind of renunciation and letting-go that is involved in the experiences referred to above is called the taking up one's *cross*. It is no coincidence that Rahner's examples have to do with self-emptying and renunciation since, for him, every authentic experience of grace is in some way a participation in the death of Jesus[29]. Renunciation (*Entsagung*) occurs when a person "radically submits to God's disposal, [is] seized and overpowered by God... when... one summons up courage (again by God's grace), embracing and surrendering one's whole existence to believe, hope, and love"[30]. Yet Rahner concedes that the taking up of one's cross is not confined to Christians alone:

> "The person who, in a hope which no longer seeks to reassure itself, relinquishes oneself in the depths of the mystery of existence, in which death and life can no longer be distinguished because they can only be grasped together, actually believes in the Crucified and Risen one, even if he or she is not aware of it (in conceptual terms)"[31].

This hopeful courage is simply another word for *faith*, which itself has two aspects[32]. There is the "ultimate courage for existence", on the one

---

27. RAHNER, *Thoughts on the Theology of Christmas*, in *TI* 3:27.

28. *Ibid.*

29. RAHNER, *Self-realization and Taking Up One's Cross*, in *TI* 9:253-57. See also his articles: *Following the Crucified*, in *TI* 18:157-70, and *Christian Dying*, in *TI* 18:252-256.

30. RAHNER, *Christian Dying*, in *TI* 18:254. See also his *Reflections on the Theology of Renunciation*, in *TI* 3:47-57.

31. RAHNER, *Self-realization and Taking Up One's Cross*, in *TI* 9:256.

32. "There can exist an 'anonymous faith' which carries with it an intrinsic dynamism and therefore an obligation to find full realization in explicit faith, but which is nonetheless sufficient for salvation even if a person does not achieve this fulfilment during their lifetime, as long as they are not to blame for this" (RAHNER, *Anonymous and Explicit Faith*, in *TI* 16:54).

hand, and "explicitly Christian faith in Jesus, crucified and risen", on the other[33]. In Rahner's view, these two factors do not simply exist alongside each other externally; ultimately, he sees them as one[34]. The peculiarity of Christian faith is that it sees in Jesus the consummation of our hope, a fulfilment also promised by God to us. This forms part of the "content" of explicit Christianity, part of that courageous faith which permits us to hope that our (negative) experiences of futility, darkness and death do not have the last word.

The explicit message of Christianity, therefore, helps us to interpret our experiences correctly. It is not a question of Christianity simply supplying a subsequent, conceptual explanation of our experiences of grace, added, as it were, as a supplementary (but unnecessary) appendix[35]. Rather,

> "the message of faith which comes in the hearing of the word opens the eyes of inner experience so that this experience may have the confidence to understand itself correctly and to accept the sweet comfort of its uncanny mystery as the real meaning of this experience"[36].

Conversely, without reference to our experience, the word of proclamation "from without" remains hollow and empty. In short, Rahner is convinced of the need to move from an anonymous experience of grace to a more explicit interpretation and appropriation of this experience in the context of Christian *faith*:

> "... Human life does of itself present a kind of anonymous Christianity, which explicit Christianity can then interpret, giving a person the courage to accept and not run away from what one experiences and undergoes in one's own life;... This would be putting into practice what St Paul said of his preaching: 'What therefore you worship (really worship!) without knowing it (as consciously and explicitly interpreted), that I preach to you' (Acts 17,23)"[37].

The "more" of Christianity, however, is not restricted solely to an increase in knowledge, or to a more reliable foundation for living. Rather,

---

33. RAHNER, *Faith as Courage*, in *TI* 18:223-224.

34. Rahner believes these two forms of courage "differ in fact only more or less as the seed differs from the flower". Hence his conviction that "it is certainly possible for a person to have that innermost faith in courageous hope for the totality of one's existence as oriented to God, to realize it freely in the commonplace routine of one's duty and love and yet inculpably to be unable to produce that courage which is required in principle from the Christian for faith in regard to Christian teaching as a whole". RAHNER, *Faith as Courage*, in *TI* 18:221-222.

35. SCHWERDTFEGER, *Gnade und Welt*, p. 370.

36. RAHNER, *Thoughts on the Theology of Christmas*, in *TI* 3:28.

37. K. RAHNER, *Mission and Grace: Essays in Pastoral Theology*, vol. 1, London and New York, 1963, p. 160.

such knowledge must lead to a specific *decision* on the part of the Christian "to abandon oneself all the more decisively to the sovereign will of God's mystery"[38]. There is, thus, a definite connection in Rahner's thought between the frequently anonymous experience of grace and the explicit acceptance of the message of faith[39].

In short, Rahner's conviction is that everyone experiences God as that mysterious reality behind the gift and summons to silence, courage, self-sacrifice, trust, etc. God is the ground of the definitive meaningfulness of the whole of human life. Nevertheless, even if we are in fundamental agreement with Rahner thus far, we could ask whether the experiences he describes are not those of a rather pious introspection. In other words, is there not here an excessive focus on the subject's "return to oneself"? Does the Christian (whether anonymous or explicit) only experience God by going inwards? If this were the case, we would be back at a rather individualistic understanding of spirituality. In the following section, we intend to show that this accusation cannot justifiably be levelled at Rahner. Rather, Christian spirituality is primarily about the following (*Nachfolge*) of Jesus; it implies a concrete imperative and a decision. Rahner has always acknowledged that he writes not from a "neutral" point of view, but from a "committed" one, that is, as a Christian who maintains that, in dealing with the ultimate issues of life, a personal Yes or No is demanded. His basic conviction – and here the influence of the *Spiritual Exercises* of Ignatius Loyola is evident – is that a person's historical life moves in freedom toward a point of *decision* in terms of either a final protest or a final acceptance of existence. The hopeful acceptance of existence is interwoven with other specific experiences in

38. "But the affirmation of an implicit Christianity is also an affirmation that this basic dynamism, like every other potentiality of the human person, cannot be content to remain implicit, but strives after its own explicitness (*Ausdrücklichkeit*) – its 'name'.... The dynamism... reaches a new degree of articulate recognition (*eine neue, höhere Stufe der Ausdrücklichkeit*) and fulfilment in the explicit confession of faith within the Church". RAHNER, *Missions*, in *Sacramentum Mundi* 4:80. See also RAHNER, *Faith between Rationality and Emotion*, in *TI* 16:60-78.

39. SCHWERDTFEGER, *Gnade und Welt*, pp. 370-371, n. 42. One of the most significant reinterpretations of grace by Rahner lies in his stress on God's universal salvific will. In contrast to the scholastic position which held that grace is scarce, and that no salvific grace existed outside the Christian sphere, Rahner argued for the universality of grace. Commenting on Rahner's Christology, J.P. GALVIN makes a similar point: "Juxtaposed to this foundational affirmation of the divine salvific will is an equally basic insistence on the indispensability of Jesus. Rahner is convinced that the indispensability of Jesus is no less essential to Christianity than the universality of God's salvific will. The difficulty lies in reconciling the two principles, which at first sight seem to contradict each other". J.P. GALVIN, *Jesus Christ*, in *Systematic Theology: Roman Catholic Perspectives*, ed. F.S. FIORENZA and J.P. GALVIN, Dublin, 1992, p. 316.

life (experiences of meaning, light, joy, love, and so on) which make an absolute claim on a person. Further, such a fundamental acceptance of existence (which does not exist only when it is explicitly talked about), entails a movement towards God[40]. Thus Christian spirituality does not primarily provide "explanations" or "instruction" or "final" answers – God is not a determinate number in the equations of people's lives.

II. Rahner's Spiritual Roots

a. The Spiritual Exercises of Ignatius

At the outset of our reflections we mentioned the danger, pointed out by Rahner, of turning the relationship with Christ into the cult of an abstract Christ-idea. Christology is not simply reflection on an idea about Jesus, but a reflection on a lived faith relationship. Rahner's conviction was that theology must be built on a living experience of faith. His own theological thinking originated from a reflection on, and the practice of, the Ignatian *Exercises*, and can be aptly characterised as a *mystagogical* theology. At issue is the question of an immediate experience of God, an experience, which has to do more with a "felt-knowledge", (a *sentire*, to use an Ignatian term), rather than with an intellectual knowledge.

Rahner considered the *Exercises* a fundamental document of the post-Reformation Church, and one which had a decisive influence on its history. In his view, the *Exercises* brought something genuinely new into the Church. While, on the one hand, Ignatius was a man of the late Middle Ages and of the "devotio moderna", on the other, he stands at the turning-point towards the age of the rational, the scientific and the technical. Moreover, the change entailed a shift from a cosmocentric worldview to an anthropocentric one[41]. The starting-point is thus the individual subject

40. Rahner does not restrict this movement to Christians alone, but acknowledges that it occurs wherever someone is faithful to the dictates of his or her conscience. Perhaps such a person may not be able to recognise this move for what it really is, or be unable to recognise its "absolutely particular" historical manifestation in Jesus Christ. Nonetheless, Christians hope both for themselves and for others that this movement will find its way through the superficiality and darkness of life to its final "eternal" goal. For the person who hears the Christian message, a new and radical situation of *choice* has been created, which can lead to the response of explicit faith.

41. This thesis is proposed by J.B. Metz, *Christliche Anthropozentrik*, Munich, 1962. In short, the modern period, in Rahner's view, can be characterised by a "turning to the subject, to subjective striving for salvation, to the subjective viewed as a task for the Church, to the attitude of reflection upon one's self,... to an existential ethic, to a 'choice' in which the subject in some sense exists by his own decision, chooses, transcends,

itself, a subject who is no longer experienced as part of an already given order of reality. Rahner portrays Ignatius as exhibiting a "subjective" approach to salvation. By this Rahner means that, in the *Exercises*, Ignatius aims at "a completely personal relationship" between Jesus Christ, the Lord of the Church, and the retreatant, who, in this way, comes to an experience of his or her calling to serve the kingdom of God and the Church[42]. Ignatius was primarily concerned with the modern person considered as a personal subject. It should not be overlooked, Rahner reminds us, that the religious path of Ignatius begins with a sub-jective experience of consolation and desolation[43].

However, the *Exercises* are not a series of pious meditations, but rep-resent an attempt, following a certain plan, to enable the retreatant to make a fundamental and free *decision* of life-long importance. Rahner interprets the *Exercises* then, primarily, in terms of a *choice* or an "elec-tion", namely, the choice of the means and the concrete way in which Christian faith can become a living reality in us. Secondly, they nor-mally take place in an environment of solitude and prayer, since the dynamic of the *Exercises* assumes a personal encounter with God. The kind of decision at issue here "cannot be deduced from the general prin-ciples of the faith or from common human wisdom alone; a decision such as this is received from God and from His grace alone in a kind of exis-tential knowledge gained in prayer"[44]. This kind of knowledge emerges from what Rahner terms a logic of existential decision, which Ignatius developed by means of his rules of choice[45]. Rahner subsequently

reflects and is... called by God... This is, in short, a turning to self-responsibility" (RAHNER, *Being Open to God as Ever Greater*, in *TI* 7:33).

42. RAHNER, *Modern Piety and the Experience of Retreats*, in *TI* 16:143. At the same time, therefore, Rahner stresses that Ignatius was a man of the Church, someone to whom the phrase "sentire cum ecclesia" could most suitably be applied. See Ignatius' *Rules for Thinking with the Church*, in *The Spiritual Exercises of St Ignatius*, nn. 352-370. We fol-low here the translation of the Exercises by L.J. PUHL, *The Spiritual Exercises of St Ignatius. Based on Studies in the Language of the Autograph*, Chicago, 1951.

43. RAHNER, *Modern Piety*, p. 140. Rahner is referring here to the *Autobiography of St Ignatius Loyola*, nn. 5-8. We follow the translation of the *Autobiography* by P.R. DIVARKAR in *Ignatius of Loyola: The Spiritual Exercises and Selected Works*, eds. G.E. GANSS et al., Classics of Western Spirituality Series, New Jersey, 1991, pp. 65-111.

44. K. RAHNER, *Spiritual Exercises*, London, 1967, p. 8. Rahner also reminds his read-ers in the Foreword (p. 8) that the true meaning of the *Exercises* only emerges from their *practice* and not from printed theological meditations. It is not that Ignatius ignores the more rational processes of reflection and decision-making, but he regards these as deriv-ative and secondary, applying when the fundamental choice is either impossible or unsuc-cessful. *The Spiritual Exercises of St Ignatius*, nn. 175-188.

45. *The Spiritual Exercises of St Ignatius*, nn. 169-189. See also RAHNER, *Modern Piety and the Experience of Retreats*, in *TI* 16:144-145. The "real heart" of the *Spiritual Exercises*, for Rahner, consists in "the existential choice and the achievement of absolute

describes this decision as the result of a solitary spiritual process. The assumption operative here lies in Ignatius' intuition that "the Creator can deal directly with the creature, and the creature directly with his Creator and Lord"[46].

Although some people may have difficulty with the feudal imagery and military language of the *Exercises*, it cannot be denied that Ignatius' aim in writing was to create disciples. In other words, Ignatius was not solely interested in personal conversion but in releasing a man or a woman for action (n. 145). Rahner would, no doubt, agree with Joseph De Guibert's description of Ignatian spirituality as a "spirituality of service" rather than as the solitary preoccupation with one's individual spiritual life[47]. This service of God, as we shall see, consists of two factors which are united, namely, a logic of existential knowledge (interpreted by Rahner in the context of the Ignatian guidelines for making an election) and a passionate love for Christ (which, for Rahner, is the aim of the meditations on the life of Jesus). Thus, we are dealing here with a combination, or better, a synthesis of enthusiasm and reason, of heart and understanding[48].

Behind the notion of choice, described above, is the attempt to discern the will of God for the retreatant. According to Rahner, Ignatius is only interested that the individual place him or herself before the Lord and ask: "What should I do?" or "What does God want from me now?"[49]

---

freedom before God (termed indifference), and the experience of the radical immediacy of God in the comfort of the 'first' and the 'second time of choice'" (p. 144).

46. *The Spiritual Exercises of St Ignatius*, n. 15. See also Rahner's *Rede des Ignatius von Loyola an einen Jesuiten von heute*, in *Ignatius von Loyola*, ed. K. RAHNER, H.N. LOOSE, and P. IMHOF, Freiburg, Herder, 1978, p. 12, where he maintains "Gott kann und will mit seinem Geschöpf unmittelbar handeln".

47. J. DE GUIBERT, *The Jesuits: Their Spiritual Doctrine and Practice*: *A Historical Study*, tr. by W.J. YOUNG, ed. G. GANSS, St. Louis, The Institute of Jesuit Sources, 1972, pp. 174-175. See also n. Ê54.

48. Note here Rahner's attempt to feel his way through this "tension of opposites" which is so characteristic of Ignatian spirituality. This is the opinion of commentators such as H. RAHNER, *Ignatius the Theologian*, tr. by M. BARRY, London, 1968, 1990, pp. 3-31, and DE GUIBERT, *The Jesuits: Their Spiritual Doctrine and Practice*. pp. 70-74. In his concluding synthesis of the personal spiritual experience of Ignatius, De Guibert states that this could be summed up in the two phrases (or tensions): "mystical invasion" and "courageous struggle". For the relevant biographical connections, see especially his first chapter, "The Personal Interior Life of St Ignatius", pp. 21-73.

49. R. BARTHES, *Sade, Fourier, Loyola*, tr. by R. Miller, Berkeley and Los Angeles, 1976, pp. 45, 48, maintains that "this interrogative structure gives the Exercises its historical originality; hitherto,... the preoccupation was more with carrying out God's will; Ignatius wants rather to discover this will (What is it? Where is it? Toward what does it tend?)". The language of interrogation developed by Ignatius is thus aimed "less at the classical question of consultations: What to do? than at the dramatic alternative by which finally every practice is prepared and determined: To do this or to do that?"

The *Exercises* thus presuppose that an existential decision can take place as a result of a personal call of God to the retreatant. Further, Rahner is convinced that if such a logic of existential decision is to remain valid today, "it must be removed from the context of the choice of a vocation in the Church and clearly expressed in terms of its general significance for human existence"[50].

This choice, this perception and acceptance of God's call effected in a personal, free decision, has two mutually related aspects: a transcendental and a categorial aspect[51]. The transcendental aspect denotes the person's radical decision or conversion to God in faith, hope and love, while the categorial aspect refers to the mediating realisation of this decision in the concrete, and implies a particular act, e.g., the choice of a way of life, the love of one's neighbour, the endurance of life's everyday trials, and so on. These two aspects cannot be separated, but neither is their reciprocal relationship a static one; rather, it is a relationship that has a history in the life (i.e., in the historical decision) of an individual. But Rahner fears it is the categorial aspect (that is, what does God want from me now?) that can too easily gain prominence. If this is the case, then the "mystagogical" dimension of the *Exercises* could be undermined. In other words, it can be overlooked that the *Exercises* constitute an initiation or a *mystagogy* into a basic experience of God[52]. To facilitate such an experience is the main task of the director of the *Exercises*. It is not a question here of a merely theoretical initiation into the essence of Christianity. The *Exercises* are and remain a matter of choice and decision in a concrete life-situation, since the conversion or *metanoia* (sometimes called by Rahner a person's fundamental option) is not just a theoretical occurrence. Rather, the initiation is to an "existentially accepted Christianity in faith, hope and love for God"[53], and not an abstract indoctrination.

---

50. RAHNER, *Modern Piety and the Experience of Retreats*, in *TI* 16:141, n. 11.

51. K. RAHNER, *The Exercises Today*, in *Christians at the Crossroads*, London, 1975, p. 71.

52. "Verstehst du schon jetzt, wenn ich sage, die Hauptaufgabe, um die alles andere zentriert ist, müsse für euch Jesuiten das Geben der Exerzitien sein. Damit sind natürlich zunächst und zuletzt nicht kirchenamtlich organisierte Kurse gemeint, die vielen auf einmal gegeben werden, sondern eine mystagogische Hilfe für andere, die Unmittelbarkeit Gottes nicht zu verdrängen, sondern deutlich zu erfahren und anzunehmen.... Aber all dieses andere sollte eigentlich von euch als Vorbereitung oder als Folgerung der letzten Aufgabe verstanden werden, die auch in Zukunft eure bleiben sollte: die Hilfe zur unmittelbaren Erfahrung Gottes, in der dem Menschen aufgeht, da' das unbegreifliche Geheimnis, das wir Gott nennen, nahe ist, angeredet werden kann..." RAHNER, *Rede des Ignatius von Loyola an einen Jesuiten von heute*, in *Ignatius von Loyola*, p. 15. (italics mine). See also RAHNER, *Christian Living Formerly and Today*, in *TI* 7:11-16.

53. RAHNER, *The Exercises today*, in *Christians at the Crossroads*, p. 73. This immediate encounter between God and the human person has, Rahner believes, special significance

b. Rahner's Interpretation of the Ignatian Election

Although he does not go into the historical background of the debate, Rahner claims that "the nature of the *Exercises* is ultimately determined by the fact that a choice, a vital decision is to be made in them"[54]. They are primarily guidelines or instructions towards a discernment of God's will, and culminate in a decision to follow that will. In other words, they are oriented not so much towards edification as towards a particular course of action[55]. Ignatius makes two significant, but unusual, claims in the *Exercises,* and it is these two claims which occupy most of Rahner's attention. The first is that a person can actually seek and find God's specific will for him or herself. The second claim is that God will "communicate Himself to the devout soul" and "deal directly with the creature,

today because: "all the societal supports of religion are collapsing and dying out in this secularised and pluralistic society. If, nonetheless, there is to be real Christian spirituality, it cannot be kept alive and healthy by external helps, not even those which the Church offers, even of a sacramental kind,... but only through an ultimate, immediate encounter of the individual with God. RAHNER, *The Immediate Experience of God in the Spiritual Exercises of Saint Ignatius of Loyola: Interview with Wolfgang Feneberg,* in *Karl Rahner in Dialogue: Conversations and Interviews 1965-1982.* tr. by H. EGAN, New York, 1986, p. 176.

54. RAHNER, *The Dynamic Element in the Church,* 89. The Spanish term "elección" can be translated as "choice" or "selection". However, most of the English literature on Ignatian spirituality retains the traditional term, "election". The essential aim of the *Exercises* has been much discussed. Broadly speaking, the main writers can be divided into two schools, the "electionists" (e.g., L. de Grandmaison) and the "perfectionists" (e.g., L. Peeters). De Grandmaison maintained that the aim of the *Exercises* is to place a spiritually minded person in a position to discern God's call clearly and to follow it generously, that is, to make a wise election of a state of life in which he or she can serve God best. L. DE GRANDMAISON, *Les* Exercices *de S. Ignace dans l'édition des* Monumenta, in *Recherches de science religieuse* XI (1920) 400-408, cited in DE GUIBERT, *The Jesuits: Their Spiritual Doctrine and Practice,* p. 123. On the other hand, Louis Peeters responded that the end and culminating point of the *Exercises* can only be a union with God which is most intimate and total. L. PEETERS, *Vers l'union divine par les Exercices de S. Ignace,* Louvain, ²1931, pp. 66 ff., cited in DE GUIBERT, *The Jesuits: Their Spiritual Doctrine and Practice,* p. 123. De Guibert himself (pp. 122-132) sees these two ends as complementary, not mutually exclusive. The end expressed in Ignatius' printed text of 1548 is to facilitate a good election. But this does not exclude the fact that he also made other uses of the text, for example, by giving the *Exercises* to those (e.g., Xavier, Favre) whose election was already made. GANSS, *Ignatius of Loyola: The Spiritual Exercises and Selected Works,* p. 390, is also in fundamental agreement with de Guibert.

55. Rahner's foundational essay on the *Spiritual Exercises* of Ignatius is *Die Logik der existentiellen Erkenntnis bei Ignatius von Loyola,* in *Das Dynamische in der Kirche* (Quaestiones Disputatae, 5), Freiburg, 1958, pp. 74-148. ET: *The Logic of Concrete Individual Knowledge in Ignatius of Loyola,* in *The Dynamic Element in the Church* (Quaestiones Disputatae, 12), tr. by W.J. O'HARA, London, 1964, pp. 84-170. The essay, however, originally appeared under the more descriptive title: *Die ignatianische Logik der existentiellen Erkenntnis – Über einige theologische Probleme in den Wahlregeln der Exerzitien des heiligen Ignatius,* in F. WULF (ed.), *Ignatius von Loyola: seine geistliche Gestalt und sein Vermächtnis (1556-1956),* Würzburg, 1956, pp. 343-405.

and the creature directly with his Creator and Lord"[56]. With regard to the first point, the question arises as to whether God's will could not be simply deduced by the use of reason within the framework of the general principles of Christian morality. Rahner's point, however, is not to undermine the role of the intellect in any such decision-making process, but to indicate how God may make known some definite will of His over and above what is shown by the use of reason.

According to the Ignatian *Exercises*, the "election" takes place at one of three times[57]. The *first* time is rather rare in that the person is so moved by God that he or she heeds His call without hesitation. In the *second* time, the retreatant reflects on the different movements of desolation and consolation in him or herself, with a view to discerning which movements come from God, and which from the evil spirit[58]. Although Ignatius is convinced that what is at issue here is a real guidance of the Holy Spirit, there is also the danger of illusion or self-deception. The suspicion of a mystical subjectivism is understandable and surfaced even in Ignatius' time. Ignatius' "Rules for the Discernment of Spirits", as well as his insistence on the counsel of a director, both of which are envisaged as integral parts of the *Exercises* were prompted by this concern[59]. It would be wrong to think that the discernment of God's will emerges simply from a type of gut feeling or instinct. Rahner insists that, while rational discursive reflection alone does not *fully* reveal this will, it would be misleading to claim that this process does not involve a "thoroughly intellectual operation of the 'intellect',... in which it is capable of apprehending values"[60]. However, it is in the *third* time of "election" that the intellect is more predominant. This time is characterised by Ignatius as one of "tranquillity", where the person, not agitated by the various spirits, considers the choice to be made in view of the end for which the person was created, that is, the greater service of

56. *The Spiritual Exercises of St Ignatius*, n. 15. In this section, our discussion of these issues is restricted to Rahner's reflections in The Logic of Concrete Individual Knowledge in Ignatius Loyola, in *The Dynamic Element in the Church*, pp. 84-170.

57. *The Spiritual Exercises of St Ignatius*, nn. 175-189.

58. "Consolation" and "desolation" are easily misunderstood terms. The Ignatian term "consolation", for example, always means spiritual consolation, which includes a tendency toward an increase of charity. Such consolation *may* bring with it a concomitant feeling of joy but this is not always the case. Hence, *any* feeling of joy, satisfaction or peace should not be too hastily interpreted as a sign of approval for some choice of action. See GANSS, *Ignatius of Loyola: The Spiritual Exercises and Selected Works*, pp. 425-426.

59. See *The Spiritual Exercises of St Ignatius*, nn. 313-336, where Ignatius provides some rules for the "First Week" of the Exercises, and further rules to aid "a more accurate discernment of spirits" more suitable to the "Second Week".

60. RAHNER, *The Dynamic Element in the Church*, p. 94, n. 9.

God. Yet, even in this third time, the retreatant expects God to guide the decision. In fact, the second and third times of election supplement each other, with Ignatius himself combining them in practice.

Ignatius' belief, then, – and this brings us to his second claim – is that, throughout the three times of election, the Creator is dealing directly with the creature and vice-versa. There is more at work here than the retreatant testing his or her capacities for a particular way of life or course of action solely by rational analysis. On the other hand, we have seen how Rahner also regards rational reflection as an indispensable element in the Ignatian discernment of spirits. The experiences of spiritual consolation and desolation are, after all, experiences with a rational structure and not merely physiological states. Indeed, Ignatius' "Rules for the Discernment of Spirits" serve to facilitate the discovery of God's will for the individual. This complex task necessitates the interpretation of one's own interior experiences or "motions" (*mociones*), which Ignatius depicts as the different movements produced in the soul. Underlying these rules, according to Rahner, is the assumption that there exist divine impulses or movements (that is, whose source is God), and which are perceived by the retreatant as a highly personal influence of God[61]. These movements include cognitive acts (e.g., thoughts, fantasies, memories), affective acts (e.g., love, desire, hate, fear, etc.) and affective feelings (e.g., lightheartedness, depression, gloominess, sweetness, etc.)[62]. Ignatius is not so much interested in all these inner movements of a person's mind and heart as such, but rather in how they can have an influence on one's Christian life in acts of faith, hope and charity. Of themselves, these movements

---

61. Rahner is aware of the highly problematical nature of this statement. Firstly, most theologians today have moved away from the image of the God of the gaps who regularly intervenes directly in creation. And, secondly, how many people automatically assume that their different interior impulses are simply to be attributed to either good or bad spirits? Many other factors (e.g., psychological, genetic, social, subconscious, etc.) are acknowledged to be at work. Rahner defends Ignatius, however, by focusing on what he considers to be the core truth of Ignatius' idea of the divine origin of certain spiritual experiences, namely the conscious experience of grace. This conscious experience of grace underpins the recognition of divine impulses (providing a "fundamental evidence and certainty"), and is presupposed by the various rules for the discernment of spirits. RAHNER, *The Dynamic Element in the Church*, p. 130.

62. J. TONER, Discernment in the Spiritual Exercises, in *A New Introduction to the Spiritual Exercises of St. Ignatius,* ed. J.E. DISTER, Minnesota, 1993, pp. 65-66. Eugen Drewermann, in an otherwise overly harsh criticism of Rahner's work, rightly underscores the importance of incorporating such movements into theological reflection. That Rahner does not discuss such movements leads Drewermann to conclude that Rahner's work is characterised by a "Bewußtseinseinseitigkeit". E. DREWERMANN, *Glauben in Freiheit oder Tiefenpsychologie und Dogmatik*, Solothurn und Düsseldorf, 1993, vol. 1, *Dogma, Angst und Symbolismus*, p. 224.

do not make someone a better or worse Christian; it all depends on how one understands and responds to them. In the present context, understanding them means to judge what is their source, that is, by what spirit they are prompted.

Rahner then explores how such experiences could be of divine origin and why they would then possess an intrinsically self-evident and self-sufficient character. A particular type of "movement" mentioned in this context by Ignatius is described as consolation without a previous cause (*consolación sin causa precedente*)[63]. The phrase "consolation without a previous cause" means for Ignatius "an invasion of God into the soul without any previous use of its own intellectual, volitional, or sense faculties"[64]. Further, since it comes from God, it is without error, though careful discernment is necessary to ascertain whether the experience is a genuine case of such consolation. Rahner concedes that in this rule (n. 330) Ignatius has left us a masterpiece of brevity but not of clarity. It is not at all clear what precisely Ignatius meant by the phrase, while Rahner's own interpretation is not without its problems either. In Rahner's view, the term "cause" refers to the "objective ground for consolation which is now consciously present and consoling"[65]. But where there is no object present to the senses, or to the understanding, or to the will, which of itself could cause consolation, then the consolation without cause is a consolation *without conceptual object*. Referring to Ignatius' description (n. 330) of the soul being drawn into the love of God, Rahner attempts to explain why "this radical love of God neither states nor presupposes any 'conceptual element' for the experience of consolation"[66]. For Rahner, what is at stake here is not the suddenness of the experience but its absence of object[67].

---

63. *The Spiritual Exercises of St Ignatius,* n. 330. The full reference is: "God alone can give consolation to the soul without any previous cause. It belongs solely to the Creator to come into a soul, to leave it, to act upon it, to draw it wholly to the love of His Divine Majesty. I said without previous cause, that is, without any preceding perception or knowledge of any subject by which a soul might be led to such a consolation through its own acts of intellect and will".

64. GANSS, *Ignatius of Loyola: The Spiritual Exercises and Selected Works,* p. 427.

65. RAHNER, *The Dynamic Element in the Church,* 132.

66. RAHNER, *The Dynamic Element in the Church,* p. 134, n. 28. In a passing reference to Bonaventure, Rahner claims that "here on earth there is an experience of the love of God which occurs without the intellect having any share in it". For a more detailed treatment of Bonaventure's contribution, see RAHNER, *The Doctrine of the 'Spiritual Senses' in the Middle Ages,* in *TI* 16:104-134.

67. Moreover, "the absence of object in question is utter receptivity to God... There is no longer 'any object' but the drawing of the whole person, with the very ground of his being, into love, beyond any defined circumscribable object, into the infinity of God as God himself... It is a question of God and God alone, precisely inasmuch as he is other

In short, when Rahner describes the experience of consolation without previous cause as "objectless", he is not referring to an unconscious experience, but to what he calls a "non-conceptual" experience of God in that the retreatant is drawn up into God's love[68]. "Without cause" thus refers to God alone, the Creator dealing directly with the creature, and not to any particular thoughts or concepts, even religious, in which God is known discursively[69].

Rahner's thesis, then, is that this experience of consolation is really an experience of transcendence elevated by grace. Normally, this experience of transcendence is only implicit as the horizon and condition of possibility of any act of the mind. But in the experience of consolation without cause, there is an "*emergence into awareness* (*ein Thematischwerden*) of transcendence and of the term to which it tends, (which) discloses a transcendence qualitatively different from the merely concomitant and implicit form"[70]. The human person is not just the subject who reaches out (pre-apprehends) in the act of knowledge towards a limitless horizon, but a subject who is also open and receptive to the infinity of God Himself. Rahner combines this twofold dimension of human transcendence when he describes how the whole of a person's being is poured into a "pure movement of receptivity" ("in diese reine Offenheit der Bewegung")[71] in the experience of consolation. In this experience of transcendence, God is present as the term of the movement. At the same time, Rahner claims that this experience of transcendence or consolation, because it is the condition of possibility of all cognition, is without error and provides the authentic guarantee for us of the term inseparable from

than any individual object, one might say inasmuch as he is the absolutely transcendent,..." RAHNER, *The Dynamic Element in the Church*, p. 135.

68. Thus, we agree with J.H.P. WONG, *Logos-Symbol in the Christology of Karl Rahner* (Biblioteca di Scienze Religiose, 61), Rome, 1984, p. 55, who claims that "it is not a question of complete absence of object but the shifting of 'focus' from the particular object to its background, which is pure dynamism of transcendence". Or, in Rahner's words, "the dynamism itself alone becomes more and more the essential". RAHNER, *The Dynamic Element in the Church*, p. 145.

69. In the eighth rule (*The Spiritual Exercises of St Ignatius*, n. 336), Ignatius mentions a second period of time (i.e., after the consolation) when the person frequently forms various resolutions and plans which derive from our reasoning and judgements. These resolutions may come from the good or evil spirit. Ignatius' point, however, is that the person "cautiously distinguish the actual time of the consolation from the period that follows it".

70. RAHNER, *The Dynamic Element in the Church*, p. 146, n. 34. "Such a transcendence is the synthesis of the intrinsic transcendent ordination of mind to being in general, and of grace which supervenes to mould this natural unlimited receptivity and make of it a dynamic orientation towards participation in the life of God himself" (pp. 144-145).

71. *Ibid.*, p. 149.

it, namely, God. Thus, he concludes that the experience of consolation supplies the ultimate ground of our knowledge of God[72].

c. Criticism and Corrections

Rahner's 1956 essay, which we have been elucidating above, has been criticised, however, for its almost complete lack of reference to Christ. In contrast, other Ignatian commentators have left us in no doubt that there *is* a definite christological dimension to the Ignatian election, even if this dimension is not apparent in Rahner's early essay[73]. Yet, the criticism of Rahner needs to be nuanced somewhat, particularly when Rahner's other, less philosophical, retreat meditations on the *Exercises* are taken into account. These writings place greater stress on the christological basis of his spirituality than do his more speculative works[74]. Rahner's retreat conferences or meditations, we believe, thus offer a necessary corrective to his essay in *The Dynamic Element in the Church*.

Underlying the necessity and importance of this christological aspect is the presupposition that the experience of God cannot be restricted solely to one's "interiority", as our discussion of Rahner's thesis of a

72. Consolation, then, in Rahner's framework, refers to the "experience of the free transcendence of the whole mind and spirit... raised by grace to the supernatural..." RAHNER, *The Dynamic Element in the Church*, p. 150, and n. 35. This "pure harmony in the depth of one's being" is experienced transcendence, and it is here, Rahner believes, that the real "certitude" of the experience lies. Peace, joy, tranquillity, etc. *may* be signs of the good spirit, but given the human capacity for self-deception, they cannot in themselves provide this certitude. Rahner nuances his claim even further when he says that the certitude at stake here is "humanly speaking of a limited and ultimately incommunicable kind which cannot be transformed into a deliberate explicit assertion in conceptual terms, (and) cannot really be certitude in the proper sense regarding our own state of grace". For a good exposition and analysis of Rahner's understanding of the election in the *Exercises*, see SCHWERDTFEGER, *Gnade und Welt*, pp. 297-344. He succinctly describes Rahner's understanding of consolation as follows: "Trost ist hier also nicht in einem äußerlich empirischen Sinn als angehängtes Begleitgefühl zur Transzendenzerfahrung verstanden, sondern in einem metaphysischen Sinn als gnadenhaft geschenktes Bei-sich-sein des Menschen im Grunde seines Wesens, insofern dieses von Gott her und auf Gott hin ist" (p. 309).

73. Referring specifically to Rahner's 1956 essay, BAKKER concludes: "Es bleibt allerdings bedauerlich, da' der Trost so wenig christologisch betrachtet wird: ist es nicht so, daß man Transzendenz erst in *Christus* erfahren kann? Dieser Aspekt tritt im Artikel nicht hervor, während er in den GH zentral ist". *Freiheit und Erfahrung*, p. 290, n. 54 (italics mine). A. DULLES makes much the same point in an important article, *Finding God's Will: Rahner's Interpretation of the Ignatian Election*, in *Woodstock Letters* 114 (1965) 139-152. The christological aspect is relevant to our study particularly in view of our earlier questions regarding the "specifically Christian" aspect of Rahner's understanding of spirituality.

74. RAHNER himself admits as much. See his *Christian Living Formerly and Today*, in *TI* 7:16, n. 12. For an example of a more speculative treatment of the topic (other than "The Logic of Concrete Individual Knowledge in Ignatius Loyola"), see RAHNER, *Theology and Anthropology*, in *TI* 9:28-45.

"pure experience of transcendence" might suggest[75]. Rather, since the incarnation, *history* must also be seen as the locus for the encounter with God[76]. Furthermore, even a cursory look at the *Exercises* reveals that the decision or election is to be made in the course of a series of meditations on the life of Christ. In his introduction to the consideration of different states of life (n. 135), Ignatius exhorts the retreatant, while *contemplating the life of Jesus,* to "begin to investigate and ask in what kind of life or in what state" God wishes to make use of him of her[77]. By "mysteries" of Jesus' life, Rahner is referring not only to events such as Christ's incarnation, crucifixion and resurrection which have a universal significance for our salvation, but also to "the ordinary, the normal, the commonplace, the boringly repetitive, what all have in common, what is insignificant", or to what he calls the "hidden life" of Jesus[78]. The point here is that the *whole* life of Jesus in all its dimensions possesses redemptive significance, and, in this sense, constitutes a "mystery". Rahner thus reflects on the salvific significance of the hidden life of Jesus, which he presents as forming a unity with all the other, more public, events of his

75. Van der Heijden, makes much the same point in his discussion of the proper *criterion* for knowing that a person's experience of God was genuine, and thus that the election was carried out correctly. Following Bakker, he warns: "Das Kriterium ist nicht mehr blo' und letztlich im inneren Kernerlebnis zu suchen, sondern in Christus". VAN DER HEIJDEN, *Karl Rahner, Darstellung und Kritik seiner Grundpositionen*, p. 220. However, the fact that van der Heijden does not include Rahner's retreat conferences in his discussion leads him to the somewhat exaggerated conclusion that the sole criterion for the early Rahner was a pure experience of transcendence. See also P. EICHER, *Wovon spricht die transzendentale Theologie? Zur gegenwärtigen Auseinandersetzung um das Denken von Karl Rahner*, in *Theologische Quartalschrift* 156 (1976) 284-295, 291.

76. "We can no longer reach God by leaving the created world or by abandoning time, space, and history; nor can we reach Him through the transcendence of our spirit toward the Absolute. He can only be reached concretely right where we ourselves are – in our flesh and blood. All grace as a participation in the inner life of God is now grace that comes from the Incarnation and therefore grace of Christ". RAHNER, *Spiritual Exercises*, 80. For a reflection on Christ as the mediator of all salvation, see Rahner's *The Eternal Significance of the Humanity of Jesus for Our Relationship with God*, in *TI* 3:35-46, where he is concerned with overcoming the "unchristian outlook and of solving the *sinful* dilemma into which original sin throws us: God *or* the world.... The Christian attitude, however, would be to honour the world as something willed and loved by God, and to do this in a properly balanced way,..." (pp. 41-42).

77. For a further collection of theological meditations on this subject as part of Rahner's contribution to a theology of the spiritual life, see his *Mysteries of the Life of Jesus*, in *TI* 7:121-201 and his article *Mysterien des Lebens Jesu*, in *LThK* VII:721-722. Our claim in this section is that by such contemplation of the mysteries of the life of Jesus, we have a counter-balance to the other main characteristic of Rahner's Ignatian interpretation, namely, that of the Creator dealing directly with the creature.

78. RAHNER, *Meditations on Priestly Life*, p. 86. See also RAHNER, VORGRIMLER, (eds.), *Mysterien des Lebens Jesu*, in *Kleines Theologisches Wörterbuch*, Freiburg, 1961, [13]1981: 287-288.

life. In so doing, he intends to underscore the gracedness of *everyday* life. It is not a question, then, of piously meditating on Jesus as an exemplary model of moral behaviour, something, he feels, the meditations on the life of Jesus in the *Exercises* are perhaps overly concerned with[79].

The reason Rahner portrays the election as *the call of Christ* can be traced to his understanding of the incarnation. God's decision for self-utterance is His basic intention for creation, and also represents a redemptive decision in regard to finite reality. In fact, Rahner presents the fundamental mysteries of Christianity – trinity, incarnation, grace, and glory – as one comprehensive mystery: that the absolute God goes out as Himself into the non-divine[80]. The incarnation, then, in this framework, is not only an event happening in a moment in time, but constitutes also the "inner entelechy" sustaining creation from the very beginning[81]. Creation and incarnation are two moments or phases of the *one* process of God's self-giving and self-expression. God is creator in as much as He willed to be the giver of grace. In other words, the presupposition is that the world was created to receive God's self-communication. In teasing out the meaning of the incarnation, of what it means to say "the Word became flesh", Rahner's accent is on how the *created* reality with its process of becoming is the reality of the Word of God[82]. Moreover, it is incorrect, he claims, to hold that we cannot know any details of the historical Jesus which would be of significance for theology and faith. Otherwise, we simply end up with a contemporary form of fideism, an attempt to emancipate oneself from the burden of history. Instead, Rahner underlines the intrinsic link between faith and history, and, more specifically, asserts that the historical event of Jesus can be seen as the *ground* of faith:

> "Catholic faith and its dogmatics as they have been understood up to now, and also as they will have to be understood in the future, remain indissolubly

---

79. RAHNER, *Mysterien des Lebens Jesu*, in *LThK* VII: 722.

80. "This self-communication comes to be in incarnation and grace,... that is to say, incarnation and divinisation of all reality... are connected. This one incarnatory-engracing, transfiguring, divinising, self-communication of God to the world, which is created in this decision for his own utterance, reveals precisely what we call the mystery of the Trinity: from this standpoint too the redemptive-historical ('economic') Trinity and the inner, immanent Trinity are intrinsically one". RAHNER, *Meditations on Priestly Life*, pp. 74-75.

81. RAHNER, *FCF*, p. 197. It is beyond our scope here to present a detailed outline of Rahner's Christology. Instead, we confine our discussion to his meditations on the incarnation, and, in particular, on the hidden life of Jesus in the *Exercises* (nn. 101-109, 134, 271). For a synthetic but comprehensive outline of Rahner's Christology, see *FCF*, pp. 176-321; and K. RAHNER, W. THÜSING, *A New Christology*, New York, 1980, pp. 3-14.

82. RAHNER, *Spiritual Exercises*, p. 105.

bound up not only with the historical existence of Jesus of Nazareth, but also with the historical events of a specific kind which took place during his life"[83].

These comments on the meaning of the incarnation serve as a background to Rahner's Ignatian meditations on the theological and spiritual significance of the hidden life of Jesus. It is only through meditating on the life of Jesus, he argues, that the retreatant will find the ultimate criterion for making an election[84]. We have seen how the discovery of the right way of following Christ in the *Exercises* is ultimately the result of an individual, personal decision. This "call" to discipleship, however, only takes place when the retreatant is drawn into the concrete historical life of Jesus. A concrete assimilation to Christ takes place which, by the same token, is also a participation in the inner life of God. The "imitation" of Christ at issue here does not, as we have said above, consist in the observance of certain moral maxims, but rather "in a true entering into His life and in Him entering into the inner life of the God that has been given to us"[85]. In short, then, the purpose of the meditations on the life of Jesus "is to discover the imperative in the life of Jesus that applies to me alone, and then to make the choice to carry it out in my life"[86].

83. RAHNER, *Remarks on the Importance of the History of Jesus for Catholic Dogmatics*, in *TI* 13:201.

84. "The Lord is the ultimate standard; there is none higher than he, since the ultimate standard of necessity is revealed to us just in this actual person. For it is just here that the Logos became man and not simply any man, but this man, so that we cannot really accept a division in the life of Jesus between what is important for us and what can be left aside". RAHNER, *Meditations on Priestly Life*, p. 81.

85. RAHNER, *Spiritual Exercises*, p. 118. In fact Rahner goes even further. Given that the Word of God entered the world in a "tangible and public epiphany of grace, and not just as an anonymous historical force", then one can conclude that Christian spirituality "must attain the same level of publicity that He has; it must relate itself explicitly (with the help of Scripture and tradition) to the 'historical' Jesus; it must understand itself as a part of His 'fullness'; in a word, it must be 'ecclesial'!" (p. 117).

86. *Ibid.,,* p. 127. Later, Rahner adds: "The purpose here in these meditations is to place ourselves in a real, not just abstract, relationship to the event of Jesus' life being considered by means of a salvation-historical and salvation-bringing remembrance. This relationship will bring us the grace necessary to follow Christ.... What takes place in a narrower, sacramental sense in the sacrifice of the Mass, also occurs in a very true sense in the faith-penetrated remembrance of the other events of Jesus' life: And this remembrance is not a mere speculative treatment of Jesus' history – in it, the grace of a definite mystery is revealed and offered to the one praying". RAHNER, *Spiritual Exercises*, p. 162.

Although the evangelists give only marginal consideration to the "pre-history" (or hidden life) of the Messiah, – the assumption seems to be that this first part of Jesus' life is not particularly significant for us in that it was so ordinary – Rahner nevertheless discovers a number of characteristics of his hidden life. See RAHNER, *Meditations on Priestly Life*, pp. 86-98 and in *Spiritual Exercises*, pp. 121-25; and pp. 151-168. These christological meditations, we believe, not only complement our previous exposition and discussion

III. Conclusions

Our discussion of Rahner's appropriation of Ignatian spirituality has centred around the difficult process of discerning God's will, and the related issue of consolation. Further, our analysis revealed certain tensions with which Ignatius, Rahner, and even the retreatant himself or herself have had to grapple. One such tension is that between the role of rational analysis and the place of a Christian enlightenment or "illumination" in the process of making an election. Secondly (and this applies especially to Rahner's Ignatius interpretation), there is the tension between the transcendental and the categorial aspects of the decision to follow the call of God. In fact, our exposition and discussion of Rahner's position indicate that these two aspects (the transcendental and the categorial) cannot be separated; rather, they mutually complement each other. Moreover, in Rahner's study of the theological problems involved in the Ignatian rules of election, the accent is firmly on the transcendental dimension, whereas, in his Ignatian retreat meditations, the categorial dimension comes to the fore. With regard to a criterion for discovering God's will, it is a question of whether there exists a *synthesis* between the attitude of receptivity and openness to God, on the one hand, and the concrete object of election, on the other[87]. Both the experience of consolation without cause and the meditation on the life of Jesus go hand in hand. Therefore, the fact that consolation without cause (as an "immediate" experience of God) has a wordless and non-conceptual character does not exclude a christological interpretation[88].

of Rahner's Ignatian interpretation, but also offer another insight into his understanding of spirituality.

87. RAHNER, *The Dynamic Element in the Church*, 158-160. If this is the case, true spiritual joy (i.e., "peace", "tranquillity", "quiet") ensues. *The Spiritual Exercises of St Ignatius*, n. 333.

88. In his reply to A. DULLES' article (*Finding God's Will: Rahner's Interpretation of the Ignatian Election*, in *Woodstock Letters* 114, 1965, 139-152), Rahner responded to the criticism that his 1956 essay seemed deficient in its failure to accentuate the Christological dimension of the Ignatian election. See K. RAHNER, *Im Anspruch Gottes. Bemerkungen zur Logik der existentiellen Erkenntnis*, in *Geist und Leben* 59 (1986) 241-247. The article arrived in the USA on 31 January 1969, but was only published posthumously in German. In his response, Rahner acknowledges the central role of the christological dimension in the Ignatian theology of choice: "Diese Dimension gibt es natürlich. Und sie ist bei Ignatius in den Exerzitien durch all die Betrachtungen des Lebens Jesu und auch durch die Betrachtungen der zwei Fahnen usw. sehr deutlich gegeben und praktiziert" (p. 244). Further, he concedes that in his own essay he has not discussed this dimension in any detail. Yet he maintains that this dimension is present in an unthematic way, since all grace is the grace of Christ: "Aber diese Dimension ist da... weil alle Gnade unter den verschiedensten Hinsichten... Gnade Christi ist und darum auch die Gnade, die als 'Trost' das Wahlgeschäft bestimmt und prägt, immer als Gnade Christi

Following on the above, it is clear that although there is a quite *personal* experience of God at the heart of Rahner's conception of spirituality, this is not synonymous with a *private* experience. He has on more than one occasion drawn attention to the deleterious effects for Christianity, of the focus on individual sanctification, for example, the neglect of socio-political issues[89]. This notion of spirituality as at once both personal and relational is, we believe, also Ignatian-inspired. Indeed, we have drawn attention to Rahner's writings on two aspects of Ignatian spirituality – two factors which are united, namely, a logic of existential knowledge (interpreted by Rahner in the context of the Ignatian guidelines for making an election) and a passionate love for Christ (which, for Rahner, is the aim of the meditations on the life of Jesus).

An authentic spirituality, in Rahner's view, then, always involves *both* a mystical *and* a societal component. Both these components form a unity just as the love of God and love of neighbour constitute a unity. The solitary mysticism, whereby the creature and the Creator interact directly, is only possible, however, for a person who loves his or her neighbour[90]. Hence, love of neighbour is not just a consequence of, but a precondition for, our relationship with God. The mystical component, we have seen. has to do with an immediate experience of God mediated, for example, through the Ignatian *Exercises*. At the same time, spirituality – understood as the practice of Christianity, or discipleship (*Nachfolge*) – also has a societal component[91]. Influenced by his former pupil and friend, J. B. Metz, Rahner came more and more to see how the socio-political backdrop of human life must also be taken into account in any contemporary understanding of spirituality[92]. Our purpose in offering a

unter all diesen Rücksichten zu denken ist und sonst die ganzen Exerzitien gar nicht verständlich werden" (pp. 244-245).

89. For example, see his interview, *Following Christ Today*, in *Karl Rahner in Dialogue*, PP. 181-185.

90. IMHOF, BIALLOWONS, eds., *Karl Rahner in Dialogue*, p. 183. While he does not deny the political dimension of Christianity, this dimension does not occupy pride of place for Rahner: "Es gibt zu wenig Menschen, die daran denken, daß im letzten Verstand nicht Gott für sie, sondern sie für Gott da sind. So im allgemeinen theologischen Geschwätz des Alltags gehöre ich gerade zu den 'anthropozentrischen' Theologen. Das ist *letztlich* ein absoluter Unsinn. Ich möchte ein Theologe sein, der sagt, da' *Gott* das Wichtigste ist, da' wir dazu da sind, in einer uns selbst vergessenden Weise ihn zu lieben, ihn anzubeten, für ihn da zu sein, aus unserem eigenen Daseinsbereich in den Abgrund der Unbegreiflichkeit Gottes zu springen". RAHNER, *Karl Rahner im Gespräch* 2: 166.

91. *Following Christ Today*, in *Karl Rahner in Dialogue*, pp. 181-185.

92. "For it has always been clear in my theology that a 'transcendental experience' (of God and of grace) is always mediated through a categorical experience in history, in interpersonal relationships, and in society. If one not only sees and takes seriously these necessary mediations of transcendental experience but also fills it out in a concrete way, then one already practices in an authentic way political theology, or in other words, a

defence of Rahner's theological approach, however, is to counter a common misunderstanding, namely, that Rahner *exclusively* pursues a transcendental method which then leads to an insensitivity to social problems and to an ineffectiveness in the realm of political and social change[93]. Rather, Rahner exhibits a twofold theological method, or better, a method that incorporates both transcendental and historical reflection. Admittedly, transcendental reflection always runs the risk of failing to take into account the historical dimensions of theological reality[94]. In so emphasising the self-communication of God to the human person in the transcendental dimension of their being, it can be overlooked that such a self-communication also has a history, "and this is at once the single history of both salvation and revelation"[95]. And Rahner, for his part, while consistently arguing for the ever-present interaction of experience and reflection, or for the reciprocal interdependence of transcendental and historical reflection in theology, nonetheless concentrates more on the transcendental moment[96]. Combining the core experience at

practical fundamental theology. On the other hand, such a political theology is, if it truly wishes to concern itself with God, not possible without reflection on those essential characteristics of humankind which a transcendental theology discloses. Therefore, I believe that my theology and that of Metz are not necessarily contradictory". RAHNER, *Introduction*, to J. BACIK, *Apologetics and the Eclipse of Mystery*, Notre Dame, 1980, p. x.

93. This awareness is evident as far back as Rahner's 1966 address to the conference on "Christian Humanity and Marxist Humanism", where Rahner explicitly states that "theology must always be 'political' theology... The theologian is aware that, according to Christianity, salvation is achieved not only within the explicitly religious sphere but in *all* dimensions of human existence,... where one loves in an absolutely responsible manner, serves one's neighbour selflessly and willingly accepts the incomprehensible nature and disappointments of one's existence, hoping ultimately to embrace its as yet unrevealed meaningfulness.... In this sense, the whole of the human sphere is religious and the whole of the religious sphere is divine". This lecture reveals Rahner's twin emphasis on God as the absolute future of humankind as well as his insistence on "the sober service of 'political' love". RAHNER, *Christian Humanism*, in *TI* 9:188-189. Rahner's awareness of a political dimension to *spirituality* is also in evidence at this time. See his *Christian Living Formerly and Today*, in *TI* 7:19, where the term "politische Frömmigkeit" is used (though this is unusually translated into English as "the 'political' form of religion"). I am also indebted here to some insightful comments on Rahner's dialectical method by L.J. O'DONOVAN, *Orthopraxis and Theological Method in Karl Rahner*, in *CTSA Proceedings* 35 (1980) 47-65, and by M.V. MAHER, *Rahner on the Human Experience of God: Idealist Tautology or Christian Theology?*, in *Philosophy & Theology* 7 (1992) 127-164.

94. According to MAHER, *Rahner on the Human Experience of God*, in *Philosophy & Theology* 7 (1992) 148, Metz's critique of Rahner highlights "the need to develop a method for the dialectic (the dialectic *between* the transcendental analysis of human experience oriented toward and by Mystery *and* the attending (dialectically) to the pluralism of social, cultural and historical positions)".

95. RAHNER, in *FCF*, p. 141.

96. "es gibt wenig philosophische, anthropologische und theologische Probleme, die schwerer richtig und ausbalanciert beantwortet werden können als das Verhältnis von

the heart of the *Spiritual Exercises* (a personal encounter with God) with the *Praxisbezogenheit* of Rahner's later writings, we can conclude that Rahner's spirituality has both a mystical and a societal component – even if the latter element was not always brought sharply into focus[97].

Throughout this essay we have sought to show what Rahner describes as the abiding significance of Jesus for Christian faith[98]. Rahner is convinced that the Church's entire christological teaching can be derived from the fundamental significance of Jesus "for us". This conviction goes hand in hand with the belief that Jesus and his salvific work have made it possible to arrive at an immediacy to the true God. In this respect, Jesus is the unassailable witness – the one who effects that to which he gives witness. We note here, too, a mutual complementarity between the anthropological and christological foci of Rahner's theology[99]. What this means is that, for Rahner, the fundamental or basic statements about Christianity must be related to the intrinsic structure of the human person. By intrinsic structure, Rahner is referring to a finality or dynamism which a person has (at least unthematically, and imparted by God) towards God's self-communication. A transcendental Christology then appeals to a person and asks him or her whether they can freely accept and appropriate such an orientation[100]. The transcendental enquiry at issue here, far from being an abstract, ahistorical process, represents an attempt to *correlate* the historical event of God's saving self-revelation and communication in Christ with the basic structures of

---

Transzendentalität und Geschichte. Insofern bin ich gar nicht verwundert, wenn man mir nachweisen will, da' dieses schwierige Verhältnis in meiner Theologie nicht umfassend und ursprünglich genug reflektiert wird.... Transzendentalität ist für mich immer Transzendentalität, die *in* konkreter und letztlich unableitbar Geschichte zu sich selbst kommt". RAHNER, *Herausforderung des Christen*, pp. 130, 136.

97. In other words, spirituality is not just about experience; it also entails a concrete lived *practice*. A common criticism of Rahner's transcendental method in this regard is that his method is insensitive to social problems and ineffectual in the area of social change. See, for example, J.B. METZ, *Faith in History and Society: Toward a Practical Fundamental Theology*, tr. by David Smith, New York, 1980, pp. 161-168.

98. "But for Christian faith Jesus, his life and the accomplishment of his death, is nothing other than God's definitive invitation to this surrender [by which we allow ourselves to be seized in faith, hope, and love] and the irrevocable promise that this surrender is really accomplished through God's powerful love and not ultimately by the efforts of our own goodwill". RAHNER, *Christianity's Absolute Claim*, in *TI* 21:180. See also, K. RAHNER, *Our Christian Faith: Answers for the Future*, tr. F. McDONAGH, London, 1981, pp. 85-104.

99. RAHNER, *Theology and Anthropology*, in *TI* 9:28.

100. RAHNER, in *FCF*, pp. 208-209. "It specifies and vindicates the universal significance of the particular event of Jesus Christ by specifying and vindicating the conditions of its possibility". J.C. ROBERTSON, Jr. review of *FCF* in *Religious Studies Review* 5/3 (July 1979) 193.

human existence and history[101]. It is the task of an authentic transcendental theology to elucidate the connection or correlation, in order to render Christian faith intelligible. As we mentioned earlier, it is only by showing how the concrete, historical events of salvation history really correspond to the basic structures of the human condition can Christianity claim to affect the human person at the ultimate level of their existence and subjectivity[102].

Marist Fathers   Declan MARMION
89 Lower Leeson Street
Dublin 2
Ireland

101. For a helpful discussion of Catholic methods of correlation in fundamental theology, along with an insistence on the need for some form of transcendental reflection in theology, see D. TRACY, *The Uneasy Alliance Reconceived: Catholic Theological Method, Modernity, and Postmodernity*, in *Theological Studies* 50 (1989) 548-570.

102. RAHNER, *Reflections on Methodology in Theology*, in *TI* 11: 100. See also J.R. SACHS, *Transcendental Method in Theology and the Normativity of Human Experience*, in *Philosophy & Theology* 7 (1992) 213-225.

The backdrop to our reflections throughout this article has been the separation between religious experience and intellectual reflection, broadly described in terms of a separation between spirituality and theology. Rahner's assumption has always been that theological reflection must be built on a living experience of faith. For all his emphasis on the ineffable God, Rahner did not stop at pure negation but used this as a springboard into the search for unity with the transcendent. He has taken seriously the dictum *lex orandi, lex credendi* (the law of prayer establishes the law of belief), and shown that the specific way Christians pray, meditate and contemplate constitutes an important element for theological reflection. In so doing, he has made a significant contribution towards overcoming the mutual marginalization between religious or spiritual experience and the theological academy.

But spirituality is not just about experience; it also entails a concrete lived *practice*. We mentioned a common criticism of Rahner's transcendental method in this regard, namely, that his method is insensitive to social problems and ineffectual in the area of social change. Against this, we emphasised how Rahner increasingly sought to complement his transcendental approach with an incorporation of a more historical perspective – testified, for example, in his choice of theological topics. If we agree that Rahner considered the transcendental method to be only one part of theology, albeit a necessary one, we also concur with his view that Christians today no longer accept theological propositions of faith which have no apparent connection with their own understanding of themselves. Thus Rahner could agree with the characterisation of his theology as a "transcendental anthropology", as long as this description did not give the impression that he had bracketed the complicated question of the relation between transcendence and history.

CHRISTOLOGY FROM THE UNDERSIDE OF HISTORY:
THE CASE OF JON SOBRINO

Fifteen years ago I wrote an article in Dutch on the orthodox character of Sobrino's christology[1]. The occasion was Cardinal Ratzinger's private study on liberation theology that had just appeared (or leaked out) in the review *30 Giorni* (March 1984). Since the point I made in that article has never reached the English-speaking world, I shall briefly dwell on it in the first part of this essay, and then proceed to evaluate some critical reviews of Sobrino's christology which more recently have seen the light of the day. The underlying assumption is that "Sobrino's theology of the Reign of God (the quintessence of his christological reflections) has remained basically the same from his writings in the early 1970s to the last"[2]. Part one then deals with Sobrino's orthodoxy, and, more in particular, attempts to disprove one of Ratzinger's arguments concerning Sobrino's alleged use of Marxist-inspired hermeneutics. Part two focuses on the same hermeneutics and their alleged lack of biblical foundation – an accusation voiced this time not by the Vatican but by theological and biblical scholars.

I. MARXIST-INSPIRED HERMENEUTICS?

1. Sobrino under attack from Rome

That Jon Sobrino ran into trouble with the Vatican is not very well known. The reason is clear: it never came to a straightforward condemnation as was the case with Leonardo Boff. Nonetheless, at various times he was requested to clarify his basic ideas and to bring them in line with generally accepted, mainstream christologies. Warnings were issued to him through the Jesuit curia: he had better keep in line with 'orthodoxy'. Sobrino thus had to 'defend' himself. This frame of mind is already evident in the Preface to the English edition of *Cristología desde América*

---

1. G. DE SCHRIJVER, *De orthodoxie van de bevrijdingstheologie*, in *Streven* 51 (1983-84) 771-784.
2. P. CHITTINAPPILLY, *The Reign of God in the Theology of Jon Sobrino. Analysis and Critical Assessment*, unpublished licentiate thesis, K.U. Leuven, 1997, p. 3. This thesis was completed under my direction. I make use of it as a valuable source for criticisms leveled against Sobrino, especially in the second part of this article.

Latina (*Christology at the Crossroads*). The preface to the Spanish edition of 1976, phrased by the 'Center for Theological Reflection' in Mex-
ico which published the book, is rather unpretentious. It mainly mentions that Sobrino's work is one of the first christologies having
originated from Latin America, and that compared to Boff's christology[3]
which came out a few years earlier, it has a more radical methodological
focus thanks to its twofold rootedness. It is, first of all, "historically
positioned" in the life of the historical Jesus and, secondly, it has been
"constructed from the Latin American situation of oppression, injustice,
and exploitation"[4]. The preface to the English edition, dated January
1978, and written by the author himself, offers a much more elaborated
text, meant to preclude possible misreadings of the corpus.

In this preface it is stated that, strictly speaking, there is nothing completely new in the book ("much of the conceptual backdrop is drawn
from current European christologies"). What makes it special is "the
way in which the various data about Jesus are structured, the stress
placed on certain aspects rather than others, and the basic intention to
give a new direction to Christology"[5], adapted to the world of the poor
who constitute the majority in the Latin American subcontinent. After
this prudent assessment, Sobrino goes on to highlight the ecclesial character of his book, its focus on the *sequela Christi* fleshed out in the present historical setting, and its basic assumption that the following of
Jesus is the royal road to make us realize, in an experiential way, the
depth of the Trinitarian mystery. His christology is ecclesial in that it
takes its point of departure in the Christian community life (the 'church
of the poor'), without ruling out the importance of a christology based
on conciliar and papal pronouncements. It is a historical christology in
that it takes seriously the hermeneutical circle between a Christian praxis
of love and the life commitment of Christ, a circularity which leads to
the 'following of Jesus' in the concreteness of history. It is, thirdly, a
Trinitarian way of thinking because it sees in Jesus' commitment to the
Reign of God an expression of his filial relation to the Father, in the
unity of the Spirit: "Maintaining the mystery of the Father is fundamental to Jesus, as is maintaining the view that the Father is the ultimate
mystery"[6].

---

3. L. BOFF, *Jesus Cristo Libertador*, Petrópolis, Vozes, 1972.
4. *Preface to the Spanish Edition*, in J. SOBRINO, *Christology at the Crossroads*, New
York, Orbis Books, 1978, p. xii.
5. *Preface to the English Edition*, *ibid.*, pp. xix- xx.
6. *Ibid.*, p. xxiii.

Similar cautious remarks literally abound in the next book, *Jesús en América Latina*, published in 1982, which, besides two new chapters, contains a series of articles written between 1978 and 1980. The insertion of these two new chapters is significant because in them Sobrino apparently responds to some objections that had been voiced against him by the Congregation of the Doctrine of the Faith. The objections mainly relate to the absence of a high christology, to the prevalence of orthopraxis over orthodoxy, and to the notion of the Reign of God which would only allow for an implicit confession of the divinity of Christ. At any rate the book was submitted to the scrutiny of Juan Alfaro, s.j., of the Gregorian University, a task entrusted to him by Pedro Arrupe, then superior general of the Jesuits[7]. Alfaro's report was published in the January-April issue of the *Revista Latinoamericana de Teología*[8].

This report, dated January 17, 1984, offers a benevolent review of Sobrino's book, pointing out, firstly, that the author wanted to clear up misunderstandings, and, secondly, to answer questions that had been raised about his book *Cristología desde América Latina*. Therefore, it is said, Sobrino starts his new book with a chapter entitled "The Truth about Jesus Christ" (thus referring to a concern of the Puebla Conference). This chapter is a preamble, so to speak, to the rest of the book; it contains an important clarification of his theological method. Sobrino affirms that no christology can afford not to take into consideration what the dogmas stipulated about the eternal consubstantiality of the Logos with the Father, a consubstantiality which found its 'natural' extension in the Logos incarnate and his filial obedience to the Father. On the other hand, although a Christology conceived from a Latin American perspective pays high respect to these dogmatic statements, its pastoral method rather consists in assimilating the historical praxis of Jesus – through the 'following of Jesus' in the actual vicissitudes of history – as a potent (mystagogic) means to make the believers understand what Jesus' divine mission, as well as his special relationship to the mystery of the Father, is all about: "Because dogmatic statements are limit statements they cannot be understood, even at the noetic level, without retracing the steps leading to their formulation. Accordingly, although Latin American Christology knows and admits from the outset the truth of the dogmatic formulations, it insists on re-creating the process that led to them, beginning with Jesus of Nazareth, and, further, holds that the

7. Sobrino dedicated the book to Pedro Arrupe.
8. J. ALFARO, *Análisis del libero 'Jesús en América Latina' de Jon Sobrino*, in *Revista Latinoamericana de Teología*, January-April, 1984, pp. 103-120.

re-creation of this process is the best way to come to an understanding of the formulas"[9].

In his review of the second chapter entitled: "The Significance of the Historical Jesus in Latin American Christology", Alfaro underlines that here as well, some important methodological insights have been formulated. (i) The question is, indeed, how to bridge the historical distance between the 'then' and the 'now' – between Jesus' commitment to the Reign of God and the Latin American Christians' endeavor to make human history advance towards the direction of the Reign of God. While European scholars for the most part are engaged in effecting a fusion of two different cultural horizons (Gadamer), Sobrino is rather of the opinion that such a fusion can only be brought about on a practical level; and this the more so because the hermeneutical interest has shifted from a focus on the 'Christ of faith' to the historical Jesus: "From a point of departure in the historical Jesus, 'praxis' has yielded up the element needed to span the historical distance; hence we hear today of praxic, liberative, and even revolutionary hermeneutics. Whatever be the achievements of these various hermeneutics, they all point to the discipleship of Jesus as the way to the attainment of an understanding of Jesus as the Christ; and at all events they are demanded by Jesus, the content of Christology"[10].

(ii) Related to this methodological standpoint is the next consideration. The history of Jesus and the Latin American reality illuminate each other. The situation in Latin America is such that the materially poor are deprived of justice; they see their most fundamental rights violated. People are slaughtered, tortured, and massacred; many of them just 'disappear', picked up by national security forces. At the same time they continue offering resistance, fighting for their rights, which brings them to a situation of persecution[11]: "The similarity of the two situations with respect to a basic point – their misery, repression, oppression, and death – makes it possible for the current situation and the history of Jesus to enjoy a common theological focus. The parallel may appear minimal, but the nucleus of this focus is the horizon of the life and death of human beings and, in the case of Jesus' history, his service to life and his struggle against death"[12]. What

9. J. SOBRINO, *Jesus in Latin America*, Maryknoll, NY, Orbis Books, 1987, p. 19. Quoted also in J. ALFARO, *art. laud.*, p. 106.
10. J. SOBRINO, *Jesus in Latin America*, p. 57.
11. *Ibid.*, p. 61.
12. *Ibid.*, p. 72. Cf. J. ALFARO, *art. laud.*, p. 108.

is more clearly understood, on the basis of this common ground, is the content of the Reign of God, the 'Good News' Jesus announces: God is in favor of life and repudiates all sorts of infringement on life in its plenitude.

The rest of the book, as already stated, is composed of a collection of articles already published earlier. From these pages, Alfaro remarks, two important theses can be gleaned which logically flow from the above-mentioned principles: (i) the God of the reign is a 'partial' God: he sides with the poor and the oppressed and takes up their defense against their oppressors. Jesus is engaged in a struggle for the true mediators of God, debunking the powers that abuse God's name in order to establish their own empire (the anti-reign): "The eschatological horizon of Jesus' mission is the kingdom of God, a kingdom of life for everyone. But, in order for it to be a reality it must be shared in by those who for centuries have been deprived of life in its various forms: the poor and the oppressed. Hence, Jesus' proclamation is 'partial'"[13] (ii) For Jesus, the Reign of God and the God of the reign are ultimate values. His whole life is geared towards this 'ultimacy', to the life giving mystery that inhabits the depths of reality and empowers his sons and daughters with a transformative love in the midst of history: "To Jesus, the ultimate mystery of life transcends concrete life... Jesus had the inner conviction that love exists in the ultimate depths of reality, that is in relation to that love that human beings truly live, and that their life is truly life when they give life to others, when they love them"[14]. Jesus' filial relationship to the Father is anchored in, and revealed through, his dedication to this ultimate mystery.

Alfaro, whose scheme of rendering Sobrino's basic ideas I have been following, concludes his report by stating that nothing of what Sobrino has put forward is unorthodox. If there are special accents in his presentation of Jesus, this is mainly due to his 'doing christology' from the context of Latin America. This makes his approach 'limited' but, in terms of pastoral theology, very fruitful. At any rate, to accuse Sobrino of Marxism would do violence to the truth: "In his reflection on the situation of the Latin American people Sobrino never makes use of the Marxist analysis of society nor gets inspiration from any ideology alien to Christianity. His reflection always takes place within the Christian specificity"[15].

---

13. J. SOBRINO, *Jesus in Latin America*, p.106. Cf. J. ALFARO, *art. laud.*, p. 113.

14. J. SOBRINO, *Jesus in Latin America*, p. 124. Cf. J. ALFARO, *art. laud.*, p. 110

15. "En su reflexión sobre la situación del pueblo latinoamericano Sobrino no recurre nunca al análisis marxista de la sociedad, ni se inspira en ninguna ideología ajena

2. Ratzinger's 'private study' on Liberation Theology: A case of overkill

I still recall the day when a friend of mine handed me an article by Cardinal Ratzinger published in the Italian review *30 Giorni*. There are indications that this review had published it without Ratzinger knowing it so that one can speak, in a sense, of a leaked document[16]. The article was given the provocative title of "I'm Going to Explain to You what Liberation Theology is About"[17], and is commonly regarded now as Ratzinger's 'private study' on these matters.

I was intrigued by this private study, and for several reasons. Ratzinger, first of all, drew a distinction between genuine theologies of liberation, and Marxist-inspired ones, the latter being spread not only in Latin America, but also in India, Sri Lanka, the Philippines, Taiwan, and Africa, and not only by Catholic but also by Protestant authors. This observation only served to lay down his verdict: "Liberation theology (in the Marxist sense) seeks to create from its premises a new universality by which the classical separations of the churches should loose their importance"[18]. What worried him more, though, was the fact that the authentic magisterium of the Catholic Church was, in a sense, discredited by this new approach. For as soon as the magisterium would dare to voice critical remarks against liberation theology's method, it would be accused of siding with the rich. This uncomfortable situation, it was stated, flowed forth from the new hermeneutics that were now in vogue. The liberation theologians placed great emphasis on the preaching and

al cristianismo. Su reflexión se desarolla siempre dentro de lo christiano". See J. ALFARO, *art. laud.*, p. 119.

16. J. RATZINGER–V. MESSORI, *Entretien sur la foi*, Paris, Fayard, 1985, p. 207: "On avait déjà rendu publique – par une indiscrétion des journaux – la réflexion dans laquelle Ratzinger expliquait sa position personnelle de théologien sur ce sujet (la théologie de la libération)".

17. J. RATZINGER, *Vi spiego la teologia della liberazione*, in *30 Giorni*, March 1984, pp. 48-55. This text is, in fact, the Italian translation of J. RATZINGER, *Presupuestos, Problemas y desafíos de la 'teología de la liberación'* published in the Peruvian Review *Oiga*, January 23, 1984, and later also in *Tierra Nueva*, 49 (April 1984), pp. 93-96; and 50 (July, 1984), pp. 95-96. An English translation appeared in the September 18 edition of *Catholicism in Crisis,* and can also be found in A. HENNELLY, *Liberation Theology. A Documentary History*, New York, Orbis Books, 1990, pp. 367-374 (J. RATZINGER, *'Liberation Theology'*, March 1984). A German translation was published in *'Die neue Ordnung'* (August, 1984), and can also be found in N. GREINACHER, *Konflikt um die Theologie der Befreiung*, Köln, Benzinger Verlag, 1985, pp. 133-145 (Kardinal Joseph RATZINGER, *Die Theologie der Befreiung*). A French translation of the text is included in J. RATZINGER–V. MESSORI, *Entretien sur la foi*, Paris, Fayard, 1985, pp. 213-232 (*Un texte de 'théologien privé'*). I mention those various editions because they display some variations in their presentation. I will take up this problem again later.

18. J. Ratzinger, *''Liberation Theology' (March 1984)*, in A. Hennelly, *Liberation Theology. A Documentary History*, New York, Orbis Books, 1990, p. 368.

deeds of the 'historical Jesus' (disconnected, so to speak, from the 'Christ of faith'), while at the same time maintaining that the praxis of people engaged in base communities ('the church of the poor') was the privileged access to grasp the true meaning of Jesus' message.

Given this alarming situation, Ratzinger thus deemed it necessary to delve into the presuppositions of liberation theology. A first presupposition is that the Marxist analysis of history and of society is regarded as the only analysis with a scientific character. This means concretely that the world is "interpreted in the light of a structure of class struggle", so that "the only possible choice is between capitalism and Marxism"; and also that "all reality is political and must be justified politically". The second presupposition is that not the church hierarchy but the "lived reality and the experiences of the 'community' determine now the understanding and the interpretation of Scriptures". Only praxis allows for a correct interpretation. In this way, however, the conciliar idea of the people of God has been transformed "into a Marxist myth". If one adds to this the third presupposition, then the reasoning comes full circle: The concept of history has taken the place of salvation history: "History is the authentic revelation, and therefore the true hermeneutical instance". Permanent truths have been replaced with the dialectics of history, a stance liberation theologians tend to justify by having recourse to a Marxist materialist philosophy in which – Ratzinger underlines – "history has assumed the role of God"[19].

To illustrate some of these presuppositions, Ratzinger specifically enters into a discussion with two Latin American authors who are mentioned by name[20], Gustavo Gutiérrez and Jon Sobrino. Two passages from Gutiérrez are quoted without mention of the book or the books they are taken from, and this to make clear to what extent liberation theology wagers on class struggle and turns all things into politics.

As far as Sobrino is concerned, more citations are given to which the number of the page is added each time but not the title of the book in question. The accusations here relate to liberation theology reducing salvation history to the dynamics of history. "We have now reached the fundamental concepts of the content of the new interpretation of Christianity. Because the contexts in which the different concepts appear are

19. *Ibid.*, pp. 371-372.
20. This is the case for the versions published in *30 Giorni,* and *Oiga,* and the respective translations that are based on them. The version published in J. RATZINGER–V. MESSORI, *Entretien sur la foi,* Paris, Fayard, 1985, pp. 226-227 (J. RATZINGER, *Un texte de 'theologien privé'),* however, omits the names and uses instead the periphrasis: "a certain Latin American theologian says…".

diverse, I would like to quote some without any claims of a synthesis.
We can begin with the new interpretation of faith, hope, and charity.
Concerning faith, for example, J. Sobrino affirms that 'the experience
Jesus has of God is radically historical'. 'His faith is converted into
fidelity'. As a consequence, faith in God has basically been replaced
with 'fidelity to history'" (143-144)[21]. The text continues with a further
quote from Sobrino (a sentence which I am going to discuss at length
below): *"'Jesus is faithful to the profound conviction that the mystery of
men... is really (the) ultimate'"* (144). To then lay down the verdict:
"Here one sees the fusion between God and history which allows one to
preserve for Jesus the formula of Chalcedon, even if it has a completely
changed meaning"[22]. To surreptitiously give a new – read: Marxist –
interpretation of Chalcedon smacks of heresy, especially if one clothes
this interpretation with the language of orthodoxy: "Ignacio Ellacuria on
the dust jacket of the book affirms that Sobrino 'says again...that Jesus
is God', adding, however, immediately that 'the true God is only the one
who is revealed historically and scandalously in Jesus and in the poor
who continue his presence. Only one who maintains these two affirmations is orthodox'"[23].

I wanted to know more about the references to Sobrino and the context from which they were taken. But how would I be able to get more
information? With the instinct of a detective I set to work. The only
clues I had were the page numbers added in brackets to the citations, and
Ellacuría's laudatory words on the dust jacket of the book from whence
the citations came. Now, just by chance I was reading these days Jon
Sobrino's book *Jesús en América Latina* in the Salvadorian edition[24]
(aside from this, there is also another Spanish edition by *Sal Terrae*,
Santander, 1982). Driven by curiosity and encouraged by the intuition of
a successful outcome, I checked whether a recommendation by Ellacuría
figured on the dust jacket, and to my bewilderment I saw that this was
indeed the case[25]. I then looked up pages 143-144 and instantly found

---

21. J. Ratzinger, *'Liberation Theology' (March 1984)*, in A. Hennelly, *op. cit.*,
p. 372.
22. *Ibid.*, p. 372 (Italics mine).
23. *Ibid.*, pp. 372-273. Ellacuría's text (on the dust jacket) reads as follows: "(Jon
Sobrino) dice de nuevo, aunque de forma más profunda y elaborada, que Jesús es Dios,
pero añadiendo immediatamente que el Dios verdadero es sólo el que se revela histórica
y escandalosamente en Jesús y en los pobres quienes continúan su presencia. Sólo quien
mantiene tensa y unitariamente estas dos afirmaciones es ortodoxo".
24. I had bought the book some months earlier when I was in Central America.
25. Ellacuría's text also figures on the dust jacket of the *Sal Terrae* edition.

out that Ratzinger had been consulting *Jesús en América Latina* in the *Salvadorian* edition. So, by a stroke of fortune, I was now sufficiently equipped to study the wider context in which the excerpted citations had to be placed. I was able to examine whether, on the basis of these citations, it really could be demonstrated that Sobrino's christology had a Marxist ring to it. It was on the basis of this comparison that I wrote my Dutch article that came out in June 1984. But before broaching the point I made there, I would like to first quote the words with which Ratzinger attacked Sobrino's 'Marxism'. The text reads as follows:

"Hope is interpreted as 'confidence in the future', and as work for the future; in that way, it is subordinated again to the domination of the history of the classes. Love consists in an 'option for the poor', that is, it coincides with an option for class struggle... In my opinion one can recognize very clearly here the mixture of the fundamental truth of Christianity and the fundamental non-Christian option which makes this thought so seductive. The Sermon on the Mount is, in reality, a choice on the part of God in favor of the poor. But the interpretation of the poor in the sense of Marxist, dialectical history and the interpretation of a partisan choice in terms of class struggle, is a move towards 'other genres' (*eis allo genos*) in which the contrary is presented as identical. The fundamental concept of the preaching of Jesus is the 'kingdom of God'. This concept is found again at the center of the theologies of liberation, read, however, against the background of Marxist hermeneutics. According to Sobrino the kingdom cannot be understood spiritually or universally in the sense of an abstract eschatological reserve. It must be understood in a party form an turned towards practice. Only if we start with the praxis of Jesus, and not theoretically, is it possible to say what the kingdom means – that is 'to work in the historical reality that surrounds us, to transform it into the kingdom'" (166)[26].

When pondering those and similar texts, I began to suspect that what Ratzinger was doing was a real case of overkill. To me it was not clear at all that Sobrino had defined Jesus' praxis in terms of a straightforward transformation of historical reality into the kingdom of God (in the way Marxists seek to transform historical reality into a not yet given 'new creation', as the final fulfillment of the dialectics of history). Sobrino's statement is much more nuanced. According to him "Jesus' practice, in as far as it is practice, i.e. in as far as he endeavors to have his deeds work on the historical reality that surrounds him in order to transform this reality into a given direction, *indirectly but efficaciously reveals*

---

26. J. RATZINGER, *'Liberation Theology' (March 1984)*, in A. HENNELLY, *op. cit.*, p. 373. This English version has the curious expression "the interpretation of the choice of a party", which I changed into "the interpretation of a partisan choice" which is more in line with the Spanish and Italian editions.

what is at stake in the Reign of God"[27]. Here, to be sure, an emphasis is placed on the endeavor to change historical reality towards a certain direction; but this change for the better is not said to be simply identical with the Reign of God. It only allows us to perceive how that which the biblical testimonies deem important for the drawing near of the kingdom of God is indirectly but efficaciously revealed in this practice. These theological dialectics of revelation seems to be closer to Bonhoeffer than to Marx. This is what I set out to prove in my Dutch article, the central part of which I am going to present again in the next section[28].

3. An old text revisited. Bonhoeffer instead of Marx

For my text of 1984 concerning Ratzinger's overkill, the quotation marks before and after each paragraph indicate that it is a literal translation. Why I deemed this literal rendering important will become clear at the end of this section. The text reads as follows:

> When analyzing the elements (allegedly) responsible for liberation theology's deviation, Ratzinger first of all points to the theological vacuum that has been created after the Second Vatican Council. The doors had been opened widely for letting alien influences enter. Human sciences (psychology, sociology, and hermeneutics) infiltrated Christian thinking, whereas also Marxism and neo-Marxism (Bloch, Horkheimer, Adorno, Habermas, Marcuse) began to exert their lure[29]. That these influences are present, is certainly true, but must they necessarily be assessed in the negative? Could it not be the case that Christianity has inevitably grown out of Aquinas' unproblematic synthesis between an incarnation spirituality with its schemes of 'man's participation in God', on the one hand, and Aristotelianism with its inner-worldly focus on virtuous life, on the other, to enter a new synthesis with modern social sciences in search for the meaning of life and virtue in a society that has lost its former homogeneous character? Will Christianity not have to make a 'leap' towards fleshing out its religious commitment in the midst of a society that, primarily for cultural and not so much for religious reasons, has become fragmented and conflict-ridden? At any rate, the believer will have to traverse the 'whole length' of the secular domain, in order to discern what is healthful in it and what stifling – and by doing so reach maturation in 'discerning the spirits'.

27. J. SOBRINO, Jesús en América Latina, San Salvador, UCA editores, 1982, p. 166: "La práctica de Jesús, en cuanto praxis, es decir, en cuanto intenta operar sobre la realidad histórica circundante para transformarla en una determinada dirección, revela, indirecta pero eficazmente, de qué se trata en el reino de Dios".

28. G. DE SCHRIJVER, art. laud., pp. 777-781.

29. J. RATZINGER, 'Liberation Theology' (March 1984), in A. HENNELLY, op. cit., p. 369.

Now it is this latter attitude and not Marxism or neo-Marxism that prevails in Sobrino. This can be shown with the help of the dialectics of 'the ultimate' and 'the penultimate' which Dietrich Bonhoeffer has developed in his *Ethics*, and which Sobrino has espoused to describe Jesus' fidelity to human history as the concrete norm for fidelity to his divine mission. Bonhoeffer, to be sure, is a theologian who did by no means integrate sociology of knowledge or any form of Marxism into his thinking. He rather stands out in his thoroughgoing reflection on the secular tasks of the Christian as Christian.

In his zeal to trace Marxist elements, Ratzinger drops a reference to Bonhoeffer when citing a sentence from which he wants to show that Sobrino is not orthodox. I quote this sentence and put the omitted passage in italics: 'Jesus is faithful to the profound conviction that the mystery of the life of men, *a mystery that is in favor of the life of men*, is really the ultimate'[30]. From this truncated text Ratzinger concludes that Sobrino has degraded Jesus' faith in God to just a faithfulness to history, a history that moreover is seen as dynamically striving towards the attainment of an inner-worldly *eschaton* ('a hypothetical future', as Ratzinger calls it'). With Sobrino, however, this sentence must be placed in the context of the following considerations: Jesus' life commitment is based on the conviction that 'there is something ultimate in the depth of reality that is in favor of men' and which ought to be upheld at any price[31]. Whoever lives up to this mystery, 'knows' that he has to espouse a lifestyle 'in favor of the others' (*el ser en favor de otros*: Bonhoeffer's pro-existence). The complete sentence thus conveys the following message: Jesus is faithful to the profound conviction that the mystery of life (God) stands up for human beings so that they may live, and that this mystery is something ultimate, something – the text continues – 'that cannot be put into question in spite of all the appearances against it'[32]. And a bit further we come across the notion 'penultimate' which, just as for Bonhoeffer, stands in a dialectical relationship to the 'ultimate': 'The ultimate mystery warrants the earnestness of the penultimate'[33], i.e. of the seriousness of our commitments in the secular realm.

There is thus no reason at all to attribute to the term 'the ultimate' a utopian, futuristic content, filled in with a purely inner-worldly orientation. Once engaged in this direction, Ratzinger remarks, 'one begins to destroy

---

30. J. SOBRINO, *Jesús en América Latina*, p. 144: "Jesús es fiel a la profunda convicción de que el misterio de la vida de los hombres y para los hombres es realmente lo último, lo que no se puede poner en duda a pesar de todas las apariencias en su contra". Cf. with Ratzinger's truncated version: "Jesus is faithful to the profound conviction that the mystery of the life of men... is really (the) ultimate" (J. RATZINGER, *'Liberation Theology' (March 1984)*, in A. HENNELLY, *op. cit.*, p. 372).

31. J. SOBRINO, *Jesús en América Latina*, p. 145: "Sólo hemos pretendido apuntar a que la radicalidad de la vida y la praxis se basan en su radical convicción que en el fondo de la realidad existe algo último, que es en favor de los hombres, y que hay que mantener a cualquier precio".

32. See the complete text, footnote 30.

33. J. SOBRINO, *Jesús en América Latina*, p. 145: "El misterio último es la garantía de la seriedad de lo penúltimo".

the present, in favor of a hypothetical future'[34]. Yet, to be precise, the 'ultimate' coincides with the very experience of God in the here and now, an
experience that requires us to impart a God-inspired acuity to our actions
and feelings; and this not just in the small sector one would like to preserve
as one's religious compartment, but *also* in these domains within secular
culture (economics, jurisprudence, and politics) which obey, for the worst
or for the best, their own logic, and which also come to bear on the way in
which modern people form their personality... Because of this formative
character the 'secular domain' is not something that can be ignored, though
it is only the 'penultimate'. Everybody, also the religious person, appropriates his normative ethical awareness by engaging in secular commitments.
But these commitments must allow themselves to be broadened and sharpened through one's contact with the 'ultimate'. Only then will our inner-
worldly commitments acquire a religious acuity, a religious acuity which is
not given any chance to prosper, if we are only busy with religious concerns disconnected from the secular: 'The length of the penultimate must
every time be traversed anew for the sake of the ultimate'[35]. Immersion
into secular affairs is simply indispensable for the sake of 'what ultimately
matters'. What really needs to be done is to 'fortify the penultimate with a
more emphatic proclamation of the ultimate, and also to safeguard (keep
alive) the ultimate by taking due care of the penultimate'..[36]..

I have dwelt on Bonhoeffer because of his undeniable influence on
Sobrino, particularly in the latter's framing of the Jesus-figure. Because
Jesus lives in close contact with that 'profundity in reality which stands up
for human beings', therefore 'God is not for him something that has been
added to historical (secular) life, and much less something that is opposed
to it. Jesus invokes God in order to radicalize the historical setting, and to
uphold that core of the inexhaustible and non-manipulable mystery that
makes itself translucent in the historical setting'[37]. Just like Bonhoeffer,
Sobrino lets the 'yes' to the 'ultimate' – to the non-manipulable mystery
that affirms life – be accompanied by an unconditional 'no'. Jesus perceives God's will as a call to an unconditional 'yes' and to an equally
unconditional concomitant 'no'. He ties this to a process of discernment.
"The first step in discerning is precisely to hear God's clear 'no' to the
world of sin that dehumanizes human beings – a sin which has nothing
mysterious about it – and, above all, to uphold this 'no' through the whole
length of history, without trying to silence or to soften this voice with
absolutely nothing at all, not even – as it often happens – with apparently
orthodox theodicies. The second correlative step consists in hearing God's
'yes' to a world that ought to be reconciled and, above all, to uphold the

34. J. RATZINGER, *'Liberation Theology' (March 1984)*, in A. HENNELLY, *op. cit.*,
p. 373.
35. D. BONHOEFFER, *Ethics* (1941), ed. E. BETHGE, New York, 1978, p. 125.
36. D. BONHOEFFER, *Ethics* (1941), p. 142.
37. J. SOBRINO, *Jesús en América Latina*, p. 145: "En este sentido Dios para Jesús no
es algo añadido a la vida histórica y mucho menos algo que se oponga a la vida histórica.
Jesús invoca a Dios para radicalizar lo histórico y mantener lo que de misterio inagotable
e inmanipulable se deja traslucir en lo histórico".

utopia of this 'yes' as a task never to be abandoned, not even when history with great frequency radically questions it[38].

This way the framework has been given within which Sobrino places the partisan option for the poor. The severe and debunking tone that accompanies the latter is nothing but Bonhoeffer's 'no', inculturated this time into the social context of Latin America. The mystery of the God of life does not allow one to keep silent when confronted with the degradation and oppression of human life. Secular oppression is a religious matter. The Christian ought to debunk, denunciate, and stand up, when he sees how certain groups of people "set themselves up as absolute judges of the 'ultimate', thus dehumanizing their fellow-men"[39]. They have to make their voices heard in the realm of the 'penultimate' in the name of the 'ultimate'.

Here, I stop quoting from the text I wrote years ago in order to add some considerations about its eye-opening character and its possible effects. When elaborating on the argumentation above, I was convinced that I had made a point. Was it, indeed, so certain that Sobrino had drawn his major inspiration from Marxist sources? The least one can say is that there are serious doubts. So I rather felt proud of my modest achievement. Yet, in the meantime my critical study had, in a sense, become pointless, and this for the following reason.

If I am not mistaken, it was during the course of 1986 that a student of mine came to my office and asked for some more information about Ratzinger's 'private study'. I started telling him how I had unearthed some misreadings in that study, especially concerning the question of the 'ultimate' and 'the penultimate'. Having explained this, I, in a self-assured way, stood up and took from one of the shelves of my library Vittorio Messori's interview with Ratzinger; for I knew that the cardinal's 'private study' was reprinted in this book. I immediately found the passages in which Sobrino's orthodoxy was put into question, such as "'His faith is converted into fidelity'. As a consequence, faith in God

38. *Ibid.*, p. 157: "El primer paso para discernir es, por tanto, oír el claro 'no' de Dios al mundo de pecado que deshumaniza al hombre, y no tiene nada de misterioso, y sobre todo mantener ese 'no' a lo largo de la historia, sin intentar acallar o endulzar esta voz absolutamente con nada, ni siquiera – como es frecuente – con teodiceas aparentemente ortodoxas. El segundo paso correlativo es oír el 'sí' de Dios a un mundo que tiene que ser reconciliado y, sobre todo mantener la utopía de ese 'sí' como tarea inabandonable, aún cuando la historia con gran frecuencia la cuestiona radicalmente". For the 'yes' and the concomitant 'no' in Bonhoeffer, see *Ethics* (1941), *op. cit.*, p. 219: "It is the 'yes' to creation, atonement and redemption, and the no of condemnation and death pronounced against life that has fallen away from its origin, its essence, and goal. But no one who knows Christ can hear the 'yes' without the 'no', or the 'no' without the 'yes'".

39. J. SOBRINO, *op. cit.*, p. 145: "Cuando los hombres se erigen en absolutos jueces de lo último deshumanizan a otros hombres".

has basically been replaced with 'fidelity to history'". But, to my surprise and dismay, I was by no means able to put my finger on the passage I had been critiquing in my article. I could hardly believe my eyes: the text crucial to me – "'*Jesus is faithful to the profound conviction that the mystery of men... is really (the) ultimate*'" [40] – had simply disappeared from the new edition, without leaving any trace of the surgical removal that had taken place (there were surely no indications that the document had been shortened)[41].

Is this a reason for rejoicing or for sadness? I suspect that Ratzinger must have heard of some criticism leveled against his position concerning the ultimate, and that embarrassed by it, he or one of his advisers (or a staff member) had deemed it convenient to remove the disputed passage[42]. At any rate, the "abyss (Bultmann speaks of a grave)"[43] that separates the 'then' and the 'now' reappeared in a new context, that of the test of orthodoxy.

II. WEAK EXEGETICAL BASIS?

Once cleansed of the suspicion that it might have been using Marxist-inspired hermeneutics, Sobrino's christology with its clear option for the materially poor as the privileged inheritors of the kingdom, is apparently not immune to further objections. As a matter of fact, independent of Roman investigations, this christology also came under attack from the side of scholars who pointed to the weakness of its exegetical basis. This is the topic I briefly want to explore in the next pages: suppose that

---

40. J. RATZINGER, *'Liberation Theology' (March 1984)*, in A. HENNELLY, *op. cit.*, p. 372.

41. J. RATZINGER, *Un texte de 'theologien privé'*, in J. RATZINGER–V. MESSORI, *Entretien sur la foi*, Paris, Fayard, 1985, pp. 226-227: "(a) Au sujet de la foi, par exemple, un théologien sud-américain affirme: l'experience que Jésus a de Dieu est radicalement historique. 'Sa foi se convertit en fidélité'. Par conséquent, on substitue fondamentalement à la foi 'fidélité à l'histoire. (b) Ici a lieu cette fusion entre Dieu et l'histoire qui permet de conserver la formule de Chalcédoine sur Jésus, même si c'est dans un sens complètement transformé". The omitted sentence should have come between (a) and (b). In this version the name of Sobrino was replaced with the circumlocution 'a certain South American theologian affirms'; whereas the indication of the page numbers in brackets has been removed. The latter is also the case with the English and German translations mentioned in footnote 17.

42. V. Messori maintains that the version of the 'private study' in his edition is integral: "Revenons donc à ce texte 'privé' qui a précédé *l'Instruction* de l'automne 1984. Les pages suivantes (*en italiques*) le reproduisent intégralement" (J. RATZINGER–V. MESSORI, *Entretien sur la foi*, *op. cit.*, p. 213).

43. J. RATZINGER, *'Liberation Theology' (March 1984)*, in A. HENNELLY, *op. cit.*, p. 370.

Sobrino's christology is orthodox, which I think it is, can it for this reason stand the test of scientific biblical studies?

1. Sobrino's exegesis as proof-texting

As early as 1983 Michael Cook made some critical remarks about Sobrino's starting point for christology, notably the historical Jesus. More in particular, he questions the indiscriminate use Sobrino makes of the notion historical. Sobrino, it is argued, attempts to present a biography of Jesus which mainly focuses on the (Marcan-based) transition between two stages: "the springtime in Galilee and the crisis in Galilee that led to Jerusalem; the latter involving a real shift for Jesus himself in terms of his understanding of his mission"[44]. This is, indeed, what Sobrino developed: Jesus initially inaugurated the kingdom with active deeds of power, but in the second stage, he was compelled to "display a love fraught with suffering". The threat of persecution had become a reality. These two stages find their application in Christian discipleship: "discipleship no longer means following Jesus in his messianic function. It now means following his own person in all its scandalous concreteness, following him even to the cross"[45].

I confine myself to just rendering three major statements put forward by Cook. (i) Sobrino mainly follows the Gospel of Mark. Now, in this gospel, the dramatic deepening of Jesus' fidelity to the Father is given full weight, and this as a model to be internalized by Jesus' disciples today: their commitment to the kingdom will also call forth opposition and persecution[46]. (ii) But, Cook asks, is this presentation of the life of Jesus not primarily exhortative and kerygmatic, instead of offering a historical account of the events: "It strikes me", Cook says, that what Sobrino "means by historical is kerygmatic... We know that Jesus remained faithful to the Father because the Father raised him from the dead and so vindicated him against his enemies. This is a theological, not a historical statement, insofar as it is talking about the action of God as vindication of Jesus"[47]. (iii) Exegetical studies show that the dramatic transition from stage one to stage two in Jesus' life "is at least structurally, pure Mark"[48]. Is it not the case

44. M. COOK, *Jesus from the other side of history: Christology in Latin America*, in *Theological Studies* 44:2 (1983), p. 273.
45. J. SOBRINO, *Christology at the Crossroads, op. cit.*, p. 118.
46. M. COOK, *art. laud.*, p. 274: "Unquestioniably, for Mark, who Jesus is is inextricably intertwined with who we are as disciples".
47. *Ibid.*, p. 273.
48. *Ibid.*, p. 274.

that Sobrino's approach, in that it bases itself on Mark's version of
the Jesus story, "wants to claim too much about the historical Jesus
without much evidence"[49]?

Cook then ventures to ask whether Sobrino's emphasis on the praxis
of Jesus (examined with the eyes of faith) does not have a typically Latin
American flavor to it. His answer is clear: If Sobrino is not, in the first
instance, interested in the historical truth of Jesus, he is, on the other
hand, passionately concerned about the faith praxis that spurs on Latin
American Christians to stand up for the cause of the downtrodden. This
commitment is situated in a very concrete historical setting, and this
explains Sobrino's preference for the term 'historical'. What counts for
him is that Jesus' praxis and his fidelity to the Father may find a continuation in the Latin American Christians' commitment to the cause of the
poor, all the more so that there are "structural similarities" between the
'then' (the persecuted Jesus) and the 'now' (oppression in Latin America): "I suspect", Cook concludes, that the perception of these similarities "is the real motive for the incessant appeal to the historical Jesus".
But he is quick to add that "for the sake of theological discussion, clarity on this question is needed, i.e. one cannot use the term 'historical '
indiscriminately"[50].

At this juncture John Meier, the author of *A Marginal Jew: Rethinking the Historical Jesus* (1991), joins in with further criticism in an article published in 1988. He first starts with a gesture of benevolence (*cap-
tatio benevolentiae*) by stating that Jon Sobrino's christology has been
"forged in the furnace of oppression, violence, and the need for a liberating praxis and theology in El Salvador", and that it represents "a fierce
drive to make academic theology speak to and be responsible to the
lived Christianity of a suffering people yearning for liberation from
political, social, and economic enslavement". But he then introduces a
distinction with far-reaching consequences: Insofar as this christology,
he says, shares the concern for the liberation of the poor from enslavement, it is able to produce a powerful discourse. Yet, insofar as it
engages in the "discourse and trappings of academic scholarship, thus
choosing to play the academic game", it must allow itself to be "judged
by the rules of the game"[51]. According to these rules what has to be

49. *Ibid.*, p. 272.
50. *Ibid.*, p. 274.
51. J. MEIER, *The bible as a source for theology*, in *The Catholic Theological Society
of America* (Proceedings of the Forty-Third Annual Convention, Toronto, June, 15-18,
1988) 43 (1988), p. 2: "They (Sobrino and Segundo) have chosen to take up the discourse and trappings of academic scholarship, complete with learned footnotes and references to noted exegetes to bolster their positions and debate their confreres".

probed is whether Sobrino has succeeded in incorporating the 'quest for the historical Jesus' into his christology. Against this background four major objections come to the fore.

(i) In his *Christology at the Crossroads* Sobrino admits that the exegetical grounding of his christology could have been more solid. In fact, Meier observes, this work is more a matter of hermeneutics than of serious exegesis. The leading authors referred to are Bultmann, Rahner, and Pannenberg, whereas only scattered references are made to a handful of German exegetes, with a total neglect of North American specialists in historical research. For Meier it is unforgivable that a christology that claims to be based on the historical Jesus fails to critically discuss "the criteria we are to use to discern the authentic material": "At times, the historical Jesus seems to be the Jesus insofar as he fits into Sobrino's program of liberation theology", which makes – Meier provokingly adds – that "we are not all that far from the proof-text use of Scripture in the old Catholic manuals of dogmatic theology"[52]. In Sobrino's new book, too, *Jesus in Latin America*, the concept of the 'historical Jesus' "continues to remain fuzzy". It is mostly equated with "a christology that emphasizes the humanity of Jesus or Jesus' earthly career", without asking which facts in this career can be historically verified[53]. This lack of precision can be shown with respect to two major statements Sobrino holds dear: first, that the poor are the privileged addressees of the Kingdom, and second, that primarily the Pharisees are to be blamed for Jesus' execution.

(ii) As far as the economically poor are concerned, it is highly debatable, Meier argues, that they are the sole individuals whose concerns Jesus took to heart: "Sobrino constantly emphasizes Jesus' partisanship and favoritism towards the poor, the oppressed and the sinners. These various groups tend to be lumped together as the object of Jesus' favor, and solidarity with them is seen as the cause of opposition to Jesus and finally of his death. Yet E.P. Sanders, in his fine book *Jesus and Judaism* points out that it is illegitimate to treat all these groups as one"[54]. The argument immediately focuses on Jesus' trial and the reason(s) for his crucifixion. Hardly are there indications, he says, that Jesus' dealing with the economically poor may have caused a major

---

52. *Ibid.*, p. 3.
53. *Ibid.*, p. 4.
54. *Ibid.*, p. 4. With reference to E.P. SANDERS, *Jesus and Judaism*, Philadelphia, Fortress, 1985.

scandal, since concern for the weak is a recurrent theme in the Old Testament literature. What really provoked anger, among rich and poor alike, was Jesus' free offer of forgiveness to public sinners, to those considered to have broken away from Judaism. Among these sinners figure the tax collectors, who were all but economically deprived; one could even call them 'oppressors' to use Sobrino's vocabulary. It is thus more prudent to posit that Jesus has offended "*many* sincere and zealous Jews" from all strata of the society of his time. Moreover, if one looks at the final clash, Jesus' attack on the temple, it is evident that this gesture not only alienated the Jerusalem priests but also the average Jewish believer: "Just as it is too simplistic to say that all of Jesus' audience was economically poor, so it is too simplistic to say that Jesus offended only the rich and the powerful"[55]. Meier acknowledges that the precise reasons why Jesus was arrested and crucified are by no means clear. He finds it grotesque, however, that Sobrino omits probing into the discussions that historians and exegetes engage in about such a highly complicated matter. Without any hesitancy Sobrino "proceeds to reconstruct the scenario of Jesus' Jewish and Roman trials, complete with a trial before the Sanhedrin" (in his eyes the Jerusalem priests and Pharisees are the false mediators of the kingdom). This naiveté makes one wonder whether he is just not 'proof-texting' to bolster the 'preferential option for the poor'.

(iii) Sobrino knows about redactional tendencies in the gospels, but he draws no conclusions from this insight. Because of this neglect, he unfortunately does not avoid the pitfall of anti-Semitism. In one of the passages of *Jesus in Latin America*[56] it is argued that the Johannine gospel makes the whole Jewish people and not just the Jewish leaders responsible for the persecution of Jesus. At this juncture Meier sarcastically asks whether Sobrino has forgotten that when John speaks about the 'Jews', in a negative sense, he only means the hostile authorities in Jerusalem. What is still more debatable, however, is that in the same Johannine context he points out that the Pharisees were famed for their excommunicating those who acknowledged Jesus as Messiah. Not only is this a redactional arrangement by the author of the fourth gospel, but in the meantime historical research has demonstrated that "the presentation of the Pharisees as *the* ultimate power in Judaism, before whom even the rulers must tremble, is a post-A.D. 70 picture and hardly

55. *Ibid.*, p. 4.
56. J. SOBRINO, *Jesús en América Latina, op. cit.*, p. 135.

reflects the historical Pharisees of Jesus' days. Contrary to Sobrino the Pharisees probably had nothing to do as a group with Jesus' death"[57].

(iv) According to Sobrino Latin American christology is not primarily interested in determining data about Jesus with exactitude: "its interest rather consists in discovering and historically insuring the basic structure of Jesus' practice and preaching" to be able to understand "the internal historicity of his person"[58]. To perceive the internal historicity of Jesus (what he stood for) is precisely what matters for Latin Americans committed to the cause of the downtrodden, and this leads – in terms of method – to the acceptance of a mirror relation between Jesus' commitment and that of the church of the poor[59]. Sobrino feels justified in using this procedure because he is convinced that the Latin American communities are replicating the first Christian communities that produced the gospels. Meier, now, decries this thesis as "naiveté once removed". The New Testament writings confront us with a plurality of Jesus portraits, and not just with one monolithic Jesus. This observation leads to the final verdict: "One is left wondering how, if at all, the Bible has really been a source of theology for Sobrino – or for liberation theology in general"[60]. Is this not again, I would retort, a case in point of sheer overkill?

2. What if exegesis were to hold a veto power over the business of theology?

Presumably, the editorial board of the proceedings of the Catholic Theological Society of America must have been embarrassed with Meier's demolition of liberation theology's biblical basis. At any rate, the board found it necessary to also publish what obviously seems to be a paper read by a respondent, Jon Nilson, who took up the defense of the accused. The title of the contribution in question is *A Response to John P. Meier.*

Nilson takes seriously Meier's accusations but at the same time contemplates that what is at stake in them is the future of a possible dialogue between exegetes and systematic theologians. He therefore posits the problem, in all its acuity, as follows: "In its starkest terms, the most significant question posed by Professor Meier's paper is this: Do the

57. J. MEIER, *art. laud.*, p. 5.
58. J. SOBRINO, *Jesus in Latin America*, pp. 73-74 (quoted by Meier).
59. J. SOBRINO, *Jesus in Latin America, op. cit.*, pp. 74-75 (quoted by Meier): "To anyone living and suffering history on the South American continent it seems altogether probable that 'Jesus was like that'".
60. J. MEIER, *art. laud.*, p. 7.

methods of historical criticism hold a veto power over anything which liberation theologians (or any theologians, for that matter) may say about the 'historical Jesus'?" He knows why he is framing the question this way. For if the answer is 'yes', which appears to be Meier's position, then "an impasse – indeed, an unbridgeable chasm – (is going to) inevitably separate the liberation theologians from the exegetes"[61]. But is such a situation really desirable? Have not North American theologians, supposing they have indeed assimilated the fine points of exegetical foundations, something to learn from their Latin American confreres? And is the same not true for specialists in historical research?

The point Nilson is hinting at is the particular experience of the Latin American theologians. They are not only living amidst a situation of distress but are also risking their lives just by writing about the message and deeds of Jesus of Nazareth. Is it not the case, Nilson continues, that specialists in the quest of the 'historical Jesus' are often overlooking the actual faith experience of the believers, as a second important source for doing christology? Looked at with the eyes of faith, some deeper dimensions in Jesus' life practice can be discerned which pure scientific knowledge is most probably unable to uncover: "When we North Americans read liberation theology, we are overhearing an anguished communal exploration of the good news Jesus embodies and proclaims. Those explorers attend to but refuse to be governed by what Professor Meier calls 'the rules of the academic game'. Injustice, oppression, suffering, and death: these constitute the main lenses through which the Gospels are read in Latin America, not the methods of historical criticism"[62]. To be sure, Nilson invites the liberation theologians to pay more attention (in as far as their interdisciplinary research allows this) to the findings of historical research. But he also invites the other party to take cognizance of the specific *locus theologicus* liberation theologians are exploring: the liberating presence of God in the world of the poor.

Instructive as Nilson's *A Response to John P. Meier* may be, his call for taking seriously the believers' experience stands somewhat in need, I think, of being complemented by a deeper probing into the method of historical research. What I mean by this will become clearer below, when I address the question of 'value-free' exegesis. But before tackling this question, I would like to briefly return to Meier's comments on Sobrino.

---

61. J. NILSON, *A response to John P. Meier*, in *The Catholic Theological Society of America (Proceedings of the Forty-Third Annual Convention), Toronto, June, 15-18, 1988)* 43 (1988), p. 15.

62. *Ibid.,* p. 16.

Meier has, without doubt, made a point by showing that Sobrino's neglect of consulting more exegetical studies concerning John's treatment of the 'Jews' has landed him, unwittingly perhaps, in the camp of anti-Semitism. Now, intrigued by this issue, I looked up in Sobrino's new book on christology, *Jesus the Liberator* (Spanish edition 1991) the passages dealing with Jesus' trials to see whether he had readjusted his insights. I was very pleased to observe that this was indeed the case. When commenting on 'persecution in John's Gospel' for example, Sobrino writes: "John's Gospel is the one which shows with the greatest wealth of detail that persecution followed Jesus throughout his life. In the passages I shall quote in this section, 'the Jews' frequently appear as those responsible. In fact, however, Jesus' main enemies are not the Jews in general, but the Pharisees – associated on five occasions with the 'chief priests'. In the passion it is the chief priests who are the main enemy, though they have also been mentioned earlier, and from John 18:3 onwards it is only the chief priests, without the Pharisees, who appear as Jesus' deadly enemies". And he continues: "From a historical point of view, the Pharisees' responsibility is exaggerated, and reflects the church situation after AD 70, when the church distanced itself from the synagogue; on the other hand the responsibility attributed to the priestly aristocracy is historical"[63].

Thus Sobrino has seized the opportunity to delve deeper into historical questions, although as he himself declares his concern is rather with the practice-oriented issue of the struggle between the anti-kingdom and the kingdom: "The account in the political trial, and even more in the religious trial, is extremely controversial from a historical point of view, and I can add nothing to clarify it. My analysis here will be in terms of the model I put forward above. The divinities and their mediations are at war, and so therefore are the mediators... Jesus' trial is also the trial of his God"[64]. This enmity comes to the fore, in the first instance, in Jesus' trial before the chief priests (who rejected his rebellious picture of God); subsequently, and to prolong this, in the political trial where Jesus was presented as posing "a greater thread to the existing society and to its socio-political organization than Barabbas"[65].

63. J. Sobrino, *Jesus the Liberator*, Kent, Burns & Oates, 1993, p. 198; with reference to R. Aguirre, *Jesus y la multitud a la luz del evangelio de Juan*, in *Estudios Eclesiasticos* 128-129 (1980), p. 128.

64. *Ibid.*, p. 204. See also *ibid.*, p. 206: "The anti-Kingdom (a society structured round the Temple in this case) actively rejected the Kingdom and its mediators, actively rejected the mediator".

65. *Ibid.*, p. 209.

One may presume that Meier would be satisfied with the more accurate historical data Sobrino has inserted in his picture of Jesus' trial. However I am not convinced that he would be content with Sobrino's staging of a battle between the anti-reign and the reign. This terminology, inspiring as it may be for Christians engaged in a struggle for justice, would find no mercy in Meier's eyes. I would counter, however, by asking whether what Meier has to say about the poor (their minimized role in the historical Jesus drama) is in turn also that convincing? And more specifically, does it invite to a 'praxis'? To broach this subject one has to turn to Meier's work itself, and here I am left with mixed feelings.

As far as the two volumes of *A Marginal Jew* are concerned, I, on the one hand, cannot but admire their methodological rigor. This rigor makes Meier say that throughout these volumes he purposely eschewed "any highly speculative theory that 'explains it all' in favor of a judicious weighing of evidence in order to arrive at modest but fairly secure conclusions about what the historical Jesus did and said"[66]. Yet, on the other, I cannot help but feeling that, in spite of this zeal for neatly reconstructing historically reliable facts, he at times seems to follow a hidden agenda which precisely consists in the removal of models for committed discipleship today.

His rigorous method both allows and encourages him to eliminate any position that he deems to fall into extremes (but as I will make clear below: these corrections also seem to follow a certain hidden agenda). I start by giving two examples of rejected positions and the way this rejection is accounted for. (a) Instead of holding (as Dodd does) that Jesus' preaching of the Kingdom went in the direction of a realized eschatology[67], Meier argues that Jesus most probably did not abandon the basic scheme of his mentor, John the Baptist, namely the proclamation of the imminent coming of the eschatological kingdom, and that it is only within this scheme (which implies that Jesus baptized) that one has to place the scenes depicting some joyful anticipations of this final event. Such anticipations are the miracles (the sick are healed), the proclamation of 'good news' to the poor (the sorrowful rejoice) and the table fellowship with tax collectors and sinners (God is also merciful to the religiously marginalized)[68].

---

66. J. MEIER, *A Marginal Jew: Rethinking the Historical Jesus*, Volume II: *Mentor, Message, and Miracles*, New York, Doubleday, 1994, p. 1049.

67. *Ibid.*, p. 350: "...already an approach such as C.H. Dodd's, which tries to collapse the message of the parables of the historical Jesus into a completely realized eschatology, must be seen with suspicion".

68. *Ibid.*, p. 154: "Jesus' miracles, his proclamation of good news to the poor, his expansive fellowship with the not-so-poor yet religiously marginalized toll collectors and

At this juncture the three anticipations are kept apart, but in the next example I am going to discuss, there is an attempt to bring about a certain hierarchy among them. I now tackle this matter. (b) When discussing the position of exegetes who see in Jesus' miracles and exorcisms the major reason why the priestly establishment in Jerusalem, with Caiaphas as the high priest, was after him[69], Meier does not want to exclude that these acts where only an 'aggravating circumstance'. The real reasons lay elsewhere, he says, and relate to what one might call the overall pattern or 'Gestalt' of Jesus: "as popular preacher and teller of parables, *plus* authoritative interpreter of the Law and teacher of morality, *plus* proclaimer and realizer of the eschatological kingdom of God, *plus* miracle worker actualizing his own proclamation"[70]. In this light, he continues, one should not ask what was *the* reason why Caiaphas wanted Jesus arrested and executed, but instead take as a working hypothesis that there was a convergence of reasons: "The imploding reasons that moved Caiaphas to action no doubt included: Jesus' proclamation that the definitive kingdom was soon to come and put an end to the present state of affairs...: his claim to authoritatively teach the will of God for people's lives, even when this seems in certain instances to run counter to provisions in the law of Moses, his ability to attract a large following...; his practice of a special rite of baptism...; and his freewheeling personal conduct that expressed itself in table fellowship with toll collectors and sinners. Taken together this was disturbing enough"[71].

I have quoted these passages at length for they are crucial in order to unearth some hidden agenda the examination of which I now begin. As a matter of fact, I have no problem with the proposal to admit of a convergence of reasons that led to Jesus' execution. The difficulty arises when I see that the miracles are said to provide just an 'aggravating circumstance', whereas other 'implosive reasons' are given prominence. To be sure, Meier is not concealing why he is doing this. His aim is to reconstruct the historical facts, set free as it were from the redactional

---

sinners all testify to and to some degree actualize God's definitive coming in power to save his people Israel – in other words the kingdom of God"; and *ibid.*, 155: "...the Son of Man bringing in the joy of the kingdom in the teeth of opposition".

69. *Ibid.*, pp. 626-627: "Some scholars look to Jesus' miracles as a major explanation of why he was finally executed... Hollenbach even goes further (by holding that) Jesus' first exorcism led inevitably to his crucifixion... In my opinion, though, we should leave open the possibility that the miracles were an 'aggravating circumstance' leading to Jesus' death".

70. *Ibid.*, p. 624.

71. *Ibid.*, pp. 627-628.

staging of the evangelists. Practically all the evangelists set great store
by Jesus' miracles by saying that that they caused various parties to plot
Jesus' death, yet in the texts about the trial miracles do not figure in the
list of accusations[72]. Confronted with this strange given, the 'historian
Meier' has to weigh which of the two versions is more probable in its
truth-claim, for credit should not immediately be given to the literary
composition of an evangelist. Granted that this is a serious problem, I
nevertheless ask myself whether the 'reconstructer Meier' is not somewhat underplaying the importance of the miracles in Jesus' life as a
whole, especially when one associates them (as he does elsewhere) with
the topic of the good news proclaimed to the poor. At this juncture, it
looks as if their importance must be downplayed so as to strengthen the
logical coherence of the reasoning concerning the trial[73].

Logic is commendable, but one can also press things too much into a
logical scheme, with the effect that the reasoning used to this end turns
out to be too schematic, if not arbitrary. I give two examples where this
might be the case: (i) The miracles are said to be not that ominous for
Jesus because they did not, after all, harm anybody (think of the many
deeds of healing); on the contrary, they benefitted those healed[74]. True,
to perform miracles is not in itself a criminal act; yet it can be viewed as
offensive by the officials, as something that indirectly undermines their
authority. And this the more so, I would add, as the deeds of healing
were intimately connected with Jesus announcing the good news to the
poor (a – considerable?[75] – amount of his followers). By reducing the
importance of the miracles in the list of accusations, is not Meier also
downplaying their significance in the ministry of Jesus to the poor? That
for me is the basic question. In a footnote to his study of the Q Beatitudes he makes this link: the proclamation of the good news to the poor
is an important part of Jesus' ministry, and this, he continues, is confirmed by the reply that is given to the disciples of John the Baptist;

72. *Ibid.*, p. 626: "…all the evangelists are at pains to tie their Gospels together as literary works having coherent plots by signaling early on in their stories that Jesus' miracles caused various parties to plot his death… Yet, when we finally do come to the arrest
and trial(s) of Jesus, we hear nothing about miracles as a reason for execution".
73. *Ibid.*, p. 628. Meier states that only in the context of the multiple major causes the
miracles acquire "a much more ominous and dangerous coloration than they would have
if seen in isolation".
74. *Ibid.*, p. 626: "Since the gospel records no miracle of Jesus that directly harms or
punishes a person, indeed since the gospel miracles are almost entirely beneficient in their
effects, it is difficult to see how deeds like healing the sick and freeing people from the
power of demons could be considered criminal".
75. The examination of the followers will be one of the topics to be treated in the
Third Volume.

with an allusion to Isa 61:6 various miracles are recited culminating in the statement: 'And the poor have the good news preached to them'[76]. But Meier is then quick to add that the poor are not the only ones to whom Jesus addressed his message: "All that is said above should not be taken to mean that *every* follower of Jesus was literally poor or that Jesus never addressed anyone but the poor"[77]. Similar restrictions also come to the fore elsewhere: "We begin to see why Jesus was not interested in and did not issue pronouncements about concrete social and political reforms... He was not proclaiming the reform of the world; he was proclaiming the end of the world"[78].

(ii) Meir's second volume is well structured, too well perhaps. It takes its starting point in the relationship between the ministry of John the Baptist and that of Jesus, to then examine, in a second step, the special input of Jesus (traveling preacher, miracle worker). In passing the direction is set for the third volume in which the good or bad reception of Jesus' message will be studied, together with a detailed analysis of the trial(s). This structure – including its starting point and end point – is so solid that all other data we can gather about the historical Jesus shuld be able to fit into this structure, according to a scale of importance[79]. My question, however, is whether this rigid structure does not lead to extreme value judgments that could have been avoided by means of a less inflexible scheme. My question again relates to the place of the poor in Jesus' ministry. One gets the impression that Jesus' table fellowship with tax collectors and sinners is regarded as being far more important (for him and, in extrapolation, for the church) than his dealing with the poor. Indeed, if the starting point is the comparison with the activities of John the Baptist (tax collectors, and prostitutes came to him to be baptized)[80], then one may expect that in Meier's reconstruction this group of people will be given a comparable significance in Jesus' ministry. If one takes into account, secondly, that one of Meier's central questions is to

76. *Ibid.*, p. 385: "That Jesus saw an important part of his ministry to be proclaiming the 'good news' of the coming kingdom of God to the poor – the very thing he is doing in the Q beatitudes – is confirmed by the reply to the disciples of John the Baptist (Mat 11:2-6; Lk 7:18-23). The reply, after reciting various miracles, reaches the climax of its narration of Jesus' ministry with an allusion to Isa 61:1: 'And the poor have the good news preached to them'. As we was in Chapter 13 there is good reason for taking the substance of this pericope as historical".

77. *Ibid.*, p. 385.

78. *Ibid.*, p. 331.

79. At times the difference gets blurred between things important in judicial matters and things important in the order of salvation.

80. *Ibid.*, p. 169.

figure out, in terms of judicial weight, what have been the convergent reasons for Jesus' execution, then it is evident again that primacy will be given to his company with the (not so poor) publicans rather than with the poor. The text I am about to quote, speaks for itself: "His (Jesus') *bon vivant* existence with robbers and sinners was therefore something more scandalous and ominous than a mere matter of breaking purity rules dear to the *haberim* or the Pharisees". The breaking of purity rules was the practice of the "so called people of the land (the *amme ha'ares*)", the "simple and uneducated Jewish masses who did not have the time, learning, nor means to follow the punctilious observances"[81], in short, the poor.

To sum up. As far as the rejection of present eschatology (Dodd) was concerned, no hierarchy was needed (rejoicing poor and repentant sinners are, each in their own way, anticipations of the eschatological kingdom). But when it comes to the trial(s), such a hierarchy apparently matters. Considering this 'special topic' as provisionally resolved, however, Meier in his general conclusion to the second volume returns to, and amplifies, the grand scheme he started with. Jesus is presented as the new embodiment of Elijah, the wonder worker *par excellence* of the Old Testament (no allusion is made any more to Isa 61,1: And the poor have the good news preached to them). What has been atypical of John the Baptist now becomes typical of Jesus. Jesus is so powerful a miracle worker, in the perspective of the end of the world, that he is even able to raise the dead (Lazarus). He is the enigmatic eschatological figure we are historically confronted with, and – here comes the verdict – who cannot be domesticated by contemporary preachers, be it in the style of emotional Jesus piety ('my sweet Lord') or in the style of socio-political reforms undertaken in the name of Jesus. The eschatological Jesus "stands in stark contrast to one popular portrait of the historical Jesus found in literature today: Jesus was a kindhearted rabbi who preached gentleness and love in the spirit of Rabbi Hillel. This domestication of a strange first-century marginal Jew bears a curious resemblance to the domestication of Jesus undertaken by Thomas Jefferson some two centuries ago. The advantage and appeal of the domesticated Jesus is obvious: He is instantly relevant to and usable by contemporary ethics, homilies, political programs, and ideologies of various stripes. In contrast, a first-century Jew who presents himself as the eschatological prophet of the imminent arrival of God's kingdom, a kingdom that the prophet makes present and effective by miracles reminiscent of Elijah and

81. *Ibid.*, p. 149.

Elisha, is not so instantly relevant and usable". And yet this is the 'authentic' Jesus retrievable by modern historical research[82].

What if exegetes (historians) were to hold a veto right over theology? It would imply that their historically reconstructed Jesus cannot possibly be regarded as a source for religiously inspired ethics or social praxis. This seems to be the core reason why Meier blames Sobrino for not having a solid grounding in the historical Jesus. But is this bleak perspective ('imitation of Christ', forget it!) any better than Sobrino's attempt to come up with a Latin American christology which allegedly lacks a historical foundation?

CONCLUSION

In this article I pursued a modest goal, namely, to demonstrate, first of all, that seemingly convincing arguments propounded in order to place Latin American christologies in an unfavorable light are, in turn, not free of flaws. And, secondly, that a dispute mounted against a certain type of christology is itself not always free of value judgments that follow a hidden agenda in their reasoning. In putting forward these two points, I am not saying that Sobrino's christology is impeccable. But to reject it basically on ideological grounds (an aversion to orthopraxis, or an aversion to models of imitation of Christ), is, in my view, highly questionable.

Faculty of Theology   Georges DE SCHRIJVER
Katholieke Universiteit Leuven
St. Michielsstraat 6
B-3000 Leuven

---

82. *Ibid.*, p. 1045.

RADICAL CHRISTOLOGIES?
AN ANALYSIS OF THE CHRISTOLOGIES OF
JOHN HICK AND PAUL KNITTER

John Hick and Paul Knitter are among the best known religious pluralists. Their collaboration as editors of *The Myth of Christian Uniqueness*[1] clearly identified them with the pluralist position that claims that
Christ may not be the only savior and Christianity is not the sole vehicle
of salvation. Their work has advocated pluralism, shaped its theological
formulation, and responded to criticisms generated from within and outside of the scholarly Christian community. They are often classified
together, interpreted and analyzed as having a similar, if not an identical,
theology of religions. While it is true that Hick and Knitter have similar
ideas about the pluralism of religions and its impact on Christian theology, they do have significant differences that are increasingly identifi-
able in their recent writings. I intend to chronicle those differences and
argue that Hick has become more firmly entrenched in his position, and
to some degree more radical in defense of his position against critics,
while Knitter has softened his version of pluralism and modified his
thinking in the light of criticism. The result is what I will call a "hard
pluralism" for Hick for which he makes few concessions to critics, and
a "soft pluralism" for Knitter which he has adjusted significantly in the
light of criticism and now borders on inclusivism.

I. A PRELIMINARY WORD ON JOHN HICK

Preliminary to the comparison of Hick and Knitter, it is important to
address a fundamental issue in the work of John Hick and the readings
of Hick by both his critics and sympathizers. That issue is whether
Hick's work is Christian theology, even a theology of religions, or
whether it is philosophy of religion. I think that much of the criticism of
Hick's pluralistic hypothesis has understood his effort to be a Christian
theology of religions. According to Hick, this is not what it is. Distinguishing clearly that his work on pluralism is philosophy of religion and

---

1. J. HICK and P.F. KNITTER (eds.), *The Myth of Christian Uniqueness: Toward a Pluralistic Theology of Religions*, Maryknoll, NY, Orbis, 1987.

not theology will help to clarify much of the discussion surrounding it. A number of articles debating the merits and deficiencies of John Hick's work leads me to address some of the issues within this debate[2]. His work on christology, most fully articulated in *The Metaphor of God Incarnate*[3], however, is constructive theology demonstrating that Hick moves fluidly between roles as philosopher of religion and theologian.

The subtitle of *The Myth of Christian Uniqueness*, "Toward a Pluralistic Theology of Religions", as well as elements of Hick's individual contribution "The Non-Absoluteness of Christianity", have added to the confusion of the theology versus philosophy of religion claims. In his chapter Hick, supporting a move to pluralism, wrote of a "theological Rubicon" which the contributors to the book were facing and being asked to cross. The substance of this metaphorical crossing of the Rubicon is, briefly summarized, the move from the exclusivist position in which one needs explicitly to be a Christian in order to be saved, or the inclusivist position in which Christ is the savior of all persons whether or not they are Christians or acknowledge Christ, to the pluralist position which accords salvific parity to all of the major traditions without reference to Christ or Christianity for salvation/liberation/fulfillment. The very language of a theological Rubicon places the work in a theological perspective. In the article Hick briefly chronicled the history of the Christian disposition that salvation exists only within Christianity (the exclusivist position) and the slightly more open successive position that salvation is available to all religious persons through the merits of the death and resurrection of Christ who came to save all humankind (the inclusivist position). He made it clear that his contribution is as a Christian when he wrote: "[I] am writing here as a Christian specifically about our Christian attitude to other religions, and accordingly I shall be concerned with Christian rather than with other forms of religious absolutism"[4]. This in itself is not necessarily subject to misinterpretation as it is quite acceptable for a Christian to write philosophy of religion

---

2. Among them are: J. HICK, *Straightening the Record: Some Response to Critics*, in *Modern Theology* 6:2 (1990) 187-195; S.B. TWISS, *The Philosophy of Religious Pluralism: A Critical Appraisal of Hick and his Critics*, in *The Journal of Religion* 70:4 (1990) 533-568; T.R. STINNETT, *John Hick's Pluralistic Theory of Religion*, in *The Journal of Religion* 70:4 (1990) 569-588; G. LOUGHLIN, *Prefacing Pluralism: John Hick and the Mastery of Religion*, in *Modern Theology* 7:1 (1990) 29-55; J. HICK, *A Response to Gerard Loughlin*, in *Modern Theology* 7:1 (1990) 57-66.

3. J. HICK, *The Metaphor of God Incarnate*, London, SCM, 1993.

4. J. HICK, *The Non-Absoluteness of Christianity*, in *The Myth of Christian Uniqueness*, p. 18; see also p. 24 for a similar instance in which Hick refers to himself as a Christian.

that focuses on Christian claims. However, it is the final paragraph of Hick's chapter that could engender some confusion. It reads:

> Finally, in this chapter I have been treating the question of the place of Christianity within the wider religious life of humanity as a topic in Christian theology.... But when one stands back from one's own tradition to attempt a philosophical interpretation of the fact of religious pluralism one has to take full account of nonpersonal as well as of personal awareness of the Ultimate. I have tried to do this elsewhere; but it was not necessary to complicate this study, as an intra-Christian discussion, in that way[5].

This passage is ambiguous regarding the perspective from which Hick is writing. Is he standing back from his own acknowledged tradition of Christianity in order to do philosophical analysis of some of the claims of that tradition vis-à-vis other religious claims and traditions, or is he standing within the tradition of Christianity as a voice not only from, but also in some unofficial way for, that tradition? It appears that his treatment of Christianity is as one from that tradition who analyzes the claims of the tradition philosophically and not one speaking for that tradition as a theologian. But his further nuance that this is an "intra-Christian discussion" which need not be complicated by philosophical interpretations may confuse the reader.

Such ambiguity is further suggested by his discussion of christology in the article. To examine philosophically the claims of classical christology is one enterprise; to offer an alternative interpretation via an inspiration christology is another, *theological*, enterprise. By an inspiration christology Hick, following closely the work of D.M. Baillie[6], suggests that God's grace was at work in Jesus' human nature in a perfect way. Following Geoffrey Lampe[7], Hick suggests that God inspired the human spirit of Jesus in such a unique way that Jesus represents the full realization of the relationship between God and humankind. An inspiration christology does not rely on or include the claim of two natures in one person. Hick thinks that this inspiration christology is a more comprehensible understanding of the nature of Christ and recommends that it replace the traditional Chalcedonian explanation of christology of two natures in one person which he finds incomprehensible.

In instances such as this one, Hick blurs the lines between philosophy of religion and theology. For while it is certainly proper for philosophy of religion to analyze the concepts and claims of a particular theological

---

5. *Ibid.*, 34.

6. D.M. BAILLIE, *God Was in Christ*, London, Faber and Faber; and New York, Charles Scribner's Sons, 1948.

7. G. LAMPE, *God as Spirit*, Oxford, Clarendon Press, 1977.

tradition such as Christianity, it is generally not the role of philosophy of religion to offer alternative constructive positions which are designed to reshape the tradition from within. Occasionally Hick engages in such internal reconstructions and thus takes upon himself the task of the theologian whose charge is to speak for and from within the tradition and not simply about the tradition. In so doing he opens himself to legitimate criticism from theological sources.

Turning to Hick's own writings, it is possible to determine what constitutes philosophy of religion and what distinguishes it from theology, particularly philosophical theology. In his small, widely read book, *Philosophy of Religion*, Hick distinguishes philosophy of religion from natural theology and apologetics. Natural theology attempts the rational demonstration of the existence of God, and apologetics attempts the "philosophical defense of religious beliefs" while philosophy of religion is "philosophical thinking about religion"[8]. Among other things, it studies the concepts of the religions. Hick describes philosophy as a second-order activity which stands apart from its subject matter. It is also important to note that in that work he claims that it need not, but can be, undertaken from a religious standpoint. It is obvious that Hick approaches philosophy of religion in his work from a religious standpoint and a commitment to the fundamental religious claim that some transcendent (unspecified) exists. This is why he terms his project in *An Interpretation of Religion* as "the development of a field theory of religion from a religious point of view"[9]. However, while his religious commitment is that of a Christian, his philosophical analysis of religion and the religions is not specifically Christian. Thus he is attempting what he calls "a religious but not confessional interpretation of religion"[10].

The reason it is so important to clarify the perspective from which he is writing is that many Christian theologians have criticized his work, specifically *An Interpretation of Religion*, as if it were Christian theology when it is not. It is perhaps the fact that Hick dismisses the projectionist theories of religion as credible in favor of a transcendent referent

8. J. HICK, *Philosophy of Religion*, fourth edition, Englewood Cliffs, NJ, Prentice Hall, 1990, p. 1.

9. J. HICK, *An Interpretation of Religion: Human Responses to the Transcendent*, New Haven, Yale, 1989, Preface, ix.

10. *Ibid.*, 1. The grounds for such an enterprise have been questioned by a number of critics who claim essentially that it is impossible to be religious in a generic sense without being confessional with its implications of particularity theologically, historically and culturally. Kenneth Surin in his contribution to *Christian Uniqueness Reconsidered*, *A 'Politics of Speech': Religious Pluralism in the Age of the McDonald's Hamburger*, argues against the effectiveness of a "decultured" and "placeless" assessment of religion Maryknoll, NY, Orbis, 1990, pp. 192-212.

which religious experience confirms, that allows one to think of Hick's work as philosophical theology more than philosophy of religion.

Sumner Twiss has offered one of the most tightly written defenses of Hick to date[11]. Employing Lindbeck's cultural-linguistic and propositional-realist categories, Twiss lays out Hick's structure as a combination of noncognitivist and cognitivist dimensions in order to avoid one-sided misreadings. He argues that these normally incompatible categories are woven throughout Hick's work in such a manner as to create a seamless garment. Twiss then goes on to argue (against Netland and Corliss[12]) for the adequacy of Hick's hermeneutics and epistemology, and the coherence of his postulate of a Divine Noumenon. In upholding the hermeneutics employed by Hick, Twiss defends the use of second order language and reflection on a particular tradition's first order language and self-understanding. In other words, he claims that Hick's pluralistic hypothesis that espouses the core unity of the religions in regard to the Real, is *Hick's hypothesis* and is not, and need not be, understood as an account of each religions' self-understanding or description. If Hick's is an explanatory hypothesis rather than a descriptive one, as Twiss, drawing upon the insights of Wayne Proudfoot[13], argues, then Hick is justified in employing his own language and formulation of what the religions are claiming about the Real. This is, I think, a valid and helpful analysis of Hick's project, one which responds to the objections of several critics. It is also one that supports the understanding that Hick has developed a hypothesis and not a definitive description and that this work is philosophy of religion and not theology or specifically, a theology of religions, as some incorrectly read it.

However, after this lucid defense of Hick's method Twiss himself criticizes Hick for not distinguishing clearly between those instances when he is writing as a Christian theologian and those in which he is writing as a philosopher of religion. This criticism is understandable given two factors: 1) the corpus of Hick's writings up until *An Interpretation of Religion*, and 2) Hick's consistent epistemological defense of the legitimacy of religious belief in all of his work including *An Interpretation of Religion*. In this regard Twiss is correct in defending Hick, against such critics as Paul Griffiths and Delmas Lewis, on the issue of the in-principled

---

11. S. TWISS, *The Philosophy of Religious Pluralism: A Critical Appraisal of Hick and His Critics*, in *The Journal of Religion* 70:4 (1990) 533-568.

12. See G.A. NETLAND, *Professor Hick on Religious Pluralism*, in *Religious Studies* 22 (1986) 289-301; R. CORLISS, *Redemption and Divine Realities: A Study of Hick and an Alternative*, in *Religious Studies* 22 (1986) 235-248.

13. Cf. W. PROUDFOOT, *Religious Experience*, Berkeley and Los Angeles, University of California Press, 1985.

cognitivity of religious language. Hick continues to claim that religious language is neither non-sense nor self-referential, but that it makes claims to an external referent which is transcendent. The claim is that such a referent exists; it does not specify the content of that referent.

One could claim that the confusion between philosophy and theology (or fusion of the disciplines of philosophy and theology) continues in *An Interpretation of Religion* because in it Hick is attempting "the development of a field theory of religion from a religious point of view"[14] or a "religious interpretation of religion"[15], but it is clear to me from other evidence internal to the work that it is a philosophy of religion and not a theology of religions. Hick states that he is proposing a "philosophical ground-plan" as a "philosopher of religion"[16]. The fact that there is no specific treatment of christology in this work is further evidence that Hick is not writing Christian theology. There is extensive treatment of the soteriological aspects of religion and of the process of salvation /liberation /fulfillment, but this is not a study restricted to Christian categories or experience. It is an examination of this phenomenon across the religions. Hick makes this clear when he states: "... that a philosopher of religion must today take account not only of the thought and experience of the tradition within which he or she happens to work, but in principle of the religious experience and thought of the whole human race"[17]. While he acknowledges that he identifies with the Christian tradition, his philosophy of religion is an attempt to reflect on the broader religious experience of humankind across the traditions.

II. HICK'S CHRISTOLOGY

Hick's work on christology, however, is clearly theological. In *The Metaphor of God Incarnate*[18], he rejects traditional christology as defined by the councils and suggests his own christological formulation. This formulation is not entirely new, as Hick relies on predecessors such as Baillie, H. H. Farmer and Geoffrey Lampe. However, Hick's christology is controversial, rejecting some long established and widely held principles of christology such as the dogma of two natures in one person and the atonement theory.

---

14. HICK, *An Interpretation of Religion*, Preface, XIII.
15. *Ibid.*, 1.
16. *Ibid.*, Preface, XIII.
17. *Ibid.*
18. J. HICK, *The Metaphor of God Incarnate*, London, SCM, 1993.

Further he is attempting to understand and interpret christology in the light of different and sometimes competing claims by other religions. All of this is within the parameters of philosophy of religion. If, however, he attempts to revise the claims of the Christian tradition, even in conjunction with a philosophical appraisal of the claims of that tradition, then he is no longer properly engaged in the discipline of philosophy of religion but has crossed over into theology. In instances in which he is proffering a theological, and specifically Christian opinion, I think that his ideas should be accepted or resisted on the grounds of theological thinking.

In *The Metaphor of God Incarnate*, Hick suggests theological positions that once were sacrosanct may now be implausible or even offensive. As an example of radical change, he cites the "extra ecclesiam nulla salus" position held by Christianity from the time of Cyprian until the later half of the twentieth century when this position was abandoned by most mainline Christian churches. He argues that similar change should occur in christology which now must be understood in the light of greater knowledge of other religions. The implications of this rethinking are significant. For Hick, it means that Christ was not pre-existent and that God and Christ are not identical. Therefore, the Chalcedonian language of two persons in one nature is inaccurate and Christ represents one manifestation of God among several of equal measure. Hick contends that the dogma of full humanity and full divinity at one time abiding in Jesus has never been given an adequate explanation in the literal sense and can only make sense metaphorically. Hick admits that it is difficult to define "metaphor" precisely but he describes it as non-literal or figurative speech that transfers meaning from one term to another. Before the councils at Nicea and Chalcedon, the language of incarnation was devotional, ecstatic or liturgical (or some combination) that was transformed into technical theological language by the councils' attempts to precisely define its meaning. Hick writes:

> The essential difference, then, between the literal and metaphorical ways of speaking of divine incarnation is that whereas the first can (at least in intention) be spelled out as a physical or psychological or metaphysical hypothesis (or a mixture of these), the second cannot be so translated without destroying its metaphorical character. And my thesis concerning the Christian doctrine of incarnation is that as a literal hypothesis it has not been found to have any acceptable meaning[19].

---

19. *Ibid.*, p. 106. Several theologians have challenged Hick on this point including Gavin D'Costa and myself, see *A Question of Final Belief: John Hick's Pluralistic Theory of Salvation*, London: Macmillan and New York, St. Martin's, 1989. Roger Haight, while not necessarily agreeing with Hick's conclusions, agrees that the doctrines have

He does not wish to deny the continued power of Christ as an example of one who trusted completely in God, but he does want to leave behind the dogmatic formulations that this fact has given rise to historically; namely Incarnation, Trinity and Atonement. According to Hick, such rethinking will free Christianity from its dogmatic shackles to see itself as one genuine spiritual path among others.

Hick has not derived his christology in a void. He readily admits his reliance on a tradition in liberal theology that originated with Schleiermacher, Strauss and Harnack, all of whom argue, in various ways, for Jesus' unique God-consciousness that enabled his charismatic presence and prophetic voice to be effective. Aided further by contemporary research on the historical Jesus that emphasizes his Jewishness and puts Jesus in the context of the social conditions of his times, Hick interprets him as an extraordinary prophet who spoke authentically in the name of God, called people to repentance, and announced the coming of the reign of God but was not himself God. The claim to divinity came not from Jesus but from the early Christian community. He interprets the resurrection as "an inner spiritual experience" among Jesus' disciples and not as an "outer sense experience"[20]. Thus, the historical Jesus never understood himself as God incarnate, was not God incarnate and only became "God incarnate" by the well-intended but erroneous interpretations of the Christian community that succeeded his life on earth. The metaphor "Son of God" became a metaphysical claim that was codified by the councils of Nicea and Chalcedon. To add credibility to the claim, the church wrongly held that the councils themselves were divinely guided.

Hick sums up the development in classical christology thus: "In the case of 'Son of God' language, then, we have what was in the ancient world a widely used and readily understood metaphor, though subsequent Christian theology was to treat it as having a literal meaning"[21]. He further argues that the literal interpretation has led Christianity into a number of pitfalls, including anti-Semitism, colonialism, and patriachalism. Whether the doctrine of the incarnation is literally true or not, the history of effects confirm that it has given rise to unchecked hubris on the part of Christians who have an inflated sense of ownership of the religious dimension because they believe that God himself founded their religion. Christians suffer from a superiority complex that has led them either to ignore the other major religious traditions or to treat them as

given rise to much criticism. See *The Situation of Christology Today* (BETL, 69), 1993, p. 320.

20. *Ibid.*, 25.
21. *Ibid.*, 42.

inferior. According to Hick, the root of this complex lies in a christology that gives Christians a claim on God that no other religion can equal.

Hick, as we shall see is also true of Knitter, is open to the possibility that there have been other "incarnations" of God besides Jesus. The difference between them is that Hick proposes that this is an actuality and not simply a probability or merely a possibility as Knitter holds[22]. Hick contends that judging by the transformation from self-centeredness to Reality [God] – centeredness evident in individuals from all of the major traditions, it is reasonable to conclude that other religions have been equally salvific for their adherents as Christianity has been for its followers.

Hick is neither timid nor apologetic about his position on christology. He is not attempting to appease critics (of whom there are many), to ingratiate himself to the Christian community, or to adjust his views to make them more acceptable to either the theological or ecclesial communities. Such intransigence has led many to criticize Hick severely, seeing his work as a genuine threat to the continuity and authority of the Christian theological tradition or to dismiss him as so far to the left as to be unworthy of serious consideration.

III. PAUL KNITTER'S CHRISTOLOGY

Paul Knitter takes a different approach from Hick. It appears that he is anxious to respond positively to critics, wants to be accepted within the mainstream Christian community and is willing to adjust his views in order to be more acceptable to theologians and the wider community of believers. In both of Knitter's recent books *One Earth Many Religions*[23] and *Jesus and the Other Names*[24], he begins with autobiographical introductions with similar content. One may wonder who or what influenced Knitter and Orbis Press to publish two works in close proximity in which the first twenty-two pages duplicate each other. Why begin with a confessional tone? Who is Knitter trying to convince or reassure – himself, his critics in the theological community, the Maryknolls who run Orbis Press and who have traditionally been dedicated to missionary

---

22. Cf. J. HICK, *Five Misgivings*, in L. SWIDLER and P. MOJZES (eds.), *The Uniqueness of Jesus: A Dialogue with Paul F. Knitter*, Maryknoll, NY, Orbis, 1997, p. 80.

23. P.F. KNITTER, *One Earth Many Religions: Multifaith Dialogue and Global Responsibility*, Maryknoll, NY, Orbis, 1995.

24. P.F. KNITTER, *Jesus and the Other Names: Christian Mission and Global Responsibility*, Maryknoll, NY, Orbis, 1996.

work[25], his colleagues at Xavier University, the Vatican, or the Christian community at large? The further content of the books confirms that Knitter is attempting to move his theology of religions more toward the center, particularly by adjusting his christology.

Let us look at the evidence for this shift. Some of the impetus comes from Knitter's partial dissatisfaction with the exclusivist-inclusivist-pluralist categories. Indeed, he admits wanting to "clarify and correct particular arguments"[26] found in his previous book *No Other Name?*[27] He continues to call himself a pluralist (though he now prefers to say that he is doing correlational theology) even as he intends to modify his position in response to critics. It is these modifications that indicate a new direction for Knitter – a direction that leads him to engage in apologetics, to make universal truth claims and to address the Christian community at large as well as theologians.

In these works he intentionally separates himself from other theologians (for example, Hick) because it is problematic when "all 'liberation' or 'pluralist' theologians are stuffed into the same drawer, even though there are distinctive, sometimes opposing, differences among them"[28]. Knitter is explicitly addressing the importance for him to include eco-human justice and liberation in his theology of religions, but differences in christology also figure heavily in his analysis. In these books, as well as in the volume *The Uniqueness of Jesus*[29], Knitter attempts to answer critics of his earlier work *No Other Name?*, his joint work with Hick (*The Myth of Christian Uniqueness*[30]) and even defend (he contends) Hick's *An Interpretation of Religion*[31]. Knitter appears stung by the criticism, which he calls "sobering". He backtracks on some of his earlier claims. For example, in *No Other Name?* he advocates a non-normative theocentric christology. In *Jesus and the Other Names* he concedes: "Truth that is nonnormative cannot go anywhere, like a sailboat without wind. So the critics insist (and I have to agree

25. *Jesus and the Other Names* is dedicated to his friends in the Society of the Divine Word, Knitter's former religious community that is directed to missionary work.

26. *Ibid.*, 8.

27. P.F. KNITTER, *No Other Name?: A Critical Survey of Christian Attitudes Toward the World Religions*, Maryknoll, NY, Orbis, 1985.

28. KNITTER, *Jesus and the Other Names*, p. 16.

29. L. SWIDLER and P. MOJZES (eds.), *The Uniqueness of Jesus: A Dialogue with Paul F. Knitter*, Maryknoll, NY, Orbis, 1997.

30. J. HICK and P.F. KNITTER (eds.), *The Myth of Christian Uniqueness*, Maryknoll, NY, Orbis, 1987.

31. J. HICK, *An Interpretation of Religion: Human Responses to the Transcendent*, New Haven, Yale, 1989.

with them) that any truth claim worth its salt must be normative"[32]. It seems that he is trying to reassure the Christian community and his theological critics that he is still a part of the fold. Again, now defending the unique role of Jesus, he writes: "The intent of this [correlational] model is not to dismantle or replace the unique significance of Jesus, but to understand it in such a way that Christians will be genuinely open to the God who is present beyond Jesus"[33]. While not denying his pluralist leanings, he reassures the Christian community that he is one of them who shares in their religious practice, even if he interprets Jesus differently from many others within the Christian community. He writes: "Speaking as a pluralist theologian, I also speak as a Christian who is nourished as the eucharistic table..."[34].

Curiously, in one section of the book Knitter describes Jesus as universal, decisive and indispensable[35]. He explains these distinctions, however, not as pertaining to Jesus himself but to his message; "he is not God's total, definitive, unsurpassable truth, but he does bring a universal, decisive, indispensable message"[36]. In *The Uniqueness of Jesus*, he writes: "I ... am not questioning *whether* Jesus is unique, but only *how*"[37]. Knitter appears to be mixing his previous incarnation as a moderate pluralist with his more recent incarnation as a radical inclusivist. If it is Jesus himself who is indispensable, then Knitter is defending a traditional view articulated by the early christological councils and taught regularly by the church. If, however, he is arguing that it is the message of Jesus that is indispensable, then he is defending a Bultmannian Christ of faith approach to christology that insists that the *kerygma* is essential but the messenger is secondary. Nonetheless, Knitter does not say that Jesus is the only such incarnational manifestation of God. In fact, he makes it plain that he believes that it is possible that God acted in a similar way in others besides Jesus.

Knitter distinguishes between the philosopher or historian of religion and the theologian in his response to the assembled critics in *The Uniqueness of Jesus,* claiming that the theologian is committed to the promotion not only of scholarship but of faith[38]. In this sense Knitter believes Christianity is intrinsically missionary. Some see his work as

32. KNITTER, *Jesus and the Other Names*, p. 55.
33. *Ibid.*, 42.
34. *Ibid.*, 14.
35. *Ibid.*, 76-80.
36. *Ibid.*, 79.
37. P.F. KNITTER, *Five Theses on the Uniqueness of Jesus*, in L. SWIDLER and P. MOJZES (eds.), *The Uniqueness of Jesus*, 1997, p. 3.
38. *Ibid.*, pp. 145-182.

oriented too much toward evangelizing, others not enough so. He sees *dialogue* as mission. Yet he believes the truth revealed in Jesus remains indispensable for those who have come to know it (i.e. Christians). He straddles a fine line between inclusivist and pluralist ideas and sometimes it is difficult to know just what exactly he means to convey to the scholarly community.

Perhaps Knitter's approach can best be characterized as a dialogical one. What interests him most is dialogue. He modifies his christology in order to promote a more fruitful dialogue among the religions. He insists on social justice and a balanced ecology in the light of what each religion is able to contribute to the well being of humankind and the world. S. Mark Heim makes this point distinguishing Knitter from Hick who is a philosopher of religion and Wilfred Cantwell Smith who is an historian of religion. Each of them is interested in forging a new path which the religions can tread together but each has a method for doing so different from the others[39]. Knitter's thinks neither in terms of philosophy like Hick nor history like Smith but in terms of dialogue and more specifically theological dialogue. This is his focus and unique contribution.

To his credit, he is willing to listen to those who oppose him, to rethink his position and change elements of it when he is convinced of the merits of criticism or counter-positions. These are important qualities for someone who grounds his theology in dialogue. To some degree it makes his theology more difficult to stereotype or even pin down. But it confirms that Knitter is listening seriously, is open to argument and is willing to change his mind if the evidence and argument appear convincing to him. Every theologian could find such a methodology instructive.

IV. MOVING IN DIFFERENT DIRECTIONS

Hick's criticism of Knitter in the volume *The Uniqueness of Jesus* points to the ambiguity in Knitter's work that I am attempting to single out. While Hick agrees in general with Knitter's five theses[40] (with the

39. See S. Mark HEIM, *Salvations: Truth and Difference in Religion*, Maryknoll, NY, Orbis,1995.
40. The five are: 1) Given the nature and history of christology, previous understandings of the uniqueness of Jesus can be reinterpreted. 2) Given the ethical imperative of dialogue, previous understandings of the uniqueness of Jesus must be reinterpreted. 3) The uniqueness of Jesus' salvific role can be reinterpreted in terms of truly but not only. 4) The content of Jesus' uniqueness must be made clear in Christian life and witness. This

exception of number four), he charges that the explanations Knitter offers are "… ambiguous, capable of being understood in both pluralist and inclusivist ways"[41]. I think that Hick's criticism is accurate. To appease his critics, Knitter presents a "softer" version of pluralism. Hick charges that Knitter has watered down his version of pluralism until it is virtually indistinguishable from inclusivism. One of the differences between Hick and Knitter is that Knitter holds that it is possible that other religions are equally salvific as Christianity, while Hick argues (on what grounds it has never been clear to me other than the roughly equal production of saintly people within all of the major religious traditions) that the religions do in fact exhibit salvific parity. Knitter holds for the possibility; Hick says it is a reality, not merely a possibility or even a probability. Hick argues that the revelations of other religions are equally universal in their applicability to salvation as is the Christian claim that Jesus saves. Of Knitter's assertion that the gospel message is "indispensable" (in a way different from other revelations of which Knitter says it is only *probable* that they too are indispensable), Hick writes: "I appreciate that it will play well with the traditionally orthodox". In other words, by trying to appease his critics he has surrendered the controversial tenets of pluralism stripping his theory of its potency and settled for a soft pluralism that looks like another form of inclusivism. Perhaps the key difference that underlies all of the differences between Hick and Knitter is concisely summarized by Hick: "His chosen mission is within and to the church". Hick's mission, while not eschewing churches or the community of ordinary believers completely[42], is not directed ecclesially. Hick noted elsewhere, "… the official structures of the mainline churches are not today particularly hospitable to controversial ideas" while "the academic world is a much more open field for the testing of ideas in vigorous controversy"[43]. Yet Hick is not completely divorced from the impact of his work on

content, however, will be understood and proclaimed differently in different contexts and periods of history. Today, the uniqueness of Jesus can be found in his insistence that salvation or the Reign of God must be realized in this world through human actions of love and justice. 5) The orthodoxy of this pluralistic reinterpretation of the uniqueness of Jesus must be grounded primarily in the ability of such a reinterpretation to nurture a holistic Christian spirituality, that is, a devotion to and a following of Jesus. The proposed understanding of Jesus as God's truly but not only saving word does meet this criterion.

41. J. HICK, *Five Misgivings*, p. 79.

42. In *The Metaphor of God Incarnate*, he indicates that his audience is Christians who are dissatisfied with "uncriticized traditional ideas" and those who either have left the church or never professed Christianity although they remain interested in religious issues, p. 13.

43. J. HICK, *A Christian Theology of Religions: The Rainbow of Faiths*, Louisville, KY, Westminster, 1995, pp. 3-4.

churches as he makes clear in the final chapter of *The Metaphor of God Incarnate* which he titles "What Does This Mean for the Churches"? He suggests that his theology advances Christianity's self-understanding in a non-traditional way. It puts Christians' belief in Jesus into a global context in which that belief stands side by side with the beliefs of different religious traditions who hold other figures as central to the liberation/salvation process. It is therefore, not so much the denial of tradition (although there is undoubtedly an element of this is Hick's work) as it is an attempt to make sense of Christian claims in the light of contemporary experience and knowledge.

Hick and Knitter have each altered their christologies and theologies since the publication of *The Myth of Christian Uniqueness*. But those alterations are leading them in different directions – Hick towards an entirely new form of Christianity (some would say it is no longer Christianity) devoid of its classical christological claims and Knitter towards a Christianity grounded in the practical as evidenced by his liberation based christology. The risk for Hick is that the Christian community (scholarly and practicing) will see him as no longer Christian and ignore his potential contribution to the conversation about Christ and other religions. Knitter risks losing the possibility of making a unique contribution by accommodating too many critical voices and no longer saying anything clear and distinct about Christ and Christianity or their relation to other religions.

Georgetown University   Chester GILLIS
Washington, DC 20057
U.S.A.

THE GOD OF RELIGIOUS PLURALISM AND CHRISTOLOGY

Christian theology has traditionally claimed that in the historical figure of Jesus the Christ, God has, in a unique and final way, disclosed himself to humanity. This revelation of God, in the person of Jesus Christ, is definitive and complete once-for-all. As such, Jesus occupies a central, unique place such as no other religion attributes to its founder. It is the mystery of Jesus Christ himself, not just his message that is at the center of faith. As Jacques Dupuis states, in Christianity "the Message and the Messenger blend into one. Christianity is a religion of a person, the Christ"[1]. As the Second Vatican Council stresses, "Christ is 'the way, the truth, and the life' (Jn. 14:6) in whom God has reconciled all things to himself... and in whom men [women] find the fullness of their religious life"[2]. Christ remains the *norma normans non normata*, that is, the norm above all other norms.

In contrast to this view, the so-called pluralist school of theologians, represented by, among others, John Hick, Wilfred Cantwell Smith and Paul Knitter[3], preach a "a new model of truth" – *pluralism* – which moves away from the insistence on the "finality of Christ", recognizing many other "teachers", "liberators" and "saviours" "*with* Jesus" and "many other religious paths, *with* Christianity"[4].

1. J. Dupuis, *Jesus Christ at the Encounter of the World Religions,* Maryknoll, NY, Orbis Books, 1991, p. 94.

2. Vatican Council II, *Nostra Aetate*, no. 2. See A. Flannery, O.P., (ed.), *Vatican II: The Conciliar and Post-Conciliar Documents*, Grand Rapids, MI, Eerdmans, 1975, p. 739.

3. I wonder whether one can still call Paul Knitter a pluralist theologian in the sense of one who acknowledges that other saviors can indeed be as efficacious as Christ. Knitter, who advocated a non-normative Christology, has now changed his position. He writes, "No longer would I want to advocate a 'non-normative christology', for that seems to imply that the encounter with God through Jesus cannot really be decisive insofar as it cannot really give us norms with which to direct our lives and take our stands". P. Knitter, *Five Theses on the Uniqueness of Jesus*, in L. Swidler & P. Mojzes, *The Uniqueness of Jesus: A Dialogue with Paul F. Knitter*, Maryknoll, NY, Orbis Books, 1997, p. 9, no. 13. Further, Knitter writes that "it is not necessary to proclaim God's revelation in Jesus as *full, definitive*, or *unsurpassable*". However, Knitter continues, "Christians must announce Jesus to all peoples as God's *universal, decisive*, and *indispensable* manifestation of saving truth and grace". *Ibid.*, pp, 8, 9. Emphasis original. This position is far removed from the kind of non-normative christology that Knitter advocated before. Knitter calls himself, however, a "pluralist Christian". *Ibid.*, p. 14, n. 20. Hick calls Knitter's position "a half-hearted or less than half-hearted pluralism". Hick, *Five Misgivings*, in *The Uniqueness of Jesus*, p. 81.

4. P. Knitter, *Towards a Liberation Theology of Religion*, in J. Hick & P. Knitter (eds.), *The Myth of Christian Uniqueness: Towards a Pluralistic Theology of Religions*, Maryknoll, NY, 1987, p. 197. Emphasis original.

The pluralists have a "democratic"[5] idea of God which enables them (i) to take leave of the traditional claim regarding the definitive character of Christ, and (ii) to affirm the independent validity of other religious traditions. In what follows I would like to reflect on the pluralists' concept of "God". A clear examination of their idea of God is imperative, because their interpretation of Jesus Christ, the God-incarnate, in whom Christians believe and whom they proclaim, will depend upon their understanding of what God is. I would propose to analyze their concept as follows.

First, I will take, among pluralists, John Hick and Wilfred Cantwell Smith as representative and analyze their concept of God. Hick, following Immanuel Kant's distinction between the noumenon and phenomena, just one aspect of Kant's complex theory of forms and perception, postulates a "God", not to explain the universe, but as an answer to "mutually conflicting" religious claims. Smith, following his study of the history of religions, postulates a "God" to explain the religious history of humanity as "one continual encounter" with the transcendent ultimate mystery. The postulated God is explained, by both of them, in such broad terms so as to include both the personal and impersonal gods and absolutes of different faiths.

Second, I will show how such a concept of God allows them to understand and to recognize the major world religious traditions as effective contexts of salvation, and, more importantly, to water down traditional orthodox Christology. I also will show, that in the final analysis, these two, the philosophical theologian, Hick, and the history-minded-theologian, Smith, do not differ very much in their understanding of "God". I am of the view that the "God" of pluralists, or, better the God of pluralism, acts, at best, as a philosophical ultimate. I contend that the pluralists fail to give a theological content to their God. In my view, what makes God significant for us is what is theologically said about God and not otherwise. God, for the Christians, is best defined in the Cross, and the Cross was possible because God became human.

---

5. T. MERRIGAN, *The Anthropology of Conversion: Newman and the Contemporary Theology of Religions*, in I. KER (ed.), *Newman and Conversion*, Edinburgh, T.&T. Clark, 1997, p. 120. Chester Gillis, an advocate of the pluralist paradigm, writes that the "pluralist position envisions a fairer God". C. GILLIS, *Pluralism: A New Paradigm for Theology*, Louvain, Peeters Press, 1993, 171. I contend that that "fairer God" is a vacuous concept and hence unnecessary for religious believers.

I. The Pluralist Understanding of God

John Hick and the Real

John Hick developed a global, pluralistic, philosophical theology in which the major world religions are understood to be variously related to the same divine Reality. Hick postulates an ultimate transcendent Reality – the Real[6] (as he calls it) – which, being beyond the scope of our human concepts, cannot be directly experienced as it is in itself but only as it appears in terms of our various human thought-forms. Employing Kant's distinction between the noumenon and phenomena, Hick writes that the Real, or the Real *an sich*, which exits beyond human perception nevertheless appears as phenomenal images in various religious traditions.

That Real, Hick claims, is *beyond,* and at the same time *behind* the *personal* and *impersonal* conceptions of the deities of both the theistic and non-theistic religious traditions of the world. However, the Real *in itself* is neither *personal* nor *impersonal*. The Real is *the* Ultimate, that is, the one which "transcends everything other than itself but [which] is not transcended by anything other than itself"[7]. Such an ultimate cannot be said to be "one or many, person or thing, substance or process, good or evil, purposive or non-purposive"[8]. The Real, then, is "no *thing*, but not nothing"[9]. No human "categories can be applied, either positively or negatively, to the noumenal"[10]. It "transcends all our thing-concepts, including our religious thing-concepts"[11].

---

6. Hick, in his early years, employed the term "God" to refer to the transcendent. But as he realized that the word "God" is essentially a theistic term, he began to employ the term "the Real" to denote the transcendent. Hick also acknowledges as much. See Hick, *Straightening the Record*, in *Modern Theology* 6 (1990) p. 191.

7. J. Hick, *The Real and Its Personae and Impersonae*, in L.Tessier (ed.), *Concepts of the Ultimate*, London, Macmillan, 1989, p. 143.

8. J. Hick, *An Interpretation of Religion*: *Human Responses to the Transcendent*, New Haven, CT, Yale University Press, 1989, p. 246. See also J. Hick, *The Rainbow of Faiths*: *A Christian Theology of Religions*, Westminster, John Knox Press, 1995, p. 60. As Keith Ward remarks, if "nothing at all can be said of the Real, then one cannot say that some expressions are more authentic manifestations of it than others. Indeed, we cannot say anything is a manifestation of it at all since that would make it a causal substratum". K. Ward, *Religion and Revelation*, Oxford, Clarendon Press, 1994, p, 311. See also K. Ward, *Truth and the Diversity of Religions*, in *Religious Studies* 26 (1990) 1-18.

9. Hick, *An Interpretation of Religion*, p. 246.

10. Hick, *The Real and Its Personae and Impersonae*, p. 156.

11. Hick, *An Interpretation of Religion*, p. 246. In the West, the thought that God is finitely experienced in various partial and inadequate ways is classically expounded by Aquinas. According to Aquinas we can say that God is, for example, good – "not in the sense in which we say of a human being that he or she is good, nor on the other hand in a totally unrelated sense, but in the sense that there is in the divine nature a quality that is

Such a Real, according to Hick, is authentically experienced as "a range of both theistic and non-theistic phenomena" in the world's religious traditions. This claim, that the Real is authentically experienced as the various phenomena of the world religions, does not mean, Hick insists, that "the Real *an sich* has the characteristics displayed by its manifestations". That is to say, then, that one cannot attribute the characteristics of, say, God the Father of Christianity, "love and justice", or the characteristics of the Brahman of Hinduism, "consciousness and bliss", to the Real *in itself*. However, these characteristics, that is, the love and justice of the heavenly Father and the consciousness and bliss of Brahman are different aspects of the Real as manifested within human experience. What is intended by Hick, then, is a strong distinction between the Real *an sich* and the various phenomenal interpretations/manifestations of the Real. In other words, then, according to Hick, no concept can be applied to the noumenal real[12]. "The Real *an sich* cannot be spoken about in human terms"[13]. "Our language can have no purchase" on the postulated noumenal reality, the Real[14]. Hick, however, qualifies this by drawing our attention to and differentiating between the "logical" and "substantial" properties of the Real *an sich*. The "substantial" properties such as "being good", "being powerful", and "having knowledge" cannot be applied to the noumenal Real. Only such "purely formal and logically generated properties" as "being a referent of a term" and "being that to which our substantial concepts do not

limitlessly superior and yet at the same time analogous to human goodness". Aquinas wrote: "We cannot grasp what God is, but what He is not and how other things are related to Him". *Summa contra Gentiles* I:30: 4, in A. PEGIS, *On the Truth of the Catholic Faith: Summa contra Gentiles*, Garden City, NY, Image Books, 1955, p. 141. In the East, the same thought is expressed in negative statements like "*neti, neti*, not this, not this". *Brhadaranyaka Upanishads* IV: 5: 15, in RADHAKRISHAN, *The Principal Upanishads*, London, George Allen and Unwin, 1969, p. 286. Hick also, to some extent, takes the *via negativa* in explaining the nature of the Real.

12. By saying this, he is proposing a version of "strong ineffability". This is Keith Yandell's expression, quoted in HICK, *An Interpretation of Religion*, 239. Hick also recognizes that strong ineffability has been criticized as incoherent because it involves the impossible attempt to refer to something that supposedly does not even have the property of "being able to be referred to". Though he dismisses this as a "logical pedantry", Hick nevertheless employs this approach to explain the Real. HICK, *An Interpretation of Religion*, p. 239

13. HICK, *The Rainbow of Faiths*, p. 59. To say that "the Real cannot be spoken about in human language is already to have said something about it in human language – namely that it cannot be spoken about it in human language". Hick sees this as a "a logical triviality with no significant consequences". *Ibid*. However, God or the Real, as the object of religious experience, can be expressed only in human terms. Though we cannot comprehend what God or the Real is, what is theologically said about God makes God significant.

14. HICK, *An Interpretation of Religion*, p. 350.

apply" can be said of or attributed to the noumenal Real. More specifically, then, we cannot say that the Real is good, powerful, loving and intelligent. We can only say that the Real is the "referent" of the terms good, powerful and loving[15].

Strictly speaking, then, the Real *an sich,* transcending all our concepts, remains unknown. This unknown Real *an sich* "is being differently conceived, and therefore differently experienced, and therefore differently responded to from within our several religio-cultural ways of being human"[16]. This does not mean that all the religions "are all the same, or that they all say the same thing". We are not considering, insists Hick, that "any and every conception of God or of the transcendent is valid, still less all equally valid"[17]. All religious expressions of the ultimate reality are "expressed in imperfect human analogies, but none is the truth, the whole truth, and nothing but the truth"[18]. "Christianity is not the only religion which sees God as active on earth and as participating in the historical process". In different ways, and in different manners, the transcendent is seen at work in the other various religious traditions. The divine Incarnation in Jesus, "is one way, but not the only way", of picturing God's presence in this world[19]. In this view, Jesus becomes the "supreme spiritual guide" for Christians and Christianity is but "*one* authentic context of salvation"[20]. "God is greater and more many-sided than either our individual or our separate community experiences" of God. Hence, we can never form a fully adequate conception of God's nature.

This view of Hick reflects what E. Troeltsch, "the father of historical relativism", pointed out. Troeltsch held that although the "Absolute" is present to and manifest in all of history, no historical manifestation of the Absolute can be regarded as absolute. Christianity is "absolute" for Christians, and other world faiths are likewise "absolute" for their own adherents. Christianity, then, must be viewed as "a purely historical, individual, relative phenomenon"[21]. Christians must recognize that the

---

15. This is a self-defeating argument. If God the Father of Christianity is an authentic manifestation of the Real, must not, then, God the Father's attributes have their analogical counterparts in the Real itself? If the Real does not have a nature in itself, can, then, the Real be a "referent" of something that is evil? We analyze these questions in the next part.

16. HICK, *An Interpretation of Religion,* p. 14; J. HICK, *Metaphor of God Incarnate,* London, SCM Press, 1993, p. 140.

17. J. HICK, *God and the Universe of Faiths,* London, Macmillan, 1973, p. 141.

18. *Ibid.,* 140; *Metaphor,* 146.

19. HICK, *Metaphor,* p. 153.

20. *Ibid.,* p. 163.

21. E. TROELTSCH, *Christian Thought: Its History and Application,* London, University of London Press, 1923, p. 22. In his *The Absoluteness of Christianity and the History of Religions,* Richmond, John Knox Press, 1971, Troeltsch writes that "nowhere is Christianity the

many others "may experience their contact with the Divine Life [God] in a quite different way, and may themselves also possess a religion which has grown up with them, and from which they cannot sever themselves so long as they remain what they are"[22]. Hick, to illustrate more or less the same idea more clearly, uses the parable of the blind men and the elephant[23], and implies that all images of the divine "express some aspect or range of aspects" of the divine and yet none by itself "fully and exhaustively" corresponds to the infinite nature of the transcendent God. In sum, then, God or the Real is the ultimate transcendent reality, which, being beyond human concepts, is "reflected" in the world's religious traditions[24]. Christianity is but one way, and Jesus is but one saviour amongst others. God/the Real is the author of the world.

Wilfred Cantwell Smith and the Transcendent

In the writings of Wilfred Cantwell Smith, we deal with a historian's assessment of both Christianity and non-Christian religions. Smith, too, like Hick, claims that the religious experience of the world is entering a new phase — a phase of religious pluralism. After a careful study of the histories of religions, Smith constructs a "world theology", a theology that is neither Christianity-centered nor Christ-centered; but unabashedly God-centered, theocentric[25]. Like Hick, Smith too substitutes God for Christ at the center of the universe. Smith himself writes, "I wonder

---

absolute religion, an utterly unique species free of the historical conditions that comprise its environment at any given time... The Christian religion is in every moment of its history a purely historical phenomenon, subject to all the limitations to which any individual historical phenomenon is exposed, just like the other great religions". *Ibid.*, 71, 85.

22. TROELTSCH, *Christian Thought: Its History and Application*, 26.

23. Hick uses a parable said to have been told by Buddha. A group of blind men, who never encountered an elephant, touched some parts of the animal. Each individual claimed that his own account of the animal was true and that therefore all others were false. In fact, all of them were true, but each referred only to one aspect of the total reality. HICK, *God and the Universe of Faiths*, p. 140.

24. W.C. SMITH, in his *The Meaning and End of Religions*, New York, Mentor Books, 1964, argued that "religion" is a Western concept, not to be found in other, especially Eastern religions. This was a welcome idea to Hick. Smith argued against the idea that "religions" are mutually exclusive ideological communities, and maintained that with the exception of Islam, it was not until the seventeenth century that such a concept of religion took shape. *Ibid.*, p. 22. This idea of Smith influenced Hick considerably. See HICK, *God and the Universe of Faiths*, 101.

25. See A. RACE, *Christians and Religious Pluralism*, London, SCM Press, 1983, pp. 100-103; H. COWARD, *Pluralism: Challenge to World Religions*, Maryknoll, NY, Orbis Books, 1985, p. 32, M. ABE, "*There is no Common Denominator For World Religions:*" The Positive Meaning of This Negative Statement, in *Journal of Ecumenical Studies* 26 (1989) 80, P. ALMOND, *Wilfred Cantwell Smith as Theologian of Religions*, in *Heythrop Theological Review* 76 (1983) 335.

whether I need shrink from saying: if Christians insist that Christ is the center of their lives, it is time that we rediscovered that God is the center of the universe"[26].

But unlike Hick, Smith does not have a specific name for the transcendent reality. Some times he uses the term "God" and in some other places he employs the term "transcendent" to denote the ultimate. Smith, at times, also uses the categories of his own tradition – the Christian, to explain his postulated God. This does not mean that Smith's concept of God is like that of the Christians. In any case, Smith's God should not be identified with the loving Father of Christianity. I shall now attempt to explain how Smith understands God.

For Smith, everything that can be subsumed under the generic term, "religion", and everything that is peculiar to each and every particular religious tradition, points to "the transcendent, indeed infinite, truth ('God'), beyond history and continuingly contemporaneous" with it[27]. This infinite transcendent God has played a "comparable role" in all the religious traditions. Smith says, "I myself – after studying the history of the Islamic and the Christian movements and having friends in both groups – am not able to think of any reason that one might reasonably have for denying that God has played in human history a role in and through the Quran, in the Muslim case, comparable to the role in the Christian case in and through Christ"[28]. Thus, for Smith, God who is in the center of the universe has revealed God-self in and through all major religious traditions, and there is nothing in any religious tradition and certainly in the Judeo-Christian tradition which makes it definitive or normative. This transcendent can be best described following the *Yogavasistha*, the Hindu scared text which talks about transcendent Brahman as follows: "Thou are formless. The only form is our knowledge of Thee". This formless transcendent, whose form, then, is given by the believer, is something or someone that "impinges" on – that has an effect on, that makes an impression on – persons of faith. In the final analysis, however, this transcendent is totally ineffable.

> The Transcendent transcends. He/She/It transcends all our grasp of it, intellectual and others; including our grasp of and response to revelation. He/She/It transcends the concept, and category, 'God', though that concept has played, for theists, a mighty and marvelous role in large sectors of

26. W.C. SMITH, *Towards a World Theology*, Philadelphia, PA, Westminster, 1981, p. 177, W.G. OXTOBY (ed.), *Religious Diversity: Essays by Wilfred Cantwell Smith*, New York. Harper and Row, 1976, p. 9, and W.C. SMITH, *The Meaning and End of Religion*, New York, Mentor, 1964, p. 181.

27. SMITH, *Towards a World Theology*, p. 157.

28. SMITH, *Idolatry*, in *The Myth of Christian Uniqueness*, p. 64.

human history.... God has used – has richly used – the concept 'God' to enter into human lives. He/She/It has also, of course, used other concepts – and many symbolic forms other than concepts – to do so[29].

For Smith, then, "God" is merely a human expression of that which remains, in itself, ultimately ineffable: "'God' as a term is the name of the concept by which we Muslims, Christians, and some Hindus and others, when we speak English, have traditionally conceptualized what, unconceptualized, may perhaps, very lamely be called 'transcendence'"[30]. "Whether articulated in a great or in an unsophisticated conceptual pattern, or not articulated, our knowledge of God – the intellectual's knowledge, and too that of the cobbler – is the form in which ideationally God appears to each of us, less or more richly". No such form is, for Smith, either "final or complete. No such form is negligible"[31]. No one can have a "complete knowledge of the transcendent". For, the transcendent is "mystery" beyond all forms, always exceeding our grasp of it. It is such a transcendent ineffable mystery who saves people. "Christians He [She, It] has saved through Christ's death and resurrection...; Buddhists He [She, It] has saved through the teachings of the Buddha...; Jews He [She, It] has saved through the Torah...; Hindus He [She, It] has saved, inspired, encouraged, made creative through the poetry of the Gita ... God has participated more richly in human affairs, man [humanity] has participated more diversely in God"[32].

29. SMITH, *Religious Pluralism in Its Relation to Theology and Philosophy – and of These two to Each Other*, in R. CULLY (ed.), *The Three Loves: Philosophy, Theology, and World Religions,* Atlanta, GA, Scholars Press, 1994, p. 179.

30. SMITH, *On Dialogue and Faith: A Rejoinder*, in *Religion* 3 (1973) p. 110; *Towards a World Theology*, pp. 184-185; ID., *Questions of Religious Truth*, London, Gollancz, 1967, p. 36; ID., *Belief and History*, Charlottesville, University Press, 1977, p. 99.

31. SMITH, *Idolatry*, p. 56.

32. SMITH, *Towards a World Theology*, pp. 171-172. S. Samartha prefers to use the term "Mystery" to refer to the transcendent. He argues that terms such as "Brahman" and "God", used to denote the "mystery", are "culturally-conditioned". The ultimate Mystery is "ineffable" and any claim on the part of any "one religious tradition community to have exclusive or unique or final knowledge becomes inadmissible". S. SAMARTHA, *The Cross and the Rainbow*, in *The Myth of Christian Uniqueness*, p.77. For Samartha, then, the Christian claim that Jesus is the Christ of God "can remain normative to Christians everywhere", but "to make it 'absolutely singular' and to maintain that the meaning of the Mystery is disclosed *only* in one particular person at one particular point, and nowhere else, is to ignore one's neighbors of other faiths who have other points of reference". *Ibid.*, p. 76. For Samartha, then, "all religion can participate in and reflect this mystery", but none can own it. Samartha argues further that the statements like "Brahman is sat-cit-ananda" and "God is triune, Father, Son and the Holy Spirit" "could well be regarded as two responses to the same Mystery in two cultural settings". It is the culture, for Samartha, and also for Hick, that gave raise to different names and forms of the one ineffable mystery. *Ibid.*

Every theological system or idea, for Smith, is "a response" to God. As a response, every theological system is "finite, is mundane, is a human construct"[33]. Religions of the world, or better, the "cumulative traditions" of the world, "seen in world-history perspective", "are temporal, contingent, mundane, while their significance lies in their role as mundane intermediaries between humankind and God"[34]. These are the external expressions – the creeds, cults, beliefs – that have nourished and continue to nourish the faith of individuals. It is a mistake, then, "to identify one's own 'religion' or tradition with God, or with absolute truth; to regard it as divine, rather than as an avenue to, or from, the divine". These cumulative traditions are not same, but different, though not conflicting. "Religious statements at their best ... have been expressions of personal or corporate involvements, tentative but joyous, inadequate but exuberant, human but transcendence-oriented. To approach them with sympathy is to hear them not as claims but as echoes, to see them not as moon but as fingers pointing to the moon"[35]. Scripture, "a human activity", should guide us, argues Smith, towards a "more sensitive awareness of what it means to be human"[36]. The transcendent lies beyond the scriptures of the world traditions, and no religion can claim to reveal the transcendent absolutely or comprehensively.

Such a transcendent impinges on persons of faith. Here, we have to explain how Smith understands "faith". Smith describes faith almost exclusively in personal terms. Faith can be described as the "adjectival quality of a person's living in terms of transcendence"[37]. Faith is a "global human quality"[38] which "lifts one above the merely mundane and the immediate, and means that one may be always in part but is never totally simply a product or a victim of circumstance"[39]. Faith has, in the words of Mark Heim, "no uniform cognitive content but instead consists in an

---

33. SMITH, *Idolatry*, p.56.

34. *Ibid.*, p. 59. Instead of using the term "religion", Smith prefers to use the term "cumulative tradition" by which he means "the entire mass of overt objective data that constitute the historical deposit, as it were, of the past religious life of the community in question". W.C. SMITH, *Meaning and End of Religion*, p. 141.

35. SMITH, *Conflicting Truth-Claims: A Rejoinder*, in J. HICK (ed.), *Truth and Dialogue in World Religions: Conflicting Truth Claims*, Philadelphia, PA, Westminster, 1974, p. 159.

36. SMITH, *What is Scripture? A Comparative Approach*, London, SCM Press, 1993, p. 2. Scripture consists of ways in which a community feeds on and in turn enriches its own traditions, making them fruitful for future generations.

37. SMITH, *Meaning and End of Religion*, pp. 141, 342,

38. SMITH, *Towards a World Theology*, p. 171

39. SMITH, *Faith and Belief*, pp. 142, 129; *Towards a World Theology*, pp. 170, 176.

existential disposition"[40]. "It is an orientation of the personality, to oneself, to one's neighbor, to the universe; a total response; a way of seeing the world and of handling it; a capacity to live at more than a mundane level; to see, to feel, to act in terms of, a transcendent dimension"[41].

Faith, then, is grounded in – may be a response to – God, the transcendent. It is constituted, in part, by the context from which it arises. Smith writes, for example, that "historical criticism shows that the faith of any person, however open it may be to transcendence and the infinite, however much it may be a divine gift, however ideally absolute, yet in actual fact has always been limited by psychological, sociological, and other contextual factors, by the knowledge and the temperament and the situation of the man and woman whose it is"[42]. There is no such thing as the Christian or the Islamic or the Hindu faith. Faith is personal and varied. All persons of faith, he avers, do nevertheless share something. That something, he says, is neither a tradition nor their personal faith. Rather, it is "that to which they respond, the transcendent itself"[43].

In sum, then, as Lesslie Newbigin comments,

> It is clear that in Smith's view 'The Transcendent' is a purely formal category. He, she, or it may be conceived in any way that the worshiper may choose. There can therefore be no such thing as false or misdirected worship, since the reality to which it is directed is unknowable.... Any claim for uniqueness made for one concept of the Transcendent, for instance the Christian claim that the Transcendent is present in fullness in Jesus (Colossians 1:19), is to be regarded as wholly unacceptable. There are no criteria by which different concepts of the Transcendent may be tested. We are shut up to a total subjectivity: the Transcendent is unknowable"[44].

Religions, as historical realities, must be acknowledged as effective and valid paths to salvation. Therefore, the idea that only one's own faith has the truth while all others have no or only relative truth is inadmissible. For Hick, truth is not "essentially a matter of either-or. It is either this or not this: it can be both"[45]. In Smith's words, "in all ultimate matters, truth lies not in an either-or but in a both-and"[46]. For Knitter, "all

---

40. S.M. HEIM, *Salvations: Truth and Difference in Religion*, Maryknoll, NY, Orbis Books, 1995, p. 55.

41. SMITH, *Towards a World Theology*, p. 113.

42. SMITH, *Faith and Belief*, p. 131; *Towards a World Theology*, p. 168.

43. SMITH, *The Meaning and End of Religion*, p. 192.

44. L. NEWBIGIN, *The Gospel in a Pluralist Society*, Grand Rapids, MI, Eerdmans, 1989, pp. 159-161, 168-170.

45. HICK, *A Philosophy of Religious Pluralism*, in F. WHALING (ed.), *The World's Religious Traditions: Current Perspective in Religious Studies. Essays in Honour of Wilfred Cantwell Smith*, Edinburgh, T.&T. Clark, 1984, p.164.

46. SMITH, *The Faith of Other Men*, New York, New American Library, 1963, p.17.

religious experience and all religious language must be two-eyed, dipolar, a union of opposites"[47]. Thus, for the pluralists, the truth of religions is relative, culturally conditioned, dipolar and evolves in what Hick calls a *truth-seeking dialogue*. Therefore, it does not seem to be reasonable to claim that one religion is partial, or inferior to another religion. That is why Smith urges the Christians towards a certain "theological surrender", that is, Christians "will have to be willing to let go of their traditional beliefs that their religion or even their Christ is superior to and normative for all others"[48]. As Hick says, and Smith would whole-heartedly

---

47. P. KNITTER, *No Other Name?: A Critical Survey of Christian Attitudes Toward the World Religions*, Maryknoll, NY, Orbis Books, 1984, p. 221. Knitter attributes "a relational uniqueness" to Jesus Christ, which means that "Jesus is unique", and so also are other unique religious figures". *Ibid.*, pp. 171-172. In other words, Knitter wants us to recognize "what God has done in Jesus without...[insisting] that God has done it *only* in Jesus". A kind of a theocentrism that Knitter advocated remains open to the possibility "of other sons and daughters who have incarnated God's grace and truth for others". P. KNITTER, *Jesus and Other Names,* Maryknoll, New York, Orbis Books, 1996, p. 43. The words of Schillebeeckx remind us of the same point. Schillebeeckx writes, "The revelation of God in Jesus, as the Christian gospel proclaims it, does not mean that God absolutizes a historical particularity (be it even Jesus of Nazareth). From the revelation in Jesus we learn that no single historical particularity can be called absolute and that therefore, because of the relativity present in Jesus, every person can encounter God outside of Jesus, especially in our worldly history and in the many religions that have arisen from it". E. SCHILLEBEECKX, *The Church: The Human Story of God*, New York, Crossroad, 1990, p. 184.

48. SMITH, *Towards a World Theology*, p. 175. G. Kaufman writes that historical consciousness leads to the difficulty, if not the impossibility, of judging the truth claims of another religion from the perspective of one's own culture and religion. For Kaufman, "none of us – Christians or non-Christians – possesses absolute truth". Since there is no way of arriving at *the* truth other than *a* truth, one has to abandon the claim of being the *only true* or *highest form* of religion. Such an abandonment would allow us "to live together fruitfully, productively and in peace in today's complexly inter-connected world". Therefore, Christians "taking other faiths, other life-orientations, with full seriousness", must "break the grip of the absolutistic commitments that have characterized much [of] traditional Christian faith and theology", enabling themselves to encounter "other significant religious and secular traditions in *their own terms*" instead of defining them in Christian terms. G. KAUFMAN, *Religious Diversity, Historical Consciousness, and Christian Theology*, in *The Myth of Christian Uniqueness*, pp. 13. 3, 4, 14. Langdon Gilkey offers "a more cautious, dialectical endorsement of historical consciousness". Attempting to interpret all religions as particular expressions of a "perennial religious/philosophical center, or, as Frithjof Schuon terms them, exoteric manifestations of an esoteric heart", Gilkey observes that "each particular religion is true and yet relative, a true revelation for that community, relative to other true revelations for other communities, and relative to the Absolute that each only partially and so somewhat distortedly manifests". In every religion, then, there is "a *relative* manifestation of the *absolute* meaning". Therefore, religions carry "*relative absoluteness*" and no one can make claims of finality for Christianity or for Christ, because "no one revelation is or can be the universal criterion for all the others". "No cultural logos is final and therefore universal". L. GILKEY, *Plurality and Its Theological Implications*, in *The Myth of Christian Uniqueness*, pp.43, 48.

agree, it is reasonable to appeal to Sir Aurobindo's "logic of the Infinite":
all we can say about the ultimate reality is much more a matter of "'both-
and' than 'either-or'"[49]. God is the mysterious transcendent reality.

The God of Pluralism and the God of Christians

Hick is a Christian, though others call him an "ecumenical theist",
meaning that that Hick is "almost as comfortable worshipping in a
Hindu temple as a Christian church"[50]. Smith is also a Christian.
However, Smith speaks as a historian of religions, and Hick as a
philosopher of religion. They both detach themselves from their tradition, Christianity, and talk for all the traditions. Their God, though in
the center of the religiously pluralistic world, should not be identified
with any particular concept of the divine. Emphasizing the distinction
between *God a se* and *God as known*, a theme quite common to many
religions, Smith and Hick like to keep God as a remote principle, as a
God-above-all-other-gods. This nameless, formless, contentless ultimate being is, according to them, the Source of all and is the same
God worshipped as the loving father of Christianity, as Adonai in
Judaism, as Allah in Islam, as Ekoamkar in Sikhism and as Ram and
Krishna in Hinduism. Given this view of God, religions are seen as
"incomplete" versions of something "utterly ungraspable". Then it is
hard to see, as Anthony O' Hear writes, "how one could in all good
conscience continue to worship in, say, a Christian church or a Muslim mosque"[51]. This is unacceptable for committed believers. Besides
diluting the truth claims of various religious traditions, the pluralists
do not give adequate emphasis to the historical factors shaping the
world religions. Besides, the pluralist insistence that we cannot know
anything about the real gives way to a kind of agnosticism – "transcendental agnosticism" that affirms "the transcendent divine reality
over against naturalistic positions, while refusing to state that the

49. J. HICK, *The Outcome of Truth: Dialogue into Truth*, in *Truth and Dialogue*,
pp. 152-153; *God and the Universe of Faiths*, pp. 148-149.
50. H. HEWITT, *Problems in the Philosophy of Religion*, London, Macmillan, 1991,
p. xiii.
51. A. O'HEAR, *The Real or the Real? Chardin or Rothko,?* in M. McCHEE, (ed.),
Philosophy, Religion and the Spiritual Life, Cambridge, Cambridge University Press,
1992, p. 56. While specifically referring to the "radical agnosticism" present in Hick's
idea of the Real, O' Hear writes: "I can, indeed, see nothing in Hick's account to rule out
a Real whose ultimate nature was not, say, closer to Nietzchean will-to-power than to a
Catholic Sacred Heart". He further asks, "what is there in the notion of the unknowable,
transcendent Real to rule out the possibility that our idea of a compassionate divinity is
simply the ultimate fantasy of a deluded humanity whose final fate is to be broken on the
wheel of existence?" *Ibid.*, p. 57.

eschaton may eventually be theistic rather than non-theistic, in however minimalist a sense"[52].

The God of pluralists, or the God of pluralism (GP) is neither personal nor impersonal. Being beyond these categories, it is seen as an abstract metaphysical principle out there. The God of religions (GR) is either personal or impersonal. The God of Christianity (GC) is a personal being who acts in history to redeem humanity.

GP is arrived at by religious experience and history. Hick's Real, like Smith's transcendent, can be apprehended in any way the worshiper may choose. There are no criteria to judge the validity of that concept. We are indeed shut up within a total subjectivity. GR is known through various prophets, teachers, and avatars. GC is not known by human speculation but by revelation. GC has chosen to reveal Himself to us through Jesus Christ, the second person of the Holy Trinity.

GP is beyond the modes of human conceptuality and demands nothing from believers. GR demands worship and obedience. GC, besides being the object of our worship and obedience, is the ultimate goal of our life.

It is true that "God" by the very definition remains mysterious and unknown. It is true that, as Gregory of Nyssa said, "God is the name 'Above every name'"[53]. It is also true, as M. Eliade wrote, that "God is without name, for no one can comprehend anything about him [her]"[54]. God can be validly referred to as "the Absolutely Different" (Kierkegaard), "the Numinous" (Rudolf Otto), "the Infinite" (Schleiermacher), "the Wholly Other" (K. Barth), "the Holy Mystery" (K. Rahner), "the Real" (Hick), "the transcendent" (Smith). As Paul Tillich wrote, there can be a "God above the God of theism"[55]. Or as Gordon Kaufman claimed, there can be a distinction between the "Real God" and the "available God"[56]. Or, as Hick and Smith claim, the Real/the Transcendent could well be the only true God, as a God-above-all-Gods.

52. D'COSTA, *John Hick and Religious Pluralism: Yet Another Revolution*, in *Problems in Philosophy of Religion*, p. 28.

53. Gregory of Nyssa, *Against Eunomius*, Book 1, chapter 42, in P. SCHAFF & H. WACE (eds.), *A Select Library of Nicene and Post-Nicene Fathers of the Christian Church*, vol. V, *Gregory of Nyssa*, trans. William Morre and Henry Austin Wilson, Grand Rapids, MI, Eerdmans, 1979, p. 99.

54. M. ELIADE, *A History of Religious Ideas*, Chicago, IL, University of Chicago Press, 1985, p. 200.

55. P. TILLICH, *The Courage to Be*, New Haven, CT, Yale University Press, 1952, p. 190.

56. G. KAUFMAN, *God the Problem*, Cambridge, MA, Harvard University Press, 1972, p. 86.

However, we contend that it is not enough to say that there is a God above the God of theism, a Real God, the Real and the God *a se* that is totally beyond the realm of human concepts. What is most important for a believer is to give a "content" to the God *a se*. Because, as Tillich said, God "is what concerns us ultimately"[57]. What meaning could the ineffable, unspeakable God *a se* have for us finite human beings? God *a se,* as a philosophical ultimate, can at the most satisfy some philosophers. But the challenge is to give the philosophical ultimate a theological content. A mere insistence upon the Real, a god above all other gods and absolutes, is unnecessary for a believer. Rather, that which is significant is what is said theologically about the God *a se*. We can ask what purpose the Demiurge of Plato's Timaeus and the unmoved mover of Aristotle's metaphysics actually serve? What is so significant about the "God above the God of theism" of Tillich or the Real God of Kaufman? In the same way, what is meaningful about Hick's concept of the Real for a religious believer? What can Smith's transcendent offer for a Muslim or Buddhist?

Religions are not interested in, as T. Z. Lavine stresses, the God of enlightenment who "after creating the world and setting it in motion according to the laws of geometry and mechanics... does not interfere with the mechanical clockwork of the universe"[58]. Such a notion of God stresses God's aseity (the idea that God exists from himself) but not the all-surpassing love and infinite tender care that is part and parcel of Christian revelation. For Christians, God is no longer the infinite supreme being beyond world history, but is rather "the Infinite in the finite"[59]; God is not "the static Infinite" but a dynamic Infinite that "emerges" out of the void and also "rushes into" to fill the void[60].

Christianity proclaims that God is not only a benevolent creator and Ruler but is also a compassionate Redeemer. God is not only a provider but is also the Saviour of humanity. Biblical faiths insist that God – who is utterly transcendent and at the same time radically immanent – freely acts in history and does not just tower above history. The God of the Bible is both the "wholly Other" and the "Infinitely Near". Our God "is both God transcendent and God *with* us and *for* us"[61]. Our God is never

57. P. TILLICH, *Systematic Theology*, vol. 1, Chicago, IL, University of Chicago Press, 1951, p. 12.

58. T.Z. LAVINE, *From Socrates to Sartre: The Philosophic* Quest, New York, Bantam, 1984, p. 117.

59. F. SCHLEIERMACHER, *On Religion: Speeches to Its Cultured Despisers*, trans. John Oman, New York, Harper and Row, 1958, p. 237.

60. SATPREM, *Oneness and the Teaching of Sri Aurobindo*, in J. WHITE (ed.), *What is Enlightenment?*, Los Angels, Jeremy P. Tarcher, 1984, pp. 111-112.

61. D. BLOESCH, *God the Almighty: Power, Wisdom, Holiness, Love*, Carlisle, The Paternoster Press, 1995, p. 24.

immanent without being transcendent, just as God does not remain transcendent without making Godself, for our sake, immanent. God is, as Moltmann stresses, not an almighty despot but an all-encompassing Spirit that upholds and nurtures us. "What He [God] *is* is not almighty power; what He [God] *is* is love"[62]. Though God does not need the world, God creates the world out of God's bounty and remains with the world in its struggle for fulfillment and happiness. As Josef Van Ess writes, Jesus' life and work make it clear that God "is a phil-anthropic (loving humanity) and sympathetic (co-suffering) God, 'down here with us'"[63]. As K. Ward writes, the relation of the Christian God to creation is seen as "involving the transformation of the finite into the infinite life of God"[64].

Christianity also teaches a "twin truth" about this God: "that there is a God whom men [women] can reach, and there is a corruption in their nature which renders them unworthy of Him [God]". It is crucial for us to keep both truths before us. "Knowledge of one alone causes either the pride of philosophers who have known God but not their misery, or the despair of atheists who know their misery but not their Redeemer". It is in our knowledge of Jesus Christ that we grasp both truths at once, namely, that we have access to God and that we creatures are in need of forgiveness and reconciliation. Such a God is always a "hidden God" but there is an escape from our blindness through Jesus Christ, "apart from Whom all communication with God has been cut off"[65].

> If the God of Jesus Christ reveals himself [Godself] in a way that He [God] has chosen, through an elect people or through the incarnation of a savior, this does not mean that…[God] has given man [humanity] a better theosophy or a new theology to put beside so many other conceptions of the divine; on the contrary, it means that [God] has freed man [humanity] from every theosophy and every idolatry[66].

In Christ, God took the initiative to reveal Godself to humanity. In contrast to the God of pluralists, the personal God of Christianity has a

---

62. J. MOLTMANN, *The Trinity and the Kingdom*, trans. Margaret Kohl, San Francisco, CA, Harper and Row, 1981, p. 197. See also *The Spirit of Life*, trans. Margaret Kohl, Minneapolis, MN, Fortress, 1992, pp. 272-273.

63. J. VAN ESS, *The Image of God and Islamic Mysticism* in H. KÜNG (ed.), *Christianity and the World Religions: Paths to Dialogue and with Islam, Hinduism, and Buddhism*, Garden City, NY, Doubleday, 1986, p. 95.

64. K. WARD, *The Concept of God*, in P. BYRNE & L. HOULDEN (ed.), *Companion Encyclopedia of Theology*, New York, Routledge, 1995, p. 343. See also K. WARD, *Religion and Revelation*, Oxford, Clarendon Press, 1994, pp. 127-129.

65. Pascal, quoted in R.MCBRIEN (ed.), *Catholicism*, Minneapolis, MN, Winston Press, 1981, pp. 310-311.

66. P.THÉVENAZ, *God of Philosophers and God of the Christians*, in *Studies in Religion* 5 (1976) 338.

Heart, and is moved and stirred by God's own "free power" to relieve our distress[67]. It would be a "bad deal to trade in the God of Jesus for an unknown God [of pluralism]"[68]. The God of pluralism, a remote princi-ple, is unnecessary for believers. We believe in a God, the God of Jesus Christ who is the Father of all. For us, God is defined in the Cross. And the Cross was possible because God became *human*.

Bishop's House   Arul PRAGASAM
Britto Nagar
Melur Road
Sivagangai-623 650
Tamil Nadu
India

---

67. K. BARTH, *Church Dogmatics* vol. 2, Edinburgh, T.&T. Clark, 1956, p. 499.

68. C.H. PINNOCK, *Response to John Hick*, in D.OKHOLM & R. PHILLIPS (eds.), *More Than One Way?: Four Views on Salvation in a Pluralistic World*, Grand Rapids, MI, Zondervan, 1995, p. 62. See also Pinnock's *A Wideness in God's Mercy: The Finality of Jesus Christ in a World of Religions*, Grand Rapids, MI, Zondervan, 1992.

A NON-SACRIFICIAL INTERPRETATION OF CHRISTIAN REDEMPTION?

René Girard, the well-known French cultural philosopher, has explicitly stated that "the sacrificial interpretation of Jesus' Passion must be criticized and exposed as a most enormous and paradoxical misunderstanding"[1]. Girard demands a non-sacrificial interpretation of Christ's death. Should we heed his call?

Proclaiming a non-sacrificial interpretation of Christian redemption will not cause a big sensation in modern society or even in many religious communities. Sacrifices, in general, and blood sacrifices, in particular, disgust most of our contemporaries. Nevertheless, in Christian theological circles, especially those connected to churches that are committed or are related to a Roman Catholic and sacramental understanding of faith, one should at least be alarmed. Denial of a sacrificial understanding of redemption means that Christ's cross should not be understood as an atoning sacrifice for our sins and that the Holy Eucharist is not a real sacrifice.

Before we decide on this, we need to ascertain what is meant by sacrifice. I will discuss this in the first part of my article. In the second part, I will consider the consequences of the arguments reviewed. In the third part I will identify, on the basis of what sacrificing has turned out to be, the conditions under which a metaphorical or spiritual use of sacrificial language may be legitimate.

The investigation of the meaning of sacrifice for Christian redemption involves several questions. In our time and in our (western) culture, these questions are usually addressed with great reluctance. The connection between redemption and sacrifice is not self-evident. The first thing we must do is enumerate and discuss the reasons for this reluctance. By doing so, many questions, including that of the definition of sacrifice, will be answered.

---

1. R. GIRARD, *Des choses cachées depuis la fondation du monde,* Paris, Bernard Grasset, 1978; the quotation is from the English edition: R. GIRARD, *Things Hidden since the Foundation of the World*, Standford CA, Stanford University Press, p. 180.

I. Reasons for the reluctance to sacrifices

There are several reasons why the connection between redemption and sacrifice is only accepted with the greatest possible reluctance. The first reason is that there is no agreement on a definition of sacrifice and what it effects. Even in theological and ecclesiastical circles, no common definition is in use. Many men and women associate different ideas with sacrifice and, for this reason, discussions and arguments are very confusing. The second reason is immediately linked with this confusion. Sacrifices are associated with violence and blood and therefore considered to be at variance with both the contents of the Gospel and modern understanding. The last reason is the disagreement between exegetes on the question of whether or not Jesus' death was a sacrifice, whether or not his followers considered it to be a sacrifice, and whether or not it should (still) be considered to be a sacrifice, as Girard clearly thinks it should not.

A definition of sacrifice

The field of cultural anthropology offers many definitions of sacrifice. It is not easy to choose one of them as a starting-point and a criterion. For although all of them claim to describe objectively the phenomena of sacrificial practice, they are either too much focused on their own theory of sacrifice or their definition derives from particular cultures and consequently cannot be used for clarification of, for instance, the way early Christians considered Jesus' death to be a sacrifice. Girard is an example of a cultural anthropologist who is convinced of his theory, that mimesis is an all pervading characteristic of human behavior. It causes conflicts between the rivals which can only be solved by a cooperative violent action against a third party, the scapegoat. This pattern of occasional historical outbursts of violence, necessary to appease the conflicting party, is repeated in a controllable fashion in ritual sacrifices. So, in the opinion of Girard, violence and the sacred always go together in the act of sacrificing[2]. Nancy Jay focuses on the relationship between sacrifice and maintenance of a male-dominated social order. She shows how blood sacrifice enables men to "both appropriate and transcend women's reproductive powers – it is 'birth done better'"[3]. Her provocative conclusion is that

---

2. R GIRARD, *La violence et le sacré*, Paris, Bernard Grasset, 1972.

3. K RAAB, *Nancy Jay and a feminist psychology of sacrifice*, in *Journal of Feminist Studies in Religion* 13 (1997) 75-89, esp. 78; Raab refers to N. JAY, *Throughout Your Generations Forever. Sacrifice, Religion, and Paternity*, Chicago/London, The University of Chicago Press, 1992, p. xxiv.– I owe these references to my colleague Dr. Maaike de Haardt.

precisely those traditions which practice the Eucharist as sacrifice also refuse to ordain women[4]. These are all valuable contributions to the investigation of the broad field of sacrificial rituals. As a starting-point or a criterion, however, they are too wedded to a specific view on the matter.

On the other hand, bias is also present in the definitions theologians and exegetes use in their interpretations. Some, like the Lutheran theologian Joachim Track, foresee the end of all sacrifice[5]; others, like the exegete Marcus Barth[6] or the Methodist patristic scholar Frances Young[7], tend to reject some part of the sacrificial practice or language, claiming they do not belong to the Christian vocabulary, while using other parts to uphold the validity claim of Christian sacrificial language.

My choice has been to start, rather arbitrarily, by adopting J.H.M. Beattie's multidimensional description of sacrifice[8]. He tries to gather as many relevant "bare bones" to get "at least a minimal preliminary notion" of sacrifice (32). He later extends this notion by referring to recent ethnological material. According to Beatti, the necessary elements of sacrifice are: that sacrifice is (1) a rite, with (2) a victim and (3) the intention to bring about both communication with gods or spirits and a change in the participants (32). I shall comment on each of these elements.

(1) The ritual aspect of the sacrifice, the dramatic performance as Evans-Pritchard labels it (quoted by Beattie, 35) is essential. Though there may have been sacrifices outside a cultic place, in a family setting for instance, there was from the beginning a ritual, a dramaturgical prescription of words and actions that form a fixed scenario for the act of sacrificing. Again following Evans-Pritchard, Beattie enumerates four acts or stages of this dramatic performance: the presentation of the victim to the Godhead; the consecration of the victim to the Godhead; the invocation or prayer, and finally, the immolation or slaughter of the victim. Often there is also a shared feast, the commensality or eating

4. JAY, *Throughout Your Generations* (n. 3), p. 126.

5. J. TRACK, *Das Opfer am Ende. Eine kritische Analyse zum Opferverständnis in der christlichen Theologie*, in R RIESS (ed.), *Abschied von der Schuld? Zur Anthropologie und Theologie von Schuldbewußtsein, Opfer und Versöhnung* (Theologische Akzente, 1), Stuttgart/Berlin/Köln/Mainz, Verlag W.Kohlhammer, 1996, 140-167.

6. M. BARTH, *Was Christ's Death a Sacrifice?*, in *Scottish Journal of Theology, Occasional Paper* 9 (1961) 1-55.

7. F. YOUNG, *Sacrifice and the Death of Christ*, London, SCM Press, 1975.

8. J.H.M. BEATTIE, *On Understanding Sacrifice*, in M.F.C. BOURDILLON / M. FORTES (eds.), *Sacrifice*, London, Academic Press, 1980 pp. 29-44. Subsequent references to this source appear parenthetically in the text.

together (33-34). If this ritual, specifically, the ritual in the cult or
liturgy, should prove to be vital, one can, from this point of view, ask,
whether Jesus' execution on the cross is a real sacrifice.

(2) For Beattie, the killing or immolation of the living victim is an
integral part of the sacrifice. The slaughtered animal is, in the opinion of
many investigators, a vicarious sacrifice, that is: the victim, usually a
domestic animal, is killed instead of the sacrificer himself. This is part of
an exchange. Either the sacrificer hopes to attain something, e.g., good
fortune, or he wants to expiate some offense. In exchange, he offers the
sacrifice. Blood stands for life; the blood of the animal signifies the life
of the sacrificer (34; 41; 43).

(3) The goal of the sacrifice is communication with gods, spirits or,
more generally, powers. The participants want to acquire closer contact
with, or, on the contrary, ward off (evil) powers. The intended change in
the participants is either an increase of power or a catharsis, a purifica-
tory effect (37-39). Frances Young has divided this category – she calls
them sacrifices for sin – into three types: the expiatory type which
intends removal of pollution and the cleansing of sins; the propitiatory
type that tries to buy off the anger of the offended God or to placate
him; and finally, the aversion type, which Evans-Pritchard calls the
apotropaic type (38) and by which the evil powers are to be driven from
the sacrificers[9]. I have gone into some details here, because the sacrifices
for sin, the piacular sacrifices, are to many people nowadays what sacrifices are really about.

One could, of course, discuss the merits of this definition. It can be
considered to be too artificial, as it relies on diverse ethnographic material. But it in every way suits our purposes: it shows how complex sacrifice is. Moreover, by stressing the ritual, bloody, and propitiatory elements, it is a good illustration of the second reason why people are so
reluctant to use sacrificial language in Christian redemption: Sacrifices
are, to our modern minds, simply disgusting.

The aversion to sacrifice

Sacrificial language and sacrificial images are common in the history
of Christian spirituality and theology. In Roman Catholic liturgy, the
Holy Eucharist is celebrated as a sacrifice[10] and in Protestant, especially
pietist, communities, there has been a special devotion to Christ's

---

9. YOUNG, *Sacrifice* (n. 7), pp. 119-121.
10. Cf. *Catechism of the Catholic Church*, Liguori, Libreria Editrice Vaticana, 1994,
nr. 1365.

wounds and his precious blood[11]. Although not explicitly related to a sacrificial practice, the specific Roman Catholic devotion to the Sacred Heart of Jesus was a sign of the presence of sacrificial motifs in popular spirituality. I say, 'was', because there is a definite decline in the veneration of all the attributes connected with Christ's death as a sacrifice. As J.S. Whale has remarked, "modern man finds the very idea (of sacrifice) revolting, on more than one ground"[12]. Frances Young shows in two modern novels – now classics – that the theme of sacrifice plays a key role, but she, too, has to confess that only by actualizing the concept of sacrifice considerably can the meaning of it be demonstrated and the repulsion to it reduced slightly[13].

Blood and the concept of violence are the biggest obstacles to many faithful to accept sacrifice as a means for salvation and redemption. It is seen as something that does not fit in with the idea of God, which Jesus has given to us. To many, the God who does not need the blood of bullock or goat, lamb or pigeon, is what Jesus has taught us about his Father. Direct access to God without rituals is, for many, the major difference with the Old Testament. Whether this is true, is a question we still have to discuss.

This direct access is also opposed to the idea of substitution which is inherent in all kinds of sacrifices for sin. Immanuel Kant long ago formulated in philosophical terms the main objection against vicarious satisfaction: Guilt is not "a transferable commitment, that can, like a debt, be given to somebody else[14]." Kant expressed this in the terms of the Enlightenment, in which personal responsibility was extremely valuable. But it is also in line with the spirit of our time to carry one's own sins rather seek their removal by somebody from outside. This applies not only to the faithful, but also to theology. Sacrifices with violence, blood, and substitution seem to many theologians to run counter to what Jesus meant in his Gospel. Is sacrifice really the exclusive or predominant way in which Jesus himself and the New Testament interpreted his death?

---

11. For many hymns in the protestant tradition, these are favourite topics. Cf. K. P. JÖRNS, *Der Sühnetod Jesu Christi in Frömmigkeit und Predigt. Ein praktisch-theologischer Diskurs*, in *Zeitschrift für Theologie und Kirche, Beiheft*, 8 (1990) 70-93.

12. J.S. WHALE, *Victor and Victim. The Christian Doctrine of Redemption*, Cambridge, Cambridge University Press, 1960 p. 42.

13. YOUNG, *Sacrifice* (n. 7) pp. 101-131; the novels are: John Steinbeck's *To a God Unknown* and William Golding's *Lord of the Flies*.

14. I. KANT, *Die Religion innerhalb der Grenzen der bloßen Vernunft*, ed. K. Vorländer (Philosophische Bibliothek, 45), Hamburg, Felix Meiner Verlag, 1990, p. 77 (B 95).

Sacrifice and New Testament

In his famous 1941 essay on demythologization, Rudolf Bultmann defended the proposition that "this mythological interpretation (of the cross as a vicarious expiatory sacrifice), in which sacrificial images and a juridical theory of satisfaction intermingle, cannot be accepted any longer"[15]. Nowadays opposition to the sacrificial interpretation or the cross is no longer restricted to Protestant theologians. In general terms, Karl Rahner and Edward Schillebeeckx have pointed out that the exclusive stress on the sacrificial interpretation is not in accordance with the testimony of the New Testament[16]. Prominent Catholic exegetes and systematic theologians such as Rudolf Schnackenburg, Otto Knoch and Wilhelm Breuning have asked: "Is the idea of Jesus' expiatory death the only way to understand salvation through Jesus"[17]? They point to the theology of St. Luke, in which the imitation of the way of Jesus means salvation. Many other exegetes call attention to the non-sacrificial role of the cross and death of Jesus in the Gospel of St. John. The late German Catholic exegete, Josef Blank, went so far as to propose that Jesus was put to death because of his opposition to the Jerusalem sacrificial Temple cult[18]. So, one might say that on the question of whether or not, according to the New Testament testimony, humankind is redeemed by a sacrifice, there is no unanimity amongst exegetes.

To demonstrate the dispute in more detail, I shall now turn to the theses which some Tübinger scholars have put forward in clear opposition to Bultmann's rejection of redemption by Jesus' vicarious sacrifice[19]. These so-called 'Tübinger Antithesen' have found justification for their

15. R. BULTMANN, *Neues Testament und Mythologie. Das Problem der Entmythologisierung der neutestamentlichen Verkündigung*, in *Kerygma und Mythos*, I, Hamburg, [5]1967, pp. 15-48, esp. 42.

16. R. SCHENK, *Opfer und Opferkritik römisch-katholischer Theologie*, in ID., (ed.) *Zur Theorie des Opfers. Ein interdisziplinäres Gespräch* (Collegium Philosophicum, 1), Stuttgart-Bad Cannstatt, Friedrich Frommann Verlag – Günther Holzboog, 1995 pp. 193-250, esp. 240-248.

17. R. SCHNACKENBURG, O. KNOCH and W. BREUNING, *Ist der Gedanke des Sühnetodes Jesu der einzige Zugang zum Verständnis unserer Erlösung durch Jesus Christus?*, in K. KERTELGE (ed.), *Der Tod Jesu. Deutungen im Neuen Testament* (Quaestiones Disputatae, 74), Freiburg/Basel/Wien, Herder, 1976, pp. 205-230.

18. J. BLANK, *Weißt du, was Versöhnung heißt? Der Kreuztod Jesu als Sühne und Versöhnung*, in J.BLANK & J.WERBICK (eds.), *Sühne und Versöhnung* (Theologie zur Zeit, 1), Düsseldorf, Patmos Verlag, 1986, pp. 21-91.

19. For a review of the 'Tübinger Antithesen' cf. I.U. DALFERTH, *Die soteriologische Relevanz der Kategorie des Opfers. Dogmatische Erwägungen im Anschluß an die gegenwärtige exegetische Diskussion*, in *Jahrbuch f. Bibl. Theol.* 6 (1991) 173-194, and by W. STEGEMANN, *Der Tod Jesu als Opfer? Anthropologische Aspekte seiner Deutung im Neuen Testament*, in RIESS (ed), *Abschied von der Schuld* (n. 5), pp. 120-139.

views in a careful examination of post-exile sacrificial practice in the Jerusalem Temple. They interpret the ritual, cultic sacrifices as a means to pay off the death penalty that is inflicted on sinners. They point to an analogy in juridical matters. In juridical disputes, a ransom can be agreed upon by the conflicting parties instead of the actual punishment. Such a settlement, *kofèr* in Hebrew, may also be reached between God and sinful men or women in the act of sacrificing. Jesus' death on the cross is in the light of this sacrificial practice seen as a ransom (cf. Mc 10,45). Humankind is redeemed by the sacrifice Jesus offered on the cross as an atonement for their sins.

Helmut Gese, Otfried Hofius, Peter Stuhlmacher, and Bernd Janowski[20], the main defenders of the 'Tübinger Antithesen', have argued again in favor of the plausibility and importance of Jesus' cross as a sacrifice. It is, however, vitally important to notice that the proponents of these theses base them on their study of second Temple sacrifices. They have established a new understanding of these sacrifices. First, they explicitly stress the atoning implication of all sacrifices. Then they point out that the atoning effect of the sacrifice is due to the initiative of God. In profane, juridical disputes, only the party that has suffered damage could agree upon a settlement by way of expiation, that is, by paying a ransom. In the communication between God and sinners, it is also God who accepts the sacrifice as expiation. So, there is no question of men or women placating and pleasing God by sacrificing and in this way actually 'buying' redemption or reconciliation. Finally, in this interpretation, substitution plays an important role. The sacrificial victim takes the place of the sacrificer or the one who orders the sacrifice. The killing is only a means to provide the blood, that is, a sign of life, given in place of the life of the sinner[21].

Three reactions to these theses show, on the one hand, how complicated the exegetical situation is, and, on the other hand, how gradually the concept of sacrifice can be cleared of the theological objections that hinder its use as an interpretation of Jesus' life and death.

---

20. Cf. H. GESE, *Die Sühne*, in ID., *Zur biblischen Theologie. Alttestamentliche Vorträge,* Tübingen, J.C.B. Mohr (Paul Siebeck), [3]1983 pp. 85-106; O. HOFIUS, *Sühne und Versöhnung. Zum paulinischen Verständnis der Kreuzestodes Jesu,* in W. MAAS (ed.), *Versuche, das Leiden und Sterben Jesu zu verstehen,* München/Zürich, 1983, pp. 25-46; P. STUHLMACHER, *Sühne oder Versöhnung? Randbemerkungen zu Gerhard Friedrichs Studie "Die Verkündigung des Todes Jesu im Neuen Testament",* in U. LUTZ & H. WEDER (eds.), *Die Mitte des NT. Einheit und Vielfalt neutestamentlicher Theologie* (FS E. Schweizer z. 70. Geb), Göttingen, Vandenhoeck & Ruprecht, 1983 pp. 291-316; B. JANOWSKI, *Sühne als Heilsgeschehen* (WMANT, 55), Neukirchen-Vluyn, Neukirchener Verlag, 1982.

21. H. GESE, *Die Sühne* (n. 20), pp. 97-98.

Ingold Dalferth has, as a systematic theologian, reacted strongly against the dogmatic way in which the Tübinger put forward their sacrificial interpretation of Jesus' death. He argues that there is a definite devaluation of the use of sacrificial language in the New Testament and in Early Christianity[22]. Therefore, it is unjustified to maintain that only the category of expiatory sacrifice expresses adequately the salvific meaning of Jesus' death. Dalferth demonstrates that St. Paul, contrary to what the Tübinger assert, has broken up the soteriological significance of the sacrificial model. The cross can only be said to be a sacrifice by way of paradox[23].

Adrian Schenker, a Catholic Old Testament exegete from Fribourg, fully agrees with the interpretation of the Old Testament sacrifices as a form of ransom (Sühne), but, to him, Jesus' death is not a ransom in exchange for the punishment that humankind has deserved for its sins. The ransom's goal was to prevent the killing. Evidently, Christ's death on the cross did not. Schenker questions the specifically atoning effect of Christ's death[24]. Wolfgang Stegemann also claims that there is no evidence that Jesus' cross is to be understood as an atonement for sins[25].

The Swiss Jesuit Raymund Schwager, professor of systematic Theology in Innsbruck rejects, in a polemic with Schenker, the entire idea of a sacrificial interpretation. As a – critical – follower of René Girard, he considers sacrifices essentially as reproductions of the historical action by which guilt is transferred to an innocent victim in order to bring an end to rivalry and conflict. Whatever theologically correct concept of sacrifice may have been developed in the course of time, the violent origin of sacrifice is preserved. Jesus' death is not a sacrifice[26]. Jesus' reaction to his opponents who put him to death exposes the scapegoat mechanism underlying all sacrifices and as such indicates the end of all sacrificing as an instrument of salvation and atonement[27]. In the opinion of Schwager, the salvific effect of Christ's death consists precisely in the abolition of sacrifice[28].

22. Cf. I.U. DALFERTH, *Christ Died For Us: Reflections on the Sacrificial Language of Salvation*, in W. SYKES (ed), *Sacrifice and Redemption: Durham Essays in Theology*, Cambridge, Cambridge University Press, 1991, pp. 299-325.

23. DALFERTH, *Die soteriologische Relevanz* (n. 19), p. 119.

24. A. SCHENKER, *Versöhnung und Sühne. Wege gewaltfreier Konfliktlösung im Alten Testament. Mit einem Ausblick auf das Neue Testament* (Biblische Beiträge, 15), Freiburg/Schw., Verlag Schweizer. Kath. Bibelwerk, 1981, p. 125.

25. STEGEMANN, *Der Tod Jesu* (n. 19), p. 122.

26. R. SCHWAGER, *Versöhnung und Sühne. Zur gleichnamigen Studie von Adrian Schenker*, in *Theologie und Philosophie* 58 (1983) 217-225.

27. R. SCHWAGER, *Brauchen wir einen Sündenbock? Gewalt und Erlösung in den biblischen Schriften*, München, Kösel Verlag, 1978, pp. 196-219.

28. R. SCHWAGER, *Christ's Death and the Prophetic Critique of Sacrifice*, in A.J. MCKENNA (ed.), *René Girard and Biblical Studies* (Semeia, 33), Decatur, GA, Scholars Press, 1985, pp. 109-123, esp. 119-121.

II. Interlude: Sacrificial Language in Spite of Objections?

Assessing the results of our explorations so far, I am, it seems, forced to the conclusion that there is no connection between Christian redemption and sacrifice. Nobody doubts that, as stated in the Christian Creed, Christ's death has effected salvation. But no Creed states explicitly that this salvific death was a sacrifice or that only the interpretation of this death as a sacrifice turns it into the cause of Christian salvation. Consequently, there does not seem to be any necessity to use sacrificial language in connection with Christian redemption. Why hold on to it then? There seem to be more arguments against than in favor of it.

I would agree that Christ's death on the cross was not a sacrifice in the strictly ritual and cultic sense. Nor can it be denied that no sacrifices are offered in Christian worship, no violence is applied, no animal or human being is ritually killed, and no real blood is shed. In fact, early Christianity objected strongly to sacrificing as a part of its religious life[29]. Nevertheless, it would be unwise to just do away with all references to sacrificing when trying to identify the causes of Christian redemption. In favor of this cautious standpoint, I submit a few considerations which may justify a further investigation of a careful and balanced use of sacrificial language and imagery.

(1) Generally speaking, religion is understood as communication with the transcendental dimension of life. This communication is often interrupted. Men and women fail to live up to the conditions that enable them to be in harmony and unity with the transcendent and divine. In many religions, sacrifices are a common means not only to stimulate good contacts with the divine, but also to make up for the interruptions. They are ideally the expression of deep feelings of gratitude, dependency, and guilt. Ritual rigidity and crude violence may obscure these feelings, but sacrifices are very strong reminders of adequate religious relations.

(2) Sacrificing was common in Jesus' Jewish background and was a general practice in the Roman world up to the fourth century. It is not surprising that in this religious climate Jesus' death was interpreted as a sacrifice, as can be witnessed in several passages of the New Testament. As one – not necessarily the most elevated and certainly not the exclusive – interpretation of what happened at Calvary, the concept of salvation through Jesus' sacrifice on the cross may claim our attention.

(3) In our civilized culture, sacrifices are despised as primitive. We often tend to forget how thin and fragile the layer of our culture and civilization

---

29. Cf. F. YOUNG, *Opfer IV: Neues Testament und Alte Kirche,* in *TRE* 25 (1995), 271-278, esp. 271: Frühchristliche "Opferkritik".

is. In times of disorder, war, and panic, we are only steps away from sacrificial practices. This is not a plea for regression to ritual sacrifices. On
the contrary. However, the fact that sacrificial language and symbolism
are seemingly so remote from modern people and so harmful to their
religious feelings, is no valid argument to banish it from theological
reflection. There is in the practice of sacrificial offering a strong
reminder of forgotten truths: the truth of evil that needs to be averted,
the defilement that should be wiped away. But also the value of giving
back to God what we have received and of receiving forgiveness, reconciliation and unity in return.

Therefore, I want to save the real meaning of sacrifice, leaving aside
the ugly and violent aspects, and to connect expiation, atonement, reconciliation, and salvation with the death of Christ. His death, violent
though not a ritual sacrifice, shows how much reconciliation and
redemption has cost. The cost of his death "for us" has the value of a
sacrifice. The heavy burden of disrupted relations and the cost of their
reparation give theology the right and the obligation to use the metaphor
of sacrifice to express the process of Christian redemption.

III. The Spiritual and Metaphorical Understanding of Sacrifice

What exactly is meant by a spiritual understanding of sacrifice? Often
this qualification is applied to justify continuing use of sacrificial language. According to R. Daly, a Jesuit scholar, "spiritualization is a term
so open to different and even opposing meanings that it can hardly be
defined adequately"[30]. However, the general sense may be taken to be a
shift from the material actions or ritual performances to the inner or ethical significance of sacrifice. I would not go as far as that. There is a use
of sacrifice that is between the real sacrifice and the ethical interpretation. It is the metaphorical use of sacrifice.

In this final part, I shall first present an interpretation of Christian
redemption in which a spiritual and metaphorical concept of sacrifice
has an important, but not a decisive impact. I shall then move on to what
I consider to be the heart of Christian redemption: God's continuing
interest in the salvation of humankind throughout history and especially
in the incarnation, life, and death of his son, Jesus Christ. This movement of God's condescension towards humankind has its parallel in
humanity's elevation towards God through the self-offering of Christ.

30. R. Daly, *The Origins of the Christian Doctrine of Sacrifice*, Philadelphia,
Fortress Press, 1978, p. 6.

He is the intercessor between God and humankind, even more: he is the representative of God with humanity and of humanity with God. This substitution theory lies at the basis of Christian understanding of sacrifice. I shall call this the incarnational interpretation of redemption. I shall conclude this article by summarizing the outcome of the argument.

Sacrifice as an important metaphor of atonement

Some would like to call the non-literal and non-ritual understanding of sacrifice the truly spiritual or symbolic interpretation, but I prefer to describe it as a metaphor. A metaphor is, as Janet Soskice has put it, "speaking of one thing in terms which are seen to be suggestive of another"[31]. Sacrifice is, in this sense, used as a model to refer to something that is situated in another semantic field. I suggest that the metaphor sacrifice expresses a specific side of Christ's atoning work. The metaphor of the battlefield denotes the victory over evil powers, in particular, God's adversary, the devil; the metaphor of the court of justice refers to the guilt and punishment of the sinner, taken over by Christ in his vicarious satisfaction. The metaphor of sacrifice, in its turn, deals with the purification of pollution and defilement[32]. The blood of the vicarious victim is meant to wipe or wash away whatever has gotten in the way of communication with God. As Helmut Gese, the main proponent of the Tübinger 'Antithesen,' remarks, the goal of atoning sacrifice is to achieve incorporation into the sacred[33]. Metaphors are not invented to answer the question of how exactly this incorporation takes place. Metaphors only suggest images. They appeal to imagination. So, it is not appropriate to maintain that we are redeemed and reconciled by a metaphorical sacrifice and then to ask, *who* has offered *what* to *whom*. In that case, Christ's sacrifice would be an allegory and not a metaphor.

So, as a metaphor, Christ's death is not a real sacrifice. In fact, the interpretation of Christ's passion and death as a sacrifice is not possible unless essential features of the sacrificial practice and ritual are ignored or viewed in a way that is different from the way they are normally seen. The most important change, of course, is the identification of sacrificer and victim. Falk Wagner calls this "the inversion of a transitive cultic sacrifice into a transitive-intransitive christological

31. J.M. Soskice, *Metaphor and Religious Language*, Oxford, OUP, 1985, pp. 23; 49.
32. Cf. C. Gunton, *The Actuality of Atonement: A Study of Metaphor, Rationality and the Christian Tradition*, Edinburgh, T&T Clark, 1988, pp. 53-141.
33. Gese, *Die Sühne* (n. 20), p. 98.

self-sacrifice"[34]. The self-offering of Jesus should also not be pressed too hard. Otherwise the self-offering (Rom 5,6-11) will look like a suicide. Or, in the case that it is the Father who ultimately delivers up his son for us (Rom 8,32), the ugly image arises of a Father who wants the death of his son. If the self-offering of Christ is taken to be the essence or, for that matter, the spiritual meaning of the metaphor of sacrificial redemption, a series of vital aspects of Christian belief will be seen in proper perspective. I shall devote some attention to two important consequences.

(1) Speaking of redemption by Christ's sacrifice for us is not restricted to the moment of his death or to his actual suffering. All phases of his life can be interpreted as the self-offering of Jesus Christ.

(2) This sheds light on a controversial point. During the Council of Trent, a hotly debated issue was whether the Last Supper was a true sacrifice or not. In the final decree, it is only stated that Christ has instituted a visible sacrament. With these words the Council "carefully refrains from declaring that the Last Supper was... in itself or by itself, a sacrifice"[35]. But it was simultaneously declared that the Eucharist is a real sacrifice, though without the spilling of blood. This leads to the conclusion that the sacrifice of the Holy Mass is the repetition of Christ's expression during the Last Supper of his willingness to sacrifice himself "for us" (Mt 26,26-29 par; 1 Cor 11,23-26). No new sacrifice is offered in Holy Eucharist, nor is there a sacrificer other than Christ himself, the priest acting sacramentally *in persona Christi*[36]. Metaphor and sacrament turn out to be closely connected. Although sacrificial language in connection with the Eucharist remains a source of misunderstanding, there is in ecumenical declarations, as the recent study of Elisabeth Hönig shows, a growing consensus on this point[37].

---

34. F. WAGNER, *Die christliche Revolutionierung des Gottesgedankens als Ende und Aufhebung menschlicher Opfer,* in SCHENK (ed), *Zur Theorie des Opfers* (n. 16), pp. 251-279, esp. 254.

35. J.F. McHUGH, *The Sacrifice of the Mass at the Council of Trent,* in S.W. SYKES (ed), *Sacrifice and Redemption: Durham Essays in Theology,* Cambridge, CUP, 1991, p. 175. Cf. D.N. POWER, *The Sacrifice we offer. The Tridentine Dogma and its Reinterpretation,* Edinburgh, T.&T. Clark, 1987, pp. 94-133, esp. 132; D. POWER, *The Eucharistic Mystery: Revitalizing the Tradition,* New York, Crossroad, 1992, pp. 257-263.

36. Cf. J. PIERCE, *The Eucharist as Sacrifice: Some Contemporary Roman Catholic Reflections,* in *Worship* 69 (1995) nr.5, 394-405.

37. E. HÖNIG, *Die Eucharistie als Opfer nach den neueren ökumenischen Erklärungen,* Paderborn, F. Schöningh, 1989; cf. Th. SCHNEIDER, *Opfer Jesu Christi und der Kirche. Zum Verständnis der Aussagen des Konzils von Trient,* in K.LEHMANN – E. SCHLINK (eds.), *Das Opfer Jesu Christi und seine Gegenwart in der Kirche. Klärungen zum Opfercharakter des Herrenmahles* (Dialog der Kirchen, 3), Freiburg i.Br. / Göttingen, Herder / Vandenhoeck & Ruprecht, 1983, pp. 176-195.

To sum up the conclusions of the argument: taking the interpretation of Christ's sacrifice as a metaphor clears the way to hold on to the spiritual significance of the sacrificial language of redemption, to concentrate on the special character of Jesus' self-offering, and to keep, under certain conditions, using sacrificial language in Christian worship.

Sacrifice and substitution

If it is correct that metaphors, by the images they use, are only suggestive of the reality they denote, none of the metaphors of redemption or atonement can claim exclusivity, for none of them denotes *all* aspects of Christian redemption. The metaphor of the altar and the sacrifice deals, strictly speaking, only with purification and entrance into the sacred. But sacrifices can also refer to victory on the battlefield, as the so-called sacrifices of aversion do; or to punishment or atonement for guilt, which is the competence of the court of justice. These are the expiatory and propitiatory aspects of sacrifice Gese has in mind when he claims that sacrifices are not just a substitute for the punishment the sinner deserves. They are, in his interpretation of Judaic sacrificial ritual cult, the sign that God accepts the sacrifice instead of the life of the sinner, who has, in sinning, gambled his life away[38]. The sacrifice stands for the total existence of the sinner (Existenzstellvertretung[39]). Schenker applies this to Jesus' self-offering and interprets it as the acceptance and taking over of the guilt of his fellow-men and women, inspired by "a rare brotherly solidarity and friendship"[40].

Consequently, the sacrifice which redeems and reconciles us has to do with substitution. This goes further than intercession. Jesus is not merely the negotiator between God and humankind in need of reconciliation. He takes our place and dies "for us." Sacrificial connotations are certainly implied in the "for us" formulas. But even more significant is the fact that Jesus gives or offers his life *in our place*. The substitution element that is inherent in practically all sacrifices is stressed by St Paul[41]. The

---

38. GESE, *Die Sühne* (n. 20), pp. 86; 97.

39. P. STUHLMACHER, *Existenzstellvertretung für die Vielen: Mk 10,45 [Mt 20,28]*, in ID., *Versöhnung, Gesetz und Gerechtigkeit. Aufsätze zur biblischen Theologie*, Göttingen, Vandenhoeck & Ruprecht, 1981 pp. 27-42; B. JANOWSKI, *Auslösung des verwirkten Lebens. Zur Geschichte und Struktur der biblischen Lösegeldvorstellung*, in *Zeitschrift für Theologie und Kirche* 79 (1982) 25-59.

40. SCHENKER, *Versöhnung und Sühne* (n. 24), p. 126.

41. R. BIERINGER, *Traditionsgeschichtlicher Ursprung und theologischer Bedeutung der Hyper-Aussagen im Neuen Testament*, in F. VAN SEGBROEK e.a. (eds.), *The Four Gospels 1992*. Festschrift Frans Neirynck (BETL, 100), Leuven, University Press / Uitgeverij Peeters, 1992, pp. 219-248.

Catholic theologian Karl-Heinz Menke, who has written a voluminous book on substitution, maintains that substitution is a key concept of Christian life and a basic category for theology[42]. He identifies Christ's self-offering on the cross and the absolute solidarity with sinful humankind, which forces him to take unconditionally their place[43].

Not only is Christ's death on the cross a sign of his self-offering on behalf of and in the place of sinners, making up for their sins and reconciling them with God. He also takes the place of God in human history. The cross is the ultimate consequence of the incarnation of God in history. For St. John, the sending of the son by the Father into this world was enough to show his unconditional saving love (Jn 3,16). For St. Paul, the incarnation of God's love culminated in the cross, which occasionally is described as the sacrifice Christ or his Father offers on behalf of salvation (Rom 3,25, 1 Cor 5,7). This means a complete change in the economy of sacrificing. Not only is it God's initiative rather than that of the sacrificer that brings about the effect of the sacrifice, as the Tübinger 'Antithesen' would have it, the identification of God and the victim in Christ's self-sacrifice causes yet another revolution, a revolution in our understanding of God, as Falk Wagner, following the example of Jürgen Moltmann, has phrased it[44].

In order to spell out the consequences of this revolution, it is essential to realize how, in the testimony of both the first and the second testament, God has related himself to humankind. It appears that, from the beginning, God has had a continuing interest in the well-being of humankind. Redemption, in other words, has always been a matter of personal interest and relationship. According to the stories handed down to us in Scripture, the loving acts of God prevail over his judgment. Langdon Gilkey has described God's actions in terms of God's providence. There is reason for wrath, but in the end Gilkey ascertains a kind of cycle in which judgments again and again provides the opportunity to see the redemptive forces in history. The history of God with humankind is ultimately a history of salvation[45].

Similarly, Raymund Schwager has described Jesus' life and death as a drama of salvation. In this drama, God, Christ and his opponents clash. But in the end Jesus identifies himself in the act of self-offering with his

42. K.-H. MENKE, Stellvertretung. Schlüsselbegriff christlichen Lebens und theologische Grundkategorie, Einsiedeln/Freiburg, Johannes Verlag, 1991.

43. K.-H. MENKE, Das Gottespostulat unbedingter Solidarität und seine Erfüllung durch Christus, in Internationale katholische Zeitschrift Communio 21 (1992) 486-499.

44. WAGNER, Die christliche Revolutionierung (n. 34), pp. 269-274.

45. L. GILKEY, Reaping the Whirlwind: A Christian Interpretation of History, New York, Seabury Press, 1976, pp. 239-270.

opponents and turns judgment and wrath into the mystery of God's trinitarian self-revelation. The self-revelation, depicted by Schwager as a drama, comprises the incarnation of God in Jesus Christ and the lasting presence of Christ's self-offering in the ecclesiastical community through the Holy Spirit. The commemoration and the re-enactment of this drama in the liturgy and in common life means salvation. Drama takes the place of sacrifice[46].

I have sought to argue that Girard's demand for a non-sacrificial interpretation of Chris's death is partly to be welcomed. It draws attention to the fact that the cross was in no way a real, ritual sacrifice, offered to God to appease him or to quell his wrath. On the other hand, however, I have argued that a total rejection of sacrificial language would deprive Christian faith and theology of a means to penetrate into the heart of the history of Christian salvation. Used as a metaphor, sacrificial language and imagery is able to show the generosity of Christ's self-offering "for us" as an implication of the incarnation of divine love in human history. I am aware that my argument has restricted itself to Jesus' cross and its interpretation. The demonstration of the legitimacy or the helpfulness of a partly non-sacrificial and a partly sacrificial understanding of the redemption in which all Christians are involved demands the effort of a critical hermeneutics in our post-Enlightenment and post-modern time. This effort can only be successful when we are open to a pluralistic approach[47] to the interpretation of Jesus' life and death as the starting-point of Christian redemption. One is as justified in speaking of the myriad ways of expressing our salvation, as one is in speaking of the myriad Christ.

Theologische Faculteit   Nico SCHREURS
Katholieke Universiteit Brabant
TFT, Postbus 9130
5000 HC Tilburg
The Netherlands

46. R. SCHWAGER, *Jesus im Heilsdrama.Entwurf einer biblischen Erlösungslehre* (Innsbrucker Theologische Studien, 29), Innsbruck / Wien, Tyrolia Verlag, pp. 203-287.
47. DALFERTH, *Die soteriologische Relevanz* (n. 19), 182.

CHRISTOLOGICAL IMPLICATIONS OF THE ECUMENICAL AGREEMENT ON JUSTIFICATION

INTRODUCTION

During the past decade remarkable ecumenical results have been achieved regarding the doctrine of justification. A case in point is especially the North American and German Lutheran-Roman Catholic dialogues[1]. The result of these two dialogues together formed the basic material for a third document: *Church and Justification* issued by the international Lutheran-Roman Catholic Joint Commission[2]. On the basis of the agreement reached in these documents the Lutheran World Federation and the Vatican came to a Joint Declaration on the Doctrine of Justification, officially signed in Augsburg (Germany) on 31 October 1999. At this congress on christology I shall not deal in detail with the contents of this agreement[3]. My point is rather the question of the christological implications of this soteriological agreement. What kind of christology will this ecumenical agreement imply? This agreement is already labelled as the most important historic ecumenical step of this century, overcoming a more than four and half centuries old division in the Western church. Hence, my question is: What kind of christological consequences must we draw from this agreement in the field of soteriology?

---

1. Cf. H.G. ANDERSON – T.A. MURPHY – J.A. BURGESS (eds), *Justification by Faith: Lutherans and Catholics in Dialogue, VII*, Minneapolis, Augsburg, 1985, pp. 13-74 (Common Statement) and K. LEHMANN – W. PANNENBERG (eds), *The Condemnations of the Reformation Era: Do they still divide?*, Minneapolis, Fortress, 1989, pp. 29-69 (Justification).

2. Cf. Lutheran-Roman Catholic Joint Commission, *Church and Justification. Understanding the Church in the Light of the Doctrine of Justification*, Geneva, Lutheran World Federation, 1994. See for an extensive evaluation of the results of the ecumenical dialogues on justification, M.E. BRINKMAN, *Justification in Ecumenical Dialogue: Central Aspects of Christian Soteriology in Debate* (IIMO Research Publications No.45), Zoetermeer, Meinema, 1996 and for an summarizing article on the basis of this study, ID., *Justification in Ecumenical Dialogue: An Assessment of the Results*, in *Exchange* 26 (1997) 40-60.

3. The text is to be found in, for example, *Joint Declaration on the Doctrine of Justification: A Commentary by the Institute for Ecumenical Research, Strasbourg*, Strasbourg, Ecumenical Institute, 1997, pp. 51-71.

The Biblical Message of Justification

The Joint Declaration mentions five points which summarize the 'Biblical message of Justification'. I shall quote a shortened version of these five points:

1. Together we hear the gospel that 'God so loved the world that he gave his only Son, so that everyone who believes in him may not perish but may have eternal life' (Jn 3,16). This good news is set forth in Holy Scripture in various ways. In the Old Testament we listen to God's word about human sinfulness.... and human disobedience.... as well as of God's 'righteousness'.... and 'judgement'....
2. In the New Testament diverse treatments of 'righteousness' and 'justification' are found.... In Paul's letters also, the gift of salvation is described in various ways.... 'Christ has set us free' (Gal 5,1-13....); 'reconciled to God' (2 Cor 5,18-21); 'peace with God' (Rom 5,1); 'new creation'(2 Cor 5,17).... Chief among these is the 'justification' of sinful human beings by God's grace through faith (Rom 3,23-25), which came into particular prominence in the Reformation period.
3. Paul sets forth the gospel as the power of God for salvation of the person who has fallen under the power of sin, as the message that proclaims that 'the righteousness of God'.... grants justification (Rom 3,21-31).... Justification becomes ours through Christ Jesus 'whom God put forward as a sacrifice of atonement by his blood, effective through faith' (Rom 3,25)....
4. Justification is the forgiveness of sins...., liberation from the dominating power of sin and death....and from the curse of the law....
5. The justified live by faith that comes from the Word of Christ.... and is active through love...., the fruit of the Spirit.... But since the justified are assailed from within and without by powers and desires.... and fall into sin...., they must constantly hear God's promises anew, confess their sins...., participate in Christ's body and blood, and be exhorted to live righteously in accord with the will of God....

Important Decisions

One of the most important decisions made in this text is the admission that there are in the New Testament 'diverse treatment of righteousness and justification' and that even in Paul's letters 'salvation is described in various ways'. Here the text refers to different concepts like, for example, freedom, reconciliation, peace and new creation. This recognition of a variety of salvation concepts in the New Testament is fully in accordance with the analysis of the well-known Lutheran ecumenist Harding Meyer of the contribution of his church to the ecumenical dialogues. His conclusion is that even if the doctrine of justification can be considered as a decisive interpretation of the centre of the gospel, this does not rule out other decisive interpretations of the salvation event to which other church traditions refer preferably[4].

With regard to my question on the christological impact of this agreement my first conclusion can be that this ecumenical text does not point to one exclusive interpretation of the salvation event in Christ. The recognition of a broad spectrum of salvific words in the language of the New Testament can be regarded as one of the most concrete results of modern New Testament scholarship. The frequent references in recent ecumenical texts to the publications of New Testament scholars such as, for example, the Presbyterian James Dunn, the Roman Catholic Karl Kertelge and John Fitzmyer and the Lutheran John Reumann are an instructive indication of this impact[5]. That means that we can already nuance the importance of our main question on the christological impact of this ecumenical agreement on justification. Whatever our answer will be, it is only the answer to the impact of one soteriological 'model'. There are more soteriological 'models' to be articulated.

In their Joint Declaration on justification Roman Catholics and Lutherans, nevertheless, share the conviction that the message of justification directs us in a special way towards the heart of the New Testament witness to God's saving action in Christ: it tells us that, as sinners, our new life is solely due to the forgiving and renewing mercy which God imparts as a gift and which we receive in faith and can never merit in any way. That means that, although this soteriological model is not the only one, it is definitively a model that touches the heart of the gospel. And that gives yet again a certain weight to our question on the christological impact of this agreement.

CHRISTOLOGICAL IMPLICATIONS?

The text itself refers only in rather vague terms to the implied christology. The most explicit reference we quoted above in the sentence

4. Cf. H. MEYER, *The Doctrine of Justification in the Lutheran Dialogue with Other Churches*, in *One in Christ* 17 (1981) 86-116, p. 116.

5. Cf. J.D.G. DUNN, *Unity and Diversity in the New Testament: An Inquiry into the Character of Earliest Christianity*, London, SCM, 1977; K. KERTELGE, *'Rechtfertigung' bei Paulus. Studien zur Struktur und zum Bedeutungsgehalt des paulinischen Rechtfertigungsbegriffs* (Neutestamentliche Abhandlungen, Neue Folge, 3), Münster, Aschendorff, 1967; J. REUMANN – J.A. FITZMYER, *Scripture as Norm for our Common Faith*, in *Midstream* 30 (1993) 81-107 and J. REUMANN (ed.), *'Righteousness' in the New Testament: 'Justification' in the United States Lutheran-Roman Catholic Dialogue*, Philadelphia, Fortress/New York, Paulist, 1982.

'Justification becomes ours through Christ Jesus "whom God put forward as a sacrifice of atonement by his blood, effective through faith"' (Rom.3,25). In this sentence we are confronted with a quotation of one of the most well-known bible texts which grounds the classic doctrine of justification as articulated especially in the Lutheran confessional writings. Although thus, I have to repeat it, this Joint Declaration does not give one exclusive interpretation of the Gospel, it is nevertheless obvious that this focus on the justification model pushes us in the direction of a specific approach of our salvation, namely a judicial approach[6].

Having arrived at this point we can put our question more specifically and ask: Does the judicial context of the doctrine of justification necessarily imply a judicial satisfaction christology like that of Anselm? In order to answer this question I propose to proceed in the following way. First, I shall deal with the, in my opinion, legitimate judicial context of this doctrine. Secondly, I hope to show that there are more adequate christological concepts to give account of this context than only the Anselmian one.

Christianity has often been blamed for imposing an unreasonably great feeling of guilt on humanity. One of the main spokesmen of this reproach is the French Roman Catholic historian Jean Delumeau. He wrote a 'cultural history of sin' of the Western-European society of the 13th to the 18th century. Delumeau speaks of a 'religion of anxiety' and observes 'that no civilisation had ever attached as much importance to guilt and shame as did the Western world'[7]. In Delumeau's interpretation the doctrine of justification in its 16th century form represents the logical, though extreme, end of a long desolate road through pessimism: 'The result was a type of preaching that spoke more of the passion of the Saviour than of His Resurrection, more of sin than of pardon, more of the Judge than of the Father, more of Hell than of Paradise'[8]. I shall not criticize Delumeau's historical description of the Western European society of that time. I am inclined, however, to criticize his analysis of the exclusively religious causes of this widespread fear. In medieval society there were a lot of fear generating circumstances like illness, wars, hunger, etc. It seems to me unfair to blame only one of these factors for being the most influential one[9].

6. Cf. O.H. PESCH, *Gerechtfertigt aus Glauben. Luthers Anfrage an die Kirche* (Quaestiones Disputatae, 97), Freiburg/Basel/Wien, Herder, 1982, p. 46. Pesch points here to the 'constitutive' rol of the office of the 'judge'(Richter) in this doctrine.

7. J. DELUMEAU, *Sin and Fear: The Emergence of a Western Guilt Culture 13th-18th Centuries*, New York, St. Martin's, 1990, 27.

8. *Ibidem*, 557.

9. See for wellknown descriptions of the multiplicity of fear generating circumstances in the Middle Ages e.g. J. HUIZINGA, *The Waning of the Middle Ages: A Study of the*

Besides this historical objection I should like to point to the intention of one of the main promulgators of this doctrine, Martin Luther. It was his great discovery that God's righteousness is definitely and insepara-bly connected with Christ's righteousness, i.e. His mercifulness. Luther was convinced of the liberating power of the justification in Christ and hence he interpreted the Cross of Christ as liberation of anxiety, as real freedom[10]. His favourite bible texts were Romans 8,15 and Galatians 4,31–5,1: 'The Spirit you have received is not a spirit of slavery leading you back into a life of fear, but a Spirit that makes us sons, enabling us to cry "Abba! Father!"' and 'You see, then, my brothers, we are no slave-woman's children; our mother is the free woman. Christ sets us free, to be free men. Stand firm, then, and refuse to be tied to the yoke of slavery again'.

However much, however, one may disagree historically on the harm-ful or liberating impact of this doctrine, it is at least a historical fact that this doctrine presupposes a strong consciousness of guilt. And this pre-supposition immediately raises the question whether such a conscious-ness still exists in our present-day culture and what effects it may have on the articulation of our faith, our life, etc.

FIRST THESIS: A FAIR CONSCIOUSNESS OF GUILT

My first thesis is that it is very salutary to admit a fair consciousness of guilt. Of course, there are overwhelmingly many examples of the paralysing and destructive effects of the cultivation of an unfair con-sciousness of guilt, often stimulated by the church. Modern literature abundantly testifies to this. Calling guilt 'guilt', however, confronting a person with the consequences of his own decisions and acts and accus-ing him of being 'guilty', accountable, responsible, etc. belongs to one of the main characteristics of righteous, human behaviour. It is one of the main aspects of human dignity. It calls upon a person to render account, in freedom of choice, of his personal responsibility in solidarity

---

Form of Life, Thought and Art in France and the Netherlands in the XIVth and XVth Cen-turies, New York, Doubleday 1954 and B. TUCHMAN, *A Distant Mirror: The Calamitous 14th Century*, New York, Knopf, 1978[11].

10. Cf. H.A. OBERMAN, *Luther. Mensch zwischen Gott und Teufel*, Berlin, Severin/Siedler, 1983[2], p. 161: 'Luthers Entdeckung ist darin völlig neu, dass er sieht, wie Gottes Gerechtigkeit mit der Gerechtigkeit Christi untrennbar vereint und darin aufgegangen ist'. The same holds true for Calvin. Cf. W.J. BOUWSMA, *John Calvin: A Sixteenth Century Portrait*, New York/Oxford, Oxford University, 1988, p. 45: 'The goal of the Christian life prominently included the relief of anxiety'.

with fellow human beings. This typically human situation of accountability makes a famous novel like Franz Kafka's *The Trial* have such a
worldwide impact as an impressive and heartbreaking description of the
universal human condition, continuously challenged by the question:
'Where is the judge?', 'Where is the Court?'.

This form of accountability should not be dismissed as outdatedly
medieval. Even the medievalist Delumeau states in the 'Introduction' to
his study *Sin and Fear*: 'We of the late 20th century have more reason
than ever to exercise prudence when tempted to pass a verdict of
"guilty" on the ecclesiastics of the past. Our era constantly speaks about
liberating itself from guilt feelings without noticing that, in the entire
history of guilt, the accusation of others has never been as strong as it is
today'[11]. On account of the many genocides and massacres in our era,
our era cries out about guilt. There is every reason for an effective,
repeated call for a tribunal at the International Court of Law in The
Hague in order to call those responsible to account. It is especially on
this point of accountability that modern liberation theology and the doctrine of justification meet, because this doctrine points to individual
responsibility and prevents one from escaping into a collectivistic alibi.
This form of individuality is pre-eminently the condition for real solidarity and demonstrates how closely the question of guilt is linked up
with the question of justice[12].

The development of a pure sense of guilt by a fair distinction between
real incapacity and reprehensible guilt is an important task for the church
in our modern culture. In the gap between the generations, the wave of
divorces and the many forms of addiction (alcohol, drugs and tobacco)
in modern Western culture, consciousness of guilt has grown considerably. The treatment of feelings of guilt, however, is no longer centred
around the church but around psychiatry. Psychiatrists have replaced
pastors. Nowadays, the forum over against which we wish to be granted
justice is, in contrast to the classic doctrine of justification, no longer
God, but one's own conscience and other people's judgement. The question may then be raised over against whom man is better off: over
against himself and his fellow humans, or over against God? A question
that cannot be answered without thinking of King David's outcry at the
end of his life: 'Let us fall into the hands of the Lord, for his mercy is
great; and let us not fall into the hands of men' (2 Sam.24,14). The
growing rapprochement between psychiatry and theology, however,

11. J. DELUMEAU, *Sin and Fear*, 5.
12. Cf. M.E. BRINKMAN, *Justification in Ecumenical Dialogue*, pp. 37-55 ('The Challenge of Ethics: Justification and Social Justice').

might well be an indication that psychiatry will not be a terminal station for the struggle with our feelings of guilt.

Therefore, the question may be asked whether the culture of guilt, brilliantly described by Delumeau, was indeed so artificially stimulated by the church. Might not the position be defensible that every era has its own fears and feelings of guilt and that the theology of every time has to deal with these real feelings? A positive answer to this question can function as a bridge between a 16th century doctrine and our modern culture. In order to build such a theological bridge I am inclined to describe the doctrine of justification in three, more or less permanent steps of reflection:

1. Our human existence presupposes an authority that calls us to account.
2. We can only for a very small part justify ourselves over against this authority.
3. We believe that the authority that calls us to account is the same as the one that can acquit us.

SECOND THESIS: A NON-ANSELMIAN CHRISTOLOGY OF THE RIGHTEOUS JUDGE

In this last, third step of reflection, we arrive at the point where the implied christology becomes crucial. And here it is the right and proper moment to articulate my second thesis, namely that the horizon of judgment which is indispensable for the doctrine of justification can only be theologically adequately articulated on the basis of the confession of the unity of the work of Jesus Christ as a unity of judgment and mercy. Only in this close connection of judgment and mercy can we speak of justification as liberation. The central motif of the doctrine of justification is the emphasis on God's undeserved merciful turning towards us, as sinners. The intention of this doctrine is to invite us to participate in the salvation founded in Christ's vicarious suffering and death. Personal and communal involvement in this liberating once-for-all event evokes the fundamental experience of divine forgiveness and acceptance.

This interpretation of the meaning of justification leads to criticism of the classic question of 'How can I find a gracious God?'. In this question the impression is created that God should receive something from us in order to be placated, whereas in contrast to this the essence of justification lies in the very fact that God grants us something, namely his forgiving love. We do not turn to God, but God turns in Christ to us. Hence, so Melanchton, one of the great Lutheran Reformers, states: being declared righteous means: being accepted by the merciful God as sinners[13]. This experience of divine acceptance as a gift profoundly determines the Christian experience of freedom. Only where a person dies and rises with Christ, can we speak of real self-acceptance as a sinner who has died and risen. In this manner, the *sola gratia* is an experience of life that relativizes all experience of possession and makes us say with Paul: 'Who makes you, my friend, so important? What do you possess that was not given you? If then you really received it as a gift, why take credit yourself?' (1 Cor.4,7).

The central christological concept of which the doctrine of justification is an interpretation is that of the participation in Christ's death and resurrection. To hear and to believe the word of justification is to die and be raised in him. So justification is not a conditional 'if-then' statement, but a causal 'since-then' and a 'because-therefore' pronouncement: Since Jesus died and rose, your sins are forgiven and you are righteous in the sight of God[14]. Keywords are here: representation and participation. Christ represents us before God and God before us. And especially in his Cross this representation has a vicarious once-for-all character which excludes mere repetition, but includes full participation. In our baptism we die and rise with him and are liberated from the burden of our sinful collectivistic and individualistic past.

Hence, my conclusion is that there are good reasons to continue our speaking about salvation in the terminology of the law court. The judge, however, is an extraordinary one. He is the judge who himself is judged in our place[15]. God judges us by identifying himself entirely with us in his son. He himself is totally involved in this judgment. This total identification of God with us brings about our justification. This christology of God's identification with us points to a form of representation which can only be interpreted as an inclusive one. Its implies our participation, our involvement in his death and resurrection,

---

13. See the text of one of the Lutheran confessional writings, Melanchton's *Apology of Confession*, IV, 71/72 and 116 in *Die Bekenntnisschriften der evangelisch-lutherischen Kirche*, Göttingen, Vandenhoeck & Ruprecht, 1986, 174 and 183.

14. Cf. G.O. FORDE, *Justification by Faith – A Matter of Death and Life*, Philadelphia, Augsburg, 1982, 21-37, pp. 36-37 and 24.

15. Cf. for this expression, K. BARTH, *Kirchliche Dogmatik*, IV/1, Zurich, Zollikon 1953, 231-311 ('Der Richter als der an unserer Stelle Gerichtete'). See for the contrast to Anselm, C. GUNTON, *Yesterday & Today: A Study of Continuities in Christology*, London, Darton et al., 1983, pp. 179-181.

symbolized in our baptism[16]. It implies our moral rebirth as acquittted people. So this soteriological 'model' of justification encompasses God's solidarity as well as our human accountability.

I.I.M.O.   Martien BRINKMAN
Heidelberglaan 2
Transitorium ll k. 825b
3584 CS Utrecht
The Netherlands

---

16. Cf. W. PANNENBERG, *Systematic Theology*, II, Grand Rapids, Eerdmans, 1994, pp. 429-437 ('Representation and Liberation').

CHRISTUS POSTMODERNUS
AN ATTEMPT AT APOPHATIC CHRISTOLOGY

From the outset of the Christian era, the central place of Jesus Christ in Christianity has evoked much theological reflection and controversy, and this remains the case in our days of postmodernism and plurality. What is the truth about Christ? How does he fulfill his role of being 'the way, the truth, and the life' (Jn 14,6). In a recent article in *Concilium*, Pierre Gisel wrote the following: "The christological truth presupposes that one dissociates oneself from every christolatry, precisely because of the truth which it reveals, concerning God as well as concerning human beings"[1]. Consequently, Jesus Christ is better considered not so much as the divine founder of Christianity but as its continual central point of reference. He is *locus* of revelation and mediation: "body and shape in which the human and the divine, the divine and the human [...] appear, are linked to each other or are 'mediated'"[2]. In this manner, Jesus is 'Jesus Christ'. Moreover, he is neither the substitute for God, nor a super-man, but the (ultimate) reference to God (Father, Spirit). Whoever praises the person of Jesus Christ, because of himself, without heeding the essential linkage to the twofold theological problem of the truth and identity of God, and the truth and identity of human beings, yields to the seduction of (christolatric) absolutism.

This seduction of absolutizing Christ is only one part of the story. In the wake of (modern totalizing) master narratives, which for the most part have lost all plausibility, and in view of the generally acknowledged plurality of world religions, Christian claims about Jesus would seem to be under attack. These claims are addressed especially to the definitive character of the revelation which occurred in Jesus Christ and his uniqueness as mediator of salvation, or to phrase it differently: the divinity of the human being Jesus Christ. In Christian circles too, nowadays, truth claims can no longer easily withstand a tendency towards relativization. For, in the eyes of many contemporaries, all religions are equal. Hence, no religious founder can be privileged. Jesus Christ must then be regarded as a religious genius like Buddha or Mohammed – human beings at the origin of a world religion, praiseworthy but nothing

---

1. P. GISEL, *De grenzen van de christologie of de bekoring van de absoluutheid*, in *Concilium* (1997) 1, 75-85, p. 76 (my translation).
2. *Ibid.*, p. 78 (my translation).

more. At the other end of the religious spectrum, the reactive rise of diverse fundamentalisms expressing absolute truth claims about Jesus Christ, represent a major consequence of this relativization of what is considered to belong among the central truths of Christianity.

This situation, being challenged and tempted by both absolutism and relativism, leaves theology with some serious questions about the self-perception of Christianity and the centrality of Jesus Christ. The old answers appear to be inadequate. In our so-called postmodern condition, theology seems in need of new patterns of thought, a new approach to address the challenges of Christianity's self-perception and the centrality of Jesus Christ herein, thus engaging in a new *fides quaerens intellectum*. A large number of contemporary theologians dedicate their research to this endeavor.

On other occasions, I have already proposed the model of an 'open narrative' as an adequate paradigm to situate Christianity after the fall of master narratives in the postmodern condition[3]. In what follows, I will first briefly sketch the main lines of this model; afterwards, starting from this model, I will focus especially on a contextually plausible conception of the central place of Jesus Christ within Christianity, a conception which also yields some indications regarding the hermeneutical position of Christian theology.

CHRISTIANITY AS AN OPEN NARRATIVE

The model of the 'open narrative' is based on patterns of thought developed by critical postmodern philosophers[4]. In their critique of the

---

3. See the references in the following footnotes.

4. These include the French philosophers of difference, such as J.-F. Lyotard, J. Derrida, M. Foucault, etc. These paragraphs are inspired by some of Lyotard's thoughts; see *La condition postmoderne. Rapport sur le savoir*, Paris, Minuit, 1979 (transl. *The Postmodern Condition. A Report on Knowledge*, Manchester, Manchester University Press, 1984); *Le différend*, Paris, Minuit, 1983 (transl. *The Differend. Phrases in Dispute*, Manchester, Manchester University Press, 1988); *Le postmoderne expliqué aux enfants. Correspondance 1982-1985*, Paris, Galilée, 1986 (transl. *The Postmodern Explained: Correspondence 1982-1985*, Minneapolis, University of Minnesota Press, 1993); *L'inhumain. Causeries sur le temps*, Paris, Galilée, 1988 (transl. *The Inhuman: Reflections on Time*, Cambridge, Polity Press, 1991). See also: *Peregrinations. Law, Form, Event*, New York, Columbia University Press, 1988. For a theological evaluation, see my *Theologie na het christelijke grote verhaal. In het spoor van Jean-François Lyotard*, in *Bijdragen. Tijdschrift voor filosofie en theologie* 55 (1994) 269-295 (with a summary in English), and my *Bearing Witness to the Differend: A Model for Theologizing in the Postmodern Context*, in *Louvain Studies* 20 (1995) 362-379.

grand or master narratives, these philosophers resolutely discard every hegemonic identification of the truth with a particular narrative. Having become conscious of the finitude, the particularity and the contingency of existence, no one can claim to have access to Truth-as-such. One does not possess truth; absolute truth claims are no longer plausible. From now on, the space for Truth-as-such is left empty. Of course, this must not stop us speaking about truth. Although one indeed is unable to take hold of the truth, one can, so to speak, remain in it, or relate to it. This happens when one vigilantly holds on to the tension between the always contextually determined articulation of particular truth claims and the irreducible inarticulate Truth-as-such – i.e., when one is aware of the unsurpassable gulf between one's own particular narrative and the *in se* inexpressible Truth to which it bears witness. Truth, then, can no longer be regarded in terms of appropriation but as relational – no longer as something one can acquire.

For J.-F. Lyotard, the 'event' implies a fundamental questioning of each articulation of truth. Such an event can be characterized as a happening of difference, in the sense of a 'differend' experienced in the interruption of a particular discourse or narrative by that which can never be grasped by the narrative itself. With this term, Lyotard points to the experience of a breach caused by the paradoxical situation in which one feels unable to express the full richness of Truth with a word, a phrase, a narrative, and senses at the same time the urgency to testify to it. After/through the event, one can not not-speak, even if one is conscious that words necessarily fail. For, due to the contemporary critical consciousness, Truth rather appears in speech as an empty place which may never be filled up. Its appearance in speech qualifies, and if necessary, criticizes, truth claims. Nevertheless, it also provokes testimony to truth, albeit an impossible testimony, because, due to the particular and contextual nature of language, it is always in a sense closing the event. In this regard, one can say that the event as an experience of difference results from a sensibility for the unutterable word, the non-expressible phrase, the inconceivable thought. Lyotard then argues for a philosophy which starts from a sort of contemplative openness for the event and bears witness to it, refusing to weaken or negate it in hegemonic thought patterns. So doing, philosophy testifies to that which does not lend itself to expression in words. Instead of a grand or master narrative, in our view, postmodern philosophy strives to become an open narrative: an always particularly and contextually embedded openness to, and testimony to the irreducible heterogeneity which accompanies human attempts at truth.

It is my conviction that – within a theological perspective – this radical hermeneutic position is very recognizable to those mindful of the *deus semper major*. In speech we refer to God but we do not lay hold of God. This religious insight thoroughly relativizes every pretension of this speech. At the same time, it actually points to its seriousness. After all, it is only via our ever-particular language that we are able to make reference to God: language is unmistakably the way to God – and thus not to be belittled – even if one has to admit that it does not reach God. Consequently, for the religious consciousness, a Christian narrative is not an autonomous and static entity; it never contains the truth itself but is an ever contextually anchored expression of the relationship of the believer to God who is truth[5]. In other words: a Christian narrative, and theology as its reflexive moment, is the expression of the relationship between the word (our words) and the Word (the Logos), between articulation in tradition (traditions) and the inarticulateness of the original Traditio[6]. To stand in this tension is to be prevented from slipping into a hegemonic truth-story, with absolute truth claims.

As a result, Christian narratives can never afford to fossilize. They must be engaged in a continuing process whereby every articulation is ultimately put under critique by the interruptive experience of the event, by the inexpressible which always breaks up each new expression. Each word is a word too little and a word too much. In a Christian perspective 'event' is the happening of grace, a grace-experience in which God reveals Godself as inexhaustible Love, to which every human expression and answer in word and deed necessarily falls short. From within itself, by the event of grace, in which the ungraspability of God is revealed, the Christian narrative is challenged to open itself, i.e., to respect and bear witness to the event of grace – though being conscious that such a witness inevitably fills in the openness.

Since the Christian narrative, or, Christian tradition, in the way it has reached us – primarily in the form of texts and stories – is not identical with God, but is indeed the way to God, the main issue in reading the traditional texts is not the word itself but the relationship of the word to the Word[7]. From this perspective, tradition is recognized as an ongoing

---

5. See my *De weg, de waarheid en het leven. Religieuze traditie en waarheid in de postmoderne context*, in *Bijdragen. Tijdschrift voor filosofie en theologie* 58 (1997) 164-188 (with a summary in English).

6. See my *Tradition, (De)Canonization, and the Challenge of Plurality*, in A. VAN DER KOOIJ en K. VAN DER TOORN (eds.), *Canonization and Decanonization* (Studies in the History of Religions, 82), Leiden, Brill, 1998, 371-378.

7. See also my *Between Relativizing and Dogmatizing: A Plea for an Open Concept of Tradition*, in *East Asian Pastoral Review* 32 (1995) 327-340.

recontextualization process of this relationship. Time and again believers have sought for clues in their personal and communal, historically developing and changing context in order to give form in word and deed to the experience of grace as inexhaustible divine gift of love. And theology for its part – as *fides quaerens intellectum* – looked for patterns of thought to express reflexively what has been held in faith.

In what follows, I would like to use the thought patterns of the model of the 'open narrative' to elaborate theologically, in a contextually plausible way, the central place of Jesus Christ within the Christian narrative. As my starting point I take the christological dogma of Chalcedon, a dogma which, as Karl Rahner pointed out already in 1954, must not only be considered an 'Ende' of a process of christological doctrinal development, fixing orthodoxy, but, at the same time an 'Anfang' for further reflection – which he pursued by means of his transcendental-theological method[8]. In the next section, I will examine the status of the Chalcedonian formula itself. Afterwards, I will relate its status to its content. Then I will answer the question of what it can mean to Christians, who within the framework of the Christian narrative feel engaged by a religious sensibility which has become definitively apparent in Jesus Christ, to profess of this Jesus Christ that he is both God and human. In the last section, I draw some conclusions towards a contextually anchored methodological apophasis in christology.

THE STATUS OF THE CHALCEDONIAN CHRISTOLOGICAL FORMULA

Christians from the fourth century professed at Nicaea (325) and Constantinople (381) that the one Lord Jesus Christ, the Son of God, is consubstantial with the Father (ὁμοούσιος τῷ πατρί), that this Lord Jesus Christ became human, was crucified under Pontius Pilate and buried, and, according to the testimony of Scriptures, rose on the third day[9]. In the fifth century, they further expressed the specificity of Jesus Christ by professing that Jesus is – simultaneously and yet distinctly – God and human. The Council of Chalcedon (451) professed that the Lord Jesus

---

8. Cf. K. RAHNER, *Chalkedon – Ende oder Anfang?*, in A. GRILLMEIER & H. BACHT (eds.), *Das Konzil von Chalkedon. Geschichte und Gegenwart. III. Chalkedon heute*, Würzburg, Echter, 1954, 3-49.

9. Cf. H. DENZINGER, *Kompendium der Glaubensbekenntnisse und kirchlichen Lehrentscheidungen*, 37th corrected and enlarged edition by P. HÜNERMANN, Freiburg/Basel/Rome/Wien, 1991, p. 63 (nr. 125) and pp. 83-84 (nr. 150). See also: N. TANNER, *Decrees of Ecumenical Councils*, 2 vols., Washington DC, Georgetown University Press, 1990, vol. 1, p. 5 and p. 24.

Christ is one and the same Son, at the same time perfectly and truly God, and perfectly and truly human, according to his divinity consubstantial with the Father, and according to his humanity consubstantial with us, except for sin. Somewhat further in the text the council fathers proclaimed that Christ is known "in two natures (ἐν δύο φύσεσιν), which undergo [in their union] no confusion, no change, no division, no separation (ἀσυγχύτως, ἀτρέπτως, ἀδιαιρέτως, ἀχωρίστως)". Unlike their union, the essence of both natures is not dissolved but preserved, and this in one person (μία ὑπόστασις), namely the Son, God, the Word, the Lord Jesus Christ, as taught by the prophets, instructed by Jesus Christ himself, and as handed down to us by the council fathers of Chalcedon in their profession of faith[10].

In view of a correct understanding, one ought to investigate the specific status of the Chalcedonian formula, 'one person acknowledged in two natures'. In fact, this formula is a – professed – dogmatical and doctrinal statement which was meant to conclude (but, as history shows, reopened) a conflictual process of reflection. The formula is a doctrinal expression, belonging to theological discourse. In the context of the time, the council fathers intended to bear witness to the mysterious reality of faith with which they were confronted in faith, profession, and preaching. Therefore, they used in a creative way the reflexive patterns of the time which were available to them. This creative process of recontextualization resulted in a metaphorical statement, allowing them to refer to that which had not been put into words before, that for which no one had a language; at least no language which offered, in the context of their time, in light of the reigning reflexive framework, enough doctrinal stability to express the specificity of the historical human being Jesus, called in faith the Christ, the Son of God, Logos-incarnate. This was done in such a way that, against monophysitism and Nestorianism, both Jesus' historical humanity and his professed divinity were really acknowledged. And this metaphorical statement worked (historically), to a certain degree. It succeeded in signifying in a contextually plausible way the mystery of Jesus Christ as perceived in faith – in other words: it was a striking evocation of the religious sensibility of the Christians (i.e., theologians) of the time.

The metaphorical power of the formula stemmed from the fact that the Fathers, in using the terminology available, kept vivid what in general

---

10. DENZINGER, *Kompendium*, pp. 142-143 (nr. 302); TANNER, *Decrees*, p. 86. For a dogma-historical explanation of these doctrinal professions and a basic bibliography, see C. ANDRESEN, *Handbuch der Dogmen- und Theologiegeschichte*. Band I. *Die Lehrentwicklung im Rahmen der Katholizität*, Göttingen, Vandenhoeck & Ruprecht, 1982.

theological terms can be called the tension between the inexpressible mystery of faith which resists articulation, and the historical context determining all articulation; as religious language, the formula is rather an expression of this tension than its neutralization and, accordingly, it interrupts theological and religious discourse, rather than discursively completing it. But, of course, this metaphorical power only remains active if this tension can be preserved. And this can be done in two ways[11].

(1) When metaphorical language becomes most current in (or is completely adopted by) a particular vocabulary, the metaphors implied risk becoming dead metaphors. In, and from, the context in which they appear, they are provided with a specific, generally accepted and determined meaning. Metaphors have then become closed in themselves; they no longer really interrupt; they no longer succeed in referring beyond the discourse in which they play their role. In the case of religious metaphors, they lose the ability to bear witness to the indefinable – yet defined – religious sensibility to the ungraspable Other, to which the Christian narrative ultimately testifies. A dead metaphor leaves the tension between inexpressibility and expression behind. In fact, once become closed in itself, the metaphorical formula, 'one person in two natures', functions only within theological discourse, and this no longer as an interruptive metaphor, but instead as an argument, an unproblematical element to be situated in the logical unfolding of a theological systematical exposition. Or the metaphor completely turns to stone, as happened with the title 'Christ', which has become a sort of name to indicate the One whom Christians regard as the center of their narrative.

Language, on the other hand, which succeeds in vividly maintaining the tension between inexpressible mystery and contextual articulation, escapes from the ever-threatening process of closing the metaphor. Accordingly, one consciously attempts to be present in this process, and warns – simultaneously criticizing and testifying – against the consequences of complete closure. One of the options in this regard is the creation of new metaphors, with the intention of pointing at the tension revealed in the old metaphorical formula.

(2) The threat of dying metaphors is only one problem theology has to face. Beyond this, one has to take into account that any metaphorical dynamism is strictly related to the context in which metaphors appear and live. This is of major importance when contexts change. We noticed

11. These observations are partly inspired by Donald Davidson's theory of metaphor, especially as received by Richard Rorty (see R. RORTY, *Contingency, Irony, and Solidarity*, Cambridge, Cambridge University Press, 1989, pp. 14 ff.).

already that religious language, because of that which it intends to express, is in need of a process of adjustment when contextual shifts occur. More specifically the vocabulary and the tension evoked in it necessitate recontextualization. If one does not succeed in recontextualizing, the tension disappears and only dated meaningless language remains, which in the end alienates because it is unable to refer to that which is revealed in the tension. In such cases theology degenerates into a closed and strictly argumentative discourse, not only without a beyond, but also without contextual rootedness. 'One person in two natures', then, no longer evokes a religious sensibility for the distinctive status of Jesus Christ, but becomes mere a disengaged definition[12].

In support of this argument I wish to point to the following formal elements which accentuate strongly the witnessing, referring character – versus a more argumentative, defining and determining character – of the Chalcedonian dogma. First of all, this council statement – however doctrinal it may seem – is primarily a credal formula, and not as such a defining description of a state of affairs. A creed implies a bringing to verbal expression of an engagement, of a being gripped, a turning towards someone to whom one stands in an (asymmetrical) relation, and thus always implies submission and receptivity. In the vocabulary of the model of the open narrative: a profession of faith is intrinsically related to a contemplative basic attitude. In professing, one intends to put into words that which reveals itself in the space of this contemplative openness.

A second element pointing to the witnessing character of the Chalcedonian formula, consists of the manifest paradox expressed in the dogmatical wording – a paradox which does not define from within the current discourse but refers beyond. This paradox is strongly accentuated by the

12. See for this also: E. SCHILLEBEECKX, *Breuken in christelijke dogma's*, in IDEM et al. (eds.), *Breuklijnen. Grenservaringen en zoektochten*. FS T. Schoof, Baarn, 1994, 15-49, esp. pp. 26 e.v. (= *Ruptures dans les dogmes Chrétiens*, in *ET-Bulletin* 8 (1997) 1, 11-38, esp. pp. 21-31). Schillebeeckx develops the idea that it is also thanks to ruptures and shifts in dogmatic formulas, that dogmas can remain true. He analyzes the tension between religious sensibility, testimony, and context, and provides six reasons which relativize an 'immobility of dogma'. The first reason Schillebeeckx provides is of immediate relevance to our subject: the expressive but context-dependent power of language necessarily causes ruptures in our understanding when contexts change. Schillebeeckx gives the following example: the meaning of 'person' and 'nature' at Chalcedon is immensely different from what we understand by these in our days. In his opinion, the Chalcedonian definition, when literally repeated in our time, would be heretical and involve a hocus-pocus-language. "In the eyes of a modern human being, a being which shares the human nature is consequently also a *human person*. This is something which undoubtedly does not contradict Chalcedon as such, but the neo-chalcedionianism derived from it, and which is dominant in many Christian churches" (pp. 30-31, my translation).

four verbal adverbs: (ἀσυγχύτως, ἀτρέπτως, ἀδιαιρέτως, ἀχωρίστως). Concerning the simultaneously held divinity and humanity of Jesus Christ, it is affirmed that both natures are not fused, are not changed in their union, but at the same time that they are neither two non-related parts of a larger whole, nor separated from each other[13]. Both terms, which in current language are considered to be opposites, are affirmed of the same Jesus Christ, without lifting the irreconcilability[14].

THE CHRISTOLOGICAL DOGMA DOES WHAT IT EXPRESSES AND EXPRESSES WHAT IT DOES

The paradox just referred to, calls for further investigation. Apart from the formal observation that it really is a paradox, it appears that – on the level of meaning and significance – the formula intends to think transcendence and immanence, God and humanity, as mutually related; in fact, it is concerned with putting in a reflexive manner this relation, or mediation, between God and world, in which Christians find themselves situated, and which they know to be present in the person of Jesus Christ. Neither monophysite nor Nestorian positions could sustain this tensile relationship to the very end, and destroyed the paradox. For it is precisely in the paradox that the opportunity is provided to bear witness to that which as such cannot be grasped in words.

The christological dogma is central to the Christian narrative because it attempts to *express* what, as a formula, it *does*. The christological dogma not only consists of a reference to the religious truth which took shape in Jesus Christ, but offers at the same time the method of this reference. In this regard, it is worthwhile to recall Richard Schaeffler's observation in *Religion und kritisches Bewußtsein* that religious discourse, as a world- and self-critical consciousness, gives expression to the being phenomenon, the being-not-God of the world and religion[15].

---

13. A more complete elaboration of the meaning of these terms can be found in P. KNAUER, *Die chalkedonische Christologie als Kriterium für jedes christliche Glaubensverständnis*, in *Theologie und Philosophie* 60 (1985) 1-15, pp. 10-11.

14. W. PFÜLLER argues in reference to G. Sauter for the importance of 'aporia' in theological discourse: "Endet Chalcedon aporetisch, dann ist es immer noch die Frage, ob dies nicht unumgänglich oder gar theologisch angemessen ist" (*Plädoyer für eine 'nach-klassische' Christologie*, in *Freiburger Zeitschrift für Theologie und Philosophie* 39 (1992), 130-154, p. 137 – I do not assent to all of the claims defended in this article). The reference to G. SAUTER is to *Grundzüge einer Wissenschaftstheorie der Theologie*, in ID. (ed.), *Wissenschaftstheoretische Kritik der Theologie*, München, 1973, 211-232, pp. 238 ff.: 'Die Aporie: angemessenes Reden von Gott'.

15. See R. SCHAEFFLER, *Religion und kritisches Bewußtsein*, Freiburg, Alber, 1973.

Precisely in examining the proper conditions – the non-identity between world and God –, religious discourse bears witness to God. In this way, the christological dogma expresses not only the relation between God and world (language), and thus the nature of our speaking about God, but is also already a bearing witness to the inexpressible God. Simultaneously, it attempts to be an expression of both the method and content of the Christian narrative. As Knauer states: the christological dogma of Chalcedon is the criterium for all understanding of the Christian faith[16].

This, however, on the condition that one succeeds with an adequate recontextualization. We can indeed attempt to investigate and reappropriate the Christian metaphysics of being from antiquity, and thus try to understand the Chalcedonian dogma in its context. But this metaphysics is no longer able to elucidate reflexively our contemporary condition. Moreover, it no longer functions as the contextual background of our sensibility and language.

A RECONTEXTUALIZATION OF THE CHALCEDONIAN DOGMA IN THE POSTMODERN CONTEXT

In the meantime, that context has changed dramatically. Nowadays the credal formula 'one person in two natures' is repeated as a doctrinal statement, in a way which, especially in view of current post-metaphysical thought patterns, must be conceded to be a decontextualized way. Only a serious recontextualization which departs from the religious sensibility expressed in our contemporary context – and, in the case of theology, in current reflexive frames – could restore to this dated credal formula its power to refer beyond, so that it may again testify to this religious sensibility. With this, I refer not to the 'original' referring potential, which could never be retrieved from its context, but to a new evocation of the tension between word and Word (Logos), between articulation and the resistance to articulation – a witness of the event of grace, as this is perceived in the contemporary religious sensibility. We proceed as follows.

The christological dogma of Chalcedon (451) – Jesus Christ is simultaneously, unconfused but not separated, both God and human – did not function on its own, but was understood as a further elaboration of the first ecumenical councils of Nicaea (325) and Constantinople (381). On these occasions, the council fathers formulated the dogma of the Trinity

16. Cf. P. KNAUER, *Die chalkedonische Christologie*, pp. 10-11.

and professed their faith in the one God, Father, Son, and Spirit (one God in three persons). Chalcedon reflected upon the second person of the Trinity[17]. The questions facing the council fathers focused upon what later[18] came to be called the hypostatic union: how is one to understand that the second person of the Trinity, the Son, the Logos, while being God, is also a human being in Jesus Christ? (I have already mentioned the conflictual context of this thematic, namely, nestorianism and mono-physitism). It is important to notice that the starting point of reflection is thus the divine Logos, the second person of the Trinity, who, as the Nicene-Constantinopolitan symbolum teaches, is consubstantial with the Father (ὁμοούσιος τῷ πατρί). In other words: the problem which the council fathers were facing can, in our context today, be described as the problem of thinking the mutual relation between universality and particularity, taking into account that one starts from universality. More specifically, how can one say of the universal God, the Son – 'through whom all things came to be' – that He is at the same time a particular human being? Focused adequately, the real problem is that of the particularity of the human being Jesus Christ. If God becomes human, what of that humanity[19]? And in coping in a creative-metaphorical way with the vocabulary then available, evoking the paradox of 'one person in two natures', the fathers succeeded in relating particularity to universality in such a way that the former was not completely absorbed by the latter.

In the contemporary context we observe rather an inversion in the christological discussion. It appears that the main theme is no longer the reflexive clarification of particularity in the light of universality, but the opposite: how can one think of universality in a context where 'particularity' is more prominent? Indeed, the relation between particularity and universality has changed as regards the Chalcedonian problem. The postmodern condition, understood as radicalized modernity, is analyzed

---

17. In the conciliar acts, the definition of the doctrine of the 'two natures' follows after the creed of Nicaea-Constantinople.

18. Cf. L. ULLRICH, *Hypostatische Union*, in W. BEINERT (ed.), *Lexikon der katholischen Dogmatik*, Freiburg/Basel/Wien, Herder, 1987, 276-282, p. 278. The 'hypostatic union' was officially mentioned for the first time at the second council of Constantinople in 553.

19. Compare for example how G. MÜLLER in the *Lexikon der katholischen Dogmatik* (note 16), defines 'incarnation' (p. 286): "I[nkarnation] ist die Bezeichnung für die fundamentale Tatsache des christlichen Glaubens, daß der dreieinige Gott in der Person des ewigen Wortes, als der ewigen Selbstaussprache des Vaters, eine menschliche Wirklichkeit sich unmittelbar angeeignet hat, um durch sie als er selbst in der Schöpfung anzukommen zum Heil des Menschen. I[nkarnation] kann den *Akt der Annahme* der menschlichen Natur durch das Wort Gottes bezeichnen wie auch das *bleibende Angenommensein*".

in terms of radical historicity, contingency, particularity and plurality. In such a framework, the universality acknowledged by Christians in Jesus Christ constitutes a problem. The concrete-particular, historically situated, contingent life-story of Jesus of Nazareth, called the Christ by the Christian narrative, is to these same Christians – especially after the pleas for a christology-from-below – in the first place, and with (relatively) few problems – the narrative of the human being Jesus of Nazareth, of whom it is said that he is at the same time God. Moreover, this happens within a context in which one has become conscious of the plurality of narratives, including religious narratives and, at the same time, of the often exaggerated hegemonic pretensions of many of these narratives. In this light, the christological problem does not appear as the problem of the second person of the Trinity, God the Son, who became a human being, but rather as the human being Jesus, called the messiah, and proclaimed God by the Christians. In other words: how can one think universality starting from particularity? A recontextualization of the Chalcedonian christological dogma should answer this question.

A good example of the fact that the questions have changed is given by the Flemish systematic theologian, Jef De Kesel, in his attempt to interpret the 'ὁμοούσιος' of Nicaea[20]. According to De Kesel, the consubstantiality of the Son with the Father does not say as much about Jesus Christ, as it does about the essence of God. It is not appropriate to think about Jesus as starting from God – the opposite is true. "The essence of God cannot be spoken about adequately without making reference to the historical and human event of Jesus. An immense intervention in the concept of God is here at stake: with regard to its content, God's essence is determined by the life, death and resurrection of Jesus Christ [...] After Him and because of Him, one must think and speak differently about God"[21].

How, then, is the particular human being, Jesus, both human and God? As has been said, the christological dogma of Chalcedon did not merely express the simultaneous humanity and divinity of Jesus Christ, but pointed also to the tensile relation in which they stand towards each other. The dogma indeed refers to 'one person in two natures', but the four verbal adverbs accentuate the paradoxical character of this union of divinity and humanity: to be sure, both natures are distinct from one

---

20. Cf. J. DE KESEL, *Hoe is Uw naam, waar zijt Gij te vinden? Over the verantwoording van het christelijke geloof*, Tielt, 1988, pp. 191-193. Also Peter Hünermann accentuates this shift (P. HÜNERMANN, *Jesus Christ. Gottes Wort in der Zeit. Eine systematische Christologie*, Münster, 1994).

21. DE KESEL, *Hoe is Uw naam*, p. 192 (my translation).

another, but not separated (ἀχωρίστως); on the one hand, they are not confused (ἀσυγχύτως), but on the other, they cannot be considered to be parts of a larger whole (ἀδιαιρέτως); and moreover, both of them preserve in their mutual relationship their own integrity (ἀτρέπτως). The sentence following upon these four adverbs even underlines this tensile relationship: by the union, the difference between both natures is not lifted, but the distinctness is preserved[22]. Precisely this being related of the divinity with the humanity, and of the humanity with the divinity enables the christological dogma of Chalcedon, when recontextualised, to bear witness to the mediation in Jesus Christ between God and human being, and to the relation between God and world (language).

In his own person, Jesus Christ signifies what we have called the relation between Word (Logos) and word – the mutually being related of Word (Logos) and word. The Logos incarnated in the word, becomes signified in the word, but does not identify itself with the word. The word 'evokes', thereby determining the indeterminable Logos, and precisely in this determining distinguishes itself from the Logos. The word never becomes Logos, but is the way to the Logos[23]. To affirm that Jesus Christ is both God and human, means proclaiming that in person, life, speech, and deeds, he was *the definitive hermeneutics of God, but that he – himself being God – only can be approached in a radical-hermeneutical way.* He is the definitive revelation of God, and this precisely in the paradoxical relation of God and humanity established in his person because, as a person, he gives expression to the tension between the word and the Word (Logos). In as far as Jesus Christ is a signification of the divine reality, the same religious hermeneutical-critical proviso applies to him as to all other religious discourse. The 'ὁμοούσιος' of the Son indeed implies, then, that precisely in his person, life and words, Jesus Christ is considered by believers to be the definitive signification (revelation) of God – 'Whoever sees me, sees the Father' (cf. Jn 14,9) – but it implies at the same time that his person, life and words, being signification of God, can only be known as the word about the Logos, while standing in a relationship to the Logos. In other words: God's superfluous love has been revealed in a particular life story that does not exhaust this love, but nevertheless signifies it in a definitive way. As a particular life story, Jesus's narrative, entangled by particularity, bears witness to the universality of grace, which as such can never be articulated.

22. Cf. H. DENZINGER, *Kompendium*, p. 143.
23. See R. Schaeffler's considerations about the religious word as phenomenon, both unveiling and veiling God's divinity. Cf. R. SCHAEFFER, *Religion und kritisches Bewußt-sein*, pp. 31ff.

In this way, one can conclude that a recontextualization of the Chalcedonian dogma does reveal the structure of the open narrative within
Christianity. Jesus Christ, in person, expresses the relationship between
word and Word (Logos). Precisely this – and here Christianity confronts
its very specificity – makes him the paradigm of the 'open narrative'[24].

TOWARDS A METHODOLOGICAL APOPHASIS IN CHRISTOLOGY

One outcome of the recontextualization of the Chalcedonian christological dogma is that any authentic theological discourse about Jesus
Christ will shape itself as an 'open narrative'. Precisely because of the
'definitiveness' of Jesus' revelation of God, he is – i.e., his person, life,
and words, and the Christian narrative about him – only approachable
within the terms of an 'open narrative'. Our words about the Lord Jesus
Christ are a discourse which ventures to enter the tension between the
word and the Word (Logos). This implies that the question of *the* meaning of Jesus Christ – and this question is not without importance, since
christology presupposes and implies soteriology (the 'for our salvation'
of the creeds is at stake) – can only be answered within the framework
of an 'open narrative'.

This consciousness – in our context made explicit in the terminology
of the model of the 'open narrative' – appears to be alive already from
the beginning, in the first narrative witnesses of what we might call the
Jesus Christ-event. Our sources regarding Jesus, i.e., the Gospels, were
meant to be testimonial literature, and certain elements in these sources,
such as (some) parables, arguments, and stories were clearly intended to
underline sharply this witnessing character – understood in terms of the
tension between the word and the Word. That is why the gospels, as

24. It could be made clear that Jesus Christ in his person, life, words, and deeds is
indeed paradigmatic for the model of the 'open narrative'. In his life and his life story
Jesus bears witness to the event of grace; he holds contemplation and kerygma, openness
and testimony, together in an exemplary fashion (*par excellence*). In his openness towards
the Father, his contemplative basic attitude, and his bearing witness to the grace appearing within this contemplative openness, he writes his life story as an open narrative, as
witness to the event of grace by which he willingly allowed his narrative be interrupted.
Moreover, he became himself an event of what in a Jewish vocabulary is called resurrection – the interruption of the narrative of suffering, and death – and, in as far as this was
told and retold in the Christian Jesus-narrative, he also became witness to this event. In
fact, the event of the resurrection revolutionizes the violently closed narrative of life and
death. As 'open narrative' Jesus Christ always refers beyond himself. For another account
of this, see L. BOEVE, *Een christologie van de onderbreking*, in J. HAERS and T. MERRI-
GAN (eds.), *Christus in veelvoud. Pluraliteit en de vraag naar eenheid in de hedendaagse
christologie* (Didachè: geloof en religie), Leuven, Acco, 1999, 91-112.

narratives of and about Jesus Christ, in the same way as the Chalcedonian dogma, do (are) what they narrate, and narrate what they do (are). Only as 'open narratives' do they testify to Jesus Christ as the 'open narrative'. The fact that the early Church found it necessary to canonize four of them, illustrates this remarkably well.

Hence, the Gospels support the affirmation made in the recontextualization of Chalcedon, namely, that Jesus Christ is the definitive hermeneutics of God, but – as far as he is proclaimed God – he can only be approached hermeneutically. The term 'incarnation' signifies this tensile relation between the particular, context-determined word and the indeterminate Word (Logos). The dynamic of the 'open narrative' between word and Word (Logos) took flesh in Jesus Christ.

The radical features of the hermeneutics urged by the recontextualised Chalcedonian dogma strongly evoke the current philosophical (and theological) interest in apophatic or negative theology. Philosophers of difference use the apophatic method to stress the non-foundational, non-groundable nature of our thinking and to emphasize the ever-withdrawing, ungraspable character of the irreducible remainder of difference, or otherness at the borders of our thinking, preventing this thinking from coming to absolute truth, from realizing full presence. Apophatic theology leads, or gives expression, to the sensibility of a limit, which thus opens a narrative from the inside[25]. In this perspective, apophasis is considered in their writing a philosophical notion, more a matter of method, without a theological outcome. The fruits of the 'via negativa' are the experience of indifferent difference, not the divine Otherness, kataphatically revealed as the God of love, in whom Christians profess their faith[26]. Nowadays, theologians can hardly expect philosophers to conclude their discourse with the Christian God[27]. Nevertheless, given the fact that

25. See, for example, J.-F. Lyotard's interest in the proscription of images in Jewish thinking, and Derrida's reflections on Pseudo-Denis' *Mystical theology*. Cf. J. F. LYOTARD, *Heidegger et les Juifs,...* (tr. *Heidegger and the Jews,....*); J. DERRIDA, *Comment ne pas parler. Dénégations*, in IDEM, *Psyche. Inventions de l'autre*, Paris, Galilée, 1987, 535-595. See also I.N. BULHOF & L. TEN KATE (ed.), *Ons ontbreken heilige namen. Negatieve theologie in de hedendaagse cultuurfilosofie*, Kampen, Kok Agora, 1992.

26. In this sense one could say, as Jean-Luc Marion said at a conference on religion and postmodernism (Villanova University, Sept. 25-27, 1997) that deconstructivists like Derrida perform the deconstruction of a type of deconstructionism (negative theology). Cf. J.D. CAPUTO & M.J. SCANLON (eds.), *God, the Gift and Postmodernism* (The Indiana Series in the Philosophy of Religion), Bloomington/Indianapolis, Indiana University Press, 1999.

27. Consider the objections of J. Derrida to J.-L. Marion's phenomenology of the donation, ultimately leading to the God-Giver, as revealed in the Christian tradition (cf. J.-L. MARION, *Die sans l'être*, Paris, PUF, 1991).

apophatical theology is a part of the Christian tradition, it is probably obvious that theologians carefully study how negative theology functions in contemporary philosophical reflection as an attempt at non-metaphysical thinking. This must be done, not to adopt this philosophical usage merely as if it is theology, but to engage it in the recontextualisation pursued at present[28]. In view of our christological elaborations, we may contend that, as a matter of fact, the same apophatical impetus is structurally present in the radical hermeneutics stemming from the tensile relation of the word to the Word (Logos), from the perception of Christ as the paradigm of the 'open narrative'[29]. Because of the Word (Logos), the word is both kataphasis and apophasis, or more precisely, kataphasis conditioned by apophasis. Precisely this combination opens, what we could call, a third way in which the Word (Logos) is referred to, no longer in either kataphatic affirmation or apophatic negation, but in 'de-negation' or (in French) 'de-nomination', which overcomes both affirmation (predication) and negation (suspension of predication): words about the Word (Logos) no longer function propositionally but pragmatically. In other words, theology and, from our perspective, christology, does not involve a metaphysics of presence, nor of absence, but of present absence, revealed in the tension between the word and the Word (Logos). In the word, the Word (Logos) is present by its withdrawal (what Pseudo-Denis referred to as 'hyper-ousia'). Precisely this constitutes the nature of the Word (Logos), and leaves the word really word.

To conclude: it ought to be clear that the model of the 'open narrative' is not only given from the context laid upon the Christian narrative, but, once acquired, is rediscovered as the basic structure at the heart of Christianity. The attempt to match this model and Christianity reverses into a real theology and, for our purpose, a real christology of the 'open narrative'. Doing theology thus no longer falls prey to fundamentalist truth claims or relativist indifference, to christolatry or to religious relativism. By recontextualising the Christian narrative in dialogue with contemporary critical consciousness, Christianity realises, by means of its apophatical impetus, the relational dimension of truth, and critically dissociates itself both from narratives of hegemonical appropriation of truth and relativist dismissals of any truth claim. Hereby, one takes as

28. The ideas proposed here are influenced by J.-L. Marion's presentation referred to in note 27. See also his *Prolegomènes à la charité*, Paris, Éditions de la différence, 1986; and *Dieu sans l'être*.

29. Cf. the paradoxical title of Derrida's *Sauf le nom*, Paris, Galilée, 1993 (save the name, or, except for the name).

one's starting point, on the one hand, the contextual and particular setting of the Christian narrative (or rather, narratives), and, on the other
hand, the inexhaustible experience of grace in Jesus Christ. More specifically, one begins from a necessary, but at the same time, fruitful mutual
relation between both, which allows us to recontextualise the claims of
Christianity in a non-hegemonic way.

Faculty of Theology   Lieven BOEVE
Katholieke Universiteit Leuven
St. Michielsstraat 6
B-3000 Leuven

INDEX OF NAMES

ʿABDALLAH IBN Aṭ-TAIYIB 283 285
ʿABDĪŠŪ OF NISIBIS 281 283
ABE M. 540[25]
ABISHIKTANANDA 244
ABŪ RĀ IṬAH 277-282
ADAMS J.L. 370[62]
ADORNO T.W. 100[2]
AGUIRRE R. 513[63]
ALAND B. 189 207[2]
ALAND K. 183[23] 189
ALBANESE C. 321[20]
ALFARO J. 495[8] 496[9.12] 497[13-14] 498[15]
ALLARD M. 281[28]
ALMOND P. 13[19] 540[25]
AMALORPAVADASS D.S. 226[9]
AMATO A. 117[24]
AMERY J. 400[5]
AMIR Y. 144[33]
AMISHAI-MAISELS Z. 392[25]
ʿAMMĀR AL-BAṢRĪ 283
AMOAH A. 305[81] 306 307[87] 308[91] 309 311[103]
ANATOLIOS K. 210[11] 212[14]
ANAWATI G.C. 275[1]
ANDERSON G. 320[14]
ANDERSON H. 50
ANDERSON H.G. 567[1]
ANDRESEN C. 582[10]
ANDREWS C.F. 244
ANSELM St. 570 574[15]
ANTIOCHUS 183
APFELBACHER K.-E. 358[26] 375[79]
APPIAH-KUBI K. 290[15] 300[60]
AQUINAS St. Thomas 36[7] 207[3] 224[8] 231[13] 232 237[6] 241[11] 331-332 333[4] 334 335[7.10] 336[12] 337-339 340[27] 341[29] 342[31] 343[32-33] 346[39] 347 394-395 502 537[11] 538[11]
ARISTOTLE 275 277 282 502
ARIUS 200
ARNAL W.E. 48[16]
ARRUPE P. 495
ASHTON J. 178[3] 189
ATHANASIUS St. 198-199 207[1] 208 210[11] 211-212 213[17] 214-216

AUGUSTINE St. 110[9] 162[11] 332
AUROBINDO 247

BACHT H. 438[21] 581[8]
BACIK J. 489[92]
BADARAYANA 235
BADGER C. 210[11] 212[16] 213
BAILLIE D.M. 76[61] 523[6] 526
BAKKEN K. 207[3]
BAKKER 483[73] 484[75]
BALDRIDGE W. 320[14]
BALJON J.M.S. 178[3] 181[14] 186
BALL D.M. 157[75]
BARCLAY J. 148[50]
BAREAU A. 253-254
BARNES T.D. 210[11]
BARR D.L. 385[7]
BARR J. 58
BARR R.R. 301[63] 466[10]
BARRETT C.K. 181[14] 186
BARRY M. 476[48]
BARTH K. 12 106 113 116[22] 118[25] 119 349 350[3] 434[7] 547 550[67] 574[15]
BARTH M. 553[6]
BARTHES R. 476[49]
BARTON J. 58
BASILIDES 195
BATTLOGG A. 466[10]
BAUCKHAM R. 135[6] 147[47-48]
BAUER W. 178[3] 179[5.7] 181[14] 183[23] 186-187 189
BAUM G. 382[2] 391[24] 400 401[9]
BAUR J. 291[18]
BEA A. 448[56]
BEASLEY-MURRAY G.R. 178[3] 181[14.17] 186
BEATTIE J.H.M. 553[8] 554
BEBAWI G. 212[15]
BECK A.B. 190
BECK M. Scott 45[1]
BECK P. 318[9]
BECKER G. 376[80]
BECKER J. 181[14] 186
BECKLEY R. 463[1]
BEDIAKO K. 294[31] 312[106]
BEINERT W. 115[21] 587[18]

BELL L. 324
BELSER 178[3] 181[15]
BENNETT ELDER L. 385[7]
BENSE W.F. 370[62]
BERENBAUM M. 384[4-5] 413[55]
BERGER P. 10[16]
BERGMAN J. 145[36]
BERNARD J.H. 181[14.16] 186[28] 189
BERRY T. 318[9]
BETHGE E. 101[5] 114[19] 504[35]
BEYREUTHER E. 182[20] 189
BIALLOWONS H. 465[6] 488[90]
BIERINGER R. 150[55] 563[41]
BIHLMEIER K. 113[15]
BILLERBECK P. 181[14] 188
BLACK C.C. 165[20]
BLACK Elk N. 325-326
BLACKELY T.D. 294[37]
BLANK J. 163[15] 164[17-18] 165[20] 171[42] 173[48] 181[14] 186 556[18]
BLEISTEIN R. 440[30] 441[32] 451[69]
BLIGH J. 180[12] 181[16] 182[19] 189
BLINZLER J. 165[20]
BLOCH E. 101[3]
BLOESCH D. 548[61]
BOCKMUEHL M. 66[14]
BODENSTEIN W. 373[75] 375[79]
BODZIN H. 269[7]
BOEVE L. 590[24]
BOFF L. 493 494[3]
BOISMARD M.-É. 178[3] 181[14] 186
BONAVENTURE St. 324 481[66]
BONHOEFFER D. 101[5] 114[19] 503 504[35-36] 505[38]
BONNER G. 208[5]
BORG M.J. 50 51[23] 66[14.16] 69 79[80]
BORGEN P. 181[14] 189
BORNKAMM G. 47[8]
BOROWITZ E. 390
BOROWSKY I.J. 393[27]
BOTTERWECK G.J. 145[37]
BOURDILLON M.F.C. 553[8]
BOUSSET W. 148[51] 365[35]
BOUWSMA W.J. 571[10]
BOWDEN J. 59[49] 401[10]
BOWKA 433[2]
BRAKKE D. 210[11] 214[18]
BRAUN F.-M. 178[3] 188
BRETON C. 117[24] 144[33] 145[39]
BRETON S. 139[14.15]

BRETT M.G. 142[26]
BREUNING W. 556[17]
BREWER K.W. 134[4]
BRINKMAN M.E. 567[2] 572[12]
BROCK S. 202[3]
BRODIE T.L. 178[3] 186
BROWN J.E. 318[9] 321[19] 325[30]
BROWN R.E. 52[27] 80[83] 148[51-52] 160[7] 162[13] 164[18] 170[41] 181[14.16] 182[19] 186[28]
BRUCE F.F. 50
BRÜCKNER R. 141[22] 187
BSTEH A. 126[17]
BUCKLEY M. 4[4]
BUDDHA 22 251-254
BÜCHSEL F. 178[3] 186
BUJO B. 294[34] 296[41] 297-299
BULHOF I.N. 344[35] 591[25]
BULUS MARCUZZO G. 281[27]
BULTMANN R. 46 58-59 163[15] 164[17-18] 165[20] 171 173[47] 178[3] 181[14.17] 186 506 509 556[15]
BURGER C.H.A. 177[3] 180[12] 181[16] 187
BURGESS J.A. 567[1]
BURRELL D. 335[10]
BUTTERWECK C. 210[11]
BYRNE P. 549[64]

CAHILL M. 49[19]
CALVIN 571[10]
CAMPLANI A. 213[17]
CAMPS A. 123[4]
CAMUS A. 268
CANOBBIO C. 85[12]
CAPUTO J.D. 591[26]
CARDINAL H. 315[2]
CARLSON J. 67[17]
CARSON D.A. 178[3] 179[5] 180[10] 181[14] 187
CARTER S. 18[27]
CASEY M. 66[14]
CASEY P.M. 148[51] 178[3] 179[5] 189
CASPAR R. 275[2]
CELAN P. 400[6]
CELSUS 147[48] 192-193
CERBELAUD D. 154[68]
CEULEMANS F.C. 178[3] 187
CHAPMAN M.D. 365[24]
CHARLESWORTH J.H. 49[18] 50 382
CHIROVSKY A. 214[21]
CHITTINAPPILLY P. 493[2]
CHOPP R. 394 395[32]

CLARKE A.D. 137[10] 146[44] 157[75]
CLASSEN J.H. 349[1]
CLAYTON J.P. 73[47] 349[1] 355[19]
CLEARY B. 316[4]
CLEMENT OF ALEXANDRIA 167[29] 208
CLENDENIN D.B. 208[7] 216[24]
CLIFFORD J. 26[46]
CLOONEY F. 27[49] 29[52]
COAKLEY S. 349[1] 370[64] 375[79]
COBB J. 27[49] 29[53] 88[17] 257[16] 262 434[9]
COGGINS R.J. 51[21]
COOK M. 507[44.46] 508
COOK R. 324[26]
COHEN A. 403[17]
CONGAR Y. 84[7] 116 127[20]
CONTRERAS E. 211[13]
CONZE E. 258[18]
CORLUY J. 177[3] 187
CORLISS R. 525[12]
CORNILLE C. 62[5] 124[10] 215[22]
COSMAO V. 316[5]
COWARD H. 540[25]
COX J.L. 321[17]
CROSSAN J.D. 48 50 52[28] 55 66[14] 71[42] 436[16]
CULLY R. 542[18]
CULPEPPER R.A. 165[20] 179[4] 184[25] 189
CUPITT D. 72[44]
CUTLAND A. 322[23]

DALFERTH I. 556[19] 558[22-23] 565[47]
DALMAIS I.-H. 207[2]
DALY R. 560[30]
DAMASCENE St. JOHN 232 275
DANIÉLOU J. 116
DANTE 271
DAUER A. 164[17] 165[20]
DAVEY F.N. 187
DAVIDSON D. 583[11]
DAVIES A. 382[2]
DAVIES A.T. 388[16]
DAVIES B. 466[11]
DAVIES D. 7[10]
DAVIES W.D. 177[1] 189
DAVIS C.J. 148[51]
DAVIS S.T. 38[19]
D'COSTA G. 14[20] 19[30] 27[47] 29[52] 62[5] 85[12] 116[23] 124[10] 125[14] 547[52]
DEBASSIGE B. 323-324

DE BONAGUIDO P. 324
DE CHARDIN T. 446[46]
DE GRANDMAISON L. 478[54]
DE GUIBERT J. 476[47.48] 478[54]
DE HAARDT M. 129[28] 552[3]
DE JONGE M. 66[14] 148[50.51] 178[3] 187
DE KESEL J. 588[20.21]
DE LACEY D.R. 151[57]
DE LAGARDE A.P. 365[35]
DE LÉON LUIS 331-337 338[19.21] 339[23] 340[25] 341[29-30] 342[31] 343-345 346[39] 347
DELLING G. 142[24] 144[33]
DELORIA V. 320[14]
DE LUBAC H. 116 429[90.93]
DELUMEAU J. 570[7] 572[11] 573
DEMKE C. 146[40]
DE MOOR D. 137[12]
DENAUX A. 155[71]
DENZIGER H. 459[116] 581[9] 582[10] 589[22]
DE RIJK L.M. 336[12]
DERRIDA J. 578[4] 591[25.27] 592[29]
DE SCHRIJVER G. 493[1] 502[28]
DESJARDINS M. 48[16]
DES PRES T. 400[7]
DEVER W.G. 137[9]
DE WETTE W.M.L. 180[12] 187
DI BERARDINO A. 207[2] 208[5]
DIETRICH D.J. 396[33]
DINGJAN F. 127[19]
DINOIA J.A. 6[8] 7[10] 8[13] 11[17] 17[24] 18[26] 123[4.6]
DISTER J.E. 480[62]
DIVARKAR P.R. 475[43]
DODD C.H. 179 180[8] 181[14] 182[17] 183[20] 189 514[67]
DOMITIAN 162
DOWNING F.G. 66[14]
DRESCHER H.G. 349[1] 374[77] 376[80]
DREWERMANN E. 480[62]
DREWERY B. 209[7] 210[10]
DUBOIS M. 387[13] 388
DUFFY, S. 19[30] 26[45]
DUKE P.D. 184[25] 189
DULLES A. 483[73] 487[88]
DUNGAN D.L. 189-190
DUNN J.D.G. 35[4] 66[14] 155[70] 569[5]
DUPREZ A. 177[1] 178[3] 180[12] 189
DUPUIS J. 83[1-2] 84[6] 87[15] 88[16] 89[18-19] 90[21] 94[26-27] 95[28-29] 124[10] 125[12] 127[21] 266[3] 535[1]

DUQUOC C. 91[23]
DYCH W. 464[4] 466[11]

ECK D. 125
ECKARDT A.R. 390[20] 392
ECKHART M. 26
EDELMAN D.V. 137[12]
EGAN H. 443[40] 464[3] 465[6] 478[53]
EICHER P. 484[75]
EICHHORN A. 365[35]
ÉLA J.M. 299[56] 300[59] 301[61.63-64.67] 302[68] 303 304[78] 313[110]
ELIADE M. 547[54]
ELLACURIA I. 500[23.25]
ELLIS P.F. 178[3] 187
ENDEAN P. 433[1] 434[7] 445[44] 464[3]
ENSOR P.W. 181[14] 189
EPHREM THE SYRIAN 200
EPP E.J. 47[9]
EUSEBIUS 162[12]
EVANS C.A. 66[16]
EVANS C.S. 61[3]

FABELLA V. 304[79] 305[81] 307[87-89] 308[91] 311[103]
FACKENHEIM E. 383
FAIVRE D. 137[12]
FANON F. 395
FARMER H.H. 526
FARMER J. 453[76]
FARRUGIA E. 433[2]
FAVRE 478[54]
FEENEY L. 9[14]
FEINER J. 443[40]
FERRARA D. 74[50] 75[56]
FEUERBACH L. 267-268
FEUILLET A. 152[62]
FINKENRATH G. 182[20] 189
FIORENZA F. 390 473[39]
FISCHER K.P. 464[3]
FITZMYER J.A. 151[56] 569[5]
FLANNERY A. 535[2]
FORDE G.O. 574[14]
FORTE B. 99[1] 115[21]
FORTES M. 553[8]
FORTNA R.T. 190
FOUCAULT M. 578[4]
FRANK A. 399
FRANKL V. 399-400

FREYNE S. 49 436[16]
FRIEDLANDER H. 384[5]
FUETER P. 294[28]
FULLER R.H. 148[51]
FUNK R. 53[29]

GADAMER, H.-G. 23
GALVIN J.P. 65[12] 435 436[14.16] 473[39]
GANDHI M. 47
GANSS G.E. 475[43] 476[47] 479[58] 481[64]
GAUDEL J.-M. 275[3]
GAVENTA B.R. 190
GEORGE M. 207[2]
GEORGI D. 49 50[20]
GESE H. 557[20-21] 561[33] 563[38]
GIBELLINI R. 289[10-11] 291[19] 292[21] 300[59] 301[64] 311[104]
GIBLIN C.H. 146[40]
GILBY T. 237[6]
GILKEY L. 20[36] 62[6] 545[48] 564[45]
GILL S. 321[20]
GILLIS C. 536[5]
GIRARD R. 551[1] 552[2] 558 565
GISEL P. 349[1] 577[1]
GNILKA J. 168[37] 178[3] 187 436[16]
GNUSE R.K. 136[9] 137[11]
GODDARD H. 264[2]
GODET F. 180[12] 187
GOGARTEN F. 375[79]
GOLDING W. 555[13]
GOLDINGAY J.E. 137[10] 140[17] 142[26] 143[29] 144[32]
GORIS H.J.M.J. 331[1]
GOTTWALD N.K. 137[9]
GOULDER M. 74[52]
GRAF F.W. 349[1] 365[38]
GRAF G. 277[13-15] 279[22] 280[23] 281[27.29] 282[36]
GRANT J.W. 326[34]
GRANT R.M. 146[44]
GRAU G. 384[5]
GREENBURG I. 413[55]
GREGORY OF NAZIANZE 207[1]
GREGORY OF NYSSA 207[1] 547[53]
GREINACHER N. 498[17]
GRESHAKE G. 113[14]
GRIENER G.E. 349[1] 356[21] 364[34]
GRIFFITH S.H. 275[5]
GRIFFITHS B. 14[20] 244

GRIFFITHS P. 7[12] 15[23] 28[50] 525-526
GRILLMEIER A. 438[21] 581[8]
GROSHEIDE F.W. 178[3] 187
GUMKOWSKI J. 384[6]
GUNKEL H. 365[35]
GUNTON C. 561[32] 574[15]
GUTIERREZ G. 47 499

HAAG E. 137[12]
HADDAD R. 280[24]
HAENCHEN E. 181[14] 187
HÄRING H. 129[29] 134[4]
HAERS J. 590[24]
HAIGHT R. 33[3] 76[63] 77[63] 90[20] 401[11] 436[16] 527[19]
HALL D.J. 388[16] 389 390 392[26] 401 405 408[37] 409[38]
HARRIS M.J. 148[52]
HARVEY V.A. 370[65]
HAUERWAS S. 393[27]
HAVEL V. 391[22]
HAYEK M. 278[17] 284[42.44] 285[49]
HEBBELTHWAITE B. 74[52] 78[70]
HEGEL G.W.F. 100 108 109[8] 112[11.12] 353 367 373 377 417[3]
HEGESIPPUS 162
HEIDEGGER M. 106 469[19]
HEILER F. 244[16]
HEIM S.M. 24[41] 123[4.6] 125[15] 532[39] 543 544[40]
HENDRIKSEN W. 178[3] 179[5.7] 187
HENGEL M. 50 58[46] 59 152[61] 159[1] 165[20.21] 166[24] 171[40]
HENNELLY A. 498[17.18] 500[21] 501[26] 502[29] 503[30] 504[34] 506[40.43]
HERMOGENES 194-196
HERTZBERG H. 321[16]
HESCHEL A. 387 389 407-408
HESS H. 214[19-21]
HEWITT H. 546[50]
HICK J. 6[10] 9 19[30] 20[36] 35[7] 62[5-6] 63[6] 65[10] 66[16] 68[19-20.23] 69[25] 70 71[39] 72-75 76[59-63] 77[63-70] 78[70-76] 79[78] 80-81 82[86] 83 85[12] 116[23] 123[5-6] 124[9] 133[1] 134 261 349 350[4.6] 351[8-9] 352 377[83] 378[88] 379[91] 434[8] 521[1] 522[2-4] 523 524[8-9] 525 526[14.18] 527[19] 528 529[22] 530[30-31] 531-532 533[41.43] 534 535[3-4] 536 537[6-11] 538[11-14] 539[16-19] 540[23-24] 541 542[32] 543[35] 544-545 546[49.51] 547-550

HIGHWATER J. 318[9]
HILL D. 160[6] 164[19]
HILLESUM E. 399
HÖNIG E. 562[37]
HOFFMEISTER J. 112[11]
HOFIUS O. 557[20]
HOLLENBACH 515[69]
HOLLER C. 326[32]
HOLTZMANN H.J. 177[3] 180[12] 181[14] 187
HOLTZMANN O. 177[3] 187
HOLZ T. 149[53]
HONEN 256
HORKHEIMER M. 100[2] 102
HORSLEY R. 52[26] 66[14]
HOSKYNS E.C. 178[3] 187
HOULDEN J.L. 51[21] 549[64]
HOWARD-BROOK W. 161[8] 165[20.23] 172[44] 178[3] 184[26] 186[27] 187
HOYE W.J. 335[10]
HÜNERMANN P. 581[9] 588[20]
HUIZINGA J. 570[9]
HULTKRANTZ A. 321[20]
HUMBERT G.J. 324[27]
HUNTER H. 74[48]
HURTADO L.W. 142[24] 144[34] 145[38] 147[47] 152[63]

IBUKI Y. 173[49]
IGGERS G.G. 373[76]
IGNATIUS OF ANTIOCH 113[15] 114[18]
IGNATIUS OF LOYOLA 474 475[42.44] 476[48.49] 477 479[59] 480[61] 482[69]
IMHOF P. 440[30] 465[5] 476[46] 488[90]
IRENAEUS St. 84[8] 192 196-197 322

JANOWSKI B. 557[20] 563[39]
JASPERS K. 68[23]
JAY N. 552[3] 553[4]
JEANROND W. 436[16]
JEFFERSON T. 518
JENSEN E. 161[9]
JEREMIAS J. 47
JILEK W. 317[7]
JÖRNS K.P. 555[11]
JOHN PAUL II Pope 327 391 395-396
JOHNSON L.T. 48 51[25] 57 58[43]
JONES H.S. 183[21] 190
JOSEPHUS 151[59]
JÜNGEL E. 114[17]
JUSTIN 4 9 193-194 198 322

KABASÉLÉ F. 294[28.33]
KÄHLER M. 46-47 51 58
KÄSEMANN E. 47
KAFKA F. 572
KAFTAN J. 366 367[47]
KALSKY M. 129[28]
KANT I. 10 78[70] 104 367 373 536-537 555[14]
KASPER W. 332[3] 350[6] 417[1.3] 419[14]
KASTNER K. 161[9]
KAUFMAN G. 545[48] 547[56] 548
KAVOLIS V. 396[34]
KAYLOR R.D. 66[14]
KECK L. 46[6] 125[13]
KEE H.C. 393[27]
KEEL H.-S. 259[19]
KEEL O. 137[12]
KEENAN J. 250[4] 251 259[22] 260
KEIL C.F. 177[3] 187
KELLENBERGER J. 62[6]
KELLY J.N.D. 154[66]
KELSEY D. 32[2]
KENNY A. 336[12]
KER I.T. 62[5] 536[5]
KERN W. 122[3] 426[71]
KERTELGE K. 556[17] 569[5]
KESHUB CHENDER SEN 222
KESSLER A. 190
KEULERS J. 178[3] 181[14] 187
KEYSSNER K. 141[22]
KHALIL SAMIR S. 275[5] 277[8-11.13.15.16] 278[17-19] 279[20] 280[23] 281[25] 283[38.41] 284[47]
KHODR G. 80[83] 85[13]
KHOURY P. 281[30]
KIERKEGAARD S. 117 374
KING J. Norman 468[17]
KIRBY J. 287[1]
KIRMIS F. 179[5] 190
KITAGAWA J.M. 115[20] 254[12]
KLEE H. 177[3] 187
KLINGER E. 440[30] 441[32] 451[69]
KLOFUTAR L. 177[3] 180[12] 187
KNABENBAUER I. 178[3] 187
KNAUER P. 585[13] 586[16]
KNIGHT H. 384[4]
KNITTER P. 6[9-10] 19[30] 20[36] 30[55] 62[5-6] 63[6] 64[7.9] 66[15-16] 67[17] 68 69[26-31] 70[33-38] 71[40-42] 72-74 75[56] 76 79[79-80] 80[81-83] 81[84-85] 83 85[12-14] 116[23] 123[4-5] 124[8-9] 133[1-2] 134 261 345[36] 346[37.39] 349 350[4] 351 352[12-13] 377 378[85] 379[95] 418[4] 521[1] 522-528 529[23-24] 530[27-28.30] 531[32.37] 532-534 535[2.4] 545[47]
KNOCH O. 556[17]
KÖRNER B. 427[76] 429[90.93]
KOESTER C.R. 177[1] 190
KOHL M. 549[62]
KOLIÉ C. 294[36]
KOPFENSTEINER T. 30[54]
KREINER A. 62[5]
KRETZMANN N. 336[12]
KRIEGER D.J. 69[31]
KROTZ L. 317[6]
KRYSTAL H. 402[13]
KÜCHLER M. 177[1] 190
KÜNG H. 11[18] 62[5] 89[19] 128[24] 134 549[63]
KUMA A. 287[1] 307
KUSCHEL K.-J. 129[29] 134[4]
KUSS O. 165[20]
KYUNG C.H. 436[16]
KYSAR R. 167[33] 178[3] 187

LABUSCHAGNE C.J. 140[18] 141[21] 142[23.25] 143[27-28.31]
LAFONT G. 106 113[14] 334[6]
LAGRANGE P.-J. 178[3] 181[14] 187
LAMOTTE E. 251[6] 252[7] 253[11] 254[13]
LAMOUILLE A. 178[3] 181[14] 186
LAMPE G.W.H. 73[47] 74[49.51] 75[73-57] 76 208[4] 523[7] 526
LANDRON B. 278[18-19] 280[24] 281[29.32] 283[38-39] 284[43.45] 285[50]
LANDSHUT S. 102[6]
LANG H. 137[12]
LANGER L. 400[8] 403[15] 404[18] 405[21]
LAPIDE P. 404[19]
LARCHET J.C. 207[3]
LAROQUE E. 316[4]
LASSON G. 109[8]
LAVINE T.Z. 548[58]
LAVOIE S. 325[31]
LEACH G.P. 324[27]
LEE D.A. 178[3] 181[17] 190
LEE J. 436[16]
LEEMANS J. 211[12]
LEIBNIZ 375[79]
LEHMANN K. 350[6] 417[3] 562[37] 567[1]
LEMAIRE T. 315[2]
LEMCHE N.P. 137[9]
LÉON-DUFOUR X. 178[3] 181[14] 182[19] 187

LE SAUX H. 249 250[1]
LESSING G.E. 67[17]
LESZCZYNSKI K. 384[6]
LEUZE R. 127[22] 269[8] 350[6]
LEVENSON J.D. 142[26] 145[37]
LEVI P. 400[4] 406[29] 407[30] 409
LEVINAS E. 102
LEVISON J. 48
LEWIS D. 525-526
LIBERATORE A. 448[56]
LIDDELL H.G. 183[21] 190
LIGHTFOOT R.H. 178[3] 181[14] 187
LINDARS B. 178[3] 180[12] 181[14] 182[18] 187
LINDBECK G. 78[76] 79[76] 346[39] 525
LITTEL F.H. 386[11]
LOCKE H.G. 386[11]
LÖHRER M. 443[40]
LOGISTER W. 125[11]
LOHFINK G. 417[1]
LOHSE E. 181[14] 190
LOISY A. 181[14] 188
LONERGAN B. 57 334
LONG C. 13[19] 115[20]
LONG C.H. 254[12]
LOOSE H.N. 476[46]
LOUGHLIN G. 77[67] 522[2]
LUCIAN 147[48]
LUDWIG R.A. 67[17]
LÜCKE F. 177[3] 188
LÜDEMANN G. 365[35]
LUKAS R.C. 384[5]
LUTHER M. 117 207[3] 256 270 391 571
LUTZ U. 557[20]
LYMAN J.R. 193[1]
LYOTARD J.-F. 578[4] 579 591[25]

MAAS W. 557[20]
MACGREGOR J. 178[3] 181[14] 188
MACK B. 66[14]
MACRAE G. 47[9]
MACRORY J. 178[3] 188
MADHVA 235 238 243
MAGESA L. 289[9] 295[39] 306[84] 307[90] 309[96] 310[102]
MAHER 489[94]
MAḤYĪ AD-DĪR AL-IṢFAHĀNĪ 283
MAIER A. 177[3] 179[5.7] 188
MALEBRANCHE 375[79]
MANNERMAA T. 445[44]

MANUEL G. 319[11]
MARCUS G. 26[46]
MARION J.-L. 591[26.27] 592[29]
MARSHALL B. 333[4] 434[7]
MARSHALL I.H. 148[51]
MARTIN A. 210[11]
MARTYN J.L. 167[31]
MARX K. 102[6]
MASTIN B.A. 178[3] 181[14] 188
MAURICE E. 433[2] 465[7]
MAXIMUS THE CONFESSOR 207[3] 322
MAY G. 193[1]
MBITI J. 288[4] 290[13] 292 293[23]
MCBRIDE S.D. 139[16]
MCBRIEN R. 549[65]
MCCHEE M. 546[51]
MCCREADY D. 78[70]
MCDONAGH F. 490[98]
MCGRATH A. 67[17] 73[46]
MCGRAVE B. 4[5]
MCHUGH J.F. 562[35]
MCINNES V.A. 408[36]
MCKENNA A.J. 558[28]
MEEKS W. 165[20] 167[30] 173[46] 178[3] 186[27] 190
MEIER J.P. 48 54[32] 57 59[48] 61[1.4] 66[14] 436[16] 508[51] 509 510 511[57-60] 512-513 514[66] 515 516[73] 517-519
MELANCHTON P. 574[13]
MELTZER E.S. 78[72]
MÉNARD C. 117[24]
MENKE K.-H. 564[42-43]
MERRIGAN T. 62[5] 65[11] 69[32] 71[41] 133[1] 377[82] 536[5] 590[24]
MESSORI V. 498[16-17] 499[20] 505 506[41-42]
METZ J.B. 166[27] 381[1] 393 394[298] 395 460[119] 474[41] 488 489[94] 490[97]
METZGER B.M. 154[69]
MEUSER E. 440[30]
MEYER B.J. 57[42]
MEYER H. 568 569[4]
MEYER H.A.W. 177[3] 180[12] 181[16] 188
MEYNELL A. 25[43]
MICHALSON G.E. 370[65]
MIGNE J.-P. 114[18]
MILBANK J. 27[47]
MILLEN Rochelle L. 391[21]
MILLER J. 319[11]
MILLER R. 476[49]

MOHAMMED 263-272
MOJZES P. 62[6] 133[1] 418[22] 530[29] 531[37] 535[3]
MOLARI C. 85[12]
MOLLAT D. 178[3] 188
MOLONEY F.J. 181[14] 190
MOLTMANN J. 375[79] 389[17-18] 390 400 401[10] 405[20.22] 406 407[31-32] 408[34.36] 410[44] 549[62] 564
MOONEY J. 327[36]
MOORE J. 394[30]
MOOS M.F. 337[15]
MORGAN R. 371[69]
MORRE W. 547[53]
MORRIS L. 178[3] 179[5.7] 188
MOSSE G. 383 384[3]
MOULE C.F.D. 74[52] 148[51]
MÜLLER G. 587[19]
MUGAMBI J.N.K. 289[9] 306[84] 307[90] 309[96] 310[102]
MULLER M. 238[7]
MUÑOZ IGLESIAS L. 340[26]
MURPHY T.A. 567[1]
MUSSNER F. 165[20]

NAGEL T. 275[4]
NASIMIYU-WASIKE A. 306[84] 307[90] 309[96] 310[101-102]
NECKEBROUCK V. 62[5] 124[10]
NEHER A. 118[27]
NEIRYNCK F. 190
NESTORIUS 269 271
NETLAND G.A. 525[12]
NEUNER J. 62[5]
NEWBIGIN L. 544[44]
NEWMAN J.H. 22[39] 23[39]
NEYREY J.H. 178[3] 181[14] 190
NIEBERGALL F. 367[49]
NIEBUHR H.R. 46[5]
NIELSEN J. 275[5] 277[8] 278[19]
NIETZSCHE F. 385-386
NIEUWENHUIS J. 186[28] 188
NILSON J. 511 512[61]
NILSSON M.P. 145[35]
NORRIS F.W. 207[3]
NOTH M. 136[8]
NOWAK K. 373[76]
NYAMITI C. 289[11] 291[19] 292[21.22] 293[26] 294[32] 311[104]
NYANAMOLI 251

OBAJE Y. 312[108]
OBERMAN H.A. 571[10]
O'COLLINS G. 143[30] 149[54] 153[64] 343 344[34]
O'DAY 178[3] 181[17]
ODEBERG H. 180[12] 181[14.16-17] 182[17] 188
O'DONOHUE J. 294[34]
O'DONOVAN L. 33[3] 437[17-18] 489[93]
ODUYOYE M. 304[79] 305[80-81] 306 307[87-89] 308[91] 309 311[103]
OGDEN S.M. 15[23] 18[28] 20[36] 33[3]
O'HARA W. 451[69] 478[55]
O'HEAR A. 546[51]
OKHOLM D. 550[68]
O'LEARY J. 261 262[25]
OLIVELLE P. 236 239[9] 143[14]
OPITZ H.G. 214[19]
OPSAHL P.D. 387[12]
ORIGEN 4 192-193 196 199-200
OTTO R. 547
OVERHAGE P. 446[47]
OXTOBY W.G. 541[26]

PAIRMAN J. 299[56]
PANIKKAR R. 64[9] 77[63] 125 222[6] 223 244 261 434[8]
PANNENBERG W. 105[7] 268[6] 370[65] 509 567[1] 575[16]
PARRATT J. 291[17] 292[20] 293[27] 294[28-29]
PATRICK D. 137[12]
PAUL OF BŪŠ 277-284
PAWLIKOWSKI J. 385[7] 391[21.23] 402 407[33] 410 411[45.47] 412[54] 413-415
PECK M.S. 45
PEELMAN A. 315[1] 319[13] 320[14] 321[16.21] 322[22] 324[25] 325[28-29] 326[35]
PEETERS L. 478[54]
PEGIS A. 538[11]
PELIKAN J. 47[10]
PÉNOUKOU E.J. 288 289[8]
PÉRIER A. 277[11]
PERKINS D. 404[19]
PERKINS P. 80[83]
PERKINSON J. 90[22]
PERRY S. 299[56]
PESCH O.H. 570[6]
PETER A. 123[4]
PETERSON E. 142[25]
PETIT J.-C. 117[24]
PETTERSEN A. 210[11]

PFÜLLER W. 585[14]
PHAN P. 436[16]
PHILLIPS R. 550[68]
PHILO 151[58] 180[13] 181[14] 193-194
PIERCE J. 562[36]
PIERIS A. 79[79] 84[9] 85[10] 227[10] 436[16]
PINBORG J. 336[12]
PINNOCK C.H. 550[68]
PLATO 194-195
PLATTI E. 278[19] 279[21] 280[24] 282 283[37]
PLINY THE YOUNGER 147[48] 148[49]
PLOTINUS 197
PLUMMER A. 177[3] 188
PLUTARCH 194
POBEE J. 294[30] 308 311 312[105.108]
POKORNÝ P. 148[51]
POLLEFEYT D. 64[8] 133[1]
POPE-LEVISON P. 47
POPKES S.W. 110[10]
PORPHYRY 192
POSPIESZALSKI K. 384[6]
POTTMEYER H.-J. 426[71]
POWER D.N. 562[35]
PROUDFOOT W. 525[13]
PSEUDO-DIONYSIUS 208
PUHL L.J. 475[42]
PUTMAN H. 280[23] 281[27.30.31]
PYE M. 355[19] 371[69]

RAAB K. 552[2]
RACE A. 540[25]
RADHAKRISHNAN 247 538[11]
RAFFELT A. 469[19]
RAHNER K. 5[6] 9 14 20[34] 21[37] 24[42] 25[44] 29
   62[5] 92[24] 93[25] 104 112[13] 113 117 125
   126[17] 134 221[3] 404[19] 433[2] 434[10] 435[11-
   13] 436 437[17.19] 438[20-23] 439[24-27] 440[30]
   441[30-32] 442[33-37] 443[37-40] 444[41-43] 445[44]
   446[44-47] 447[48-51] 448[53-57] 449[57-60] 450[60-
   63] 451[67-69] 452[70-75] 453[76-80] 454[81-85]
   455[87-90] 456[94-98] 457[99-104] 458[105-111]
   459[112-118] 460[119-120] 461[121-126] 462[127-131]
   463 464[3-5] 465[6-9] 466[9-10] 467[12-15] 468[17]
   469[18-19] 470[20-26] 471[27-32] 472[33-34.36-37]
   473[38-39] 474[40-41] 475[41-45] 476[46.48] 477[50-53]
   478[53-55] 479[56.60] 480[61-62] 481[65-66] 482[67-
   68.70] 483[72-74] 484[75-78] 485[79-82] 486[83-86]
   487[86-88] 488[90] 489[92-95] 490[96-100] 491[102]
   509 547 556 581[8]

RAINBOW P.A. 152[63]
RAMANUJA 238[7-8] 243 247
RANKE 365[39]
RATZINGER J. 230 231[11] 493 498[16-18] 499[20]
   500[21] 501[26] 502[29] 503[30] 504[24] 505
   506[40-43]
REID D. 350[5]
REID J.B. 90[22]
REIKERSTORFER J. 441[30]
REINISCH L. 442[37]
REITSEMA G.W. 376[80]
RENAN E. 67[17]
RENSBERGER D. 165[20.22]
RENZ H. 349[1] 365[38]
REPGES W. 338[21]
RESCHER N. 31[1] 32[1] 37[9]
REUMANN J. 47[9] 569[5]
REYMOND B. 350[6]
RHYS DAVIS T.W. 252[8]
RIALL A. 210[11]
RICHARDSON B. 317[6]
RICKLIN T. 190
RIDDERBOS H.N. 178[3] 188
RIESS R. 553[5] 556[19]
RILEY H. 466[10]
RISSE G. 264[2]
RITSCHL A. 67[17] 364 365[35]
ROBERTSON J.C. Jr. 490[100]
ROBINSON R. 59
RÖPER A. 445[44]
RONDET H. 448[56]
RORTY R. 583[11]
ROSIER I. 336[12]
ROTH J. 413[55]
ROUSSEAU A. 84[8] 207[1]
ROVATTI P.A. 101[4]
ROWDON H.H. 151[57]
RUBENSTEIN B. Rogers 384[4]
RUBENSTEIN R.L. 384[4]
RUDDIES H. 349[1]
RUETHER R. 400-401 412[54] 413[56] 414[57-58]
   415
RUNIA D.T. 189
RUOKANEN M. 128[27]
RYAN M. 386[11] 390

SACHS J.R. 491[102]
SACHS LITTELL M. 384[4]
SAEBO M. 147[46]

SALM L. 437[17]
SAMARTHA S. 127[18] 542[32]
SAMBOU E. 288[7]
SAMUEL V. 294[31]
SANDERS E.P. 48 53[30] 54 57[40] 66[14] 181[14] 509[54]
SANDERS J.N. 178[3] 188
SANKARA 235
SANKS H. 33[3]
SANON A. 288[7] 294[38] 295
SATPREM 548[60]
SAUTER G. 585[14]
SAWYERR H. 293[27] 294[28-29]
SCANLON M.J. 591[6]
SCHAEFFLER R. 585[15] 589[23]
SCHÄUBLIN C. 207[2]
SCHAFF P. 46 547[53]
SCHANZ P. 177[3] 179[5] 188
SCHECHTER R. 386[10]
SCHEFFCZYK L. 211[13]
SCHENK R. 556[16] 562[34]
SCHENKER A. 558[24] 563[40]
SCHILLEBEECKX E. 19[31] 21[38] 35[5] 67[18] 116 124 216[12] 332[3] 545[47] 556 584[12]
SCHINELLER P. 20[35]
SCHLEIERMACHER F. 67[17] 68 368 371 528 547 548[59]
SCHLETTE H.R. 117
SCHLIER H. 162[10.13] 165[20] 166[26] 170[39]
SCHLINK E. 562[37]
SCHMIDT-LEUKEL P. 62[5] 123[4]
SCHNACKENBURG R. 163[14] 165[20] 171[41] 178[3] 181[14] 188 556[17]
SCHNEIDER T. 562[37]
SCHOCKENHOFF E. 115[21]
SCHÖNMETZER A. 459[116]
SCHOFFELEERS M. 294[37]
SCHOLTZ G. 373[76]
SCHOONENBERG P. 127[21]
SCHOOT H.J.M. 338[20] 339[11]
SCHOPPMANN C. 384[5]
SCHOTTROFF L. 165[20] 167 168[35]
SCHREITER R.J. 37[8] 288[7] 289[8] 292[21-22] 293[26] 294[28.33.36.38] 295[39-40]
SCHREURS N. 125[11]
SCHÜSSLER-FIORENZA E. 33[3] 48[14-15] 66[14] 129[28] 381[1] 393[28] 394[29.31] 395[32]
SCHULZ S. 178[3] 179[5] 188
SCHUON F. 545[48]

SCHWAB R. 3[1]
SCHWAGER R. 418[4] 558[26-28] 564 565[46]
SCHWEIKER W. 30[54]
SCHWEITZER A. 45 46 67[17]
SCHWENDIMANN F. 448[56]
SCHWERDTFEGER N. 445[44] 470[23] 472[35] 473[39] 483[72]
SCOTT D.C. 222[4]
SCOTT R. 183[21] 190
SCOTUS 340[27]
SCROGGS R. 146[40] 148[50]
SCULLION J.J. 137[12]
SECKLER M. 426[71]
SEGUNDO 508[51]
SENIOR D. 163[16] 174[50]
SESBOÜÉ B. 153[65]
SHAKYANUMI 261
SHANKARA 215
SHARMA A. 78[70]
SHECHTER R. 385-386
SHERMAN F. 387[12] 388
SHERWIN-WHITE A.N. 148[49]
SHINRAN 256
SHORTER A. 294[35]
SHWEDER R.A. 399[1]
SIDEBOTTOM E.M. 184[25] 190
SIEBENROCK R. 465[9]
SIMPSON J.E. 208[6]
SMALLEY S.S. 184[25] 190
SMITH D. 490[97]
SMITH J.Z. 321[17]
SMITH M.S. 137[12]
SMITH W.C. 64[9] 532 535-536 540[24] 541[26-28] 542[29-32] 543[33-39] 544[41-43.46] 545[48] 546
SNOW J. 322
SOARES-PRABHU G. 226[8]
SOBRINO J. 493[2] 494[4] 495 496[9-10] 497[13-15] 498-501 502[27] 503[30-31.33] 504[37] 505[39] 506 507[45] 508[51] 509 510[56] 511[58-59] 512 513[63] 514-519
SOCRATES 198
SONG C.-S. 436[16]
SOSKICE J. 561[31]
SOUGA T. 304[79] 305 307[88]
SPICQ C. 183[24] 190
STÄHLIN G. 179[5.6] 182 190
STANTON G.N. 51[21]
STARKLOFF C. 326[33]
STAVROPOULOS C. 216[24]

STAVROU M. 211[13]
STEELY J.E. 148[51]
STEGEMANN W. 556[19] 558[25]
STEINBECK J. 555[13]
STEINMETZ P. 321[16] 325[31] 326[32]
STELTENKAMP M. 326[32]
STEWART O. 327[36]
STINNETT T.R. 522[2]
STOLINA R. 464[3]
STOLZMAN W. 321[16] 322[24]
STRACHAN R.H. 181[14] 188
STRACK H.L. 181[14] 188
STRANGE G.R. 214[21]
STRANSKY T. 320[14]
STRAUSS D. 67[17]
STRAWSON 333[4]
STRUTHERS MALBON E. 385[7]
STUDER B. 207[2] 208[5]
STUHLMACHER P. 66[14] 557[20] 563[39]
SUCHOCKI M. 6[10]
SUERMANN H. 277[7]
SUGDEN C. 294[31]
SUGIRTHARAJAH R.S. 37[8] 48[13]
SULLIVAN, F. 9[14] 18[26]
SUNDBERG A.C. 190
SUNDKLER B. 293[27]
SURIN K. 27[47] 524[10]
SUZUKI D.T. 254[14] 255 [15]
SWEET J. 148[50]
SWIDLER L. 29[53] 62[6] 64[9] 68[19] 71[43] 72[43] 73[45] 133[1] 529[22] 530[29] 531[37] 535[3]
SYKES S.W. 73[47] 558[22] 562[35]
SYMMACHUS 146

TAL U. 385[8.9] 390-391
TALAL ASAD 26[46]
TANENBAUM M.H. 387[12]
TANNER K. 334[4] 581[9] 582[10]
TAPPA L. 307[89]
TAUBES J. 165[20]
TAYLOR J.V. 288[5]
TAYLOR M. 443[40]
TEN BOOM C. 399[2]
TEN KATE L. 344[35] 591[25]
TERTULLIAN 77[73] 194-196
TESSIER L. 537[7]
THEISSEN G. 66[14]
THEOBALD C. 436[16]
THEODOSIUS 146

THEOPHILUS OF ANTIOCH 195 198
THÉVENAZ P. 549[66]
THIBAUT G. 238[7]
THIEL J. 15[22]
THOMA C. 388[15]
THOMAS J.C. 182[17] 190
THOMAS O.C. 350[7]
THOMPSON C.P. 339[24] 340[27] 341[29] 342[31]
THOMPSON M.M. 184[25] 190
THOMPSON W. 404[18]
THOMPSON W.M. 58[45]
THOMSON D.L. 294[37]
THOMSON R.W. 207[1] 214[19]
THÜSING W. 151[60] 440[30] 485[81]
TILLICH P. 67[17] 215 547[55] 548[57]
TILLMANN F. 178[3] 181[14] 188
TINKER G. 321[18]
TOMSON P.J. 170[38]
TONER J. 480[62]
TORRES S. 290[15] 300[60]
TRACK J. 553[5]
TRACY D. 27[48] 29[51.53] 346[38] 381[1] 393[28] 394[29.31] 395[32] 491[101]
TRAJAN 147
TREAT J. 320[14-15] 321[18]
TROELTSCH E. 349[1-2] 350[5.7] 351-353 354[17-18] 355-357 358[26] 359 360[28] 361-362 363[31] 364[34] 365[36-37] 366[46] 367[48-49] 368 369[57.60] 370[62.64-65] 371[68-70] 372[72-75] 373 374[78] 375[79] 376[80] 377-378 379[91] 380 539[21] 540[22]
TROUPEAU G. 281[28]
TUCHMAN B. 571[9]
TURNER D.H. 321[17]
TUTU D.M. 291
TWELFTREE G.H. 66[14]
TWISS S. 522[2] 525[11]
UKPONG J.S. 292[21]
ULLRICH L. 587[18]

VALKENBERG P. 129[29]
VAN BAVEL T.J. 332[2]
VAN BEECK F.J. 14[21] 20[34] 67[17]
VAN BEEK W.E.A. 294[37]
VAN BUREN P. 382
VAN CANGH J.-M. 137[12]
VAN DE HOOGEN T. 128[24]
VAN DEN BUSSCHE H. 178[3] 181[14] 188
VAN DER HEIJDEN 484[75]

VAN DER KOOIJ A. 580[6]
VAN DER MERWE B.J. 142[25]
VAN DER TOORN K. 580[6]
VAN DE SANDT H. 125[11]
VAN ESS J. 549[63]
VAN LIN J. 123[4]
VAN SEGBROECK F. 563[41]
VATTIMO G. 101[4]
VECSEY C. 321[16]
VERGOTE A. 146[45]
VERMES G. 66[14]
VICEDOM G.F. 288[4]
VOIGT G. 178[3] 188
VON BALTHASAR H.U.   116 417 418[5.7]
    419[14] 420[20-21] 421[29.32-33] 422[41-43] 423
    424[51-52.57] 425[62] 426[68.72.75] 427[77-81]
    428[82-86] 429[87.90-96] 430[97-99] 431[101-102]
    432[103-104] 463[1-2]
VON FUNK F.X. 113[15]
VON HARNACK A. 46 47 73[46] 76 354[17]
    371[70] 528
VON HÜGEL F. 350[7]
VORGRIMLER H. 469[19] 484[78]
VORLÄNDER 555[14]
VROOM H. 127[22] 128[23]

WACE H. 547[42]
WAGNER F. 561 562[34] 564[44]
WALLACE A. 327[36]
WALLS A. 313[109.111]
WALTER P. 115[21]
WALTERS A. 318[9]
WARD K. 75[56] 537[8] 549[64]
WARRIOR R.A. 320[14]
WATKINS M. 319[11]
WATT W.M. 275[4]
WEAVER W.P. 49[18]
WEDER H. 557[20]
WEIL S. 202
WEINER E.S.C. 208[6]
WEISS B. 180[11-12] 181[15] 188
WEISS J. 46 67[17]
WENGST K. 167[32]
WERBICK J. 556[18]
WESSELS A. 47[12]
WESTCOTT B.F. 178[3] 180[12] 181[14.15] 189
WHALE J.S. 555[12]
WHALING F. 544[45]
WHITE J. 548[60]

WIESEL E. 388-389 405[21]
WIJSEN F.J.S. 129[29]
WIKENHAUSER A. 178[3] 181[14] 189
WILFRED F. 220[2]
WILKEN R.L. 4[3] 46[3]
WILLIAMS A.N. 207[3]
WILS J.-P. 128[24]
WILSON H.A. 547[53]
WILSON P. 391[22]
WILSON R.A. 401[10]
WILTVLIET T. 129[28]
WINTER B.C. 137[10] 146[44] 157[75]
WINTER B.W. 150[55]
WINTER C. 146[44]
WISSINK J. 344[35]
WITHERINGTON B. 49[17] 50 51[22] 66[13-14]
    178[3] 186[27] 189
WITSCH N. 349[1]
WITTGENSTEIN L. 7[11]
WITTSTADT K. 440[30]
WOJCIECHOWSKI F. 315[2]
WONG J. 92[24] 433[2-3] 434[8-9] 439[15] 440[30]
    448[56] 455[92] 482[68]
WRIGHT C.J.H. 137[10] 140[17] 142[26] 143[29]
    144[32]
WRIGHT G.E. 141[20]
WRIGHT J.H. 90[20]
WRIGHT N.T. 46[4] 54[33] 55 56[39] 66[14]
WULF F. 478[55]
WURST G. 190
WUST P. 376[80]
WYRWA D. 207[2]

XAVIER 478[54]

YAḤYĀ IBN ʿADĪ 277 280-283
YANDEL K. 62[6] 538[12]
YOUNG F. 193[1] 197[2] 553[7] 554[9] 555[13]
    559[29]
YOUNG G. 317[8]
YOUNG W.J. 476[47]

ZAEHNER R.C. 243[13]
ZAHLAUER A. 464[3]
ZAHN T. 180[12] 181[14.16] 189
ZEHNER J. 128[27]
ZENGER E. 137[12]
ZIRKNER H. 269[8]
ZULEHNER P.M. 469[18]

BIBLIOTHECA EPHEMERIDUM THEOLOGICARUM LOVANIENSIUM

SERIES I

* = Out of print

*1. *Miscellanea dogmatica in honorem Eximii Domini J. Bittremieux*, 1947.

*2-3. *Miscellanea moralia in honorem Eximii Domini A. Janssen*, 1948.

*4. G. PHILIPS, *La grâce des justes de l'Ancien Testament*, 1948.

*5. G. PHILIPS, *De ratione instituendi tractatum de gratia nostrae sanctificationis*, 1953.

6-7. *Recueil Lucien Cerfaux. Études d'exégèse et d'histoire religieuse*, 1954. 504 et 577 p. FB 1000 par tome. Cf. *infra*, n°s 18 et 71 (t. III).

8. G. THILS, *Histoire doctrinale du mouvement œcuménique*, 1955. Nouvelle édition, 1963. 338 p. FB 135.

*9. *Études sur l'Immaculée Conception*, 1955.

*10. J.A. O'DONOHOE, *Tridentine Seminary Legislation*, 1957.

*11. G. THILS, *Orientations de la théologie*, 1958.

*12-13. J. COPPENS, A. DESCAMPS, É. MASSAUX (ed.), *Sacra Pagina. Miscellanea Biblica Congressus Internationalis Catholici de Re Biblica*, 1959.

*14. *Adrien VI, le premier Pape de la contre-réforme*, 1959.

*15. F. CLAEYS BOUUAERT, *Les déclarations et serments imposés par la loi civile aux membres du clergé belge sous le Directoire (1795-1801)*, 1960.

*16. G. THILS, *La «Théologie œcuménique». Notion-Formes-Démarches*, 1960.

17. G. THILS, *Primauté pontificale et prérogatives épiscopales. «Potestas ordinaria» au Concile du Vatican*, 1961. 103 p. FB 50.

*18. *Recueil Lucien Cerfaux*, t. III, 1962. Cf. *infra*, n° 71.

*19. *Foi et réflexion philosophique. Mélanges F. Grégoire*, 1961.

*20. *Mélanges G. Ryckmans*, 1963.

21. G. THILS, *L'infaillibilité du peuple chrétien «in credendo»*, 1963. 67 p. FB 50.

*22. J. FÉRIN & L. JANSSENS, *Progestogènes et morale conjugale*, 1963.

*23. *Collectanea Moralia in honorem Eximii Domini A. Janssen*, 1964.

24. H. CAZELLES (ed.), *De Mari à Qumrân. L'Ancien Testament. Son milieu. Ses écrits. Ses relectures juives* (Hommage J. Coppens, I), 1969. 158*-370 p. FB 900.

*25. I. DE LA POTTERIE (ed.), *De Jésus aux évangiles. Tradition et rédaction dans les évangiles synoptiques* (Hommage J. Coppens, II), 1967.

26. G. THILS & R.E. BROWN (ed.), *Exégèse et théologie* (Hommage J. Coppens, III), 1968. 328 p. FB 700.

27. J. COPPENS (ed.), *Ecclesia a Spiritu sancto edocta. Hommage à Mgr G. Philips*, 1970. 640 p. FB 1000.

28. J. COPPENS (ed.), *Sacerdoce et célibat. Études historiques et théologiques*, 1971. 740 p. FB 700.

29. M. DIDIER (ed.), *L'évangile selon Matthieu. Rédaction et théologie*, 1972. 432 p. FB 1000.
*30. J. KEMPENEERS, *Le Cardinal van Roey en son temps*, 1971.

SERIES II

31. F. NEIRYNCK, *Duality in Mark. Contributions to the Study of the Markan Redaction*, 1972. Revised edition with Supplementary Notes, 1988. 252 p. FB 1200.
32. F. NEIRYNCK (ed.), *L'évangile de Luc. Problèmes littéraires et théologiques*, 1973. *L'évangile de Luc – The Gospel of Luke*. Revised and enlarged edition, 1989. x-590 p. FB 2200.
33. C. BREKELMANS (ed.), *Questions disputées d'Ancien Testament. Méthode et théologie*, 1974. *Continuing Questions in Old Testament Method and Theology*. Revised and enlarged edition by M. VERVENNE, 1989. 245 p. FB 1200.
34. M. SABBE (ed.), *L'évangile selon Marc. Tradition et rédaction*, 1974. Nouvelle édition augmentée, 1988. 601 p. FB 2400.
35. B. WILLAERT (ed.), *Philosophie de la religion – Godsdienstfilosofie. Miscellanea Albert Dondeyne*, 1974. Nouvelle édition, 1987. 458 p. FB 1600.
36. G. PHILIPS, *L'union personnelle avec le Dieu vivant. Essai sur l'origine et le sens de la grâce créée*, 1974. Édition révisée, 1989. 299 p. FB 1000.
37. F. NEIRYNCK, in collaboration with T. HANSEN and F. VAN SEGBROECK, *The Minor Agreements of Matthew and Luke against Mark with a Cumulative List*, 1974. 330 p. FB 900.
38. J. COPPENS, *Le messianisme et sa relève prophétique. Les anticipations vétérotestamentaires. Leur accomplissement en Jésus*, 1974. Édition révisée, 1989. XIII-265 p. FB 1000.
39. D. SENIOR, *The Passion Narrative according to Matthew. A Redactional Study*, 1975. New impression, 1982. 440 p. FB 1000.
40. J. DUPONT (ed.), *Jésus aux origines de la christologie*, 1975. Nouvelle édition augmentée, 1989. 458 p. FB 1500.
41. J. COPPENS (ed.), *La notion biblique de Dieu*, 1976. Réimpression, 1985. 519 p. FB 1600.
42. J. LINDEMANS & H. DEMEESTER (ed.), *Liber Amicorum Monseigneur W. Onclin*, 1976. XXII-396 p. FB 1000.
43. R.E. HOECKMAN (ed.), *Pluralisme et œcuménisme en recherches théologiques. Mélanges offerts au R.P. Dockx, O.P.*, 1976. 316 p. FB 1000.
44. M. DE JONGE (ed.), *L'évangile de Jean. Sources, rédaction, théologie*, 1977. Réimpression, 1987. 416 p. FB 1500.
45. E.J.M. VAN EIJL (ed.), *Facultas S. Theologiae Lovaniensis 1432-1797. Bijdragen tot haar geschiedenis. Contributions to its History. Contributions à son histoire*, 1977. 570 p. FB 1700.
46. M. DELCOR (ed.), *Qumrân. Sa piété, sa théologie et son milieu*, 1978. 432 p. FB 1700.
47. M. CAUDRON (ed.), *Faith and Society. Foi et société. Geloof en maatschappij. Acta Congressus Internationalis Theologici Lovaniensis 1976*, 1978. 304 p. FB 1150.

48. J. KREMER (ed.), *Les Actes des Apôtres. Traditions, rédaction, théologie,* 1979. 590 p. FB 1700.

49. F. NEIRYNCK, avec la collaboration de J. DELOBEL, T. SNOY, G. VAN BELLE, F. VAN SEGBROECK, *Jean et les Synoptiques. Examen critique de l'exégèse de M.-É. Boismard,* 1979. XII-428 p. FB 1000.

50. J. COPPENS, *La relève apocalyptique du messianisme royal. I. La royauté – Le règne – Le royaume de Dieu. Cadre de la relève apocalyptique,* 1979. 325 p. FB 1000.

51. M. GILBERT (ed.), *La Sagesse de l'Ancien Testament,* 1979. Nouvelle édition mise à jour, 1990. 455 p. FB 1500.

52. B. DEHANDSCHUTTER, *Martyrium Polycarpi. Een literair-kritische studie,* 1979. 296 p. FB 1000.

53. J. LAMBRECHT (ed.), *L'Apocalypse johannique et l'Apocalyptique dans le Nouveau Testament,* 1980. 458 p. FB 1400.

54. P.-M. BOGAERT (ed.), *Le livre de Jérémie. Le prophète et son milieu. Les oracles et leur transmission,* 1981. *Nouvelle édition mise à jour,* 1997. 448 p. FB 1800.

55. J. COPPENS, *La relève apocalyptique du messianisme royal. III. Le Fils de l'homme néotestamentaire.* Édition posthume par F. NEIRYNCK, 1981. XIV-192 p. FB 800.

56. J. VAN BAVEL & M. SCHRAMA (ed.), *Jansénius et le Jansénisme dans les Pays-Bas. Mélanges Lucien Ceyssens,* 1982. 247 p. FB 1000.

57. J.H. WALGRAVE, *Selected Writings – Thematische geschriften. Thomas Aquinas, J.H. Newman, Theologia Fundamentalis.* Edited by G. DE SCHRIJVER & J.J. KELLY, 1982. XLIII-425 p. FB 1000.

58. F. NEIRYNCK & F. VAN SEGBROECK, avec la collaboration de E. MANNING, *Ephemerides Theologicae Lovanienses 1924-1981. Tables générales. (Bibliotheca Ephemeridum Theologicarum Lovaniensium 1947-1981),* 1982. 400 p. FB 1600.

59. J. DELOBEL (ed.), *Logia. Les paroles de Jésus – The Sayings of Jesus. Mémorial Joseph Coppens,* 1982. 647 p. FB 2000.

60. F. NEIRYNCK, *Evangelica. Gospel Studies – Études d'évangile. Collected Essays.* Edited by F. VAN SEGBROECK, 1982. XIX-1036 p. FB 2000.

61. J. COPPENS, *La relève apocalyptique du messianisme royal. II. Le Fils d'homme vétéro- et intertestamentaire.* Édition posthume par J. LUST, 1983. XVII-272 p. FB 1000.

62. J.J. KELLY, *Baron Friedrich von Hügel's Philosophy of Religion,* 1983. 232 p. FB 1500.

63. G. DE SCHRIJVER, *Le merveilleux accord de l'homme et de Dieu. Étude de l'analogie de l'être chez Hans Urs von Balthasar,* 1983. 344 p. FB 1500.

64. J. GROOTAERS & J.A. SELLING, *The 1980 Synod of Bishops: «On the Role of the Family». An Exposition of the Event and an Analysis of its Texts.* Preface by Prof. emeritus L. JANSSENS, 1983. 375 p. FB 1500.

65. F. NEIRYNCK & F. VAN SEGBROECK, *New Testament Vocabulary. A Companion Volume to the Concordance,* 1984. XVI-494 p. FB 2000.

66. R.F. COLLINS, *Studies on the First Letter to the Thessalonians,* 1984. XI-415 p. FB 1500.

67. A. PLUMMER, *Conversations with Dr. Döllinger 1870-1890.* Edited with Introduction and Notes by R. BOUDENS, with the collaboration of L. KENIS, 1985. LIV-360 p. FB 1800.

68. N. LOHFINK (ed.), *Das Deuteronomium. Entstehung, Gestalt und Botschaft / Deuteronomy: Origin, Form and Message*, 1985. XI-382 p. FB 2000.
69. P.F. FRANSEN, *Hermeneutics of the Councils and Other Studies*. Collected by H.E. MERTENS & F. DE GRAEVE, 1985. 543 p. FB 1800.
70. J. DUPONT, *Études sur les Évangiles synoptiques*. Présentées par F. NEIRYNCK, 1985. 2 tomes, XXI-IX-1210 p. FB 2800.
71. *Recueil Lucien Cerfaux*, t. III, 1962. Nouvelle édition revue et complétée, 1985. LXXX-458 p. FB 1600.
72. J. GROOTAERS, *Primauté et collégialité. Le dossier de Gérard Philips sur la Nota Explicativa Praevia (Lumen gentium, Chap. III)*. Présenté avec introduction historique, annotations et annexes. Préface de G. THILS, 1986. 222 p. FB 1000.
73. A. VANHOYE (ed.), *L'apôtre Paul. Personnalité, style et conception du ministère*, 1986. XIII-470 p. FB 2600.
74. J. LUST (ed.), *Ezekiel and His Book. Textual and Literary Criticism and their Interrelation*, 1986. X-387 p. FB 2700.
75. É. MASSAUX, *Influence de l'Évangile de saint Matthieu sur la littérature chrétienne avant saint Irénée*. Réimpression anastatique présentée par F. NEIRYNCK. *Supplément: Bibliographie 1950-1985*, par B. DEHAND-SCHUTTER, 1986. XXVII-850 p. FB 2500.
76. L. CEYSSENS & J.A.G. TANS, *Autour de l'Unigenitus. Recherches sur la genèse de la Constitution*, 1987. XXVI-845 p. FB 2500.
77. A. DESCAMPS, *Jésus et l'Église. Études d'exégèse et de théologie*. Préface de Mgr A. HOUSSIAU, 1987. XLV-641 p. FB 2500.
78. J. DUPLACY, *Études de critique textuelle du Nouveau Testament*. Présentées par J. DELOBEL, 1987. XXVII-431 p. FB 1800.
79. E.J.M. VAN EIJL (ed.), *L'image de C. Jansénius jusqu'à la fin du XVIIIᵉ siècle*, 1987. 258 p. FB 1250.
80. E. BRITO, *La Création selon Schelling. Universum*, 1987. XXXV-646 p. FB 2980.
81. J. VERMEYLEN (ed.), *The Book of Isaiah – Le livre d'Isaïe. Les oracles et leurs relectures. Unité et complexité de l'ouvrage*, 1989. X-472 p. FB 2700.
82. G. VAN BELLE, *Johannine Bibliography 1966-1985. A Cumulative Bibliography on the Fourth Gospel*, 1988. XVII-563 p. FB 2700.
83. J.A. SELLING (ed.), *Personalist Morals. Essays in Honor of Professor Louis Janssens*, 1988. VIII-344 p. FB 1200.
84. M.-É. BOISMARD, *Moïse ou Jésus. Essai de christologie johannique*, 1988. XVI-241 p. FB 1000.
84A. M.-É. BOISMARD, *Moses or Jesus: An Essay in Johannine Christology*. Translated by B.T. VIVIANO, 1993, XVI-144 p. FB 1000.
85. J.A. DICK, *The Malines Conversations Revisited*, 1989. 278 p. FB 1500.
86. J.-M. SEVRIN (ed.), *The New Testament in Early Christianity – La réception des écrits néotestamentaires dans le christianisme primitif*, 1989. XVI-406 p. FB 2500.
87. R.F. COLLINS (ed.), *The Thessalonian Correspondence*, 1990. XV-546 p. FB 3000.
88. F. VAN SEGBROECK, *The Gospel of Luke. A Cumulative Bibliography 1973-1988*, 1989. 241 p. FB 1200.

89. G. THILS, *Primauté et infaillibilité du Pontife Romain à Vatican I et autres études d'ecclésiologie,* 1989. XI-422 p. FB 1850.
90. A. VERGOTE, *Explorations de l'espace théologique. Études de théologie et de philosophie de la religion,* 1990. XVI-709 p. FB 2000.
91. J.C. DE MOOR, *The Rise of Yahwism: The Roots of Israelite Monotheism,* 1990. *Revised and Enlarged Edition,* 1997. XV-445 p. FB 1400.
92. B. BRUNING, M. LAMBERIGTS & J. VAN HOUTEM (eds.), *Collectanea Augustiniana. Mélanges T.J. van Bavel,* 1990. 2 tomes, XXXVIII-VIII-1074 p. FB 3000.
93. A. DE HALLEUX, *Patrologie et œcuménisme. Recueil d'études,* 1990. XVI-887 p. FB 3000.
94. C. BREKELMANS & J. LUST (eds.), *Pentateuchal and Deuteronomistic Studies: Papers Read at the XIIIth IOSOT Congress Leuven 1989,* 1990. 307 p. FB 1500.
95. D.L. DUNGAN (ed.), *The Interrelations of the Gospels. A Symposium Led by M.-É. Boismard – W.R. Farmer – F. Neirynck, Jerusalem 1984,* 1990. XXXI-672 p. FB 3000.
96. G.D. KILPATRICK, *The Principles and Practice of New Testament Textual Criticism. Collected Essays.* Edited by J.K. ELLIOTT, 1990. XXXVIII-489 p. FB 3000.
97. G. ALBERIGO (ed.), *Christian Unity. The Council of Ferrara-Florence: 1438/39 – 1989,* 1991. X-681 p. FB 3000.
98. M. SABBE, *Studia Neotestamentica. Collected Essays,* 1991. XVI-573 p. FB 2000.
99. F. NEIRYNCK, *Evangelica II: 1982-1991. Collected Essays.* Edited by F. VAN SEGBROECK, 1991. XIX-874 p. FB 2800.
100. F. VAN SEGBROECK, C.M. TUCKETT, G. VAN BELLE & J. VERHEYDEN (eds.), *The Four Gospels 1992. Festschrift Frans Neirynck,* 1992. 3 volumes, XVII-X-X-2668 p. FB 5000.

SERIES III

101. A. DENAUX (ed.), *John and the Synoptics,* 1992. XXII-696 p. FB 3000.
102. F. NEIRYNCK, J. VERHEYDEN, F. VAN SEGBROECK, G. VAN OYEN & R. CORSTJENS, *The Gospel of Mark. A Cumulative Bibliography: 1950-1990,* 1992. XII-717 p. FB 2700.
103. M. SIMON, *Un catéchisme universel pour l'Église catholique. Du Concile de Trente à nos jours,* 1992. XIV-461 p. FB 2200.
104. L. CEYSSENS, *Le sort de la bulle Unigenitus. Recueil d'études offert à Lucien Ceyssens à l'occasion de son 90ᵉ anniversaire.* Présenté par M. LAMBERIGTS, 1992. XXVI-641 p. FB 2000.
105. R.J. DALY (ed.), *Origeniana Quinta. Papers of the 5th International Origen Congress, Boston College, 14-18 August 1989,* 1992. XVII-635 p. FB 2700.
106. A.S. VAN DER WOUDE (ed.), *The Book of Daniel in the Light of New Findings,* 1993. XVIII-574 p. FB 3000.
107. J. FAMERÉE, *L'ecclésiologie d'Yves Congar avant Vatican II: Histoire et Église. Analyse et reprise critique,* 1992. 497 p. FB 2600.

108. C. BEGG, *Josephus' Account of the Early Divided Monarchy (AJ 8, 212-420). Rewriting the Bible*, 1993. IX-377 p. FB 2400.
109. J. BULCKENS & H. LOMBAERTS (eds.), *L'enseignement de la religion catholique à l'école secondaire. Enjeux pour la nouvelle Europe*, 1993. XII-264 p. FB 1250.
110. C. FOCANT (ed.), *The Synoptic Gospels. Source Criticism and the New Literary Criticism*, 1993. XXXIX-670 p. FB 3000.
111. M. LAMBERIGTS (ed.), avec la collaboration de L. KENIS, *L'augustinisme à l'ancienne Faculté de théologie de Louvain*, 1994. VII-455 p. FB 2400.
112. R. BIERINGER & J. LAMBRECHT, *Studies on 2 Corinthians*, 1994. XX-632 p. FB 3000.
113. E. BRITO, *La pneumatologie de Schleiermacher*, 1994. XII-649 p. FB 3000.
114. W.A.M. BEUKEN (ed.), *The Book of Job*, 1994. X-462 p. FB 2400.
115. J. LAMBRECHT, *Pauline Studies: Collected Essays*, 1994. XIV-465 p. FB 2500.
116. G. VAN BELLE, *The Signs Source in the Fourth Gospel: Historical Survey and Critical Evaluation of the Semeia Hypothesis*, 1994. XIV-503 p. FB 2500.
117. M. LAMBERIGTS & P. VAN DEUN (eds.), *Martyrium in Multidisciplinary Perspective. Memorial L. Reekmans*, 1995. X-435 p. FB 3000.
118. G. DORIVAL & A. LE BOULLUEC (eds.), *Origeniana Sexta. Origène et la Bible/Origen and the Bible. Actes du Colloquium Origenianum Sextum, Chantilly, 30 août – 3 septembre 1993*, 1995. XII-865 p. FB 3900.
119. É. GAZIAUX, *Morale de la foi et morale autonome. Confrontation entre P. Delhaye et J. Fuchs*, 1995. XXII-545 p. FB 2700.
120. T.A. SALZMAN, *Deontology and Teleology: An Investigation of the Normative Debate in Roman Catholic Moral Theology*, 1995. XVII-555 p. FB 2700.
121. G.R. EVANS & M. GOURGUES (eds.), *Communion et Réunion. Mélanges Jean-Marie Roger Tillard*, 1995. XI-431 p. FB 2400.
122. H.T. FLEDDERMANN, *Mark and Q: A Study of the Overlap Texts*. With an *Assessment* by F. NEIRYNCK, 1995. XI-307 p. FB 1800.
123. R. BOUDENS, *Two Cardinals: John Henry Newman, Désiré-Joseph Mercier*. Edited by L. GEVERS with the collaboration of B. DOYLE, 1995. 362 p. FB 1800.
124. A. THOMASSET, *Paul Ricœur. Une poétique de la morale. Aux fondements d'une éthique herméneutique et narrative dans une perspective chrétienne*, 1996. XVI-706 p. FB 3000.
125. R. BIERINGER (ed.), *The Corinthian Correspondence*, 1996. XXVII-793 p. FB 2400.
126. M. VERVENNE (ed.), *Studies in the Book of Exodus: Redaction – Reception – Interpretation*, 1996. XI-660 p. FB 2400.
127. A. VANNESTE, *Nature et grâce dans la théologie occidentale. Dialogue avec H. de Lubac*, 1996. 312 p. FB 1800.
128. A. CURTIS & T. RÖMER (eds.), *The Book of Jeremiah and its Reception – Le livre de Jérémie et sa réception*, 1997. 332 p. FB 2400.
129. E. LANNE, *Tradition et Communion des Églises. Recueil d'études*, 1997. XXV-703 p. FB 3000.

130. A. DENAUX & J.A. DICK (eds.), *From Malines to ARCIC. The Malines Conversations Commemorated*, 1997. IX-317 p. FB 1800.
131. C.M. TUCKETT (ed.), *The Scriptures in the Gospels*, 1997. XXIV-721 p. FB 2400.
132. J. VAN RUITEN & M. VERVENNE (eds.), *Studies in the Book of Isaiah. Festschrift Willem A.M. Beuken*, 1997. XX-540 p. FB 3000.
133. M. VERVENNE & J. LUST (eds.), *Deuteronomy and Deuteronomic Literature. Festschrift C.H.W. Brekelmans*, 1997. XI-637 p. FB 3000.
134. G. VAN BELLE (ed.), *Index Generalis ETL / BETL 1982-1997*, 1999. IX-337 p. FB 1600.
135. G. DE SCHRIJVER, *Liberation Theologies on Shifting Grounds. A Clash of Socio-Economic and Cultural Paradigms*, 1998. XI-453 p. FB 2100.
136. A. SCHOORS (ed.), *Qohelet in the Context of Wisdom*, 1998. XI-528 p. FB 2400.
137. W.A. BIENERT & U. KÜHNEWEG (eds.), *Origeniana Septima. Origenes in den Auseinandersetzungen des 4. Jahrhunderts,* 1999. XXV-848 p. FB 3800.
138. É. GAZIAUX, *L'autonomie en morale: au croisement de la philosophie et de la théologie*, 1998. XVI-739 p. FB 3000.
139. J. GROOTAERS, *Actes et acteurs à Vatican II*, 1998. XXIV-602 p. FB 3000.
140. F. NEIRYNCK, J. VERHEYDEN & R. CORSTJENS, *The Gospel of Matthew and the Sayings Source Q: A Cumulative Bibliography 1950-1995*, 1998. 2 vols., VII-1000-420* p. FB 3800.
141. E. BRITO, *Heidegger et l'hymne du sacré*, 1999. XV-800 p. FB 3600.
142. J. VERHEYDEN (ed.), *The Unity of Luke-Acts*, 1999. XXV-828 p. FB 2400.
143. N. CALDUCH-BENAGES & J. VERMEYLEN (eds.), *Treasures of Wisdom. Studies in Ben Sira and the Book of Wisdom. Festschrift M. Gilbert*, 1999. XXVII-463 p. FB 3000.
144. J.-M. AUWERS & A. WÉNIN (eds.), *Lectures et relectures de la Bible. Festschrift P.-M. Bogaert*, 1999. XLII-482 p. FB 2400.
145. C. BEGG, *Josephus' Story of the Later Monarchy (AJ 9,1–10,185)*, 2000. X-708 p. FB 3000.
146. J.M. ASGEIRSSON, K. DE TROYER & M.W. MEYER (eds.), *From Quest to Q. Festschrift James M. Robinson*, 2000. XLIV-345 p. FB 2400.
147. T. RÖMER (ed.), *The Future of Deuteronomistic History*, 2000. Forthcoming.
148. F.D. VANSINA, *Paul Ricœur: Bibliographie primaire et secondaire - Primary and Secondary Bibliography 1935-2000*, 2000. XXV-544 p. BF 3000.
149. G.J. BROOKE & J.D. KAESTLI (eds.), *Narrativity in Biblical and Related Texts*, 2000. Forthcoming.
150. F. NEIRYNCK, *Evangelica III: 1992-2000. Collected Essays*, 2000. Forthcoming.
151. B. DOYLE, *The Apocalypse of Isaiah Metaphorically Speaking*, 2000. XII-473 p.
152. T. MERRIGAN & J. HAERS (eds.), *The Myriad Christ*, 2000. XIV-605 p.
153. M. SIMON, *Le catéchisme de Jean-Paul II*, 2000. Forthcoming.
154. J. VERMEYLEN, *La loi du plus fort*, 2000. Forthcoming.

PRINTED ON PERMANENT PAPER • IMPRIME SUR PAPIER PERMANENT • GEDRUKT OP DUURZAAM PAPIER - ISO 9706

ORIENTALISTE, KLEIN DALENSTRAAT 42, B-3020 HERENT